WRITING, READING, AND RESEARCH

Several Selections from the Same Anthology (Cross-Referencing)

Baker, Susan W. "Biological Influences on Human Sex and Gender." Stimson and Person 175-91.

Leifer, Myra. "Pregnancy." Stimson and Person 212-23.

Stimpson, Catherine R., and Ethel Spector Person, eds. Women: Sex and Sexuality. Chicago: U of Chicago P, 1980.

An Article in an Encyclopedia or Other Reference

A well-known reference work:

Harmon, Mamie. "Folk Arts." The New Encyclopaedia Britannica: Macropaedia. 15th ed. 2002.

"Morrison, Toni." Who's Who in America. 60th ed. 2006.

"Yodel." The Shorter Oxford English Dictionary. 5th ed. 2002.

A lesser-known reference work:

Hames, Raymond. "Yanomamö." South America. Vol. 7 of Encyclopedia of World Cultures. Boston: Hall, 1994.

A Preface, Introduction, Foreword, or Afterword

Bradford, Barbara Taylor. Foreword. Forever Amber. By Kathleen Winsor. 1944. Chicago: Chicago Review, 2000.

PERIODICALS AND NEWSPAPERS

An Article in a Magazine

Block, Toddi Gutner. "Riding the Waves." Forbes 11 Sept. 1995: 182+.

Fletcher, Winston. "The American Way of Work." Management Today Aug. 2005: 46-49.

Schwartz, Deborah F. "Dude, Where's My Museum? Inviting Teens to Transform Museums." Museum News Sep./Oct. 2005: 36-41.

An Article in a Journal

Pages numbered continuously throughout the volume:

Gerson, Lloyd P. "What Is Platonism?" Journal of the History of Philosophy 43 (2005): 253-76.

Each issue begins on page 1:

Anderson, Rebecca, and Jane Puckett. "The Usefulness of an Online Platform for Capturing Literacy Field Experiences: Four Lessons Learned." Reading Instruction & Research 23.4 (2005): 22-46.

An Article in a Newspaper

Cauvin, Henri E. "Lawyers Seek Release of U.S. Detainee in Iraq." Washington Post 31 Aug. 2005: A19.

Leonhardt, David. "Defining the Rich in the World's Wealthiest Nation." New York Times 12 Jan. 2003, natl. ed.: sec. 4: 1+.

Ranii, David. "Adding a Different Symbol." News and Observer [Raleigh] 9 Sep. 2005: 3D.

An Editorial

"Oil for Food as Usual." Editorial. Wall Street Journal 9 Sep. 2005: A16.

A Letter to the Editor

Brewer, Jack. Letter. U.S. News & World Report 5 Sep. 2005: 16.

A Review

Benfey, Christopher. "An Illustrated Woman." Rev. of The Tattoo Artist, by Jill Ciment. New York Times Book Review 21 Aug. 2005: 8.

Glenn, Kenny. Rev. of Man on the moon [film]. Premiere Jan. 2000: 20.

Rev. of Going to the Territory, by Ralph Ellison. Atlantic Aug. 1986: 91.

Stearns, David Patrick. Rev. of The Well-Tempered Clavier, by J. S. Bach [CD]. Angela Hewitt, piano. Stereophile Dec. 1999: 173+.

OTHER SOURCES

An Audio Recording

Dickinson, Dee. Creating the Future: Perspectives on Educational Change. Audiocassette. Minneapolis: Accelerated Learning Systems, 1991.

Mahler, Gustav. Symphony No. 7. Michael Tilson Thomas, cond. London Symphony Orch. CD. RCA Victor, 1999.

Shuster, George N. Jacket notes. The Poetry of Gerard Manley Hopkins. LP. Caedmon, n.d.

A Film, DVD, or Video Recording

A theatrical video:

Downfall. Dir. Oliver Hirschbiegel. Screenplay by Bernd Eichinger. Newmarket Films, 2005.

All About Eve. Dir. Joseph L. Mankiewicz. Perf. Bette Davis, Anne Baxter, and George Sanders. Fox, 1950. DVD. Studio Classics, 2003.

A nontheatrical video:

The Classical Hollywood Style. Program 1 of The American Cinema: Prod. New York Center for Visual History. Videocassette. Annenberg/CPB, 1995.

A Lecture

Granetta, Stephanie. Class lecture. English 315. Richardson College. 7 Apr. 2006.

Kamenish, Eleanor. "A Tale of Two Countries: Mores in France and Scotland." Public lecture. Friends of the Public Library. Louisville, 16 Apr. 2006.

A Pamphlet

Golden Retriever Club of America. Prevention of Heartworm. N.p.: GRCA, 2006.

Who Are the Amish? Aylmer, Ont.: Pathway, n.d.

An Interview

Clements, Caroline M. Personal interview. 15 July 2005.

Maher, Bill. Interview with Terry Gross. Fresh Air. Natl. Public Radio. WHQR, Wilmington, NC. 9 Aug. 2005.

(continued on next page)

Trump, Donald. "Trump Speaks." Interview with Aravind Adiga. <u>Money</u> Feb. 2003: 28.

A Television or Radio Program

<u>The Crossing</u>. Dir. Robert Harmon. Screenplay by Sherry Jones and Peter Jennings. History Channel. 1 Jan. 2000.

Garcia-Navarro, Lourdes. Report on illegal immigration. <u>All Things Considered</u>. Natl. Public Radio. 8 Sep. 2005.

An Unpublished Essay

Strickland, Allen. "Identical Twins: Born to Be Alike?" Essay written for Prof. Lisa Gorman's English 12 class. Summer term 2005.

An Unpublished Letter

Cilano, Cara. Letter to Author. 5 Mar. 2006.

An Unpublished Questionnaire

Questionnaire conducted by Prof. Barbara Waxman's English 103 class. Feb. 2006.

INTERNET AND ELECTRONIC SOURCES

An Online Book

Calvin, William H. <u>How Brains Think: Evolving Intelligence Then and Now</u>. New York: Basic Books, 1996. 1 Oct. 2005 <http://www.williamcalvin.com/bk8/>.

Conrad, Carl W. <u>A Brief Commentary on the Book of Mark</u>. 2004. 1 Oct. 2005 <http://www.ioa.com/~cwconrad/Mark/>.

Wollstonecraft, Mary. <u>Vindication of the Rights of Women</u>. 1792. Bartleby.com, 1999. 1 Oct. 2005 <http://www.bartleby.com/144/>.

A Part of an Online Book

Speed, Harold. The Visual Memory. <u>The Practice and Science of Drawing</u>. 1913. Project Gutenberg, 2004. 1 Oct. 2005 <http://www.gutenberg.org/files/14264/14264-h/14264-h.htm#CHAPTER_XVIII>.

A Print Periodical (Newspaper, Magazine, or Journal) Accessed on the Publication's Web Site

Hopfensperger, Jean. "Wal-Mart Debate Gains Momentum across Minnesota." <u>Minneapolis Star Tribune</u> 12 Sep. 2005. 1 Oct. 2005 <http://www.startribune.com/stories/1405/5608958.html>.

Hopkins, Philip F., et al. "Black Holes in Galaxy Mergers: Evolution of Quasars." <u>Astrophysical Journal</u> 630.2 (2005): 705-15. 1 Oct. 2005 <http://www.journals.uchicago.edu/ApJ/journal/issues/ApJ/v630n2/62521/62521.html>.

Hosenball, Mark. "Iraq: Planning for Pullout." <u>Newsweek</u> 19 Sep. 2005. 1 Oct. 2005 <http://msnbc.msn.com/id/9285511/site/newsweek/>.

A Nonprint Periodical Accessed on the Publication's Web Site

"Cellular's Unhappy Customers." <u>Red Herring</u> 7 Sep. 2005. 1 Oct. 2005 <http://www.redherring.com/>.

A Work Accessed in an Online Database

Ernst, Steve. "Pandemic Fever." <u>Bioscience Technology</u> July 2005: 6. <u>InfoTrac OneFile</u>. 1 Oct. 2005 <http://infotrac.galegroup.com/>.

Parks, Noreen. "Dolphins in Danger." <u>Science Now</u>, 17 dec. 2002: 2-3. <u>Academic Search Elite</u>. Ebscohost. 1 Oct. 2005 <http://web3.epnet.com/>.

"Ukraine Foreign Minister Says 'No Alternative' to Constructive Ties with Russia." <u>Global News Wire</u> 28 July 2005. <u>LexisNexis Academic Universe</u>. 1 Oct. 2005 <http://web.lexis-nexis.com/universe>.

An Online Encyclopedia Article

"Humpback Whale." <u>Encyclopaedia Britannica</u> 2005. Encyclopaedia Britannica Online. 1 Oct. 2005 <http://0-search.eb.com.uncclc.coast.uncwil.edu/eb/>.

An Online Review

Ebert, Roger. Rev. of <u>The Constant Gardener</u>, dir. Fernando Meirelles. <u>RogerEbert.com</u> 1 Sep. 2005. 1 Oct. 2005 <http://rogerebert.suntimes.com>.

An Organization's Web Site

<u>The Coral Reef Alliance</u>. "Major Mesoamerica Initiative Underway." 1 Oct. 2005 <http://www.coralreefalliance.org/parks/mar/>.

A Course Web Page

Reilly, Colleen. English 204: Introduction to Technical Writing. Course home page. U of North Carolina Wilmington. Spring 2003. 29 Apr. 2003 <http://people.uncw.edu/reillyc/204/>.

An Academic Department Page

Dept. of English home page. U of North Carolina Wilmington. 10 Mar. 2003 <http://www.uncwil.edu/english/>.

A Personal Web Page

Hemming, Sally. Home page. 1 Oct. 2005 <http://www.sallyhemming.com>.

Weblog (Blog) or Online Posting

Lessig, Lawrence. "Gifts from the Other Side." Weblog entry. <u>Lessig Blog</u> 11 Sep. 2005. 1 Oct. 2005 <http://www.lessig.org/blog/>.

Newlin, Keith. "McTeague's Tooth." Online posting. 22 Mar. 2003. 1 Oct. 2005 <http://people.uncw.edu/newlink/tooth.htm>.

Computer Software

<u>ChemSketch</u>. Vers. 8.0. Software. 2005 <http://www.acdlabs.com/download/chemsk.html>.

<u>Twain's World</u>. CD-ROM. Parsippany, NJ: Bureau Development, 1993.

E-Mail

Wilkes, Paul. E-Mail to Author. 29 dec. 2005.

WRITING, READING, AND RESEARCH

SEVENTH EDITION

Richard Veit
Christopher Gould
University of North Carolina, Wilmington

PEARSON
Longman

New York Boston San Francisco
London Toronto Sydney Tokyo Singapore Madrid
Mexico City Munich Paris Cape Town Hong Kong Montreal

Senior Sponsoring Editor: Virginia L. Blanford
Senior Marketing Manager: Sandra McGuire
Production Manager: Bob Ginsberg
Assistant Editor: Rebecca Gilpin
Project Coordination, Text Design, and Electronic Page Makeup: GGS Book Services, Inc.
Cover Design Manager: John Callahan
Cover Designer: Maria Ilardi
Cover Illustration: Courtesy of Getty Images, Inc.
Senior Manufacturing Buyer: Alfred C. Dorsey
Printer and Binder: R. R. Donnelley & Sons Company
Cover Printer: Coral Graphic Services

Library of Congress Cataloging-in-Publication Data

Veit, Richard.
    Writing, reading, and research / Richard Veit, Christopher Gould.—7th ed.
        p. cm.
    Includes bibliographical references and index.
    ISBN 0-321-39437-2
        1. English language—Rhetoric. 2. Research—Methodology. 3. Academic writing.
    4. College readers. I. Gould, Christopher, 1947-II. Title.
    PE1408.V45 2006
    808′.042—dc22

                                                                              2006004455

Please visit us at www.ablongman.com

ISBN 0-321-39437-2

1 2 3 4 5 6 7 8 9 10—DOH—09 08 07 06

Contents

To the Instructor

Writing, Reading, and Research, Seventh Edition, reflects the assumption that the three activities in its title are central to a college education. Every college student must be able to access information and ideas, analyze and synthesize them, and communicate the resulting knowledge to others.

What is more, writing, reading, and research are so closely and symbiotically related that they should be studied together. We believe that the research paper should not be seen (though it often is) as one among many isolated writing tasks, distinguished chiefly by its intricate search protocols and citation formats. Research, in the broader sense that we envision, includes activities both large and small. Every task involving sources is a research activity, whether it be reading a textbook, using a library, searching the Internet, asking questions, taking notes, or writing a summary analysis in response to an essay-exam question. A textbook, as we see it, should reflect this inclusive definition, engaging students in the rewards and excitement of research writing while preparing them to do it well.

It follows that students need to develop and refine the many skills involved in college research. Writing an essay based on library sources, for example, employs a wide range of skills that, in our experience, many first-year college students have not yet mastered. Most basic of all is active critical reading. Students need to employ efficient strategies to read with perception and understanding, to analyze and critique what they read, and to make productive use of the information and ideas that arise from their reading.

For these reasons, we believe that writing, reading, and research skills should be taught and practiced together. A composition course that prepares students for the tasks they will actually face during their college and professional careers can and should be a unified whole. That unity is the principle that informs this book.

Developing the skills of writing, reading, and research is a process that can be divided into successive stages. We have attempted to take a common-sense approach to this process by introducing concepts sequentially. Although each chapter has its own integrity, each also builds on the concepts developed in preceding chapters.

In general, our book moves from simpler to more complex tasks—from working with a single source to connecting multiple sources, from comprehension to analysis and critique, from paraphrase and summary to synthesis—before presenting the more advanced and creative aspects of writing, reading, and research.

We have pursued several specific goals in writing this book:

- Broadening the traditional notion of undergraduate research
- Presenting the processes of research in a practical sequence

- Blending the best features of a theoretically informed rhetoric, an interdisciplinary reading anthology, and a research guide
- Creating a text that instructors will find serviceable as a teaching resource and that students will find lively, readable, and instructive as a guide to research writing
- Supplementing assignments with student responses, illustrating the processes that lead to a finished product
- Providing helpful and engaging exercises, frequent opportunities to write, and many occasions for discussion and critical response.

New to This Edition

The guided, sequential approach—always the hallmark of this textbook—remains intact in this edition, as does the abundance of examples, activities, and sample student papers. As always, however, we have tried to provide new tools and resources for students. In this edition, we have included almost thirty new readings that provide flexible, contemporary resources for assignments, as well as six student samples. New "Guidelines" sections throughout summarize important strategies for writing, revising, and incorporating research into writing. Finally, a wealth of new exercises appear throughout the book to provide expanded opportunities for student practice.

Supplements

An extensive instructor's manual offers suggestions for using *Writing, Reading, and Research* in the classroom. It provides an overview of each chapter and suggested assignments, along with responses to the in-text exercises and the questions that follow the end-of-chapter readings.

Acknowledgments

Our greatest debt is to our students, from whom we have learned most of what we know about teaching composition. In particular, we wish to thank the student writers who shared their notes and experiences in this edition: Millicent Lambert, Allen Strickland, Courtney Holbrook, and Ellie Stephens.

We also thank the following reviewers, whose wise and thoughtful suggestions made an immeasurable contribution to the seventh edition: Desire Baloubi, Shaw University; Amy Beaudry, Quinsigamond Community College; Nancy Brown, Lourdes College; and Andrew Lamers, Bakersfield College.

Finally, we thank our editor, Virginia Blanford, assistant editor, Rebecca Gilpin, our production manager, Bob Ginsberg, and others at Longman who have been involved with this new edition, as well as our friends and colleagues at the University of North Carolina, Wilmington.

RICHARD VEIT
CHRISTOPHER GOULD

PART I

Chapter 1

Writing, Reading, and Research

1 Introduction to Writing, Reading, and Research

A college education does more than just introduce you to current information about a field of study. It also teaches you how to find that information, how to analyze and evaluate it, and how to place it in specific contexts alongside other, sometimes conflicting, information. In short, a college education invites you to learn and think on your own. The sum of knowledge in any field is too vast and the world is changing too rapidly for an education that merely imparts facts and statistics. Instead, an education worthy of the name helps you develop skill and confidence in finding, interpreting, assessing, and synthesizing what you are expected to know, both now and after you graduate. Professionals, technicians, executives, and other educated adults who have developed and refined these skills are more likely to contribute new ideas and to communicate discoveries within their fields.

Nearly all the courses you take, whether in biology, accounting, theology, or forestry, presuppose certain skills and knowledge. The most important of these—the ones most vital to success in college as well as your career—involve writing, reading, and research. As a fluent writer, an alert reader, and a resourceful researcher, you enjoy enormous advantages. This book is designed to help you assume these roles.

Writing, reading, and research are not mysterious or unusually difficult. You have been reading and writing for years, and whether you realize it or not, you perform certain kinds of research all the time, both in and out of school. For example, when you were deciding which college to attend, you probably conducted research by examining college catalogs, visiting Web sites, consulting with your guidance counselor, talking with friends, or traveling to several campuses. In fact, if you found and read a catalog and then wrote an application essay, you used all three skills.

Since writing, reading, and research are interrelated activities, it makes sense to study them together. Research often involves finding what others have written, reading it, and then writing in response. Even as you write, you frequently read what you have written, deciding whether further research, organizational changes, or further editing is needed. And finally, what you have written about your research becomes someone else's reading.

WRITING

Writing is a complex process that includes various subskills, from the basics of handwriting and spelling to the subtler nuances of tone and organization. Unlike the ability to speak, acquired in early childhood without formal instruction, writing skills are developed later, usually in school. Time and practice gradually lead to competence, and although most of us master the fundamentals easily enough, no one ever *completely* perfects the craft of writing. Even the most admired authors, after years of accomplishment, continue to learn from experience and refine their craft. Although a course in composition or a book like this can help you improve your writing, repeated practice remains the best teacher.

The essence of writing is *options;* writers continually make choices. Even on those rare occasions when you know exactly what to say, you still confront a vast array of options. You must choose an organizational plan, gauge the level of formality that best suits the occasion, determine the most effective strategies for opening and closing your text, and decide which facts, arguments, or supporting details are most appropriate. Even the selection of individual words often involves considering a number of synonyms.

In one sense, choice makes writing difficult. Too many options can be overwhelming. Even accomplished authors are familiar with writer's block: staring at the blank page or computer screen, agonizing over what to say next. And while there are compensating periods when words seem to flow, the text that "writes itself" is a fiction. Nevertheless, experienced writers persevere through moments of frustration, confident in the strategies they have developed for generating ideas and overcoming obstacles.

Fortunately, choice brings opportunities as well as difficulties. Creative choices are, after all, what make writing an art, rather than just a competency. As writers, we are not word mechanics churning out assembly-line products. We are artisans, using our imagination, experience, and talent to create, from the unlimited options available to us, texts that are both functional and original. Writing allows us to communicate ideas and information in ways that are profound, funny, provocative, or highly persuasive. Despite, or perhaps because of, the demanding work and hard choices that writing involves, the sense of achievement we derive from creating a work uniquely our own can be great, even exhilarating.

Writing Habits and Strategies

Skilled writers devote considerable time to the preliminary stages of composing before they try to produce a complete, polished draft. They do not, however, all follow the same routine, nor do they, as individuals, pursue a uniform approach to every writing task. In fact, one of your goals in this course should be to discover which procedures lead to the best results in specific situations: a timed essay exam vs. an informal response to assigned reading vs. a research paper due at the end of an academic term. In the following passage, Nancy Sommers, a scholar who has studied writing processes for nearly thirty years, discusses her experiences as a writer and a teacher of writing:

> I stand in my kitchen, wiping the cardamom, coriander, and cayenne off my fingers. My head is abuzz with words, with bits and pieces of conversation. I hear a phrase I have read recently, something about "a radical loss of certainty." But, I wonder, how did the sentence begin? I search the air for the rest of the sentence, can't find it, shake some more cardamom, and a bit of coriander. Then, by some play of mind, I am back home again in Indiana with my family, sitting around the kitchen table. Two people are talking, and there are three opinions; three people are talking, and there are six opinions. Opinions grow exponentially. I fight my way back to that sentence. Writing, that's how it begins: "Writing is a radical loss of certainty." (Or is it uncertainty?) It isn't so great for the chicken when all these voices start showing up, with all these sentences hanging in mid-air, but the voices keep me company. I am a writer, not a cook, and the truth is I don't care much about the chicken. Stories beget stories. Writing emerges from writing. . . .
>
> If I could teach my students one lesson about writing it would be to see themselves as sources, as places from which ideas originate, . . . all that they have read and experienced—the dictionaries of their lives—circulating through them. I want them to learn how sources thicken, complicate, enlarge writing, but I want them to know too how it is always the writer's voice, vision, and argument that create the new source. I want my students to see that nothing reveals itself straight out, especially the sources all around them. But I know enough by now that this . . . ideal can't be passed on in one lesson or even a semester of lessons.
>
> Many of the students who come to my classes have been trained to collect facts; they act as if their primary job is to accumulate enough authorities so that there is no doubt about the "truth" of their thesis. They most often disappear behind the weight and permanence of their borrowed words, moving their pens, mouthing the words of others, allowing sources to speak through them unquestioned, unexamined.
>
> At the outset, many of my students think that personal writing is writing about the death of their grandmother. Academic writing is [from their point of view] reporting what Elizabeth Kübler-Ross has written about death and dying. Being personal, I want to show my students, does not mean being autobiographical. Being academic does not mean being remote, distant, imponderable. Being personal means bringing their judgments and interpretations to bear on what they read and write, learning that they never leave themselves behind even when they write academic essays. . . .
>
> With writing and with teaching, as well as with love, we don't know how the sentence will begin and, rarely ever, how it will end. Having the courage to live with uncertainty, ambiguity, even doubt, we can walk into all those fields of writing, knowing that we will find volumes upon volumes bidding *us* enter. We need only be inventors, we need only give freely and abundantly to the texts, imagining even as we write that we too will be a source from which other readers can draw sustenance.

Notice how Sommers, a published scholar, grapples with the same self-doubts and frustrations that beset less experienced writers. But, after years of practice and reflection, she has come to view these distractions as an inevitable stage in a process that almost always produces an acceptable draft. In fact, she has learned to exploit the potential of distractions. For example, Sommers understands that ideas and isolated bits of language come to mind at unexpected, sometimes inconvenient moments—while you cook, exercise, shower, or try to go to sleep. Proficient writers do not disregard or try to postpone these moments of invention and discovery, which more typically result from deliberate contrivance rather than spontaneous inspiration. Notice how Sommers, recalling an experience evoked by the perplexing phrase, "Writing is a radical loss of certainty," has to "fight [her] way back" to the topic at hand. She understands that personal associations and experiences are not irrelevant distractions during the early stages of composing. Sommers therefore embraces "uncertainty, ambiguity, even doubt," confident that insightful ideas and fluent language will eventually emerge.

The chief difference between experienced writers and most first-year college students is that the former, like Sommers, have learned to break down the complexity of writing by approaching it in manageable stages, so that what starts out as an awkward exploration ends up, several stages later, as a polished essay or a crafted report. Writers who strive for early perfection are usually doomed to frustration. Polish and clarity evolve over time through patient drafting and redrafting. Although composing is seldom easy for anyone, skillful writers rely on the routines they have developed over time. They know that with patience and persistence, good ideas, graceful sentences, and appropriate vocabulary will come. Like these writers, you too can learn to settle down to the hardest part of writing—getting started.

EXERCISES | Writing Habits and Strategies

1. In each of the following passages, a published author talks about the craft of writing. As you read each passage, take note of anything that relates to your own writing processes.

   a. With a blank [Microsoft] Word document before me, I waited for the right words to come. I had always found that getting started was one of the hardest parts of technical writing, and that was certainly holding true now. I decided to skip the introductory matter for the time being and jump right into documenting the software's functions. This material didn't seem to require as much creativity, and it was something I could tackle bit by bit.

      Over the next few months I slowly, and sometimes painfully, documented each function of the program. Half the battle was simply trying to understand what I was writing about. The program's interface certainly left something to be desired, and my lack of building knowledge was a definite obstacle. Oddly enough, even the programmers didn't have a complete grasp of their creation. To top things off, I had to learn RoboHelp and attempt to produce a written and on-line document simultaneously. Until now there had been no online help, so this was another blank slate I had to fill all on my own.

      —Alina Rutten, "How I Became a Goddess"

   b. I've handwritten all my books. I like to handwrite because I find that I think differently when I do so. Computers are seductive in that you feel that you don't have to edit and rework as much because the printed text can look so good, and if you have a good printer it looks even better. So for me the stages tend to be that I work something through in my head, and then I start writing it. And I work a lot with question outlines because the question-and-answer format is one I like a lot and use often in writing essays. I think: "What kind of questions do I envision myself and another audience wanting to know, say, about this film or about this issue?"

—bell hooks, "bell hooks and the Politics of Literacy: A Conversation"

c. Only the very young and the very old may recount their dreams at breakfast, dwell upon self, interrupt with memories of beach picnics and favorite Liberty lawn dresses and the rainbow trout in a creek near Colorado Springs. The rest of us are expected, rightly, to affect absorption in other people's favorite dresses, other people's trout.

And so we do. But our notebooks give us away, for however dutifully we record what we see around us, the common denominator of all we see is always, transparently, shamelessly, the implacable "I." We are not talking here about the kind of notebook that is patently for public consumption . . . ; we are talking about something private, about bits of the mind's string too short to use, an indiscriminate and erratic assemblage with meaning only for its maker.

—Joan Didion, "On Keeping a Notebook"

d. Writing isn't hard; no harder than ditch-digging.

—Patrick Dennis

After reading these passages, write for twenty minutes about how you compose papers and other academic assignments that involve writing. Try to draw comparisons and contrasts between the routines you have developed and those of the writers cited above.

2. Exchange your writing in small groups and discuss similarities and differences.

In this book we assume that you have completed a course in college or high school that introduced you to stages of the writing process. Nevertheless, we think it useful to review a sequence of composing strategies that many seasoned writers have adapted to their own individual needs and preferences. Remember that since occasions for writing differ, this is not a rigidly uniform sequence of "steps"; those who use it productively make adjustments. The main thing to keep in mind is that there are no shortcuts to effective writing.

Several times in this book, we present papers that college students have written in response to assignments in their composition classes. In this chapter, you will read a paper by Millicent Lambert, a first-year college student who addressed the assignment detailed below. In addition, to illustrate the composing processes that led to her polished draft, we have recorded the evolution of Millicent's paper from her first encounter with the assignment through the proofreading of her final draft. (Also, we have provided several other examples of this type of essay, sometimes referred to as a *profile,* at the end of this chapter.)

Research involves deciding what you want to know, focusing your investigation, and then making discoveries about a topic. Later in this course you will engage in *secondary research*, finding out what other researchers have already learned and reported. Library research is an example. The paper you write in response to this assignment, on the other hand, involves *primary research*, gathering information firsthand, through direct observation.

Here is the assignment in brief: *Investigate a place or activity, discovering as much as you can through careful, persistent observation; then report your discoveries in an engaging, informative paper.*

The following suggestions and guidelines should be helpful:

- Choose an organization, office, building, or outdoor locale where a particular activity takes place. Examples include a health-food cooperative, art gallery, community festival or pageant, hospice, auction, or farmer's market.

- Select a place or activity that is relatively unfamiliar to you. If you describe something you know well, you may be influenced by unconscious preconceptions and thus take for granted or overlook details that an outsider would find unusual and interesting. For this assignment, it is important that you observe and write as an *objective reporter*, not as a participant or insider.

- Take careful note of what goes on, particularly anything that might not be obvious to the casual observer. Notice how people act, how they respond to each other, their behavior, and the unspoken rules that operate within the context.

- Adopt one of two methods of gathering data: be an unobtrusive "fly on the wall," listening and watching others who are generally unaware of your presence; or be an inquiring reporter, talking to people and asking questions.

- Return to the site as often as necessary until you understand your subject thoroughly. Take copious notes during or immediately after each visit.

- Write about the institution/activity and about your personal experiences during your visit(s). Report what *you* see and feel free to use the word *I* in your report. You can state what you expected or intended to find, what you actually discovered, and how your views were changed or reinforced by the observation.

- Do not devote much space to obvious or surface details about the place or activity you describe. Try not to tell readers things they may already know. Get behind the obvious and describe what *really* is going on.

- Describe what you witnessed during your observation(s) rather than generalizing about what happens on typical occasions. Use specific details.

Submit prewriting, notes, and preliminary drafts along with the final version of your paper.

After you have read Millicent Lambert's polished essay and followed her progress through the several stages that led to it, the nature and requirements of this assignment should become clearer to you. Notice that the assignment calls for something beyond purely personal writing. That is, the instructor asked members of the class to draw on sources outside their own opinions and past experiences; they were expected to rely on direct observation and, possibly, to conduct an interview or informal survey. This procedure might involve visits to several sites or repeated observations of a single site.

To be a fair, open-minded observer is not necessarily to assume a completely detached, impersonal stance toward a topic. In fact, when you read Millicent's essay, you will find that she became personally involved with what she was writing about, her observation of an eighth-grade class. The assignment on page 8 calls for a type of writing not completely different from the personal essays that Millicent had written in high school, nor from the more formal research-based writing she would do later in her composition course. Although the assignment does not call for a traditional research paper—the kind that cites library sources and uses formal documentation—it does involve a particular type of research. (Later chapters of this book explain other methods of research in greater detail.)

Audience and Purpose

Whenever we engage in discourse—that is, whenever we converse, write a letter, give a speech, compose an essay, or participate in any other type of transaction involving language—we adapt our words and style of delivery to our intentions. Imagine, for example, overhearing a dialogue between a male and a female college student who meet at a party. The conversation might begin with little more than customary phrases of introduction, followed by routine questions about hometowns, majors, interests, and tastes in music. Nevertheless, an astute observer would recognize in this dialogue certain subtle attempts to manipulate a familiar ritual for complex purposes. Each speaker may be trying to gauge the degree of his or her attraction to the other, to make an impression, and to advance (or perhaps to slow down or even to end) the progress of a relationship. Like these speakers, all of us, since early childhood, have become skilled at adapting language behavior to specific situations. So it is when we write.

Effective writers carefully consider their reason (*purpose*) for writing and the persons (*audience*) that they hope to inform, persuade, entertain, or otherwise influence. These considerations affect a wide range of decisions involving language, because there is no multipurpose style or structure that suits every writing task. To illustrate, consider the following excerpt from the Declaration of Independence:

> We hold these truths to be self-evident, that all men are created equal. . . .

Now contrast it with this excerpt from H. L. Mencken's comic paraphrase, "The Declaration of Independence in American":

> All we got to say on this proposition is this: first, me and you is as good as anybody else, and maybe a damn sight better. . . .

Both passages are widely admired, but since they address different audiences and purposes, they exemplify vastly different styles. In the original version, Thomas Jefferson hoped to justify American independence to the world and to persuade fellow colonists of the necessity of armed rebellion. In contrast, Mencken wanted to amuse readers while making a point about language; therefore, his writing is informal and humorous. Each style suits the writer's goals, but neither would have been appropriate in the opposite situation, nor for the assignment that Millicent Lambert received from her instructor.

Millicent's purpose and audience were defined by the assignment on page 8. She was expected to report, from a personal point of view, information and impressions that would engage the interests of a particular audience of readers. She understood that her instructor wanted to simplify the task by defining that audience as readers like herself. However, she could not entirely ignore the fact that her instructor—who would be reading and responding to her paper—was an important part of her audience as well.

With these considerations in mind, Millicent began her research and writing, the stages of which are traced in the following pages. As you read these pages, you can judge how effectively she took into account the demands of her purpose and audience. The final draft of Millicent's paper appears on pages 11–18.

Lambert 1

Millicent Lambert

15 March 2005

Ms. Kate Tully

Eighth Grade Revisited

As I walked down the hall wearing my college sweatshirt and wind pants, I heard the bell ring. It was my first day of class and I was late. Would the students be seated in rows, quietly listening to the teacher, as I entered the classroom for the first time? I had no idea how I would be perceived by these students. Here I was, a twenty-year-old college sophomore trying to pose as an eighth grader. Have times changed? Are the kids just like they used to be? I was scared as I opened the door to Ms. Hobson's classroom. My heart was pounding and my palms were sweaty; I was about to discover what it's like to be an eighth grader in a large public school.

As I took a seat near the back of the room, Ms. Hobson was standing at the chalkboard, wearing a red blazer and khaki pants; she was a small woman, about five feet, four inches, whose smile seemed heart-warming and compassionate. Introducing me to the class, she said, "Students, this is Millicent. She's just moved here, so let's make her feel welcome as she adjusts to her new surroundings." After this introduction, the class carried on with their reading assignment, and I went outside for a moment to talk with the teacher.

In the small Christian academy that I attended, students were expected to carry on with their work without engaging in any horseplay, even when the teacher wasn't present. But in this room full of hyperactive teenagers, the talking and giggling started almost immediately, clearly audible in the hallway where we were standing.

I had met Ms. Hobson the day before to discuss the purposes of my observation. I'd read articles about teenage cliques, "queen bees," concealed weapons, and drugs. Now that I was contemplating a career in public education, I wondered whether I was prepared for what lay ahead for me, if not as a teacher, then perhaps as a parent. I wanted to learn firsthand whether large public schools are as unruly as the media often portray them, and I hoped to discover whether today's thirteen-year-old is as difficult to understand, to relate to, or simply to manage as I'd been led to believe.

Ms. Hobson had conceded that her students were hard to open up to and told me that masquerading as an eighth grader wouldn't be easy. Now I wasn't sure how to interact with these students--how I should talk with them or whether they would want to talk with me at all. I felt the urge to run

Lambert 3

down the hall and give up on the idea of going back to eighth grade. However, I had to write a paper that required primary research.

By the time the bell had sounded for lunch, I was anxious to talk with someone. The students gathered their lunchboxes and made their way slowly to the cafeteria, the girls on one side of the hall, the boys on the other. It was easy to see that most of the girls were preoccupied with physical appearance. Their hair and nails were carefully groomed; they dressed fashionably in designer brands; their makeup looked flawless. They seemed older than their actual age.

Ashley, a cute girl in a light pink turtleneck, silver hoop earrings, and soft pink lipstick, offered a friendly smile. Accompanied by three other girls, she reminded me of my friends in middle school. I remembered our lunchroom conversations about boys and using makeup to hide our blemishes. I began to feel more comfortable, realizing that no matter how much time had passed, eighth graders may be fundamentally the same. Sensing my nervousness, Ashley invited me to join her and the others. I was eager to know them better, but I also worried about how much they would want to find out about me. Could I pull off this undercover act without being detected?

Lambert 4

"How long have you been friends?" I asked casually.

"We've known each other since kindergarten. Laura transferred in last year, but now she's a member of the group."

"A member?"

"Yes," Ashley explained, "part of our circle of friends."

Carrie, another member of the group, turned to me and asked, "So do you have a boyfriend?"

I was stunned. I'd just met these girls, and the first thing they wanted to know about me was whether I had a boyfriend! Unsure of what to say and anxious to avoid complications, I responded, "Well, actually no, I'm not seeing anyone right now."

"Oh really," Laura replied archly. Then all four girls started laughing.

Confused and embarrassed, I asked whether all of them had boyfriends. They responded almost in unison, "Of course we do." My first unspoken thought was, "Well excuse me for asking!" Then I remembered that it was Ashley who had first opened up to me, and I was surprised and ashamed at how quicky I'd allowed myself to get drawn into the competitiveness and insecurity.

My thoughts were interrupted by the boys at an adjoining table, who had begun throwing grapes in our

Lambert 5

direction. Just as I turned to look, one of them, named Brad, stood up and aimed directly at me. I was so startled when the grape hit my shoulder, that, without thinking, I picked it up and threw it back at him. Although this immature gesture aroused laughter, one of the girls at my table was evidently annoyed by it. At first, I thought she was embarrassed by the spectacle, but it quickly became clear that she was used to being the center of attention and resented this intrusion. "I just can't stand Brad; he can be so obnoxious," she announced, as if no one could recognize that they secretly liked each other. Or maybe I was the only one who did.

After lunch, we all went back to class, and Ms. Hobson began reading us a story from the literature textbook. Many of the students paid no attention to her at all. When the whispering and laughter got too loud to ignore, Ms. Hobson stopped abruptly and asked what was so funny. But after some momentary embarrassment, it wasn't long before the disruptions started back up.

As soon as she'd finished reading, Ms. Hobson tried to initiate a discussion of the theme of revenge in the story. "Who should you try to get revenge on?"

A boy near the back of the room blurted out, "I get revenge on the people I hate." Coming from a thirteen-year-old, this sounded eerie and foreboding, yet I sensed that it was more of a self-dramatizing pose than a warning. Probably he was angry at one of his classmates.

Ms. Hobson went on: "The only people you should try to get revenge on are the ones who do good for you." Her point was that whenever a person does something to help you, you should return the favor. Trying to get even with someone who has hurt you is pointless, since you end up hurting yourself.

By now it was 2:15, and there was still one assignment left for the day. We arranged our desks in a semicircle in order to face each other. I sat between two boys who at first seemed quiet and passive. But as soon as the teacher turned her back, the boy on my left threw a paper airplane across the room. Hearing a whisper of laughter in the background, Ms. Hobson said, "Whatever you're doing needs to stop before I turn around." She then introduced a topic for discussion, "When you think of yourself, what makes you proud?"

I was very curious to know how some of the students would respond to this topic, but for the first minute or so the room was completely silent. Finally, one of the girls seated near the middle of the semicircle raised her hand and said, "I'm proud that I'm a good cheerleader." Suddenly,

Lambert 7

everyone in the room wanted to speak. "I'm proud to be on the basketball team"; "I'm proud because I make good grades." One member of the class turned to me and asked what made me proud. I wasn't sure what to say. So I sat there for a few seconds before finally saying, "I'm proud because I'm a good friend."

As the conversation continued, I found myself wanting to reveal my true identity. With ten minutes left before the announcements would start coming over the intercom, Ms. Hobson turned to the class and said, "Students, Millicent has something to tell you."

The class became very quiet as I walked up to the podium at the front of the room. I began: "Today has been a really amazing day. It was my first day here at this new school, and you've made me feel so welcome. I was nervous about coming today, but for different reasons than you may think. The truth is that I'm a twenty-year-old college student who wanted to see what it would be like to be in eighth grade again." The class started laughing in amazement. They didn't seem angry with me for tricking them; they loved the idea that I wanted to come back to the eighth grade.

I stayed around after the bell to answer many questions. Students wanted to know what college is like and

Lambert 8

what kinds of experiences I'd had in high school. It was exciting because I felt that I was really connecting with the students, probably because I too had been an eighth grader, and I had an idea of where they were coming from.

I learned a lot from my observations. I found out that eighth-grade students are not very different from what they were when I was their age. They face the same issues as they try to fit in. They're under constant scrutiny--by their parents and teachers, but mostly by their peers. Their friendships are more important to them than anything else, but even these are often fragile and insecure. The influence of peers is pervasive and at times insidious, as I discovered in the cafeteria, where I found my adult self throwing a grape at a thirteen-year-old boy. Often they don't recognize their own neediness, or if they do, they can't acknowledge it. Their classroom behavior is not a sign of disrespect so much as it is an indication of their doubt that teachers can relate to emotional issues that they themselves don't fully understand. Most of all, I came away with the hope that I can somehow allay those doubts and really make a difference in the lives of students. Without that hope, I could never undertake the challenges of teaching middle school.

Millicent's paper is one of a wide variety of possible responses to the assignment on pages 11–18. It is a polished piece of writing, but it did not start that way. The following pages trace the stages of her research and writing, which culminated in the essay you have just read. These stages include *prewriting, composing a first draft, peer review, revision,* and *editing.*

Prewriting

Drafting a paper is easier when you have an idea of what you want to say. Before you begin a first draft, it makes sense to pursue strategies that can help you generate or discover ideas and put them in writing. These strategies include *brainstorming, mapping, freewriting, collecting data,* and *outlining.* Millicent used all five in a sequence that helped her get started.

Brainstorming

Writers, business people, and scientists often unlock their thinking through *brainstorming,* a way of bringing to mind as many ideas about a topic as possible. Brainstorming not only provides raw material to work with; it also arouses creativity. You can brainstorm out loud or on paper. One way is to write down all the words or phrases about a topic that come to mind, listing them on the page, one after the other as they occur to you. Don't evaluate them or worry about whether they're consistent with each another. Sometimes you must pass over three or four—or even a dozen—useless ideas before a good one comes along. The purpose is to bring associations together in your mind, like rubbing sticks to create a spark.

When Millicent's instructor presented the assignment on page 8, she asked the class to brainstorm possible topics. Here is an excerpt from the list that Millicent produced:

```
–Campus areas
        Arboretum
        Post office
–Occupations
        Taxi driver
                Hours? Safety?
        Walking tour guide
        Lifeguard (Tony)
        Bridgetender
                How many are left?
                How do you qualify and apply?
        Ferry pilot
        Travel agent
        Veterinary assistant
```

-Occupational Sites
    Senior center
    Assisted-living facility
        What types of daily activities?
        What kinds of relationships do residents form with each other?
        With staff members?
    Day-care center/preschool
    Public schools

Millicent jotted down ideas as they came to mind, without rejecting anything as inappropriate, unworkable, or silly. She wrote quickly, not worrying about punctuation or spelling. She wrote entirely for her own benefit, and some of the names and items on her list made sense only to her. But you can see her mind at work—and the way brainstorming helped her thought processes gather momentum, with one idea provoking another. The list shows her train of thought, moving from campus locations, to unusual occupations, to occupational sites in general, to educational sites in particular, which was the eventual focus of her paper.

EXERCISE | **Brainstorming**

Choose a friend or classmate as a writing partner. While you generate a list of *the most creative or effective* television commercials, ask your partner to brainstorm a list of *all* television commercials. After ten minutes, compare lists to see which one contains more interesting or promising items for an essay on television advertising. Can you draw any inferences about effective brainstorming—what contributes to it and what may impede it?

Mapping or Clustering

Mapping involves making ideas concrete, putting them in black and white so you can look at them and see their relationships. Basically, you want to make patterns of words and phrases that radiate out from a central concept. When they do this, writers are often surprised how the linking process generates new ideas. Sometimes, the visual pattern itself can suggest an essay's basic organization. As in brainstorming, it is better to jot down ideas quickly, without trying to evaluate them.

From her brainstorming notes, Millicent found that she was focusing on public schools, which she further explored in the map shown in Figure 1.1. Each of the areas of public education that she listed led to a variety of ideas, and, in the

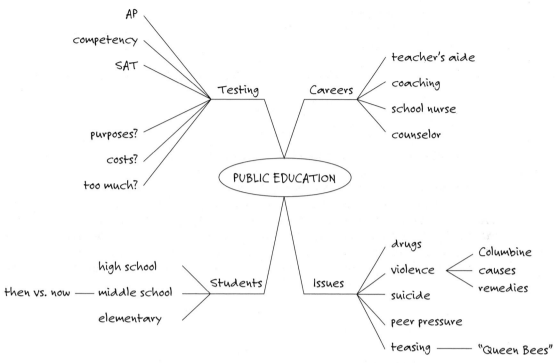

Figure 1.1 Millicent Lambert's map.

process of filling out the map, Millicent came up with several interesting ideas for her paper.

Some of the paths her mind took turned out to be dead ends ("Testing," e.g.), but others were promising leads. She considered careers in public education as well as a variety of social issues affecting schools. Also on her map was the idea of how students may have changed over time, which for Millicent proved to be the most promising of all. Notice, however, that one item under a different category ("Queen Bees") may also have contributed to her planning, since it appears in the final draft of her essay.

Freewriting

After an unfocused prewriting strategy like brainstorming or mapping, a good way to develop more focused ideas is to *freewrite*. Begin writing about your topic at a steady, comfortable pace, jotting down whatever comes to mind; then continue, without stopping, for perhaps ten or fifteen minutes. Don't reject any ideas; simply let them flow. Don't worry about spelling, punctuation, or even coherence.

Freewriting is not for others to read; its purpose is to help you explore your topic and come up with ideas to use later. Millicent's ten-minute freewriting looked like this:

> Middle school then and now. Aren't kids of the same age basically the same no matter where they live or when? Maybe but there are <u>some</u> differences. Foreign exchange students show us that. Everything I read about violence, drugs, and peer pressure in schools seems to assume that it wasn't always like this. It wasn't that way in my school, but that's more related to its size and the type of school it was.
>
> Or was it all that different?! I don't really have any way of knowing, and here I am thinking about teaching without much of a clue. The classes I see in movies (like <u>Dangerous Minds</u>) seem very intimidating. Is it really like that, and could I survive, let alone accomplish anything?
>
> So let's see, I could interview a teacher, counselor, principal, or someone who's student-teaching. There are a couple of people in my neighborhood who teach. I could talk to one of them. But this all seems a little stale, really—not really the kind of first-hand observation that the assignment calls for. But would I even be allowed into a school, and even if I were, the kids would know that they're being watched. Like they say about observing a roomful of four-year-olds—it's no longer a roomful of four-year-olds when there's an adult observing them.
>
> I can't help wondering if I could get away with it—pretending to be a student in middle school.

This is typical freewriting—rambling, conversational, uncensored. If it were clearly organized and carefully edited, it would not be authentic. Beginning with several possibilities in mind, Millicent used freewriting to focus her thinking. As she freewrote, she considered talking with one of her neighbors who work in public schools. Millicent went on to consider the possibility of observing a middle-school class, but her freewrite seems to dismiss the idea as impractical. Later, however, when Millicent talked with a neighbor who works as a school counselor, she found him enthusiastic about the idea of actually posing as an eighth grader. The neighbor encouraged Millicent to talk with one of the teachers in his school, and he offered to make an appointment for her with Ms. Hobson. At this point, Millicent became more enthusiastic about her project, beginning to feel confident that she had found a topic that would not just fulfill the assignment but also engage her interests and those of her readers.

Collecting Data

Millicent called Ms. Hobson, who cheerfully agreed to talk with her about her project. By the end of their conversation a few days later, Ms. Hobson had persuaded Millicent that posing as an eighth grader, while challenging, was something she could carry off convincingly. Ms. Hobson emphasized the importance of accepting her students on their own terms, resisting any impulse to judge them overtly. Millicent anxiously awaited the following day, when she would put her acting skills to the test.

Knowing that her credibility would be compromised if any of the students saw her take notes, Millicent knew that she would have to rely on memory. She managed, however, to record some of her impressions right after lunch, while Ms. Hobson was reading to the class. Following are a few of those jottings:

Ms. Hobson
  —red blazer, khaki pants
  —short—5' 4" maybe
  —warm smile, soft but authoritative voice
Lunch
  —boys and girls separate, opposite sides of hall
  —girls' physical appearance—MAJOR concern
      hair, nails, designer clothes, makeup
      look older than they really are
  —Ashley
      pink turtleneck, pink lipstick, silver hoops
      Carrie & Laura: "members of the group," "circle of friends" since k
      "Do you have a boyfriend?" (Carrie)
  —Brad
      grapes
      "I can't stand him. He can be so obnoxious" (love/hate?)
      Or did she just need to remain the center of attention?

These jottings—supplemented by more copious notes recorded after the school day had ended—illustrate several kinds of note-taking:

- **Listing details.** Knowing that her essay would benefit from concrete descriptive details, Millicent took careful notes about everything she observed. Her first cluster of notes, for example, includes details about Ms. Hobson's appearance and mannerisms.

- **Recording events.** In a second cluster of notes, Millicent recorded her perceptions and interactions with students. Here, as elsewhere, she used a form of shorthand, omitting details that she knew she could fill in later.

• **Interviewing.** Although Millicent couldn't interview students, she managed to capture and record a few short quotations. Knowing that she had to get as much information and as many ideas into writing as quickly as possible, she relied on a few phrases that left a particularly strong impression (e.g., "members of the group," "circle of friends"). Nonetheless, she usually contented herself with conscientious efforts to paraphrase what people said. If, on the other hand, she had been granted the opportunity to quote anyone at length about specific facts, matters of opinion, historical context, or anything else demanding strict accuracy, thoroughness, and objectivity, Millicent would not have been justified in taking this approach. As it is, she used quotations sparingly, only when a speaker's words were memorable and more telling than a paraphrase might have been.

• **Analysis and interpretation.** At several points during her visit, Millicent formed interpretations of what she was observing. At one point she wrote, "Or did she just need to remain the center of attention?" Observations like these are often the most valuable part of note-taking, since they highlight what you have learned. They also may help you find a focus for your paper.

Outlining

Good notes furnish raw material for your paper, but at this stage that material is very raw. Later, when you compose a draft, you must *select* which parts to use (good notes typically contain two or three times as much material as the writer ultimately includes) and decide how to *organize* them. For some writers, selecting and organizing lead to an **outline.** However, since writing does not consist of separate, distinct "steps" in a sequence, and since many decisions about selecting and organizing are best made while composing a draft, few writers try to produce a detailed outline at this point. Some, however, may sketch a brief, informal outline before drafting—if only to arrive at a very general notion about how to select and organize material. Regardless of whether you adopt this approach, you should feel free, as you compose, to alter organizational plans whenever you encounter new ideas or recognize a better way to structure your emerging draft. Millicent Lambert drew up this brief outline before beginning her first draft:

> Visiting Middle School
> Preliminary Meeting with Ms. Hobson
>   My purposes/aims
>   Her enthusiasm and encouragement
>   Her concerns/advice
> Morning
>   Anxieties
>   First impressions
>   Reading assignment
>   Noisiness and rowdy behavior

Lunch
    Ashley and her group
    Love/hate relationships between boys and girls
    Brad and the Queen Bee
Afternoon
    Story about "revenge"
    Group discussion about being proud of yourself
Unmasking

This outline helped Millicent get started on a first draft—a valuable impetus. But she was not a slave to it, and as you will see, she had already refined it when she wrote the draft reprinted on pages 27–33.

Composing a First Draft

If you have explored a topic in your mind and on paper through prewriting and have taken good notes, you have a head start. You are now ready to begin a first draft. As you compose this draft, keep your prewriting plans in mind, but remain flexible. Since you are still discovering ideas in this preliminary version, try not to worry about spelling, punctuation, or usage. The time to make these corrections comes later, when you edit a revised draft. Pausing at this stage to check punctuation or spelling is counterproductive because it often interrupts composing. Unlike freewriting, however, a first draft should be arranged in paragraphs, and the ideas should be supported with examples, reasons, or illustrations.

Millicent polished her draft and brought the revision to class. Her instructor paired students and asked them to respond to each other's drafts following detailed guidelines.

| **Peer Review** | **GUIDELINES** |

Read your partner's draft from beginning to end as you might read an article in a magazine or newspaper—to understand what the writer has to say, engaging with ideas and information presented. Don't look for problems in content, organization, or usage. After this first reading, describe in one or two sentences the draft's impact on you as a reader—what it makes you think about, how it makes you feel, what questions it raises. Then briefly state the writer's purpose as you see it—how you think she or he wants to influence readers. If you recognize some general way that the draft's organization or content doesn't suit that purpose, call attention to it constructively. The important thing is to offer helpful, supportive comments without being insincere or patronizing. After this initial response, reread analytically, examining content and organization. Comment briefly in the margins on whatever arouses your interest or attention. Often, the most useful comments point to details that arouse questions or cause confusion. Consider in particular how various parts of the paper advance or digress from what you consider to be the author's purpose. When both you and your partner are finished, return the drafts, read each other's review, and discuss both for as long as necessary.

As you read Millicent's draft on the following pages, notice her classmate's brief marginal notes and the longer comment written at the end.

Lambert 1

Millicent Lambert

15 March 2005

Ms. Kate Tully

Glad to Call Them Friends

As I walked down the halls wearing my college
sweatshirt and wind pants, I heard the bell ring. It was my
first day of class and I was late. Would all the students
be seated in rows, quietly listening to the teacher, as I
entered the classroom for the first time? I had no idea how
I would be accepted among these students. Here I was, a
twenty-year-old college sophomore going back to figure out
what it's like to be an eighth grader. Have times changed?
Are the kids just like they used to be? I was scared as I
opened the door to Ms. Hobson's classroom. My heart was
pounding and my palms were sweaty; I was about to see what
it's like to be an eighth grader in the twenty-first
century.

As I took a seat near the back of the room, Ms. Hobson
was standing at the chalkboard, wearing a red blazer and
khaki pants; she was a small woman standing about five
feet, four inches, whose smile seemed heart-warming and
compassionate. Introducing me to the class, she said,
"Students, this is Millicent. She just recently moved to
town, so let's make her feel welcome as she adjusts to her

Your opening engages my interest.

It sounds like she introduced you as a member of the class. I'm confused.

Lambert 2

new surroundings." After this introduction, the class
carried on with their reading assignment, and I went
outside for a moment to talk with the teacher. Presumably,

Do you really believe this?

whenever the teacher leaves the room, students are expected
to carry on with their work without engaging in any
horseplay. But this was a classroom full of hyperactive
teenagers whose attention was hard to hold for five minutes
under the best of circumstances, let alone when the teacher
was outside the room. The talking and giggling started
almost immediately, clearly audible in the hallway where we
were standing.

I had met Ms. Hobson the previous day, when I
discussed with her the purposes of my observation. She had
told me that her students were hard to open up to and that
masquerading as an eighth grader wouldn't be easy. The truth
was that I wasn't really sure how to interact with these
students--how I should talk with them or whether they would
even want to talk with me. At that moment, I wanted to run

Oh, now I get it. Up till now I wasn't sure why you were attending the class.

down the hall and give up on the idea of going back to
eighth grade, but I had a paper to write, and that was an
assignment that required primary research.

By the time the bell had sounded for lunch, I was
anxious to talk with someone. The students gathered their
lunchboxes and made their way slowly to the cafeteria, the

Lambert 3

girls on one side of the hall, the boys on the other. They
were at that pivotal stage of love-hate relationships. It
was obvious that physical appearance was a preoccupation
for most of the girls, and they all seemed older than
their actual age.

How so?

Ashley, a cute girl in a light pink turtleneck, silver
hoop earrings, and soft pink lipstick, offered a friendly
smile. Walking with three other girls, she reminded me of
my friends in middle school. I remembered our lunchroom
conversations about boys and ways of using makeup to hide
our imperfect complexions. I began to feel more comfortable,
realizing that no matter how much time had passed, eighth
graders are fundamentally the same. Sensing my nervousness,
Ashley invited me to join her and the others. I was eager
to know them, but I also worried about how much they would
want to find out about me. Could I pull off this
undercover act without being detected?

"How long have you been friends?" I asked casually.

"We've known each other since kindergarten. Laura
transferred in last year, but now she's a member of the
group."

Dialogue is a nice change of pace here.

"A member?"

"Yes," Ashley explained, "part of our circle of
friends."

Lambert 4

All four of the girls acted as though they were best friends. Carrie, another member of the group, turned to me and asked, "So do you have a boyfriend?"

I was taken aback. I'd just met these girls, and the first thing any of them wanted to know was whether I had a boyfriend! Unsure of what to say and wanting to avoid complications, I responded, "Well, actually no, I'm not seeing anyone right now."

"Oh really," Laura said archly, and then all four girls started laughing.

Confused and embarrassed, I asked whether all of them had boyfriends. They responded almost in unison, "Of course we do." My first unspoken thought was, "Well excuse me for asking!"

My thoughts were interrupted by some boys at an adjoining table who had begun throwing grapes in our direction. Just as I turned to look, one of them, named Brad, stood up and aimed directly at me. I was so startled when the grape hit my shoulder, that I picked it up and threw it right back at him. Although this gesture of defiance aroused a good bit of laughter, one of the girls at my table was evidently annoyed by it. At first, I thought she was embarrassed by the spectacle, but it quickly became clear that she was use_ to being the center of attention and resented this intrusion. "I just can't stand

Lambert 5

Brad; he can be so obnoxious," she announced, as if no one recognized that they secretly liked each other. Maybe no one else did.

After lunch, we all went back to class, and Ms. Hobson began reading us a story from the literature textbook. Many of the students were paying no attention to it at all. When the whispering and laughter got too loud to ignore, Ms. Hobson stopped abruptly and asked what was so funny. Though they were embarrassed momentarily, it wasn't long before the disruptions started back up again.

As soon as she'd finished reading, Ms. Hobson tried to initiate a discussion of the theme of revenge in the story. "Who should you try to get revenge on?"

A boy near the back of the room blurted out, "I get revenge on the people I hate." Coming from a thirteen-year-old, this sounded eery and foreboding, yet I sensed that it was a self-dramatizing expression of transitory anger.

Ms. Hobson went on: "The only people you should try to get revenge on are the ones who have done good for you." Her point was that whenever a person does something to help you, you should return the favor. Trying to get even with someone who has hurt you is pointless, since you end up hurting yourself.

By now it was 2:15, and one assignment was left for the day. We arranged our desks in a semicircle in

order to face each other. I sat between two boys who at
first seemed quiet and passive. But as soon as the teacher
turned, the boy on my left threw a paper airplane across
the room. Hearing laughter in the background, Ms. Hobson
said, "Whatever you're doing needs to stop before I turn
around." She then introduced a topic for discussion,
"When you think of yourself, what makes you proud?"

I was very curious to know how some of the students
would respond to this topic, but for the first minute or so
the room was completely silent. Finally, one of the girls
seated near the middle of the semicircle raised her hand and
said, "I'm proud that I'm a good cheerleader." Suddenly,
everyone in the room wanted to speak. "I'm proud to be on
the basketball team"; "I'm proud because I make good grades."
One member of the class turned to me and asked what made me
proud. I wasn't sure what to say! So I sat there for a second
before finally saying, "I'm proud because I'm a good friend."

As the conversation continued, I found myself wanting
to reveal my true identity. With ten minutes left before the
announcements would come over the intercom, Ms. Hobson
turned to the class and said, "Students, Millicent has
something to tell you."

The class became very quiet as I walked up to the
podium at the front of the room. I began, "Today has been a
really amazing. It was my first day here at this new school,

Lambert 7

and you've made me feel welcome. I was nervous about coming today, but for different reasons than you may think. The truth is that I'm a twenty-year-old college student who wanted to see what it would be like to be in eighth grade again." The class started laughing in amazement. They weren't angry with me for tricking them; they loved the idea that I wanted to come back to the eighth grade.

I stayed around after the bell to answer many questions. Students wanted to know what college is like and what kinds of experiences I'd had in high school. It was exciting because I felt that I was really connecting with the students, probably because I'd been an eighth grader and knew where they were coming from.

I learned a lot from my observations. I found out that eighth-grade students are not very different from what they were when I was their age. They still face the same issues as they try to find a place to fit in. Their friendships are more important to them than anything else, and they view teachers as respected authority figures.

I'm not seeing respect for teachers. Omit this?

Millicent,

What a great idea for a topic and what a lot of effort you've put into making it work! I can't get over how you actually fooled the students.

If I had to name one thing that leaves me a little confused at the end of your paper, I guess it would be your attitudes about the eighth graders. At first, you seem put off by their rowdiness in class, and although I suppose their behavior may be disrespectful—if not disruptive—it doesn't really surprise me. Neither does the cliquishness of the girls, nor their fixation on boys and boyfriends. (Is that maybe because I have two younger sisters?) But I get the sense that some of this surprises you, maybe even bothers you at first. I know it's been six or seven years since you were in eighth grade, but is it really that long? What about your experience as an eighth grader was different? your personality? your parents' expectations? the type of school you attended?

So, when I get to the end of the paper, I'm not prepared for the conclusions you reach. When you say that the eighth graders are not very different from what you were at their age, I'm surprised. Can you tell me more about some of the issues that affect them as they try to fit in? Do they really view teachers as authority figures, as you say they do in your last paragraph? I'm not really seeing that in your paper.

At a more specific level, I like the way you open with your anxieties about meeting the class and pulling off the hoax. I think it would have been less effective to start out by telling what you wanted to learn and how you'd planned out your visit with the teacher a day before. But it took a while for me to catch on to what was happening. I wondered whether you were student teaching or just coming in as a normal observer. I think you might want to get this out in the open sooner—in the first couple of sentences if possible. It might create some suspense. Also, can you provide a better sense of what you hoped to accomplish beyond carrying out a class assignment? Are you considering a career in teaching? Are you just curious about whether things have changed? Are you wondering how it might have felt to go to a middle school very different from the one you attended?

Don't get me wrong, this is the paper I wish I'd written! I really would look forward to reading your revision of it if that's OK with you.

Peer Review

As you can see by comparing Millicent's editing draft with her final paper, she benefited from the careful **peer review** of her classmate Kevin. Most experienced writers are eager, even greedy, for this kind of feedback. By the time you complete a draft for others to read, you should have read it and reread it so often that you can no longer view it objectively. A fellow student can help you see this draft through her or his eyes, enabling you to gain a fresh perception of it.

A peer reviewer's principal task is to give you a sense of how a detached reader might respond to your draft. When you read and comment on another person's writing, you should not think of yourself as a teacher or judge. Instead, be yourself and respond as honestly and helpfully as you can. Notice several important features of Kevin's response to Millicent's paper:

- **Holistic response.** The longest comment is a final *holistic* response, reflecting on the entire draft—the writer's intentions and how the draft makes an impact on one reader—rather than addressing isolated details. Kevin provides, in a few sentences, two indispensable kinds of feedback: telling the writer, truthfully but tactfully, what took place in his mind as he read the draft ("When I get to the end of the paper, I'm not prepared for the conclusions you reach") and suggesting only one or two possibilities for revision (e.g., "Can you provide a better sense of what you hoped to accomplish beyond carrying out a class assignment?").

- **Respect for the writer's ownership.** Kevin's comments are tentative, not directive. When he thinks a particular revision may be needed, he asks questions rather than dictates how to change the draft (e.g., "Do you really believe this?").

- **Attention to positive features.** Kevin notes the best features of the text without being insincere or patronizing. He is supportive ("Your opening engages my interest") while letting Millicent know where he has difficulties ("It sounds like she introduced you as a member of the class. I'm confused").

- **Little concern for mechanical errors.** The respondent gives scant attention to lapses in style or mechanics. Occasionally, a reviewer will point out an error that may escape the writer's attention (e.g., *use to*, a misspelling that appears twice in the draft), but that is far less relevant now than providing other kinds of help. (Proofreading for awkward sentences and mechanical correctness is important later, when you can enlist the assistance of an alert editor.)

- **Comments fall into several categories:** *proposals for revision* (e.g., "Maybe omit this?"), *responses to the writer's strategies* (e.g., "Dialogue is a nice change of pace here"), *descriptions of the reader's response* (e.g., "Oh, now I get it. Up till now I wasn't sure why you were attending the class"), and *requests for clarification or amplification* (e.g., "How so?"). Although each type of comment can be helpful, those near the end of the list tend to be more useful in "opening up" a draft by allowing the writer to remain in charge of revising his own draft.

By far the most useful of Kevin's comments were those that encouraged Millicent to reconsider her overall aims:

> Can you provide a better sense of what you hoped to accomplish beyond carrying out a class assignment? Are you considering a career in teaching? Are you just curious about whether things have changed? Are you wondering how it might have felt to go to a middle school very different from the one you attended?

These comments helped resolve a dilemma revealed in the final paragraph of Millicent's draft. When she began thinking about her topic, Millicent had focused on meeting the demands of an assignment. And although she had clarified her notions of audience and purpose before writing a draft, her final paragraph revealed uncertainties about what to conclude from her observations. Kevin, viewing Millicent's draft from a more detached perspective, recognized these uncertainties and offered several suggestions. By expressing curiosity about her conclusions, Kevin encouraged Millicent to consider various possibilities. Consequently, her final draft includes an expanded conclusion that more clearly addresses the purposes of her project.

Revision, however, involved more than just adding new material at the end of a first draft. Millicent now reconsidered her entire paper in light of her clarified intentions. In the third paragraph of her revision, for example, she introduces the idea that her experience as a middle-school student in a small private school may influence her perspective. Another important change appears in the following paragraph, which is much more specific about the writer's aims.

Revising

Careful, deliberate revision distinguishes accomplished writers from novices. Experienced writers devote time to rereading, changing words, rearranging sentences and paragraphs, adding new material, and rewriting. Some drafts require more revision than others.

A few things about revision hold true for almost any successful writer. First, you need feedback from an alert, objective respondent. You yourself may be that respondent, provided that you can step back and view your work as a detached reader. After you have completed a draft, let it sit (for a few days if possible, but at least overnight) so you can see it from a fresh perspective. Many writers like to read their work aloud, either for themselves or for someone else. Some discover ideas as they recopy or retype what they have written, since this allows them to read their work slowly and attentively. Frequently, however, the most valuable help comes from a trusted friend or classmate who reads your draft and offers suggestions. This is the kind of help Millicent Lambert received from her classmate Kevin during a peer-review session.

Since writers are not all alike, they adopt different strategies for revision. Some revise all at once. They write a draft all the way through and then compose a revised draft, followed by a third, and so on. Others engage in ongoing revision, altering one sentence or paragraph again and again before moving on to the next. Millicent Lambert falls somewhere in between. She composed her drafts on a word processor and made frequent changes as she proceeded. But she printed out complete drafts several times and made changes with a pencil before entering them into her word processor. Here is a revision of the second paragraph of her preliminary draft:

As I took a seat near the back of the room, Ms. Hobson was standing at the chalkboard, wearing a red blazer and khaki pants; she was a small woman, ~~standing~~ about five feet, four inches, whose smile seemed heart-warming and compassionate. Introducing me to the class, she said, "Students, this is Millicent. She's just ~~recently~~ moved ~~to town~~ here, so let's make her feel welcome as she adjusts to her new surroundings." After this introduction, the class carried on with their reading assignment, and I went outside for a moment to talk with the teacher. ¶ In the small Christian academy that I attended ~~Presumably, whenever the teacher leaves the room~~, students ~~are~~ were expected to carry on with their work without engaging in any horseplay, even when the teacher wasn't present. But, in this ~~was a class~~ room full of hyperactive teenagers, ~~whose attention was hard to hold for five minutes under the best of circumstances, let alone when the teacher was outside the room.~~ The talking and giggling started almost immediately, clearly

As you can see by comparing Millicent's two drafts, this type of rephrasing was only part of her revision process. She also changed the title of her paper, while adding a few details elsewhere (like her description of the girls standing in the hallway outside the cafeteria).

Writers often reassess their basic goals during revision. They consider the readers they are addressing, how they want those readers to respond, and how they can provide more and better evidence to support their aims. Revision means *seeing again*, and often the best way to accomplish this is to look at your concluding paragraphs to see whether they reflect the same purpose as earlier parts of your draft. Writers often discover or revise their purpose as they compose a first draft, and it is not unusual for the last parts of that draft to reflect an emerging aim that the opening paragraphs do not anticipate. This was the case for Millicent.

Before completing a final draft, Millicent sketched another brief outline—one that reflects the aims of that draft:

Eighth Grade Revisited

Introduction
    Anxiety
    Description of Ms. Hobson
    First impression of the class
The aims of my observation
Descriptions of students
    Girls: Ashley and her circle
    Boys: Brad and the "Queen Bee"
Afternoon
    Story about revenge
    Class discussion about pride
Revealing my true identity
    Students' responses
My conclusions
    Insecurity of adolescents
    Importance of friends
    Peer pressure

Editing and Proofreading

Finally, you need to edit and proofread your revised draft. This involves deleting imprecise or inappropriate words and phrases as well as carefully checking punctuation and spelling. After editing and proofreading, you are ready to print another copy of your paper and give it a final review for errors. Though the spell-check feature of your word-processing program identifies many mistakes, it overlooks others (e.g., word substitutions like *then* used for *than*). Therefore, you should give your paper a careful proofreading as well.

Developing Your Own Writing Routines

Writing has been compared to swimming, woodworking, and other such skills. Basically, this comparison is valid and reassuring; college students *can* indeed develop their writing abilities to the point of proficiency. However, writing differs from many other skills—long division, for instance—in that it involves very few dependable rules, all of which are mastered at an early age (e.g., beginning every declarative sentence with a capital letter and closing it with a period). Well-meaning teachers sometimes hope to reduce writing to a set of rules or admonitions such as "Never open a sentence with a conjunction" or "Never use the words *you* and *I* in an essay." However, most experienced writers have found these dictates unreliable (frequently disregarding those just mentioned) because they have learned that writing is seldom systematic, orderly, or predictable. This is not to say that their approach is haphazard. Knowing that trial and error is inefficient, these writers rely on a repertoire of procedures, which may include brainstorming, mapping, freewriting, and other techniques described in earlier parts of this chapter.

Throughout this book you will encounter guidelines for addressing various writing tasks. Keep in mind that these guidelines do not work in the same predictable way for every individual. They will not produce a single best response to a given assignment. They should, however, encourage you to experiment with approaches that experienced writers have used to get past the moments of writer's block that everyone encounters. To discover which ones can help you under which circumstances, engage in as many as possible, merely going through the motions at first if necessary. Over time, you may come to rely on a few standbys that minimize anxieties brought on by the interplay of the complex skills involved in writing for academic purposes.

Writing an Essay That Incorporates Primary Research   **GUIDELINES**

Prewriting

1. Read the writing prompt carefully and ask your instructor to explain anything that isn't clear.

2. Use brainstorming, mapping, freewriting, or all three to discover a suitable topic and to clarify the purpose of your essay.

Collecting Data

1. Having chosen an appropriate topic—a person, institution, or location to profile—reserve enough time to observe it thoroughly and to reflect on what you have observed.

2. Employ as many techniques for collecting data—listing details, recording events, interviewing, analyzing and interpreting information—as your topic permits.

Composing a Preliminary Draft

1. Consider starting with an informal scratch outline.

2. Try not to perfect your preliminary draft as you compose. Strive for fluency rather than correctness; get your ideas down as quickly as you can without focusing on spelling, punctuation, or usage.

Profiting from Peer Review

1. Before submitting your draft for peer review, read over it carefully and try to remedy any obvious problems with organization or clarity. If necessary, compose a second draft incorporating necessary changes.

2. Discuss your peer reviewer's response to your draft. In particular, make sure that each of you has a clear understanding of the purpose of your essay.

Revising, Editing, and Proofreading Your Essay

1. Take into account the response of peer reviewer(s), but keep in mind that you ultimately own the essay.

2. Adopt a revision strategy that you can be comfortable with–"all-at-once" revision, "ongoing" revision, or something in between.

3. Adopting the stance of a critical reader, look for lapses in clarity and concision.

4. Don't place unqualified trust in word-processing features such as grammar or spell checks.

 READING

Reading demands active participation. Without the alert engagement of a reader, words on a page have no meaning. Only you can bring them to life. Your ability to interpret words, your knowledge of how sentences and paragraphs are put together, your past experiences with reading and with life, your current mood—all these work together to make your reading of an essay, a poem, or even a recipe different from those of other readers.

Reading Habits and Strategies

No one else reads exactly as you do. In some ways, reading is a very personal activity. No matter what you read—even a textbook like this one—it is unlikely that anyone else will interpret it exactly as you do. Even among classmates with similar backgrounds, responses are not often the same. Since no one is an exact duplicate of anyone else, each person's reading experience is unique. Furthermore, even the same reader may experience the same text very differently on separate occasions.

In the following passage, Wendy Lesser, editor of the literary journal *Threepenny Review*, illustrates this point in a description of her reading habits:

> Nothing demonstrates how personal reading is more clearly than rereading does. The first time you read a book, you might imagine that what you are getting out of it is precisely what the author put into it. And you would be right, at least in part. There is some element of every aesthetic experience, every *human* experience, that is generalizable and communicable and belongs to all of us. If this were not true, art would be pointless. The common ground of our response is terrifically important. But there is also the individual response, and that too is important. I get annoyed at literary theorists who try to make us choose one over the other, as if *either* reading is an objective experience, providing everyone with access to the author's intentions, *or* it is a subjective experience, revealing to us only the thoughts in our own minds. Why? Why must it be one or the other, when every sensible piece of evidence indicates that it is both?
>
> Rereading is certainly both, as I was to discover. You cannot reread a book . . . without perceiving it as, among other things, a mirror. Wherever you look in that novel or poem or essay, you will find a little reflected face peering out at you—the face of . . . the original reader, the person you were when you first read the book. So the material that wells up out of this rereading feels very private, very specific to you. But as you engage in this rereading, you can sense that there are at least two readers, the older one and the younger one. You know there are two of you because you can feel them responding differently to the book. Differently, but not entirely differently: there is a core of experience shared by your two selves (perhaps there are even more than two, if you include all the people you were in the years between the two readings). And this awareness of the separate readers within you makes you appreciate the essential constancy of the literary work, even in the face of your own alterations over time, so that you begin to realize how all the different readings by different people might nonetheless have a great deal in common.

You may note some similarities between Lesser's characterization of reading and Nancy Sommers's description of writing (page 5). Both Lesser and Sommers examine literate acts that engage both individual creativity and interaction with others. Both talk about mediating between free associations of recollected experience and the completion of a task (publishing an essay or getting to the end of a story). Most importantly, though, both Lesser and Sommers stress the *active* nature of reading and writing: readers do much more than retrieve information, and writers do not simply transcribe facts and ideas from useful sources.

Interpreting Texts

We have seen that writing practices differ among individuals and vary according to purpose and audience. The same is true of reading; there is no single best way to read. When we encounter the short, precise sentences in a set of directions, we want to find out how to do something quickly and efficiently, like programming a VCR. When we pick up a poem or a short story, however, we have other aims and expectations. Instead of looking for information or instruction, we want to derive pleasure from the way words and images are used, to engage with sympathetic characters, or to enjoy a suspenseful plot. To participate fully and actively in this type of reading, we must connect our values and experiences with an imaginative text.

Audience

What you get out of reading depends on what you bring into it. For example, if you bring an extensive background in music to the following passage, you will get much more from it than the average reader:

Passage written for an audience of musical experts

> Although Schoenberg sometimes dreamed of serialism as a reassertion of German musical hegemony, he more commonly thought of it as a purely formalistic ordering device, and most American serialists share that view. So [did] the Soviets, with their crude denunciations of "formalism." But just as with psychoanalysis, dismissed by its opponents as a web of metaphors conditioned by time and place, serialism can be considered narrowly Viennese and, by now, dated. And not just dated and extraneous to an American sensibility, but out of fashion.
>
> —John Rockwell, *All-American Music*

Even if all the names and terminology were explained, most readers would still find this passage obscure. Actually, though, its level of difficulty depends on the reader. To thousands of music experts, the meaning is clear, but to those who do not bring musical expertise to the reading, not much emerges. Evidently, the passage is aimed at a small, informed **audience** of readers. If you were reporting on musical trends for a wider audience, you would not quote this passage from John Rockwell's book, at least not without clarification.

Consider now another passage that addresses a somewhat wider audience, readers of the *Chronicle of Higher Education,* most of whom are university professors and administrators with backgrounds in a variety of academic fields:

Passage written for a highly educated audience without musical expertise

> About three years ago, I tried an experiment with a group of scholars and artists. . . . "As you know," I said, "I write about classical music. Suppose I named the main styles in musical composition since serialism. Would any of you understand what I was talking about?" "No," said everybody, and I can't say I was surprised.
>
> Something odd has happened to classical music. Somehow, it—and most notably its advanced, contemporary wing—has unhitched itself from the wider world of art and culture. Readers of the *Chronicle* might know about contemporary painting, or films or novels, or (the younger readers, anyway) ambient music or alternative rock. But I'd be surprised if they were familiar with current classical composers. . . .
>
> Serial music—conventionally thought to be the high-water mark of musical modernism—may have been, at least in America, both a cause and a symptom of this breach. It was pioneered in Europe in the 1920s, by Arnold Schoenberg, the composer who (very loosely speaking) did for music what abstract painters did for painting, and who is defended in a recent book, *Arnold Schoenberg's Journey* . . . , by Allen Shawn. Just as abstract painters gave up painting faces, objects, and scenes, Schoenberg began by writing music without familiar chords and melodies. More crucially, he gave up repetition and regular rhythms, and instead wrote complex pieces with unexpected contours and an irregular pace.
>
> —Greg Sandow, "Serialism as a Museum Piece"

The author of this passage, who also writes for the *Wall Street Journal* and *Village Voice,* starts by reassuring readers that many well-educated people don't know much about recent classical music. Then, before trying to explain serialism, he provides some historical context and draws an analogy to modern painting, which probably is more familiar to most educated adults. Unlike John Rockwell, who addresses a musically sophisticated audience, Greg Sandow targets readers who know less about music in particular, but are generally conversant with history and the arts.

Many other writers adapt language and content to a still wider audience of readers with varied backgrounds. For example, the following passage describes a collection of unconventional musical instruments designed and built by visionary composer Harry Partch. The author of the passage, Allan Ulrich, is the classical music and dance critic for the *San Francisco Examiner,* a daily newspaper with a large circulation. Ulrich is reviewing an exhibition of Partch's work for readers of the *Examiner's* Sunday supplement:

> There are the visionaries and then there are the cranks. Somewhere in that wispy zone of shadow separating the two, in that spiritual limbo for which we lack a precise word, posterity has deposited Harry Partch (1901–74)—composer, instrument builder, philosopher, multiculturalist, great California-born creative maverick.
>
> The twenty-five instruments devised and constructed by Partch . . . reflect his obsession with the ancients, not merely in their names—Kithara I and Kithara II, Chromelodeon—but in his belief that they should affect an area beyond human consciousness. The enormous Marimba Eroica, individually hung Sitka spruce blocks laid over cave-like resonators the size of the piano, emits four low tones, the lowest of which is not audible to the human ear. That you can also feel Partch's music has no doubt endeared him to a younger generation; vibes and all that. . . .
>
> What the "Sounds like Art" Festival should accomplish is to place Partch in some kind of context. He may have been one of the greatest American individualists; still, he has spawned a generation of composer-instrument makers who feel free to journey down their own paths. The Bay Area's Beth Custer and Matt Heckert, Los Angeles' Marina Rosenfeld and the German-born, Seattle-based artist who goes by the sole name of Trimpin, will all add their distinctive constructions to this project.
>
> Here, perhaps, is where the Harry Partch legacy truly resides. Idiosyncrasy may have ventured, ever so timorously, into the mainstream of American music, but the current remains as unpredictable as ever.
>
> —Allan Ulrich, "American Visionary"

Passage written for a general audience

Even readers without much musical knowledge or interest can derive something from this passage. Although Ulrich introduces information unfamiliar to most of us, he uses informal language and relies on concepts (e.g., vibes) that most adults can readily understand.

Tacit Knowledge

Interpretation is influenced by more than just the vocabulary of a particular text, the length of its sentences, or the educational credentials of the reader. It also depends on the amount of **tacit knowledge** that writers and readers share—that is, how much a writer can safely assume that readers understand without explanation.

For example, almost any reader knows what a DVD is without a parenthetical decoding of the abbreviation. On the other hand, few people other than public-school teachers and administrators in North Carolina can be expected to know that an LEA is a local educational agency or school district. However, educators who frequently use the term LEA in their professional discourse would be distracted by a memo that continually refers to "local educational agencies," just as most newspaper readers would be distracted by a column that repeatedly refers to "digital video discs."

Context

Interpretation is also affected by context. Removed from the sports page of a newspaper in the Southeast, the headline "Yellow Jackets Overcome by Green Wave" is ambiguous at best. Similarly, the headline "High Budget Hopes Give Footsie a Fillip" may seem clear to a reader of the financial pages of the London *Daily Mail,* but outside that context, it would perplex most educated Americans, including many experienced investors.

Successful reading, then, depends not only on knowledge and skill, but also on the reader's familiarity with context and the writer's ability to assess the needs and expectations of a particular audience. It depends on what the writer and the reader bring to a text. Good readers are alert and flexible. For them, reading is as creative a process as writing—and as varied.

Efferent and Aesthetic Approaches to Reading

The late Louise Rosenblatt, a pioneer in the study of reading processes, draws a distinction between *efferent reading* and *aesthetic reading*. When readers need information, they adopt an efferent stance: they just try to grasp what a text is saying. When they adopt an aesthetic stance, readers pursue unique personal engagement with a text (usually a work of literature). When the first edition of this book appeared, in 1985, many English teachers assumed that nearly all students enter college already proficient at efferent reading. As a result, reading assignments in first-year English courses were often confined to literary texts. Reading, to the extent that it was taught at all, involved mastery of the aesthetic stance described in the final paragraph of the excerpt from Wendy Lesser's essay (page 41).

As teachers and textbook authors, we remain skeptical of these assumptions. Therefore, in Chapter 2, as well as in various other parts of this book, we explain and illustrate strategies that facilitate efferent reading. Nevertheless, as enthusiastic, life-long readers of literature, we do not discount the value of aesthetic reading in the daily lives of educated adults. Nor do we approach these two types of reading as totally distinct, let alone incompatible. In fact, your response to most of the selections in this book will be enriched by your ability to move smoothly and productively between both types of reading.

Problems arise when students restrict themselves to one type of reading or adopt a stance unsuited to the situation at hand. When you read a textbook to acquire information, for example, you overlook style, tone, and figurative language.

If a friend accidentally swallowed a poison, you would search the back of the bottle for an antidote and read rapidly, perhaps aloud: "Do not induce vomiting. Have the victim drink two quarts of fresh water." Needless to say, you would not comment to the victim about the author's prose style: "Hey, Phil, listen to these short, precise sentences!" Under these circumstances you want only information.

At the opposite extreme, if you were asked to respond to the following poem, a haiku by Bashō, a seventeenth-century Japanese poet, gathering information would not be your aim:

> *The ancient lagoon*
> *A frog jumps*
> *The splash of the water.*

These lines invite you to respond to images. You do not read them to increase your knowledge of amphibian behavior or marine ecology. And though experienced readers of poetry may respond differently than novices, each reader's aesthetic response is personal and unique. One reader may recall a childhood experience. Another may simply derive a sense of peace and beauty. A third reader, familiar with Zen Buddhism, may have a more philosophical response. This reader may note a contrast between the poem's first line (an image of eternal stillness) and the second (a momentary action), finding in the last line, where the two contrasting images merge, an insight into timeless truth. Someone unused to reading such an open-ended text may find it puzzling and ultimately useless.

Interpreting Texts   **EXERCISE**

To test the validity of what we have said about interpretation, see how your responses to two very different passages compare with those of other readers. Reread the passage about Harry Partch on page 43 and state in a sentence or two what you consider its main idea to be.

Now read the following haiku by another Japanese poet, Buson, and write an equally brief interpretation of it:

> *On the bell of the temple*
> *rests a butterfly,*
> *asleep.*

Express your personal response to the poem, even if you feel it is not very insightful. (Keep in mind that a single "correct" interpretation of such a poem probably does not exist.)

Compare your responses with those of classmates. Do they differ? Is there more agreement about interpreting the prose passage as opposed to the poem? How do you account for any differences? Even with the passage about Harry Partch, is there room for difference?

Responding to Reading

Most of the reading you will do in this book lies somewhere between the objective prose of how-to instructions and the subjective language of poetry. It requires active, alert participation. When you conduct research, you cannot read a source without being critically aware of both the information it presents and the author's attitude, purpose, and reliability.

In addition to exercises that engage writing, reading, and research, most chapters in this book conclude with several longer texts, followed by questions about ideas and interpretations that the readings may arouse. Deliberate response to these texts demands care and persistence because, just as good writing involves revision, good reading entails rereading.

When you discuss the reading selections in this book, you will find that your responses often coincide with those of classmates, but there also will be legitimate differences. You may form interpretations that others do not share or understand, and readers often resist interpretations that diverge from their own. Nevertheless, this is inevitable; reading affirms both the connectedness of communities and the differences that distinguish us as individuals.

The best way to respond to reading is to write about it. Writing stretches our thoughts by encouraging us to connect one idea with another. And because it is visible, writing helps us see what we mean. It also helps us become clearer, more logical, and more concrete. As you learned earlier in this chapter, freewriting is a method of open-ended response that invites us to jot down whatever comes to mind through focused (or unfocused) thought. Freewritten responses to reading may evoke personal associations, observations about style, restatements of what the author is saying, or any other thought or feeling that comes to the tip of the pen.

EXERCISES | **Responding to Reading**

1. Each of the following short texts presents difficulties in interpretation for at least some readers. Read each one carefully, then freewrite about it for five minutes. Remember, freewriting is not bound by rules (other than writing steadily for a given period of time).

   a. This sign was posted in a clothing store:

      Kindly spare us the discomfort of refusing requests for refunds.

   b. These personal ads were published in a community newspaper:
      • M, 44, clean, sporty, original equipment, runs great, seeks F that needs a lift.
      • F, 28, black and glossy, seeks confidential WM, very giving, who's bound for whatever.
      • Mistress Marcy seeks playmate.
      • Ornery, self-sufficient, prof SWF, mid 40's, seeks man with integrity. If you're not honest, don't bother.

c. The following advertisement appeared in the "Help Wanted" section of the *Nassau Guardian*, a widely circulated daily newspaper in the Bahamas:

> The Firm Masterminds Historians, Scientists, Financiers, Philosophers, Senior Pastors, Bankers, Solicitors, Doctors (1998) Inc.
>
> Wisdom / Reversals / Expulsions / Nulls & voids available via discernments laws & sciences/disengagements laws & sciences to discern / Expel / Call out / Shutdown / Reverse / Null & void / Secret or suspected child molesters / incestors / False pastors / mistressings / Homosexuality / Wife beaters & spousal batterers etc. IF you can establish just cause which is Mandatory! We cleanse homes / Marriages / Businesses / Churches. Rates are $750 to $2,500 per hour.

d. Following is an entry from the *New York Times* column "Metropolitan Diary":

> On a trip to the post office in early December, I asked the clerk, a young Asian woman with a fairly heavy accent, what she had other than holiday stamps. She replied that she had flags, John Wayne, and Mozart.
>
> Surprised but delighted, I asked for two sheets of Mozart and paid my bill. She slipped the stamps into an envelope and slid them to my side of the window.
>
> On my way out, I decided to see if I could discern why the United States Postal Service had decided to honor the Austrian composer with a stamp.
>
> A peek in the envelope revealed that I had purchased two sheets of stamps dedicated to Moss Hart.

e. The following entries were posted on the Website starbucksgossip. typepad.com:

- You've gotta be out of your damned mind to tip at Starbucks. It's already near $4 a coffee. Lord forbid if I'm buying for my girlfriend. Maybe add a pastry. Now I'm at $11 for two coffees and a donut??? I'm supposed to tip on top of that? Hell NO!
- Starbucks is McDonald's in green—nothing more. People who work there don't DESERVE a tip. If you want to tip them, fluffy bunnies and good graces to you.
- I've been a Starbucks counter employee for two years. Perusing the entries in this debate, I note a degree of free-floating hostility that requires some corrective comment. If we as service employees "ask" for a tip by putting a tip jar out, in what way are we harming, harassing, or even annoying anyone? Obviously we are not doing any of those things; thus the anger directed by some of the above commenters must have its source elsewhere. I think I know what that is: the "upscale" lifestyle we purvey. Having traveled widely in Europe, I cannot help but note, by contrast, how instinctually resentful the average American is of anything—be it a person, a restaurant, or a product—that bespeaks deviation in any degree from the utilitarianism that dominates American commercial culture. Certain rarefied enclaves excepted (Manhattan's Upper East Side, for instance), American aesthetic values start and end with the middlebrow— that's where the customers are. A place like Starbucks—that tries for a kind of pseudo-bohemian elegance (and speaks in foreign tongues of "latte" and "grande," etc.)—inevitably confuses and disturbs the Average Man, threatening his faith in an equal entitlement to the trough. In short, this tipping

"controversy" is masking the true hidden battle of our times: Will we or will we not grow up?

2. Exchange freewrites in groups of four. Are there differences? If so, how can you explain them? Have one member of your group list the types of difficulty that these selections present—for example, ambiguities (perhaps intentional), assumptions about the tacit knowledge of readers, unfamiliar or unclear context.

Reading Response Groups

Thus far, we have presented reading as a process that engages individual, independent thought as well as literal understanding. Specifically, we have stressed the idea that readers often *create* meaning rather than passively *receive* it from a "determinate" text—one that supposedly elicits a single accurate interpretation that coincides with the author's intentions. In order to dispel the notion that reading amounts to little more than *retrieving* information and ideas that writers have *put* into their texts, we have emphasized the autonomy of individual readers—their privilege to interpret what they read.

Granted that autonomy, one might plausibly interpret the passage by Allan Ulrich on page 43 as a satirical jab at avant-garde music. To go a step further, another person might view it as a parody of museum reviews—a mischievous hoax at the expense of literal-minded readers. While most of us would consider that a peculiar response, a carefully selected group of like-minded readers might accept it as an inventive, possibly useful, interpretation—though one that the author probably did not anticipate. But most reasonable people will agree that there are limits. It is unlikely, for example, that any community of readers would entertain the possibility that Ulrich is denouncing avant-garde music as an elitist conspiracy launched by multinational corporations. Such an interpretation is too eccentric to be plausible.

The autonomy of individual readers, then, can be exaggerated. Reading, like writing, is not a completely solitary activity. It is, instead, a *social* process, and readers often benefit from the responses of peers just as Millicent Lambert did when she revised her essay.

The following transaction among three experienced readers demonstrates the collaboration of a **reading group**, two or more individuals who share, often in writing, their personal responses to a text. Although they vary in size, most groups consist of three to six members. Your instructor may place you in a reading group and assign specific tasks, often called **prompts**, for you and your partners to address. (On the other hand, students in the same class may create reading groups of their own, and collaboration is sometimes spontaneous and unfocused.)

The following assignment is designed to initiate discussion and collaborative response to a short magazine article. Take a moment now to read it, along with the article itself, which follows.

| **Freewriting Prompt** | **ASSIGNMENT** |

Read "A Short History of Love," an article from *Harper's*, a magazine of opinion concerned with political and cultural issues. (Before publication, the article was delivered as a paper at an academic conference cosponsored by the Columbia University Psychoanalytic Center and the Association for Psychiatric Medicine.) As you read, use your pencil to mark important or noteworthy ideas and to record any reactions or personal associations that come to mind. Keep your writing brief, using shorthand as much as possible, and try not to pause for more than a few seconds in perhaps three or four places at most. Then read the article again, this time looking more closely at how Lawrence Stone presents the history of romantic love and draws conclusions about it. After this second reading, freewrite for twenty minutes in response to the article's ideas. In particular, consider whether you agree with the author's suggestion that there is something dangerous or unhealthy in contemporary attitudes about love. Bring this freewriting to class next time, prepared to share it with other members of your reading group.

PRACTICE READING

A Short History of Love

Lawrence Stone

Historians and anthropologists are in general agreement that romantic love—that usually brief but intensely felt and all-consuming attraction toward another person—is culturally conditioned. Love has a history. It is common only in certain societies at certain times, or even in certain social groups within those societies, usually the elite, which have the leisure to cultivate such feelings. Scholars are, however, less certain whether romantic love is merely a culturally induced psychological overlay on top of the biological drive for sex, or whether it has biochemical roots that operate quite independently from the libido. Would anyone in fact "fall in love" if they had not read about it or heard it talked about? Did poetry invent love, or love poetry?

Some things can be said with certainty about the history of the phenomenon. The first is that cases of romantic love can be found in all times and places and have often been the subject of powerful poetic expression, from the Song of Solomon to Shakespeare. On the other hand, as anthropologists have discovered, neither social approbation nor the actual experience of romantic love is common to all societies. Second, historical evidence for romantic love before the age of printing is largely confined to elite groups, which of course does not mean that it may not have occurred lower on the social scale. As a socially approved cultural artifact, romantic love began in Europe in the southern French aristocratic courts of the twelfth century, and was made fashionable by a group of poets, the troubadours. In this case the culture dictated that it should occur between an unmarried male and a married woman, and that it either should go sexually unconsummated or should be adulterous.

By the sixteenth and seventeenth centuries, our evidence becomes quite extensive, thanks to the spread of literacy and the printing press. We now have love poems, such as Shakespeare's sonnets, love letters, and autobiographies by women concerned primarily with their love lives. The courts of Europe were evidently hotbeds of passionate intrigues and liaisons, some romantic, some sexual. The printing press also began to spread pornography to a wider public, thus stimulating the libido, while the plays of Shakespeare indicate that romantic love was a concept familiar to society at large, which composed his audience.

Whether this romantic love was approved of, however, is another question. We simply do not know how Shakespearean audiences reacted to *Romeo and Juliet*. Did they, like us (and as Shakespeare clearly intended), fully identify with the young lovers? Or, when they left the theater, did they continue to act like the Montague and Capulet parents, who were trying to stop these irresponsible adolescents from allowing an ephemeral and irrational passion to interfere with the serious business of politics and patronage?

What is certain is that every advice book, every medical treatise, every sermon and religious homily of the sixteenth and seventeenth centuries firmly rejected both romantic passion and lust as suitable bases for marriage. In the sixteenth century, marriage was thought to be best arranged by parents, who could be relied upon to choose socially and economically suitable partners. People believed that the sexual bond would automatically create the necessary harmony between the two strangers in order to maintain the stability of the new family unit. This assumption is not, it seems, unreasonable, since recent investigations in Japan have shown that there is no difference in the rate of divorce between couples whose marriages were arranged by their parents and couples whose marriages were made by individual choice based on romantic love.

In the eighteenth century, orthodox opinion about marriage began to shift from subordinating the individual will to the interests of the group, and from economic or political considerations, toward those of well-tried personal affection. The ideal marriage was one preceded by three to six months of intensive courting by a couple from families roughly equal in social status and economic wealth; that courtship, however, took place only with the prior consent of parents on both sides. But it was not until the Romantic movement and the rise of the novel, especially the pulp novel of the nineteenth century, that society accepted a new idea—that it is normal and indeed praiseworthy for young men and women to fall passionately in love, and that there must be something wrong with those who fail to have such an overwhelming experience sometime in late adolescence or early adulthood. Once this new idea was publicly accepted, the arrangement of marriage by parents came to be regarded as intolerable and immoral.

Today, the role of passionate attachments between adults is obscured by a new development: the saturation of the whole culture—through every medium of communication—with the belief that sexuality is the predominant and overriding human drive, a doctrine whose theoretical foundations were provided by Freud. In no past society known to me has sex been given so prominent a role in the culture at large, nor has sexual fulfillment been elevated to such preeminence in the list of human aspirations—in a vain attempt to relieve civilization of its discontents. We find it scarcely credible today that in most of Western Europe in the seventeenth century, in a society in which people usually married in their late twenties, a degree of chastity was practiced that kept the illegitimacy rate—without contraceptives—as low as two or three percent. Today, individualism is given such absolute priority in most Western societies that people are virtually free to act as they please, to sleep with whom they please, and to marry and divorce when and whom they please. The psychic (and, more recently, the physical) costs of such behavior are now becoming clear, however, and how long this situation will last is anybody's guess.

Here I should point out that the present-day family—I exclude the poor black family in America from this generalization—is not, as is generally supposed, disintegrating because of the very high divorce rate—up to fifty percent. It has to be remembered that the median duration of marriage today is almost exactly the same as it was a hundred years ago. Divorce, in short, now acts as a functional substitute for death: both are means of terminating marriage at a premature stage. The psychological effects on the survivor may well be very different, although in most cases the catastrophic economic consequences for women remain the same. But the point to be emphasized is that broken marriages, stepchildren, and single-parent households were as common in the past as they are today.

The most difficult historical problem regarding romantic love concerns its role among the propertyless poor. Since they were propertyless, their loves and marriages were of little concern to their kin, and they were therefore more or less free to choose their own mates. By the eighteenth century, and probably before, court records make it clear that the poor often married for love, combined with a confused set of motives including lust and the economic necessity to have a strong and healthy assistant to run the farm or the shop. It was generally expected that they would behave "lovingly" toward each other, but this often did not happen. In many a peasant marriage, the husband seems to have valued his cow more than his wife. Passionate attachments among the poor certainly occurred, but how often they took priority over material interests we may never know for certain.

Finally, we know that in the eighteenth century—unlike the seventeenth—at least half of all brides in England and America were pregnant on their wedding day. But this fact tells us more about sexual customs than about passionate attachments: sex began at the moment of engagement, and marriage in church came later, often triggered by the pregnancy. We also know that if a poor servant girl was impregnated by her master, which often happened, the latter usually had no trouble finding a poor man who would marry her, in return for payment of ten pounds or so. Not much passion there.

Passionate attachments between young people can and do happen in any society as a byproduct of biological sexual attraction, but the social acceptability of the emotion has varied enormously over time and class and space, determined primarily by cultural norms and property arrangements. We are in a unique position today in that our culture is dominated by romantic notions of passionate love as the only socially admissible reason for marriage; sexual fulfillment is accepted as the dominant human drive and a natural right for both sexes; and contraception is normal and efficient. Behind all this lies a frenetic individualism, a restless search for a sexual and emotional ideal in human relationships, and a demand for instant ego gratification.

Most of this is new and unique to our culture. It is, therefore, quite impossible to assume that people in the past thought about and experienced passionate attachments the way we do. Historical others—even our own forefathers and mothers—were indeed other.

The responses of the reading group, which appear below, have been edited to remove crossed-out phrases, spelling errors, and other distractions that appear in the original versions.

Janet's freewriting

The author wants us to think more critically about romantic
love, perhaps even to view it as unnecessary. Too many of us
assume that living without romantic love is to be deprived.
Stone wants us to examine and question that assumption. He
addresses readers familiar with Shakespeare and Freud
and comfortable with terms like orthodox opinion and ego
gratification. He assumes an audience already a bit
cynical about romance and passionate love. I think the
reader most receptive to Stone's ideas has lost any idealism
about such matters and is willing to believe that passion
is not necessary, maybe unhealthy, in long-term
relationships. The essay is for people more likely to sneer
at Valentine's Day than to search for just the right
greeting card.

Stone's point is that passion, romance, and sexual
fulfillment are less crucial to happiness than our culture
conditions us to believe. He argues that poets and
playwrights created romantic love and that Freud added
the notion that sex is an overriding drive. The presumed
need for passionate attachments has been constructed by a
culture in which the individual comes first and the needs
of the group are relegated to a distant second. Stone
warns that addiction to romance places us at peril, and
he lists the increase of sexually transmitted diseases,
divorce, depression, and even mental illness among the
results.

Stone supports his ideas with evidence from history, with particular attention to the mass distribution of novels, the Romantic movement, and the influence of Freud. There's a gradual change in tone as the reading progresses. After the first few paragraphs, I expected a scholarly, informative piece with no earth-shaking point to it. But by the time I was finished, I realized that Stone was on a soapbox. As the essay develops, I get the picture of an embittered prude manipulating history to argue against something he either doesn't want or can't have.

Alex's freewriting

Stone asks readers to consider a cultural norm in an unfamiliar and unconventional way. The trappings of romantic love so permeate our daily lives that we assume there's something wrong with an adolescent or young adult who doesn't experience the feeling. So Stone asks us to set aside this conditioning for a moment and to entertain the idea that a thing we all "know" to be natural and proper really isn't. Also he wants us to see that there's something at stake. I'm not sure he wants to alarm us and alter patterns of behavior, but he does want us to think about the consequences of our beliefs and to get a debate going. I think he makes two important points. First, love may be a form of learned behavior. Second, because of historical developments (democracy and individualism, invention of mass media, Freudian psychology), romantic love has run rampant and poses certain dangers.

I think Stone is addressing a well-educated, broad-minded audience--the sort of people who subscribe to <u>Psychology Today</u>. Ironically, that type of reader, like the people who perpetuated the concept of romantic love prior to the eighteenth century, are an elite. An essay like this is probably leisure reading for such persons. I think Stone envisions a reader who prides herself on being an independent, tough-minded skeptic--someone who isn't taken in by bunk just because it's popular or "nice." An iconoclast, I guess you could say. I'm not sure whether Stone is <u>addressing</u> this type of audience so much as he is <u>conjuring it up</u>.

I see a contradiction. In paragraph one, Stone mentions the uncertainty of "scholars" (psychologists?) about whether love is "culturally induced" or "has biochemical roots." If it's biochemical, aren't historians and anthropologists mistaken in the view that Stone attributes to them? Or are psychologists less certain about this than scholars in other fields? Does Stone express himself poorly, or am I reading carelessly? Stone introduces more specific support in paragraph five, referring to the divorce rate in Japan. It's interesting, though, that he relies on emotionally charged language in his next-to-last paragraph: words like <u>frenetic</u>, <u>restless</u>, and <u>demand</u>. This seems out of keeping with the rest of the essay, which sounds more scholarly.

The essay is chronologically ordered, tracing the history of romantic love. But beneath that, I see a question-answer approach. Stone opens with a problem or dilemma, and the first paragraph ends with two questions. The next paragraph opens with "Some things can be said with certainty," and Stone lists those things. Paragraph four then opens with "another question," and that question leads to two more. Paragraph five goes back to certainty, beginning with "What is certain is that...."

Agnes's freewriting

Stone reminds an audience of psychoanalysts of the history
of romantic love. He assesses where we stand today, with
tremendous pressures to seek and insist upon sexual
fulfillment. For me, it's not clear whether Stone sees
romantic love and sexual love as the same thing. Stone fails,
probably on purpose, to give a detailed explanation of how
"love" took the place of arranged marriage and how, through
"saturation of the whole culture," sexual gratification was
encouraged, even idealized. The chips seem to go down when he
examines the influences of Freud. Is he trying to discredit
the Freudian theory of human sexuality, now taken for granted
in some circles? Is that the reason for the sly allusion to
Freud's justification of neurosis, <u>Civilization and Its
Discontents</u>? Stone seems to say that we pay a heavy price for
license and excess. Is he trying to upset the Freudians? To
urge therapists to stress social values rather than
individual desires as they guide their patients out of a
self-induced wilderness?

   Stone is speaking to a group of professionals interested
in new ways of thinking about mental illness and its
treatment. The allusion to <u>Romeo and Juliet</u> isn't so
important, since every high schooler has read the play. The
troubadours are less familiar, but anyone who's heard of Bing
Crosby or Perry Como has heard the term. So I think Stone is
flattering his audience without really demanding much of
them. It seems scholarly, but is it really? His tone is
earnest, though bias slips in near the end. There's not a
great deal of hard evidence. Frankly, I think this essay
could be adapted for the <u>Parade</u> section of the Sunday paper

```
with only minimal editing. After all, we're all interested in
what makes us tick, and all the emphasis on the demons of
instant gratification, license, and unfettered individualism
would hit home with people trying to figure out what's gone
wrong with their relationships. Why not say something about
the psychic toll taken by adulterous liaisons or arranged
marriages?
```

"A Short History of Love" is not an obscure or difficult text, yet each of these readers responds to it a bit differently. One difference involves their interpretations of the author's purpose. Janet sees Stone as "an embittered prude manipulating history to argue against something he either doesn't want or can't have." Alex seems more inclined to take the article at face value, simply as an attempt to provoke thought and debate. Agnes seems annoyed, believing that Stone wants to display knowledge and flatter the self-image of his readers.

Other differences emerge. Alex is analytical, examining the structure and language of the article—down to the author's choice of specific words. Agnes refers to things outside the text (from the title of a book by Freud to the names of popular singers during the 1940s). Janet falls somewhere in between: She records personal associations, such as the reference to greeting cards, while noting Stone's ideas and the order in which he presents them. Both Alex and Agnes pose questions, interrogating the text as well as their own responses to it.

Although other differences can be found, an important point emerges: The personality, interests, and thinking style of each individual affect his or her reading of "A Short History of Love." None of the readings is inherently better than the others; on the contrary, the best reading would be informed and enriched by all three perspectives. It would benefit from Janet's speculations about the author, Alex's analysis of language and structure, and Agnes's skepticism. This formidable array of skill and perspective is something that no single member of the group possessed as an individual.

The sharing of freewritten responses is not always an end in itself. Instructors may ask groups to address an issue or problem introduced by a reading. For example, reading groups might receive the following guidelines after having freewritten in response to "A Short History of Love."

GUIDELINES	**Group Work**

Read your freewriting aloud to members of your group. As you listen to others read, take note of any interesting observations, but be particularly alert to the following:

- Do group members feel that the origins of romantic love are mainly cultural or biological?

- Do they see any unhealthy obsession with romance, sex, or individualism in modern society? Do they share Stone's sense of alarm or urgency?
- Did anyone in your group connect what Stone calls "frenetic individualism" and the desire for immediate self-gratification with other areas of life?

After all group members have read their freewriting aloud, try to reach some consensus regarding these questions:

- Has Stone identified a serious social problem that needs to be addressed?
- What is the most plausible way to resolve the tensions that Stone outlines?
- Does extreme individualism and the desire for self-gratification contribute to other social problems? If so, which ones?

Reading groups strive for consensus—or at least mutual understanding— rather than a single authoritative interpretation. After Janet, Alex, and Agnes had read their freewritten responses aloud, they discussed each other's ideas and observations. For example, Alex remarked on Janet's belief that as Stone gets further into his topic, he sounds more like a soapbox orator than a scholar. Alex connected that idea with something he had noted about the tone of the article—that "emotionally charged language" appears in the next-to-last paragraph. Janet's point thus helped Alex see the language of one paragraph as part of a broader pattern. Janet, on the other hand, benefited from Alex's narrower focus on words in a specific segment of the text. Not only was her perception reinforced by what Alex noted, but also she found supporting evidence for what had been only a vague impression about the author's tone.

As Janet, Alex, and Agnes proceeded to discuss each other's responses, a number of similar transactions ensued. Agnes took issue with Janet's and Alex's notion that Stone wishes to alter public behavior. She reminded her partners that Stone's article was delivered as a paper at an academic conference and that his primary audience was psychoanalysts rather than a randomly selected group of single men and women. Acknowledging that they had overlooked that fact, Janet and Alex modified their interpretation of Stone's purpose. Later, influenced by her partners' doubts about Stone's authority in fields other than history, Janet grew skeptical herself. All continued their discussion for about fifteen minutes.

At the end of this and many of the following chapters, you will be invited to work in reading groups, engaging in a similar process of collaborative response and inquiry. When you do so, try to adopt the constructive approach exemplified by these three readers.

 ## RESEARCH

Many students expect research to be an excruciating ordeal, and the idea of THE RESEARCH PAPER looms in student mythology as the academic equivalent of a root canal.

Fortunately, the myth is wrong. Research needn't be a tedious ordeal, though it can be for those who begin without knowing what they are doing or why. *Research* is nothing more than finding out what you need to know. If you are good at it—if you have learned a few elementary skills—it can be useful and satisfying; it can even be fun.

You are already skilled in certain kinds of research. Right now, for example, if you wanted to find your dentist's telephone number, you could easily do so, even though your phone book contains thousands of names. Your research skills enable you to find out what movies are showing on television tonight and the current price of Raleigh mountain bikes. Research in college involves additional skills that are equally useful and not any more difficult to acquire. These skills not only help you become a competent college researcher, but also prove useful after you graduate.

Research takes many forms, from looking up the definition of a word to conducting an opinion poll. Depending on what you want to find out, you may ask the opinions of experts, undertake fieldwork or laboratory experiments, interview eyewitnesses, analyze photographs, or observe the behavior of people who don't know they're being watched. This more observational type of research is the kind that Millicent Lambert conducted for her essay. Other research methods—those explained and illustrated in this book—involve written sources. You can discover general information in reference works such as encyclopedias and almanacs. More specific information and ideas can be found in magazines, newspapers, journals, pamphlets, books, and Web sites. Your college library and computer databases are two valuable resources for conducting this type of research.

The skills you develop as a researcher provide personal benefits outside of college. For example, knowing how to use the library can help a pharmacy major locate a summer job. Or it can help consumers find out which videorecorders are most reliable. Unlike these more private kinds of inquiry, the research you perform as a college student has a more public purpose. It may be part of a larger project in which you share your findings with other scholars, communicating what you have learned through *research writing*.

In short, any organized investigation can be called research, and any writing you do as a result—from poetry to scientific reports—may be called research writing. Research is an important academic skill because college students rarely begin a major assignment with all the information they need. When you write about personal feelings, research is unnecessary; no one is likely to challenge expressions of feeling. However, if you write about dating customs of the early twentieth century, you must rely on more than feelings or casual conversation. Since readers expect your writing to be dependable and accurate, research is indispensable.

Not all good writing, of course, is research writing. Your responses to the readings on pages 46–48, for example, are probably based on personal reflection and opinion rather than research. For the same reason, the following passage would not qualify as research writing:

> Since I decided to marry at the age of twenty-three, I've been made to feel as if a career is no longer a viable option. . . .

> I've been accused of misrepresenting myself during college as someone trying to earn an MRS degree rather than an education. When "feminist" friends hear that I am taking my husband's name, they act as if I'm forsaking "our" cause. One Saturday afternoon, a friend phoned and I admitted I was spending the day doing laundry—mine and his. Her voice resonated with such pity that I hung up.
>
> New York City, where we live, breeds much of this antagonism . . . but I've also experienced prejudice in my hometown in Colorado. At a local store's bridal registry, I walked in wearing a Columbia University sweatshirt and the consultant asked if I'd gone to school there. On hearing that I'd graduated ten months earlier, she explained that she had a daughter my age. "But she is very involved in her career," she added, presuming that I, selecting a silver pattern, was not.
>
> —Katherine Davis, "I'm Not Sick, I'm Just in Love"

Though this personal account is well written and honest, it does not report research. Instead, it is a personal reflection that is not based on sources or systematic inquiry. If, however, the author had cited quotations and facts gathered from formal interviews with experts or friends, had found and reported published scholarship relating to marriage and family, or had cited the opinions of feminist scholars, then her essay would have been based on research rather than personal reflection. This is what we mean by research writing—locating and citing sources.

Distinguishing Features of Research Writing

EXERCISE

Would you call Millicent Lambert's essay "Eighth Grade Revisited" an example of research writing? Explain. Are any parts of that essay based on research? Could the essay be made more convincing through additional research? If Millicent wished to incorporate more research into her essay, what kinds of research would you recommend?

 ## READING SELECTION

Following is an excerpt from a recently published book, *Reading Don't Fix No Chevys: Literacy in the Lives of Young Men*. The authors, both university professors of English education, report the findings of their study of forty-nine adolescent males from a variety of ethnic, socioeconomic, and geographical backgrounds. Included in the excerpt are references to *Flow: The Psychology of Optimal Experience*, a book by adolescent psychologist Mihaly Csikszentmihalyi. Numbers cited in parentheses designate pages in Csikszentmihalyi's book.

Going with the Flow

What Boys Like to Do and Why They Like to Do It

MICHAEL W. SMITH AND JEFFREY D. WILHELM

1   Csikszentmihalyi (1990a) begins his book with a simple premise: that "more than anything else, men and women seek happiness" (p. 1). Everything else for which we strive, he argues—money, prestige, *everything*—is only valued because we expect (sometimes wrongly) that it will bring us happiness. Csikszentmihalyi has spent his professional life studying what makes people happy, more specifically by examining the nature of flow, "the state in which people are so involved in an activity that nothing else seems to matter" (p. 4).

2   He offers eight characteristics of flow experience that we think can be usefully collapsed into four main principles:

- A sense of control and competence
- A challenge that requires an appropriate level of skill
- Clear goals and feedback
- A focus on the immediate experience

These principles resounded throughout all of our data.

3   What we found in our study is that all of the young men with whom we worked were passionate about some activity. They experienced flow. But, unfortunately, most of them did not experience it in their literate activity, at least not in school. . . .

A SENSE OF COMPETENCE AND CONTROL

4   According to Csikszentmihalyi (1990a), when people describe flow experiences, they typically talk about a sense of competence and the feeling of control that stems from having developed sufficient skills so that they are able to achieve their goals. . . .

5   Again and again we heard boys talk about how a feeling of competence kept them involved in an activity. Again and again we heard boys exclaim that they would quickly give things up if they did not gain that competence. That's why it was so striking that only two boys made a link between accomplishment and reading. . . .

6   The boys also discussed the importance of feeling control. This came out clearly in their discussion of school. Csikszentmihalyi (1990a) notes that "knowledge that is seen to be controlled from the outside is acquired with reluctance and it brings no joy" (p. 134). The boys in our study seemed to concur . . . in their discussions of reading and of writing.

7   Here's Chris talking about writing:

A lot of times with writing I get excited, especially when the teacher doesn't give you a limitation. Like with _____, we did a lot of writing assignments with poems and whatnot and that really caught my interest because you could write about whatever you wanted to write about.

8   Guy echoed his point:

I like writing without having any guidelines to follow, just where you have to do your own thing. I might not mind having a guideline as [to] how long it has to be, but I don't like having a topic to write about, just to make up my own story.

According to some of the boys, what was true for writing was also true for reading.   **9**
Joe noted the importance of control over his reading:

> I don't like it if I have to read it, but if I read it on my own then it would probably
> seem a little better. . . .

A CHALLENGE THAT REQUIRES AN APPROPRIATE LEVEL OF SKILL

As Csikszentmihalyi (1990a) notes, "By far the overwhelming proportion of optimal   **10**
experiences are reported to occur within sequences of activities that are goal directed
and bounded by rules—activities that require the investment of psychic energy, and
that could not be done without the appropriate skills" (p. 49). He explains: "Enjoyment comes at a very specific point: whenever the opportunities for action perceived
by the individual are equal to his or her capabilities" (p. 52). We found that the
young men in our study gravitated to activities that provided the appropriate level of
challenge. . . .

The emphasis on an appropriate level of challenge . . . marked their discussions of   **11**
reading in interesting ways. Some of the boys wistfully recalled reading *Goosebumps*
books that they had found interesting but that were now too easy. But more often the
boys talked about feeling overmatched by reading. Haywood put it this way:

> Ah, well I like a book that isn't, isn't easy but not so difficult that you don't under-
> stand what is going on. Ah, because if you are reading a book that doesn't make sense
> to you then you just, you know, "Well I don't know how to read this" and then you
> have [a] negative attitude and you don't concentrate and you don't really gain any-
> thing from the experience.

Ricardo provided a specific example: **12**

> Ah, I don't like reading plays because it's hard, it's just everything is talking and . . .
> when you've done a page you have to look back and say OK, this person is talking to
> that person.

The potential impact of feeling "overmatched" is clear as we recall the comments   **13**
in our discussions with the boys about the importance of competence and control.
The young men in our study wanted to be challenged, but they wanted to be challenged in contexts in which they felt confident of improvement, if not success. If the
challenge seemed too great, they tended to avoid it, instead returning to a domain in
which they felt more competent. . . .

CLEAR GOALS AND FEEDBACK

The importance of clear goals and feedback is intimately associated with the two char-   **14**
acteristics of flow experiences that we have discussed so far. First, without a clear sense
of a goal, it seems impossible to have a sense of competence. Second, it is impossible to
identify an appropriate level of challenge. As Csikszentmihalyi (1990a) points out,
sports and games provide goals and feedback by their very nature: a tennis player wins
or loses a point, a lacrosse player scores a goal or is scored upon, a video game player
moves up to a new level or loses the game. . . .

This emphasis on immediate feedback has important consequences for reading.   **15**
Reading extended texts such as novels is not likely to provide quick and clean feedback, but reading short informational texts, such as magazines and newspapers, does.

16   For example, in the activity interviews, when boys spoke of their enjoyment of reading, most spoke about how they valued it as a tool they used to address an immediate interest or need. Here's Timmy talking about what he reads on the Internet:

> Well, I like to go to the sports and stuff [']cause I like to see, I like sports a lot . . . I like to see what is going on and what's, like, who won the games and . . . I like to go to NASCAR and I like NASCAR a lot so. I like to see what is happening and they are like [mumble] it is just fun to ah, find out.

And Mark talking about reading a golfing magazine:

> 'Cause ah, it's probably the best golf magazine out there and it, I mean it just tells you ways and shows you pictures on how you can improve your swing, and if you slice the ball, it teaches you how to hook the ball so it goes straight, and it ah shows you what new balls come out that are fit for you and new clubs that would fit you and just different things like that.

And Bam on reading the newspaper:

> Like, if you find something that happened around your neighborhood, "Oh, I didn't know that happened. I should read it." Stuff like that. I didn't know my friend went to jail because he tried to rob somebody. I didn't know that until I read the paper. They put his name there in the paper.

And Maurice on reading his driver's education book:

> That was something that I thought was interesting because it helps me. It helps me to put my seat belt on because before, if they see me without a seat belt on, they couldn't do anything about it unless you were actually stopped and they saw you without a seat belt on. But now, if they see you, they can just stop you like that. So that's helping me put my seat belt on at all times, and it's keeping me out of ticket trouble, keeping points off my license.

And Barnabas on reading about video games:

> Some of the stuff be frustrating. All the magazines I read, they say how they made the game too hard. It's true. They made the game too hard. And, sometimes, I beat the game already and I want to see what all the secret stuff was. I mean, it tells you where all the secret stuff is, but I still got to find them myself. That's all. I'm just asking for a little map.

17   The boys we cite here could be described as taking an efferent (Rosenblatt, 1978) stance in their reading. Or perhaps it's more accurate to say that they choose texts that reward an efferent reading. Csikszentmihalyi (1990a) provides a lens through which to understand that choice. Efferent reading by its nature provides an opportunity for clear and immediate feedback that aesthetic reading does not. If you're looking for in formation and you find it, you know that your reading is successful: You can beat the game, fix the electrical problem, or hit the ball straighter. . . .

A FOCUS ON THE IMMEDIATE EXPERIENCE

18   The implications of the way that boys valued reading become even clearer in light of the final characteristic of flow experiences. The *sine qua non* of flow experiences is that people are so focused on what they are doing they lose awareness of anything outside the activity. Csikszentmihalyi (1990a) speaks of this quality in a number of ways: the merging of action and awareness, concentration on the task at hand, the loss of self-consciousness, and the transformation of time. In his study, a young basketball player

provides testimony: "Kids my age, they think a lot . . . but when you are playing basketball, that's all there is on your mind—just basketball. . . . Everything seems to follow right along" (p. 58).

The young men in our study spoke in ways that resonate with the words of this   19 basketball player. They valued their favorite activities for the enjoyment they took from the immediate engagement in those activities, not for their instrumental value. The boys played sports because they enjoyed them, not to win a scholarship or to impress others. They played music or rapped because they enjoyed being engaged in that way. And when they engaged with other media, they did so because it made them laugh or kept them on the edge of their seats. Unlike their experience with reading, their focus was on the moment, not on the instrumental value of the activity. . . .

THE IMPORTANCE OF THE SOCIAL

Although Csikszentmihalyi's (1990a) work helped us understand our boys' activity   20 ratings, it wasn't fully explanatory. Csikszentmihalyi notes that "Another universally enjoyable activity is being with other people" (p. 50), yet as he admits, socializing appears to be an exception to the rules for flow that he posits. What wasn't an exception was how important socializing was to the young men in our study. . . .

The boys talked about how their friendships allowed them to be themselves. What   21 they seemed to mean was that they could talk more intimately with friends. Only two of them alluded to friends as a protection against the pressure of being male in a specified way. Both of those who did were very involved with the arts, and they seemed to see girls as more accepting of their artistic inclinations. Pablo put it this way:

> I guess boys are more—they judge you. They think you have to be a big macho man in order for you to hang out with them. I mean, not all boys, but a lot of 'em, and I guess girls accept you more, for who you are, and I guess it depends on person to person, but that's what I've found.

But this was decidedly a minority opinion. . . .   22

The friendships occasionally affected the boys' literate lives. Gohan had two   23 friends with whom he shared poetry. Mark checked the Internet or the newspaper to keep up with the hockey scores not because of his interest but because his friends would expect him to know. Neil's friendship circle was characterized by long discussions of movies by favorite directors. . . .

Their friendships also affected their attitudes toward school. Of the twenty-one   24 who talked about liking school, nineteen said they did so because of the social dimension of schooling. Buster's sentiments provide a summary of this viewpoint:

> Probably my favorite part of going to school is the social aspect. I don't know, I guess I just like interacting with my friends and stuff. I mean, that's probably my favorite part about school. As far as classes go, there's certain classes I really don't like and some that are OK, but . . . probably my favorite part of school is seeing my friends.

In contrast, only two boys talked about valuing school because they loved to   25 learn. . . .

SIGNIFICANT DEPARTURES

As we noted previously, virtually all of the boys noted that reading played a part in   26 their lives outside school, but only seven spoke of the enjoyment they received from reading extended text[s] outside of school, which seems to us to be the conventional understanding of what it means to be a reader. Of these seven, two were primarily readers of history and five of novels, though two of the novel readers talked especially of their interest in historical fiction.

27   These seven boys provided a number of reasons for their enjoyment of books. Stan worked the hardest to articulate his feelings:

> I like reading books because they let you think about certain things that have happened, or they . . . I wouldn't say I want to get away from the world, but it's kind of an escape, like watching TV but it's better than TV. You can't really—like reading a book is—watching TV is, like, no comparison to reading a book because reading a book you can get right into it and all that stuff, and I'm not quite sure what makes a book good, just it has to be sort of interesting. I mean it's different for, you know, certain people. Certain people like certain things. I like a lot of books, I like books that sort of keep you on your toes, books that make you think, controversial books, just a little bit of everything I think.

Stan's last statement resonates with previous ones we've cited on the importance of challenge. Suspense and the drive to figure out the "puzzle" a book provides were important. He raises other key points as well, including the need to be able to enter a book. We took this to mean that he was able both to visualize the story world and to see things from the perspectives of others. Like Stan, the [other] boys who were readers spoke of a desire to be engaged in the big ideas they encountered in reading. . . .

28   Our attention to students' likes and dislikes . . . doesn't mean that we are simply saying, "Just give them reading that relates to their interests." The boys' interests were sufficiently different that doing so would mean a class could never read a common text. Rather, we are saying that if we understand why they like what they like, we can work to create the conditions that will make students more inclined to engage in learning what they need to know. These conditions are those of "flow" experiences: a sense of control and competence, an appropriate challenge, clear goals and feedback, and a focus on the immediate.

Freewriting

Freewriting helps you focus your thoughts about what you read. Write a full page in your journal or notebook, recording your reactions to "Going with the Flow," along with any thoughts that the passage arouses. Write at your normal pace about whatever comes to mind. Because this writing is not for others to read, try to put your ideas on paper without stopping to polish your writing or to correct errors. Though free to record any thoughts that relate to the reading, you may wish to respond to some of the following questions: Do the authors' findings accord with your experience as a high-school student? Do they confirm, contradict, or alter your perceptions of adolescent males? What findings do you suppose a similar study of adolescent girls might produce? Do you think the attitudes and literate behaviors of previous generations of adolescent boys would have been different from those that Michael W. Smith and Jeffrey D. Wilhelm report? Do their findings have any social implications?

Review Questions

1. What four principles do Smith and Wilhelm cite as characteristic of flow experiences?

2. How do efferent and aesthetic responses to reading differ? How does the distinction between these two responses relate to the boys that Smith and Wilhelm interviewed?

3. In what respects do the seven boys who read longer texts outside of school differ from others?

Discussion Questions

1. Which of the quoted comments about reading or writing experiences do you most identify with? Which do you least identify with?

2. In another part of the article from which the excerpt on page 5 was drawn, Nancy Sommers quotes Ralph Waldo Emerson: "One must be an inventor to read well." What evidence for that assertion do you find in "Going with the Flow"?

3. Do you think that Smith and Wilhelm overvalue aesthetic reading or undervalue efferent reading? If so, how and why?

Writing

1. In a dictionary, look up any of the following words with which you are unfamiliar:

premise (paragraph 1)   optimal (paragraph 10)   *sine qua non* (paragraph 18)

2. Interview four or five classmates or friends about how they use literacy in their daily lives (school, work, leisure) and how they feel about reading and writing. Use the information you gather to confirm or modify Smith and Wilhelm's conclusions.

WRITE, READ, and RESEARCH the NET

1. *Write:* Using one or more of the prewriting strategies discussed and illustrated on pages 19–25, record your thoughts, observations, or personal experiences regarding the empowerment that comes with reading and writing well or the disempowerment that often accompanies illiteracy.

2. *Read:* Review the following Web site:
english.cla.umn.edu/literacy_lab/bookshelf/bookshelf.htm.

3. *Research:* Using the Internet, find articles and other sources that relate to changing definitions of literacy and the political and social implications of how we define this term. Draft an outline and summary of your findings.

ADDITIONAL READINGS

Most of the following selections illustrate a type of writing that the assignment on page 8 (the one to which Millicent Lambert responded) is designed to elicit.

The first two selections, articles from the *New York Times* and a Canadian newspaper, the *Globe and Mail*, address the topic of literacy, introduced in "Going with the Flow." A final selection, "The Holly Pageant," details the customs and conventions surrounding a familiar event that is governed by rigidly enforced, yet often unspoken, rules of behavior.

Making Fairy Tales into Learning Tools

RICHARD ROTHSTEIN

1   Most people recognize the importance of reading stories to toddlers, who can then learn how books work (for example, that a line of text proceeds from left to right), how letters form words, and how narrative flows.

2   But literacy is only one benefit of storytelling. Another is the chance for children to identify with fanciful characters who try to work out conflicts with others and within themselves. If very young children can't do this in the safety of an adult's lap, the later costs to them and to society can be greater than poor reading skills.

3   Can any of this loss be made up later? A storybook program at a San Antonio juvenile prison suggests that it may never be too late.

4   Three people came together to create the program. Celeste Guzman works for Gemini Ink, a group that seeks opportunities for creative writers to give workshops in schools, seniors' centers, shelters for battered women, and prisons. Glenn Faulk, a prison officer at the Cyndi Taylor Krier Juvenile Correctional Treatment Center, designs activities for violent youths while they serve their sentences. Grady Hillman, a poet, trains artists and writers to teach in community settings.

5   Their plan evolved slowly, with few of its possibilities apparent at first. Youths at the Krier juvenile prison are expected to perform public service. Mr. Faulk proposed to several that rather than mow lawns at the courthouse or pick up trash on the highway, they write children's books that could be donated to a library at a battered-women's shelter. He thought the idea might be particularly attractive to youths who had themselves fathered children before being imprisoned. He also knew that in writing children's stories, the youths would be forced to abandon their tough-guy street language.

6   Ms. Guzman then recruited Mr. Hillman to run a writing workshop for seven juvenile offenders who volunteered. He began each session by reading a children's book aloud, expecting to teach story structure and character development. But it soon became apparent that the storytelling had another, unanticipated effect: the six young men and one young woman, none of whom had lived healthy childhoods that included adults' reading stories, were enjoying the tales themselves.

7   Their favorite, Mr. Hillman said, was *Millions of Cats*, by Wanda Gag. It is an "ugly duckling" kind of story in which an old woman wants to pick a single cat as a pet, from millions of cats who hope to be selected. Her choice is unexpected, a cat who has been least aggressive in seeking her favor.

Mr. Hillman surmised that the story was popular because the youths had spent their adolescence driven toward arrogance and feigning toughness. The notion that humility might have a reward was surprisingly attractive to them.   8

Mr. Hillman's own favorite was *The Tale of Peter Rabbit*, by Beatrix Potter. Because Peter disobeys his mother's rules, he is trapped in Mr. McGregor's garden. Peter's predicament becomes progressively worse, but he ultimately resolves it and escapes to the security of home. This, Mr. Hillman thought, might be a parable for the young offenders' own lives.   9

The workshop's explicit goal was the youths' contribution of their work to the community. Each of them wrote a story. Some were fanciful, like a tale about a wizard who can't spell and whose wishes are therefore fulfilled improperly: when he wants a bath, he spells *bat*, and so instead of getting a bath, he gets a bat that chases him around his cave. Some stories were more realistic, like one about a girl who has to accept that she is shorter than others.   10

Ms. Guzman had the storybooks printed, and in May the youths read their stories aloud at a prison meeting to which their parents were invited. Now, as the young offenders earn behavior points that make them eligible for supervised trips away from the center, they will be permitted to perform readings for children on the outside.   11

Thirty years ago, literacy programs were more common in adult and juvenile prisons alike, because reading and writing skills were thought important for future employment. Some adult programs included "bibliotherapy," using literature to explore psychological problems as a step to rehabilitation.   12

But today, prisons give more emphasis to punishment, protection of the community, and restitution. The San Antonio program is an exception to that trend, though not the only one. Mr. Hillman now hopes to train writers around the country to use storybooks with youthful offenders. If all children heard fairy tales when they were small enough to sit on laps, though, perhaps fewer would have to do so in prison.   13

Hackers Devise Their Own Language Literacies

RUSSELL SMITH

The recent National Endowment for the Arts survey about reading habits in the United States has depressed a lot of people. Everyone is blaming television and the Internet for the widespread decline in reading. There is a contradiction in this thought: Television may well be a factor, but the Internet, as my colleague Ian Brown has already pointed out, is still largely text-based, and spending time there involves hours of reading.   1

How the Internet could make people stupider is hard to see. The people who spend all their time on the Internet—hackers—are about the most intelligent generation of people since the population at large could communicate in rhyming poetry.   2

Consider leetspeak, the code or cipher that hackers and on-line gamers use to communicate in secret under the gaze of law enforcement and mere lamers like me and you. Leetspeak (which comes from *elite*) relies on humor and improvisation, and on layers of reference and is a new kind of language in several startling respects. It consists of slang words—such as *warez* for pirated software, or *woot* for cool or excellent— which are then transliterated into numbers and symbols. The numbers and symbols are visual puns or icons for the letters represented. For example, the letter *e* is written as a *3* (which looks like a capital *e* when read backwards), *a* as a *4*, *l* as a *1*, *s* as a *5*, *o* as a *0*. Letters are also created by assembling typographical symbols, as in ASCII art—for   3 example, *r* can be written as *p|* or *|2* or just *2*. My name could be written *2(_)55311 $\Mi7[-]* or *P\u$$31L 5miT#*. The variations are endless and depend largely on how many strange characters you can conjure from your computer's hidden sets.

4   There have been underworld dialects in existence forever, from Cockney rhyming slang to children's pig Latin, and they have had the same function: They are both an area of play and a mechanism for exclusion. Leetspeak is both but takes a new form. Where street slangs are entirely oral—they have no written form—this one is *only* written, and never spoken; many of its typographical extravagances cannot be spoken at all. This language is a cipher on top of a jargon: in other words, the slang words, already incomprehensible to outsiders, are further rearranged into symbols. This is not, as is commonly said, "postliterate"; it is in fact *purely* literate; indeed it is, like the play of sounds and shapes that makes up the best poetry, *literary*.

5   Further textual play consists in alternating upper- and lower-case letters and in deliberately misspelling words. *Porn* will often be written *pr0n, the* will be *teh*. These are mostly just appropriations of common errors. To *own*, for example, which in gaming slang means to defeat, will be written *pwn* because the *p* and the *o* are side by side on the standard keyboard and are often mistyped. But these jokes also stem from a pattern of evasion which is designed to fool not just people but machines. This "fat-finger" typing is exactly what spammers do to circumvent the filters on your e-mail: they make the word readable to a human intelligence, which can adjust for errors and see the word as it should be, but not to a search engine, which has no such flexibility. (This is why all those Viagra and porn ads get through to your computer if they just put spaces or hyphens into the telltale words. Song titles are often deliberately misspelled on Kazaa to deceive the sweeping searches of record-industry narcs.) Useless suffixes also delight leetspeakers. The letters *xor* often represent an *x* or a hard *c* sound. The word *hacker* is often written as *haxor*. Why *xor*? Because that string of letters is an inside joke to computer programmers.

6   Ask a real hacker to explain some of these jokes and you are in for a series of history lessons. This language has mutated more quickly than any other language in history: Each of these phrases has undergone several subtle changes in spelling in a span of only twenty years. James Reid, a programmer and former Goth who is now a computer security expert for a company called nCircle Canada (a name itself possibly leet-influenced), begins explaining the *xor* operation as "a binary operation where you take two binary strings . . . ." Then he sighs. "It's a long explanation. Just say it's a Boolean operation. The letters come from formalized logic."

7   He explains the word *woot* as a play on *root*, from "root user account"—if you have gained the root, you have taken over someone else's computer (something that in the hacker world is definitely cool). Then you change the *r* to a *w* as if you have a childlike speech impediment.

8   Reid also explained to me the evolution of the cipher word *jU4r3z*. It comes from *warez*, or stolen software. There is a Mexican town called Juarez whose name sounds similar . . . so, merely for humorous effect, you replace *warez* with *Juarez* and then you replace some letters with numbers. Apparently every hacker in the universe can read this stuff like English.

9   Reid calls this repeated mutation of mutations a "continuum of obfuscation." He sees it as "iterative"—a concept from postmodernist cultural theory in which a series of linguistic or syntactic operations on a word or phrase produces a slight variant on the last. This is the tradition of lexical invention which gives us, for example, Derrida's *difference* and *differance* and Lacan's *omelette* and *hommelette* and all those other clever French idea-puns.

I guess this makes my point pretty clear: So much for the decline of literacy among the computer generation.   10

By the way, a project is underway to transliterate the Bible into leet, at www.christianhacker.org/html/NHV.html.   11

The Holly Pageant

LAVONNE ADAMS

Everything is ready. The fire trucks and ambulances have been moved outside, floors have been swept, chairs have been placed in orderly rows. At seven o'clock, the Holly Pageant is scheduled to begin.   1

Armed with a green metal cash box and a rubber stamp for the patrons' hands, I take my seat behind the folding table to the left of the front door. I watch as the girls and their parents arrive, chattering excitedly, arms laden with garment bags, shoe boxes, makeup cases, curling irons. The mothers greet each other, size up the competition, push compliments from their tongues—"Oh, you look so pretty tonight!"—"What a beautiful dress!"—"I love what you've done to your hair!"   2

Barbara, one of the pageant organizers, arrives. She is in charge of acquiring the judges from the "Certified Judges List," a product of the judging seminars held every year in Raleigh. Each year, she assiduously sets the judge's table with a white tablecloth, glasses of water, and bowls of snack foods. Once the judges arrive, she ushers them into the radio room, where they remain sequestered until the pageant commences. She stands at that door, as anxious as a presidential body guard.   3

I have heard rumors of corrupt judges, bribed by overanxious mothers at other pageants, yet have been assured that these judges are not told the names of the contestants until they are handed the programs.   4

Barbara's four-year-old son runs up to her, yanks impatiently on her arm, whispers something in her ear. She glances around anxiously, frowns as she takes his hand, then disappears in the direction of the bathroom. The inner sanctum has been left unguarded. I take advantage of the opportunity. Unobtrusively, I walk toward the radio room, cautiously turn the knob, ease open the door, and slip inside. The judges look up, startled . . . perturbed. Once I explain why I am interested in talking to them, they smile, settle back in their chairs, obviously relieved. They agree to let me interview them after the pageant. I slip back outside.   5

The Holly Pageant is a tradition in this small North Carolina town, a social event rivaled only by the yearly parish "reunion" at the town's largest Baptist church. The Holly Ridge Volunteer Fire Department and Rescue Squad officially adopted the pageant a few years ago, after a group of local citizens abandoned it. There was much debate that night. Since I was a new member, I felt unsure of my local standing, so I kept my mouth firmly closed. The other female members had stars in their eyes; the men had dollar signs. "This," one of them declared, "could be financially rewarding." He saw it as a means of breaking the endless cycle of barbecue dinners and bake sales. He was proven right: the department cleared approximately $1,400 that first year.   6

The theme for this year's program is "Rock around the Clock." Mounted on the wall directly opposite the front door is a large black and white poster featuring a caricature of two "jitter-buggers," the male sporting a fashionable crew cut, the ponytailed female wearing a poodle skirt, bobbie socks, and saddle oxfords. The stage is done in a 1950s motif, a reminder of an age of American innocence. Black 45-rpm records   7 and oversized red musical notes are plastered on the white walls. All the props are surrounded with a gold tinsel garland, the kind used to decorate Christmas trees. Everything is supposed to shine in the harsh white glare of the spotlights.

8   I hear music, applause, the introduction of this year's emcee, a popular local disc jockey. The entertainment is beginning.

9   "Notice how carefully she walks—so ladylike," says the emcee. She is referring to Tiny Miss contestant number two, who is carefully placing one patent-leather clad foot in front of the other. With every step, her fluffy pink iridescent party dress shimmers.

10   The Tiny Miss contestants are three to five years old—there are four of them this year. Glenda, another of the pageant organizers, told me that there was no contestant number one; she dropped out after the third night of practice—simply refused to continue.

11   "It's time for our former Tiny Miss to present her portrait to Chief Duane Longo. Duane?" calls out the emcee.

12   Traditionally, each of the outgoing queens presents the department with a framed photograph—twinkling eyes, smile, and crown preserved for posterity. Duane walks toward the stage, bouquet of roses lying awkwardly across his left arm. Each footstep resounds from the plywood platform that functions as the stage. The Tiny Miss Holly is staring at his knee caps. He kneels. They look at each other uncertainly for just a moment, then swap the flowers for the photo. The little girl wraps her free arm around his neck, briefly buries her face against his shoulder.

13   "Awww," I hear from a woman in the audience, "isn't that sweet!"

14   Duane leaves the stage a flattering shade of crimson.

15   The four Tiny Miss contestants return to the stage. One is hiding behind the emcee; the rest are waiting expectantly, anxious smiles frozen on their faces.

16   "And your new Tiny Miss Holly is contestant number . . . three!"

17   The audience cheers, screams, whistles. A crown is placed upon a small head.

18   "When she grows up," the emcee tells the audience, "she wants to be a cheerleader."

19   I remember when they crowned last year's Tiny Miss Holly. One contestant, who stood to the winner's right, folded her arms across her chest, stamped her foot, eyebrows lowered over a fierce angry glare, bottom lip stuck out petulantly. For just an instant, I feared for the physical safety of the new little queen, afraid the other girl was going to hit her. As the twinkling crown was placed carefully upon the winner's blonde curls, her competitor burst into tears.

20   "How embarrassing for her mother," whispered a voice in the crowd.

21   There is a brief intermission. I see one of the defeated contestants standing next to the stage. She's surrounded by friends and family. Her father is talking softly to her as she hangs her head dejectedly. I move closer, catch the funereal terms of the adult voices as her parents pat her shoulder consolingly. "You looked real pretty, honey"—"You did a good job"—"You'll be ready for them next year."

22   The pageant continues with the introduction of the Little Miss contestants, ages six to nine, a bit older than the Tiny Miss contestants. These young girls appear on stage one at a time wearing incredible concoctions of satin, lace, taffeta, beads, and rhinestones: fairy-tale visions from our youth. The women in the audience gasp, sigh, exclaim enthusiastically over the beauty of each dress. Contestant number one steps onto the stage wearing a stunning teal-green party dress, appliquéd with a combination of rhinestones, pearls, and sequins.

"Contestant number one," reads the emcee, "enjoys shrimping with her daddy."   23

I sit down in a chair recently vacated by one of the covey of visiting queens,   24
winners of other local pageants. To my left sits a stately, composed woman who is
scrutinizing the proceedings. I ask her if she is the mother of the queen whose seat I
just appropriated. "No," she answers, pointing to yet another queen who is getting
ready to entertain the crowd. "That's my daughter."

As we discuss pageants in general, I ask her about the cost of the clothing.   25

"You can't wear a sack, you know. This is based on more than talent and poise.   26
You can put the most talented, beautiful girl up there, but if her dress is not competitive . . . well . . . ." She leaves the sentence unfinished, raises her eyebrows, looks at me
knowingly. She then describes a dress she saw at another pageant: floor-length black
velvet with white satin flowers, spaghetti straps, $15-a-yard rhinestone trim. Total
cost, $2,500.

She points to the owner of that dress, who later entertains the crowd with a   27
"Dixie/Battle Hymn of the Republic" medley. Tonight she is wearing a royal-blue
sequined cocktail dress. I am disappointed that she has not worn the black gown, as
I've never seen a dress that cost $2,500.

My curiosity piqued, I head backstage to track down the owner of the blue party   28
dress. I walk into the combination meeting room and kitchen, now transformed into
a massive dressing room, the smell of makeup, hair spray, perfume, and hot bodies
hanging thick in the air. One teen contestant is in the kitchen area, practicing her tap
routine on a sheet of plywood meant to protect the new linoleum floor, purchased
with proceeds from last year's pageant. I look around the room, searching for that
particular child, or rather that particular dress, in the confusion. I spot her on the far
side of the room. As I work my way toward her, I dodge the hyperactive contestants
and the tense chaperons who dress the girls and have them on stage at all the appropriate times. Once I catch up to her, I ask the woman I assume to be her mother, "If
it's not too personal, would you mind telling me how much you spent on that dress?"
I pause to gauge her reaction, then add encouragingly, "It's absolutely gorgeous."

To the mother's right stands a woman who has been acknowledged periodically   29
throughout the evening as being instrumental in helping several contestants with both
their dance routines and their hairdos. She is dressed in a pink lace, pearl-studded tea
gown, blonde hair and makeup flawless. The mother pauses uncertainly, looks to this
woman for support.

"Why do you want to know?" the woman growls. A feral look comes into her eyes;   30
her demeanor becomes aggressive, yet with an oddly defensive undertone.

I catch myself taking a step backward, totally unprepared for the hostility in her   31
voice. I straighten my back, refuse to be intimidated, wonder if she thinks I'm a spy for
a competitor. I explain, "I'm a writer. I'm working on a story."

I wait as she stares me up and down, then nods to the mother before once again   32
turning her back on me.

"Three hundred and fifty dollars," states the mother.   33

While Glenda stressed that this year's parents have not been as competitive as   34
those in years past, by the time you figure in the costumes and the dance lessons, it's
about a $2,000 investment for each contestant. This year the pageant has a total of
fifteen contestants.

Before the crowning of the new Little Miss, the former Little Miss makes her final   35
appearance on stage. Tradition. With tears in her eyes, she waves farewell to her admirers. Well-wishers step forward with balloons and bouquets of flowers as a pre-taped

message plays, "I want to thank God for giving me the opportunity to be Little Miss Holly . . . and Uncle Roger for letting me use his Corvette to ride in the parades."

36   My daughter says that several years ago the winner of the Little Miss competition wore her full-length dress to school the day after the pageant.

37   "And she wore her crown, too!" she adds emphatically.

38   "The sash?" I ask.

39   "Yep," she says. "Her daddy stayed with her all day. He even spread out napkins across her lap at lunch. And her friends had to hold up her skirts during recess because the playground was muddy and the grass was all wet. But she still climbed on the monkey bars."

40   We have another brief intermission, then the visiting queens go up on stage one by one to introduce themselves. Our newly crowned Tiny Miss and Little Miss are allowed to join the throng. When the Tiny Miss steps up to the microphone, she says, "Hi. I'm . . . ." She panics, has obviously forgotten what to say, looks around like a cornered mouse. "Mommy!" she calls out in a frightened voice. Her mother steps up to the stage with an indulgent smile and prompts her daughter. The little girl returns to the microphone and announces her name.

41   Glenda chuckles, "If that wasn't precious!"

42   Most of the older girls, the Pre-teens and the Teens, have been in pageants before. They're familiar with the routine, know all the ins and outs, understand how to play up to the judges, an art in itself.

43   Teen contestant number one, for instance, seems to be a house favorite. She does a clogging routine entitled "Texas Tap" that brings down the house. Her talent is undeniable, her exuberance contagious. I find myself smiling and clapping in time to the music along with the rest of the audience. Unfortunately, when it comes time for her prepared speech, this contestant forgets what she was going to say, stumbles verbally. She mumbles, "Oh God," then continues the best she can.

44   A young woman to my right shakes her head, turns to me and says with resignation, "She would have had a hard time, anyway. Her gown is red."

45   My face must reflect my bewilderment.

46   "With red hair?" she adds with implied significance.

47   Obviously, the contestant is unenlightened. Redheads don't wear red. Faux pas. One just doesn't do these things.

48   Some rules in the pageant circle are even more specific. Wearing black shoes with an evening gown is forbidden, as are hats, parasols, and elbow-length gloves. Rules are rules. I have heard that one mother, in another pageant, tried to add an extra row of lace to her daughter's socks. It was specified that only two rows of lace would be allowed. The pageant's organizers solemnly handed this mother a seam-ripper.

49   According to Glenda, this pageant has done away with collective judging, the commonly accepted practice of simultaneously lining up the girls on stage, having them turn, pose in front of the judges. "We don't want them compared to one another. They stand on their own merit."

50   Teen contestant number one does not win.

51   The pageant over, I weave through the departing crowd toward the radio room, anxious to talk to the judges. There is a long line. Accompanied by their mothers, each contestant is given the opportunity to discuss her performance with the judges, find out what cost her the competition, where she lost those valuable points. It is a quiet cluster.

To my left stands one of the winners. Her mother is not waiting with her, not **52** monitoring her behavior. One of her friends walks by, teases, "Hey, you won this year. Why are *you* waiting to see the judges?"

The victor smiles, puffs out her chest with pride, swings her right hand up to her **53** forehead. She nods toward the closed door. "I just want to tell them . . . (with a saucy salute) . . . thanks!"

A mother and her daughter, one of the defeated contestants, try to slip past un- **54** noticed. Another mother looks up, asks, "Aren't you going to conference with the judges?"

"No, I'm afraid I might start crying," the first mother answers. Her daughter says **55** nothing, but her eyes are red.

After a thirty-five minute wait, I am finally able to talk to one of the judges, a man **56** named John. He's wearing a black tuxedo, sports a diamond stud in his ear, has a red carnation pinned on his lapel. He's a hairdresser, has done hair for lots of the pageants—that's how he got "hooked." Most of the judges, he explains, become in- volved when either friends or their own children enter a pageant. These judges don't get paid for their work; instead, they receive a small gift.

"Why do you do it, then?" I ask.   **57**

"I like to see the girls have a good time," he answers.   **58**

Every year I'm asked if I'm going to enter my two little girls in the pageant. Every **59** year I say no.

"Mommy," asks my youngest, "don't you think I'm pretty enough to win?"   **60**

ABOUT THE REST OF THIS BOOK

The chapters that follow in the first part of this book present an orderly progres- sion for developing your skills as a college writer, reader, and researcher. A number of chapters are concerned with reading, since an essential first step is to become a careful, perceptive reader. The early chapters are devoted to techniques and skills in reading for understanding. Later we introduce skills in reading critically and in writing analytically about a text. One area that receives special attention is read- ing argumentative writing and then writing to persuade others.

Our approach to research is systematic and incorporates several stages. We first introduce important skills that involve single sources, including paraphrase and summary. Those skills are then applied to working with multiple sources. The next step is to synthesize paraphrases and summaries of several readings.

We introduce you to various kinds of research, with particular attention to locating and using sources in the library. Our aim is to enable you to find almost any available information you are looking for. We show you how to compile infor- mation, select it, arrange and present it, and document it. In short, you will learn how to write research papers with skill and confidence.

The second part of this book, the Research Paper Reference Handbook, ex- plains the formal conventions of research writing, including lists of works cited, parenthetical notes and footnotes, outlines, and typing conventions. In addition to the MLA style used in most composition classes, two alternative formats are also explained.

We believe you will find this course rewarding and interesting. The activities you will engage in and the skills you will acquire are all eminently practical, and you will have ample opportunity to use them in the years to come. Being able to find the sources you are seeking, to read them perceptively, and to write clearly and articulately about what you have found can give you both a sense of power and a lasting satisfaction.

2 *Strategies for Reading*

Reading is one of the most useful abilities that college students can develop and improve. Of course, you already read well, since you are processing the words on this page. However, being an alert critical reader involves complex skills that we all should refine continually.

◼ INFERENCES

As you learned in Chapter 1, reading is more than just recognizing words on a printed page. It involves the ability to interpret texts by drawing *inferences*— recognizing a writer's intentions, perceiving what is implied but not stated, making connections between the ideas you read and other ideas that you bring from outside the text, and drawing conclusions. You already exercise sophisticated interpretive skills when you read, as the following hypothetical example demonstrates.

Imagine that after having missed three meetings of your psychology class, you receive the following communication from the Dean of Students' office:

> This is to inform you that this office has been notified that you have reached the maximum number of absences permitted by the instructor of Psychology 207. In accordance with University Academic Policy, further absence will cause a lowering of your course grade and may result in your failing the course. This office will continue to monitor your academic progress. Do not hesitate to contact us if we can be of any help to you.

You might form this interpretation: First, the fact that you received a formal notification from the office of a campus administrator, rather than a friendly verbal comment from your instructor, indicates a problem. The formality of the language ("This is to inform you") and the impersonal style ("This office has been notified," rather than "your teacher has told me") give you a sense that a formidable bureaucracy has its eye on you. You conclude somewhat uncomfortably that the university takes attendance seriously. In addition to the actual warning about lower grades, you also note the more vague, implied threat ("This office will continue to monitor your academic progress"), which is only partially eased by the more benevolent final sentence. Upon reading this notice, you understand that it would be unwise for you to miss any more classes if you can possibly help it.

Prior knowledge allows you to interpret the notice in this way. Your previous experience with schools and school officials, with policies and grades, and with the way people use language all lead you to a particular understanding of the notice. Of course, not every reader will respond precisely as you do to such a message, but the point is clear—your mind is actively at work whenever you read. Good readers remain alert—recognizing, understanding, comparing, and evaluating the information they encounter.

EXERCISE | **Drawing Inferences**

Imagine the following scenario. Two weeks before Election Day, Mr. and Mrs. Davis, both in their late thirties, are walking with their five-year-old daughter through a shopping mall. Suddenly a man, smiling broadly, grabs Mr. Davis's hand and shakes it vigorously. On the lapel of his suit jacket is a large button that reads, "Bob Inskip for State Senate." He says:

> Hi, folks, I'm Bob Inskip. Hope you're havin' a great day. My what a beautiful little girl! [*To the girl:*] Hello, sweetheart, do you know how much you look like your mama? [*To Mrs. Davis:*] But, wait a minute, you're too young. This has to be your little sister. [*To both Mr. and Mrs. Davis:*] You know, I'm running for State Senate, and I need the support of honest, hard-working family folks like you. I'm not one of those professional politicians, and you won't find a lot of fancy degrees tacked onto my name. But then you won't find any drug charges on my record either. Now I'm not saying anything against my opponent, who's probably a well-meaning young fella. But anybody who compares our records can see I'm a local taxpayer, businessman, and property owner who grew up the hard way without any handouts. And that's the kind of senator we need keeping an eye on those government bureaucrats. I think smart folks like you will understand the issues and vote for me, Bob Inskip. Have a good one.

In a flash, he's off grabbing another shopper's hand and introducing himself.

1. Take a few minutes to write your interpretation of what you have read. What do you learn about Bob Inskip, outside of the explicit content of his remarks to the Davises? What kind of an impression does he make on you? Is that the impression he wishes to make? Specifically, what qualities do you find in him, and what alerts you to them? Why do you think he says what he does?

2. Now think about why you were able to read the passage as you did. What previous knowledge and experiences allowed you to interpret it in that way? Would a visitor from a country with a different political tradition, say, Libya or China, interpret Bob Inskip's behavior and intentions as you have?

 ## CONTEXT

Introduced briefly in Chapter 1, *context* refers to the often complex web of circumstances surrounding almost every text or utterance. Suppose someone were to lead you blindfolded through the stacks of your college library, asking you at some arbitrary point to reach out and remove any book from one of the shelves. Still blindfolded, you flip the book open and point your finger at the open page; then, when your blindfold is removed, you begin reading. In all probability, it will take some time before the words begin to make sense—if indeed they ever do. With no idea of why or when or by whom the book was written, without any inkling of what preceded the passage you turned to, it is likely that you will misconstrue what you read. (This helps to explain why *quoting out of context* is so misleading and is therefore discouraged in all types of discourse, but especially in research writing and argument.)

When good readers approach any type of text, from a comic strip to a technical report, they form expectations about what it will say. Otherwise, even the simplest language would make little or no sense. We have all participated in or witnessed conversations similar to this: Two friends, Phoebe and Reuben, are discussing the rain clouds that loom threateningly in the western sky. Phoebe's mind then turns to an upcoming softball game and she says, "I hope they'll be able to come." Reuben, still thinking about the clouds, stares at her with a puzzled look. He cannot understand Phoebe because he is unable to place her words in the appropriate context. She is addressing one topic while he is trying to relate her words to another.

Like conversation, reading requires you to fit words into a context, which includes background information, tacit knowledge, and prior experience. For example, if you are reading the directions on the box of a frozen dinner, your familiarity with context allows you to anticipate a particular type of information, style, structure, and language. Consequently, the statement "Preheat conventional oven to 375°" makes sense.

Several elements contribute to the context of any passage you read. Imagine, for example, that you are reading the final chapter of a detective novel. In this case, context includes the following:

1. Recognition of the defining features of a particular type of text (e.g., knowing that detective novels end by solving a crime)

2. Familiarity with terms such as *homicide* and *motive*

3. Knowledge of what happened in previous chapters

All these elements allow you to anticipate what you are likely to encounter as you read. Without this context, reading is virtually impossible.

| **Analyzing Context** | **EXERCISES** |

1. To test our claim that it is nearly impossible to read without a context, see if you can draw meaning from the following passage:

. . . As the tellers passed along our lowest row on the left-hand side, the interest was insupportable—two hundred and ninety-one, two hundred and ninety-two—we were all standing up and stretching forward, telling with the tellers. At three hundred there was a short cry of joy, at three hundred and two another—suppressed however in a moment. For we did not yet know what the hostile force might be. We knew however that we could not be severely beaten. The doors were thrown open, and in they came. Each of them as he entered brought some different report of their numbers. It must have been impossible, as you may conceive, in the lobby, crowded as they must have been, to form any exact estimate. . . .

a. Are there any words in the passage that you do not know? Can you tell what the passage is describing? What guesses did you make as you read it?

b. Although its language is not especially difficult, it is likely that the passage did not make much sense to you, since you were deprived of the context that a reader would normally have. Had you encountered the passage in its original context, you would have had the following information: It is an excerpt from a letter written in 1831 by British historian Thomas Babington Macaulay. As a Member of Parliament, Macaulay had voted in favor of the important Reform Bill, which liberalized voting privileges. Along with other supporters of this legislation, he had had little hope that the bill would gain the more than three hundred votes needed for passage. Excitement grew as the tellers (clerks who counted and certified individual votes) announced their tallies.

Provided with this context, would it be easier to read the passage a second time? If so, why?

2. Imagine you have been asked to read the following process description as a test of your powers of recall. Here are the directions: Read it once, put it aside, and then write down as many specific facts as you can remember.

The procedure is actually quite simple. First you arrange things into different groups. Of course, one pile may be sufficient depending on how much there is to do. If you have to go somewhere else due to lack of facilities, that is the next step; otherwise you are pretty well set. It is important not to overdo things. That is, it is better to do too few things at once than too many. In the short run this may not seem important but complications can easily arise. A mistake can be expensive as well. At first the whole procedure will seem complicated. Soon, however, it will become just another facet of life. It is difficult to foresee any end to the necessity for this task in the immediate future, but then one can never tell. After the procedure is completed, one arranges the materials into different groups again. Then they can be put into their appropriate places. Eventually they will be used once more, and the whole cycle will then have to be repeated. However, that is part of life.

—John D. Bransford and Marcia K. Johnson, "Cognitive Prerequisites for Understanding"

Although the vocabulary and sentence structure of this passage are simple, you probably had difficulty recalling details. But suppose you had been provided the title "Doing the Laundry." Do you think you could have recalled more specific facts?

3. Now read the following narrative paragraph:

The Prisoner
Rocky slowly got up from the mat, planning his escape. He hesitated a moment and thought. Things were not going well. What bothered him the most was being held, especially since the charge against him had been weak. He considered his present

situation. The lock that held him was strong, but he thought he could break it. He knew, however, that his timing would have to be perfect. Rocky was aware that it was because of his early roughness that he had been penalized so severely—much too severely from his point of view. The situation was becoming frustrating; the pressure had been grinding on him for too long. He was being ridden unmercifully. Rocky was getting angry now. He felt that he was ready to make his move. He knew that his success or failure would depend on what he did in the next few seconds.

—John D. Bransford, *Human Cognition: Learning, Understanding, and Remembering*

Now reread the paragraph, replacing the title with "The Wrestler." Does this alter your response? Why is it possible to play with the meaning of this paragraph by changing its title? What if the paragraph opened with a summarizing sentence? From a reader's perspective, what is the value of a title and summarizing sentence?

 ## STRATEGIES FOR UNDERSTANDING

As the preceding exercises demonstrate, familiarity with context makes it easier to interpret a passage. Since the context in which you place a passage depends on your knowledge, experiences, values, opinions, and interests, another reader may place the same passage in a somewhat different context and, as a result, interpret it differently.

There are skills, however, that all good readers share. They are observant of context and seek clues to enrich their understanding of it, thus refining their interpretation. In large part, readers develop this ability through practice. The more you read, the better reader you become. But it also helps to be familiar with some of the principles and strategies of good reading. You can become a better reader quickly with a little training and lots of practice.

Good readers routinely adopt various ***reading strategies***. These strategies take time—and, at first, may seem counterproductive—but they save time in the long run, since they make your reading more alert, thorough, and efficient. Choosing the most appropriate and effective strategies depends on your purposes for reading. Sometimes you read for entertainment, at other times, for information or ideas. Often you read for several different purposes at the same time. Sometimes you accept the writer's authority and strive to understand and absorb what you read. At other times, you approach a text more critically, assessing the writer's authority and the validity of her ideas. Chapter 7 presents strategies for critical reading. The focus of this chapter, on the other hand, is reading for understanding and information. The strategies that experienced readers use to understand a text include the following:

- Looking for clues in a text before starting to read it
- Responding to clues provided by the author
- Reading with a pencil
- Rereading as necessary

Surveying a Text

To understand even the simplest passage, you must first place it in an appropriate context so as to anticipate what it is likely to contain. The more you know about context, the more reliably you can anticipate and the more efficiently you will read. It is therefore useful to discover in advance as much about a text as you can. The technique is simple: *Look over what you intend to read—quickly but alertly—before you begin to read it.*

Specifically, there are several clues to look for before you begin your actual reading, as the following situation demonstrates. Suppose you are reading an issue of *Newsweek* and you come upon the "My Turn" essay that appears on the facing page. What might you do before reading it (or even as you decide whether you want to read it)?

EXERCISE   **Surveying a Text**

Look now at the *Newsweek* essay on the facing page and see how much you can gather about it *without actually reading its text*. What do you expect the topic of the essay to be? What do you guess is the writer's point of view? What allowed you to make these guesses?

Prereading

Good readers search for clues when they first encounter a text. Following are some of the sources of information that can improve your understanding of a text and enrich your interpretation of it. While specific references are to the *Newsweek* essay, these sources of information can improve your understanding of most of the reading that you do in college.

Title

It may seem obvious to begin reading a text by taking note of its title, but a surprising number of students read assigned chapters and articles without doing so. Consequently, they miss an important source of information.

Article titles, chapter headings, and newspaper headlines usually identify topics discussed in the text, helping you anticipate content. For example, the title of this chapter, "Strategies for Reading," led you to expect an explanation of how to get more from your reading. The *Newsweek* essay provides both a title, "I Can Do Anything, So How Do I Choose?" and a subtitle indicating an essay about planning for the future.

Highlighted Quotations

Important passages are often highlighted, providing clues to the central idea of a text. In the *Newsweek* essay, for instance, a statement appears beneath the author's photograph: "There are moments of self-doubt and frantic calls cross-country.

My Turn

I Can Do Anything, So How Do I Choose?

With countless options and all the freedom I'll ever need, comes the pressure to find the perfect life.

BY JENNY NORENBERG

FOR THE MOST PART, MY WOMEN friends and I were kids of upper-middle-class privilege, raised to believe that, with hard work and a little courage, the world was ours. We climbed mountains at summer camp, went to Europe on high-school class trips and took family vacations to New York City and the Grand Canyon. Our parents, like theirs before them, told their kids they could go anywhere and do anything. We took them at their word.

By the time we hit adulthood, technology and globalization had brought the world to our doorstep. Now in our mid-20s, we're unsteadily navigating a barrage of choices our mothers never had the chance to make. No one can complain about parents who started sentences with "When *you're* president ..." But we are now discovering the difficulty of deciding just what makes us happy in a world of innumerable options.

Three years ago my friends and I barreled out of the University of Wisconsin ready to make our mark on the world. Julia headed to France to teach English. I started law school in Minneapolis. Marie and Alexis searched for work in San Francisco. Bridget started an internship in D.C. Kristina landed a job in Ireland. The list goes on. Scattering to our respective destinations, we were young enough to follow our crazy dreams but old enough to fend for ourselves in the real world. At a time when our lives were undergoing dramatic changes, so was America. Three months after receiving our diplomas, the Twin Towers came crashing down. We realized that, in more ways than one, the world was scarier and more complex than we'd ever imagined.

Since graduation, we've struggled to make our own happiness. It seems that having so many choices has sometimes overwhelmed us. In the seven years since I left home for college, I've had 13 addresses and lived in six cities. How can I stay with one person, at one job, in one city, when I have the world at my fingertips?

YOUNG AND RESTLESS: There are moments of self-doubt and frantic calls cross-country. ('I don't know a soul here!')

Moving from one place to the next, bouncing from job to job, my friends and I have experienced the world, but also gotten lost in it. There have been moments of self-doubt, frantic calls cross-country. ("I don't know a soul here!" "Do I really want to be a ____?") Frustrated by studying law, I joined friends in San Francisco to waitress for a summer and contemplate whether to return to school in Minnesota. Unhappy and out of work in Portland, Molly moved to Chicago. Loni broke up with a boyfriend and packed her tiny Brooklyn apartment into a U-Haul, heading for Seattle. Others took jobs or entered grad school anywhere from Italy to L.A. Some romances and friendships succumbed to distance, career ambition or simply growing up. We all lost some sleep at one point or another, at times feeling utterly consumed by cities of thousands, even millions, knowing that even local friends were just as transient as we were.

Like so many women my age, I remain unmarried at an age when my mother already had children. She may have had the opportunity to go to college, but she was expected to marry soon after. While my friends and I still feel the pressure to marry and have children, we've gained a few postcollege years of socially accepted freedom that our mothers never had.

The years between college and marriage are in many ways far more self-defining than any others. They're filled with the simplest, yet most complex, decisions in life: choosing a city, picking a career, finding friends and a mate—in sum, building a happy and satisfying life. For me and for my group of friends, these years have been eye-opening, confusing and fabulous at the same time.

The more choices you have, the more decisions you must make—and the more you have yourself to blame if you wind up unhappy. There is a kind of perverted contentedness in certainty born of a lack of alternatives. At my age, my mother, whether she liked it or not, had fewer tough decisions to make. I don't envy the pressure she endured to follow a traditional career path and marry early. But sometimes I envy the stability she had.

Once again I've been unable to resist the lure of a new city. So, as I start my legal career in Chicago, I'm again building friendships from scratch, learning my way around a strange new place. Yes, my friends and I could have avoided the loneliness and uncertainty inherent in our journeys, and gone back to our hometowns or stayed in the college town where we had each other. But I doubt any one of us would trade our adventures for that life. I have a sense of identity and self-assurance now that I didn't have, couldn't have had, when I graduated from college. And I know someday I'll look back on this time—before I had a spouse, a home and children to care for—and be thankful for the years that just belonged to me.

NORENBERG lives in Chicago.

(I don't know a soul here!)" This allows an alert reader to infer that the author relies on friends or family members for advice and encouragement as she struggles with the normal insecurities of a person her age.

The Author

Information about an author can enrich your reading of a text. Recognizing an author's name often allows you to make predictions. The title "Teenagers and Sex" would arouse different expectations if the author were evangelist Pat Robertson as opposed to Hugh Hefner, the publisher of *Playboy*. Professional titles, academic degrees, authorship of other publications, or information about a writer's occupation and accomplishments may provide clues about her expertise or bias. Often a book will introduce its author on the flap of a dust jacket. Articles may do this in an introductory headnote, in a footnote to the first page, or on the last page.

The *Newsweek* article provides a photograph of the author, identifying her only as a resident of Chicago. Since neither her name nor her face is familiar, you may infer that the article expresses the views of a recent college graduate who is neither a professional writer nor a celebrity. References to choices and options in both the title and subtitle further suggest that the author comes from a relatively privileged background.

Past Experience

Sometimes prior reading provides clues about what to expect. A regular reader of *Newsweek* will recognize the "My Turn" column as a recurring feature of that magazine. Articles in this series typically relate the personal experiences or express the opinions of individual readers. This provides further confirmation that this is a personal essay about planning for the future.

Section Headings

Headings and subheadings are especially useful in longer passages. One effective strategy is to leaf through a text to distinguish the parts that make it up. Before reading a book, examine its table of contents; before reading an article or chapter, look for headings. Accurately predicting a text's major ideas and organization makes reading more efficient. Although the *Newsweek* article has no subject headings, a text that does can be found on pages 60–64.

Date of Publication

Knowing when a text was published can help you to evaluate it. If you need information about international terrorism, for instance, it makes an enormous difference whether a source was published in 2000 or 2005. Date of publication may also put an author's ideas and claims into perspective. As the author herself indicates in her third paragraph, the attitudes of recent graduates have changed significantly since 2001, the year she completed her college education.

Length

Noting the length of a text can give you an indication of how thoroughly the author's point is developed. It also helps to know where you stand within that development as you read.

Bold Type, Illustrations, and Captions

You can find additional clues to the contents of a book chapter by briefly examining it before you read. Words relating central concepts are often boldfaced. (Look for examples in this chapter.) Other major ideas may be illustrated in charts, graphs, drawings, or photographs and explained in captions. Open a textbook that has illustrations and see what you can learn from looking at them.

With an article like the one we have examined, it takes only a few seconds of prereading to gather most of this information. Prereading strategies amply repay the small investment of time you make in carrying them out: your mind is receptive as you begin to read, your reading is made easier, and you can read more alertly and profitably.

| **Using Prereading Strategies** | **EXERCISES** |

1. Read "I Can Do Anything, So How Do I Choose?" and determine the accuracy of the predictions you made using prereading strategies. Did these strategies enable you to read more efficiently?

2. Using as many prereading strategies as you can, explain what predictions you can make about the rest of this chapter and about the reading that appears on pages 134–41.

Responding to Textual Clues

Good writers help their readers. They anticipate who those readers are likely to be, and then they strive to be understood by them. They write clearly, using a vocabulary and style appropriate to their audience. They provide punctuation to signal pauses or to show when one idea ends and another begins. Good readers, for their part, recognize and profit from the signals they are given.

It is always easier for us to read a passage if we have a reasonably clear notion of what it is likely to be about. In a variety of ways, authors allow us to anticipate their ideas. Even inexperienced writers provide readers with various signposts to help them, as the following paragraph from a student's paper on teenage drinking demonstrates:

> Another cause of drinking among teenagers is peer pressure. They are told, "If you don't join in with everyone else, you're going to feel left out." Before you know it, they are drinking along with the rest of the crowd. Soon they are even drinking before class, at lunch, and after school. They now have a serious drinking problem.

This paragraph, taken from a rough draft, would benefit from additional development and other kinds of revision. Even so, it demonstrates some of the signposts that writers provide for readers. Previous paragraphs in the paper discuss other factors contributing to teenage drinking. The opening words of this paragraph, *Another cause*, are a **signal phrase**, indicating that a further reason is about to be introduced. The first sentence is a **topic sentence** summarizing the general point of the paragraph. Upon reading it, we can predict that the rest of the paragraph will explain how peer pressure works. The writer does just that, detailing the process of how teenagers develop a drinking problem through peer pressure, and she uses transition words or phrases like *before you know it, soon*, and *now* to show that she is describing a sequence of stages.

Notice also how your mind works as you read the following passage with numbered sentences:

> **1** Scarfe was always a tyrant in his household. **2** The servants lived in constant terror of his fierce diatribes, which he would deliver whenever he was displeased. **3** One of the most frequent causes of his displeasure was the food they served him. **4** His tea, for example, was either too hot or too cold. **5** The soup had either too much or too little seasoning. **6** Another pet peeve was the servants' manner of address. **7** God help the butler who forgot to add *sir* to every sentence he spoke to Scarfe, or the chauffeur whose tone was deemed not properly deferential. **8** On the other hand, when one of the most timid parlor maids would hesitate in speaking so as to be certain her words did not give offense, he would thunder at her, "Out with it, you stupid girl!"
>
> **9** Scarfe's wife and children were equally the victims of his tyranny. . . .

Observe how each sentence in the passage creates a context for sentences to come and so allows you to anticipate them. In the analysis that follows, we have made some assumptions about how you, or any typical reader, might respond to the passage. Take some time to examine the analysis carefully and see if you agree with it.

As you read the Scarfe passage, your mind follows a fairly predictable path. First, since sentence 1 makes a general statement, you recognize it as a topic sentence. In other words, you guess that Scarfe's tyranny is the **main idea** of the paragraph. It comes as no surprise that sentence 2 provides a specific detail about his tyranny—he terrorized servants. After sentence 2, you might expect either to learn which other members of the household Scarfe terrorized or to get more specific information about his treatment of the servants. The latter turns out to be the case. The signal phrase "one of the most frequent causes of his displeasure" in sentence 3 shows where the paragraph is heading: "one of" indicates that food is among several causes of Scarfe's anger and suggests that you may learn about others. The author makes the relationship between 2 and 3 clear by **repeating key words and phrases:** "his displeasure" in 3 recalls "he was displeased" in 2, and "they" in 3 refers to "the servants" in 2. Sentence 4 also provides a signal phrase, "for example," helping you anticipate an instance of Scarfe's displeasure. Although sentence 5 offers no explicit signal, it is phrased like sentence 4 and contains the words "either too . . . or too . . . ," suggesting a parallel purpose. In sentence 6, "another pet peeve" refers back to sentence 3, which describes the first pet peeve. Since 3 is followed by examples, you can expect the same of 6, and in fact both 7 and 8 also give specific instances of the servants' manner of address. Sentence 8 begins with the signal phrase, "on the other hand," which indicates a change in direction; that is, the sentence offers an example different from the one in 7. It says that servants could be criticized for being too deferential, as well as for not being deferential enough.

Through *topic sentences*, *repeated key words*, and *signal phrases*, writers give readers clues to make reading easier. Without having to think about it, experienced readers respond to these clues, make predictions, and read with greater ease and effectiveness as a result. Chapter 4 pays special attention to topic sentences. The remaining sections of the chapter are concerned with other reading clues.

Responding to Textual Clues	**EXERCISES**

1. Only the first sentence (sentence 9) of the second paragraph is given in the passage about Scarfe. Make some predictions about the rest of the paragraph. Do you think sentence 9 is likely to be the paragraph's topic sentence? What would you expect the rest of the paragraph to be about? How does sentence 9 relate to the preceding paragraph? Does it contain any signal words or phrases linking it to that paragraph?

2. By inventing details, complete the second paragraph, illustrating how Scarfe mistreated his wife and children. When finished, see what clues you have provided your readers.

Recognizing Transitions

Just as it is important for readers to recognize clues, it is also important for writers to provide them. Signal words and phrases make reading easier because they clarify the relationship between one sentence and another. For this reason they are also called *transitions*. They help the reader see in which direction the ideas in a passage are moving. Relationships between sentences can be classified into several general categories. The following are four of the most important relationships, together with commonly used transition words for each.

And *Signals*

And words signal movement in the same direction. They tell you that the new idea or fact will in some way be like the previous one. Here are the most common *and* signals:

and	first	similarly	furthermore
too	second	finally	what's more
also	another	indeed	moreover
then	in fact	likewise	in addition

Example: Pilbeam's wisecracks got on his classmates' nerves. He *also* angered the teacher by snoring during the metaphysics lecture.

But *Signals*

But words signal a change in direction. They tell you that the new fact or idea will be different or opposite from the previous one.

but	however	conversely	unfortunately
still	the fact is	nonetheless	notwithstanding
instead	in contrast	nevertheless	on the other hand

Example: The doctor ordered Gerstenslager to give up all spicy foods. *Nonetheless,* he could still be found most nights by the TV set, munching happily on jalapeños and pickled sausages.

For Example *Signals*

For example words signal a movement from the general to the specific. They tell you that the new fact or idea will be a specific illustration of the previous general one.

for example	for instance	specifically	to begin with

Example: Mopworth is a splendid athlete. At a high-school track meet, *for example*, she took firsts in both the low hurdles and the ten-kilometer race.

Therefore *Signals*

Therefore words signal a cause-and-effect relationship. They tell you that the new fact or idea will be the result of the previous one.

thus	therefore	accordingly	consequently
so	hence	as a result	thereupon

Example: The Godolphin twins never remembered to set their alarm clocks. *As a result,* they were always late for their eight o'clock statistics class.

EXERCISES | **Transitions**

1. The following passages are made difficult to read because signal words have been removed. Supply signal words where you feel they would be useful to clarify relationships between sentences or to make the flow of the passage smoother.

   a. The open-source movement traces its roots to 1984, when MIT computer scientist Richard Stallman quit his job in academia to start the Free Software Foundation. In the 1960s and early 1970s, virtually all software was in the public domain [i.e., uncopyrighted and marketable], and thus open for constant revision and review. By the early 1980s, nearly all new software was proprietary, or "closed-source"— its underlying code copyrighted and guarded as closely as the Coke recipe. Stallman felt that this approach hampered the free flow of ideas and ultimately delivered bad software. He devised a clever legal device known as a General Public License (GPL), or "copyleft." Software that is licensed under a copyleft is in the public domain. Any derivative works that use a piece of copylefted code must be in the public domain. The copyleft is like a virus, passing itself on to its descendants.

—Leif Utne, "Free at Last!"

b. What is Benford's Law and why is it weird? Think of a large and random set of numbers that is somehow derived from other numbers. Closing stock prices are essentially derived from a host of other numbers. Growth, cost of labor, prevailing interest rates, and so on [affect stock prices]. [There is an] amazingly large volume of numbers in [economic data]. You'd think those numbers, which are basically assembled randomly, would be spread out randomly. There'd be just as many numbers beginning with nine or four or one. That's where you'd be wrong. Some unseen and unknown universal force . . . bunches these kinds of random numbers into very predictable patterns.

—Kevin Maney, "Baffled by Math?"

Nearly every sentence in these paragraphs has an *and, but, for example,* or *therefore* relationship to the sentence before it and, presumably, could carry a signal word or phrase. But since so many signals would clutter the paragraph, you must decide where to include and where to omit them. For each signal you add, explain why it seems necessary or desirable.

2. Reread the passages above and identify other cohesive techniques (repeated words and phrases, topic sentences) that the writers have provided to help readers.

3. What transition words and phrases can you find in the article on page 81?

4. Find a passage from another of your textbooks—one that uses a variety of transitional signals. Write a brief commentary on how those signals alert readers to connections among ideas.

5. Look at the paragraph you wrote in response to exercise 2 on page 85. What transitional words and phrases did you provide? Add any others that seem necessary.

Reading with a Pencil

Students confront two basic tasks when reading for academic purposes: remaining alertly engaged and facilitating later review. Almost everyone has had the disconcerting experience of struggling to remain alert only to drift into a trance, as the eyes continue to plod across the page after the mind has wandered elsewhere. When concentration is a struggle, reading is slow, unpleasant, and ineffective. Fortunately, there is a way to read more efficiently while maintaining concentration: You can read better if you use a pencil.

Reading with a pencil involves two activities—***underlining*** and ***note-taking.*** If a book is yours, you may do both. When underlining, you highlight main ideas and significant information. When writing marginal notes, you summarize the author's ideas in your own words or jot down your own ideas and responses.

Reading with a pencil keeps the mind alert and active. When you combine writing with reading, you bring a larger area of your brain into play. Reading with a pencil also forces you to respond more actively. When you search for an author's main ideas and connect them with personal experiences or with other texts, you become more involved with what you read. When you are thinking in this manner, you are more likely to understand what you read.

Besides increasing alertness, reading with a pencil creates a useful record that provides ready access to what you have read. For example, if you have marked a textbook chapter with underlining and marginal notes, you can review the material quickly and effectively before an exam. You won't have to reread everything, since you have marked what seems most important. Moreover, by reviewing the highlighted passages, you stimulate memory and thereby recollect most of what you learned and thought about the first time through.

Just as no two people interpret or respond to a book in exactly the same way, no two readers will mark a book in the same way either. In general, people's diverse experiences provoke a multitude of associations and reactions to the same text. Likewise, even the same reader may respond differently to the same text, when her purposes for reading change.

Annotating and Underlining for Recall

Let us assume that a student in developmental psychology is about to be tested on a textbook chapter that analyzes relationships between adolescents and their parents. Seeking literal comprehension of important facts, she might annotate one excerpt from the chapter as follows:

PRACTICE READING

Relationships with Maturing Children

Diane E. Papalia, Sally Wendkos Olds, and Ruth Duskin Feldman

1   Parenthood is a process of letting go. This process usually reaches its climax during the parents' middle age. It is true that, with modern trends toward delaying marriage and parenthood, an increasing number of middle-aged people now face such issues as finding a good day-care or kindergarten program and screening the content of Saturday morning cartoons. Still, most parents in the early part of middle age must cope with a different set of issues, which arise from living with children who will soon be leaving the nest. Once children become adults, parent-child ties usually recede in importance; but these ties normally last as long as parent and child live.

ADOLESCENT CHILDREN: ISSUES FOR PARENTS

2   It is ironic that people at the two times of life popularly linked with emotional crises—adolescence and midlife—often live in the same household. It is usually middle-aged adults who are the parents of adolescent children. While dealing with their own special concerns, parents have to cope daily with young people who are undergoing great physical, emotional, and social changes.

3   Although research contradicts the stereotype of adolescence as a time of inevitable turmoil and rebellion . . . , some rejection of parental authority is necessary

for the maturing youngster. <u>An important task for parents is to accept children as they are, not as what the parents had hoped they would be.</u>

Theorists from a variety of perspectives have described this period as one of questioning, reappraisal, or diminished well-being for parents. However, this too is not inevitable, according to a questionnaire survey of 129 two-parent, intact, mostly white, socioeconomically diverse families with a firstborn son or daughter between ages 10 and 15. Most vulnerable were mothers who were not heavily invested in paid work; apparently work can bolster a parent's self-worth despite the challenges of having a teenage child. For some other parents, especially white-collar and professional men with sons, their children's adolescence brought increased satisfaction, well-being, and even pride. <u>For most parents, the normative changes of adolescence elicited a mixture of positive and negative emotions.</u> This was particularly true of mothers with early adolescent daughters, whose relationships generally tended to be both close and conflict-filled (Silverberg, 1996).

4

WHEN CHILDREN LEAVE: THE EMPTY NEST
<u>Research is also challenging popular ideas about the empty nest, a supposedly difficult transition, especially for women.</u> Although some women, heavily invested in mothering, do have problems at this time, they are far outnumbered by those who, like Madeline Albright, find the departure liberating (Antonucci & Akiyama, 1997; Barnett, 1985; Chiriboga, 1997; Helson, 1997; Mitchell & Helson, 1990). Today, the refilling of the nest by grown children returning home (discussed in the next section) is far more stressful (Thomas, 1997).

5

The empty nest does not signal the end of parenthood. It is a transition to a new stage: the relationship between parents and adult children. For many women, this transition brings relief from what Gutmann called "the chronic emergency of parenthood" (Cooper & Gutmann, 1987, p. 347). They can now pursue their own interests as they bask in their grown children's accomplishments. The empty nest does appear to be hard on women who have not prepared for it by reorganizing their lives (Targ, 1979). This phase also may be hard on fathers who regret that they did not spend more time with their children (L. B. Rubin, 1979).

6

In a longitudinal study of employed married women with multiple roles, the empty nest had *no* effect on psychological health, but cutting back on employment *increased* distress, whereas going to work full-time *decreased* it (Wethington & Kessler, 1989). On the other hand, in a comparison of stress at various stages of life, men in the empty-nest stage were most likely to report health-related stress (Chiriboga, 1997).

7

WHEN CHILDREN RETURN: THE REVOLVING-DOOR SYNDROME
What happens if the nest does not empty when it normally should, or if it unexpectedly refills? In recent decades, more and more adult children have delayed leaving home. Furthermore, the <u>revolving door syndrome</u> (sometimes called the *boomerang phenomenon*) has become more common, as increasing numbers of young adults, especially men, return to their parents' home, sometimes more than once. The family home can be a convenient, supportive, and affordable haven while young adults are getting on their feet or regaining their balance in times of financial, marital, or other trouble.

8

According to the National Survey of Families and Households, at any given moment 45 percent of parents ages 45 to 54 with children over age 18 have an adult child living at home; and three out of four 19- to 34-year-olds have lived in the parental home after turning 19 (in four out of ten cases, more than once). Thus this "nonnormative" experience <u>is becoming quite normative, especially for parents with</u>

9

There is a great deal of variation among families, but parents who work usually adjust to the empty nest more easily.

more than one child. Rather than an abrupt leave-taking, the empty-nest transition may be seen as a more prolonged process of separation, often lasting several years.

10   The way this transition plays out for parents is "strongly related to children's progress through the transition to adulthood" (Aquilino, 1996, pp. 435–436). Most likely to come home are single, divorced, or separated children and those who end a cohabiting relationship. Leaving school and ending military service increase the chances of returning; having a child decreases them.

Revolving door is more likely to arouse stress because some people view adult children living at home as a sign that they have failed as parents.

11   As common as it has become, the revolving-door syndrome contradicts most parents' expectations for young adults. As children move from adolescence to young adulthood, parents expect them to become independent. Their autonomy is a sign of parental success. As the timing-of-events model would predict, then, an unanticipated return to the nest may lead to tension. Serious conflicts or open hostility may arise when a young adult child is unemployed and financially dependent or has returned after the failure of a marriage. Relations are smoother when the parents see the adult child moving toward autonomy, for example by enrolling in college.

12   Disagreements may center on household responsibilities and the adult child's lifestyle. The young adult is likely to feel isolated from peers, while the parents may feel hampered in renewing their intimacy, exploring personal interests, and resolving marital issues (Aquilino & Supple, 1991). The return of an adult child works best when parents and child negotiate roles and responsibilities, acknowledging the child's adult status and the parents' right to privacy.

GUIDELINES   ## Annotating and Underlining for Recall

- *Mark the most important ideas.* Use underlining to outline a passage, highlighting those parts that express important ideas—topic sentences instead of supporting details, unless they too are significant. Notice that the reader does not underline anything in paragraphs 6 and 7, which illustrate a point made in the first sentence of paragraph 5:

  Research is also challenging popular ideas about the empty nest, a supposedly difficult transition, especially for women. Although some women, heavily invested in mothering, do have problems at this time, they are far outnumbered by those who, like Madeline Albright, find the departure liberating (Antonucci & Akiyama, 1997; Barnett, 1985; Chiriboga, 1997; Helson, 1997; Mitchell & Helson, 1990).

- *Don't underline too much.* Underlining nearly every sentence blurs distinctions between important concepts and minor details. Be selective, highlighting only the most important ideas and information. Of course, the amount you underline depends on what you read. A passage with heavily concentrated information may require lots of underlining. Passages that list examples or provide background may not be underlined at all. Judgment, derived through experience, offers the best guidance.

- *Mark with rereading in mind.* Underline words that clearly and briefly express important ideas. You needn't underline entire sentences if there are phrases that capture main ideas. Sometimes parts of different sentences can be connected to form a single statement, as in the following example:

In recent decades, more and more adult children have delayed leaving home. Furthermore, the underline{revolving-door syndrome} (sometimes called the *boomerang phenomenon*) underline{has become more common, as} increasing numbers of young adults, especially men, return to their parents' home, sometimes more than once. The family home can be a convenient, supportive, and affordable haven while young adults are getting on their feet or regaining their balance in times of financial, marital, or other trouble.

According to the National Survey of Families and Households, at any given moment 45% of parents ages 45 to 54 with children over age 18 have an adult child living at home; and three out of four 19- to 34-year-olds have lived in the parental home after turning 19 (in four out of ten cases, more than once). Thus this "nonnormative" experience underline{is becoming quite normative, especially for parents with more than one child.}

- *When the author's words are not convenient or clear, use your own.* If a passage is not phrased in words suitable for underlining, rephrase the main idea in a marginal note. The reader of our sample passage wrote marginal notes to summarize ideas in paragraphs 4 and 11. Capsulizing important concepts in your own words helps you understand what you read. When people talk about "writing to learn," one of the things they mean is that when students recast difficult or unfamiliar ideas in their own words, their ability to understand and recall those ideas is enhanced. In some sense, they assume ownership of concepts that may initially have seemed obscure and alien.

- *Use special symbols to signal the most important passages.* Since some of the passages you mark are more important than others, highlight them by placing symbols beside them in the margins. Stars, asterisks, checks, and exclamation or question marks make important passages stand out.

- *Mark only your own books.* Because no two readers think exactly alike as they read, no one likes to read books that other people have marked. Writing in books borrowed from the library or friends is both a discourtesy and an act of vandalism. Use stick-on notes, or make photocopies of any borrowed materials that you want to mark. Of course, you are strongly urged to mark books that belong to you.

Annotating and Underlining for Recall

EXERCISE

Like the *Newsweek* editorial on page 81, the following article concerns relationships between college students and their parents. As you read it, try to connect the views of the author, a college president, with those expressed in the *Newsweek* piece. Then reread with a pencil, annotating specific facts and concepts. Be careful to mark any passages that might help you better understand, modify, or contradict views held by the author of the *Newsweek* editorial.

PRACTICE READING

Keeping Parents off Campus

Judith R. Shapiro

Every September I join our deans and faculty to welcome first-year students and their families to the Barnard [College] campus. It is a bittersweet moment; while the parents are filled with pride, they also know they now must begin to let go of their children. Parents must learn to back off.

Confidently, with generosity and grace, most parents let their children grow up. They realize that the purpose of college is to help young people stand on their own and take the crucial steps toward adulthood while developing their talents and intellect with skill and purpose.

But this truth is often swept aside by the notion that college is just one more commodity to be purchased, like a car or a vacation home. This unfortunate view gives some parents the wrong idea. Their sense of entitlement as consumers, along with an inability to let go, leads some parents to want to manage all aspects of their children's college lives—from the quest for admission to their choice of major. Such parents, while the exception, are nonetheless an increasing fact of life for faculty, deans, and presidents.

Three examples, all recently experienced by my staff, illustrate my point. One mother accompanied her daughter to a meeting with her dean to discuss a supposedly independent research project. Another demanded that her daughter's academic transcript be sent to her directly, since she was the one paying the tuition bills. And one father called his daughter's career counselor so he could contact her prospective employers to extol her qualifications.

I have had my own awkward encounters on this front. I have met with parents accompanying their daughters on campus visits who speak in "third person invisible." The prospective student sits there—either silently or attempting to get a word in edgewise—while the parents speak about her as if she were elsewhere. I always make a point of addressing the student directly; although this initially feels as if I were talking to a ventriloquist's dummy, I find that, if I keep at it, I can shift the conversation to one between the young woman and me.

Stories abound of parents horrified by a child's choice of major and ready to do battle with faculty or deans. These parents fail to understand that passion and curiosity about a subject, coupled with the ability to learn, are the best career preparation.

We are living in times when educational pressures on families begin when children are toddlers and continue relentlessly through the teenage years. Four-year-olds may face a battery of tests to get into a desirable preschool. As they face the college admissions process, parents attuned to the barrage of media coverage believe that the best colleges accept only superhumans—a belief encouraged, admittedly, by some universities—and strive to prepare their sons and daughters accordingly. (One father even took a year off from his job to supervise the preparation of his daughter's admissions portfolio.)

By the time their children enter college, parents have become so invested emotionally in their success that they may not understand why it is crucial that they remain outside the college gates. The division of responsibility between parents and colleges during the undergraduate years is a complex matter, as is the question of how much responsibility young people should be expected to take for themselves.

We have been hearing much of late about a return to the *in loco parentis* approach that fell out of favor in the late 1960s. The same baby boomers who fought to end these restrictions want to bring them back, perhaps out of dismay that their own children may have to make some of the same mistakes that they did.

Colleges should do as much as they can to provide a safe and secure environment. More important, they must help students learn to take care of themselves and to seek guidance on life's tough decisions. Neither colleges nor parents can make the world entirely safe for our young people and, hard as it may be to accept, there are limits to our ability to control what life has in store for our children.

Parents do best when they encourage their college-bound children to reach out enthusiastically for opportunities in the classroom and beyond. And if they can let go, they will see the results that they want and deserve: young people, so full of intelligence, spirit, and promise, transformed into wonderful women and men.

Annotating to Stimulate Response

Now let's look at a passage from an essay by historian and novelist Wallace Stegner. In this case, a student in a history course has been assigned a collection of readings about public-land policy in the West. Students will discuss these readings before taking an essay exam testing their ability to make connections—to recognize points of agreement and disagreement—among the readings. The reader's annotations show that he is reading for more than just information:

PRACTICE READING

Some Geography, Some History

Wallace Stegner

1 How many now?

Within the six Rocky Mountain states there lived in 1960 less than seven million people. They were densest in Colorado, at 16.9 to the square mile, and thinnest in Nevada at 2.6. Surprisingly, they were more urban than rural. Over half of Colorado's people were packed into the ten counties along the eastern face of the Rockies; the rest were scattered thinly across fifty-three counties. More than two-thirds of Utah's population made a narrow dense band of settlement in the six counties at the foot of the Wasatch. The cause for this concentration is the cause that dictates so many aspects of Western life: water. As Professor Webb said, the West is an oasis civilization.

2 Fewer than 3 per sq. mi.!

3 Scarcity of H_2O means population is concentrated in few areas

5 Calif. isn't "West"; Fla isn't "South." Sounds like one of those writers who tells you what is and isn't Southern

Room, then—great open spaces, as advertised. In reality as in fiction, an inescapable fact about the West is that people are scarce. For comparison, the population density of the District of Columbia in 1960 was 13,000 to the square mile, that of Rhode Island 812, that of New Jersey 806, that of Massachusetts 654. By the criterion of space, California at 100 to the square mile had already in 1960 ceased to be West, if it ever was, and Washington at 42.8 was close to disqualification; but Oregon, thanks to its woods and its desert eastern half, was still part of the family at 18.4, which is less than half the density of Vermont.

4 Paradox: lots of land, not much of it livable

The natural resources of these open spaces are such as cause (heartburn) among corporations and individuals who wish the West were as open as it used to be, and were not watched over by so many federal bureaus. Now that the pineries of Wisconsin and Michigan are long gone, the Northwest holds our most valuable forests. Now that the (Mesabi) Range approaches exhaustion, Iron County, Utah, becomes a major source of iron ore; the steel industry based upon Utah ore and limestone, and Utah, Colorado, and Wyoming coal is a first step on the road that led to Pittsburgh and Gary. It has been estimated that the Upper Colorado River basin contains a sixth of the world's known coal reserves. The oil shales of Utah and Colorado, already in experimental reduction in Parachute Canyon, lie ready for the time when petroleum reserves decline. The Rocky Mountains contain most of our gold, silver, lead, zinc, copper, molybdenum, antimony, uranium; and these, depending on the market of the moment, may produce (frenzies) comparable with the gold rushes of the last century. A few years ago, on a road across the Navajo Reservation near the Four Corners, I was stalled behind an oil-exploration rig that had broken an axle fording Chinle Wash after a cloudburst. Behind me, in the hour I waited, stacked up fifteen or twenty cars and parts of three other exploration outfits. And who pulled the broken-down rig out and let us go on? A truck loaded with twenty tons of uranium ore. This on a road that only a little while earlier had been no more than ruts through the washes, ducks on the ledges, and periodic wallows where stuck travelers had dug and brushed themselves out of the sand.

Enormous potentials for energy—coal, oil, oil shale, uranium, sun. But one source, water, has about exhausted its possibilities. The Rockies form the nation's divide, and on them are generated the three great western river systems, the Missouri, Columbia, and Colorado, as well as the Southwest's great river, the Rio Grande. Along these rivers and their tributaries most of the possible power, reclamation, and flood-control damsites have been developed. Additional main-stem dams are not likely to recommend themselves to any close economic analysis, no matter how dam-building bureaus promote them, and conservationist organizations in coming years can probably relax a little their vigilance to protect the scenery from the engineers.

6 Developers suffer physically from their own greed

7 Where's this?

8 With natural resources of East and Midwest depleted, corporations eye riches of the West

9 Now the steel industry is declining. Does development start a chain of events culminating in poverty?

10 Unusual word: Erratic business cycles cause frenzies and panics

11 Precious minerals but no water

12 Paradoxes: sparsely populated but urban, great natural wealth but no water

---

This reader's annotations are more complex and varied than those of the first reader, who was more concerned with memorizing facts and understanding concepts. This reader's marginal notes fall into several categories:

- **Summary.** Notes 3, 4, 8, and 11 differ little from the marginal annotations in the excerpt from the psychology textbook. The reader is simply trying to recast Wallace Stegner's ideas in his own language.

- **Questions.** Questions help identify the "gaps" that exist in almost any text—places that cause confusion or arouse doubts and reservations, places where a reader would like more detail or explanation. In his first marginal note, for example, the reader ponders how much the population of the Rocky Mountain states has grown in the past thirty-five years. Is Stegner's assessment, published in 1969, still valid? Does Stegner foresee shifting trends in population growth? Have natural barriers to dense settlement kept the region relatively immune to radical changes brought on by development, as Stegner seems to forecast?

- **Personal reactions.** A reader may react either to the ideas presented in a passage or to the author's manner of expressing them (tone, vocabulary, bias). Note 2 illustrates the first type of reaction, which may voice agreement, disagreement, outrage, skepticism, or various other responses. (Note 2 says little more than "Imagine that!") Reactions become more complex when a reader calls on personal experience or draws connections to facts outside the text. In note 5, for example, the reader is saying something like this:

> Isn't it striking that Stegner should say that California, the westernmost of the lower forty-eight states, isn't "really" western? It reminds me of how many people say that Florida, the southernmost state, isn't "really" southern. Stegner sounds like an old-time native talking to an audience of outsiders or newcomers who don't know from western.

This note addresses the relationship between Stegner (as "speaker") and the reader (as "listener"). More specifically, the reader consciously resists the role of passive listener, one who might not question a subjective interpretation of where the West begins and ends.

Notes 6 and 10 comment on vocabulary. Specifically, they point to Stegner's tendency to describe the greed of corporations and developers in terms of illness (*heartburn*) and mental disturbance (*frenzy*). Alongside the natural abundance of the West, attempts to exploit and plunder its wealth are portrayed as symptoms of disease. Again, an alert reader recognizes a careful writer's efforts to influence interpretation and response.

- **Extrapolations.** To *extrapolate* is to take a given set of facts or ideas and to project, predict, or speculate about other facts or ideas that are not known or not provided in the text. For instance, a business executive, examining sales figures for the previous three years, might try to extrapolate how much future sales are likely to increase or decline in the coming months. Readers extrapolate when they take a writer's ideas and extend them, expand on them, or apply them in other contexts that the writer may have overlooked, suppressed, or failed to anticipate. In note 9, for instance, the reader points out that since Stegner wrote his essay, the steel industries of Pittsburgh and Gary, Indiana, have also suffered economic decline, just as the upper Midwest had earlier. This leads the reader to extrapolate an idea about business cycles—an idea that is not stated (and perhaps not even implied) by Stegner.

- **Inventories.** Sometimes readers detect recurring ideas, images, or patterns of language in a passage. Or, perhaps during a second reading, they recognize connections among their own annotations. For example, when the reader connects Stegner's use of the words *heartburn* and *frenzy* to describe corporate behavior, he is starting to make an inventory in his mind. Note 12 is an attempt to put another type of inventory into writing: The reader sees that Stegner describes the West through a series of contradictions or paradoxes.

Not every annotation you make when reading with a pencil will fall neatly into one of these categories. However, the important thing is to record thoughts and responses that come to mind as you experience a text. As readers become more proficient at this process, they start to engage in conversations or dialogues with the texts they read. In the process, they become more independent, relying less on rules and rigid categories of response.

EXERCISE | ## Annotating to Stimulate Response

Imagine that you are a student in the same history course and that you have been asked to read the following review of the book *What You See in Clear Water: Life on the Wind River Reservation*, by western writer and television producer Geoffrey O'Gara. Specifically, you are expected to draw connections between information and ideas brought forth in the passage by Stegner and those presented in the review of O'Gara's book, published more than thirty years later. Read through the review; then read it again, annotating to stimulate response. Annotate the text in a way that would help you contribute to class discussion and, perhaps, prepare you to make connections between these two readings on the same general topic.

PRACTICE READING

Not a Drop to Drink

Timothy Egan

Nearly every story about American Indians—past or present, on the reservation or off—ends the same way. We know what's going to happen because it's what always happens: the Indians lose. And nearly every story about water rights in the American West also has a predictable ending: the rich and powerful get what they want, usually aided by a huge government subsidy. So suspense is not one of the sensations a reader feels while following Geoffrey O'Gara along in his exploration of water rights and tribal intrigue in that lovely, lonely, storm-scoured rectangle in the middle of Wyoming labeled the Wind River Indian Reservation.

Water is power in the West, something Mark Twain noticed during his initial journalistic forays to the other side of the hundredth meridian: whiskey is for drinking, he wrote from Nevada, water is for fighting over. It continues to drive everything from the pathological sprawl of Phoenix to presidential-level debates over whether some dams should give way to fish. Wyoming is unique only in that the players are largely unknown outside the Mountain Time Zone, and the stakes, while enormously consequential within the small world drained by the Wind River, are unlikely to affect anyone's subdivision in a major city.

"What You See in Clear Water" is centered around a moderate-size river that draws its sustenance from snowmelt draining from an arc of ancient stone above 13,000 feet in the center of the state. The higher reaches of the valley are full of pine, fir, elk, and deer, and the lower elevations are flatter, more like the Great Plains, but cold—marginal cropland. It is hard to imagine many people wanting to live there year-round without, say, at least a good generator and maybe satellite television. The inhabitants, in fact, largely arrived by government incentive—coercion, in the Indians' case, and an exaggerated claim of irrigation-born farm riches in that of the whites.

The Indians are an odd pairing. From one side came the Eastern Shoshone, a people who roamed all over the Great Basin chasing bison and elk. Early on, they sided with whites, even helping the Army harass other tribes. They were ordered onto the reservation with their longtime enemy, the Northern Arapaho, a tribe that traces its roots to people of the Algonquian language group. Originally, the reservation was 44 million acres, probably big enough for the two tribes to sustain themselves and get along. But it has been shrunk, by Congressional mandates and real-estate schemes masquerading as Indian policy, to some 2 million acres. The whites came in the early 1900s and are the prime beneficiaries of an irrigation system drawing off the Wind River, which has cost American taxpayers more than $70 million. In one of many ironies, O'Gara, also the author of *A Long Road Home*, notes that the initial funds to build the homesteaders' water diversion came from money supposed to go to Indians.

The book chronicles a long fight—cultural, legal, and political—in which the Indians finally win from the United States Supreme Court the right to control water within the reservation, only to have that power taken away from them by a state court ruling. In some ways, the story has parallels to the South before the Civil Rights Act of 1964, when local powers essentially ignored federal law.

O'Gara is a lyrical writer when sketching pictures of the land. He is fair and evenhanded in trying to explain a complex issue freighted with emotion. He lets his characters have their say, revealing the racism of some white ranchers, and the desperation that hangs like low fog in so many reservations. . . . In the end, the Indians are left with nothing but a certain moral high ground, and, as they say in the West, you can't eat the scenery.

Keeping a Reading Journal

There are times when writing marginal notes may not be the most effective reading strategy. Perhaps you have borrowed a book from the library or from a friend, or you may want to expand the range of your responses to a particular reading (i.e., write at greater length than you would be able to do comfortably in the margins of a book). On such occasions, a reading journal is a good way to stimulate the same type of active engagement with a text that takes place when you write marginal notes.

Consider how one reader has commented on the following passage, which opens the book *Zen and the Art of Motorcycle Maintenance*. The reader is taking a course in contemporary literature and has selected Pirsig's book from a list of nonassigned readings. Asked to compose a paper that explains and develops her interpretation of the book's narrator, she decides to use a reading journal as stimulus for reflection. First read the passage and then observe how the reader reflects on it in a reading journal:

PRACTICE READING

From Zen and the Art of Motorcycle Maintenance

Robert Pirsig

What follows is based on actual occurrences. Although much of it has been changed for rhetorical purposes, it must be regarded in its essence as fact.

I can see by my watch, without taking my hand from the left grip of the cycle, that it is eight-thirty in the morning. The wind, even at sixty miles an hour, is warm and humid. When it's this hot and muggy at eight-thirty, I'm wondering what it's going to be like in the afternoon.

In the wind are pungent odors from the marshes by the road. We are in an area of the Central Plains filled with thousands of duck-hunting sloughs, heading northwest from Minneapolis toward the Dakotas. This highway is an old concrete two-laner that hasn't had much traffic since a four-laner went in parallel to it several years ago. When we pass a marsh, the air suddenly becomes cooler. Then, when we are past, it suddenly warms up again.

I'm happy to be riding back into this country. It is a kind of nowhere, famous for nothing at all and has an appeal because of just that. Tensions disappear along old roads like this. We bump along the beat-up concrete between the cattails and stretches of meadow and then more cattails and marsh grass. Here and there is a stretch of open water, and if you look closely, you can see wild ducks at the edge of the cattails. And turtles. . . . There's a red-winged blackbird.

I whack Chris's knee and point to it.

"What!" he hollers.

"Blackbird!"

He says something I don't hear. "What?" I holler back.

He grabs the back of my helmet and hollers up, "I've seen lots of those, Dad!"

"Oh!" I holler back. Then I nod. At age eleven you don't get very impressed with red-winged blackbirds.

You have to get older for that. For me this is all mixed with memories that he doesn't have. Cold mornings long ago when the marsh grass had turned brown and cattails were waving in the northwest wind. The pungent smell then was from muck stirred up by hip boots while we were getting in position for the sun to come up and the duck season to open. Or winters when the sloughs were frozen over and dead and I could walk across the ice and snow between the dead cattails and see nothing but grey skies and dead things and cold. The blackbirds were gone then. But now in July they're back, and everything is at its alivest and every foot of these sloughs is humming and cricking and buzzing and chirping, a whole community of millions of living things living out their lives in a kind of benign continuum.

You see things vacationing on a motorcycle in a way that is completely different from any other. In a car you're always in a compartment, and because you're used to it, you don't realize that through that car window everything you see is just more TV. You're a passive observer, and it is all moving by you boringly in a frame.

On a cycle the frame is gone. You're completely in contact with it all. You're in the scene, not just watching it anymore, and the sense of presence is overwhelming.

That concrete whizzing by five inches below your foot is the real thing, the same stuff you walk on; it's right there, so blurred you can't focus on it, yet you can put your foot down and touch it anytime, and the whole thing, the whole experience, is never removed from immediate consciousness.

Here are the annotations that the reader wrote in her journal:

1. Well, the title is certainly interesting, and the author's note [in italics] is amusing. Most writers probably aren't so quick to tell you that something may not be factual.

2. Funny how this starts off seeming <u>not</u> to be the sort of thing I'd choose to read: I'm not an outdoorsy person, and I've been on a motorcycle exactly once—thought I'd never walk again after thirty-four miles of it! Maybe it's guilt feelings, sitting in the car openly admitting that the scenery is OK but sort of dull after a while, something for seeing through windows. Maybe I'm not, as Pirsig suggests, old enough to appreciate it. I don't like to sweat—have a compulsion about being clean, and I'm none too secure about the idea of being inches from pavement that could skin me clean if I made one wrong move.

3. I like what he says about smelling things, though. The smell of lawns being watered, wet pavement, honeysuckle, the ocean, even rotting logs. I used to find the smell of Greyhound buses exciting—the lure of adventure. I guess the motorcycle thing is like that, though maybe both Pirsig and I have been influenced by movies. I did sort of enjoy my one and only ride on a cycle, but I've never felt safe repeating the experience.

4. The narrator seems to be hinting at something about safety and risk. He's riding with his son—surely he's no hot-dogging type; you don't risk your children that way. So the risk is something else. My boyfriend once suggested how wonderful it would be to spend the rest of your life sailing around the world. I disagreed, since I'm afraid of drowning, sharks, sunburn (too many movies again?). He added, "However long it might be." There are various kinds of risk, not all of them physical. It's sobering to think how attached I am to safety. I've certainly taken some risks in my life, though seldom physical.

5. I wonder if the narrator is talking about this a bit when he says that you become part of the scene instead of just an observer.

This response to reading lies at the opposite extreme from the notes and under-lines written in the psychology textbook. It is a highly personal response, as well as a greatly elaborated one. Of course, neither extreme (nor any one approach in between) is inherently better. Partly, it is a matter of individual preference, but mostly it is a case of tailoring your approach to your purposes for reading. The student responding to the excerpt from *Zen and the Art of Motorcycle Maintenance* is deliberately trying to explore her personal response to the character and voice of the narrator. She is doing this not because she is necessarily a more intuitive or imaginative person than the first reader; rather, she is trying to meet the demands of an academic task that calls for her subjective response to a text.

The responses in this student's reading journal fall into several categories:

- **Reactions to details outside the immediate text.** In her first annotation, the reader has attended to the author's prefatory note and reflected on the title of the book. In doing so, she draws on previous reading experiences.

- **Inferences.** In her fourth annotation, the reader begins to draw conclusions about how the narrator reveals himself as a person. This type of response will prove useful later, when she develops her thoughts into a more formal piece of writing aimed at a particular audience. Notice how the free play of seemingly irrelevant ideas in previous annotations appears to have primed the pump—to have led the reader spontaneously to focus her inquiry and form inferences.

- **Speculations.** Making an inference often arouses further reflection. In her fifth annotation, the reader extends and amplifies ideas from the previous annotation.

No list of categories will exhaust the range of responses that can appear in a reading journal. Independent of rules and formulas, experienced readers have learned to be inventive and even playful in their journal entries. However, if you have not used a reading journal before, you may want to try out some of the following suggested techniques, or *prompts:*

- Select a quotation from the reading:
  —Explain it.
  —Apply it to your life.
  —Explain precisely why it is not clear.
  —Supply a concrete illustration of one of its ideas.
  —Rewrite it so it communicates more clearly.
  —Examine its unstated assumptions.
  —Examine its logic or evidence.
  —Argue with it.
  —Examine its implications and significance.
- Make a list of words you did not know and their definitions.
- Take a long or complex passage and boil it down to key points.
- Try to pin down definitions of key terms.
- Pick out several impressive sentences or images.
- Point out internal contradictions or inconsistencies.
- Study relationships among facts, opinions, generalizations, and judgments.
- Examine the treatment of opposing views. Are they ignored? tolerated? refuted? ridiculed?
- Examine the structure or organization of the text.
- Characterize the audience that the text appears to target.

A variation on the reading journal is the **double-entry notebook**, in which the reader draws a vertical line down the middle of each page and writes the usual kinds of journal responses in the left-hand column. Later, she records further reflections on those responses in the column at the opposite side of the page. Many readers find the double-entry notebook an effective way to stimulate critical analysis by opening up a conversation or dialogue with themselves as well as with the text. Here is how some of the journal responses to the passage from *Zen and the Art of Motorcycle Maintenance* might look in a double-entry notebook:

Respond in this column to the text as you read it.	Reflect later on those responses here in the right-hand column.
I like what he says about smelling things, though. The smell of lawns being watered, wet pavement, honeysuckle, the ocean, even rotting logs. I used to find the smell of Greyhound buses exciting—the lure of adventure. I guess the motorcycle thing is like that, though maybe both Pirsig and I have been influenced by movies. I did sort of enjoy my one and only ride on a cycle, but I've never felt safe repeating the experience.	The "nature" thing is really a diversion. Not sure why, but I don't think he's going to be raving on about nature.
The narrator seems to be hinting at something about safety and risk. He's riding with his son—surely he's no hot-dogging type; you don't risk your children that way. So the risk is something else. My boyfriend once suggested how wonderful it would be to spend the rest of your life sailing around the world. I disagreed, since I'm afraid of drowning, sharks, sunburn (too many movies again?). He added, "However long it might be." There are various kinds of risk, not just physical. It's sobering to think how attached I am to safety. I've certainly taken some risks in my life, though seldom physical.	When he talks about being part of the scene, I also think of the idea that what's worth doing is worth doing well. The catch is, of course, that we can excuse any failure by saying, well, it wasn't worth doing.

continues

Respond in this column to the text as you read it.	Reflect later on those responses here in the right-hand column.
I wonder if the narrator is talking about this a bit when he says that you become part of the scene instead of just an observer.	People say that all the time—"it's stupid"—just because it turned out bad. There are a lot of people just going through the motions because they decide too quickly that the results won't be worth real involvement; so the bad outcome is predetermined.

In her double-entry notebook, this reader has managed to sustain a dialogue between Pirsig's text and the personal associations that it arouses in her mind. Notice, for example, how the first annotation in the right-hand column carries the reader from the purely personal reflection expressed in the corresponding entry in the left-hand column back to an observation about Pirsig's text. The two following pairs of entries, on the other hand, move in the opposite direction.

Successful college students learn to adjust their reading processes to address various purposes. The different strategies presented in this chapter—annotating and underlining to recall specific facts and details, annotating to stimulate response, and keeping a reading journal—can help you regulate your reading processes, making them serve the needs at hand.

CHECKLIST   Reading Strategies

Prereading

1. Survey the text, looking for clues before you start to read.
2. Try to draw inferences from the title and length of the text; highlighted quotations; sections headings; bold type, charts, graphs, drawings, and captions; information about the author; and date of publication.
3. Rely on past experience with similar texts.
4. Keeping in mind the distinction between efferent and aesthetic reading explained in Chapter 1 (pages 43–45), consider the aims of your reading: e.g., memorizing facts, discovering background information, getting the basic gist of a complicated issue, stimulating response to a text, a topic, or an argument.

Preliminary Reading

1. Look for transitional words and phrases as well as any other clues provided by the author.
2. Read with a pencil, underlining and annotating, in order to remain active and alert and to facilitate later review.

3. If your aim is to process facts and information for future recall, follow the guidelines found on pages 90–91.

4. If your aim is to stimulate response to a text, a topic, or an argument, develop your annotations along the lines illustrated on pages 93–94. Use annotations to summarize passages, to raise questions and pose possible answers, to record personal reactions, to extrapolate from the text, to develop inventories of recurrent words, images, or ideas.

Follow-Up

1. Record your recollections and responses to the text in a reading journal, using one or more of the prompts found on page 100 if necessary.

2. Respond to your own responses by keeping a double-entry journal.

3. If at all possible, give the text at least a second reading.

READING SELECTIONS

The following two articles appeared in the "Education Life" supplement to the *New York Times*. The author, Glenn C. Altschuler, is Dean of the School of Continuing Education and Summer Sessions and professor of American studies at Cornell University.

Learning How to Learn

GLENN C. ALTSCHULER

As they begin their first year of college, many students do not know how to study—in no small part because they have not been challenged in secondary school, where their transcripts are embellished by grade-point inflation.   **1**

A nationwide survey by the University of California at Los Angeles of over 364,000 students in 1999 found that only 31.5% reported spending six or more hours a week studying or doing homework in their last year of high school. That was down from 43.7% in 1987, when the question was first asked. And 40.2% said they studied fewer than three hours a week, while 17.1% owned up to studying less than one hour a week.   **2**

No surprise then that so many college freshmen who insist they know all the material wonder why their first battery of exams do not go so well. No surprise either that offering courses that teach "learning strategies" has become a cottage industry. (Professionals think the term "study skills" too narrow, and they have banished the stigmatizing word "remedial" from the lexicon of higher education.)   **3**

For the bookish, *How to Study in College*, by Walter Pauk, the standard text in the field, is available in its seventh edition, at more than four hundred pages. For those inclined to the Internet, hundreds of institutions have established Web sites with mcnuggets of advice on how to study and to advertise the services of learning strategies centers. The University of St. Thomas, in St. Paul, Minn., for example, insists that successful students commit daily MURDER (Mood, Understand, Recall, Digest, Expand, Review).   **4**

5   Over 1.6 million students are enrolled in learning strategies courses in two- and four-year colleges and universities, according to the National Association for Developmental Education; an additional 900,000 take advantage of tutoring and supplemental instruction, individually or in groups.

6   At the Learning Resource Centers at the New Brunswick, Newark, and Camden, N.J., campuses of Rutgers, about 13,000 students in 34,000 visits a year are supported in a variety of settings. They include workshops with descriptions like "Cramming for exams—and the consequences—in the social sciences" and "Identifying and understanding one's individual learning style for success in ecology courses."

7   Nonetheless, it is not easy to get the students who most need assistance to use the resources available to them. Doing so, suggests Janet Snoyer, a learning-strategies specialist at Cornell University, means "breaking down the relentless high-school mindset that 'help' is designed for laggards and ill-equipped minds." Professionals know that although they will require those with manifestly inadequate preparation to see them and will exhort all first-year students to come in early in the semester, many students will not make an appointment until they receive a disappointing grade, and others not even then.

8   Sometimes, a lack of motivation, procrastination, and difficulty managing time on the part of students are symptoms of emotional or personal distress. For such students, Ms. Snoyer says, "Study skills tips barely reach the tip of the iceberg," and a referral to peer counseling or psychological services is appropriate.

9   But for many students learning how to learn is the iceberg. Fortunately, it can be chipped away at, or even melted. Professionals begin by getting students to acknowledge that being an undergraduate is a full-time job, requiring forty hours every week including attendance in class and course-related work. Accounting for how they have spent every hour for a week or two (including snoozing and schmoozing) helps students assess their ability to set priorities, manage time and, if necessary, to create a new schedule and monitor their adherence to it.

10   When they hit the books, students should also consider where, how long, and with whom they will study. Will proximity to a telephone, television, refrigerator, friend, or potential date lead into temptation? Can extended exposure to an isolated library carrel cause narcolepsy?

11   A Cornell student, Paul Kangas, discovered that trying to study "while lying in bed was a good antidote for insomnia but not the best way to memorize a list of German vocabulary words." But no matter how conducive to studying their accommodations may be, few undergraduates work more effectively at night than during the day.

12   And even fewer can concentrate for more than ninety minutes without a break. That is why, as Michael Chen, an instructor in the Center for Learning and Teaching at Cornell, puts it, "Time between classes is prime time, not face time."

13   In his book, Mr. Pauk advises undergraduates to carry pocket work so that they can read an article or memorize vocabulary for Spanish class while waiting at the doctor's office or the airport. Even if this approach seems a bit compulsive, a specific goal—one chapter, three problem sets—and a reward when it is reached, makes study less daunting. That reward, whether it is a coffee break or an update on the Jets game, works only if it lasts no more than half an hour.

14   Although students often spend their study time alone, study in groups can be extremely helpful. Carolyn Janiak, a Cornell student, said she found that she always learned more when working with others because discussions "force me to focus on the bigger picture and argument." As she clarified her opinions, she said, she was able to memorize details as well.

Group sessions work best if each student has already reviewed (and if necessary   15
memorized) all the material required for an assignment or exam; parceling out the
work for vicarious learning is risky. Leslie Schettino, who teaches learning strategies
courses in New York State at Tompkins Cortland Community College and Ithaca College, asks members of study groups to compare lecture notes, read problems aloud,
pretend they are tutors in, say, the math lab and end a meeting only when everyone
understands the most important concepts. Often students discover that the best way
to master material is to be forced to explain it to someone else.

But groups are not for everyone. Andrew Janis of Cornell tries to study when his   16
roommate is out because "complaints about organic chemistry distract me." He plays
"quiet jazz" or turns his radio to "an AM station that is all fuzz." As he examines notes,
handouts and review sheets, he uses an online encyclopedia to help with dates and
other pertinent information.

Effective note-taking is essential. It takes time for students, who are used to high-   17
school teachers who signal them with the phrase, "Now this is really important," to
recognize the "architecture" of a lecture—the introduction and summary, inflection,
emphasis and pause, the use of *therefore*, the digression—and to figure out what is
worth taking down. Successful students read over their notes nightly, identifying the
theme and two or three crucial points. If anything is not clear, they ask the instructor
for clarification as soon as possible. To review notes for the first time the night before
an exam is to court disaster.

Notes on a text should be taken on a separate sheet of paper or a computer. Stu-   18
dents might begin by skimming to identify the "geography" of the book—its subheadings, graphs, maps, and tables, and its main lines of argument. I advise students to
throw out their highlighters: those who use them are passive learners who do little
more than paint their books yellow. Students who summarize a chapter in their own
words, in a few paragraphs, tend to understand the material better and remember it
longer. Questions might be recorded in the margin of the book, to be raised in discussions or in office hours.

Learning how to learn is not easy. It requires will and discipline, what the   19
nineteenth-century English biologist Thomas Henry Huxley called "the ability to
make yourself do the thing you have to do, when it ought to be done, whether you
like it or not."

But just about everyone can do it. And the rewards—emotional, intellectual, and   20
financial—reach well beyond a grade in a college course.

Adapting to College Life in an Era of Heightened Stress

GLENN C. ALTSCHULER

The first week of her freshman year at Cornell University, Kate Wilkinson of   1
Plymouth, Mass., made a big mistake. She agreed to play Trivial Pursuit with several
other students in her dormitory. Kate was embarrassed that she did not know what element was converted to plutonium in the first nuclear reactor, what one-time Yugoslav
republic is shaped like a boomerang, or even the longest American war. Far worse,
everyone else did (or seemed to).

Kate called her mother and, between sobs, gave voice to her fear that she was not   2
smart enough to succeed at the university.

3   While some first-year students experience little or no anxiety, most freshmen have a stress story like Kate's, be it academic or personal—about family or financial responsibilities, inadequate high-school preparation, or pressure to do well in today's increasingly competitive environment.

4   In a 1999 survey of 683 colleges and universities conducted in the first days of school by the University of California at Los Angeles, 30.2% of freshmen acknowledged that they frequently felt overwhelmed, almost double the rate in 1985.

5   The number of appointments at Cornell's counseling and psychological services has risen by 29% in the last four years. More than 40% of first-year students at Johns Hopkins University visit its counseling center.

6   According to Dr. Samuel Parrish, medical director of the Student Health and Wellness Center at Johns Hopkins, better record keeping, greater awareness of on-campus services, and additional staff and office hours account for some of the increase. And, he said, now "there is no stigma in asking for help."

7   Mental health professionals say that young adults today appear to be under much more stress than past generations were. Many of them have fewer "stabilizing forces in their lives," said Dr. David Fassler, chair of the American Psychiatric Association's Council on Children, Adolescents, and Their Families and author of *Help Me, I'm Sad*.

8   "Many live far away from their extended family, or they've moved a lot of times, so they're less connected to their neighborhoods," he said.

9   At the extreme end of the continuum, more students may be arriving on campus with diagnosed psychological problems. After documenting a rising incidence of depression among students, Harvard University issued a report last year recommending, among other steps, that more psychologists be hired, that residence assistants and tutors receive instruction on mental problems and that two rooms be set aside in every living unit for students experiencing emotional crises.

10   While academic pressure may not cause mental illness, it can act as a trigger. "Some kids have a genetic predisposition for depression and are more likely than others to get depressed," said Dr. Fassler, ticking off the warning signs—"sadness, decreased energy and appetite, loss of interest in usual activities, decreased interest in sex, any thoughts of suicide."

11   The vast majority of students, of course, are not clinically depressed but are experiencing the self-doubt and anxiety typically associated with the critical transition from high school and home to college, and will adjust. Ms. Wilkinson, for example, has made that transition and is now doing well.

12   In an attempt to minimize the trauma of freshman year, most colleges and universities supply peer counselors, residence hall advisers, faculty advisers, an academic advising center, a mental health clinic, and suicide-prevention services. At Cornell, students can call the Empathy, Assistance, and Referral Service (EARS); at the State University of New York at Albany, the Middle Earth Peer Assistance Program sponsors a telephone line, a campus radio talk show, a weekly advice column, and peer theater performances about student problems.

13   Even the traditional organized activities of freshman year—ice cream socials, wilderness-reflection weekends, wrestling parties in kiddie swimming pools filled with yogurt—have therapeutic undercurrents to help students let off steam and face the seemingly monumental task ahead.

14   Noting that students who accept stress as normal and even beneficial tend to respond more creatively to its demands, therapists, counselors, and faculty members offer a variety of advice for coping with the freshman year.

In *Beating the College Blues*, Paul A. Grayson and Philip Meilman advise students who are frequently irritable, anxious, or angry or who have difficulty sleeping to try relaxation techniques: warm baths; slow, deep breathing; meditation; guitar playing; a long walk.   15

Dr. Grayson and Dr. Meilman, who direct counseling services at New York University and Cornell, also recommend making an inventory of commitments (say, a five-course load, twenty-hour-a-week job, crew team practice at 6:00 a.m., a steady girlfriend) and personal habits (procrastinating or partying too much?) as well as impressions of college life. That exercise helps students determine whether to drop a course or change study habits. A reality check by peers and parents can also identify flawed thinking ("I'm the only person here who has not chosen a major").   16

Students tend to waste time between classes, then try to read and to write papers at night, when they are tired and are tempted to socialize. It is better to complete three to four hours of course-related work, six days a week, before dinner.   17

Students who get eight hours of sleep, get up early, and study during the day, starting with the first week of classes, do not have to scramble as the assignments pile up. (This schedule has another advantage: the first person up in the morning gets immediate access to the bathroom and a hot shower.)   18

Freshmen should get to know at least one adult on campus fairly well, starting with a faculty adviser. Alas, many students stand at the adviser's door with a hand on the knob, seeking a signature and speedy get-away, afraid to interrupt a Nobel Prize-winning experiment.   19

More often than not, those who plant themselves in a chair ready to discuss their backgrounds, their academic and professional aspirations, and uncertainties and their personal interests will get a warm response. Students who take the initiative to meet with advisers and visit professors' offices—not only after doing poorly on an exam but also to discuss a required text or ask how a professor became interested in a subject—learn that many teach better in private than in a large lecture hall. And the college, whatever its size, begins to seem far less impersonal.   20

In the midst of the forced social interaction that characterizes college life, it takes time and many false starts to make a real friend. Roommates do not have to be best friends, but they can be a freshman's first friend. Eating dinner with a roommate, even if she is only "just OK," and meeting others in the dormitory and in class will help students get through those sometimes lonely first weeks.   21

Participating in an extracurricular activity during the first semester provides contact with students who share interests. With their regular practice schedules, the marching band or rugby team may inspire discipline and efficiency.   22

Noting that Henry David Thoreau went to the woods because he wanted to live deliberately, Professor Allan Emery, who teaches English at Bowling Green State University in Bowling Green, Ohio, reminds his freshmen students to pause at least once a day to examine their lives.   23

Too often, as students drive through day after busy day, waiting to vegetate, lubricate, or unleash a primal scream on the weekend, college resembles anything but Walden Pond.   24

"Seize opportunities to reflect on life—your life and the lives of others," Professor Emery suggests, "and you will be far less likely to lose your equilibrium."   25

"That's what those well-stocked libraries, tree-lined avenues, and peaceful quadrangles are for."   26

Freewriting

Write for ten to fifteen minutes about your thoughts as you read Altschuler's articles. What do you learn from them? Which parts confirm personal experiences and observations? Are there parts that don't? Do your experiences or observations contradict any points made by the author or the experts he quotes? Can you think of other ways to develop study skills or to manage stress that Altschuler might have added to either article? Would you have approached the first weeks of college differently if you had read one or both of these articles?

Group Work

As freewrites are read aloud by each group member in turn, jot down notes whenever you hear ideas you wish to comment on or question. Discuss what you have written, taking note of similarities and differences in your responses. (For example, do you respond similarly to the assertion that entering college students usually don't spend enough time studying?) Do group members find the survival strategies discussed in these articles realistic and helpful?

Review Questions

1. How does Altschuler account for the poor academic performance of many first-year students whose academic records indicate that they are well prepared for college?
2. Why do so few students take advantage of the help offered through courses and workshops that teach study skills?
3. What factors contribute to the increasing stress that college students feel?

Discussion Questions

1. Each of these articles ends with a philosophical quotation. What do you suppose Altschuler is trying to accomplish through this technique? That is, how do you think he is trying to influence readers? Does he succeed? Are the quotations well chosen?
2. Do you see any evidence that high schools are attempting to better prepare their graduates for college life? What factors may impede their ability to do so?
3. Altschuler does not attempt to correlate size, location, or type of institution (e.g., liberal arts college, technical institute, two-year community college, research university) with the challenges that face first-year students or with the availability of services that help them meet those challenges. Is this a serious oversight? Try to speculate on what he might have found had he pursued this line of inquiry.

Writing

1. Examine your college catalog, Web site, and any brochures or other sources of information distributed among entering students or readily available to them. Take note of every type of service or facility designed to address the issues of adjustment discussed in Altschuler's articles. Write a report that assesses the adequacy of the support system at your school and how it compares with those that Altschuler refers to. You may wish to conclude with recommended changes or additions.

2. In paragraph 4 of "Learning How to Learn," Altschuler asserts that "hundreds of institutions have established Web sites with mcnuggets of advice on how to study and advertise the services of learning strategies centers." Try to locate a dozen or so of such Web sites and report what you find. Specifically, you might list frequently offered advice, unusual or innovative suggestions, and strategies most and least conducive to your individual learning style.

WRITE, READ, and RESEARCH the NET

1. *Write:* Suppose you have been asked to speak to graduating seniors at your former high school. Use one of the prewriting strategies detailed on pages 19–24 to generate ideas about what you might say.

2. *Read:* Review the two following Web sites:
   http://www.washington.edu/doit/Brochures/Academics/survival.html
   http://www.clemson.edu/collegeskills/

3. *Research:* Using the Internet, find Web sites from various colleges and universities that list and describe survival skills for entering students. Draft a report that reviews and evaluates several of these Web sites.

 ## ADDITIONAL READINGS

The following readings explore topics introduced previously in this chapter. Roland Merullo examines the needs and frustrations of college students whose cultural backgrounds and personal histories differ significantly from those of classmates whose families are college educated. The final two selections deal with academic stress and relationships between traditional-aged college students and their parents. Writing for *Newsweek*, Steven Levy argues that student blogs may offer more reliable and realistic information about campus life than popular books issued by mainstream publishers. Finally, psychiatrist Richard Kadison offers his assessment of student stress, based largely on his first-hand experience as head of Mental Health Services at Harvard University.

The Challenge of First-Generation College Students

Roland Merullo

1   A friend of mine, a dean of long standing at a prestigious Midwestern university, talks to me sometimes about her most interesting or most troubled students. She is careful to protect their anonymity, changing names and details—as I will do here—but the force of these stories is preserved. After listening to them, I am reminded again of both the psychological resilience and fragility of young adults: their apparent maturity, on the one hand, and, on the other, the fact that people in their late teens and early to mid twenties are still assembling a grown-up persona, still solidifying the belief system by which they will live, still struggling to find the place that feels like home.

2   Of all the stories that my friend, whom I will call Catherine, has told me, the one that touched me most deeply concerned a young man from just north of the United States-Mexico border. His parents were of Mexican and Indian ancestry and had immigrated to the United States before he was born. Both of them lacked advanced English skills and worked at menial jobs. They had not graduated from high school; no one in their families and no one in either their Mexican or American neighborhoods had ever attended college. Not long after settling in the United States, they gave birth to a son—Miguel, I will call him—who showed a spark of brilliance from the time he could speak, and who excelled in school from his first day.

3   Not surprisingly, by the time he reached his last years of high school, Miguel was interested in several top-rank colleges, and they were interested in him. He chose the one where my friend Catherine works, arriving there on a cool September day with thousands of other excited first-year students, all of them going about the same rounds: locating dormitory buildings, buying textbooks, taking their places in classrooms.

4   But Miguel's excitement had a shadow over it. No one he had ever been close to had lived in a college dormitory room, paid for textbooks, been left on his own with a schedule of classes and a campus map, been thrown together so intimately with thousands of strangers.

5   He made friends quickly, as many freshmen do, but none of those friends came from a world quite like his. In many ways, purely by virtue of his age and intellectual interests, he had much in common with them. But there were other, subtler ways in which he felt completely alone in his new environment, a smart refugee washed up on the shore of a luxurious island. Short and stocky, with a protuberant Mayan brow and dark skin, he did not look like any of his classmates. Their ironic humor and casual references to travel and inherited wealth, their taste in food, the upper-middle-class values by which they'd been raised, their choice of words, their speech patterns, and posture—Miguel had some acquaintance with those things, naturally. It wasn't, after all, as if he'd been brought up on Mars. And yet there was a way in which the behavior of his new acquaintances seemed alien, and gave rise, within him, to a painful friction.

6   He did not understand that friction clearly, and did not have words—in either of his languages—to describe it. Not until he failed his first course and was sent to see my friend did his real feelings peek out from beneath the shadows.

7   Catherine met with Miguel several times during his second term. Without probing, without pretending to be a therapist or a friend, she tried to help him clear away the internal obstacles that kept him from performing in his classes the way both of them knew he could. But by then he had begun to soothe his discomfort with alcohol and drugs. Soon he fell in love, desperately, and the affair drew him farther away from

his scholastic responsibilities. His talks with Catherine became islands of clarity in what was now a blurred and perilous seascape, and he sailed from one meeting to the next through winds and currents she could only imagine. Despite her generous efforts, and the intervention of school counselors, Miguel failed four courses in his second term and went back home towing his enormous potential behind him, like a smashed-up new boat.

The reason that Miguel's story struck me so profoundly was that it is a more extreme version of my own. I grew up in a working-class, mostly Italian-American neighborhood near Boston, on a street where some of the forty-eight adults had not finished high school and only one had been to college. That lone graduate was my mother, and even she had gone to school for something practical—physical therapy— rather than any kind of purely intellectual broadening. We weren't as poor as Miguel, nor as isolated, and not as likely to be the victims of racial or ethnic prejudice, but in 1969, when I left home for Phillips Exeter Academy as a junior in high school, I believe that I experienced some of what he must have felt during his year at college, and something like what thousands of American students experience every fall.   **8**

On the surface, like Miguel, I fit in well enough. I played sports, made friends, suffered no obvious psychological trauma (unlike him, I managed to pass my courses). But, despite high scores on the entrance exams and a history of A's in junior high and two years at a Catholic high school, I didn't do well for the first three terms at Exeter. The material wasn't beyond me; the teachers weren't inattentive. But the part of me that might have focused on my studies was focused instead on something invisible to me, and mysterious: in some buried psychological workshop, I was trying to find a way to weld two very different worlds.   **9**

In the Exeter world, there were no crucifixes or pictures of saints on the walls; the food was bland and unappetizing; the adults seemed almost comically reserved and proper compared with my aunts and uncles at home; my friends knew how to play bridge, how to order in expensive restaurants; some of them had been raised by nannies and had lived abroad, or at least gone with their families on exotic European vacations. My nextdoor neighbor in the dormitory used the word *guinea* once, in my presence, a fighting word back home; and, in front of the common-room television on a winter afternoon, some classmates—innocently, perhaps—chanted "Beat the wop!" when Emile Griffith fought the middleweight Italian champion Nino Benvenuti. (When Benvenuti knocked out Griffith in the later rounds, I found myself on top of a common-room table, dancing and gloating.) There were plates of brie in faculty apartments— I had never tasted it—and copies of the *New Yorker*, a magazine I'd never seen in my parents' or relatives' houses. The cartoons were puzzling to me, and the advertisements carried a whiff of snobbery that I took as a personal affront. As a scholarship boy, I was required to wait on faculty tables at dinner one out of every three terms, a practice that has since been discontinued at that school.   **10**

It would be inaccurate to give the impression that I went through my years at Exeter embittered and alone. I did not. Almost all of my memories of that place, and, later, of Boston University and Brown University, are happy ones. It would also be false to claim that class and cultural dislocation are the only, or even the primary, reasons that bright students fail to work to their potential. Indeed, at Exeter, some of the most troubled students I knew came from wealthy clans that had been sending sons to the school since before the Civil War. Those students arrived on campus with a heavy weight of expectation in their luggage, too, but it was a different kind, a different challenge. When Catherine tells me stories about students pressured by their ambitious, upper-middle-class families or students who suffer from poor health, depression, indolence, addiction, or some   **11** general post-adolescent confusion, I feel a certain basic human empathy for them, but none of the twist in my chest that Miguel's story elicited.

12   In the United States over the past thirty years, colleges have come to a better understanding both of the delicacy of young-adult psychology and of the unique predicament faced by first-generation students. Most institutions have begun to work harder to help people like Miguel make the adjustment to campus life. In the course of writing this article, I talked with administrators at a number of places, ranging from Smith College—small, private, single-sex—to the University of Texas at Austin. Both of those colleges, like so many others, offer carefully thought-out orientations designed to help students like Miguel, to soften the discordance between the ghetto, barrio, or hollow and the neatly tended lawns and careful speech patterns of academe.

13   Smith has a month-long program in July for those entering freshmen it calls "educationally disadvantaged." It pays their travel and other expenses and, in September, allows them to take a lighter course load for a term and assigns them a faculty adviser who got to know them in the July program.

14   The University of Texas at Austin has programs for transfers, first-generation college students, and others who face unusual transitions. At Austin, about 30% of these students are Hispanic, 30% African-American, 30% from poor white families, and 10% from Asian or "other" backgrounds. There and elsewhere, what they have in common is an extra weight in their backpacks, a burden composed of cultural dislocation (in some cases, just the act of leaving their families at a young age to pursue an education is culturally inappropriate); economic hardship (many of them, even those with full scholarships, feel obliged to work while in college, in order to contribute to the family income); and the inability to look to their relatives for guidance about campus life.

15   But even now there are institutions that have no such programs, or that offer only special orientations aimed exclusively at minority students. And even the colleges that go to extra lengths to identify and rescue their troubled freshmen still see people like Miguel, students with tremendous potential who seem bent on self-destruction.

16   As someone who comes from a sort of demilitarized zone between the poorest of the poor and the most comfortable of the rich, between street fights and Sophocles, I believe that I have a clear view of part of that self-destructive picture—the part that has to do with the psychological obstacles raised by movement between cultures and between economic classes. Miguel's story says a great deal to me, not only about him, or Hispanic Americans, or college life, but about the hidden damage caused by the inequities in American society. Hearing about Miguel, I thought immediately of the kinds of interior trauma experienced by someone like O. J. Simpson—raised in the projects, living in Beverly Hills. And the late comedian Freddie Prinze—who grew up in a part of Manhattan that he called "a slum with trees," became a millionaire, and then, at the height of his success, committed suicide. And Frank Sinatra, another millionaire product of a poor upbringing, rubbing shoulders with presidents one day and punching reporters the next. I thought of Dorothy Allison, Maya Angelou, and Claude Brown, who struggled to heal the wounds in themselves and bridge the gap between American worlds with language, with art.

17   The number of poor, and poorly prepared, students who succeed in college and beyond undercuts the simplistic notion that economic or educational disadvantage is an excuse for failure, violent behavior, or indulgence in drugs. For every Miguel, there are thousands of first-generation college students who take to their studies like salmon to the open sea. For every O. J. Simpson, there are hundreds of kids who grow up in housing projects, make a success of themselves in the wealthier world, and subdue whatever demons that radical transition may have spawned.

But I am fascinated by the ones who fail, and by the reasons for their failure, and **18** by the ways we might move beyond knee-jerk conservative and liberal theorizing and probe more deeply into how external success resonates, internally, for the children of the poor.

I believe it is almost impossible for those well-off educators and administrators **19** who are themselves products of educated parents to imagine what someone like Miguel actually feels when he walks across their campus; what chord is struck in him when his fellow students casually—almost innocently—make jokes, say, about the people serving and cleaning up in the cafeteria line ("wombats," we used to call them at Exeter). I believe it is difficult for those educators to comprehend, on something other than an intellectual level, that the child of the ghetto, the barrio, or the white working-class neighborhood was raised to believe that there is an oppressor just on the other side of some invisible border.

In my case, it was "the high mucky-mucks" my father worked with in his state job **20** and the people in the wealthier suburbs west of Boston. Hundreds of times in my childhood I heard comments about these faceless snobs, people who believed they were superior to us, who had things we would never have—stock portfolios, summer homes, new cars, skiing vacations, servants, the *New Yorker* on the coffee table; who were determined to keep us in the neat cage of our semi-success even as they mouthed the platitudes of American opportunity. Our litany of complaint came out of a confusion of wounded pride and frustrated ambition, but there was never any question about the existence of an enemy out there, people who were not like us and did not wish us well. How much more pervasive and powerful that litany must be for poor black, Hispanic, or American Indian boys and girls, for the daughters of white coal miners in Appalachia or the sons of Kmart clerks in western Kansas—eighteen-year-olds dropped into college life from what must sometimes seem like another universe.

And how terrible it must be when these young adults (and sometimes they are not **21** so young, having returned to school after years in the working world) suddenly find themselves on the other side of that invisible border, consorting with the enemy. Have they not become the very people their parents and peers despised? Or at least become friends with them, sharing their jokes and tastes? In the film *Good Will Hunting*, when the character played by Matt Damon leaves behind his lower-middle-class South Boston roots and ventures into the wider world—drawn by a Harvard girlfriend and propelled by his own brilliance—his friends cheer him on. The film ends, predictably, on an upbeat note. But, watching the last scenes through a surprising spurt of tears, I wondered what demons Will Hunting was carrying with him into that world. What bitter internal conflicts would he face in his twenties and thirties and middle age? What kinds of guilt, doubt, and anger? And I wonder now if any college administrator has yet devised an orientation program that will come close to healing someone like him, at that deep level.

In my own teaching life, I have encountered dozens, perhaps hundreds, of students **22** from uneducated families, three of whom stand out in memory. The first, a young man, was raised in the poorest section of northern Vermont; the second, a young woman, in a series of factory towns from central Massachusetts to western Pennsylvania; the third, an older student, had been abandoned at birth and raised by uneducated parents, among undereducated friends, in eastern New Hampshire. I spent a good deal of time with all three of them, working, as my friend Catherine did with Miguel, to clear up their confusion and redirect their energies. I listened and talked to them for hours on end, shared a few of my own experiences, helped them with papers and applications, wrote recommendations for jobs and grants, read their novels-in-progress. They responded variously, the first clinging to his bitterness, drinking, criticizing everything he saw, very nearly failing to graduate. The second set her past difficulties aside (like the ornaments on an elaborate Tibetan deity, which are said to be its lusts and angers, hammered, thanks to a lifetime of meditation and good works, into mere decoration) and created, in herself and in her writing, a beautiful blend of the toughness of her upbringing and the refinement of the learned world. The third earned his degree not long before his first grandchild was born and then set about building a successful career as a teacher.

23   In the end, as it was with those students, success or failure is mostly an individual matter, a mysterious blend of fate and will. As Dostoyevsky argued in his novels, people from all walks of life fail and succeed, act well and act badly, for reasons that no amount of scientific study can ever fully comprehend. But, for those of us, teachers and administrators, who deal with first-generation college students, perhaps it is useful simply to try to imagine the complexity of their predicament, the uniqueness of it. Perhaps it might be helpful to think about another friend of mine, someone who grew up in a large, lower-middle-class, Irish-American family and was the only one of seven children to go to college. Recently she told me that her older brothers and sisters not only had failed to read to her as a child, but had pointedly chosen not to read to her, urging her, instead, in the direction of television and toys. The clear message was that reading would bring her nothing but trouble, would link her to the oppressor in a way that the rest of the family found distasteful.

24   To those of us who value education and the richness it has brought to our lives, an attitude like that seems counterintuitive, even absurd. But for thousands of students it is part and parcel of what they carry to campus on that thrilling first day. We can counsel them, support them, talk with them without condescension or syrupy, self-conscious "generosity"; we can try to design programs that help them fulfill their potential, personally and intellectually. Many of them will make good use of our kindness and vault into the high scaffolding of the educated classes. But some—too many—will fall back into the shadows of a free and democratic society that, more and more with each passing year, builds stone walls between the well-off and the poor, decorates them with ivy, and tacks up a sign: Please Apply.

What Your College Kid Is Really Up To

STEVEN LEVY

1   Aaron Swartz was nervous when I went to interview him. I know this not because he told me, but because he said so on his student blog a few days afterward. Swartz is one of millions of people who maintain an Internet-based Weblog that allows one to punch in daily experiences as easily as banging out diary entries with a word processor. Swartz says the blog is meant to help him remember his experiences during an important time for him—freshman year at Stanford. But it also opens up a window to the rest of us.

2   Let me explain. I recently completed *I Am Charlotte Simmons*, Tom Wolfe's 676-page novel of contemporary college life, based in part on the author's research tour of several campuses, including Stanford. Critics have nitpicked on some of Wolfe's obvious miscues (pampered student-athletes thumb-twitch on Play-Station 3, which doesn't exist yet). But the larger question is whether Wolfe's status-centered, sex-crazed, subintellectual fictional Dupont University actually bears resemblance to modern campus life.

Well, there's now an excellent way for armchair anthropologists to get an answer   3
to such a question. The candid, impressionistic reports of student bloggers provide an
unfiltered picture of what college is really like these days. Take Swartz's blog, which is
popular among thousands of readers who know him as a brilliant teenage computer
whiz. Swartz shares the confusion and excitement of a shy eighteen-year-old
Chicagoan's immersion into higher education with a maturity that eludes Wolfe's
madeup brainy backwoods virgin, Charlotte Simmons. Along with Swartz, we sit
through lectures, drop in on beer bashes and obsess helplessly over the ponytailed
goddess who sits ahead of him in Sociology. In short, Swartz's genuine account of college life is considerably more nuanced (and less alarming) than Wolfe's fictional one.

A quick Web search unearths a wealth of other student bloggers around the coun-   4
try, from the quirky to the prosaic. (Worst opening line of a student-blog entry: "Today
I will tell you about my canker sores.") A couple of schools even point prospective applicants to student blogs as evidence of rich campus life. Some of the results are more
than Wolfe-worthy, like the observations of a student who checked out the Crayola
Web site to find a match for the shade of purple that she dyed her hair. Less interesting
are blogs actually assigned by professors; they seem too self-consciously crafted for
Teacher's approval.

Clearly the student blogs that tell us most about college are the ones that speak   5
from the heart. "The most interesting blogs are from normal people ranting about
their everyday lives . . . . You're not reading *about* somebody, you're actually reading
their thoughts. Thanks to the wonders of Google, it's easy to locate people in your college community who have blogs and see how people in your situation are dealing with
similar obstacles."

That last remark was from an e-mail sent to me by a woman student in Swartz's   6
dorm whose blog is a combination of Sylvia Plath and Moll Flanders. Certain entries
are fairly explicit—she doesn't want to censor herself—even though someone might
Google her youthful indiscretions twenty years hence.

Similarly, exposing his observations and emotional crises to the billion or so peo-   7
ple with Web access doesn't faze Aaron Swartz. "When we grow up," he says, "this is
going to be more normal." Swartz, however, does draw the line when it comes to readership. When he found out his parents were visiting his student blog, "I blocked their
IP address from the Web site," he says. That's a detail that Tom Wolfe would have
died for.

Pressure and Competition

Academic, Extracurricular, and Parental

RICHARD KADISON AND THERESA FOY DIGERONIMO

It seems to me that college students today are more driven to succeed than any gener-   1
ation before them—and more likely to break down. The journey can be fraught with
the developmental pressures of fitting in, getting along with roommates, exploring
sexuality, and addressing the myriad of questions that come with the transition from
adolescence to adulthood. And as if that weren't enough to handle, the pressure-
cooker atmosphere on campus is intensified by academic, extracurricular, and parental
pressures.

ACADEMIC PRESSURES

2   The kids whom I see entering college today are not strangers to academic pressure. With record numbers of high school seniors applying for a finite number of spaces at public and private colleges and universities across the country, the institutes of higher learning have become far more selective than in the past. And many kids get the message early that being good isn't good enough.

3   Consequently, during their high school years, these ambitious students have taken college-level courses and SAT and ACT preparation classes. To boost their transcripts, they have participated in internships and attended corporate and political conferences and workshops; they have led the student government, joined after-school clubs, competed in varsity athletics, and volunteered their time in community and humanitarian projects. They have taken the tough job of doing well in school and getting into college very seriously.

4   Finally, the college acceptance letter arrives in the mail, and the pressure is off. With the prize in hand come feelings of relief and exhilaration, but they are short-lived. After arriving at school, a new set of pressures and expectations appears. Now comes the push to earn top grades and distinguish one's self in order to get into graduate school or secure a good job in a very competitive market. Some students face this task with a clear agenda and plan; others arrive with a blank slate. Most begin with a combination of enthusiasm, uncertainty, and a paradoxical desire to be unique and to fit in. Without strong coping skills to face these internal and external pressures, today's college students are walking combustibles, and the competitive college environment is often the igniting match.

Gotta Get All A's

5   In high school, it wasn't too difficult for the best students to rise to the top and for even average students to get exceptional grades. But college often changes all that, striking a blow to kids whose total sense of self-worth is tied to academic achievement (and this seems to be the case more and more often).

6   I get a lot more calls lately from faculty saying, "I received an e-mail from a student saying that if she fails this course, she's going to kill herself." The reason for this desperate feeling is not so much the objective stress (such as fear of doing poorly in the class) but the subjective stress. Too many students who get a B on a test overgeneralize and assume that this one misstep will lead to a disastrous life. They feel deeply that they are failures who will never get into graduate school or be successful in their careers. There is a complete loss of perspective, especially for the brightest students. They were tops in their high schools, but now find themselves in the middle of the pack surrounded by other "perfect" students. Because this is a time of developing autonomy, they face a challenge to their preconceived view about life—*I'm supposed to be smarter and stand out.* This confusion affects their identity as they struggle with the question, *If I'm not the best, who am I?* Sadly, some decide, *I'm a failure and a disgrace.*

7   College kids who are very focused on grades in order to get into graduate school or grab top jobs tend not only to feel more stress than other students, but I believe that they also get less out of their education than those who allow themselves to be less focused and less perfect. Grade-obsessed students are less willing to explore courses that are not directly related to their major. Students have told me that they do not want to "waste" their time or risk getting a low grade in an area they are not entirely comfortable with. They don't give themselves the freedom to enjoy learning for learning's sake. (Ironically, even some students in liberal arts colleges resist a liberal education.)

This is not a problem at top-tier schools only. Students at schools of lesser renown **8** may feel even greater pressure to prove themselves. They may feel they are already at a disadvantage to students at the Ivies and need to achieve even more and accomplish even greater feats in order to compete for a place in graduate school or in the job market.

This situation robs these students of a chance to enjoy learning, which in itself is **9** a wonderful antidote for academic stress. They won't let themselves work off tension through the fine or performing arts or put things in perspective through philosophy, religion, or psychology courses. They also miss the opportunity to delve more deeply into themselves and figure out who they are and what they really want to do with their lives.

The students who suffer the most academic stress are often the very ones least **10** willing to admit to anyone at college that they are suffering. They fear that conceding even the slightest struggle will kill their chances of getting a good recommendation for graduate school or jobs. With an eye still on the prize, they try to deny the problem but pay the cost in suffering.

Gotta Work Harder

Other students are quite resilient when they get their first "unacceptable" grade and **11** vow to work even harder. For many students, however, this response makes the situation even worse:

> Ted was a business student who came from a small, rural high school. He entered a large university and immediately felt that he did not have the educational background that others students brought with them. But Ted did not despair over his first C on a term paper; he was determined to prove that he could succeed. He confronted the challenge by increasing his study time, gobbling up every free second. He gave up his morning jog, barely grabbed a snack during the day, stopped "unnecessary" socializing, and stayed up to the wee hours of the morning studying.
>
> Ted thought he was doing a good thing. He did not realize that in addition to studying, daily exercise, nutritious food, adequate sleep, and good friends are also absolutely necessary to academic success. By studying too much and too long, Ted was soon studying less and less efficiently. This increased his need to study more, setting up a dangerous cycle: the more kids study and give up exercise, food, sleep, and social interactions, the more susceptible they become to depression. . . .

THE HARD FACTS

The American College Health Association survey of 29,230 college students found these impediments to academic performance:

- Stress—29.3 percent
- Sleep difficulties—21.3 percent
- Concern for a troubled friend or family member—16.6 percent
- Depression, anxiety disorder, seasonal affect disorder—11.6 percent
- Death of a friend or family member—8.8 percent

> **TIPS FOR MENTAL HEALTH**
>
> Exercise and food feed the body and the brain so they can function at peak levels. Early stages of sleep allow us to feel rested and restored, and the later stages allow us to integrate cognitive functions so we can remember what we studied the day before. Friendships give us necessary comfort and support.

THE EXTRACURRICULAR JUGGLING ACT

12   For some students, college is a three-ring circus, and they are the jugglers. In one hand, they juggle the balls representing the demands for high academic performance; in the other, they twirl the hoops of social relationships; and in the air, they spin the pins of their extracurricular activities. Some manage to maintain the delicate balance without dropping any of the load, but for others, the act is just too difficult, and balls, hoops, and pins eventually collide.

13   Undergraduates who must master an especially difficult balancing act are the student athletes. They are often engaged in time-intensive and demanding sports activities while trying to survive the pressure all other students face as well. They try to keep up with studies while practicing their sport seven days a week. Then they scramble to keep the pieces together when their team goes on trips to away games during long seasons, causing the athletes to miss classes. Practices sometimes run through the dinner hour, adding another level of challenge in finding good nutrition and getting adequate calories to regenerate the fuel spent during practice.

14   In addition to their desire to perform well in the classroom, these students may have the added pressure of performing well on the athletic field or arena. There is usually intense competition for spots in the starting lineup. One poor practice session, a fumbled football, a bad at-bat, or poor shooting on the basketball court can quickly erode the athlete's sense of self-esteem, his or her identity as an accomplished star (which they all were in their high schools), and the ability to stay mentally strong in the midst of all the other college pressures.

15   I'll share a recent story of a football player who is a good example of how things can so easily go wrong for college athletes:

> As a high school player, Harry had won numerous division and state honors. He was heavily recruited by college coaches and decided to take an athletic scholarship to a powerhouse school three hundred miles away from his home. At the end of his first freshman semester, he packed his bags and quit school. His friends and family were shocked and wondered what could have happened to such promising talent.
>
> Harry's coach wasn't so surprised; he'd seen this happen many times before. "Harry was a good player," he says. "But he wasn't the best on my team. No matter how hard he tried, he wasn't going to be in my starting lineup as a freshman. But I have to admit, he was a hard worker. In fact, Harry put in too much time on his own in addition to our grueling team schedule. And that hurt his studies. I was told in October that he was failing two classes, and I immediately put him on mandatory study time, but that didn't help. This was a young man who was obsessed with what he saw as his failure on the field and just couldn't keep his mind on the books. I also think Harry was homesick. His dad had been his number one supporter, and without him on the sidelines, maybe Harry just felt too alone out there." Put all these factors together, and it's no longer shocking that this young man headed for the security of home.

Athletes like Harry are not uncommon. Even the ones who make the starting team **16** struggle with pressures and expectations that can make it very difficult to balance the demands of school with those of their coaches.

I recently heard of a soccer star who loves the sport and her team and coach, but **17** she finds herself under tremendous pressure during the long soccer season. She travels nearly every weekend for Division 1 games up and down the East Coast, often leaving on a Thursday (missing classes) and not getting back until late Sunday night or even Monday. She is exhausted upon her return, and she still has homework to do. That's a tough schedule for anyone.

Also notable are the disruptive schedules of members of the band, orchestra, glee **18** clubs, student drama productions, student government organizations, debate clubs, feminist and political activities, and other activities that demand not only a lot of practice and rehearsal but extensive travel time to distant and time-consuming events. Many students take their involvement in these activities very seriously, and sometimes to the breaking point. This was the case with one ambitious news editor:

> Larry had a high-achieving personality, and he tried to do it all. Larry took over as editor in chief of his college newspaper after the former editor abruptly left school. Larry knew the editorial staff was a bit disorganized and that the quality of articles had taken a dive over the past year, but he thought it would be easy to get the paper back on track. That naive assumption almost cost Larry his college degree.
>
> "The reporters had no idea what 'deadline' or 'jounalistic integrity' meant," Larry recalls with a sad shake of his head. "I would end up writing half the pieces myself and doing major rewrites on the pieces that 'borrowed' information right out of the *New York Times*. I was spending hours and hours every day (often until three or four in the morning) in the newspaper office. School work? What was that? Friends? I had no time for them, and because I was so tired and cranky, they had no time for me either. By the end of the semester, I had almost single-handedly saved the paper from disgrace, but the price was awfully high. I no longer wondered why the previous editor dropped out of school. My GPA plunged, and I ended up on academic probation. I want to be a journalist when I graduate, and so I thought this was an important life experience for me. Now I think I'll get my degree first and then jump into the real world of newspaper reporting."
>
> A new editor took over for Larry the following year and no doubt is holed up somewhere right now, trying to keep the presses rolling, but at what cost?

PARENTAL EXPECTATIONS

In the 1960s and 1970s, sons and daughters openly rebelled against parental expecta- **19** tions. With peer support behind them, they had no trouble speaking out against their families' views of politics, religion, and moral values. But it seems to me that the children of the new millennium are not so outspoken about their own needs and goals and pay the price in increased stress.

Many in this college generation have been raised in a culture of conformity and **20** high expectations. Parents have given their children every opportunity to enrich themselves, to excel, to become superkids. In highly structured and supervised environments, they give and give and give more than any generation before them. This is a positive situation in one sense: today's children have had far more exposure to after-school and Saturday morning classes in dance, art, science, politics, and computers and greater specialized focus and training in athletics and music. But as the bar continues to be raised higher and higher and the academics become more and more challenging, this culture of high expectations sets up a classic situation for stress and early burnout.

21   The situation can be particularly stressful in immigrant families. In these cases, some hopeful and ambitious parents push their kids hard to move up from just-off-the-boat working-class status to middle-class professionalism. This syndrome leaves no time or tolerance for exploring life or self.

22   It is with the best of intentions that parents raise the bar on minimum expectations. But a large number of sound studies have found that the results of this increased pressure from home have a part to play in the epidemic of mental health issues on campus.

Expecting Top Grades

23   Parents have a right to expect their children to get good grades in college. Parents who know their child is goofing off, partying too much, or dedicating far more time to perfecting video game skills than studying have good reasons to demand better. Although socializing is an important part of the college experience, the goal, after all, is to get an education.

24   Parental pressure for good grades becomes a problem when it is unrealistic. Some parents are convinced that a child who earned all A's in high school should do the same in college, but this often does not happen. The reality of a higher education finds students who earned all A's in high school quickly wracking up B's and C's in college even though they're working hard and giving full effort to their classes. They may find that the study skills and level of work that rewarded them in high school are inadequate for college studies. They need time to acclimate to the higher expectations. They need support from home that assures them that doing their best is all they can do—that sometimes the grade is not the most important thing.

25   But this message is hard to believe, never mind deliver, if the child has always been at the top of his or her class. And it's also hard for parents to judge if their children who are earning those B's and C's are really working hard:

> Geta and her parents are caught in this argument over grades, and neither side is able to concede to the other. Geta had been in the top five percent of her high school class in Florida. When she entered an elite college in the Midwest, she says she was unprepared for the academic rigors she faced and ended her first year with a B– average. Geta's parents were angry and threatened to pull her out of the college if she did not raise her grades the following semester. They had come to this country from eastern India and worked hard seven days a week in their own restaurant so that their daughter could have a good life in a profession like computer engineering or medicine. They expected Geta to focus on her studies and graduate at the top in her college class. There were no excuses to do otherwise.
>
> Geta, who had been having trouble adjusting to the academic demands of her school, found that adding her parents' demands to her stress load was more than she could handle. She failed out of school her sophomore year and returned home with an eating disorder that seemed to successfully divert her own and her parents' attention away from her academic failure and the underlying reason of unrealistic expectations.

Expecting to Share the Same Goals

26   At his graduation from Harvard Law School, my friend's joy was momentarily dimmed when his mom came up to him and said quite seriously, "It's still not too late to go to medical school." The parental expectation that children choose a certain career can be direct, as in this case, or more subtle, as in my own case. When I was in college, I became interested in Buddhism and religious studies. Although my parents didn't order

me to drop those classes, I knew they didn't like the idea. My dad grew up quite poor in Chicago and worked hard to get to medical school and then send his own son to an Ivy League school. I'm sure that to him, the idea of spending time studying religions seemed like a waste of time and money. It could not possibly contribute to my ability to earn a living when I graduated.

Fortunately, my parents remained calm while I explored subjects that were non-medical, but today many parents are more vocal in their plans for their children. On campus after campus, counselors tell of students doing poorly in courses required for medical or law school, for example, in a conscious or unconscious effort to escape from the career expectations of parents.   **27**

Some parents steer their sons and daughters toward certain careers and assume they will follow that lead without question. We all have heard the stories about the young adults who are disowned when they refuse to join the family business. We've heard about the families who pressure their children to choose occupations with social status in fields like law, medicine, or business. We all also know stories about young people who bend to the pressure to please their parents and then live with regret and personal disappointment for the rest of their lives. Some young adults do both: they earn the college degree their parents insist on and then turn away and follow their heart into another field. In many of these situations, the pressure on the young adults is more than they can handle, and soon they find themselves struggling with anxiety disorders, eating disorders, substance abuse, or depression. It is very difficult to live knowing you must choose to please those who love you or please yourself.   **28**

Expecting Close Communication and Family Togetherness

College students will feel additional stress if they and their parents disagree over how much and how often they should communicate. Certainly, parents don't expect to be cut off from information. Whether a college student is living at home or in a dorm room, parents expect to hear how he is doing, how his classes are going, what kind of grades he is getting, what friends he's making, how his professors are, and so on. But these perfectly natural expectations are notorious for causing tension between parents and their college-age children.   **29**

The college student is struggling to become autonomous and may not feel like communicating much or often. Some are just too busy to stay in touch. Others find that too much communication triggers loneliness and homesickness, and so they avoid it. And some say it pulls them back into the parent-child lectures and arguments they've grown out of. For whatever reason, it is quite common for college students to either intentionally or unintentionally put distance between themselves and their parents. Although this is their choice, they still feel the stress of parental complaints.   **30**

This disagreement over sharing oneself spills over into family togetherness time as well. Parents often tell me that because they are still supporting their child and consider her a member of the family, they naturally look forward to seeing her occasionally. The students I talk to don't always feel the same but do feel the guilt associated with this differing view.   **31**

Max confided to me that he was very excited about visiting his roommate's family over the Thanksgiving break, but had not yet told his parents about his plan. "They're going to be so angry that I'm not coming home for Thanksgiving," he admitted. But it's a five-hour car ride from the campus to my home, and Jim's house is only one hour away. But as long as my parents are paying the bills, there's no way I can make them understand that I'd rather not make the trip; they always try to guilt me into doing what they want." Max's plan was to spring this news on his parents at the last second and take off before they had a chance to make him change his plans. Obviously, he did, indeed, feel guilty.

32   Cancelling visits home may be a coping mechanism to fight off homesickness, or it may be done in the rush of a self-centered life, but either way, it is always the cause of family tension that adds on more layers of daily tension.

What Parents Don't Expect

33   Of all the many things parents tell me they expect from their children at college, I have never heard parents say that they expect them to develop emotional or mental problems. They would never think that they could be the parents of one of the thirty-eight percent of students who say they have been so depressed in the past year that they couldn't function. They can't imagine that their kids will be the ones involved in binge drinking at college, and yet we know that approximately two-fifths of college students reported drinking five drinks in a row (or four in a row for women) within the two weeks previous to the survey. Your child may be the one who is studying hard, feeling happy, and accomplishing all goals—but maybe he is not, and the expectation that all is well makes it harder to speak up.

34   Many parents also don't expect their children to seek counseling for psychological problems. Students who come to our mental health services center tell us that their parents would be upset if they found out. Their parents have given the clear message (whether stated or unstated) that their children should not talk about their back-ground or family to "strangers." They don't want counselors digging into the details of what goes on at home, and their children know it. In these cases, students struggling with mental health issues are in a troublesome bind: either respect their parents' feel-ings and stay away from mental health counseling services or seek relief from their pain, but they can't do both. That's a lot of stress.

3 *Paraphrasing*

When you *paraphrase* a statement, a brief passage, or a longer excerpt from a text, you recast information and ideas in different words. College students engage in paraphrasing almost daily. When you take notes during class, for example, you try to capture the main points of your instructor's lecture in your own words. Likewise, essay examinations often ask you to distill important concepts from lectures, reading, and class discussion. In fact, the ability to present unfamiliar information and explain complex ideas in your own language is a crucial academic skill because it helps you demonstrate knowledge and understanding.

PARAPHRASE AS A READING STRATEGY

Let's begin with the most informal, and probably most frequent, use of paraphrase. Whenever skillful readers encounter a challenging passage, they try to construct an interpretation—to reach some understanding of it. One way they do this is to paraphrase. Consider the following sentence from *Talking Power,* a book by Robin Lakoff, a scholar of language study:

> When it is important that language be forceful, we attempt to buttress it in some tangible ways.

A fluent reader might pause for less than a second to process this sentence by mentally recasting it in different terms: "When we want people to pay attention to our words, we try to back them up with something concrete." Sometimes, readers write these interpretive paraphrases in the margins; other times, they simply read further to see whether their mental paraphrase turns out to be correct. In the case of Robin Lakoff's sentence, the accuracy of our paraphrase is confirmed by an illustration that appears later in the same paragraph:

> Nowadays we often think of . . . oaths as mere words themselves, *pro forma* declarations. But they originated as dire threats. . . . The very words *testify, testimony* recall one ancient link between words and reality. They are derived from the Latin *testes,* its meaning the same as in current English. In swearing, the Roman male . . . placed his right hand upon his genitals; the implication was that, if he swore falsely, they would be rendered sterile—a potent threat.

Sometimes, a marginal paraphrase proves useful later on. If, for example, you plan to review material for an exam, paraphrasing an important idea could be helpful. There are, however, limits to how much you can fit into the margins, just as there are limits to how much time you can devote to paraphrasing, either in your head or on paper. And since a paraphrase, unlike a summary, restates every idea from its source, writers seldom paraphrase more than two or three contiguous sentences. Proficient readers, likewise, rarely recast multiple sentences in their heads, even when they encounter a challenging passage such as the following, also from Lakoff's book:

> We are not mere passive recipients of manipulative communicative strategies. Orwell and other worriers ignore the truth, whether unpleasant or happy: we all manipulate language, and we do it all the time. Our every interaction is political, whether we intend it to be or not; everything we do in the course of a day communicates our relative power, our desire for a particular sort of connection, our identification of the other as one who needs something from us, or vice versa.

Adhering to one common, though naive, bit of advice, a baffled reader might look up every unfamiliar or confusing word and try to recast the passage in simpler language. After five minutes with a dictionary, this reader might render the first sentence as follows: "We are not inactive receivers of influencing talkative plans." The same industrious reader would learn also that *Orwell* refers to George Orwell, a British novelist and essayist who lived from 1903 to 1950. But all this effort produces little clarification. To make matters worse, the strategy is even less effective in dealing with the next sentence, in which the words are familiar to almost any English-speaking adult. Here, a dictionary offers no help at all.

Efficient readers, therefore, paraphrase sparingly. Often, they delay understanding for a few sentences to see whether subsequent text provides clarification. Later in the paragraph from which we have quoted, for example, Lakoff says, ". . . We are always involved in persuasion, in trying to get another person to see the world or some piece of it our way, and therefore to act as we would like them to act." Now, the foregoing sentences become clear, and most readers will not need to return to them for paraphrasing.

This first type of paraphrase lies at one end of a spectrum on which every act of reading and interpretation might be placed; more personal types of response lie at the opposite end. When we want to explore our individual responses and connections to a text, we read and write subjectively, less concerned with literal understanding of what the writer is trying to say. But when we want to get down exactly what a sentence or passage says, we paraphrase it. The figure below illustrates the spectrum of which we speak:

Responses to Reading

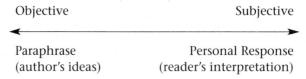

Objective   Subjective

Paraphrase   Personal Response
(author's ideas)   (reader's interpretation)

USING PARAPHRASE IN WRITING

Up to this point, we have treated paraphrase as a reading strategy—a way to understand or come to terms with concepts in academic texts. Whether performed mentally or recorded on paper, this private type of paraphrase differs from others in one important way: It is usually not accompanied by an ***acknowledgment phrase*** (e.g., "according to Robin Lakoff") or ***formal documentation*** (e.g., a parenthetical note keyed to a bibliographical entry). In other words, since this kind of paraphrase will not be read by anyone else, you are not obligated to identify its source explicitly. For example, if you wrote a marginal paraphrase of the main idea of this paragraph, you probably would not begin with "Veit and Gould say that . . . " or end with a note citing the authors' names and a page number.

Notice how we qualify this advice: A *private* paraphrase—one that *no one else* is going to read—is *usually* not accompanied by an acknowledgment phrase and documentation. However, if you were to place such a paraphrase in a notebook or index card or on a photocopied page that does not clearly identify the author, title, and location of the source, failure to acknowledge and document could prevent future use of the paraphrased ideas. If you ever wanted to cite or even refer to those ideas in any kind of writing intended for other readers (including your instructor), you would have to relocate the source and cite it appropriately. This is necessary because every public use of paraphrase—every use involving a reader other than yourself—demands acknowledgment and proper documentation.*

One public use of paraphrase involves rewording a difficult passage for an audience unfamiliar with its concepts or terminology. Legal experts often paraphrase complex, ambiguous texts such as contracts, court decisions, and legislation; and when they do so, they usually interpret as well as translate. Others may paraphrase an argument with which they disagree in an effort to demonstrate good faith and a willingness to listen and understand. Finally, in research projects particularly, writers paraphrase sources to cite important information, to place a topic or issue in context, or to support an interpretation or opinion. Subsequent sections of this chapter will consider each of these occasions for paraphrasing.

Before continuing, we must emphasize one crucial point about paraphrasing for *any* purpose. Whenever you paraphrase, you must *completely* rephrase your source, using your own words and your own style. Neither substitution of words nor rearrangement of word order produces a legitimate paraphrase of another writer's ideas. Suppose, for example, that you wanted to paraphrase the following sentence from an article about Walt Disney World written by columnist Manuela Hoelterhoff for the *Wall Street Journal:*

> I did not have a great time. I ate food no self-respecting mouse would eat, stayed in a hotel that could have been designed by the Moscow corps of engineers and

The original passage

---

*The conventions of acknowledgment and documentation are presented in subsequent chapters. In particular, the parenthetical note, a short annotation usually citing the source of paraphrased ideas or quoted words and the page(s) on which they can be found, is explained in Chapter 5. Although the scope of the present chapter is confined to techniques of paraphrasing, the significance of proper documentation should not be overlooked or minimized.

suffered through entertainment by smiling, uniformed young people who looked like they had their hair arranged at a lobotomy clinic.

The following sentence illustrates one of several acceptable paraphrases:

An acceptable
paraphrase

Visitors to Disney World can expect unappetizing food, uncomfortable lodging, and sappy young singers and dancers who all look alike.

On the other hand, the following sentence would not be an acceptable paraphrase because it merely tinkers with Hoelterhoff's sentence:

An
unacceptable
paraphrase

Don't expect to enjoy yourself. You will eat food unfit for rodents, let alone humans; sleep in a hotel that looks like a relic of the Soviet Union; and endure performances by grinning teenagers who look like they've had brain surgery.

Whenever you write a paraphrase that others will read, as in a research paper, you are bound by certain rules of fair play. Specifically, you must completely re-cast material borrowed from your source, using your own words and your own style. Failure to do so is *plagiarism*, an act of dishonesty. Unless you quote your sources exactly (either set off with quotation marks or indented as a blocked quotation), readers will assume that the language and style you use are entirely your own. You must also give full credit for a source's contribution to your writing.

Upcoming chapters will provide more detail about the use of sources in research writing, including paraphrase and quotation, citation of sources, and avoidance of plagiarism.

Paraphrasing for a Different Audience

Writers sometimes paraphrase a source in order to express its ideas more clearly for a particular audience. For example, a reference to Shakespeare might, in certain contexts, benefit from a clarifying paraphrase:

"That which we call a rose," wrote the Bard, "by any other name would smell as sweet." His point is that we should not judge people by their names or things by the words that refer to them, since names do not alter essence.

The second sentence paraphrases the first. However, it does more than just restate an idea in different words (e.g., "A rose would be just as fragrant no matter what we called it"). It goes further, stating the implicit meaning of the source—a meaning that Shakespeare left unstated.

Likewise, a newspaper reporter might want to review recent discoveries in genetic engineering. Rather than quote extensively from articles in professional journals, where such discoveries are introduced and explained to scientists, the reporter would paraphrase crucial information in familiar, everyday language. The technical vocabulary and style appropriate to an audience of professional research scientists would confuse most newspaper readers.

Specialized and General Audiences

When you write for an audience that shares knowledge about a particular field, you customarily adopt the language, or ***jargon***, appropriate to that field, even though it confuses most outsiders. (You can find a host of magazines and journals aimed at specialized audiences in the periodical section of your college library.) Writers for *Field and Stream* expect readers to understand specialized words and abbreviations relating to game animals and rifle scopes; an article in *PC Computing* would not explain the difference between RAM and ROM; and authors who publish in the scholarly journal *Linguistic Inquiry* assume that readers are familiar with terms like *anaphoric dependencies* and *surface filters*. We all have special interests that allow us to interpret texts that baffle others.

Often in research writing you must translate the specialized jargon of a source into a clearer, more accessible language that suits the needs of a general audience. Paraphrasing technical information for laypersons is therefore a useful skill for college students.

Consider two passages relating to periodicity, the rhythmic behavior exhibited in many plant and animal species. The first passage, from *Physiological Zoology*, a scientific journal, presents difficulties for most readers:

> Recent studies have provided reasons to postulate that the primary timer for long-cycle biological rhythms that are closely similar in period to the natural geophysical ones that persist in so-called constant conditions is, in fact, one of organismic response to subtle geophysical fluctuations which pervade ordinary constant conditions in the laboratory (Brown, 1959, 1960). In such constant laboratory conditions a wide variety of organisms have been demonstrated to display, nearly equally conspicuously, metabolic periodicities of both solar-day and lunar-day frequencies, with their interference derivative, the 29.5-day synodic month, and in some instances even the year. These metabolic cycles exhibit day-by-day irregularities and distortions which have been established to be highly significantly correlated with aperiodic meteorological and other geophysical changes. These correlations provide strong evidence for the exogenous origins of these biological periodisms themselves, since cycles exist in these meteorological and geophysical factors.
>
> —Emma D. Terracini and Frank A. Brown, Jr., "Periodisms in Mouse 'Spontaneous' Activity Synchronized with Major Geophysical Events"

Passage for a specialized audience

If you were researching periodicity, you might get the gist of this specialized writing. But if you wanted to report information to readers who do not share your background and interests, you would paraphrase parts of the passage in more familiar language.

In the second passage, Frank Brown recasts some of the same information for an article published in the less specialized *Science* magazine:

> Familiar to all are the rhythmic changes in innumerable processes of animals and plants in nature. . . .
>
> These periodisms of animals and plants, which adapt them so nicely to their geophysical environment with its rhythmic fluctuations in light, temperature, and ocean tides, appear at first glance to be exclusively simple responses of the organisms to these physical factors. However, it is now known that rhythms of

Passage for a less specialized but professional audience

all these natural frequencies may persist in living things even after the organisms have been sealed in under conditions constant with respect to every factor biologists have conceded to be of influence. The presence of such persistent rhythms clearly indicates that organisms possess some means of timing these periods which does not depend directly upon the obvious environmental physical rhythms. That means has come to be termed "living clocks."

—Frank A. Brown, Jr., "Living Clocks"

Though accessible to many educated adults, this passage assumes the reader's interest in scientific research (a valid assumption about people who subscribe to *Science* magazine).

Notice how Brown once again paraphrases the same basic information, this time adapting it to a still broader audience for an article published in the *Saturday Evening Post:*

Passage for a general audience

One of the greatest riddles of the universe is the uncanny ability of living things to carry out their normal activities with clocklike precision at a particular time of the day, month, and year. . . .

Though it might appear that such rhythms are merely the responses of organisms to rhythmic changes in light, temperature, or the ocean tides, this is far from being the whole answer. For when living things . . . are removed from their natural habitat and placed under conditions where no variations occur in any of the forces to which they are generally conceded to be sensitive, they commonly continue to display the same rhythms they displayed in their natural environment.

—Frank A. Brown, Jr., "Life's Mysterious Clocks"

In each of these cases, writing is adapted to the needs of a particular group of readers. The first passage targets research scientists. Consequently, the authors avoid assigning "agency"—telling who performs critical actions. They say, for example, that "*recent studies* have provided reasons" and that "organisms *have been demonstrated* to display"; they do not say "*scientists* have provided reasons" or "*we and our colleagues* have demonstrated." Although writing that does not assign agency is often harder to understand, scientists prefer this style because they consider it more objective. In the third passage, written for the *Saturday Evening Post*, the author uses simpler vocabulary (like *living things*) and explains concepts (like *controlled conditions*, described as "conditions where no variations occur in any of the forces to which [living things] are generally conceded to be sensitive").

You may wonder whether writers ever paraphrase in language more formal than that of an original source. Because the results may sound peculiar or pretentious, writers who do this often seek a comic effect. For example, in a well-known essay about misuses of language, George Orwell translates a passage from the Old Testament into modern political jargon. The original passage, from *Ecclesiastes*, reads:

I returned, and saw under the sun, that the race *is* not to the swift, nor the battle to the strong, neither yet bread to the wise, nor yet riches to men of understanding, nor yet favour to men of skills, but time and chance happeneth to them all.

Ridiculing what he calls "modern English," Orwell paraphrases the source as follows:

> Objective consideration of contemporary phenomena compels the conclusion that success or failure in competitive activities exhibits no tendency to be commensurate with innate capacity, but that a considerable element of the unpredictable must invariably be taken into account.

Orwell's aim is not to communicate the ideas or sentiments expressed in a source, but to show how a particular type of language renders them obscure and inelegant. The paraphrase draws attention to its own vocabulary and style and away from the content of its source.

The following sentence from a magazine that targets an audience of gay men presents a different situation in which a writer might paraphrase a source in more formal language:

> Chubby, fat, and obese queers suffer outcast status.

The word *queer*, used in reference to homosexuals, is traditionally a stereotypical and abusive term that still offends many readers. (However, since the author of the source is himself a gay man, clearly he does not mean to be offensive.) Words like *chubby, fat*, and *obese* also carry negative connotations—implicit meaning, as opposed to objective "dictionary" definition. Therefore, if our aim is to report ideas objectively, an appropriate paraphrase might be the following:

> According to one observer, gay men are repelled by obesity.

Some may object to this paraphrase because it substitutes intentionally strong language with euphemisms (polite equivalents for unpleasant or controversial words), blunting the impact of the original source. Therefore, a better strategy might be a carefully introduced quotation:

> Writing for *Outweek* magazine, Jay Blotcher asserts, "Chubby, fat, and obese queers suffer outcast status."

Notice that in each case, the writer stands at a distance from the paraphrased or quoted source. This is often appropriate when citing controversial or highly subjective opinions. Some textbooks, in fact, distinguish between **informative paraphrases**—those that adopt the tone of a source, reporting facts and opinions as though the writer accepted their validity—and **descriptive paraphrases**—those that take a more detached stance, *describing* a source rather than *reporting* its information or opinions without qualification. Thus, an informative paraphrase of the forgoing sentence might begin this way:

> Textbooks sometimes differentiate between informative and descriptive paraphrases. . . .

An informative paraphrase

A descriptive paraphrase, on the other hand, might open like this:

> Veit and Gould report that textbooks sometimes differentiate between informative and descriptive paraphrases. . . .

A descriptive paraphrase

Though valid, the distinction between informative and descriptive paraphrases is not emphasized in this chapter; instead, we demonstrate how and when writers may detach themselves from certain sources. (The principle will be discussed also in Chapter 12.)

EXERCISES   ## Paraphrasing for a Different Audience

1. The following sentences appear in another article about periodism, or "biological clocks," the topic addressed in preceding excerpts. This article, also by Frank Brown, was published in *Biological Bulletin*. Try to paraphrase the sentences for a general audience, similar to the one targeted in Brown's article in the *Saturday Evening Post:*

   Much has been learned, particularly in recent years, as to the properties, including modifiability, of this endogenous rhythmicity. The fundamental problem, however, that of the timing mechanism of the rhythmic periods, has largely eluded any eminently reasonable hypotheses. . . .

2. Recast the passage from the article in the *Saturday Evening Post* (page 128), adapting it to *National Geographic World*, a magazine for elementary-school-aged children.

3. Copy a passage from a textbook for one of your advanced courses that some people might find difficult. Write a paraphrase accessible to most readers.

4. The following referendum initiative appeared on ballots in New Jersey. Write a paraphrase to assist voters who are nonnative speakers of English:

   Should the "Jobs, Science, and Technology Bond Act of 1984" which authorizes the State to issue bonds in the amount of $90,000,000.00 for the purpose of creating jobs by the establishment of a network of advanced technology centers at the State's public and private institutions of higher education and for the construction and improvement of technical and engineering-related facilities and equipment as well as job training and retraining programs in high-technology fields at these institutions; and in a principal amount sufficient to refinance all or any such bonds if the same will result in a present value savings; providing the ways and means to pay that interest of such debt and also to pay and discharge the principle thereof, be approved?

Formal and Informal Writing

When you paraphrase a passage from the *Saturday Evening Post* for the readers of *National Geographic World*, as you did in the preceding exercise, you write something that sounds different from the original. After all, the two versions satisfy different purposes and target different audiences. Good writers, able to negotiate a range of styles and levels of formality, have learned to adapt what they say to specific occasions. Official documents often demand formal usage, while notes to friends call for a more casual tone. Between these extremes lies a range of stylistic levels. Examples that follow illustrate various points along this spectrum.

First is a passage from the Gospel of Saint Luke in the King James Bible, a translation undertaken by English scholars of the early seventeenth century, the age of Shakespeare:

> And it came to pass in those days, that there went out a decree from Caesar Augustus that all the world should be taxed. (And this taxing was first made when Cyrenius was governor of Syria.) And all went to be taxed, every one to his own city. And Joseph also went from Galilee, out of the city of Nazareth, into Judaea, unto the city of David, which is called Bethlehem (because he was of the house and lineage of David) to be taxed with Mary his espoused wife, being great with child. And so it was that, while they were there, the days were accomplished that she should be delivered. And she brought forth her firstborn son, and wrapped him in swaddling clothes and laid him in a manger, because there was no room for them in the inn.
>
> And there were in the same country shepherds abiding in the field, keeping watch over their flock by night. And, lo, the angel of the Lord came upon them, and the glory of the Lord shown round about them, and they were sore afraid. And the angel said unto them, "Fear not: for, behold, I bring you good tidings of great joy, which shall be to all people." For unto you is born this day in the city of David a Saviour, which is Christ the Lord. And this shall be a sign unto you: Ye shall find the babe wrapped in swaddling clothes, lying in a manger. And suddenly there was with the angel a multitude of the heavenly host praising God and saying, "Glory to God in the highest, and on earth peace, good will toward men." And it came to pass, as the angels were gone away from them into heaven, the shepherds said one to another, "Let us now go even unto Bethlehem and see this thing which is come to pass, which the Lord hath made known unto us." And they came with haste and found Mary and Joseph and the babe lying in a manger. And when they had seen it, they made known abroad the saying which was told them concerning this child.

The language of this passage is lofty and formal. Its vocabulary is elevated, even obscure in places; there are no contractions or colloquialisms (words or expressions more appropriate to conversation than public speech or writing). Still, a great many, probably most, English-speaking adults are so familiar with this narrative that it presents no real difficulties for them.

However, the following passage from *The Best Christmas Pageant Ever*, a play by Barbara Robinson, shows how this biblical passage might confuse some native speakers of English. In this scene, the mother is directing a rehearsal for a nativity play. The Herdmans—Ralph, Leroy, Claude, and Imogene—have never attended a Christian worship service:

> **Mother:** All right now *(finds the place and starts to read)*. There went out a decree from Caesar Augustus that all the world should be taxed . . . *(All the kids are visibly bored and itchy, except the HERDMANS, who listen with the puzzled but determined concentration of people trying to make sense of a foreign language.)* . . . and Joseph went up from Galilee with Mary his wife, being great with child. . . .
>
> **Ralph:** *(Not so much trying to shock, as he is pleased to understand something.)* Pregnant! She was pregnant! *(There is much giggling and tittering.)*

Mother: All right now, that's enough. We all know that Mary was pregnant. *(MOTHER continues reading, under the BETH-ALICE dialogue.)* . . . And it came to pass, while they were there, that the days were accomplished that she should be delivered, and she brought forth her firstborn son. . . .

Alice: *(to BETH)* I don't think it's very nice to say Mary was pregnant.

Beth: Well, she was.

Alice: I don't think *your mother* should say Mary was pregnant. It's better to say she was "great with child." I'm not supposed to talk about people being pregnant, especially in church.

Mother: *(reading)* . . . and wrapped him in swaddling clothes and laid him in a manger, because there was no room for them in the inn. . . .

Leroy: What's a manger? Some kind of bed?

Mother: Well, they didn't have a bed in the barn, so Mary had to use whatever there was. What would you do if you had a new baby and no bed to put the baby in?. . .

Claude: What were the wadded-up clothes.

Mother: The what?

Claude: *(pointing to the Bible)* It said there . . . she wrapped him in wadded up clothes?

Mother: *Swaddling* clothes. People used to wrap babies up very tightly in big pieces of material, to make them feel cozy. . . .

Imogene: You mean they tied him up and put him in a feedbox? Where was the Child Welfare?

To Alice (described in the cast of characters as a "prim, proper pain in the neck"), informal words like *pregnant* seem irreverent in this context. However, stage directions—the parenthetical comments in italic type—show that the Herdmans intend no irreverence. Thus, the excerpt highlights an important fact about language: As our nation grows more culturally diverse, we are less justified in assuming that any one way of phrasing information and ideas is inherently better, clearer, or more appropriate than all others.

Consider how the same Gospel passage appears in a more recent version of the Bible:

At that time Emperor Augustus ordered a census to be taken throughout the Roman Empire. When this first census took place, Quirinius was the governor of Syria. Everyone, then, went to register himself, each to his own home town.

Joseph went from the town of Nazareth in Galilee to the town of Bethlehem in Judea, the birthplace of King David. Joseph went there because he was a descendant of David. He went to register with Mary, who was promised in marriage to him. She was pregnant, and while they were in Bethlehem, the time came for her to have her baby. She gave birth to her first son, wrapped him in cloths and laid him in a manger—there was no room for them to stay in the inn.

There were some shepherds in that part of the country who were spending the night in the fields, taking care of their flocks. An angel of the Lord appeared to them, and the glory of the Lord shone over them. They were terribly afraid, but the angel said to them, "Don't be afraid! I am here with good news for you, which will bring great joy to all the people. This very day in David's town your Savior was born—Christ the Lord! And this is what will prove it to you: you will find a baby wrapped in cloths and lying in a manger."

Suddenly a great army of heaven's angels appeared with the angel, singing praises to God: "Glory to God in the highest heaven, and peace on earth to those with whom he is pleased!"

When the angels went away from them back into heaven, the shepherds said to one another, "Let's go to Bethlehem and see this thing that has happened, which the Lord has told us."

This version of the narrative uses familiar words, like *pregnant*, yet few people would consider it fundamentally less reverent than the King James version.

Paraphrasing in a Different Style

1. The following texts are *parodies*, works that adopt—and often exaggerate—the language and style of a specialized field or variety of text. After reading each, try to determine what type of language or document it parodies.

a. Postal System Input Buffer Device

Robertson Osborne

Although no public announcement of the fact has been made, it is known that the United States Post Office Department for some time has been installing Postal System Input Buffer Devices as temporary information storage units on pseudo-randomly selected street corners. Several models are in use: some older ones are still to be found painted in a color which may be described as yellow-greenish in hue, low saturation, and low in brilliance, but a significantly large proportion are now appearing in a red, white, and blue combination which seems to provide greater user satisfaction although the associational-algebra value-functions remain obscure. Access to the majority of these devices is from the sidewalk, although a recent modification (including a 180-degree rotation about a vertical centerline) makes some of them accessible from an automobile, provided that the vehicle is equipped with either (a) a passenger in normal working condition, mounted upright on the front seat or (b) a driver having at least one arm on the right-hand side which is six feet long and double-jointed at the wrist and elbow. Figure 1 shows a typical sidewalk-access model Postal Input Buffer Device.

Most normal adults without previous experience can be readily trained to operate the machine. Children and extremely short adults may find it necessary to obtain assistance from a passerby[1] in order to complete steps 4 (Feed Cycle) and 6 (Verification), or both. The machine is normally operated as described below.

---

[1] In this context, *passerby* may be defined as a member of the set of human beings having a maximized probability of occupying the event space.

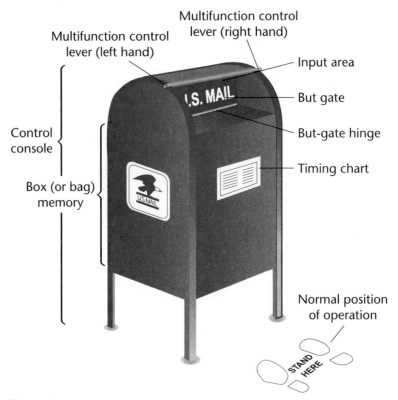

Figure 1

1. Position of Operator. Locate the Control Console (see Figure 1). Stand in front of the machine so that the control console is facing you.[2]

2. Initial Setup. Grasp the Multi-Function Control Lever (Figure 1). This lever performs several functions, each being uniquely determined by that portion of the Operation Cycle during which it is activated. The lever may be grasped with either hand. With the other hand, position the input in preparation for step 4 (Feed Cycle).

3. Start Operation. Pull the Multi-Function Control Lever toward you until it is fully extended. It will travel in a downward arc, as it is attached to a mechanical But Gate hinged at the bottom. (The But Gate, so named because it allows but one operation at a time, is specially designed to make feedback extremely difficult.) Pulling the Multi-Function Control Lever at this time accomplishes an Input Buffer Reset and Drop-Chute Clear. These actions are of interest only to the technician, but are mentioned here in preparation for the following note.

   NOTE: The lever should move freely. If it does not, the memory is full and cannot accept further information until it has been unloaded. The operator may elect to (a) wait for a Postal System Field Engineer (a "mail carrier") or (b) find another Postal System Input Buffer Device. If choice (b) is elected, refer to Description, above; also see Figure 1.

[2]The Novice Operator Trainee may prefer to face the console.

WARNING: Under no circumstances should the operator attempt to clear the unit; loss of a ring or wristwatch may result. In extreme cases, some individuals have lost thirty years.

4. Feed Cycle. Visually check to see that the input area is clear. The input area may be recognized because it is totally dark and makes a 90-degree downward turn; obstructions are hence not visible under normal circumstances. While holding the Multi-Function Control Lever in the extended position, start the input feed by manually inserting the information package.[3]

NOTE: One particularly advantageous feature of the Postal Service Input Buffer Device is that, at this stage, the address field may be mixed alphanumerics (including special characters) and may be presented to the unit in normal format (reading left-to-right and top-to-bottom), backward, or even upside down.

5. Transfer Cycle. Release the Multi-Function Control Lever. The machine will now automatically transfer the input to the delay-box memory (delay-bag in some models). The operator will soon become familiar with the typical "squeak" and "clank" signals, provided on all models to indicate satisfactory operation of the But Gate. Actual transfer of the information, however, is not signalled unless the information is very densely packed, in which case a "thump" signal may occasionally be heard.

NOTE: A "boing" signal indicates that the information is unsuited to the Input Buffer Device and that a programming error has therefore occurred.

6. Verification. Pull the Multi-Function Control Lever again (see step 3), check to see that the Input Zone (Figure 1) is clear (see step 4), and release the lever. This completes one full Operation Cycle. Additional cycles, when necessitated by large input quantities, may be initiated by returning to step 1 (above).

NOTE: Step 6 is not actually necessary for machine operation. The Postal Service Input Buffer Device has been designed to permit this step, however, to satisfy the requirements of the overwhelming "Post-Mailing Peek Compulsion," which affects most users of the unit and which has been linked by some writers[4] to the "Unsatisfied Sex-Curiosity" Syndrome.

[3]Perhaps better known to some readers as a "letter" or "postcard."
[4]Op. cit.

b. The Etiology and Treatment of Childhood[1,2]

Jordan W. Smoller, University of Pennsylvania

Childhood is a syndrome that has only recently begun to receive serious attention from clinicians. The syndrome itself, however, is not at all recent. As early as the eighth century, the Persian historian Kidnom made reference to "short, noisy creatures," who may well have been what we now call "children." The treatment

[1]The author would like to thank all the little people.
[2]This research was funded in part by a grant from Bazooka Gum.

of children, however, was unknown until this century, when so-called "child psychologists" and "child psychiatrists" became common. Despite this history of clinical neglect, it has been estimated that well over half of all Americans alive today have experienced childhood directly (Suess, 1983). In fact, the actual numbers are probably much higher, since these data are based on self-reports, which may be subject to social desirability biases and retrospective distortion.

The growing acceptance of childhood as a distinct phenomenon is reflected in the proposed inclusion of the syndrome in the upcoming *Diagnostic and Statistical Manual of Mental Disorders, 4th Edition,* or *DSM-IV,* of the American Psychiatric Association (1985).

Clinicians are still in disagreement about the significant clinical features of childhood, but the proposed *DSM-IV* will almost certainly include the following core features:

1. Congenital onset

2. Dwarfism

3. Emotional lability and immaturity

4. Knowledge deficits

5. Legume anorexia

CLINICAL FEATURES OF CHILDHOOD
Although the focus of this paper is on the efficacy of conventional treatment of childhood, the five clinical markers mentioned above merit further discussion for those unfamiliar with this patient population.

Congenital Onset
In one of the few existing literature reviews on childhood, Temple-Black (1982) has noted that childhood is almost always present at birth, although it may go undetected for years or even remain subclinical indefinitely. This observation has led some investigators to speculate on a biological contribution to childhood. As one psychologist has put it, "we may soon be in a position to distinguish organic childhood from functional childhood" (Rogers, 1979).

Dwarfism
This is certainly the most familiar marker of childhood. It is widely known that children are physically short relative to the population at large. Indeed, common clinical wisdom suggests that the treatment of the so-called "small child" (or "tot") is particularly difficult. These children are known to exhibit infantile behavior and display a startling lack of insight (Tom & Jerry, 1967).

Emotional Lability and Immaturity
This aspect of childhood is often the only basis for a clinician's diagnosis. As a result, many otherwise normal adults are misdiagnosed as children and must suffer the unnecessary stigma of being labelled a "child" by professionals and friends alike.

Knowledge Deficits
While many children have IQ's within or even above the norm, almost all will manifest knowledge deficits. Anyone who has known a real child has experienced the frustration of trying to discuss any topic that requires some general knowledge. Children seem to have little knowledge about the world they live in. Politics, art, and science—children are largely ignorant of these. Perhaps it is because of

this ignorance, but the sad fact is that most children have few friends who are not, themselves, children.

Legume Anorexia
This last identifying feature is perhaps the most unexpected. Folk wisdom is supported by empirical observation—children will rarely eat their vegetables (see Popeye, 1957, for review).

CAUSES OF CHILDHOOD
Now that we know what it is, what can we say about the causes of childhood? Recent years have seen a flurry of theory and speculation from a number of perspectives. Some of the most prominent are reviewed below.

Sociological Model
Emile Durkind was perhaps the first to speculate about sociological causes of childhood. He points out two key observations about children: 1) the vast majority of children are unemployed, and 2) children represent one of the least educated segments of our society. In fact, it has been estimated that less than twenty percent of children have had more than a fourth-grade education.

Clearly, children are an "out-group." Because of their intellectual handicap, children are even denied the right to vote. From the sociologist's perspective, treatment should be aimed at helping assimilate children into mainstream society. Unfortunately, some victims are so incapacitated by their childhood that they are simply not competent to work. One promising rehabilitation program (Spanky & Alfalfa, 1978) has trained victims of severe childhood to sell lemonade.

Biological Model
The observation that childhood is usually present from birth has led some to speculate on a biological contribution. An early investigation by Flintstone and Jetson (1939) indicated that childhood runs in families. Their survey of over eight thousand American families revealed that over half contained more than one child. Further investigation revealed that even most non-child family members had experienced childhood at some point. Cross-cultural studies (e.g., Mowgli & Din, 1950) indicate that familial childhood is even more prevalent in the Far East. For example, in Indian and Chinese families, as many as three out of four family members may have childhood.

Impressive evidence of a genetic component of childhood comes from a large-scale twin study by Brady and Partridge (1972). These authors studied over 106 pairs of twins, looking at concordance rates for childhood. Among identical or monozygotic twins, concordance was unusually high (.92), i.e., when one twin was diagnosed with childhood, the other twin was almost always a child as well.

Psychological Models
A considerable number of psychologically-based theories of the development of childhood exist. They are too numerous to review here. Among the more familiar models are Seligman's "learned childishness" model. According to this model, individuals who are treated like children eventually give up and become children. As a counterpoint to such theories, some experts have claimed that childhood does not really exist. Szasz (1980) has called "childhood" an expedient label. In seeking conformity, we handicap those whom we find unruly or too short to deal with by labeling them "children."

TREATMENT OF CHILDHOOD

Efforts to treat childhood are as old as the syndrome itself. Only in modern times, however, have humane and systematic treatment protocols been applied. In part, this increased attention to the problem may be due to the sheer number of individuals suffering from childhood. Government statistics (DHHS) reveal that there are more children alive today than at any time in our history. To paraphrase P. T. Barnum: "There's a child born every minute."

The overwhelming number of children has made government intervention inevitable. The nineteenth century saw the institution of what remains the largest single program for the treatment of childhood—so-called "public schools." Under this colossal program, individuals are placed into treatment groups based on the severity of their condition. For example, those most severely afflicted may be placed in a "kindergarten" program. Patients at this level are typically short, unruly, emotionally immature, and intellectually deficient. Given this type of individual, therapy is of necessity very basic. The strategy is essentially one of patient management and of helping the child master basic skills (e.g., finger-painting).

Unfortunately, the "school" system has been largely ineffective. Not only is the program a massive tax burden, but it has failed even to slow down the rising incidence of childhood.

Faced with this failure and the growing epidemic of childhood, mental health professionals are devoting increasing attention to the treatment of childhood. Given a theoretical framework by Freud's landmark treatises on childhood, child psychiatrists and psychologists claimed great successes in their clinical interventions.

By the 1950s, however, the clinicians' optimism had waned. Even after years of costly analysis, many victims remained children. The following case (taken from Gumbie & Poke, 1957) is typical.

> Billy J., age eight, was brought to treatment by his parents. Billy's affliction was painfully obvious. He stood only four feet, three inches, high and weighed a scant seventy pounds, despite the fact that he ate voraciously. Billy presented a variety of troubling symptoms. His voice was noticeably high for a man. He displayed legume anorexia, and, according to his parents, often refused to bathe. His intellectual functioning was also below normal—he had little general knowledge and could barely write a structured sentence. Social skills were also deficient. He often spoke inappropriately and exhibited "whining behavior." His sexual experience was nonexistent. Indeed, Billy considered women "icky."

> His parents reported that his condition had been present from birth, improving gradually after he was placed in a school at age five. The diagnosis was "primary childhood." After years of painstaking treatment, Billy improved gradually. At age eleven, his height and weight have increased, his social skills are broader, and he is now functional enough to hold down a "paper route."

After years this kind of frustration, startling new evidence has come to light which suggests that the prognosis in cases of childhood may not be all gloom. A critical review by Fudd (1972) noted that studies of the childhood syndrome tend to lack careful follow-up. Acting on this observation, Moe, Larrie, and Kirly (1974) began a large-scale longitudinal study. These investigators studied two groups. The first group comprised thirty-four children currently engaged in a long-term conventional treatment program. The second was a group of forty-two children receiving no treatment. All subjects had been diagnosed as children at least four years previously, with a mean duration of childhood of 6.4 years.

At the end of one year, the results confirmed the clinical wisdom that childhood is a refractory disorder—virtually all symptoms persisted and the treatment group was only slightly better off than the controls.

The results, however, of a careful ten-year follow-up were startling. The investigators (Moe, Larrie, Kirly, & Shemp, 1984) assessed the original cohort on a variety of measures. General knowledge and emotional maturity were assessed with standard measures. Height was assessed by the "metric system" (see Ruler, 1923), and legume appetite by the Vegetable Appetite Test (VAT) designed by Popeye (1968). Moe et al. found that subjects improved uniformly on all measures. Indeed, in most cases, the subjects appeared to be symptom-free. Moe et al. report a spontaneous remission rate of ninety-five percent, a finding which is certain to revolutionize the clinical approach to childhood.

These recent results suggest that the prognosis for victims of childhood may not be so bad as we have feared. We must not, however, become too complacent. Despite its apparently high spontaneous remission rate, childhood remains one of the most serious and rapidly growing disorders facing mental health professionals today. And, beyond the psychological pain it brings, childhood has recently been linked to a number of physical disorders. Twenty years ago, Howdi, Doodi, and Beauzeau (1965) demonstrated a six-fold increased risk of chicken pox, measles, and mumps among children as compared with normal controls. Later, Barby and Kenn (1971) linked childhood to an elevated risk of accidents—compared with normal adults, victims of childhood were much more likely to scrape their knees, lose their teeth, and fall off their bikes.

Clearly, much more research is needed before we can give any real hope to the millions of victims wracked by this insidious disorder.

2. Translate two or three paragraphs from either of the above texts into a fundamentally different type of language: informal (adapted to the readers of newspapers and popular magazines), colloquial (conversational), or slang.

3. Write a short parody similar to either of the above, imitating or exaggerating a particular type of specialized language or document.

Paraphrasing an Argument

Objectivity is difficult when you must paraphrase an argument with which you disagree. Nevertheless, fairness and accuracy allow you to present yourself as a person of integrity and good will whose views deserve careful consideration.

The need to paraphrase an argument with which you disagree may arise under various circumstances, but let's consider one of the most familiar. Suppose you want to refute a commonly held opinion. You may wish to begin by demonstrating that you understand, have considered, and respect that opinion. One obstacle may be your ***personal commitments***. Consider the following sentence from an essay by English professor Paul McBrearty, who argues for the elimination of anonymous student evaluations of college instructors:

> Anonymity in student evaluations virtually assures lowered academic standards and inflated grades. The pressures on teachers to *give* good grades so as to *get* good grades are severe, pervasive, unremitting, and inescapable.

A source that makes an argument

Though we happen to disagree with this argument, we do not consider the following a fair, objective paraphrase of the first sentence:

An unacceptable paraphrase

> Some college professors fear that students will use anonymous evaluations as a way of getting even for unfair grades.

This paraphrase states a claim that the author of the original passage is not really making. Specifically, it implies that *because* some college professors grade unfairly, they are afraid of student reprisals. What McBrearty is actually saying is that instructors should be able to grade both fairly and rigorously without fear of reprisal.

Another obstacle to paraphrase is overdependence on familiar patterns or *schemas*. Schemas are recurrent structures that help us make predictions about what a writer or speaker is going to say next. Most of the time, schemas allow us to read and listen efficiently. For example, the fourth sentence in the previous paragraph—"One obstacle can be your personal commitments"—leads most readers to expect that another obstacle will be discussed in a subsequent sentence or paragraph. A problem with schemas is, of course, that readers may take too much for granted and draw hasty assumptions about what a writer is about to say. Consider, for instance, the second sentence in the excerpt from McBrearty's article:

The original phrasing

> The pressures on teachers to *give* good grades so as to *get* good grades are severe, pervasive, unremitting, and inescapable.

At first glance, the following sentence may seem an appropriate paraphrase:

A hasty paraphrase

> Professors are tempted to bribe students with high grades.

Having encountered this claim before, a reader might be tempted to conclude that the author is preparing to make the same argument. Later in his essay, however, McBrearty asserts:

A statement made later in the same source

> Whenever student evaluations are used in any way by administrators as a basis for the denial of promotion, retention, or salary increase, or for assigning a less-than-satisfactory rating to a faculty member, the faculty member is denied the constitutional right of due process if not permitted to confront what are in effect his or her accusers.

Although we still do not find this argument valid, we must recognize that McBrearty is not suggesting that popular instructors are offering bribes, but rather that they may be responding to pressure in order to protect their jobs. Therefore, the following is a fairer paraphrase of the second sentence from the original passage:

A fairer paraphrase

> Professors fear that they will face the consequences of poor student evaluations if they grade rigorously.

Sometimes, writers must paraphrase arguments that not only diverge from their own opinions but also challenge their personal values. On these occasions, the best approach is to be explicit in attributing such an argument to its source. Suppose, for example, a writer who opposes censorship had to paraphrase the following passage from an essay by Barbara Lawrence titled "Four-Letter Words Can Hurt You":

> Obscene words . . . seem to serve a similar purpose: to reduce the human organism (especially the female organism) and human functions (especially sexual and procreative) to their least organic, most mechanical dimension; to substitute a trivializing or deforming resemblance for the complex human reality of what is being described.

A source that makes an argument

A writer might emphasize that Lawrence's argument is incompatible with her own views by engaging in what we have referred to as descriptive paraphrase. In other words, she might use an ***attribution phrase*** to distance herself from the source—perhaps "According to Barbara Lawrence" or one of these alternatives:

> In an essay often cited by proponents of censorship, Barbara Lawrence argues . . .
>
> Lawrence presents an argument often raised by those who wish to suppress pornography. . . .

Acceptable attribution phrases

On the other hand, it would not be fair to use a slanted or loaded attribution phrase like "According to radical feminist Barbara Lawrence."

Earlier in this chapter, we spoke of the rare occasion for paraphrasing a source that uses language offensive to many readers. Equally unusual is the need to cite arguments that violate the generally permissive boundaries of academic inquiry and conversation. Though scholars must respect those with whom they disagree, we sometimes encounter ideas so hateful that we feel compelled to express disapproval. A number of years ago, one of our students found a periodical in the university library that he considered abusive and insulting to gay men and women as well as to religious minorities. To voice his indignation, the student wrote to the head librarian and, hoping to get his point across, paraphrased some of the views expressed in the periodical. Considering the circumstances, he felt justified in using these judgmental attribution phrases:

> Here we find the familiar homophobic claim that. . .
>
> Overt anti-Semitism emerges later, when. . .

Judgmental attribution phrases

Determining when to express judgment about paraphrased sources—or deciding that a particular opinion is out of bounds and therefore unworthy of paraphrase—is a sensitive issue in academic communities. However, it is generally best to avoid judgmental citations of sources unless there are clear and compelling reasons for doing so.

Paraphrasing an Argument

EXERCISE

Try to paraphrase each of the following arguments. Paraphrase only the argument, which appears in italic type; preceding sentences merely provide context.

  a. The SAT has become a symbol—or, in the language of literary criticism, the objective correlative (that is, the object that correlates to the emotion)—of all the anxieties, concerns, fears, and frustrations in the college-admissions system. *The underlying issue, I am forced to conclude, is not, in fact, the test, but rather the nature, character, and degree of competition now endemic in college admissions—and in higher education generally.*

     —Lee Bollinger, "Debate over the SAT Masks Perilous Trends in College Admissions"

b. Standardized testing in public education was introduced to set a minimum standard of performance after thirty years of "education reform" was shown to be a failure—resulting in expensive schools run by educational bureaucrats who have miserably failed minority communities and inner-city students.

  Mastering standardized tests is a skill that is necessary to obtain credentials in just about any field—like it or not. Real education can easily accompany standardized tests.

     —Jeffrey Geibel, letter to the editor, *New York Times Magazine*

c. Sociologists have never demonstrated a firm connection between which college Americans attend and their success later in life.

  Ivy League graduates tend to do well financially, but it is unclear whether that reflects the added value of their elite education or merely that they were already primed for success when they applied to college.

     —Walter Shapiro, "Rejected by College of Choice? Relax"

Paraphrasing in Research Papers

As we have said earlier in this chapter, research writing often uses paraphrases sources in order to cite important information, to place a topic or issue in context, or to support an interpretation or opinion. In these cases, a writer must be careful to identify sources by name (usually in the form of parenthetical notes, which will be introduced in Chapter 6.)

  Uses of paraphrase in research writing—particularly conventions of style and documentation—will be explained in greater detail in Chapter 12. The following examples simply illustrate various contexts in research writing that might call for paraphrase.

Paraphrasing to Cite Information

Suppose you are writing a research paper arguing for curtailed consumption of red meat. Using a direct quotation, you might open your paper this way:

Quoting to cite information

In his recent book, *Beyond Beef: The Rise and Fall of the Cattle Culture*, Jeremy Rifkin cites the following facts:

> Some 100,000 cows are slaughtered every twenty-four hours in the United States. In a given week, ninety-one percent of all United States households purchase beef. . . . Americans currently consume twenty-three percent of all the beef produced in the world. Today, the average American consumes sixty-five pounds of beef per year (154).

On the other hand, you might paraphrase the source to better effect. Consider this alternative:

Better: paraphrasing to cite information

Americans are so addicted to beef that every week ninety-one percent of all families in the U.S. buy it. Because of this dietary preference, our country lays claim to nearly a fourth of the world's supply. Individually, each of us devours, on average, sixty-five pounds of beef each year, requiring a daily slaughter of 100,000 cows (Rifkin 154).

Although it may be easier simply to quote Jeremy Rifkin, there is no compelling reason to do so. Since there is nothing particularly unusual about his vocabulary or style, the basic information that he reports can be presented just as effectively in your own words.

Paraphrasing to Place a Topic or Issue in Context

Suppose that the college you attend has imposed restrictions on the use of air conditioning during summer sessions. Responding to outcries of opposition, you write an objective, researched study of the possible consequences of this unpopular measure—both its advantages as a conservation measure and its inevitable drawbacks. Recognizing the need for open-minded inquiry, you begin your report by addressing the widely held belief that air conditioning has become an indispensable comfort for nearly everyone in the United States. You might do this by paraphrasing the following passage from an essay by Frank Trippett:

> [Air conditioning has] seduced families into retreating into houses with closed doors and shut windows, reducing the commonality of neighborhood life and all but obsoleting the front-porch society whose open casual folkways were an appealing feature of a sweatier America. Is it really surprising that the public's often noted withdrawal into self-pursuit and privatism has coincided with the epic spread of air conditioning? Though science has little studied how habitual air conditioning affects mind or body, some medical experts suggest that, like other technical avoidance of natural swings in climate, air conditioning may take a toll on the human capacity to adapt to stress (Trippett 75).

A source that provides context for an issue

Your opening paragraph might begin like this:

> Although most of us regard air conditioning as an unqualified blessing if not an absolute necessity, our dependence on it carries seldom examined consequences. Author Frank Trippett enumerates some of these consequences. For one thing, air conditioning has altered notions of neighborliness, luring people away from the front porch and into air-tight rooms where they have little contact with anyone outside the family. This seclusion may contribute to certain antisocial tendencies, such as self-absorption and extreme competitiveness. Also, Trippett suggests that while it remains an unproven theory, some scientists have suggested that air conditioning impairs our ability to cope with stress (75).

A paraphrase of the source

Notice that the author of the source, Trippett, is cited at the beginning of this paraphrase rather than in the parenthetical note at the end. (The parenthetical note must be retained, however, to identify the precise location of the borrowed ideas—page 75 of the magazine in which Trippett's article was published.)

Paraphrasing to Support an Interpretation or Opinion

Suppose that you are writing a paper arguing that the recording industry has grown too powerful. In the course of your research, you find the book *Music for Pleasure: Essays in the Sociology of Pop*, in which Simon Frith, a scholar of popular culture, argues that one consequence of the recording industry's power is suppression of certain kinds of musical talent:

A source that expresses an opinion

> The industrialization of music means a shift from active musical production to passive pop consumption, the decline of folk or community or subcultural traditions, and a general loss of musical skill. The only instruments people like me can play today are their [CD] players and tape-decks (Frith 11).

A paragraph in your research paper might open as follows:

A paraphrase of the source

> One consequence of the recording industry's power is the gradual decline of amateur musical talent. Simon Frith, a scholar of popular culture, has argued that the mass marketing of CDs has discouraged music-making by amateurs and undermined regional and ethnic traditions, thus limiting the acquisition and exercise of individual talent. Says Frith, "The only instruments people like me can play today are their [CD] players and tape-decks" (11).

There are two things to note about this paraphrase. First, when you use a source to support an opinion or interpretation, you normally choose a recognized authority. You are therefore more likely to identify the source in an acknowledgment phrase rather than a parenthetical note. (Notice that the paraphrase also cites the basis of Frith's authority—his being a scholar of popular culture—though it would not do so if he were a universally recognized person like Albert Einstein or Hillary Clinton.) The other thing you may notice about this paraphrase is that it incorporates a direct quotation. Since there really isn't any way to rephrase the last sentence without losing something, it is best to quote it directly.

EXERCISE | **Paraphrasing in Research Papers**

For each of the following quotations, write a paraphrase appropriate to the situation at hand. Remember that you may choose to name the source before you paraphrase, or you may put the last name(s) of the source in a parenthetical note at the end, along with page number.

a. You are enrolled in a history course titled Robber Barons and Reformers: The United States from 1877 to 1917. A paraphrase of the following quotation can be used to introduce a research paper examining the influences of oligarchies or ruling elites during this period of American history.

Source:
A passage from page 2 of the editors' introduction to *Ruling America: A History of Wealth and Power in a Democracy*. The editors of the book are Steve Fraser, an historian and freelance writer, and Gary Gerstle, a professor of history at the University of Maryland.

Quotation:
Phrases like "ruling class" or "ruling elite" sound a discordant note. They do not sound like they belong in the vocabulary of American politics and its history. . . . There is something ineffably alien about such notions, stepchildren imported from the lingua franca of the Old World and its sedimentary layers of titled aristocrats, landed gentry, military castes, and dynastic families. It is a cherished American folk belief, after all, that classes do not exist.

b. You are enrolled in an anthropology course that introduces the aims and methods of archeology. A paraphrase of the following quotation illustrates the difficulty and urgency of identifying architectural landmarks that are not particularly old or historical and thus places zealous preservationism in some perspective.

Source:
An article by interior designer Brad Dunning in the *New York Times Magazine*. Dunning decries the demolition of a California house designed in 1963 by architect Richard Neutra, whose work is sometimes compared with that of Frank Lloyd Wright. The quotation appears on page 72.

Quotation:
Now that important modern architecture has finally achieved iconic stature, this is especially painful. Perhaps twenty years ago this wanton act might have been less shocking; the style had yet to achieve its lofty status. But at this point, when contemporary architecture has moved so far from the idealism and social engineering intended—and realized—by these surviving gems, the thought that a house of this caliber would be in jeopardy escaped even the most paranoid preservationists.

c. As a student in a course titled Writing about Music, you are asked to look into the effects of mass-marketed musical recordings on popular taste. A paraphrase of the following quotation will allow you to introduce one point of view.

Source:
An article by music critic Alex Ross in the *New Yorker*. The quotation appears on page 94.

Quotation:
Ninety-nine years ago, John Philip Sousa predicted that recordings would lead to the demise of music. . . . Before you dismiss Sousa as a nutty old codger, you might ponder how much has changed in the past hundred years. Music has achieved onrushing omnipresence in our world: millions of hours of its history are available on disk. . . . Yet, for most of us, music is no longer something we do ourselves, or even watch other people doing in front of us. It has become a radically virtual medium, an art without a face.

Effective Paraphrasing   **GUIDELINES**

The general principles set forth in this chapter can be summed up in the following guidelines:

- Paraphrasing involves a special kind of reading and response, appropriate when the occasion calls for close literal reading and accurate reporting.

- When you paraphrase a passage to make it suitable for a different audience, you should make appropriate adjustments in style, vocabulary, and degree of formality.

- When you paraphrase an argument, particularly one with which you disagree, you must be fair and objective.

- When you paraphrase a source in your research writing, you must completely recast information and ideas in your own language and style. Simple word substitution does not constitute a legitimate paraphrase; neither does rearrangement of word order.

 ## READING SELECTION

With a PhD in biology, Barbara Ehrenreich began her career as a political essayist and social critic. In researching her most recent book, *Nickel and Dimed: Surviving in Low-Wage America*, Ehrenreich worked in a variety of jobs at the minimum wage. The following essay, which describes one of her jobs, appeared in the *New York Times*.

Another Day, Another Indignity

BARBARA EHRENREICH

1   Only a person of unblemished virtue can get a job at Wal-Mart—a low-level job, that is, sorting stock, unloading trucks, or operating a cash register. A drug test eliminates the chemical miscreants; a detailed "personality test" probes the job applicant's horror of theft and willingness to turn in an erring co-worker.

2   Extreme submissiveness to authority is another desirable trait. When I applied for a job at Wal-Mart in the spring of 2000, I was reprimanded for getting something "wrong" on this test: I had agreed only "strongly" to the proposition, "All rules have to be followed to the letter at all times." The correct answer was "totally agree."

3   Apparently the one rule that need not be slavishly adhered to at Wal-Mart is the federal Fair Labor Standards Act, which requires that employees be paid time and a half if they work more than forty hours in a week. Present and former Wal-Mart employees in twenty-eight states are suing the company for failure to pay overtime.

4   A Wal-Mart spokesman says it is company policy "to pay its employees properly for the hours they work." Maybe so, but it wasn't a policy I remember being emphasized in the eight-hour orientation session all new "associates" are required to attend. The session included a video on "associate honesty" that showed a cashier being caught on videotape as he pocketed some bills from the cash register. Drums beat ominously as he was led away in handcuffs and sentenced to four years in prison.

5   The personnel director warned us, in addition, against "time theft," or the use of company time for anything other than work—"anything at all," she said, which was interpreted in my store as including trips to the bathroom. We were to punch out even for our two breaks, to make sure we did not exceed the allotted fifteen minutes.

6   It turns out, however, that Wal-Mart management doesn't hold itself to the same standard of rectitude it expects from its low-paid employees. My first inkling of this came in the form of a warning from a coworker not to let myself be persuaded to work overtime because, she explained, Wal-Mart doesn't pay overtime. Naively, I told her this was impossible; such a large company would surely not be flouting federal law.

7   I should have known better. We had been apprised, during orientation, that even after punching out, associates were required to wait on any customers who might

approach them. Thanks to the further requirement that associates wear their blue and yellow vests until the moment they went out the door, there was no avoiding pesky last-minute customers.

Now some present and former employees have filed lawsuits against Wal-Mart. **8** They say they were ordered to punch out after an eight-hour shift and then continue working for no pay. In a practice, reported in the [New York] *Times*, that you might expect to find only in a third-world sweatshop, Wal-Mart store managers in six states have locked the doors at closing time, some employees say, forcing all present to remain for an hour or more of unpaid labor.

This is "time theft" on a grand scale—practically a mass mugging. Of course, in **9** my brief experience while doing research for a book on low-wage work, I found such practices or milder versions of them by no means confined to Wal-Mart.

At a Midwestern chain store selling hardware and lumber, I was offered an eleven- **10** hour shift five days a week—with no overtime pay for the extra fifteen hours. A corporate-run housecleaning service paid a startling wage of only $6.65 an hour but required us to show up in the morning forty minutes before the clock started running— for meetings and to prepare for work by filling our buckets with cleaning supplies.

What has been revealed in corporate America . . . is a two-tiered system of moral- **11** ity: Low-paid employees are required to be hard-working, law-abiding, rule-respecting straight arrows. More than that, they are often expected to exhibit a selfless generosity toward the company, readily "donating" chunks of their time free of charge. Meanwhile, as we have learned from the cases of Enron, Adelphia, ImClone, WorldCom, and others, many top executives have apparently felt free to do whatever they want— conceal debts, lie about profits, engage in insider trading—to the dismay and sometimes ruin of their stockholders.

But investors are not the only victims of the corporate crime wave. Workers also **12** suffer from management greed and dishonesty. In Wal-Mart's case, the moral gravity of its infractions is compounded by the poverty of its "associates," many of whom are paid less than $10 an hour. As workers discover that their problem is not just a rogue store manager or "bad apple" but management as a whole, we can expect at the very least widespread cynicism, and perhaps an epidemic of rule-breaking from below.

Freewriting

Freewrite for ten to fifteen minutes about Ehrenreich's account of working conditions at Wal-Mart. You may write about anything you've learned, perhaps comparing or contrasting your own experiences as an employee with those of the author. On the other hand, you might consider whether and how this essay changes your perspectives as a customer or consumer.

Group Work

Share freewrites in your group, each member reading aloud while others are taking notes. As you listen, try to develop a list of rules (often unwritten) and expectations (often unstated) that influence employee behavior, relationships between workers and employers, and notions about ethical conduct in the workplace.

Review Questions

1. What screening techniques do Wal-Mart managers use to avoid hiring persons they consider undesirable?

2. How does Wal-Mart define "time theft"? In what sense, according to Ehrenreich, does the company itself engage in a different variety of time theft?

3. What "two-tiered system of morality" does Ehrenreich perceive in corporate culture?

Discussion Questions

1. Do you think Ehrenreich's audience, readers of the *New York Times*, is any more or less likely to shop or work at Wal-Mart than Americans in general? Does it matter? How do you think Ehrenreich hopes to influence her audience? That is, what would she like them to feel, understand, or do?

2. Is Ehrenreich challenging or appealing to the traditional American work ethic? If both, which aspects of the work ethic does her article challenge, and which does it validate?

3. While coworkers struggled to make a living, Ehrenreich was conducting surreptitious research. Does this affect her reliability as an observer or reporter? If so, how? How do you suppose her coworkers would respond to her article?

Writing

1. Citing the same kinds of information that Ehrenreich presents in her article, freewrite for at least fifteen minutes about your worst (or best) job. Using details from your freewriting along with information from Ehrenreich's article, write an essay that explains and illustrates the defining features of a bad (or good) job.

2. Each December, *Multinational Monitor* names its "Ten Worst Corporations"; in January, *Fortune* magazine releases its annual list of "The 100 Best Companies to Work for in America." Locate the appropriate issues of both periodicals for the past three years, looking either in your college library or the two following Web sites:
   <http:// www.essential.org/monitor>
   <http://www.fortune.com/fortune/lists/bestcompanies/index.html>
   Use your findings to develop criteria for evaluating a future workplace.

WRITE, READ, and RESEARCH the NET

1. *Write:* Freewrite for fifteen minutes about anything you have read, observed, or experienced regarding work in the retail sector. If this proves difficult, you may focus your freewriting on low-wage work in general or on your experiences and observations as a shopper in one or more of the larger discount chains (Kmart, Target, Wal-Mart).

2. *Read:* Consult the following two Web sites:
   <http://www.walmartstores.com/wmstore/wmstores/HomePage.jsp>
   <http://www.walmartwatch.org/>

3. *Research:* Using the index to the *Wall Street Journal*, which should be available online or in hardbound volumes in your library, scan the brief descriptions of articles listed under the heading "Wal-Mart." You may also consult the Wal-Mart homepage:
   <http://www.walmartstores.com/wmstore/wmstores/HomePage.jsp>
   Using any information you can gather about Wal-Mart's record as an employer and its response to criticism, write an essay assessing the reliability of Ehrenreich's article.

 ## ADDITIONAL READINGS

The following articles deal with low-wage employment. First is a review of Iain Levison's memoir, *A Working Stiff's Manifesto*, published a year after Ehrenreich's book, and next is a *Newsweek* article about safety issues involving part-time summer jobs for teenagers.

Get a Job

JONATHAN MILES

"In the last ten years, I've had forty-two jobs in six states," Iain Levison tells us. He can   **1**
now add "writer" to a résumé that includes film-set gofer, fish cutter, oil truck driver, cook, mover, crab fisherman, and thirty-six other job titles. Anyone who finds these numbers startling probably hasn't put in any time behind a restaurant prep line or a retail counter lately, or has missed reading Barbara Ehrenreich's *Nickel and Dimed* and Ben Cheever's *Selling Ben Cheever*, two similar recent first-person chronicles about zigzagging through the lower levels of the American workplace. As Levison notes, "a million others" could have written the same book he has, a claim worth disputing on a literary level only.

"I have become, without realizing it, an itinerant worker, a modern-day Tom   **2**
Joad,"[1] Levison writes, between pungent recountings of his on-the-clock misadventures. This revelation comes as something of a surprise to Levison, who—fresh out of college and the Army, and ripe with all the correct intentions—expected something different. "There was an unspoken agreement between me and the Fates that, as I lived in the richest country in the history of the world, and was a fairly hard worker, all these things"—a house, a wife, a serviceable car, a fenced-in yard—"would just come together eventually." In February, touting his economic proposals, George W. Bush proclaimed that jobs lead to "more independence, more self-esteem and more joy and hope." But while Bush's own job may have provided him those blessings, Levison and millions of other Americans have discovered that hourly jobs lead not to joy or to

---

[1] A migrant farm worker in John Steinbeck's novel *The Grapes of Wrath*. (Editor's note)

hope but only to different hourly jobs. "It's surviving," Levison says, "but surviving sounds dramatic, and this life lacks drama. It's scraping by."

3　　To be fair, Levison is often a lousy hire. His overeducation makes him impatient lugging other people's stuff around, even though it qualifies him for little else. From a chi-chi Manhattan grocery he steals as much Chilean sea bass as he can fit into his pants. He cooks the log books on trucking runs, blows up the head of a lawn statue he mistakes for a heating-oil tank by pumping fuel into it, and on job applications he writes "the moon" for where he went to grade school and "compulsive masturbation" for his hobbies. But this last tack, like many of his others, is reactive rather than proactive, to crib from the current corporate parlance. "They'll hire me on nothing but a drug test," he writes, so what's the use? And this, more than anything else, is what chafes him.

4　　Despite scattered grumblings, Levison's beef with his myriad employers isn't about money. "The real problem is with the expendability of us all. One human is as good as the next. Loyalty and effort are not rewarded."

5　　The last ten years have supposedly seen the demise of the "Organization Man," the archetype of employee-employer fidelity that William H. Whyte posited in his 1956 classic of that name. The breakdown of that conformist ideology has proved a boon to white-collar workers, enabling them to manage their career arcs far more independently. For the unskilled labor pool, however, it has yielded few rewards. Working the same job all your life may strike many as a nightmare out of the 1950s, but for those like Levison it sometimes sounds like a merciful dream. "I have a job," he writes glumly. "Here we go again."

6　　Unlike Ehrenreich and Cheever, who ventured into workplaces as undercover reporters, Levison is the real deal, less a correspondent than a combatant. Levison's account lacks the Michael Harrington-like[2] ambitions of Ehrenreich's book and the writerly *savoir faire* of Cheever's, but it bears an immediacy that neither of those authors can quite match. That said, "A Working Stiff's Manifesto" is at times lopsided, knee-jerk and braying; but it is also bracing, hilarious and dead on. "It wasn't supposed to be like this," Levison writes, but if there's naïveté involved (and there is), it's a communal naïveté. It's called the American Dream.

The High Cost of Summer Cash

Teenagers Are Twice as Likely as Adults to Get Hurt on the Job

Julie Scelfo and Karen Springen

1　　Soon the final school bell will ring, and four million teenagers will start their summer jobs. Aaron Janssen is one of them. Janssen, 16, is psyched to have landed a stint as a cook near his home in Iowa; working makes him feel like his dad and will help him buy a car. The job's hazards don't concern him. "Everyone knows to be careful," he says. But a working teenager can be a perfect storm of eagerness and inexperience, and here's a case in point: last week a fifteen-year-old boy died in a job-related accident while working for a Maryland landscaping firm.

---

[2]Michael Harrington (1928–89), author of *The Other America*, brought public attention to economic inequalities in America. (Editor's note)

While putting high-school students to work has obvious benefits, it also holds   2
considerable risks. Each year, more than 70,000 working teenagers end up in the emergency room because of work-related injuries, according to the National Institute for
Occupational Safety and Health. Even more worrisome are fatalities: about seventy
teens die on the job each year, mostly in farm and retail work. Government agencies
hope to cast new light on these statistics; last week the U.S. Labor Department sent
tougher child-labor regulations to the Office of Management and Budget for approval.

Is it immaturity? Lack of training? A sense of invincibility? The exact cause is of-   3
ten unclear, but last week's fatality raises all these questions. Michael Barrios was killed
after he climbed atop a mulch-spreading truck and fell in. (The Maryland Occupational Safety and Health department is investigating the death; the landscaping company did not return calls seeking comment.) Even seemingly cushy jobs can be
dangerous. In 2000 Adam Carey, 16, of Beverly, Massachusetts, landed a job at a country club. Nobody saw exactly what happened, but at some point Adam ran a golf cart
into a deck, fatally puncturing one of the chambers of his heart. "I just assumed when
you send a child into the workplace that the employer knows the law," says Adam's
mother, Maggie, who sued the club's board of directors and the golf-cart manufacturer.
Both companies declined to comment, citing pending litigation.

Public agencies and employers are taking steps to educate parents and kids. The   4
Labor Department this month launched a series of public-service announcements
called "Youth Rules!" about what kinds of jobs are appropriate for teens. In Indianapolis, a new pilot program funded by the Accident Fund Insurance Company takes teenagers to a hospital physical-therapy ward, where they put their arms in slings to feel
what it would be like if they had to maneuver with only one arm. "It was extremely
eye-opening," says Eldon Horton, a career counselor who led a recent tour for forty-
five students. "Kids think, 'I've gotten this far; nothing's happened to me. I must be
pretty invincible.'" Now when they learn about the daily grind, they may learn about
human frailty, too.

4 Reading for the Main Idea

The reading strategies presented in Chapter 2 serve a number of purposes. One of the most important is to help you see, quickly and clearly, what a writer is getting at. Normally, when readers approach a text, the first question that confronts them is "What is this about?" or "What is the *main idea*?" Being able to recognize, understand, and restate the main idea of a text is useful in carrying out a variety of academic tasks, including library research.

Defining main idea as a concept, however, is not so easy. Chapters 1 and 2 have demonstrated how individual readers *create meaning* when they bring their unique personal histories to a text. Consequently, no two readers are likely to experience a long, complex piece of writing (the novel *Moby Dick*, e.g.) in precisely the same way. In an effort to account for this diversity, one modern philosopher has declared that "every reading is a misreading." In the face of such views, you may ask how it is possible to arrive at anything like the main idea of a reading.

There is no easy answer to that question because the meaning of a written text does not belong entirely to the writer, nor entirely to the reader. Instead, readers and writers negotiate meaning collaboratively. Under ideal circumstances, this is how reading operates. But in order for the negotiation to proceed smoothly and predictably, both writer and reader must agree on and abide by certain established conventions. When you tried reading a passage in Chapter 2 that defied one of those conventions—an informative title—the collaboration between you and the writer suffered.

Basically, writers plant clues and signals, while readers respond to them in relatively consistent and predictable ways. This chapter focuses on the unwritten rules of this reciprocal process. Familiarity with these rules should help you hold up your end of the transaction between writer and reader.

 ## GENERAL AND SPECIFIC CATEGORIES

When the main idea of a written text can be captured in a sentence, that sentence is a *general* statement, broader than other statements in the same text, which are more *specific*. Distinguishing between general and specific is an important aspect of reading for the main idea. Following is a list of words that illustrates the distinction:

most general	things
	life forms
	animals
	humans
	students
	first-year students
	members of Professor Fangle's music theory class
most specific	Roscoe Jellyquack

Each item in the list is more specific, and therefore less general, than the one above it. As a category, each encompasses fewer members. The first item includes everything in the universe, while the last includes only a single individual. Roscoe belongs to each category; his dog Elmo belongs to just the first four; and Elmo's flea collar is a member of only the most general category, things.

Statements can also be arranged in general-to-specific order:

- Some people have qualities not shared by everyone.
- Jo Ann has many exceptional traits.
- Most notable is her superhuman will power.
- She can stick to her diet no matter how great the temptation.
- Monday, when I offered her a pastry, Jo Ann turned it down for an apple.

Again, each statement is a more specific instance of the statement before it. Each bears a *for example* relationship to the one it follows, and the examples cover less and less territory. The last one is a very specific, **concrete** statement, one that presents a picture you can visualize in your imagination—a particular event at a particular time involving particular people. In contrast, the first one is a very general, **abstract** statement, one that calls up an idea but not a specific event that you can see with your mind's eye. Recognizing the relationship between general, abstract statements and specific, concrete statements is essential to efficient reading.

General and Specific Categories   EXERCISES

1. Arrange the following lists in order from the most general to the most specific:

a. loafer
   footwear
   casual shoe
   Colonel Eggslump's right loafer
   garment
   product
   shoe

  b. The College of Arts and Sciences
    higher education
    Natural History of Intertidal Organisms 553
    The Marine Biology Option
    Zenith State University
    Department of Biology
    Division of Physical Sciences

  c. Madame DeShamble lacked concern for her fellow creatures.
    Madame DeShamble cut off the tails of blind mice with a carving knife.
    Madame DeShamble was a heartless person.
    Madame DeShamble was cruel to animals.

  d. Words can affect their hearers.
    The cry "Give me liberty or give me death" aroused support for independence.
    Political oratory can be particularly stirring.
    Some statements provoke people's emotions.

2. For each of the following categories, provide one that is more general and another that is more specific:

  a. chair
  b. circus performer
  c. Walter loves Connie.
  d. Parents often urge their teenaged children to do well in school.

 DEDUCTIVE AND INDUCTIVE ORGANIZATION

Within almost any passage, some statements are more general than others. Often, the way a writer arranges general and specific statements is important. Notice, for example, that the passage on page 84, which you examined in Chapter 2, contains four levels of generality. If we number those levels from 1 (most general) to 4 (most specific) and indent each level of specificity farther to the right, relationships among sentences become visible.

  1 Scarfe was always a tyrant in his household.
    2 The servants lived in constant terror of his diatribes, which he would deliver whenever he was displeased.
      3 One of the most frequent causes of his displeasure was the food they served him.
        4 His tea, for example, was either too hot or too cold.
        4 His soup had either too much or too little seasoning.
      3 Another pet peeve was the servants' manner of address.
        4 God help the butler who forgot to add *sir* to every sentence he spoke to Scarfe, or the chauffeur whose tone was deemed not properly deferential.

4   On the other hand, when one of the more timid parlor
    maids would hesitate in speaking so as to be certain her
    words did not give offense, he would thunder at her, "Out
    with it, you stupid girl."
2   Scarfe's wife and children were equally the victims of his tyranny.

The most general sentence, at level 1, presents the main idea of the entire passage—that Scarfe was a tyrant in his household. Each level-2 sentence identifies victims of his tyranny. Likewise, level-3 sentences specify the supposed provocations of these victims, and level-4 statements provide concrete examples of those provocations. For the most part, then, sentences in the passage are arranged in a general-to-specific sequence.

Unlike the Scarfe passage, the explanatory paragraph you have just read ("The most general sentence . . .") is arranged in a specific-to-general order. Its first three sentences make specific statements before the last sentence sums them up in a general conclusion.

In general-to-specific, or *deductive*, passages, the writer begins by stating the main idea in a general way, then demonstrates it with specific examples or explanations. In specific-to-general, or *inductive*, passages, the writer takes you through a sequence of discovery, with the main idea coming as a conclusion reached after specific evidence has been presented.

Deductive arrangements are far more common than inductive, although few passages are as neatly organized or as multi-leveled as the one about Scarfe.

Deductive and Inductive Passages

EXERCISES

1. Decide whether each of the following passages is arranged in a deductive (general-to-specific) or inductive (specific-to-general) order:

   a. These days who doesn't have to face the easy, breezy invasiveness of strangers in service positions? Salespeople at high-end stores who have a little too much to say about your shoes or haircut. Trainers at gyms who tell you where and when to eat and what movies to see. The owner of the bed-and-breakfast who told my nephew last week that there were no cartoons on the TV in our room because children are supposed to be doing their homework after eight o'clock. The dentist who asked a novelist friend of mine if she could get him a literary agent. Waiters who believe that touching customers, physically or emotionally, will result in higher tips.

   —Bob Morriss, "Kindness (Ugh!) of Strangers"

   b. To be auctioned on Thursday: a life jacket worn by a passenger on the *Titanic*— a victim, not a survivor. A slip of paper found with the body of another victim. A canvas bag that was filled with the belongings of yet another victim. A whistle that belonged to the relatively junior officer in charge of lifeboat number fourteen. The romanticized, Leonardo DiCaprio–Kate Winslet vision of the *Titanic*, this is not.

   —James Barron, "For Sale: Survivors of the *Titanic*"

c. Do you know someone who needs hours alone every day? Who loves quiet conversations about feelings or ideas, and can give a dynamite presentation to a big audience, but seems awkward in groups and maladroit at small talk? Who has to be dragged to parties and then needs the rest of the day to recuperate? Who growls or scowls or grunts or winces when accosted with pleasantries by people who are just trying to be nice? If you answered yes to these questions, chances are that you have an introvert on your hands.

—Jonathan Rauch, "Caring for Your Introvert"

2. The folllowing paragraph contains several levels of generality. Try to number each sentence in the same fashion as the Scarfe passage on pages 154–55.

Many great mathematical quests are exciting adventures of the mind whose completion takes years of effort but whose results are not usually of immediate practical use. Perhaps the best known is Fermat's Last Theorem, scribbled in the margin of an old book and finally proved by Andrew Wiles in 1994. Fermat wrote that he had found a "marvelous proof" of a negative statement. If you take a whole number and raise it to some power greater than two, he said, it is not possible to write that number as the sum of two nonzero numbers raised to the same power. So, say, 20,736, which is twelve to the fourth power, cannot be written as a sum of two nonzero numbers to the fourth power. In the twentieth century, much effort was directed at solving the "Hilbert Problems." Most of the problems, which were more like broad questions than like the problems one finds in textbooks, had no direct applicability. Can arithmetic contradict itself? Can one find a general method to figure out whether it is possible to find whole-number solutions to equations. Is every even number the sum of two prime numbers?

—Fernando Gouvea, "What's It Do? Nothing, but Mathematicians Relish the Quest"

3. How would you characterize the organization of the following poem?

**Lying in a Hammock at William Duffy's Farm
in Pine Island, Minnesota**

James Wright

Over my head, I see the bronze butterfly,
Asleep on the black trunk,
Blowing like a leaf in green shadow.
Down the ravine behind the empty house,
The cowbells follow one another
Into the distances of the afternoon.
To my right,
In a field of sunlight between two pines,
The droppings of last year's horses
Blaze up into golden stones.
I lean back, as the evening darkens and comes on.
A chicken hawk floats over, looking for home.
I have wasted my life.

4. Write another version of the second paragraph of the Scarfe passage, beginning with the sentence "Scarfe's wife and children . . . ," inventing details for your sentences as needed. Make the sentences in your paragraph follow this pattern: 2, 3, 4, 4, 3, 4, 4.

THESIS STATEMENTS AND TOPIC SENTENCES

Sometimes, as the preceding examples have demonstrated, writers condense the main idea of a passage into a single sentence. When one sentence states the main idea of an entire essay (or a longer text, such as a research paper or a book chapter), it is called a *thesis statement*. When a statement within a single paragraph states its main idea, it is called a *topic sentence*.

Identifying Topic Sentences

Not every paragraph has a topic sentence (in fact, fewer than half do), just as not every longer text has an explicit thesis statement. When topic and thesis sentences appear, however, they are valuable reading clues, helping readers recognize a writer's intentions and anticipate what may follow. It pays to notice them. Since a deductive arrangement is much more common than an inductive one, topic sentences appear most frequently at the beginning of paragraphs, introducing and preparing for the supporting sentences that follow. Less often, they come at the end of a paragraph, summing up or drawing conclusions from preceding statements. As you read the following paragraphs, see if you can identify topic sentences.

> The effect of an ice age is dramatic. It does not just ice up the poles but drops temperatures everywhere around the world by about ten degrees centigrade. The world's wildlife gets squeezed into a band near the equator and even here life is hardly comfortable. The vast polar ice packs lock up a lot of the earth's water, disrupting rainfall and turning previously lush tropical areas into drought-stricken deserts.
>
> —John McCrone, *The Ape That Spoke*

> In the Medieval Glass of Canterbury Cathedral, an angel appears to the sleeping wise men and warns them to go straight home and not return to Herod. Below, the corresponding event from the Old Testament teaches the faithful that each moment of Jesus's life replays a piece of the past and that God has put meaning into time—Lot turns round and his wife becomes a pillar of salt (the white glass forming a striking contrast with the glittering colors that surround her). The common themes of both incidents: don't look back.
>
> —Stephen Jay Gould, *The Flamingo's Smile*

The first paragraph opens with a topic sentence that is perfectly straightforward: *The effect of an ice age is dramatic*. This sentence facilitates reading by indicating what will follow: examples that illustrate the idea expressed in the topic sentence—in this case, with three dramatic consequences of an ice age. The second paragraph, arranged inductively, offers no such clue at the beginning. Instead, the author begins with specific evidence: He describes stained-glass representations of two biblical episodes. A topic sentence comes at the end, drawing a general conclusion from the evidence: Both episodes illustrate a common theme.

EXERCISES   **Identifying Topic Sentences**

1. Identify the topic sentences in each of the sample paragraphs in Exercise 1 on pages 155–56.

2. Identify the topic sentence in each of the following passages:

   a. [Chess champion Boris] Spassky was an urbane outsider in his own country. Unlike many Soviet grandmasters, he had never joined the Communist Party. Indeed, as a young man, he had the temerity to ask a forbidden question in public: "Did Comrade Lenin suffer from syphilis?" This earned him an official inquiry. Later, at risk to his career, he refused to sign a petition on behalf of the American Communist Angela Davis. He also flirted with Russian nationalism.

   —Gabriel Schoenfeld, "The American Opening"

   b. For the critic and historian Van Wyck Brooks, writing in the 1930s, William Dean Howells was a wise but essentially sunny New England patriot, who had absorbed enough European culture to be serious without absorbing so much of the cynical, the model of a modernized but not corrupted American author. For Alfred Kazin, in the 1940s, Howells was a democratic poet, an urban rhapsodist, a realist with a singing heart. For Lionel Trilling, writing in the 1950s, Howells was a trembling modern liberal, with a strong social conscience but a fastidious distaste for democratic ecstasies. For John Updike, in the 1980s, Howells was the original and still unvanquished prophet of the "anti-novel." Since the fate of most writers is oblivion, this is a lot of recognition.

   —Adam Gopnik, "A Critic at Large"

   c. Recent events have played into the hands of those who believe that architecture has lost its way and become—in some cases fatally—too fancy for its own good. Last week's report on the collapse in May of the Paul Andreu-designed terminal at Charles de Gaulle airport outside Paris, which killed four people, came amid the sudden critical scrutiny of and public scandals over Mr. Andreu's opera house under construction in Beijing. There were the problems with Santiago Calatrava's roof for the Olympic Stadium in Athens, which threatened the very opening of the games. The Whitney Museum of American Art dismissed Rem Koolhaas's plans for its extended galleries on the grounds that they were too bold and expensive. And in the squabble over ground zero, the only thing the competing designers seem to agree on is the need to build a Freedom Tower vastly taller than most New Yorkers would feel safe living and working in.

   —Alain de Botton, "Form Follows Inspiration"

 RESTATING THE MAIN IDEA

Because you want to understand what you read, recognizing topic sentences is more than just an exercise. To read efficiently, you must see what a writer is getting at; you must understand the main idea. A topic sentence that states the main idea neatly provides valuable help. Sometimes, however, topic sentences are not so explicit as they are in the preceding examples. As you read the following paragraphs, try to identify the writer's main idea:

> Our files show us that most men are unhappy with the state of their bodies. They would prefer to have the kind of torso that provokes oohs and ahs from admiring women. They would like to have bulging biceps that will win the respect and envy of other men. They seek the pride and confidence that comes from possessing a truly well-developed physique. They want the kind of body that any man can build by subscribing to the Jack Harrigan Dyna-Fit Program.
>
> —An imaginary advertisement

> Almost everyone has hitherto taken it for granted that Australopitheca [our female hominid ancestor who lived more than a million years ago], since she was primitive and chinless and low-browed, was necessarily hairy, and the artists always depict her as a shaggy creature. I don't think there is any reason for thinking this. Just as for a long time they "assumed" the big brain came first, before the use of tools, so they still "assume" that hairlessness came last. If I had to visualize the Villafranchian hominids, I'd say their skin was in all probability quite as smooth as our own.
>
> —Elaine Morgan, *The Descent of Woman*

In the case of the body-building ad, you may wonder whether the first or last sentence should be called the topic sentence. An argument can be made for either. The first sentence is a general statement, contending that most men are dissatisfied with their physiques. The remaining four sentences restate that contention more specifically. On the other hand, the writer's main idea is not just to describe this dissatisfaction but to provoke a response, namely to convince male readers that they should spend their money on the Dyna-Fit Program. Perhaps, then, the last sentence is more appropriately viewed as the topic sentence. Actually, though, since the main idea of the whole paragraph combines information from both the first and last sentences, supplemented by what you infer about the author's intentions, you can best capture the main idea in a general statement of your own: *Men who wish to improve their physiques should invest in the Harrigan Dyna-Fit Program.*

A similar question arises in regard to the paragraph about Australopitheca. Here, the author's main idea is stated twice—first in the short second sentence and again, more concretely, in the final sentence. But since neither sentence expresses the entire idea of the paragraph, you could once again formulate your own statement of the main idea: *Despite most people's assumption to the contrary, Australopitheca was probably no hairier than modern woman.*

Paragraphs with Implied Main Ideas

Many paragraphs have no explicit topic sentence. Often, these paragraphs deal with several different ideas joined together for convenience, as in the following example:

> [Joseph] Smith set up the first Mormon community in Kirtland, Ohio, in 1830, but persecutions drove the Mormons to Missouri and then to a spot on the east bank of the Mississippi which the Prophet named Nauvoo. At first the Mormons

were welcomed in Illinois, courted by both political parties and given a charter that made Nauvoo practically an autonomous theocracy. The settlement grew rapidly—even faster than Chicago; by 1844, with fifteen thousand citizens, Nauvoo was the largest and most prosperous city in Illinois. It was at Nauvoo that Joseph Smith received the "revelation" sanctioning polygamy, which he and the inner circle of "elders" were already practicing. Although supported by Isaiah iv. 1, "And in that day seven women shall take hold of one man," this revelation split the church. The monogamous "schismatics" started a paper at Nauvoo; Smith caused the press to be broken up after the first issue; he and his brother were then arrested by the authorities for destruction of property and lodged in the county jail, whence, on June 27, 1844, they were pulled out by a mob and lynched. Brigham Young, who succeeded to the mantle of the Prophet, and to five of his twenty-seven widows, directed retaliation; and for two years terror reigned in western Illinois. The Mormons were a virile, fighting people, but the time had come for them to make another move, before they were hopelessly outnumbered.

—Samuel Eliot Morrison, Henry Steele Commager, and
William E. Leuchtenburg, *The Growth of the American Republic*

This paragraph narrates a series of events in the early history of the Mormon church, but no one sentence summarizes everything.

Sometimes, a single-topic paragraph does not need a topic sentence because the main idea can be easily inferred from the context. Here is an example of such a paragraph:

Thin soup served in a soup plate is eaten from the side of the spoon, dipped into the liquid away from you. Thick soup may be eaten from the tip and dipped to ward you. Soup served in bouillon cups is usually sipped (silently) from the spoon until cool and then drunk—using one handle or both. Eat boneless and skinless fish with a fork, but to remove the skin or bones it is necessary to use a knife. According to the best modern practice, you may cut a piece of meat and lift it at once on the fork in the left hand to the mouth while holding the knife in the right.

—*Britannica Junior* (1956), "Etiquette"

If the authors had wanted to introduce this paragraph with a topic sentence, they might have written something like this: *Polite people follow certain rules of table etiquette when they eat.* But since preceding paragraphs undoubtedly address other aspects of etiquette, including table manners, no topic sentence is needed in this context. In many situations, however, topic sentences are useful. One common mistake of inexperienced writers is to omit such sentences when they might aid the reader.

EXERCISES   Restating the Main Idea

1. Identifying topic sentences can be useful, but the important thing is to recognize the main idea of a passage. Remember that the two do not always coincide.

   For each of the following paragraphs, try first to identify a topic sentence. If no one sentence adequately states the author's main idea, write your own one-sentence statement of that idea. Then consider whether the paragraph would have been more readable if the author had included your topic sentence. If so, should it go at the beginning, middle, or end of the paragraph?

a. Nearly twice as heavy as gold, plutonium is silvery, radioactive, and toxic. The pure metal first delivered to Los Alamos showed wildly differing densities, and the molten state was so reactive that it corroded nearly every container it encountered. Happier as a liquid than as a solid, plutonium has seven distinct crystallographic phases and the highly democratic ability to combine with nearly every other element on the periodic table. It can change its density by twenty-five percent in response to minor changes in its environment. It can be as brittle as glass or as malleable as aluminum. Chips of plutonium can spontaneously ignite at temperatures of 150 to 200 degrees Celsius. When crushed by an explosive charge, plutonium's density increases, which decreases the distance between its nuclei, eventually causing the metal to release large amounts of energy—enough to vaporize a city.

—David Samuels, "Buried Suns"

b. Larry Wald . . . owns a Fort Lauderdale bar called the Cathode Ray Club. Faced with a ban on smoking in taverns, Wald spent months devising an alternative to banishing smokers to the street. He puzzled out which liqueurs would combine to make the Nicotini [cocktail] more like a smoky sensation in the back of your throat than a stinging shot of hooch; fiddled with the amounts of tobacco for the infusion process (an effort that, he says, kept him "high as a kite" until he struck the right balance); and even searched out which *blend* of tobacco to deploy, since the ordinary loose variety lacked enough nicotine kick. The end product was an all-too-healthy-looking clear fluid (spurring customers to doubt whether there was nicotine present)—so Wald added food coloring to give the drink that unmistakable amber hue that says "toxic."

—Marshall Sella, "The Nicotini"

2. In the following passages, topic sentences have been replaced by ellipses (. . .). Using context to infer the main idea of each, try to guess what the topic sentence might be.

a. . . . Folks with high blood pressure and no muscle tone look on as the sinewy and buff row, run, and scale their way around tropical islands on television. Couples who haven't exchanged a meaningful word for days pay close attention as Dr. Phil advises the quarrelsome on how to put the magic back in their marriages. As the rate of restaurant dining rises and home cooking falls, viewers are glued to the Food Network, watching hollandaise coalesce and homemade bread rise in a TV kitchen set.

—Anna Quindlen, "The Jackson Twelve Performs"

b. Commander, Cavalier, Armada, Titan, Pilot, PT Cruiser, Intrepid, Magnum, Charger, Marauder, Galant, Lancer, Red Line, Trailblazer, Escape, Excursion, Expedition, Crossfire, Vanquish. The longest-lasting military name is Chevrolet's Corvette, named fifty years ago for a type of high-performance World War II destroyer. Today, the car is far more famous than the warship.

—*New York Times*, "What's in a Name?"

3. Like an inductive paragraph, which ends by stating a conclusion, many scientific experiments can be called inductive, in that they lead to discovery. So too the

following might be called an inductive exercise because it asks you to draw conclusions from your discoveries.

a. From books, magazines, or other kinds of texts, find one paragraph that begins with a topic sentence and another that ends with a topic sentence. Transcribe (or photocopy) them both and bring them to class.

b. Examine an example of each of the following:
   - college-level textbook
   - novel
   - biography
   - newspaper article
   - magazine article

From each, select ten paragraphs at random and see how many (1) begin with a topic sentence, (2) end with a topic sentence, (3) have a topic sentence imbedded within, (4) have an implied topic sentence, or (5) have no unifying concept at all.

c. Now draw some conclusions from this experiment: How easy is it to find topic sentences? When they occur, where are topic sentences most likely to be placed? Are certain types of writing more likely than others to make use of topic sentences? If so, why? Can you draw any general conclusions about how writers construct paragraphs?

Detecting Implications

The preceding section of this chapter demonstrates how paragraphs can have topic sentences that are implied rather than explicitly stated. In such cases, discerning the main idea is left to the reader. But that is only one of many tasks involved in comprehension. Writers also leave gaps in the meaning they wish to communicate, and they expect alert readers to fill them in.

Even in everyday conversation, we do not always state everything we mean. Consider, for example, the ***implication***, the unstated but intended meaning, in the following conversation between two students:

COLIN: I signed up for Professor Sneederbunk's course.

DANEEN: I hope you've got a large supply of caffeine tablets.

Without saying so explicitly, Daneen is implying that Professor Sneederbunk's course is difficult and requires long, late study hours. For Colin to understand her, he must draw connections, relying on past experience with college life and with how people use language. A less sophisticated listener, say, an eight-year-old, might not be able to bridge the gap between what Daneen says and what she actually means.

Being a sophisticated listener or reader demands skill at drawing inferences. Not everyone derives the same meaning under the same circumstances. Gaps can often leave messages open to more than one interpretation. In the preceding example, Colin was probably already aware of the reputation of Professor Sneederbunk's course and therefore understood exactly what Daneen meant. But someone else overhearing her remark might draw a different conclusion, inferring perhaps that Professor Sneederbunk's classes are so boring that students have difficulty staying awake. Successful communication depends on knowing your audience and adapting your message so that they can infer what you mean.

Writers also rely on implications. Consider the following paragraph, taken from an essay about the bizarre treatment the author receives because he is blind:

> For example, when I go to the airport and ask the ticket agent for assistance to the plane, he or she will invariably pick up the phone, call a ground hostess and whisper: "Hi, Jane, we've got a seventy-six here." I have concluded that the word *blind* is not used for one of two reasons: either they fear that if the dread word is spoken, the ticket agent's retina will immediately detach, or they are reluctant to inform me of my condition of which I may not have been previously aware.
>
> —Harold Krents, "Darkness at Noon"

The writer expects us to infer that a "seventy-six" is an airline code for a blind passenger. He also assumes our understanding that ticket agents whisper into phones because they do not want people in the vicinity, including Krents himself, to hear what they say. Earlier in his essay, Krents writes, "There are those who assume that since I can't see, I obviously also cannot hear." Having read this, a reader can infer that the whispering agents foolishly imagine that Krents will neither hear nor understand their words. The final sentence of the paragraph demands even more sophistication in drawing implications. Krents probably expects readers to infer a meaning that can be spelled out like this:

> The agents don't really believe they will go blind if they say the word, and Krents isn't sincere when he suggests that they may. The agents also can't really think that Krents doesn't know that he is blind. But as silly as either conclusion would be, the real reasons behind the agents' behavior are almost as absurd: they apparently think of blindness as a condition too embarrassing to be spoken of to a blind person. They aren't giving Krents credit for being able to notice that they are evading the topic. Worse, they aren't even able to realize that a blind person is a human being with the same capacities for hearing and thinking as anyone else.

You can easily see that the passage, with its unspoken implications, is far more effective than it would have been if Krents had spelled out everything he meant. By causing us to think for ourselves and to draw conclusions, Krents enlists us as partners in creating meaning. That sense of partnership makes us more receptive to his purpose in writing. After reading the paragraph, you might draw the following, more general conclusion:

> Perhaps I, the reader (now that I see the airline agents' behavior as ridiculous), should give some thought to how I treat blind people or others with disabilities.

Drawing inferences is an important part of reading, and good readers are as alert to implied meaning as they are to that which is explicitly stated.

| **Detecting Implications**

1. What might you infer from the following bits of overheard conversation?

   a. A well-dressed couple in their twenties are dining in an elegant restaurant.

      Man: But darling, you've never given brandy a *chance.*

      Woman: Well excuse the hell out of me, Mister Connoisseur.

   b. *Investor:* Are you suggesting that I sell my shares of Pushmore Pharmaceuticals? Broker (quoting Shakespeare): There is a tide in the affairs of men, which, taken at the flood, leads on to fortune; omitted, all the voyage of their life is bound in shallows and in miseries.

2. Though the words in each of the following passages express a relatively clear and explicit meaning, they don't explain everything that was on the author's mind. What inferences can you draw as you read each passage?

   a. Although the characters are now portrayed more realistically than at any time in the past six decades, remember that there are limits to how far they (and you) can go. At times, the Hardys experience doubts about their personal and professional activities, but these introspective moments are necessarily limited, due to the fast pace of their action-filled lives. There's nothing that could drive Frank or Joe to tears because they're too gutsy and determined to behave that way. Dialogue no-no's include long speeches, cursing, vulgar references, and taking the Lord's name in vain (including the term *jeez*). For example: Positive, upbeat: "Wow!" "All right" "Great!" "Believe it!" Negative, sarcastic: "Rats!" "Yeah, right," "Yeah, yeah," "Yuck!" "Oh, *boy.*" Grunts and groans can be substituted for expletives when a character is undergoing a great deal of stress or pain. So when someone slashes Frank's hand with a knife, he can say "Unnnh!" instead of "#&@*#!" You can also use a character's name in place of an unacceptable phrase. Frank can say, "Joe, you messed up," instead of, "Damn it, you messed up." Finally, despite the necessity for wholesome expletives, please omit terms such as "damn," "shucks," "goody," and positive sounding "*oh, boys.*" As mentioned previously, this is a modernized series, with a healthy dose of realism.

      —"The Writer's Guide to Hardy Boys Rack Books," reprinted in *Harper's* magazine

   b. As intrepid as the executives at Viacom [who paid themselves more than $50 million dollars each when the company recorded annual loss of $17.5 million] but more innovative in his grasp of virtual reality than the accountants at Enron, Bernard Ebbers, the former chief executive of World-Com, conceived of an $11 billion swindle by thinking as far outside the box as did the Wright Brothers and Thomas Edison. Fearless on the threshold of the unknown, he ventured over the horizon into the kingdom of imaginary numbers and found gold where none was known to exist. At least twenty thousand people lost both their jobs and their pensions, but how else did America settle the Great Plains if not in the company of dead or dying Indians? Nor did Ebbers flinch in the face of adversity when brought into court on charges of criminal fraud. As forthright as the young George Washington contemplating the stump of the chopped-down cherry tree, Ebbers made no attempt to hide behind the screen of a lawyer's weaseling lies. "I don't know about technology," he said, "and I don't know about finance and accounting."

      —Lewis H. Lapham, "Be Prepared"

A FURTHER COMMENT ON PARAGRAPHS

We reemphasize the point that relatively few paragraphs contain explicitly stated topic sentences. The paragraph is actually a less structured unit of text than is often supposed. Most writers usually do not plan paragraphs as they compose. Instead, they often use the paragraph break as a form of punctuation—sometimes to signal a new idea or a change in direction, sometimes to provide emphasis. At other times, long topics may be divided rather arbitrarily into paragraphs, to provide pauses and to make a text appear less formidable.

Eye appeal is frequently a factor in paragraphing. Essays written in a sprawling handwriting are likely to have (and need) more paragraph breaks than typed essays. Newspapers, because of their narrow columns, contain shorter paragraphs than those found in most books. Psychologists have discovered that readers find material easiest to process when it is divided into short to medium-length paragraphs.

For all these reasons, no two writers create their paragraphs in exactly the same way. Given passages such as those featured in the following exercise, from which all paragraph breaks have been removed, any two professional authors or writing instructors chosen at random will probably disagree about where the breaks belong.

Supplying Paragraph Breaks   EXERCISES

1. Paragraph breaks have been removed from the following passages. Decide where you would put them and indicate your choices, using the paragraph symbol (¶). Remember that there are different yet appropriate responses to this exercise.

   a. Where is the "official" birthplace of Route 66? This question has been asked many times over the years, and now we finally have the answer. On October 20, 1925, the Joint Board on Interstate Highways issued its "final" report that selected the system of roads to be known as United States Highways. The report designated 75,884 miles of road as the interstate system, with each road given a specific routing and number. The report was approved by the Secretary of Agriculture on November 18, 1925, forwarded to the American Association of State Highway (and Transportation) Officials (AASHTO) and accepted at their annual meeting. The Joint Board was then dissolved, and the Executive Committee of AASHTO was empowered to make "minor" changes in the recommended system "as appeared necessary or desirable." Between November 1925 and final approval of the system on November 11, 1926, the committee acted on 132 requests, many of which were not minor, resulting in changes to the route numbers and expansion of the system to 96,626 miles. This is the story of one of those changes.
   —James R. Powell, "The Birthplace of Route 66"

   b. Inevitably there were some lapses of judgment, but in general the sheer scale of the American landscape made it relatively easy to tuck a superhighway away unobtrusively among its folds. Problems arose where scale changes required a more delicate touch. This was often the case along coastlines, for example, where highway planners understandably wished to provide scenic drives with views of the ocean. Sometimes this was achieved brilliantly, as in Monterey and San Luis Obispo counties, California, where California's Route 1 (not part of the Interstate System) snakes gracefully above the Pacific, affording spectacular vistas of Big Sur and Carmel without in any way interfering with the grandeur of the landscape. Farther north along the Pacific coast, however, there are too many instances of highways encroaching clumsily on beach areas, some of these roads being built on landfills that have altered for the worse the relationship between land and sea. The California Highway Commission permitted the razing of centuries-old redwoods to facilitate the construction of the Redwood Freeway, while in a number of instances national and state parks have been disfigured by thoughtless routing. In general, though, the rural sections of the Interstate System can be considered a success. The real problems occurred when the superhighways approached cities and penetrated the urban fabric itself.

—Christopher Finch, *Highways to Heaven: The AUTO Biography of America*

2. Compare your responses to the first exercise with those of classmates. Was there general agreement about the number of paragraph breaks you supplied? Did you agree with the authors of the two passages (who, as it happens, presented them in five paragraphs and one paragraph, respectively)? What conclusions might you draw from this exercise?

 ## READING SELECTION

The following article was published in February 2002, just as a series of books about aggressive behavior among girls and women began to gain public attention. Margaret Talbot is a frequent contributor to the *New York Times Magazine*, where the article originally appeared.

Girls Just Want to Be Mean

MARGARET TALBOT

1   This focus on the cruelty of girls is, of course, something new. For years, psychologists who studied aggression among school children looked only at its physical and overt manifestations and concluded that girls were less aggressive than boys. That consensus began to change in the early 1990s, after a team of researchers led by a Finnish professor named Kaj Bjorkqvist started interviewing eleven- and twelve-year-old girls about their behavior toward one another. The team's conclusion was that girls were, in fact, just as aggressive as boys, though in a different way. They were not as likely to engage in physical fights, for example, but their superior social intelligence enabled them to wage complicated battles with other girls aimed at damaging relationships or reputations—leaving nasty messages by cell phone or spreading scurrilous rumors by e-mail, making friends with one girl as revenge against another, gossiping about someone just loudly enough to be overheard. Turning the notion of women's greater empathy on its head, Bjorkqvist focused on the destructive uses to which such emotional attunement could be put. "Girls can better understand how other girls feel," as he puts it, "so they know better how to harm them."

Researchers following in Bjorkqvist's footsteps noted that up to the age of four   2
girls tend to be aggressive at the same rates and in the same ways as boys—grabbing
toys, pushing, hitting. Later on, however, social expectations force their hostilities un
derground, where their assaults on one another are more indirect, less physical, and
less visible to adults. Secrets they share in one context, for example, can sometimes be
used against them in another. As Marion Underwood, a professor of psychology at the
University of Texas at Dallas, puts it: "Girls very much value intimacy, which makes
them excellent friends and terrible enemies. They share so much information when
they are friends that they never run out of ammunition if they turn on one another."

In the last few years, a group of young psychologists, including Underwood and   3
Nicki Crick at the University of Minnesota, has pushed this work much further, observing girls in "naturalistic" settings, exploring the psychological foundations for nasti-
ness and asking adults to take relational aggression—especially in the sixth and seventh
grades, when it tends to be worst—as seriously as they do more familiar forms of bullying. While some of these researchers have emphasized bonding as a motivation, others
have seen something closer to a hunger for power, even a Darwinian drive. One Australian researcher, Laurence Owens, found that the fifteen-year-old girls he interviewed
about their girl-pack predation were bestirred primarily by its entertainment value. The
girls treated their own lives like the soaps, hoarding drama, constantly rehashing trivia.
Owens's studies contain some of the more vivid anecdotes in the earnest academic literature on relational aggression. His subjects tell him about ingenious tactics like leaving the following message on a girl's answering machine—"Hello, it's me. Have you
gotten your pregnancy test back yet?"—knowing that her parents will be the first to
hear it. They talk about standing in "huddles" and giving other girls "deaths"—stares of
withering condescension—and of calling one another "dyke," "slut," and "fat" and of
enlisting boys to do their dirty work.

Relational aggression is finding its chroniclers among more popular writers, too.   4
In addition to Wiseman's book, this spring will bring Rachel Simmons's *Odd Girl Out:
The Hidden Culture of Aggression in Girls*, Emily White's *Fast Girls: Teenage Tribes and the
Myth of the Slut*, and Phyllis Chester's *Woman's Inhumanity to Woman*.

In her book, the twenty-seven-year-old Simmons offers a plaintive definition of   5
relational aggression:

> Unlike boys, who tend to bully acquaintances or strangers, girls frequently attack
> within tightly knit friendship networks, making aggression harder to identify and in-
> tensifying the damage to the victims. Within the hidden culture of aggression, girls
> fight with body language and relationships instead of fists and knives. In this world,
> friendship is a weapon, and the sting of a shout pales in comparison to a day of some-
> one's silence. There is no gesture more devastating than the back turning away.

Now, Simmons insists, is the time to pull up the rock and really look at this seething
underside of American girlhood. "Beneath a façade of female intimacy," she writes,
"lies a terrain traveled in secret, marked with anguish and nourished by silence."

Not so much silence, anymore, actually. For many school principals and counselors   6
across the country, relational aggression is becoming a certified social problem and the
need to curb it an accepted mandate. A small industry of interveners has grown up to
meet the demand. In Austin, Tex., an organization called GENaustin now sends counselors into schools to teach a course on relational aggression called Girls as Friends,
Girls as Foes. In Erie, Pa., the Ophelia Project offers a similar curriculum, taught by
high-school-aged mentors, that explores "how girls hurt each other" and how they can
stop. A private Catholic school in Akron, Ohio, and a public-school district near

Portland, Ore., have introduced programs aimed at rooting out girl meanness. And Wiseman and her Empower Program colleagues have taught their Owning Up class at sixty schools. "We are currently looking at relational aggression like domestic violence twenty years ago," says Holly Nishimura, the assistant director of the Ophelia Project. "Though it's not on the same scale, we believe that with relational aggression, the trajectory of awareness, knowledge and demand for change will follow the same track."

7   Whether this new hyper-vigilance about a phenomenon that has existed for as long as most of us can remember will actually do anything to squelch it is, of course, another question. Should adults be paying as much attention to this stuff as kids do, or will we just get hopelessly tangled up in it ourselves? Are we approaching frothy adolescent bitchery with undue gravity or just giving it its due in girls' lives? On the one hand, it is kind of satisfying to think that girls might be, after their own fashion, as aggressive as boys. It's an idea that offers some relief from the specter of the meek and mopey, "silenced" and self-loathing girl the popular psychology of girlhood has given us in recent years. But it is also true that the new attention to girls as relational aggressors may well take us into a different intellectual cul-de-sac, where it becomes too easy to assume that girls do not use their fists (some do), that all girls are covert in their cruelties, that all girls care deeply about the ways of the clique—and that what they do in their "relational" lives takes precedence over all other aspects of their emerging selves.

8   Nowadays, adults, particularly in the upper middle classes, are less laissez-faire about children's social lives. They are more vigilant, more likely to have read books about surviving the popularity wars of middle school or dealing with cliques, more likely to have heard a talk or gone to a workshop on those topics. Not long ago, I found myself at a lecture by the best-selling author Michael Thompson on "Understanding the Social Lives of Our Children." It was held inside the National Cathedral on a chilly Tuesday evening in January, and there were hundreds of people in attendance—attractive late-forties mothers in cashmere turtlenecks and interesting scarves and expensive haircuts and graying but fit fathers—all taking notes and lining up to ask eager, anxious questions about how best to ensure their children's social happiness. "As long as education is mandatory," Thompson said from the pulpit, "we have a huge obligation to make it socially safe," and heads nodded all around me. He made a list of "the top three reasons for a fourth-grade girl to be popular," and parents in my pew wrote it down in handsome little leather notebooks or on the inside cover of Thompson's latest book, *Best Friends, Worst Enemies*. A red-haired woman with a fervent, tremulous voice and an elegant navy blue suit said that she worried our children were socially handicapped by "a lack of opportunities for unstructured cooperative play" and mentioned that she had her two-year-old in a science class. A serious-looking woman took the microphone to say that she was troubled by the fact that her daughter liked a girl "who is mean and controlling and once wrote the word *murder* on the bathroom mirror—and this is in a private school!"

9   I would never counsel blithe ignorance on such matters—some children are truly miserable at school for social reasons, truly persecuted and friendless and in need of adult help. But sometimes we do seem in danger of micromanaging children's social lives, peering a little too closely. Priding ourselves on honesty in our relationships, as baby-boomer parents often do, we expect to know everything about our children's friendships, to be hip to their social travails in a way our own parents, we thought, were not. But maybe this attention to the details can backfire, giving children the impression that the transient social anxieties and allegiances of middle school are weightier and more immutable than they really are. And if that is the result, it seems particularly unfortunate for girls, who are already more mired in the minutiae of relationships than boys are, who may already lack, as Christopher Lasch once put it,

"any sense of an impersonal order that exists independently of their wishes and anxieties" and of the "vicissitudes of relationships."

I think I would have found it dismaying if my middle school had offered a class 10
that taught us about the wiles of Marcie and Tracie: if adults studied their folkways, maybe they were more important than I thought, or hoped. For me, the best antidote to the caste system of middle school was the premonition that adults did not usually play by the same rigid and peculiar rules—and that someday, somewhere, I would find a whole different mattering map, a whole crowd of people who read the same books I did and wouldn't shun me if I didn't have a particular brand of shoes. When I went to college, I found it, and I have never really looked back.

And the Queen Bees? Well, some grow out of their girly sense of entitlement on 11
their own, surely; some channel it in more productive directions. Martha Stewart must have been a Q.B. Same with Madonna. At least one of the Q.B.'s from my youth—albeit the nicest and smartest one—has become a pediatrician on the faculty of a prominent medical school, I noticed when I looked her up the other day. And some Queen Bees have people who love them—dare I say it?—just as they are, a truth that would have astounded me in my own school days but that seems perfectly natural now.

On a Sunday afternoon, I have lunch with Jessica Travis and her mother, Robin, 12
who turns out to be an outgoing, transplanted New Yorker—"born in Brighton Beach, raised in Sheepshead Bay." Over white pizza, pasta, cannoli, and Diet Cokes, I ask Robin what Jessica was like as a child. "I was fabulous," Jessica says.

"She was," her mother agrees. "She was blond, extremely happy, endlessly curi- 13
ous, and always the leader of the pack. She didn't sleep because she didn't want to miss anything. She was just a bright, shiny kid. She's still a bright, shiny kid."

After Jessica takes a call on her pumpkin-colored cell phone, we talk for a while 14
about Jessica's room, which they both describe as magnificent. "I have lived in apartments smaller than her majesty's two-bedroom suite," Robin snorts. "Not many single parents can do for their children what I have done for this one. This is a child who asked for a pony and got two. I tell her this is the top of the food chain. The only place you can go from here is the royal family."

I ask if anything about Jessica's clique bothers her. She says no—because what she 15
calls "Jess's band of merry men" doesn't "define itself by its opponents. They're not a threat to anyone. Besides, it's not like they're an A-list clique."

"Uh, Mom," Jessica corrects. "We are definitely an A-list clique. We are totally A-list. 16
You are giving out incorrect information."

"Soooorry," Robin says. "I'd fire myself, but there's no one else lining up for the 17
job of being your mom."

Jessica spends a little time bringing her mother and me up to date on the elaborate 18
social structure at her high school. The cheerleaders' clique, it seems, is not the same as the pom-pom girls' clique, though both are A-list. All sports cliques are A-list, in fact, except—"of course"—the swimmers. There is a separate A-list clique for cute preppy girls who "could play sports but don't." There is "the white people who pretend to be black clique" and the drama clique, which would be "C list," except that, as Jessica puts it, "they're not even on the list."

"So what you are saying is that your high school is littered with all these groups 19
that have their own separate physical and mental space?" Robin says, shaking her head in wonderment.

When they think about it, Jessica and her mom agree that the business with 20
the rules—what you can wear on a given day of the week and all that—comes from Jessica's fondness for structure. As a child, her mom says she made up games with "such

elaborate rules I'd be lost halfway through her explanation of them." Besides, there was a good deal of upheaval in her early life. Robin left her "goofy artist husband" when Jessica was three, and after that they moved a lot. And when Robin went to work for Oracle, she "was traveling all the time, getting home late. When I was on the road, I'd call her every night at eight and say: 'Sweet Dreams. I love you. Good Night.'"

21   "Always in that order," Jessica says. "Always at eight. I don't like a lot of change."

22   Toward the end of our lunch, Jessica's mother—who says she herself was more a nerd than a Queen Bee in school—returns to the subject of cliques. She wants, it seems, to put something to rest. "You know I realize there are people who stay with the same friends, the same kind of people, all their life, who never look beyond that," she says. "I wouldn't want that for my daughter. I want my daughter to be one of those people who live in the world. I know she's got these kinds of narrow rules in her personal life right now. But I still think, I really believe, that she will be a bigger person, a person who spends her life in the world." Jessica's mother smiles. Then she gives her daughter's hair an urgent little tug, as if it were the rip cord of a parachute and Jessica were about to float away from her.

Freewriting

Freewrite for ten to fifteen minutes about Talbot's account of relationships among girls in early adolescence. You may write about anything that reaffirms or challenges your own perceptions, whether they are based on personal experience, observation, or other reading. Or, you may wish to consider how serious a problem relational aggression is.

Group Work

Share freewrites in your reading group, each member reading aloud while others are taking notes. After everyone has read, try to reach some consensus about the reliability of Rosalind Wiseman as an observer and Margaret Talbot as a reporter and about the implications of relational aggression as a social problem. If your group cannot reach a consensus, try to agree on a clear presentation of conflicting views.

Review Questions

1. When and how did scholarly interest in cruelty among girls get started? What directions has it taken more recently?

2. How might adults take recent discoveries about relationships among girls too seriously? How could this affect their parenting?

3. What was Talbot like as a teenager? How have the "Queen Bees" of her adolescence developed as adults?

Discussion Questions

1. Which television programs and films depict meanness and aggression among adolescent girls? Do they usually treat it dramatically, comically, or both? Which, in your opinion, are most and least realistic?

2. What do you suppose Talbot means by the "superior social intelligence" of girls as compared to boys? Might one make a similar comparison between women and men? If so, what are some possible implications for family relationships, friendships, or the workplace?

3. Would you say that Jessica Travis is a well-adjusted teenager? Would you expect her to become a successful adult? How do you think Talbot would respond to these questions?

Writing

1. In an article published in the July 5, 2002, issue of the *Chronicle of Higher Education*, Carol Tavris takes issue with Talbot and others who have studied and written about aggressive behavior among girls and women. Locate the article in your college library. Write an essay that either affirms Talbot's claims and refutes Tavris's (or vice versa) or that attempts to reconcile views expressed by the two authors.

2. Using paragraph 18 of Talbot's essay as a model, write a short description of high-school culture and relationships as you recall them from your own experience.

3. Write an essay responding to one or more of the questions that Talbot poses in paragraph 7.

WRITE, READ, and RESEARCH the NET

1. *Write:* Freewrite for fifteen minutes about bullying and peer pressure among adolescents of both sexes.

2. *Read:* Review the two following Web sites:
   <http://www.williampollack.com/voices_intro.html>
   <http://www.msnbc.com/news/735673.asp#BODY>

3. *Research:* Using the Internet, locate Web sites that address the topics of bullying and peer pressure in junior and senior high schools. Use the information you collect to write a paper assessing whether recent books and discussions have accurately portrayed (or exaggerated) issues of safety in public schools.

 ## ADDITIONAL READINGS

The following selections further explore connections between gender and violence. First is an excerpt from the book *Real Boys' Voices* by clinical psychologist William Pollack. Pollack's book reports the results of his extensive interviews with adolescent boys regarding "the things that hurt them" and their reluctance to acknowledge them openly. Following this are two magazine articles dealing with violent crimes against victims who have, sometimes unwittingly, challenged sexual mores enforced by persons of their gender.

Listening to Boys' Voices

WILLIAM POLLACK

1   In my travels throughout this country—from the inner-city neighborhoods of Boston, New York, and San Francisco to suburbs in Florida, Connecticut, and Rhode Island; from small, rural villages in New Hampshire, Kentucky, and Pennsylvania to the pain-filled classrooms of Littleton, Colorado—I have discovered a glaring truth: America's boys are absolutely desperate to talk about their lives. They long to talk about the things that are hurting them—their harassment from other boys, their troubled relationships with their fathers, their embarrassment around girls and confusion about sex, their disconnection from parents, the violence that haunts them at school and on the street, their constant fear that they might not be as masculine as other boys.

2   But this desperate coast-to-coast longing is silenced by the Boy Code—old rules that favor male stoicism and make boys feel ashamed about expressing weakness or vulnerability. Although our boys urgently want to talk about who they really are, they fear that they will be teased, bullied, humiliated, beaten up, and even murdered if they give voice to their truest feelings. Thus, our nation is home to millions of boys who feel they are navigating life alone—who on an emotional level are alone—and who are cast out to sea in separate lifeboats, and feel they are drowning in isolation, depression, loneliness, and despair.

3   Our sons, brothers, nephews, students are struggling. Our boyfriends are crying out to be understood. But many of them are afraid to talk. Scotty, a thirteen-year-old boy from a small town in northern New England, recently said to me, "Boys are supposed to shut up and take it, to keep it all in. It's harder for them to release or vent without feeling girly. And that can drive them to shoot themselves."

4   I am particularly concerned about the intense angst I see in so many of America's young men and teenaged boys. I saw this angst as I did research for *Real Boys*, and then again in talking with boys for this book. Boys from all walks of life, including boys who seem to have made it—the suburban high school football captain, the seventh-grade prep school class president, the small-town police chief's son, the inner-city student who is an outstanding cartoonist and son of a welfare mother—all were feeling so alone that I worried that they often seemed to channel their despair into rage not only toward others but toward themselves. An ordinary boy's sadness, his everyday feelings of disappointment and shame, push him not only to dislike himself and to feel private moments of anguish or self-doubt, but also, impulsively, to assault, wound, and kill. Forced to handle life's emotional ups and downs on their own, many boys and young men—many good, honest, caring boys—are silently allowing their lives to wither away, or explode.

5   We still live in a society in which our boys and young men are simply not receiving the consistent attention, empathy, and support they truly need and desire. We are only listening to parts of what our sons and brothers and boyfriends are telling us. Though our intentions are good, we've developed a culture in which too often boys only feel comfortable communicating a small portion of their feelings and experiences. And through no fault of our own, frequently we don't understand what they are saying to us when they do finally talk.

Boys are acutely aware of how society constrains them. They also notice how it **6** holds back other boys and young men, including their peers, their male teachers, and their fathers. "When bad things happen in our family," Jesse, an astute twelve-year-old boy from a large middle-class suburb of Los Angeles, recently told me, "my father gets blocked. Like if he's upset about something that happened at work, he can't say anything and we have no idea what he's thinking. He just sits in front of the television, spends time on the Internet, or just goes off on his own. You can't get through to him at all. He just gets totally blocked." Of course, Jesse is teaming to do the same. And if we don't allow, even teach boys like Jesse to express their emotion and cry tears, some will cry bullets instead.

A NATIONWIDE JOURNEY

I began a new nationwide journey to listen to boys' voices last summer in my native **7** Massachusetts. In one of the very first interviews, I sat down with Clayton, a sixteen-year-old boy living in a modest apartment in Arlington, a medium-sized suburb of Boston. Clay introduced me to his mother and older sister, and then brought me to his attic hideaway, a small room with only two small wooden windows that allowed light into the room through a series of tiny slits. Clay decided to share some of his writing with me—poetry and prose he had written on leaves of white and yellow paper. His writings were deeply moving, but even more extraordinary were the charcoal sketches that, once he grew comfortable with my presence, he decided he would also share. His eyes downcast, his shoulders slumped inward, he opened his black sketchbook and flipped gently through the pages.

On each consecutive sheet of parchment, Clay had created a series of beautiful **8** images in rich, multicolored charcoal and pastels. "You're a talented artist," I said, expressing my real enthusiasm.

"I haven't shown these to too many people," he said, blushing. "I don't think any- **9** one would really be too interested." Clay's pictures revealed his angst, and in graphic, brutal detail. There was a special series of drawings of "angels." They were half human, half creature, with beautiful wings, but their boyish faces were deeply pained. Soaring somewhere between earth and heaven, the angels seemed to be trying to free themselves from earthly repression, striving for expression, longing to reach the freedom of the skies. They evoked the mundane world where Clayton's psychological pain felt real and inescapable, yet they also evoked an imaginary place where he could feel safe, relaxed, and free.

In our conversation, Clayton revealed that his inner sense of loss and sadness had **10** at times been so great that on at least one occasion he had seriously contemplated suicide.

"I never actually did anything to commit suicide. I was too afraid I'd end up in a **11** permanent hell . . . but that's how bad I felt. I wanted to end it all."

I thought to myself that maybe that's what these tortured angels were about—a **12** combination of heavenly hope mixed up with a boy's suppressed "voice" of pain.

Clayton then revealed "The Bound Angel," a breathtaking sketch of one of his **13** winged, half-man creatures bent over in pain, eyes looking skyward, but trunk and legs bound like an animal awaiting slaughter.

Clayton explained, "His hands are tied, and his mouth is sealed so he cannot **14** speak. He's in pain, but he has no way to run from it, to express it, or to get to heaven."

"Your angel wants to shout out his troubles to the high heavens, but he is bound **15** and gagged. He wants to move toward someone, but he is frozen in space. He needs to release his voice, but he cannot and fears he will not be heard. That's why he's so tortured."

16   "Yes, exactly," he said.

17   "I guess if he's tied up long enough," I responded, "and can't release that voice, he'll want to die, like you did."

18   "I think so," Clay said.

19   There is no reason we should wait until a boy like Clay feels hopeless, suicidal, or homicidal to address his inner experience. The time to listen to boys is now.

Bad Girls

A Brutal British Columbia Murder Sounds an Alarm about Teenage Violence

PATRICIA CHISHOLM AND CINDY E. HARNETT

1   The waterfront park where Reena Virk was viciously beaten and left to drown looks like a Canadian dream: clumps of trees dot one shore, while attractive middle-class homes line the opposite bank. Residents of Saanich, just north of Victoria, know the place as a handy getaway for jogging, boating, and family outings. But like many suburban parks across the country, it has two faces. After dark, it becomes a haunt for restless local teenagers looking for a place safe from prying adult eyes. Here, kids can engage in the typical rituals of an adolescent Friday night—exchanging gossip, smoking, maybe having a drink, or making out—usually without incident. So it probably wasn't surprising that the fourteen-year-old Virk agreed to go off to the park with a couple of acquaintances on the night of November 14, even though she had been in a nasty fight with some of their friends slightly earlier. On that occasion, another teenage girl stubbed out a lit cigarette on Virk's forehead, apparently over suspicions that the ninth-grade student had spread rumors about her. "She very much wanted to belong with the cool kids," recalls her friend Molly Pallmann. "That's because a lot of kids would bug her—I would see her crying in the hallways. Unfortunately, that led to her being killed. She was a sweet kid."

2   The horror of what happened next has sent shock waves across the country and attracted attention as far away as Sweden. Although some of the details remain unknown, it is clear that Virk was lured to the park at about ten o'clock by two teens she met while hanging out at a convenience store a few blocks away. Once out of sight of passers-by, she was set on and so viciously kicked and beaten that she suffered multiple fractures, including fractured arms and a broken neck and back. According to a sister of one of the accused, she cried out, "Help me, I love you," during the assault. When her partly submerged body was found more than a week later, a few hundred meters from where she was attacked, a few scraps of underwear was all that remained of her clothing.

3   Eight teenagers aged fourteen to sixteen—seven of them girls—now face charges ranging from second-degree murder to aggravated assault, and Canadians are asking themselves some painful, seemingly unanswerable questions. Why was a young girl, with no history of violence, viciously murdered, allegedly by her peers? Why is violence among young girls sharply on the rise? And what, if anything, can be done to halt the trend? Sibylle Artz, Director of the School of Child and Youth Care at the University of Victoria and author of *Sex, Power, and the Violent School Girl*, believes that too

often such cases are dismissed as the actions of a few bad eggs from dysfunctional families. But the behavior of many young girls, Artz suggests, is being twisted by profound cultural pressures their parents barely understand. Pressures to be sexy, to be popular—to be powerful. And when conventional methods of achieving those goals fail, more and more girls are turning to violence. "They are taking the attitude that the way to reach power is by being like males," Artz says. "If they can't get what they want, they become enforcers for the group. It's an ugly and painful thing."

That, many Canadians might respond, is an understatement. While the overall numbers remain small compared with boys, police are charging vastly more girls with violent crimes than they did ten years ago. Since 1986, two years after the Young Offenders Act became law, assault charge rates for girls in British Columbia alone have more than tripled, rising to 624 in 1993 from 178 that year. And while not all experts agree that more crimes are actually being committed—some argue that public concern over youth crime is pushing officials into making more arrests—many say there is little doubt that common and aggravated assaults are on the increase. "Except for murder, I'm convinced that things have gotten worse," says Ray Corrado, a professor at Simon Fraser University's School of Criminology. "The context of the violence has also changed. It's more random, more vicious—and it's not just in the bad parts of town." 4

Corrado cautions against jumping to the conclusion that violence among young girls is widespread. The vast majority do what young girls have always done: attend school, pursue hobbies, flirt—without getting into fights. And even among the minority who are violent, murder, Corrado notes, "is still incredibly rare." But he says there is a visibility—as well as an element of unpredictability—to teenage crime that can create a strong sense of intimidation among teens themselves. Often, such crimes occur or germinate in highly public places such as transit stops, twenty-four-hour convenience stores, parks and malls. When tensions rise—among girls, a fight can be ignited by as little as a slight over appearance or competition for a boy—things can get out of hand very quickly. "It starts with kicking and punching and they all want to be part of it," Corrado says. "Then they panic." 5

Often, the fever seems to rise because of boys. To a chilling degree, many very young girls are desperate to be mated. Sue Johanson, a Toronto-based television sex therapist, has found that young girls are becoming much more aggressive in the pursuit of boys, inundating them with calls, letters, whatever it takes to get their attention—but with decidedly mixed results. "I have more guys say to me that the only reason they had sex was because a girl came on like blockbusters and it was the only way to get rid of her," Johanson says. 6

They go by their "mall" names of Fila, Crystal, and Kat, and violence is something they accept as part of adolescent life. All three have scars on their wrists from suicide attempts; each talks about the importance of control in lives that, for the most part, are clearly out of control. The three hang out at the Storefront, a drop-in center in the Marlborough Mall in northeast Calgary that offers counseling, job placement help, and family services, as well as a place where kids can shoot pool, play a few arcade games, and watch TV. 7

"There's a pretty big reason for violence among girls," says Fila. "It's got to do with dominance and what you believe is yours. Usually it comes down to our boyfriends. First you threaten—'Don't touch him or I'll kill you.' And if that doesn't work you fight." Crystal and Kat say that clothes are also a flash point. There is even a hierarchy of most desired brands—Nike, Fila, and Adidas. Kat says clothes matter because they reflect status and membership. "It's about belonging. You want to be part of a group, a gang. It's like your family," says Kat, who is in tenth grade. As for violence, Crystal 8 says, "people don't listen if you say it nicely, so you have to put it bluntly and threaten them. And if that doesn't work, what comes next is to fight."

9   Fila, Crystal, and Kat all profess the same tastes when it comes to music and movies. They love rap: their favorite singers are Puff Daddy, Mase, and Tupac Shakur. "We like the black men and the words. They've got perfect bodies and they've got attitude," says Fila. "Yeah, and they're half-naked," adds Crystal. "They're risky. They've got this I don't care attitude, I'll just be who I am." The same kind of tastes are reflected in the movies they like, all based on gang life, such as *Gang Related*.

10   Although statistics in Calgary show no growth in the total number of violent crimes involving young girls, police say the level of threats and violence is increasing. On November 21, a group of five fifteen- and sixteen-year-olds confronted four other girls between the ages of twelve and fourteen. Two of the younger girls were assaulted at a transit stop, one punched in the face and the other threatened that she would be thrown from the train platform if they did not give up their jackets—one a Nike, the other Le Chateau. As of October 31, there had been sixteen violent offences involving adolescent girls this year. Last year during the same period, there were twenty-two, and in 1995, only seven. "There clearly is more violence being shown by young girls than was the case years ago," says Staff Sergeant Dan Dorsey. "I left the streets in 1988 to work major crime, and when I came back this year, I could see there are far more female young offenders than was the case ten years ago."

11   Dominance, control, and the sanctity of the group: they are powerful motivators. And for adolescent girls, who often suffer a calamitous drop in self-esteem with the onset of puberty, a punch-up or two may seem like a small price to pay for being part of the gang. Seventeen-year-old Jaime Denike, who attends Gladstone Secondary School in east-end Vancouver, says that among teenage girls there is strength in numbers. "In a lot of instances, it will be one girl against one girl, but all their friends will end up getting involved," she says. Adds fifteen-year-old Zoe Verbauwhede: "Every single thing becomes a big deal." The Gladstone students agree that problems between teenage girls often arise from the intense need to conform. "In school, nobody can really be themselves," Verbauwhede says. "They'll be left out. So people try to act cool." Some teachers and students have been trained in conflict resolution techniques, contributing to a relatively safe environment at Gladstone, but the girls also say there is still an unwritten code not to snitch on peers—much like many of the Saanich students who did not report Virk's murder despite widespread rumors. "No one wants to be a rat," Denike explains.

12   For those who are inescapably different, life at school can mean unrelenting misery that eventually deteriorates into habitual violence. Marie speaks bitterly of the Oshawa, Ontario, school where she was harassed from the age of eight because of her thick glasses and short, round body. Such treatment can be particularly devastating for vulnerable kids, like Marie, who come from troubled families and have spent time in foster care. For the past four months, she has spent many hours each day wrapped in a mangy sleeping bag, sitting on Yonge Street outside the Evergreen teen drop-in centre in Toronto's downtown core. Although she is five months pregnant, most nights she perches over hot air grates on city streets: she has been kicked out of all the local shelters because, as she says, her "roommates would start fights and I'd finish them."

13   Although Virk appears, at least on the surface, to have been a fairly normal schoolgirl, there are hints that she was caught in a similar, downward spiral of plummeting self-esteem. Some of her friends have acknowledged that she was self-conscious about her weight, and others have pointed out that she chafed under the rules of her parent's household—both are Jehovah's Witnesses of East Indian origin. About a year ago, she

ran away from home and was placed in foster care. And earlier this year, her father Manjit Virk was charged with two sex offenses against his daughter and one count of uttering threats. All three charges were stayed last August, and the teen later recanted; last week her family said the charges were false, made by their daughter in an attempt to gain more freedom by being relocated to a foster home.

Many prosecutors and social scientists caution against easier treatment for girls than boys. Halifax Crown Attorney Catherine Cogswell has become impatient with such an approach. "What's facing the system is how to get out the message that violence is wrong and to not deal with girls with kid gloves," she says. "I have seen parents, police officers, social workers, and judges be more lenient because the case involves a girl. I have walked away and thought, really, this is sexist." **14**

A sampling of recent Halifax-area cases vividly demonstrates the casual viciousness girls are capable of. In one recent incident, Cogswell recalls, a teenager stabbed her friend with a knife, puncturing her lung. By the time they got to court, neither could remember what the fight was about. And last year, when four boys gang-raped a classmate, a group of teens—including girls—stood by cheering. At the trial, one girl referred to the attack as "no big deal." According to her, "these things happen at school all the time." **15**

Whatever the reasons, some teenage girls clearly are experiencing acute—at times uncontainable—levels of anger and are showing far more willingness to strike out. Researchers and clinicians are also discovering a chilling lack of empathy among young girls—a quality that, until recently, appeared to be more common among adolescent boys. Miriam Kaufman, a Toronto pediatrician and author of *Mothering Teens: Understanding the Adolescent Years*, says many girls she counsels seem devoid of even a basic moral sense. "It's as if right and wrong are not even part of their experience or vocabulary," she says. Such detachment appears to have been very much present among some of those charged in Virk's death: according to the mother of one of the accused, her daughter is a habitual troublemaker utterly lacking in remorse. "If you don't like this person, beat them up. Whatever you want you can have," she says, describing her daughter's mentality. **16**

According to June Larkin, a professor of women's studies at the University of Toronto who was also an elementary schoolteacher for twenty years, girls still feel trapped in gender stereotypes, despite thirty years of feminism. Many formal barriers to women may be down, she points out, but support for girls in non-traditional roles still remains weak. The result, she says, is that "if girls can't get equal, they'll get even." That attitude may pervert the notion of true equality, but it is hardly surprising, Larkin adds. "With few other options, it's to be expected that some girls will adopt the violent behavior of dominant boys," Larkin says. She notes, however, that such tactics are almost always used against other girls. Boys, she says, are far more difficult to overpower and, in general, are impervious to insults. Girls, on the other hand, are deeply enraged by verbal attacks. Ironically, she notes, sexual put-downs, like "slut" or "whore"—the traditional language of sexism—are particularly popular with violent girls. **17**

But according to many who work with distressed young girls, there is another, equally disturbing reason for their growing love affair with violence: parental neglect. Carey MacLellan, an Ottawa lawyer who frequently defends female young offenders, believes that parents must take much more responsibility for their children. Starting with the current obsession over clothes—wearing the right, usually high-priced jacket or shoes—parents should stop encouraging children to conform to peer ideals that are based on money. "There is a real nexus now between the clothing, gang behavior, and crime," MacLellan says. "I think parents have to take responsibility for that—they are **18** the ones paying for it." MacLellan also faults adults for failing to set limits, often rationalizing that they have no way to exert authority over their kids: "I have children calling their mother 'bitch,' and the parents just sit there. I have to walk away." MacLellan is also deeply concerned about the nonchalance he sees in many teens. "These kids, no matter what their behavior, have no fear of repercussions, none."

19   They may not, but many of the eight hundred people who packed a memorial service for Reena Virk late last week certainly did. During his remarks at the service, Witness elder Richard Toews called Reena's death an "incomprehensible tragedy." The brutal slaying, he added, is a reminder that big-city crime can just as easily lurk in smaller cities like Victoria, no matter how blissful they appear. And that is a warning that might well be sounded in almost any community across the country.

STABBINGS, BEATINGS: AN UNSETTLING RECORD

20   Reena Virk's death was not an isolated act of violence involving teenage girls. Some other cases:

- In London, Ontario, police charged a thirteen-year-old girl with attempted murder last week after a nine-year-old boy at Princess Elizabeth Public School was stabbed in the neck with a knife. Police gave no explanation for what sparked the attack. The girl also faces two counts of assault with a weapon in another incident involving two of her thirteen-year-old female classmates.
- In October, an early-morning argument broke out between two men in separate vehicles on Montreal's South Shore. At an intersection, the men jumped out and began fighting. Police say one man's seventeen-year-old girlfriend stabbed the other man in the back three times.
- On July 2, a woman died after being shot in the head at her home in Boucherville, Quebec, following her fiftieth birthday party. Her seventeen-year-old daughter was charged with first-degree murder.
- On March 10, a seventy-year-old grandmother died after being stabbed repeatedly in the head and neck with a kitchen knife at her home in Buckingham, Quebec. The woman's thirteen-year-old granddaughter was charged with second-degree murder.
- In February, 1996, a fourteen-year-old Winnipeg girl allegedly assaulted a sixteen-year-old girl. Police say she was attempting to coerce the older teen into prostitution.
- In December, 1995, Alexis Bonilla, a seventeen-year-old pimp who belonged to the Latino Assassins gang, was ambushed, beaten and drowned in a creek in Burnaby, British Columbia. Three girls were charged—two were fourteen, the third sixteen. Two pleaded guilty to second-degree murder. The third teen was acquitted.
- On October 26, 1995, Sylvain Leduc, seventeen, and three other teenagers were abducted by members of Ottawa's Ace Crew gang and confined in a Nepean, Ontario, apartment. Leduc was tortured to death; the others survived. One woman, then seventeen, was charged with first-degree murder. Three adults also face the same charge. Three teenage gang members, meanwhile, have already been convicted of lesser charges, including kidnaping and assault.
- On July 8, 1995, Kulwarn Dhiman, thirty-four, picked up three teenage girls in Calgary. According to court testimony, after all four drank together for hours, Dhiman tried to force one girl to perform oral sex. He was stabbed to death. Two girls, both fourteen, were convicted of manslaughter.

- In May, 1994, a fourteen-year-old Mississauga, Ontario, girl took part in a botched robbery attempt in which a midnight stroller, Brian Harris Baylen, was stabbed to death. Her sixteen-year-old friend, Clifford Arnold Long, stabbed Baylen in the back first. Then the girl plunged a steak knife into his back as well. The girl, a victim of sexual abuse, was convicted of manslaughter. Long, tried in adult court, was sentenced to eight years.

Be a Man

KEVIN JENNINGS

When I was eight, my dad died unexpectedly of a heart attack. As the youngest of five   1
siblings (four of us boys), I looked to my brothers for guidance on how to act in this unsettling and unfamiliar territory. At dad's funeral I got the message. When I started crying, my brother Mike looked down and barked, "Stop crying. Be a man. Don't be a faggot."

While astoundingly insensitive in his timing, my brother was simply passing   2
down the code of masculinity he'd been taught. "Real men" don't show their feelings, and those men who do are faggots—which is the last thing any real man would want to be. It's a lesson I have spent nearly three decades trying to unlearn.

Many important lessons—the kind that shape our lives—are learned long before   3
college or grad school. Sadly, today's boys seem to be learning the same lesson—with far deadlier results. Consider these examples:

- On February 2, 1996, Barry Loukaitis, a sophomore at a Moses Lake, Washington, junior high school, gunned down fellow student Manuel Vela, Jr., in retaliation for months of being called "faggot." Even though a teacher and another student also died in the assault, Loukaitis was convicted of only one count of first-degree murder—because the jury saw clearly that it was only Vela that Loukaitis had planned to kill.
- On December 1, 1997, fifteen-year-old Michael Carneal killed three students and wounded five more at a West Paducah, Kentucky, high school after months of harassment following the publication of a student newspaper column in which it was rumored that Carneal was gay.
- On May 22, 1998, fifteen-year-old Matthew Santoni stabbed sixteen-year-old Jeffrey LaMothe to death in downtown Northampton, Massachusetts, after months of being called "faggot" by a group of fellow students of whom LaMothe was the ringleader.

Why haven't you heard more about these incidents? Well, sadly, homophobic ha-   4
rassment in our schools is so commonplace that it is no longer news. But surely this seemingly novel phenomenon of youth taking up firearms in response should have made headlines. And here's the real kicker. None of the boys who perpetrated these attacks identifies as gay.

What's going on here? As we begin another school year close on the heels of one   5
in which schoolyard shootings became a dreary staple of the nightly news, it's time to analyze why some young people are driven to kill. Obviously, we could prevent some killings if we restricted the ease with which anyone can get a firearm, but that would not get at the root cause of the problem. We need to own up to the fact that our culture teaches boys that being "a man" is the most important thing in life, even if you

have to kill someone to prove it. Killing someone who calls you a faggot is not aberrant behavior but merely the most extreme expression of a belief that is beaten (sometimes literally) into boys at an early age in this country: Be a man—don't be a faggot.

6   As Suzanne Pharr so eloquently explained in her landmark work *Homophobia: A Weapon of Sexism*, antigay bigotry is inextricably intertwined with the maintenance of "proper" gender roles by which little girls are supposed to be "sugar and spice and everything nice" and boys are supposed to be, well, quite the opposite. When boys take up guns to kill those who torment them with words like "faggot," we shouldn't be surprised. They're just doing what we have taught them to do. At Barry Loukaitis's sentencing, Manual Vela, Sr., had the chance to confront his son's killer and said, "You thought being called a faggot was bad; maybe 'sweetie' will sound better to you now." Like father, like son.

7   The cycle of violence starts early—in the nursery rhymes kids learn to recite; in the classrooms, where students hear antigay comments twenty-six times a day on average and where teachers do nothing an astounding ninety-seven percent of the time; and on the football fields, where coaches still use the drill "smear the queer" to teach tackling skills. In this culture boys learn early: Be a man—or else.

5 *Summarizing*

A *summary* of a text or passage is a brief distillation of its salient points—its main ideas and essential information—that excludes any supporting details, such as examples or illustrations. Summaries save time, but they serve other purposes as well, such as focusing attention and stimulating recall. A textbook chapter, for example, may end with a summary that reinforces new concepts and reemphasizes important information. A scientific or technical article may open with an *abstract*, a summary of findings that allows a reader to recognize the main point quickly and, perhaps, decide whether to proceed through the entire text. As a student, you have probably written a fair number of summaries already. A book review or "report on the literature" requires you to summarize the contents of one or more texts. A lab report contains a brief account of your experimental procedures and results. An argumentative paper (like a trial lawyer's *brief*) may conclude with a forceful summation of the evidence you have presented. Less familiar, perhaps, are the uses of summary in research writing. As you consult sources filled with detailed information and expert analysis, you must determine which is most important and relevant, recording only that on your note cards. In fact, your completed research paper is by nature a summary, a carefully condensed and focused presentation of what you have discovered during the course of an investigation.

Whenever you read, your mind engages in something like summarizing: seeking out main ideas, making connections among them (as well as drawing associations with your other experiences), and creating a framework for efficient storage in your memory. You can assist that process when you annotate your reading. For example, a student reading a textbook to learn how the human eye works might write this summary note in the margin:

> In the human visual system the initial coding of the image occurs in the *retina*, a layer of neural cells at the rear of the eyeball. The retina contains a two-dimensional layer of sensory cells, called *rods* and *cones*, which are sensitive to light. Each of these cells is a *transducer* that is capable of generating a neural signal when struck by light.
>
> —Neil A. Stillings, *Cognitive Science: An Introduction*

Rods and cones in the retina encode images

Writing the note helps the student see the main point of the passage and remember it.

SUMMARY AND PARAPHRASE

Although marginal annotations often *paraphrase*, the preceding note *summarizes:* it omits details, including definitions of terms. As you will see, summary and paraphrase share similarities in both form and function. Before introducing those similarities, however, we need to consider two ways that summary and paraphrase differ. First, unlike a paraphrase, a summary may quote a phrase or two, or even a short sentence, from the original source, provided that it is set off with quotation marks. Second, summarizing involves decisions about what is most important and what can be left out. In the following passage, a British author writes about the processing and marketing of groceries:

The original source

All these techniques, originating in the United States and vigorously marketed by American businessmen, have spread across the industrialized communities of Europe.

One of these has been a significant change in shopping habits. When food retailers still purchased their supplies in bulk—flour and sugar by the sack, tea in a chest, butter in a keg, and cheeses whole—the local store was a place of resort. It was a social center as well as a distribution point. Standard articles, prepackaged and preserved by canning or freezing in a large-scale modern factory, are distributed with more efficiency, even if with the loss of social intercourse, in an equally efficient large-scale supermarket. Hence it is reasonable to suggest that one of the effects American food technology has had on the character of European society has been to accelerate the extinction of the general store on the street corner, of the specialized butcher, baker, greengrocer, and dairy and to substitute the supermarket. Great Britain, moving forward a decade behind the United States, possessed 175 supermarkets in 1958, 367 in 1960, and 4,800 in 1970.

—Magnus Pyke, "The Influence of American Food Technology in Europe"

Notice the difference between a paraphrase and a summary of this passage. A student wishing to use the information in a research paper might paraphrase as follows:

A paraphrase of the source

New methods of processing and distributing food, developed in America and sent overseas, have brought social change to Europe. For one thing, many Europeans no longer shop for groceries as they once did when stores bought large containers of flour, sugar, tea, and butter and whole cheeses. In those days, the food store was a place to meet friends as well as to buy groceries. Though impersonal by comparison, today's supermarkets are more efficient, selling products that come individually packaged from the factory, where they have been canned or frozen to keep them fresh. Consequently, American methods have led to the gradual disappearance of butcher shops, bakeries, produce markets, and dairy stores, all of which have been supplanted by supermarkets. The number of supermarkets in Britain, which is about ten years behind trends established in the U.S., grew from 175 in 1958 and 367 in 1960 to 4,800 in 1971 (Pyke 89–90).

This paraphrase alters the writer's language, while retaining all his ideas, including examples and minor details. The following summary, on the other hand, presents only the most important ideas:

A summary of the source

American innovations in the production and distribution of food have brought supermarkets to Europe. Once a neighborly "place of resort," the corner store has been supplanted by the more efficient, though less sociable, supermarket (Pyke 89–90).

Notice that the summary omits details and examples found in the paraphrase. Nevertheless, it provides a faithful representation of the author's ideas and attitudes. You may also notice that this particular summary retains a phrase from the original source, placed in quotation marks.

A summary, like a paraphrase, makes an author's ideas clear, perhaps even clearer than they are in the original. Unlike a paraphrase, a summary may incorporate a quotation—a phrase or short sentence from the source—if it is set off with quotation marks. Both summary and paraphrase, however, must acknowledge their common source in a parenthetical note.

Summary and Paraphrase　　　　　　　　　　　　EXERCISE

A process for writing summaries follows this exercise, but you already can summarize a passage with a main idea. The following excerpt from a book review by Evan Thomas concerns the ways that U.S. Presidents devised foreign policy before the creation of the National Security Council, an advisory group that includes cabinet members and other diplomatic experts. Paraphrase the passage; then write a brief summary. Both paraphrase and summary must be written in your own words, though you may quote a short phrase or two in the summary. Avoid any reference to the author, ending both paraphrase and summary with a parenthetical note: (Thomas 9).

> During the early days of the Cold War, when America was first taking on the role of leader of the West, there was no national security staff. Policy coordination, such as it was, often occurred over lunch at the F Street Club, a WASP-y hangout a few blocks from the White House. Sometimes this informality worked. In 1947, the deputy secretary of state, Robert Lovett, laid the groundwork for the creation of NATO by bringing top secret cables over to the apartment of the Senate Foreign Relations Committee chairman, Arthur Vandenberg. The two men would have a martini and discuss the Western alliance. But sometimes casualness was a prescription for disaster. President Kennedy at first disdained bureaucratic committees, preferring to cozy up with the dashing old boys at the CIA. The result was the Bay of Pigs.

 ## WRITING SUMMARIES

One way to summarize a short passage resembles the process introduced in Chapter 4, where you created topic sentences for paragraphs with main ideas that were implied but not stated: *Read the passage once or twice until its meaning is clear, put it aside, and then write a brief summary from memory.* As the length of a passage increases, however, summarizing becomes more of a challenge. Since college students are expected to summarize a variety of texts and passages, some of which are long and complex, you can benefit from a reliable, efficient method of composing summaries. The following process can save time and minimize frustration. As in all other types of writing, time spent in the preliminary stages pays off later on.

GUIDELINES   ## Summarizing Longer Passages

- *Read carefully.* To summarize a text or a passage, you must understand it thoroughly. Read it, look up unfamiliar words, and discuss its meaning with others.

- *Read with a pencil.* Underlining and marginal notes can increase comprehension. Be selective; underline main ideas only. Use your own symbols and marginal comments to highlight important ideas. Good notes and underlining will make later review quick and easy, so it pays to concentrate the first time through.

- *Write a one-sentence paraphrase of the main idea.* If the text or passage has a thesis statement, paraphrase it. If not, state what you take to be the main idea in your own words. This statement should provide a focus for everything else in the summary.

- *Write a first draft.* Compose a miniature version of the text or passage based on portions you have underlined and marginal notes you have written. Keep this draft simple, following the order of ideas found in the original. Paraphrase where possible, although parts of the first draft may still be close to the phrasing of the original.

- *Paraphrase your draft.* Treat your draft as a passage to be paraphrased. Restate its ideas and information in your own language and style, quoting no more than an isolated phrase or two or a single short sentence if there is an idea you cannot express as effectively in your own words. Remember that a summary expresses the ideas of the text or passage smoothly and clearly as well as concisely. Provide transitions, eliminate unnecessary words, combine ideas, and clarify any confusing sentences.

To illustrate this process, let's suppose you need to summarize the following passage from pages 76–78 of *Telling It Like It Isn't*, a book by J. Dan Rothwell, a scholar of semantics, the study of how language affects the way we think. First, read it with care until you are sure that you understand it (step 1).

Once you are satisfied that you understand the passage, go back and reread it with a pencil (step 2). Following is the passage as it was marked by one reader. (Since readers differ, it is unlikely that you would have marked it in exactly the same way.)

PRACTICE READING

Stereotyping: Homogenizing People

J. Dan Rothwell

We all carry around images of what members of particular groups are like. For instance, what image is conjured in your mind for a dope smoker, New York cab driver, black athlete, college professor, construction worker? These images are often shared by others. Typically, they stress similarities and ignore differences among members of a group. These images, then, become stereotypes—the attribution of certain characteristics to a group, often without the benefit of firsthand knowledge.

Stereotypes are judgments . . . of individuals not on the basis of direct interaction with those individuals specifically . . . but based instead on preconceived images for the category they belong to. Stereotypes, however, are not inherently evil. Some stereotypes, when predicated upon personal experience and empirical data, can be valid generalizations about a group.

Some stereo-types are valid?!

There are several potential problems with stereotypes, however. First, these preconceived images of groups may produce a frame of reference, a perpetual set in our minds concerning the group as a whole. Then, when faced with an individual from the group, the preconceived image is applied indiscriminately, screening out individual differences. Individuals become mere abstractions devoid of unique qualities, pigeonholed and submerged in the crowd, a crowd that is thought to be homogeneous.

① *The group becomes more important.*

Indiscriminate application of stereotypes is particularly troublesome because stereotypes are not necessarily grounded on evidence or even direct experience. The classic study of stereotyping by Katz and Braly (1933) clearly revealed that stereotypes are often formulated in ignorance. They reflect attitudes toward labels, racial, ethnic, and others, frequently without benefit of actual contact with members of the group stereotyped. Student subjects held Turks in low esteem, yet most had never interacted with any member of this group.

A second problem with stereotypes is what general semanticists term *allness*. This is the tendency to characterize an individual or an entire group in terms of only one attribute or quality. This one characteristic becomes all that is necessary to know about a person. Once you realize that the person is a woman, or a Jew, or a Southerner, no more information is sought. This unidimensional view of a person is nothing more than a simplistic conception of an individual. You may be a Jew but also a brother, son, brilliant lawyer, charming compassionate individual, devoted father, loving husband, and so forth. Allness sacrifices complexity and substitutes superficiality. Racial and ethnic characteristics do not lend themselves to change, yet racial or ethnic labels may be the prepotent characteristic that supersedes all others. In fact, allness orientation may produce exaggerated perception of group characteristics. Secord et al. (1956) showed "prejudiced" and "unprejudiced" subjects several pictures of blacks and whites. The prejudiced observers exaggerated the physical characteristics of blacks such as thickness of lips and width of nose. Racial labels accentuated the stereotyped differences between "races" for prejudiced (allness-oriented) subjects.

②

③ *When we see stereotypes, we can't see people!!*

A final problem associated with stereotyping is that it can produce frozen evaluations. Juvenile delinquents or adult felons may never shed their stigmatizing label despite "going straight." Zimbardo and Ruch (1977) summarize studies conducted at Princeton University over several decades regarding stereotypes by

Princeton students of various ethnic groups. While the stereotypes did change, they tended to do so relatively slowly. In 1933, blacks were deemed superstitious by 84% of Princeton students, 41% in 1951, and 13% in 1967. Thirty-four years is a very long time for people to acquire an accurate image of blacks on this one item.

Summary of above

Stereotypes are thus troublesome because they are often indiscriminate, exhibit an allness orientation, and can produce frozen evaluations. Considering the pervasiveness of stereotyping in our society, one should not take it lightly. When we stereotype, we define a person, and this definition, superficial at best, can be quite powerful.

To stereotype is to define, and to define is to control, especially if the definition is widely accepted regardless of its accuracy. In a male-dominated society women may be stereotyped as empty-headed and illogical. The fact that the stereotype has persisted for years manifests the control men have over women, control that excludes women from executive positions and relegates them to mindless housekeeping duties. Women's liberation is fundamentally the struggle to define, to reject male stereotypes of females.

Vicious circle

Stereotypes are sometimes seductive, however. When women are told repeatedly that they are stupid, they may begin believing it. A self-fulfilling prophecy may develop. Low self-esteem produced from male definitions of women as unintelligent can lead to poor performance and the consequent belief that the stereotype has merit. The stereotype is thus nurtured and perpetuated. Stereotyping can thus control, insidiously imprisoning its victims in constraining roles.

SUMMARY
★

So while stereotyping isn't intrinsically evil, most stereotypes lack empirical foundations and are assertions of power and dominance over less powerful groups. Reduced to an abstraction, victims of stereotyping must struggle to define themselves or be content to accept roles others have carved out for them. It is little wonder our society has been experiencing turmoil.

Now write the thesis, a sentence stating the main idea of the passage (step 3):

Thesis

Stereotypes are judgments of people based on preconceived images about a group they are supposed to belong to.

Next, a first draft might look like this (step 4):

A first draft

We all carry around images of what groups are like, and these images are often shared. They stress similarities and ignore differences. Stereotypes assign certain characteristics to a group without benefit of firsthand knowledge. They are judgments of individuals based on preconceived images, not on direct interaction. However, stereotypes are not inherently evil. Some are valid.

Nevertheless, there are problems with stereotypes. When you have a preconceived image of a group, it induces a perceptual set that screens out individual differences. Indiscriminate stereotypes are not grounded on evidence and are often formulated in ignorance without actual contact. A second problem is allness: characterizing an individual or group in terms of only one attribute or quality. When you realize someone is a woman, a Jew, or a Southerner, you may not look for other information. This is a very simplistic idea of a person. It is superficial and does not account for the complexities that real people exhibit. A final problem with stereotypes is frozen evaluations: judgments that have stayed the same for a long time and change relatively slowly.

So we can see that stereotypes are dangerous because they are indiscriminate, are inclined toward allness, and give a frozen evaluation. They also define and control people if the stereotypes are widely accepted. Women, for example, have to struggle to reject men's stereotypes of females. Sometimes stereotypes are seductive. People believe these images, so they become self-fulfilling. An image can control its victims, imprisoning them in roles. Even though most stereotypes aren't valid, victims of stereotyping must either struggle to define themselves or accept the bad image others have made up for them.

The final step is to revise and proofread (step 5). Here you can concentrate on condensing, on avoiding repetition, and on focusing the sentences around the thesis. Because you are seeking economy, see if your first draft can be shortened. The result is a final draft that is, in effect, a summary of a summary, as in this final version:

> Stereotypes are perceptions of individuals based on unexamined assumptions about a group they belong to. Although some stereotypes may be valid, they often create problems. First, stereotypes prevent us from regarding people as individuals. Second, they cause us to characterize people or groups on the basis of only one superficial attribute, a problem known as *allness*. Third, stereotypes become frozen and take years to change. When these false images are widely accepted, they define and therefore control people so thoroughly that unless victims struggle to disprove a stereotype, they often subscribe to it themselves (Rothwell 76–78).

The final draft

Writing Summaries

EXERCISES

1. Using the process outlined on page 184, summarize the following passage from "Forty Years in the Sand," an article by Karl E. Meyer in *Harper's*. Close your summary with a parenthetical note citing the name of the author and page 9, where the passage appears.

   The British created Iraq in 1918, confident it would become a beacon of enlightenment unto the Middle East, that it would nurture moderate Arab regimes, that its monarchs would serve as peacemakers between Zionists and Arabs in Palestine, and that it would anchor the region in the wider interests of a far-flung empire. The experiment persisted for forty years, and it failed.

   The United States has occupied Iraq for more than two years now. Our stated ambition there is to "spread freedom," nurture moderate Arab regimes, act as a peacemaker between Israel and its neighbors, and anchor the region in the wider interests of American national security. Yet the lessons of Britain's failure have eluded the American promoters of Operation Iraqi Freedom, who remain strangely uncurious about Great Britain's chastening moment in the Mesopotamian sun.

   Historical parallels are slippery; still, it is not often that one nation has the benefit of learning from the blunders of another so similar to it, with much the same goals, in the very same country, and within just a few decades of its own attempt. If Britain's experiment in Iraq offers a harbinger of things to come, will it take thirty-eight more years before Americans learn the same lessons?

2. Summarize the following portion of an essay concerning changes in the Scholastic Aptitude Test (SAT), from page B14 of an issue of the *Chronicle of Higher Education.*

The College Board's New Essay Reverses Decades of Progress Toward Literacy

Dennis Baron

Those of us who took the SAT remember what we got on that test, even if we took it long ago. On the other hand, few of us recall our high-school GPA, and the permanent record that was supposed to follow us forever has vanished without a trace. But the score that propelled us into the college of our choice, or kept us out, stays with us, surfacing at cocktail parties or when our children or our students ask, "Whadja get?" as they begin to worry about the SAT's ability to open the doors of the college of their choice.

The SAT hasn't changed dramatically since I took it forty-five years ago (my scores are none of your business), but now and then it has been overhauled, at least on the surface. On March 12 some 330,000 American high-school students took the newly revised SAT, expanded to include a writing sample. Exit polls report the following responses to the latest version of America's high-stakes college-entrance exam:

- The College Board found strong student enthusiasm for the test, with few complaints from parents.
- In contrast, Stanley Kaplan saw widespread discontent over the SAT's increased length and difficulty, with the essay proving particularly worrisome.
- FairTest, a longtime test watcher, charged that the new SAT is little more than the old test grown a size larger so that the multimillion-dollar nonprofit College Board, which owns the test, can raise prices, exploit proctors and graders, and increase the salaries and bonuses paid to its executives.

It doesn't take a psychometrician—that's a vocabulary word you won't find on the SAT; it means "someone who cooks up standardized tests"—to tell you that comments like those correlate very highly with the interests of the speakers who make them, proving that in testing, as in crime, we can get the right answer by asking *cui bono?*—literally "who benefits?" but loosely rendered into the English of late capitalism as "follow the money."

The College Board benefits from changing its test to keep up with changing educational times, while plugging in to the national testing frenzy to protect its market share. In addition, the Kaplans and the *Princeton Reviews* and the rest of the test-prep industry scare test takers into cram courses on essay writing, raising the companies' bottom line while they help students raise their scores. And critics who argue that the SAT assesses neither knowledge nor potential, that it reinforces social stratification instead of creating avenues for mobility, benefit from catching the brief media flurry surrounding the rollout of a new test, even though those critics must also acknowledge that testing has such a stranglehold on the American consciousness that no one really cares whether their objections are valid.

The comments of those most directly involved in education, teachers and students, are also predictable. Teachers seldom agree about curriculum, and those interviewed about the new SAT seem evenly divided for or against the essay. It either does or does not give students an opportunity to think critically and write the kind of impromptu, timed theme on a surprise topic that the College Board seems to think they will encounter regularly in college and later on in their careers.

And students, whose lot is ever to complain, gripe that the test is too long, the breaks too short, and there isn't enough time to finish. Some test takers liked the essay, others didn't. Many weren't used to writing by hand, and most agreed that the general nature of the topic—on March 12 students on the East Coast had to discuss majority rule, while students in the West dealt with the role of creativity in the modern world—together with the time constraint of twenty-five minutes for planning and execution all but guaranteed a response that was both formulaic and unreflective.

Because I write and teach about writing, I have my own concerns about the SAT essay test. It makes up only thirty percent of the new and "improved" writing section—that section is worth 800 of the new SAT's total score of 2400 points—and is nothing more than the old, optional SAT II writing test repackaged as a mandatory part of the SAT I. Furthermore, more than two-thirds of a student's "writing" score comes not from writing prose but from identifying sentence and paragraph errors by way of multiple-choice questions. That method is no different from the SAT's earlier attempts to gauge writing knowledge indirectly.

The students are right that responses to general essay prompts in the new test are almost certain to be formulaic, and that those essays that don't fit the five-paragraph mold are likely to be rated down by graders looking for an easy peg to hang a score on. SAT test-preparation guides, whether online or in print, stress the importance of a simple four- or five-paragraph structure. They encourage students to begin with a catchy opener; to demonstrate their literacy by offering supporting examples from literature, not pop culture or personal experience; and to dazzle graders by throwing in a few obscure vocabulary words.

Such advice is counterproductive, since (1) formulas like the five-paragraph essay, while common enough "in vitro," in school and on standardized tests, rarely occur "in vivo," in the more natural world of personal and on-the-job writing; (2) literary examples may demonstrate that the writer is also a reader, but they may not always be the best examples to support an argument; and (3) the average student can't deploy sesquipedalian words appropriately.

 ## USES OF SUMMARY

Thus far we have said little about why a writer might summarize a text or a passage, beyond the obvious reason of saving the reader's time. Basically, however, summary serves most of the same purposes as paraphrase. The marginal note beside the textbook passage on page 181 shows how summary, like paraphrase, can help you understand and internalize complex and important ideas. Likewise, you can use summary to make a challenging passage accessible to others who may be unfamiliar with its terminology and concepts. (Our summary on pages 182–83 of Magnus Pyke's account of European grocery shopping provides an example.)

Summarizing an Argument

Another frequent use of summary is to demonstrate understanding of a contro-versial point of view or argumentative text. Suppose you need to summarize the following excerpt from an essay about nonsexist language written by conservative columnist William Safire:

A source that makes an argument

> It makes sense to substitute *worker* for *workingman* . . . , *firefighter* for *fireman*, and *police officer* for *policeman*. Plenty of women are in those occupations, and it mis-leads the reader to retain the old form. . . .
>
> But do we need *woman actor* for *actress*, or *female tempter* for *temptress?* And what's demeaning about *waitress* that we should have to substitute *woman waiter* or the artificial, asexual *waitron?* We dropped *stewardess* largely because the occu-pation was being maligned—a popular book title suggesting promiscuity was *Coffee, Tea, or Me?*—a loss that also took the male *steward* out the emergency exit, and now we have the long and unnecessarily concealing *flight attendant*. We were better off with *steward* and *stewardess*.
>
> The abolition of the *-ess* suffix tells the reader or listener, "I intend to con-ceal from you the sex of the person in that job." Thus, when you learn that the *chairperson* or *chair* is going to be Pat Jones or Leslie Smith, or anyone not with a sexually recognizable first name like Jane or Tarzan, you will be denied the infor-mation about whether that person is a man or a woman.
>
> Ah, that's the point, say the language police, sex-eraser squad: it should not matter. But information does matter—and does it really hurt to know? What's wrong with *chairwoman* or *Congresswoman?* Let's go further: now that the anti-sexist point has been made in this generation, wouldn't it be better for the next generation to have more information rather than less?

Regardless of whether you agree with these views, you probably would employ an attribution phrase, rather than just a parenthetical note, to call attention to their source. Notice how the underlined phrases in the following summary do that:

A summary with attribution phrases

> <u>Some purists argue</u> that certain forms of nonsexist language are awkward and un-necessary, contributing little if anything to gender equity. <u>These writers contend</u> that occupational titles like *flight attendant* and *waitron* are awkward or silly and that they conceal relevant information about people's identities. <u>One such critic, William Safire, believes</u> that the injustices of sexist language have been suffi-ciently addressed already and that some traditional job designations should be retained (10).

EXERCISE | **Summarizing an Argument**

Write a summary of the following argument excerpted from another editorial by Safire. Since your summary will refer to the author by name, the closing parentheti-cal note should indicate only that the passage appears on page A17.

> As every bigamist should know, *polygamy* is the condition of having more than one spouse at the same time, while *polyandry* is sex-specific—the marriage of a woman with more than one man.

I estimate that 98% of the 30,000 bigamists are males with plural wives, which means that there are probably fewer than 600 polyandrists in active practice today, presumably in a conservative ratio of one woman to two men. These 200 women and their 400 husbands (whose identities are unknown to snooping neighbors) deserve a discreet salute for quietly pioneering America's future lifestyle.

One woman, in the security of being doubly beloved and beneficiaried, can surely provide life-extending companionship to two men. And when one husband passes on, either to his Maker or to some gold-digging bimbo, the long-lived polyandrist would still have the remaining man for mutual comfort and support.

The Polyandry Movement, first espoused in this space five years ago, met an underwhelming response. Aberrant fogies like me, married nearly forty years to one woman, are selfishly disinclined to share, but two generations from now—given the woeful diminution of exclusive marriage commitment and the lengthening of life—the two-husband home may be the bedrock of the newest morality and the salvation of what's left of the American family.

Summarizing in Research Papers

Summary serves the same purposes as paraphrase in research writing: to cite important information, to place a topic or issue in context, and to support an interpretation or opinion. (It is, of course, equally important to use parenthetical notes to identify summarized sources.) The following examples illustrate these occasions for using summary in research writing.

Summarizing to Cite Information

Suppose you are writing a research paper about homelessness. One of your sources, an article by David Levi Strauss, cites the following facts:

> "Home" has increasingly become a site of violent conflict and abuse. Half of all homes are "broken" by divorce; many more are broken by spousal abuse. Child abuse in the home is a national epidemic. Poverty kills twenty-seven children every day in America. Ozzie and Harriet are dead, and the Cosbys don't live around here.
>
> Every year in the United States a million and a half kids run away from home. Many of them end up on city streets. Right now, today, there are some thirty thousand kids living on the streets of New York City. Contrary to popular belief, most of them run away not because they want to but because they have to; because even the streets are safer than where they're running from, where many of them have been physically and sexually abused by their families. Even so, they are not running *to* anything but death. Nationwide, more than five thousand children a year are buried in unmarked graves.

A source that cites information

A summary of these facts might be useful in a paragraph that dispels misconceptions about homeless people, including the belief that they are primarily adults who have made poor choices. Your summary might look like this:

> One of the most brutal facts about homelessness is the number of victims who are minors. Driven from their families by domestic violence, huge numbers of children (30,000 in New York alone) have taken to the streets, vainly hoping to find safety. Thousands of them die (Strauss 753).

A brief summary

Basically, this summary presents facts, including one statistic. Though obliged to identify your source in a parenthetical note, you probably would not cite the author's name in an acknowledgment phrase, since there is nothing about the manner in which you present these facts that is uniquely his. If, on the other hand, you wanted to quote a bit, you probably would employ such a phrase. A slightly longer summary, then, might look like this:

A longer summary quoting the source

> One of the most brutal facts about homelessness is the number of victims who are minors. One reason is a dramatic increase in domestic violence, especially in poor neighborhoods. As journalist David Levi Strauss puts it, "Ozzie and Harriet are dead, and the Cosbys don't live around here." Strauss points to some alarming facts: on any given day, thirty thousand children are homeless in New York City; thousands of homeless children die every year in the United States (753).

Summarizing to Place a Topic or Issue in Context

Suppose that a member of the student government on your campus has voiced opposition to Black Culture Week, arguing that such an event is unwarranted without a comparable celebration of white European culture. If you wished to examine and refute this familiar argument in a research paper, you might wish to demonstrate that most white Americans know far less about African cultures than they suppose—certainly a great deal less than most African Americans know about western European culture. In the course of your research, you locate a book review by Neal Ascherson, which includes the following paragraph:

A source that provides context for an issue

> This is a book perfectly designed for an intelligent reader who comes to the subject of Africa reasonably fresh and unprejudiced. Unfortunately, those are still fairly uncommon qualifications in Europe. The first category of baffled consumers will be those who until yesterday spent much energy denying Africans their history. They did not quite say, like [one] Cambridge professor, that Africa had no history at all. They said that anything ancient, beautiful, or sophisticated found on the continent could have had nothing to do with the talentless loungers incapable of making a decent cup of tea or plowing in a straight line. The ruins of Great Zimbabwe had been built by the Phoenicians; the Benin bronzes were probably Portuguese; and all ironwork was Arab. A more sophisticated version of this line was that although Africa had made a promising start, some unknown disaster or lurking collective brain damage had immobilized Africans halfway down the track. This meant, among other things, that the history and archaeology of Africa belonged to the Europeans, who had dug it up and were alone able to understand it. Back to Europe it went and there, to a great extent, it remains.

A summary of this passage would allow you to place Black Culture Week in a different context from the one in which your fellow student views it. Consequently, your paper might include a paragraph like this somewhere in its introduction:

A paragraph summarizing the source

> Black Culture Week is more than just an occasion for celebrating African heritage. It is an opportunity to dispel some of the demeaning misperceptions and stereotypes that diminish respect or even curiosity among white Americans. Among these is the belief, held by many educated people of European descent,

that Africa has no native history or culture at all—that whatever artifacts are found there were brought by non-Africans, who are also the only people capable of understanding or appreciating their beauty or significance (Ascherson 26). Black Culture Week, therefore, is not so much a matter of promoting African heritage as it is a matter of correcting pervasive misinformation so that educated people can decide whether to study a field that many assume to be nonexistent or unworthy of serious attention.

Summarizing to Support an Interpretation or Opinion

When we discussed the paraphrasing of arguments in Chapter 3, we examined various ways of citing the source of a debatable point of view. Specifically, we looked at these options:

- Stating an argument without an attribution phrase, but putting both the author's name and appropriate page number(s) in a parenthetical note.

- Identifying the source with an attribution phrase and leaving only the page number(s) in the parenthetical note. (Attribution phrases that might be used to introduce a paraphrase of Barbara Lawrence's argument appear on page 141.)

- Expressing judgment about the credibility of the source in an attribution phrase. (Judgmental attribution phrases used in a letter to a library director appear on page 141.)

The effects of attributing an opinion to its source are equally important in the case of summary. Consider the following passage from an essay by Charles R. Lawrence, III, a professor of law at Georgetown University. Lawrence argues that racial insults are not protected by the constitutional guarantee of free speech when they occur on college campuses.

If the purpose of the First Amendment is to foster the greatest amount of speech, racial insults disserve that purpose. Assaultive racist speech functions as a preemptive strike. The invective is experienced as a blow, not as a proffered idea, and once the blow is struck, it is unlikely that a dialogue will follow. Racial insults are particularly undeserving of First Amendment protection because the perpetrator's intention is not to discover truth or initiate dialogue but to injure the victim. In most situations, members of minority groups realize that they are likely to lose if they respond to epithets by fighting and are forced to remain silent and submissive.

A source that expresses an opinion

    Courts have held that offensive speech may not be regulated in public forums such as streets where the listener may avoid the speech by moving on, but the regulation of otherwise protected speech has been permitted when the speech invades the privacy of the unwilling listener's home or when the unwilling listener cannot avoid the speech. Racist posters, fliers, and graffiti in dormitories, bathrooms, and other common living spaces would seem to clearly fall within the reasoning of these cases. Minority students should not be required to remain in their rooms in order to avoid racial assault. Minimally, they should find a safe haven in their dorm rooms and in all other common rooms that are part of their daily routine.

I would also argue that the university's responsibility for insuring that these students receive an equal educational opportunity provides a compelling justification for regulations that insure them safe passage in all common areas. A minority student should not have to risk becoming the target of racially assaulting speech every time he or she chooses to walk across campus.

If you were arguing in favor of a speech code that prohibits racial insults, you could cite Lawrence's claims by summarizing the passage as follows:

A paragraph summarizing the source

The First Amendment was designed to protect the free exchange of ideas, but racial insults are designed to injure or intimidate others, to discourage rather than promote discussion. It would be different if minority students were able to walk away from such insults, but when they occur in dorms and other university buildings, offended students are compelled to endure them (Lawrence B1).

If you wanted to add the weight of authority to this opinion, you might introduce your summary with an attribution phrase—for example, "Georgetown University law professor Charles Lawrence concludes that . . ." or "Some legal experts argue that. . . ."

If, on the other hand, you disagreed with Lawrence, you certainly would introduce your summary with an attribution phrase—perhaps, "Professor Charles Lawrence expresses views typical of those who argue that protecting the interests of minorities takes priority over preserving unrestricted free speech," You might even consider a more judgmental attribution phrase—for example, "Professor Charles Lawrence rationalizes the abridgment of free speech, presenting it as a means of promoting equality and justice."

EXERCISE | ## Summarizing in Research Papers

Write a summary of each of the following passages—one that is appropriate to the given situation. Remember that you may either identify the source at the beginning of your summary or put the last name(s) of the author(s), along with page number(s), in a parenthetical note at the end.

a. *Source:*
The following passage appears on page 60 of an article by Pat Wingert, staff writer for *Newsweek*. The article discusses a growing tendency among students to take more than the traditional four years to complete an undergraduate degree.

Situation:
Enrolled in a course titled Psychology of Marriage and Family, you are writing a research paper about the causes of stress in relationships between parents and their adult children. Specifically, you want to identify and document recent trends.

Passage:
It used to be that kids went to college for four years. But most students today take about five years to graduate. The problem is particularly bad at public universities,

where, on average, only half the students get out in four years—compared with eighty percent of private-school kids. At the University of Michigan, fully sixty-five percent graduate on time. But at UCLA, only forty-two percent graduate in four years, and less than a third of the students in the Texas university system do. These long-timers have become a nightmare for university administrators, who over the next decade will need to make room for the biggest crop of incoming freshmen since the baby boom.

b. *Source:*

The following passage opens an article by Jane Gross on page 1 of a recent issue of the *New York Times.*

Situation:

You are writing a research paper about assisted living for a course titled Recent Issues in Gerontology. You want to introduce your topic by dispelling the notion that assisted living is an unqualified blessing for dependent seniors.

Passage:

Everyone complains about the food. Nobody wants to sit with the misfits. There are leaders and followers, social butterflies and loners, goody-goodies, and troublemakers. Friendships are intense and so are rivalries. Everybody knows everybody else's business. Except for the traffic jam of wheelchairs and walkers, the dining room at the Atria assisted living community here might as well be a high-school cafeteria.

Mary Mercandante, 88, has an explanation for the restive, gossipy environment when old people are forced to live under one roof, even in a top-notch place like this. "Nobody wants to be here," said Mrs. Mercandante, who has lived in the residence for all of its five years and has a gold key to prove it. Phil Granger, a chipper 84-year-old newcomer, agrees that no one welcomes assisted living's stark reminder of mortality. "There's everything anybody could want here," said Mr. Granger, who spreads good cheer by dispensing hard candy, except to diabetics and those with dementia, who might choke. "The only thing wrong with this place is that we're all old. We remember what we used to do and can't do anymore."

c. *Source:*

The following passage appears on page 7E of a newspaper essay by Blake Hurst, a Missouri farmer.

Situation:

You are writing a research paper for a course titled Environmental Economics. You wish to examine the feasibility and possible consequences of subsidizing the farming and marketing of organic foods in the United States. A summary of the following passage will allow you to introduce one point of view about your topic.

Passage:

We farmers are the original conservatives, extremely slow to adopt new technologies of any kind. But we're faced with physical problems that don't have easy solutions. Weeds must be killed, plants require nourishment, and people need food that's safe and affordable.

In response to those realities, we have adapted the latest technology to our ends. To ignore these facts in favor of requiring more "natural" foods would raise the price of what we eat and decrease the variety available to consumers. That may suit upper-class professionals and the so-called slow food movement, but it will serve the middle class poorly and devastate the poor.

GUIDELINES | **Effective Summarizing**

The general principles set forth in this chapter can be summed up in the following guidelines for effective summarizing:

- Like paraphrasing, summarizing calls for close literal reading, but it also involves recognizing main ideas—distinguishing them from minor points and illustrative details.
- Like a paraphrase, a summary is written in your own language, although it may contain a short quotation or two—never more than a single sentence.
- Although there is no single correct way to compose a summary, one useful method is detailed on page 184.
- Summaries serve the same basic functions in research writing as paraphrases do.

READING SELECTION

Following is a chapter from the recent book, *Amazing Grace: The Story of America's Most Beloved Song.* The words to "Amazing Grace" were written in 1748 by John Newton, the captain of a slave vessel, inspired by his miraculous deliverance from a violent storm at sea. Although Newton continued to trade slaves, his hymn became an anthem for abolitionism and, later, for various other human-rights issues.

Understanding Grace

STEVE TURNER

1   The spread of "Amazing Grace" could be viewed as slow but relentless, the natural consequence of being in a growing number of hymnals and of being conveniently positioned when significant forms of communication were invented. In the early part of the nineteenth century it was included in an average of two hymnals each year: By the end of the century this had increased to an average of eight. Since 1900 it has benefited from the advent of the phonograph, radio, television, and portable tape recorder.

2   A more accurate picture would be to see its development as episodic; the writing of the words in 1772, the addition of the music in 1835, and the absorption into secular culture in 1970. Significantly, these stages coincided with major spiritual upheavals in American life, each of which resulted in "Amazing Grace" being understood in a different way.

3   The first of these was the revival later known as the Great Awakening, which started in Massachusetts under the preaching of Jonathan Edwards and continued under George Whitefield and others. Although Newton wasn't one of its converts, the Calvinistic theology that was its heritage had a profound effect on his intellectual and spiritual development, and in this respect "Amazing Grace" was a product of the Great Awakening.

Whitefield, whom Newton admired so much, died before "Amazing Grace" was   4
written, but he would have approved its theme of salvation through the undeserved
favor of God. Yet while Whitefield was quite aggressive in denouncing non-Calvinistic
theology as not merely off the mark but "anti-Christian," Newton showed a generosity
of spirit, believing that "hatred of sin, thirst after God, poverty of spirit, and dependence on Christ" were the marks of a believer regardless of his position on secondary
theological issues. "If I thought a person feared sin, loved the word of God, and was
seeking after Jesus," he wrote in 1775, "I would not walk the length of my study to
proselyte (sic) him to the Calvinistic doctrines. Not because I think them mere opinions, or of little importance to a believer—I think the contrary—but because I believe
these doctrines will do no one any good till he is taught them of God."

The next boost to "Amazing Grace" had come during the Second Great Awakening,   5
when it appeared in *Southern Harmony* attached to "New Britain" and became part of the
shape-note music revolution. Despite being known as the Second Great Awakening, this
revival was not a replica of what had happened under Edwards and Whitefield. The leaders tended to be less educated (and often proud to be so since they thought it showed
their power as preachers came directly from God rather than from natural gifts), the sermons less scholarly and the responses to them more extremely physical and emotional.
It was also guided by a different theology. The emphasis had subtly shifted from God
choosing people to people choosing God, from Calvinism to Arminianism.

The knock-on effect of this change would be profound, leading in the twentieth   6
century to the worst excesses of televangelism, audience manipulation, and bumper-
sticker theology. If the task of the preacher was not merely to present the gospel and allow the spirit to convict but to elicit a decision, then any technique that changed
minds was legitimate. Under these circumstances the "altar call" and the "anxious seat"
were introduced. Preachers became more theatrical. Music began to play an important
part in working on the emotions. Gipsy Smith, the evangelist that Edwin Othello Excell
worked with after the death of Sam Jones, was given the following advice early in his
ministry: "Always sing before you preach. The song is the gimlet that makes the hole
for the nail to go in. Sometimes if you don't sing you might split the board."

Although "Amazing Grace" was Calvinistic, the theological distinctives were   7
buried in its sinews rather than tattooed on its skin. There was nothing in it that an
Arminian would find objectionable. When Newton referred to himself as a "wretch," it
was with total depravity in mind, but an opponent of this doctrine, such as the evangelist Charles Finney who called it "anti-scriptural and nonsensical dogma," could
take it to mean a feeling of despondency. Likewise, "I once was lost, but now am
found" was meant by Newton to emphasize his inability to save himself and therefore
his utter dependence on God, but it could be taken to mean: "I once felt confused and
unsure of my direction in life, but now I feel as thought I am on the right path."

Although the Second Great Awakening occupied the first half of the nineteenth   8
century, its effects were felt throughout. Sam Jones, an evangelist who stressed moral
reformation more than spiritual regeneration, was a direct descendent as were Moody
and Sankey with their carefully stage-managed campaigns. During this period Excell
removed Newtons's most explicitly Calvinistic lines ('But God, who called me here
below . . .') and replaced them with the "ten thousand years" stanza. As the Methodist
son of a German Reformed Church pastor, it's hard to believe that he wasn't aware of
the theological significance of his editing.

The most recent fillip to "Amazing Grace" came not in the midst of a Christian   9
revival but during the new consciousness movement that gathered momentum in
the 1960s and 1970s. Embracing disciplines as varied as yoga, sound-color healing,

geomancy, astrology, rebirthing, and Mind Control, there was no single worldview, as there had been with the Awakenings, but there was a basic shared belief in the need for personal transformation through accessing a higher source of energy. The human problem was not original sin but limited consciousness. Salvation came not through divine rescue but through mind expansion and the awareness of previously hidden powers.

10   Converts to New Age practices were excited by the prospect of tangible, speedily obtained results. Astrological guidance, unlike prayer, didn't require holy living to be effective. Yogic bliss, unlike the biblical "peace that passeth all understanding," could be achieved through correct technique rather than repentance and obedience. The salvation offered by Christ was fully realized only at death, whereas inner healing could be fully realized only in life. Tom Wolfe, in his classic essay "The Me Decade," called it "the third great religious wave in American history, one that historians will very likely term the Third Great Amakening."

11   It was in this climate that "Amazing Grace" first flourished as a pop song, and it's surely no coincidence that the story of Judy Collins's recording begins at an encounter group in New York. In the era of transformative therapies "Amazing Grace" was no longer automatically perceived as a song about the mercy of God but as a celebration of human potential. Wretchedness was no longer a fatal spiritual condition leading to exclusion from heaven but an inability to realize self-worth. (Joan Baez and Odetta had already switched to singing "saved a soul like me.") Grace was not an amazingly supernatural act but a perception-shaking jolt, one frequently induced by altering the body's chemistry.

12   Newton had written it as a testimony to his own rottenness and God's graciousness. It was now being interpreted to mean that we can achieve whatever we want given the right degree of determination. This view was promoted by the psychologist M. Scott Peck in his phenomenally popular *The Road Less Traveled* (1978), in which he combined psychological insight with pseudo-Christian spirituality. The concept of grace was important to Peck and he devoted a quarter of his book to a discussion of it, prefacing the section with four stanzas of "Amazing Grace."

13   A Christian vocabulary was used and Bible verses were quoted but Peck's analysis of the human condition was far from Christian. In his opinion, the central human problem was laziness. We could receive grace if only we did something about it. Pure evil, he argued, was merely "laziness carried to its ultimate, extraordinary extreme." He sounded almost orthodox when stating that grace was a gift of God, but then he qualified it by claiming that we were all potential gods. So where was the gift of grace to be found? The answer was that it is hidden in the ninety-five percent of our consciousness of which we are unaware. "If you want to know the closest place to look for grace," he wrote, "it is within yourself. . . . To put it plainly, our unconscious is God. God is with us. We were part of God all the time."

14   Although released two years before Peck's book was published, the "Amazing Grace" rewritten by New Wave singer Jonathan Richman captures the same spirit. Newton was lost, but Richman just feels that way. Newton gets saved, but Richman just gets to feel good. Grace pursues Newton, but it's inside Richman all along.

> *Well, amazing grace, how sweet the sound*
> *Which brings my joy back again.*
> *Sometimes I've worried so much, felt so lost, but then I always feel found,*
> *And I should know by now that grace is something that's always within.*

If we all possess grace and yet it remains hidden from most of us, an effort of the   15
will or a sudden illumination is required to access it. If Peck is right, grace will favor
those who are determined and resilient, those who are able to focus their energies to
embark on the journey within. This thinking gave rise to the assumption that grace is
something bestowed upon those with grit and self-control, life's champions rather
than life's losers. Grace is the overcoming of obstacles, the rising to any challenge, the
fulfilling of potential.

A TV commercial for the John Hancock Mutual Life Insurance Company used dur-   16
ing the opening and closing ceremonies of the 1996 Atlanta Olympics emphasized this
understanding. It told the stories of four American athletes who had triumphed over
adversity to become Olympic gold medalists. Brief sequences of each athlete were followed by captioned details of the hardships they had overcome. "One of twenty-two
children, Wilma Rudolph wore a leg brace from age six to ten, a victim of rheumatic
fever," said one. "Incredibly, she became the world's fastest woman, winning three
gold medals at the 1960 Rome Summer Games." The only sound during the whole
commercial was an edited recording of Judy Collins singing "Amazing Grace."

The implication was clear. The wretchedness each one had experienced was a   17
physical or social handicap, and the grace that had saved them was contained within
their own determination to succeed. That's what made a champion. All that was required was a vision and the inner strength to follow it. A quote from Jesse Owens,
which closed the sequence, said, "Everybody should have a dream."

The commercial won praise from the advertising industry and according to a *USA*   18
Today viewers' poll was the third most popular spot in the Olympic coverage. To Steve
Burgay, John Hancock's head of advertising, it was an inspired choice not only because
it was a song that already had a deep resonance but because it embodied the Olympic
ideal. "If you look at what these athletes accomplished, it had to do with amazing
grace," he said. "It had to do with more than just their bodies. It had to do with their
spirits. I think that's why people felt that it was a perfect match. You have to have a
certain kind of spirit and spirituality to accomplish what these people accomplished.
That's why 'Amazing Grace' seemed to go hand in hand with their stories."

Some felt "Amazing Grace" was not so much about inner resolve as it was about a   19
moment of mental clarity when a person sees his or her life's meaning and purpose.
Often they related it to forms of intense awareness, such as those experienced during
Zen satori, trance states, and drug highs; Joan Baez, who has been performing the song
for almost forty years, confessed that she was not sure what the word *grace* meant.
"I've never thought about it, but it sounds like the loveliest way to say a form of enlightenment or a form of real gratitude, of giving. It's a state I would like to be in for
more than thirty seconds a day."

If *grace* is another word for this kind of illumination, the blindness of "Amazing   20
Grace" must refer to our limited consciousness. Normal life has a dulling effect. The
range of small things that we have to deal with each day clutters our perceptions.
Grace has a neurological effect on us, allowing us to see clearly, even if only momentarily. During this time we perceive things as they really are and are able to make the
appropriate decisions.

In a sermon on "Amazing Grace," Unitarian Universalist minister Roberta Finkel-   21
stein of Sterling, Virginia, asked what grace is for those who don't believe it originates
with God. "Grace is still a very personal and subjective experience. It is something
indescribable that happens to us when we least expect it, when we haven't asked for
it, and certainly when we don't merit it. Whatever it is, we are transformed by the

experience in the here and now, and sustained by its memory later on. It is what life surprises us with."

22   A related understanding was that "Amazing Grace" is about the loss of ego and the recognition that we are all part of an energy force. What that force is, was of no great concern. This was the thinking of liberal Protestant theologian Paul Tillich, who wrote: "It (grace) strikes us when, year after year, the longed-for perfection of life does not appear, when the old compulsions reign within us as they have for decades, when despair destroys all joy and courage. Sometimes at that moment a wave of light breaks into our darkness, and it is as though a voice were saying: 'You are accepted, accepted by that which is greater than you, and the name of which you do not know.' Do not ask for the name now; perhaps you will find it later." In what appears to be a similar spirit Judy Collins declared, "'Amazing Grace' is a song about letting go, bottoming out, seeing the light, turning it over, trusting the universe, breathing in, breathing out, going with the flow."

23   This is grace as the experiencing of the interconnectedness of things, the mystical state in which the individual sees herself as a molecule in a universal dance of molecules. In her book *States of Grace: The Recovery of Meaning in the Postmodern Age*, Charlene Spretnak defines a state of grace as "consciousness of the unity in which we are embedded" and argues that people can experience this either unexpectedly or through performing a ritual that invites it. "Experiencing grace involves the expansion of consciousness of self to all of one's surroundings as an unbroken whole, a consciousness of awe from which negative mind-states are absent, from which healing and groundedness result. For these reasons grace has been deemed 'amazing.'"

24   Understood like this the force that we are to submit to is anonymous. Grace comes by admitting our limitations and abandoning ourselves to the energy that suffuses the universe in the belief that it has our best interests at heart. This involves total trust because the energy that creates and nurtures may turn out to be the same energy that destroys and inflicts suffering. Judy Collins: "We're always in the path of this power and my own feeling is that agnostics, atheists, spiritual people and devoted church-goers alike all have the same experience because it is talking about forces unseen which are always around us."

25   "Amazing Grace" had global implications for some. They considered it anthropocentric to think of grace only in terms of how it benefits us as humans. There needed to be consideration of how all life could be transformed through international peace, animal welfare, and environmental protection. This touched on the meaning of grace as "elegance of proportion." Amazing grace would take place when everything was in its right relationship with everything else. "Grace means harmony," said Pete Seeger. "Isn't the law of gravity throughout the universe a kind of harmony or the way the ninety-three elements combine throughout the universe or the way that mathematics works? There's harmony there."

26   Seeger's contribution to Ed Sanders's *New Amazing Grace* consisted of four lines that expressed this view:

> *From quarks to stars, there's grace we know*
> *The grace of MC square*
> *And endless more, above, below*
> *We feel the grace is there.*

27   A campaign by the World Wildlife Fund used photographs of dolphins, penguins, a polar bear, and a panda with the slogan, "Amazing Grace . . . Don't Let It Vanish

Without a Trace." As a magazine ad, this was perplexing, Was Grace the name of the penguin or the polar bear, and was this a campaign to prevent their extinction? But a supporting sixty-second TV commercial in which the opening of "Amazing Grace" was played over a collage of images of the natural world made the intention clear. Over dissolving shots of giraffes and African sunsets an unidentified voice described how the planet has given life to more than ten million species: "An amazing place. Truly amazing grace." *Grace*, in this sense, was not a supernatural rescue but a balanced and unexploited natural world. The commentary ends by appealing for help so that "we can keep this planet in a state of grace."

The most widespread understanding of "Amazing Grace" was that it celebrated a general sense of preservation; it was a song about being kept from danger and blessed with good things. The most common contemporary uses of the word *grace* is in the phrase "There but for the grace of God go I," said on seeing someone fall victim to a misfortune. The person saying it usually means: "It could have been me. But it wasn't. And I'm grateful." 28

What would John Newton think of these contemporary interpretations? As someone keen to endorse the good, even if eventually pointing out the bad, I think he would agree that grace bears all of the above characteristics. Grace had opened his eyes. Grace had motivated him. "How unspeakable our obligations to the grace of God!" he wrote to a friend shortly after moving to Olney. "What a privilege it is to be a believer! They are comparatively few, and we by nature were no nearer than others. It was grace, free grace, that made the difference." 29

Grace restrained evil and promoted harmony. He could see examples of God's wisdom and love in nature. After visiting a museum display of then-remarkable mechanical toys, he commented: "Not withstanding the variety of their motions, they were all destitute of life. There is unspeakably more wisdom and contrivance in the mechanism of a butterfly or a bee, that flies unnoticed in the fields, than in all his apparatus put together. But the worlds of God are disregarded, while the feeble imitations of them which men can produce gain universal applause." 30

Grace had protected him before his conversion in his narrow escapes from death. "It extends to the minutest concerns," he wrote to a young girl in 1783. "He rules and manages all things, but in so secret a way that most people think he does nothing when, in reality, he does all." 31

But he would have made an important distinction. General, or "common," grace, extended to all creation but it was special grace that "saved a wretch like me." Although both came from God, they were not to be confused. The grace that through conscience stopped people from being as evil as they could be, would not inevitably lead on to repentance. For that to take place required saving grace. "The convictions of natural conscience, and those which are wrought in the heart by the Holy Spirit, are different, not only in degree, but in kind. The light of a glow-worm and of the sun do not more essentially differ." 32

He believed that everyone benefited from common grace but relatively few benefited from saving grace. He used his own conversion as an example of the difference. His crewmates on the *Greyhound* endured the same Atlantic storm and were brought safely to Loch Swilly (common grace), but only for Newton did the experience lead to spiritual transformation (saving grace). "No one else on board was impressed with any sense of the hand of God in our danger and deliverance," he wrote. "No temporal dispensations can reach the heart unless the Lord himself applies them. My companions in danger were either quite unaffected, or soon forgot, but it was not so with me. 33

I was not any wiser or better than they, but the Lord was pleased to vouchsafe me peculiar mercy."

34   Of all the recent understandings of grace, the two that are most similar in appearance to saving grace, or "amazing grace" as Newton phrased it, are the relinquishing of the ego and mental clarity. Grace, Newton frequently stressed, can only begin when efforts to save ourselves have been abandoned. Yet "throwing yourself on the mercy of God" is not the same as blind surrender to the powers of the universe. Newton saw his submission as being to a knowable being, with a personality and a will, who, because of the crucifixion, had the power to forgive and restore.

35   "We are never more safe, never have more reason to expect the Lord's help, than when we are most sensible that we can do nothing without him," he wrote. "This was the lesson Paul learnt—to rejoice in his own poverty, and emptiness, that the power of Christ might rest upon him. Could Paul have done anything, Jesus would not have had the honour of doing all.

36   "This way of being saved entirely by grace, from first to last, is contrary to our natural wills. It mortifies self, leaving it nothing to boast of, and, through the remains of an unbelieving legal spirit, it often seems discouraging. When we think of ourselves so utterly helpless and worthless, we are too ready to fear that the Lord will therefore reject us whereas, in truth, such a poverty of spirit is the best mark we can have of an interest in his promises and care."

37   Spiritual illumination came as a result of this saving grace and wasn't a requirement for it. You were enlightened because you were saved, not saved because you were enlightened. He didn't discount the value of reason but believed that because it had been corrupted it was unable to accept the verdict that it was corrupt. Only a mind renewed by grace could agree with the doctrine of total depravity and want to repent and follow Christ. Without this renewal, the teachings of Christianity not only appeared ridiculous but were morally offensive. "When the heart is changed, and the mind enlightened, then reason is sanctified," he argued. "[It] renounces its curious disquisitions, and is content humbly to tread in the path of revelation. This is one difference [between faith and rational assent]—assent may be the act of our natural reason, faith is the effect of immediate Almighty power."

38   Grace wasn't a onetime experience for Newton. He attributed his daily protection, his desire to live obediently, and his future hopes to grace. "Amazing Grace" began with the hour he first believed but continued through the dangers, toils, and snares, through death and on into eternity. "The grace of God has a real influence upon the whole man," he once wrote. "It enlightens the understanding, directs the will, purifies the affection, regulates the passions, and corrects the different excesses to which different persons are by constitution or habit inclined."

39   When Newton preached to inmates of a London prison in 1775, he took as his text the words of Paul: "Here is a trustworthy saying that deserves full acceptance: Christ Jesus came into the world to save sinners of whom I am the worst." Some of the men were awaiting execution. He told them the story of his life and "gained their attention more than I expected" (1 Timothy 1:15).

40   As he preached he found himself crying and noticed many of the prisoners also in tears. "Had you seen their present condition and could you hear the history of some of them, it would make you sing, 'O to grace how great a debtor!'" he later wrote. "By nature they were no worse than the most sober and modest people, and there was doubtless a time when many of them little thought what they should live to do and suffer. I might have been, like them, in chains, and one of them have come to preach to me, had the Lord so pleased."

This is the paradox at the heart of "Amazing Grace." Someone as naturally corrupt   41
as any condemned prisoner "sunk in sin, and lost to shame" had been chosen to be
blessed. If he had possessed an unimpeachable reputation or had lived the life of an as-
cetic, he might have been tempted to think that salvation was his just desert. But he
was running from all that was good and godly when he was finally forced to his knees.
He had been given what he didn't deserve. This was, by definition, amazing. This was,
by definition, grace.

Two years after composing "Amazing Grace" he wrote: "That I was ever called to   42
a knowledge of his salvation, was a singular instance of his sovereign grace. That I
am still preserved in the way, in defiance of all that has arisen from within and without to turn me aside, must be wholly ascribed to the same sovereignty. If, as I trust,
he shall be pleased to make me a conqueror at last, I shall have a peculiar reason to
say, 'Not unto me, not unto me, but unto thy name, O Lord, be the glory and the
praise!'"

It's fitting that of all the millions of words that Newton spoke, preached, and   43
wrote (his selected works alone total almost four thousand pages) it should be the
handful that make up "Amazing Grace" that have endured because this was not only
the story of his life but the essence of his message. He was a man appalled at the
depths of his sinfulness and amazed at the heights of God's mercy.

It's impossible to know his story and not to wonder how he would feel if he were   44
to be transported into the twenty-first century and hear the lines he wrote in his attic
at Olney being sung on the street corners of London, in the folk clubs of New York, at
the Brandenburg Gate in Berlin, on the mountainsides of Kenya, and in the secret
churches of China; to hear the phrases he put together coming from the mouths of
rock singers, mourners, antiglobalization protesters, and Christian worshipers of every
denomination in every country in the world.

What he might say is indicated, I believe, in a passage he wrote toward the end of   45
his life. "Perhaps the annals of thy church scarcely afford an instance in all respects so
singular. Perhaps thy grace may have recovered some from an equal degree of apostasy,
infidelity, and profligacy: but few of them have been redeemed from such a state of
misery and depression as I was in, upon the coast of Africa, when thy unsought mercy
wrought for my deliverance.

"But, that such a wretch should not only be spared and pardoned, but reserved to   46
the honour of preaching thy gospel, which he had blasphemed and renounced, and at
length be placed on a very public situation, and favoured with acceptance and usefulness, both from the pulpit and the press; so that my poor name is known in most parts
of the world, where there are any who know thee, this is wonderful indeed! The more
thou hast exalted me, the more I ought to abase myself."

Freewriting

In your notebook, write for ten to fifteen minutes about the thesis of Steve Turner's
chapter—that "Amazing Grace" has served as both an agent and an index of spiritual awakening during crucial periods in American history (including the Civil
War, which Turner addresses in another chapter of his book). You may wish to consider the influence of other songs, like "The Battle Hymn of the Republic" or "We
Shall Overcome," the anthem of the Civil Rights Movement, or various other
songs that have been appropriated in the cause of social change, advertising, or

propaganda. To what extent do songs influence history? To what extent do historical events establish and perpetuate the popularity of particular songs?

Group Work

Share freewrites in your reading group, each member reading aloud while others are taking notes. As you listen to each other read, try to develop a consensus about whether Turner is justified in declaring that "Amazing Grace" is "America's most beloved song."

Review Questions

1. To what three "spiritual upheavals in American life" does Turner connect the history of "Amazing Grace"?

2. How, according to Turner, did the New Age spirituality of the late twentieth century differ from traditional Protestantism in defining grace?

3. How did John Newton distinguish between "common grace" and "saving grace"?

Discussion Questions

1. Although Turner does not accuse any person or group of distorting John Newton's message, he seems to find some appropriations of "Amazing Grace" more fitting than others. Do you think he is too inclusive or not inclusive enough?

2. Do you sense that Turner approves or disapproves of the life insurance commercial referred to in paragraphs 16–18? What words or phrases suggest what his attitude might be?

3. Do you sense that Turner approves or disapproves of the advertisement for the World Wildlife Fund, referred to in paragraph 27? What words or phrases suggest what his attitude might be?

Writing

1. Brainstorm a list of hymns and anthems that might compete with "Amazing Grace" for the distinction of being America's most beloved song. Choose one, research its history on the Internet, and report your findings in a short essay.

2. Locate and read one of the texts that Turner refers to in this chapter (e.g., Tom Wolfe's essay "The Me Decade" or M. Scott Peck's *The Road Less Traveled*). In the case of a book-long text, you might read only the first and last chapters. Write an essay that expands, clarifies, or disputes Turner's representation of that text.

WRITE, READ, and RESEARCH the NET

1. *Write:* Freewrite for fifteen minutes about the appropriateness of television commercials referred to in Discussion Questions 2 and 3, above.
2. *Read:* Review the following website:
   http://www.amazinggracewholefoods.com
3. *Research:* Using the internet, locate other websites that use "Amazing Grace" as a trade name for products or services. Write an essay that supports or rejects the appropriation of sacred or patriotic music for commercial purposes.

 ADDITIONAL READINGS

The following selections extend the topic of popular—if not iconic—music and its relationship to cultural history. First is a condensation of the final chapter of *Sweet Freedom's Song: "My Country 'Tis of Thee" and Democracy in America,* co-authored by Stephen J. Hartnett and the late Robert James Branham. Hartnett, a musician and poet, teaches speech communication at the University of Illinois. Branham was a professor of rhetoric at Bates College. The authors trace the history of the British national anthem and its American counterpart, often referred to by its opening line: "My country, 'tis of thee." Next, Steve Turner, author of *Amazing Grace: The Story of America's Most Beloved Song,* looks at the evolution of rock 'n roll after Woodstock.

"America," "God Save the Queen," and Postmodernity

ROBERT JAMES BRANHAM AND STEPHEN J. HARTNETT

The 1831 premiere of Samuel Smith's "America" in Boston's Park Street Church fea-   1
tured a well-drilled children's choir and the moral pretensions of temperance[1] activists gathered to celebrate a properly righteous July Fourth unsullied by the drunken revelry of their social inferiors. For much of the rest of the nineteenth century the song was employed in a variety of similarly ceremonial but also frequently oppositional occasions. Whether using Smith's original lyrics in dignified celebrations of the nation or any number of the hundreds of parodied variations used to protest the nation's failures, most of the grassroots activists using "America" held the song to be an iconic symbol of American identity. One might argue about whether the promises and ideals of "sweet freedom's song" had been filled and were cause of celebration or whether in fact they had been buried beneath generations' worth of hypocrisy and fear and were cause for protest, but it was generally agreed that democracy was an evolving experiment and that using one's politics, both individually and collectively, was a healthy and productive way of making sure that the nation continued to learn (albeit it slowly,

[1]The temperance movement was an effort to discourage the consumption of alcoholic beverages and to outlaw their sale. (Editor's note)

painfully slowly) how to be more true to its foundational principles. Thus, while "America" was a universally popular *and* contested song, one senses that the myriad groups appropriating it shared the assumptions that democracy was serious business and that participating in political struggle—particularly via song—was part of what it meant to be an American.

2   The gradual development of mass media led, however, to the production of a culture awash in an almost infinite number of images, sounds, and commodities, hence to the creation of a world in which very little is agreed on, let alone shared as an icon worth fighting for. Not surprisingly, "My Country, 'Tis of Thee," played a central role in the evolution of this situation, for it was among the first songs recorded and sold on a mass scale, contributing to the production of what scholars now refer to as "the culture industry." The first commercial recordings were developed in 1889 for use in phonograph parlors, where patrons paid a nickel, spoke the name of a song into a tube, and listened to their selection through a separate tube connected to a phonograph in the room below. In 1890, North American Records developed the first cylinder duplication machinery. Jules Levy, who billed himself "the world's greatest cornet player" and was the first major musician to be exclusively recorded, scored a number-one hit with his 1893 version of "America," as did the Columbia Mixed Double Quartet in 1916. Two different versions, one by "March King" John Philip Sousa's band, charted in 1905. Sousa then included the song in his collection *National, Patriotic, and Typical Airs of All Countries*, which became the standard text for American service bands for the next fifty years. . . .

3   But the culture industry is not monolithic, as both its products and its means of mass marketing have always been open to appropriation by groups of all political and religious persuasions. For example, in 1910, the Mormon Tabernacle Choir achieved national celebrity through the release of their recording of twelve hymns and patriotic songs, including "America." Just twenty-three years earlier, the Mormons had been considered un-American by Congress, which had forced legal and social reforms through the Edmunds-Tucker Act. In response to such persecution, the Choir's recordings blended church songs and patriotic anthems to assert their patriotism. Perhaps as a nod to the complicated costs and benefits of this quintessential example of assimilation, "America" has been regularly featured in the Choir's concerts ever since. The sense that "America" was the nation's unofficial hymn—a claim that . . . was pushed forcefully by the song's author, Samuel Smith—thus merged nicely with the new means of production and distribution enabled by the recording industry. It is wonderfully appropriate, then, that the 25,000-voice choir of the evangelist Billy Sunday recorded "America" in 1918. The song was then included in *Songs for Service*, the popular evangelistic hymn collection compiled by Sunday's musical director, Homer Rodeheaver. Thus, by the early twentieth century, "America" had crossed many contexts—secular and scared, home and stage—to become a staple element of American public life and a touchstone for the discussion of what it means to be an American. One is forced to wonder, however, if the ever-accelerating capability for mass-producing recorded songs and corresponding songbooks—all fetching fancy profits as commodities—has come to the point where there are simply too many objects of consideration for any one of them to fire the collective imagination the way "God Save the King" and then "America" did from roughly 1750 through 1932.

4   The fact that one can discuss national songs and immediately think of "America" is evidence of the foreshortening of our national sense of history and tradition, which in turn closes off options for cultural productions and protest. Indeed, . . . "America" has been sung for the past 260 years *mostly* as a vehicle of protest. One wonderful

example of how our forebears used "America" to lampoon a nation rocketing along on what many thought was a fast track to destruction was George S. Kaufman and Morrie Ryskind's 1931 Broadway musical *Of Thee I Sing*. With its title drawn from Smith's "America," *Of Thee I Sing* lampooned campaign politics in the midst of the Depression. Candidate John P. Wintergreen is elected to the presidency by ignoring the social catastrophes all around him, instead playing up his romance with Mary Turner, who has promised to marry him if he wins. His campaign song (written by George and Ira Gershwin) turns Smith's "America" into a wickedly ironic pop hit:

> Of thee I sing, baby,
> You have got that certain thing, baby.
> Shining star and inspiration
> Worthy of a mighty nation,
> Of thee I sing! . . .

At a time when political leaders seemed incapable of dealing with the country's   5
social problems, *Of Thee I Sing* used "America" to parody vacuous political sloganeering and to caricature the decline of democratic politics into a deadening distraction of romantic and patriotic spectacle.

Four years after *Of Thee I Sing* opened on Broadway, sixteen-year-old Ella Fitzgerald   6
recorded a similar parody of Smith's "America" with the Chick Webb Orchestra. Her "Vote for Mr. Rhythm," released at the height of the Depression, describes an imaginary feel-good candidate:

> Everyone's a friend of his.
> His campaign slogan is:
> "Change your woes
> Into a-wo-de-ho."
> Vote for Mr. Rhythm,
> Let freedom ring,
> And soon we'll be singing,
> Of thee I swing.

With its platform of promised good times, Fitzgerald's "Vote for Mr. Rhythm" is played over the closing credits of D. A. Pennebaker's revealing documentary of the 1992 Clinton presidential campaign, *The War Room*. A song performed as an ironic critique of feel-good politics during the depression is thus revised as an equally ironic critique of feel-good politics in the age of the Teflon presidency.

Whereas Smith's 1831 "America" sings of proud citizens whom we know first   7
gathered to sing the song in a choral form in a temperance gathering in a church, this 1935 parody (and its 1992 appropriation) speaks of cynical citizens who come to recognize democracy as a lark, a romp, "a-wo-de-ho" that leaves the masses swinging. Following Fitzgerald's 1935 "Vote for Mr. Rhythm" and the Gershwins' 1931 title song from *Of Thee I Sing*, "America" was used in the second half of the twentieth century mostly as a humorous prop symbolizing political naïveté and the surreal politics of conventioneers' straw hats and slogan-adorned banners. Indeed, it would appear that the song has become either a token of lost innocence, immediately identified as nostalgic musical quotation, or an object of merciless pastiche in which a song's promises are not only no longer taken seriously but lampooned as the deluded rhetoric of hopelessly idealistic dreamers. . . .

8   For example, Charles Gross's musical soundtrack to Everett Aison's 1968 film *Post No Bills* uses eleven comical variations on "America" (including bluegrass, Dixieland, and cocktail-lounge versions). The ten-minute film opens with a shot of a beautiful lake surrounded by trees; the camera pans to a billboard with the exhortation "Drink Beer!" In the next image, a lone man (Bob Brady) tears down the billboard and burns it, then moves on to destroy another. A police officer catches him in the act and arrests him. As he exits the courthouse after sentencing, he is met by a crowd of cheering supporters who are holding signs protesting billboards. They lift him on their shoulders and carry him to a bar to celebrate by drinking beer, the very activity urged by the billboard he had destroyed. He becomes a celebrity and appears on a television talk show; as he is applauded by the mindless studio audience, he smiles and lights a cigarette. The film ends with this bitter image dissolving to a shot of the protagonist's image displayed on a billboard with the slogan "Smoke the Rebel's Cigarette." Gross's multiple variations on "America" are dispersed throughout the film. Thus, in the year of the assassinations of Kennedy and King, the Tet Offensive, and the riotous Democratic National Convention in Chicago, Smith's song is used to illustrate the voracious banality of a nation in which protest and patriotism have been absorbed as little more than the raw material for corny sloganeering and commercial kitsch. Gross's point would appear to be clear: democracy has become little more than a joke, a façade for consumerism—believing in the promises and possibilities of democracy amounts then to a kind of naïve sentimentalism as outdated as "America."

9   A similar critical use of the song may be found in Chip Lord's 1981 video short *Get Ready to March!* Newly inaugurated president Ronald Reagan is shown waving to the crowd at a parade while the text rolls by explaining that the president's proposed budget for the National Endowment for the Arts will be less than the allocation for military bands. The brilliant soundtrack accompaniment is a trumpeter stumbling through "America," thus symbolizing the perilous predicament of the arts in an age of unprecedented military expenditures. Addressed to an implied audience whose opposition to Reagan has been outvoted, Lord's video concludes with the admonition: "Get Ready to March!" America the nation and "America" the song are here mutually botched by Reagan's headlong rush into barbarism. While Aison's *Post No Bills* and Lord's *Get Ready to March!* offer wickedly biting commentaries, they also illustrate the paradoxical role of "My Country, 'Tis of Thee" in postmodernity. Indeed, whereas prior generations of activists used the song both to criticize the nation and to celebrate its utopian promises, in these two films the song stands as little more than an outdated symbol, a throwback, a decayed reminder of just how completely democracy has slid into meaninglessness. In this sense, then, Aison's and Lord's appropriations of "My Country, 'Tis of Thee" recall "Bitter" Ambrose Bierce's[2] despair. But whereas Bierce and his Gilded-Age contemporaries bemoaned a nation sinking beneath the weight of gross political corruption and deadly capitalist exploitation, our postmodern predicament is generally understood, for better or worse, as more properly cultural, as a result of the incredible multiplicity of images and sounds and tastes and other commodities. . . .

10   One final observation is in order regarding the incomprehensible, almost comically obscene use of "America" for commercial purposes. The list here could be extended at will, but one example will suffice; in this case, the guilty party is AT&T. In a full-page ad in the *New York Times*, complete with a full-size picture of a cordless phone

---

[2]Ambrose Bierce (1842–1914) was a writer of fiction, satirist, and social critic. (Editor's note)

painted in the Stars and Stripes, large letters announce "Two Hundred More Reasons to Let Freedom Ring." Smith's original version of the song . . . was complicated by a variety of tricky intentions and subtle exclusions, yet there is no doubt that he envisioned his song speaking of *political* freedoms. In 1831 "let freedom ring" was a call for the realization of the nation's then-and-still radical promises of justice and equality for all. But in 2000 the phrase "let freedom ring" is a call for a "fifty-dollar-cash-back" deal that, when you sign on to the AT&T juggernaut, includes "NO ROAMING, NO LONG-DISTANCE CHARGES." One cannot imagine a more representative example of the conflation of politics with commerce, of the confusion of the individual's consumption with the community's political obligations.

In contrast to the . . . vulgar advertising version of AT&T, our sense is that one of   11
the most significant factors in the long popularity of "My Country, 'Tis of Thee" is the simple beauty and inescapable presence of the human voice. At the April 1997 Central States Communication Association Conference in St. Louis, for example, Bob [Branham] presented some of the materials in this book to a packed room of fellow historians, rhetorical critics, and music lovers. While Bob told the story of the song, complete with slides and video, friends read some versions of the song while I and others sang some of the variations of the song. The presentation was greeted with something I have never seen before at an academic conference: a standing ovation, complete with some members of the audience crying. It would seem that even the most ironic of postmoderns still want to love their country, still thrill at the sheer depth and wonder of a historical story when well told, and still cherish the simple pleasure of hearing their friends and colleagues and neighbors burst out in a good song—"My country, 'tis of thee, / Sweet land of Liberty, / Of thee I sing," indeed.

The Dream Is Over

STEVE TURNER

In 1969 everyone involved in what was becoming known as "rock culture" believed it   1
looked as though redemption was indeed drawing nigh. The mutant beings that Timothy Leary promised would result from widespread LSD consumption had arrived. The Golden Age prophesied by the gurus was about to dawn. The lost secrets of earlier ages were being uncovered. The Garden of Eden was about to be regained.

There was a call to return to values, many of which could have been endorsed by   2
the early Christian church. People were not to be judged by their outward appearance but by the content of their hearts. Greed, gossip, violence, prejudice, and hypocrisy were to be exposed as hideous sins. Natural beauty was to be celebrated. Brotherhood and sisterhood were to be enjoyed. Communal living was to be encouraged. Above all, there was to be love.

For a while young people the world over appeared united in their appreciation of   3
these simple values and in their avowed rejection of materialism. The most significant conduit for these ideas was rock 'n' roll. Without rock 'n' roll the news about LSD would have taken a long time to travel from New York and San Francisco to Tokyo, Peking, Moscow, London, and Paris. How many would have heard of an Indian guru or an English magician without an introduction by the Beatles or the Rolling Stones?

It wasn't the music alone that spread the word, but the attendant culture of news-   4
papers, magazines, books, events, happenings, festivals, and posters. Interviews with musicians regarded as spokesmen were awaited with anticipation. What will Lennon

have to say about the revolution? What is Jagger's stand on Marxism? Does Dylan think psychedelics are necessary to spiritual growth?

THE WOODSTOCK SPIRIT

5   The event that now stands as a consummation of all this religious yearning was the Woodstock Music and Art Fair, mounted in upstate New York during August 1969. Much of the festival was an orgy of self-congratulation, with newspaper and radio reports of the chaos caused by the sudden influx of people being gleefully quoted from the stage. The owner of the land on which the festival was held announced, "If these are the kids who are going to inherit the world, I don't fear for it." The organizers modestly promoted the "Aquarian Exposition" as "Three Days of Peace and Music."

6   Over that three-day period half a million young people gathered on rough farmland in the Catskill Mountains to listen to some of the era's best rock 'n' roll acts—including Jimi Hendrix, the Who, the Band, the Grateful Dead, Santana, and Joe Cocker. Social order was maintained, without the assistance of outside security forces or riot police. The fences broke down early on, so that it became a free festival. The sanitation gave out, there was hardly enough food, it rained—but there was no stampede, no violence, and no abuse.

7   There were hundreds of "freak outs" from badly produced LSD, there was one birth and one death (from a heroin overdose), but none of the problems expected from such massive crowds and inadequate facilities. The young people's remarkable behavior inspired amazement and delight. "We're all feeding from each other," said one overwhelmed stage announcer. "We must be in heaven, man!"

8   John Sebastian, whose Lovin' Spoonful had been among the pioneer folk-rock bands, had arrived not expecting to play. Slightly stoned and wearing a tie-dyed jean jacket, he was the embodiment of the wide-eyed, groovy, Lennonesque hippie who believed that the kingdom had come but who had been rendered partially inarticulate by the glory of it all. When he was finally coaxed on stage, he gazed out over the solid mass of humanity and marveled, "Far out! Far around! Far down! Far up! You're truly amazing. You're a whole city. And it's so groovy to come here and see all you people living in tents. A flop-house is all you need if you've got love, I tell you."

9   The myth of Woodstock was the same myth that Scott McKenzie's "San Francisco" had promoted two years before: "There's a whole generation / With a new explanation." It was suggested that this was a generation "come of age," able to coexist without the frictions of greed and enmity and free of the interfering hand of the law. These were people who needed only to obey the dictates of their own pure hearts.

10   The subsequent Warner Brothers film, which was to become most people's experience of Woodstock, was edited in such a way that it appeared to endorse the idea of a return to primal innocence. Fans wallowed in mud like newly discovered tribespeople, as if to show that cleanliness was no longer next to godliness. Newly acquainted couples wandered off naked into the long grass to copulate without shame. Good vibrations and happy smiles abounded. Calling for a return to the Garden of Eden, Joni Mitchell wrote "Woodstock," a song that suggested the festival was evidence of an evolutionary surge forward.

11   But Woodstock lasted for only a weekend. For many attenders it was nothing more than a chance to see acts like Jefferson Airplane, Janis Joplin, and Crosby, Stills & Nash for free. It was naive to speculate on great changes in human nature simply because a well-behaved audience had imbibed free rock 'n' roll. Change the circumstances, change the crowd, change the setting, and you could equally well have ended up with a disaster.

The "peace and music" line was upheld because people desperately wanted to believe a change had come. In the decade of Vietnam, assassinations and urban riots, they wanted to prove themselves capable of a new way of living. Drugs, meditation, and the good thoughts inspired by music made them feel as though they had all the love that was needed to bring the world back from the brink. Woodstock was a microcosm of the coming order.   12

END OF THE DREAM

Yet Woodstock fever was short-lived. Within four months came the first of several   13
blows to the notion that a human remedy for sin had been discovered. On a California racetrack, the Rolling Stones were to give a free concert. To illustrate the point that the new generation didn't need the law, it was suggested that instead of security guards, Hell's Angels, the original "noble savages" of postwar American subculture, would serve. It was a symbolic gesture, using society's outlaws to uphold law. These guards wouldn't be paid in cash, but in beer.

But everything that had gone right at Woodstock went wrong at Altamont. Before   14
the day arrived, local astrologers were warning of an ominous conjunction of the planets. On the day itself, bad LSD was producing surges of violence through the crowd. When the Rolling Stones began to play "Sympathy for the Devil," some Hell's Angels knifed a black teenager to death in view of the stage. Mick Jagger turned to his band, saying, "Something very funny happens when we start that number."

In the ensuing commotion Jagger pathetically tried to restore order. His whole   15
message had been based on individual morality—"I'm free to do what I want any old time" ("I'm Free")—and now he was having to play headmaster. "I mean, like people, who's fighting and what for? Hey, people! I mean, who's fighting and what for? Why are we fighting? Why are we fighting? We don't want to fight. Come on. Who wants to fight? I mean, like every other scene has been cool . . ." Confronted with the unacceptable face of evil, His Satanic Majesty was powerless, appealing fruitlessly to reason in the heat of violence, calling not for righteousness but for coolness. It was a terrifying evening, and a sobering vision for those who saw *Gimme Shelter*, the documentary record of the event. On Jagger's next tour of the United States, observers later noted, he wore a large crucifix around his neck.

Although only another rock festival, Altamont is now regarded as the beginning   16
of the end of the utopian dreams of the 1960s. The idea was dawning that maybe the new generation was no different from the old generation; it just had longer hair, a more varied sexual life, and a different range of preferred drugs. "There's nothing in the streets / Looks any different to me," wrote Pete Townshend in the Who single "Won't Get Fooled Again"; "Meet the new boss / Same as the old boss." "Nothing happened except that we all dressed up," commented John Lennon. "The same bastards are in control, the same people are running everything, it's exactly the same. They hyped the kids and the generation."

Other events crowded in to confirm the idea. The deaths, within two years of   17
Brian Jones, Janis Joplin, Jim Morrison, and Jimi Hendrix intensified the general mood of depression, not just because these musicians had been removed as figureheads but also because in each case an uninhibited lifestyle had been responsible for the death.

The breakup of the Beatles amid considerable acrimony not only removed the one   18
group that appeared to unify rock culture but also raised a poignant question: if even the legendary composers of "All You Need Is Love" can't see eye to eye, can *anyone* get along?

THE MANSON LOGIC

19   Equally significant were the series of murders carried out in Los Angeles during 1969 by the Charles Manson "family." Manson had picked up on the dream of a new dispensation, was a regular user of LSD, had dabbled in religion, wrote songs, played guitar, lived in a commune, and idolized the Beatles. Yet Manson had strange dreams. He saw John, Paul, George, and Ringo as the four horsemen of the Apocalypse and took his LSD vision of everything as God to terrifying logical conclusions.

20   Manson argued that as we are all God, it's no crime for one part of God to stick a blade into another part of God. The only moral consideration is whether you feel love as you do it. Love is all you need. He reasoned, "If God is one, what can be evil?" Having instructed his followers to destroy their egos, usually with drugs, he then had them murder for him as they awaited the final holocaust out of which only he and his chosen few would emerge to start the world anew.

21   Where most people paddled, Manson dived in deep. Where most traveled light, he accumulated baggage, until his head was filled with all the fragmented, half-digested philosophies of hippiedom. What was particularly chilling about Manson, though, was the logic. Having dispensed with the idea of an objective God "out there," he jettisoned the morals associated with such a God. He raised the specter of a world of annihilated egos where the strongest ruled and nothing really mattered anyway, because all was part of the anonymous One.

22   "Charles Manson believed in the ancient Hindu assertion that, from the absolute point of view, good and evil, order and disorder, are reconciled in the One," noted R. C. Zaehner, an Oxford professor of Eastern religion. "Believing, he acted on his beliefs, and many a 'rich pig' was to meet a gruesome and untimely end because Charlie, so far from being mad, seems to have had a lucidly logical mind. He took the ambiguities and ambivalences of Indian religion as transmitted to him seriously, but drew conclusions that were the exact opposite of conclusions conventionally drawn."

DIMINISHED EXPECTATIONS

23   Thus the 1960s closed with an air of apprehension. No one wanted to let go of all the small victories of the decade, but then it was hard to believe in an imminent change in the human condition. Writer David Downing captured the mood in an essay on Crosby, Stills, Nash & Young when he commented that "no new premises have been laid down, no other path has been publicly accepted."

24   He continued, "The rejection of one set of social and personal values did not in itself create a new set. That is a long process. In the meantime you . . . create a little harmony for the world of jagged edges little changed by your understanding of it. Crosby, Stills, Nash & Young do that, and only that. No amount of talent can pull a rabbit out of no hat."

25   The spokesmen of rock 'n' roll beat a retreat into rural domesticity, clutching to the most traditional forms of security. On his first post-Beatles album, John Lennon announced, "The dream is over," and in "God" he systematically denied the "myths" of religion, politics, and rock 'n' roll. Having traveled the long and winding road of the 1960s, he could trust only "Yoko and me / That's reality."

26   In a celebrated *Rolling Stone* interview in 1970 Lennon set the tone for the new decade. "I no longer believe in myth, and the Beatles is another myth," he said. "I don't believe in it; the dream is over. And I'm not just talking about the Beatles. I'm talking about the generation thing. The dream is over. It's over and we've got to get down to so-called reality."

Getting down to "reality" characterized the new mood of resignation. Paul   **27**
McCartney retreated to his Scottish farm and forsook the "poetry" that had become associated with Beatles songs.

Bob Dylan, now looking more like a Jewish businessman than a rock 'n' roll star,   **28**
also went into the country and started writing songs that had a considerably narrower focus than anything he'd done before. The celebrated prophet-poet was now content to sing about holding each other tight "the whole night through" and to rhyme "night" with "shining bright." On the albums *Nashville Skyline* (1969) and *New Morning* (1970) he would set up problems only to have them neatly resolved in the arms of his baby.

THE EAGLES AND JACKSON BROWNE

New songwriters coming of age in the 1970s had arrived with hopes of being part of a   **29**
movement, only to find that the concerns had changed. Instead of looking outward or upward, they folded in on themselves, examining their own anxieties in the face of cultural inertia.

This mood of spiritual desolation was perhaps best captured by the Eagles and   **30**
Jackson Browne, musicians reared on sixties optimism who didn't get into the recording studio until the party was all over. The renewed search for meaning in a world stripped of illusion was to become their subject matter.

Don Henley of the Eagles observed: **31**

> The first half of the seventies has been a big escape. We'd come to the end of the sixties when there were people in the streets and everybody took acid and thought it was going to change the world. People were in shock that it really didn't change anything. I'm not saying people should let go of all their dreams and myths, but the seventies seem to have a big value gap.
>
> *Hotel California* is about trying to look at things in a different way, to go from here and try to develop a new set of values and a new thrill that is more meaningful and more valid than one just built on sand. Some of the first thrills had no base, no real root in anything.

The songs of the Eagles, with their sweet vocals and country roll, dealt rather self-   **32**
pityingly with the pilgrimage of laid-back Californians as they gorged themselves on the good things of life while hoping for the peace of mind discovered by mystics and ascetics. Even as they protested the wear and tear they suffered in the fast lane, they seemed to like telling you about the excesses they'd been through to discover the fruitlessness of it all.

Just as the writer of Ecclesiastes had complained, "Vanity of vanities, all is vanity"   **33**
(KJV), and then proceeded to chase the fleeting pleasures of life to try and prove the assumption wrong, so the Eagles took to the road, drove fast cars, chased women, accepted adulation, and downed tequila before writing such remorseful songs as "Take It to the Limit" and "After the Thrill Is Gone."

They really warmed to the theme of hollow hedonism on the concept album   **34**
Desperado (1973). The desperado of the song is a restless man who tries to slake his thirst with earthly pleasures. His problem is that the more he gets, the thirstier he becomes. Whatever fine things are laid before him, he's always yearning for what he doesn't have.

Years later I asked founding member Bernie Leadon (by now a Christian) what he   **35**
felt when he looked back on these songs.

I still think they were all very perceptive of the human condition. But ultimately they offered no answer. There have been a lot of fine blessings laid on our tables, but in the end we do want the things we can't get. Are we ever going to be satisfied? The ultimate answer must be no.

In "Hotel California" they ended up saying we're stuck, we can't get out. It's like we've got all the fast cars and credit cards, but we're trapped. We're victims of our own appetites. We're on a treadmill where we just try to satisfy our physical desires or our emotional needs and so we need more sex, more money, and more food. Then we need more exciting sex and better-tasting food. I've heard people say, "Give me more of everything and then I'll be satisfied." But ultimately you're not.

Jackson Browne was never as self-pitying, but the sense of searching for a lost dream permeates much of his work. Tucked away in his songs are references to the quest for truth and the need to be lifted to a higher level of existence.

36   It was on *The Pretender* that the subject really came into focus for him. Recognizing that a life devoid of purpose eventually immobilizes, Browne made the Pretender a sixties idealist going through a crisis of faith, needing something to believe in yet aware that his earlier dreams have receded. He decides to go for gold, to leap back into the mainstream of life, the epitome of everything he once railed against. Having started out as a bold young optimist, he finally surrenders.

EXOTIC CONVERSIONS

37   Not everyone returned to life as normal. There were those who had lost their bearings after the formless experience of drugs and yoga and who looked for more authoritarian forms of religion where your thoughts were sorted out for you ahead of time. Tired of highs, unsure of what was right and wrong, they wanted to subscribe to strict rules and put themselves under a daily discipline.

38   On an American tour with Fleetwood Mac in 1971, guitarist Jeremy Spencer went missing overnight. Four days later he turned up as a member of the Children of God, a heretical "Christian" cult that later used prostitutes to lure male converts and brainwashing techniques to retain those it already held. When the group's manager finally tracked him down, he found that Spencer had cut his hair, didn't want to rejoin Fleetwood Mac, and was from then on to be known as Jonathan.

39   "He'd been brainwashed, and it nearly killed me to see him," said a roadie who had also gone along to the Children of God commune. "He just mumbled 'Jesus loves you.' He was with about five hundred of these people and they're just like vegetables." Spencer was later allowed by the cult to record albums under his own name, with lyrics that followed the party line.

40   Only the year before, founding member Peter Green had suddenly quit Fleetwood Mac after a London concert, apparently unable to reconcile his growing social concerns with his status and lifestyle as a superstar. There has always been speculation about the role of LSD in this sudden "conversion," but Green took to giving his royalties away to charity and studying Christianity and Judaism. He has never returned to the limelight.

41   The most remarkable conversion came when Cat Stevens, a Catholic by birth, became a Muslim, abandoned his recording career, sold his gold discs, and took up life as a religious educator under the name Yusef Islam. He had been a typical product of his spiritually hungry generation, taking LSD, checking into Buddhism and meditation, playing around with numerology and astrology. Then, in 1975, as one of the superstars of the business, he was to be found saying, "I believe the only thing left in life is to fall in love totally or become spiritual," and "The only person I believe in now is God."

Four years later he was handed a copy of the Qur'an, and he converted shortly   42
afterward. "Up until that point," he says, "I felt that all religions had some facet of the
truth, but not the complete and comprehensive truth. When I read the Qur'an I realized that religion was not something you could concoct. It is either true religion, which
means that it is God's religion, or it is not God's religion. Islam means 'surrender,' and
it's God's religion."

Stevens began to adopt the white robes of Middle Eastern Muslims, prayed faith-   43
fully five times a day, and set up the Islamic Circle, an educational trust based in an old
warehouse in north London. He stopped listening to rock 'n' roll, auctioned off his
guitars because there was "some doubt about the lawfulness of playing stringed instruments," and regarded his past life as a rock star with detachment.

> I used to believe in astrology. I used to believe in I Ching. I used to believe in every-
> thing. But it deluded me into thinking I was getting somewhere. When you finally
> find the right way of living, you can't make it up yourself. If you want the freedom to
> go on making mistakes, it's up to you. If you find something that's guaranteed, that's
> going to take you where you want to go; you no longer have to exhaust yourself look-
> ing. Your final destination on this earth is the grave. So what's the point?

6 *Synthesizing*

In previous chapters, you have paraphrased and summarized isolated texts and passages. More often, research writing involves combining, or *synthesizing*, ideas and information from several sources. If, for example, you wanted to learn more about dirigibles or the early history of your hometown, you would probably consult books, articles, and Web sites. A report of what you discovered would synthesize information from those sources.

There are several techniques for synthesizing sources, the simplest of which consists of two steps: writing a separate summary of each source and then linking those summaries with transitional devices. Following is a demonstration.

A BRIEF SUMMARY REPORT

Suppose you are enrolled in an art appreciation course. Your instructor has divided the class into small groups, providing each with several brief critical appraisals of the work of a contemporary artist. Groups are expected to synthesize these sources in a summary report to be shared with the entire class. Your instructor has made it clear that for this particular assignment—unlike others that will come later in the course—you are not expected to include a list of works cited. Instead, you are to attach copies of your sources and to cite only each author's last name in parentheses at the end of the paragraph in which you summarize his or her appraisal of the artist's work.

A first step is to read carefully each of the three sources that have been assigned to your group, looking for important ideas and underlining noteworthy information.

PRACTICE READING

Brooke Cameron, Professor of Art, University of Missouri

[Thomas] Kinkade is reinventing the wheel: His work is like Currier and Ives. It presents no particular challenge; it's just a nice, nostalgic look at the little stone cottage. His only gimmick is [that] he's the painter of light. So the lights are on in the houses. But this is not exactly breaking new ground. Plenty of painters did this in the nineteenth century. He's offering a warm, fuzzy buzz for people. And if that's what they want, fine. I'm not against that, but he's gotten way more than his due.

I can't imagine why somebody would want one of these things when they could have a real Currier and Ives print. I own some, and I'm very fond of them. They're real. But no way in my darkest day would I ever consider buying a Thomas Kinkade; if I'm going to pay money for art, I want it to offer me something either that I have not seen before or that's an authentic piece of art history. When all is said and done, no one's going to remember Thomas Kinkade as an artistic innovator. They may remember him as a businessman. He's selling something that's very comfortable. There's no poetry in there—it's kitsch. He's sort of a male Martha Stewart.

Karal Ann Marling, Professor of Art History, University of Minnesota–Twin Cities

Most of his works are landscapes with little houses in them. They are suffused with nostalgia, but the people I've interviewed about them think his paintings create a sense of safety and light in a darkened world. So in a way, they're a perfect metaphor for the re-nesting of America. There's nothing controversial about his painting; there's often something religious at least in their implication. He also puts the number of Scripture verses in his pictures, and he shows his devotion to family by putting his wife's initials in the pictures. They repay close attention to detail.

I'm sitting here in my office surrounded by Thomas Kinkade picture puzzles, Thomas Kinkade calendars, Kinkade throws to put on the end of your couch. Clearly this is a major cultural phenomenon, and I thought it was interesting that no one seemed to pay any attention to it. The *New Yorker*, the snottiest of American magazines, wrote a kind of exposé—as though the rest of us didn't already know this. This is popular art, this is how it's made, and all of a sudden, all of these people who've never heard of Thomas Kinkade—presumably they never go to the mall—are insulted by this art movement they know nothing about.

I'm not so sure the critical reception is what counts in any event. People who flock to the Guggenheim don't want to see another damn thing except the Norman Rockwells. It's about time we started paying some respect to artists who manage to engage the popular imagination.

Kinkade knows what he's doing—he writes about it quite compellingly, in fact. He's seen artists such as Albert Bierstadt in the nineteenth century who used landscape painting to say great things about American westward expansion and patriotism. Bierstadt was able to bridge the gap between fine and popular art. We've lost that sensibility, and Kinkade knows about that stuff. He's not some ignorant pissant out there making velvet paintings to hang in the gas station. He's really tapped a deep wellspring of need.

Mark Pohlad, Associate Professor of Art and Art History, DePaul University

He fulfills a need for people to surround themselves with what we used to call craft, which provides for escape and is lovely, and is something that doesn't really ask questions but provides solace and something predictable. It would be so easy to trash Thomas Kinkade, but he meets some kind of need for a great many people who are bright, reasonable, and articulate.

What you can really do with Thomas Kinkade's art that you can't do with real art or great art is own it. If you like something of his work, you can buy a great Thomas Kinkade for $1,500, and he makes it really easy. In the same way, if you go to the Van Gogh exhibition, the final room is a gift shop. They seem to know that people want to have something to prove their artistic experience. There's this appetite to own things that he's good at supplying. They are clearly [in] hideous taste, but there's a sense in which a million people can't be wrong. It's really easy to shrug it off and say it's crap, the equivalent of a Schwarzenegger movie, but something has to be going on there.

One strategy for composing your group report is to summarize the sources individually and then link the summaries with transitions. Writing the summaries is easy enough, but you also need to unify the report with a theme that relates to all three sources. Certainly they all present critical appraisals of the work of Thomas Kinkade. But is there a single statement that can connect all three? Your group could start by paraphrasing the main idea of each source as we have done below:

- Kinkade may be a marketing genius, his work is so imitative that it offers little if anything to consumers, let alone serious collectors.
- In their disdain for the work of Thomas Kinkade, highbrow critics overlook its subtleties and misunderstand its societal impact.
- Regardless of its dubious value as art, Kinkade's work satisfies the needs of a great many intelligent people who enjoy and want to own paintings.

In search of a unifying theme, we can begin with these three observations:

- Few if any traditional art critics esteem the paintings of Thomas Kinkade.
- Kinkade's work is nevertheless in great demand.
- Its popularity may tell us something about the American public.

From these observations, you can discern a central idea that can provide a unifying theme for the group report: *Although many art critics denigrate the work of Thomas Kinkade, his commercial success indicates that he appeals to the tastes and values of millions of Americans.*

Writing the report now becomes easier. Group members can begin by drafting two or three sentences that introduce the topic and state a central idea, then follow them with summaries of the three sources, as in the essay that follows.

I Know What I Like. . . . But Is It Art?

The paintings of Thomas Kinkade are seen everywhere--in calendars and jigsaw puzzles and, of course, above living-room sofas. Consumers and amateur collectors appreciate their warmth, wholesomeness, and religious imagery. On the other hand, those who study and analyze art are usually more skeptical. Although many art critics denigrate the work of Thomas Kinkade, his commercial success indicates that he appeals to the tastes and values of many Americans.

The most frequent critical response to Kinkade's work is disdain. Scholars and critics often view it as so imitative and derivative of nineteenth-century art as to be unworthy of collecting or even owning. If these critics commend anything at all, it is the marketing genius of artist, who has been compared to Martha Stewart (Cameron).

There are, however, scholars and critics who take a different view. They are impressed by the minute details in Kinkade's paintings and by the artist's familiarity with canonical works of art like those of Albert Bierstadt. Those who take this view dismiss Kinkade's detractors as elitists who underestimate his sophistication and fail to recognize or refuse to respect what contributes to public popularity (Marling).

Finally, there are a few critics who, despite their distaste for Kinkade's paintings, have tried to account for its popular appeal. One explanation is that it lies in the individual's desire to own works of art. Kinkade's paintings fulfill that desire because they are affordable (Pohlad).

The debate over Thomas Kinkade probably comes down to the question of whether artistic worth is incompatible with popular appeal. Although the mass marketing of art, music, and literature has been around for more than two centuries, it seems that for some the jury is still out.

There are several things to note about this report. First, it concludes with a paragraph that extends the main idea stated in the introduction. Second, it is divided into paragraphs: one to introduce the main idea, one to conclude the paper, and one for each summary. Although this report could have been a single long paragraph, indentations assist the reader by signaling changes in topic. On the other hand, if the writers had used more or longer sources or had taken more information from each source, more paragraphs might have been needed.

Regardless of how such a report is structured, it is called ***objective*** because it presents information from sources without any overt expression of the report writers' opinions. (In Chapter 7, we consider subjective, critical reporting, in which a writer analyzes or evaluates sources.) Nevertheless, objectivity is relative. For example, this particular report skims over details about the images in Thomas Kinkade's paintings. This may reflect the report writers' personal interests and observations, or simply their assumption that readers are already familiar with the artist's work. Suppose, however, that the same three sources had been read and synthesized by someone very different from these writer—say, a business major, a devout Muslim fundamentalist, a subscriber to the *New Yorker*, or a fan of Martha Stewart's. An objective report by the business major might devote more attention to the marketing of Kinkade's art. Struck by Marling's claim that there is "something religious" about the paintings, the Muslim fundamentalist might respond to Cameron's analysis of light or Pohlad's comments about ownership in ways that others would not predict. Likewise, one who subscribes to the *New Yorker* or who reveres Martha Stewart might be influenced by remarks that other readers would consider insignificant. The point is that each of these readers, indeed all readers, unavoidably—and often unconsciously—connect what they read with other texts and with their personal experiences and interests.

In short, no synthesis is ever entirely objective. Nor is any synthesis a completely definitive report on a topic. Consider, for example, how the writers of the foregoing synthesis might change their approach after reading the following article as a fourth source.

PRACTICE READING

Not a Pretty Picture
Ruined Gallery Owners Call Painter Thomas Kinkade a Double-Dealer*

Richard Jerome, Ellen Piligian, and Alice Jackson Baughn

Thatch cottages, gardens, and gazebos, all wreathed in a gentle haze: The paintings of Thomas Kinkade offer a happy landscape for an anxious age. That quality—and Kinkade's devout Christianity—helps make him, by some estimates, the most collected American artist alive. Reproductions of his work appear in roughly one of twenty U.S. homes, adorning walls, mugs, doormats, even La-Z-Boy recliners.

The call of Kinkadia was irresistible for Thomas Baggett, III, a dentist turned Pentecostal pastor from Lake Charles, Louisiana. Baggett, 49, says he was first exposed to the artist's oeuvre four years ago at one of a national network of Kinkade galleries, this one in a Nashville mall. Mesmerized—and looking for retirement income—he and his wife, Devaney, 39, decided to become dealers. They followed a business plan calling for them to open three Kinkade stores; they were assured,

---

*This article appears on pages 115–16 of the September 8, 2003, issue of *People*.

they say, of netting more than $500,000 a year. "I was told only two dealers had ever failed," Baggett says. "One had cancer and died. The other one ended up in a mental institution."

The Baggetts have ended up in court, suing the Santa Cruz, California-based artist to cover the nest egg they say they lost on their galleries. They're not alone—ten other owners have similar legal disputes. Among the claims are that Kinkade and his publicly owned company Media Arts Group defrauded them by saturating the market with galleries and unloading inventory on discount chains. The chains then sold the artwork for far less than the galleries were obliged to charge. "The pieces we were selling for $479," Baggett says, "they were selling for $59.95."

"Customers thought we were just jacking our prices up," recalls Brian Wittman, 48, who until last year ran a Portage, Michigan, gallery with his wife, Andrea, 42. "My image of Thomas Kinkade was shattered." Once well-off, the Wittmans have struggled. Unable to find work in the same state, Brian, a super-market-chain manager, hired on with a company in Boca Raton, Florida; ex-interior designer Andrea holds a registration job for a Paw Paw, Michigan, hospital. The couple are suing for $5.4 million. Still, the Wittmans feel lucky compared with some dealers they met at a convention last year. "People were crying," says Andrea. "They lost their homes, their kids' education."

Media Arts CEO Tony Thomopoulos counters that those are rare exceptions among the nation's three hundred Kinkade gallery owners. "The vast majority," he says, "are happy and prosperous." San Diego dealer Mike Koligman, head of the national owners' association, agrees. "We've had nothing but good relations with Media Arts," he says. "We're having a good time." Thomopoulos contends that the disgruntled dealers, who bought their inventory on credit, owe the company a total of $5 million and are suing to avoid payment. He notes that Media Arts doesn't prepare business plans—that's up to the dealer (though Baggett and others used planners recommended by the company). Moreover, Thomopoulos calls charges that Media Arts "dumped" merchandise "absurd." The only exceptions, he claims, were a one-time sale at Tuesday Morning stores in December 2001 and offerings on QVC tied to Kinkade's appearances on the TV network four times a year. At the company's request, seven of the ten suits have been sent to binding arbitration, to be decided by a panel of lawyers rather than a jury; the others may go that route as well.

One thing is certain: The dispute contrasts starkly with the artist's painted world, an imaginary idyll that grew out of his hardscrabble youth in rural Placerville, California. Kinkade was five when his father walked out on his mother and two siblings. He found solace in Christianity—"I guess maybe God became the father I never knew," he once said—and in art. After attending Art Center College of Design in Pasadena in the early 1980s, he sold oil paintings out of his garage. But his trademark images—digitally reproduced, then touched up by "high-light artists"— eventually made him wealthy. Last year Media Arts, which he founded in 1990, claimed $32 million in net revenues, turning out everything from $295 lithographs to $10,000 prints on canvas—with Kinkade's blood mixed into the signatures to provide DNA for authentication purposes. In the mid-1990s he launched his network of galleries.

Four of them belonged to Jim Cote, a Michigan entrepreneur who opened his first store in 1996. He and his wife, Barbara, 52, were then worth about three million dollars and had just remodeled their six-thousand-square-foot dream house. "Everything," he says, "was rosy."

Now the bloom is off, and Cote is suing for $14.4 million. After initial success, he says, one gallery tanked, leaving him with debts totaling $500,000—and blasted illusions. "Kinkade's philosophies seemed so noble and pure," Cote says. "Now I feel he was only concerned with his own financial welfare." Divorced since 1999, he claims the failure of his business helped end his marriage. Today Cote lives in a small apartment with his dog Harry. "I'm 53 and I have nothing," he says. "I'm an eternal optimist. But right now it's a little bleak."

If the writers who synthesized the first three sources had considered this article, they might have reached a different conclusion. The four sources could, for example, be synthesized with a thesis like this: "Thomas Kinkade has aroused controversy both as an artist and as the founder of a business empire."

Although synthesis is rarely if ever a simplistic, rule-governed process, the following guidelines can assist you in composing one rudimentary type of report.

GUIDELINES | **Writing a Brief Summary Report**

1. Read each source carefully, looking for important ideas and underlining noteworthy information.
2. Write a one-sentence summary of each writer's main idea.
3. Look for a theme that links the sources. If you can find one, state it in a sentence that can serve as the thesis statement for your report.
4. Write the report:
   - Begin with your thesis statement.
   - Follow with a summary of each source.
   - Link the sources with transitional phrases.
   - End with a general concluding statement or paragraph.

EXERCISE | **Writing a Brief Summary Report**

Following are three newspaper articles published during a three-week period in 2003. Write a brief summary report on these sources using the guidelines detailed above.

Study Links Higher Speed Limits to Deaths

*Danny Hakim**

A report from the Insurance Institute for Highway Safety says increased speed limits on Interstate highways led to nearly 1,900 extra deaths in twenty-two states from 1996 to 1999.

*This article appears on page A12 of the late edition of the November 24, 2003, issue of the *New York Times*.

The report, which will be released on Monday, says people are adjusting to drive above the new limits. . . .

In 1995, the federal government repealed its speed limits—55 miles per hour, or 65 on rural Interstates—and sent authority back to the states.

Twenty-eight states have raised rural Interstate speed limits to at least 70 miles an hour. For a time, Montana had no daytime speed limits on some highways, requiring one to drive in a "reasonable and prudent manner." The state became something of a destination spot for drivers searching for an American version of the autobahn. . . .

The state also found its "reasonable" approach open to legal challenge and has since imposed a 75-mile-an-hour Interstate limit.

The Insurance Institute's report has several components. It highlights a recent study by the Land Transport Safety Authority of New Zealand, which appears to have done a more thorough study of the increased speed limits in the United States than the Transportation Department, which was essentially taken out of the business of setting speed limits by Congress.

The New Zealand study focuses on twenty-two states that raised their limits to 70 or 75 mph almost immediately after the repeal of the federal cap. Trends from those states are compared with trends in twelve states that kept their limits at 65. The study found 1,880 more deaths on the Interstates in those twenty-two states from 1996 to 1999, though the authors noted that geographical effects might have skewed the results because most of the states that went to 75 were in the West.

The institute's researchers also looked at trends in six states and five cities, some that raised limits and some that did not. The finding appears to show that drivers in states with higher speed limits drive faster.

In Maryland, where the Interstate speed limit is 65 mph, the mean speed was 66. About one percent of drivers exceeded 80 mph. By contrast, in Colorado, where the Interstate speed limit is 75, the mean speed was 76. About a quarter of drivers regularly went over 80. . . .

The consensus of most traffic safety researchers is that raising speed limits is harmful.

"Speed is central to safety," said Leonard Evans, a safety researcher who worked for General Motors for more than three decades. "The largest yearly traffic fatality decline ever recorded in peacetime in the U.S. was in 1974, the first year of the nationwide 55 mph speed limit."

Dr. Evans noted that there were other factors involved, but "a major portion of the sixteen percent decline, from 54,052 in 1973 to 45,196 in 1974, is related directly or indirectly to the speed limit change."

"Increasing speed limits reverses the process," he added.

Studies by the federal government have offered similar findings.

Of course, gauging the effect of any one issue on traffic fatality rates is not easy. For decades, death rates in the United States have been inching down as traffic safety has improved, though rates are not declining as quickly as in some other leading nations. And nearly 43,000 people died last year in traffic-related accidents, more than in any other year since 1990, partly because the nation is driving more as the population increases and suburban sprawl continues.

There are various problems, from increases in drunken driving to the widely debated effects of sport utility vehicles. Perhaps the most potent factor is that seventy-nine percent of Americans wear seatbelts, meaning twenty-one percent do not.

Although most researchers said that raising speed limits had been bad for safety, Colonel Driscoll of the Montana Highway Patrol said a speed limit that would be appropriate in New York City would not work in Montana.

"A lot of people go to the hospital in Billings," he said. "If you're in Sidney, Montana, and need to go to Billings, you have to go 270 miles. In New York, you probably have to go 2.7 miles to get to a hospital.

"You can lose a whole day going 55."

If You're a Speedster, Say 'Janklow' Slowly

Al Neuharth[**]

More than seventy-one percent of licensed drivers across the USA admitted they exceed speed limits in a poll taken this year by AAA. That is more than 138 million of us breaking the law.

This week, habitual speedster Bill Janklow, longtime and highly regarded South Dakota governor and congressman, was convicted of manslaughter. He ran a stop sign last August at more than 70 miles an hour in a 55-mph zone, killing motorcyclist Randy Scott.

Records show Janklow received twelve speeding tickets from 1990 to 1994. He always was in a hurry and often boasted of how he burned up the road.

The crash and his conviction ended more than thirty years of public service. No matter what his sentence on January 20, at age 64 Janklow's life now is about as sad as it can get.

My native state of South Dakota, where I return and drive frequently, is one of more than a dozen states where the speed limit on Interstates is 75 mph. Even so, if you travel at that legal limit, many cars and large trucks gun by you.

The magnitude of the nation's speeding problem:

- Last year, 13,713 died in speeding accidents.
- The economic cost of speeding-related crashes was $40.4 billion.

Prior to Janklow's accident, I often had a heavy foot on the pedal. Now that the enormity of his accident has sunk in, here is my early New Year's resolution, which I vow not to break: "All speed limits in cities or on the open road will be strictly observed by me, no matter how many impatient drivers in a hurry honk or holler their way past me."

I'll just keep repeating "Janklow" to myself slowly and count my blessings that I came to my senses before a tragedy like his befell me.

In the Land of the Lead Foot

Judy Blunt[***]

Westerners—especially we Montanans—are used to being lampooned as a pack of lead-footed sociopaths bent on expressing our individual and constitutional freedoms by driving as fast as we please, wherever we please, and maybe cracking a can of suds on the way.

[**]This article appears on page 13A of the December 12, 2003, issue of *USA Today*.

[***]This article appears on page A43 of the late edition of the January 12, 2003, issue of the *New York Times*.

"In Montana you don't see many posted speed limits," David Letterman, the recipient of a few speeding tickets himself, once joked. "So, when the police car pulls alongside of me, of course I immediately assumed he wanted to race." Last spring the head of a local chapter of Mothers Against Drunk Driving made national headlines with outrageous assertions that Montana drivers measure their cross-state travel in bottles of beer: a six-pack between this town and that, a case to cross the state.

With the conviction Monday of Representative Bill Janklow of South Dakota for vehicular manslaughter, the West's fondness for fast driving is again in the news, this time as part of a tragedy. Mr. Janklow sped through a stop sign near his hometown, Flandreau, South Dakota, last August and killed a motorcyclist. He has resigned from the House and faces up to eleven years in prison.

Mr. Janklow's very conviction is proof that Westerners' love of speed has its limits. But the limits are those dictated by duty and personal responsibility, not by law.

Almost three decades ago, many Western states resisted the federally imposed energy-conservation speed limit of 55 miles per hour—and for understandable reasons. On the highways, rural drivers tend to be destination drivers: business in Havre, school in Bozeman, shopping in Billings. Towns are hundreds of miles apart on roads that stretch to the horizon. Off the freeway, you can travel miles without meeting another car, and hundreds of miles without seeing one of the few dozen Highway Patrol officers scattered across thousands of miles of roadway on any given shift.

Rather than dictate a common speed, most states relied on a driver's common sense. Forced to comply with what was considered an unreasonably low national speed limit, Montana circumvented it by imposing an inconvenience fine for simple speeding—five dollars, payable at the roadside—and charging the truly reckless speeders huge fines. I grew up hearing about people who traveled across the state with a stack of five dollar bills in the glove box, but I never met anyone who did that.

When the national speed limit was lifted for rural sections of Interstates in the late 1980s, almost every state posted higher limits. Montana laws, however, simply reverted to their original "reasonable and prudent" language, requiring drivers to use good judgment in maintaining a safe speed given weather, road and traffic conditions, and the state of their vehicle.

Yet instead of becoming known for our expectation of reasonable behavior, Montana quickly gained a reputation as the place to go if you wanted to drive recklessly. The myth became reality.

Western attitudes about speed limits have always been misconstrued: we do not encourage deviant behavior so much as personal responsibility. It's an antiquated stance, this resistance to limiting individual freedom, and it is often used as evidence of our irresponsibility. For example, Montana voted down an open-container law in the last legislative session. On the highway or the back roads, driving with an open beer is still legal.

Does this encourage drunken driving? Not necessarily. Our DUI laws are appropriately harsh. We can hold individuals accountable for bad choices without limiting everyone's freedom.

Of course, debates over abstract principles will not provide any solace to the friends and family of the man Mr. Janklow killed, Randy Scott. Nor will new laws and posted limits. The laws already on the books—against speeding, running a stop sign, driving recklessly—did not stop Mr. Janklow or prevent this tragedy.

> It would be a mistake, however, to conclude from this sad affair that we Westerners are more tolerant of careless or negligent driving than people elsewhere. No matter where you live and drive, society has a right to expect one rule that cannot be legislated: reasonable and prudent behavior. And anyone who thinks reckless behavior is unique to the rural West didn't commute this morning.

 # AN OBJECTIVE REPORT ON SOURCES

Some reports focus less on a topic—on the information *within* sources—than on the sources themselves. This kind of report can be composed in much the same way as a brief summary report. The main difference is that a report on sources refers specifically to its sources, saying, in effect, "Source A says this; Source B says this; Source C says this. . . ." A report on sources can be subjective (presenting your own analysis and opinions), but for now we will consider objective reports. Following is an example.

Suppose you are reporting on two editorials that debate the issue of how to memorialize Ronald Reagan's presidency. Since your report presents the opinions of other writers, it must refer specifically to both sources. Before reading the editorials, look at their titles, at least one of which indicates the author's position. Next, try to locate each writer's thesis statement. Finally, read both editorials with a pencil, marking important information and ideas.

PRACTICE READING

Reagan Deserves Landmarks

Jim Martin *

It's a bit sad, but perhaps to be expected, that both friends and political opponents of Ronald Reagan have seized upon his death to argue publicly about the proper way to honor him.

The Ronald Reagan Legacy Project, launched in 1997 by conservative activist Grover Norquist, seeks to honor the former president by naming in his honor "significant political landmarks" in the fifty states and more than three thousand U.S. counties, "as well as in former communist countries across the world." Others would like to see his face on the ten-dollar or twenty-dollar bill. And even others would like to see his face carved on Mount Rushmore.

Columnist Marianne Means, a frequent critic of the late president during his White House years, is among those who think the rush to carve and print is all wrong. Arguing that "simply renaming objects" does little more than "make dedicated fans feel good." Ms. Means sides with the former first lady Nancy Reagan, who wants "to identify her Ronnie with a cause that can keep his legacy alive."

---

*Jim Martin is president of the Sixty Plus Association, a conservative senior citizens's advocacy group. This editorial appears in the September 17, 2004, issue of the *Morning Star*, a Wilmington, North Carolina, newspaper.

I offer two modest proposals to keep the legacy alive, both of which should make friend and foe equally happy. They represent causes with which President Reagan and President Reagan alone among our former leaders will be identified by historians.

No, Grover, champion tax-cutter that he was, Mr. Reagan is not the only tax-cutting president to occupy the White House, so I am not suggesting that we rename the Treasury Building in his honor.

But "bricks and mortar" is a good way to remember a fallen hero.

And what better way to remember Ronald Wilson Reagan than by naming all of the U.S. embassies, in all of the countries liberated from communist oppression during his administration, in the fortieth president's honor.

The list would be substantial: the Czech Republic, Estonia, Georgia, Grenada, Hungary, Latvia, Lithuania, Poland, Romania, Russia, and on and on. Thanks to Mr. Reagan's leadership, vision, and gutsy determination, tens of millions of men and women are free today because he refused to accept the status quo of the Cold War.

And while we're at it, I think it would be fitting to rename the U.S. embassies in Germany and Japan in FDR's honor.

As much as the victory over communism was Mr. Reagan at his best, so was his brave confrontation with the ravages of Alzheimer's disease. So my second proposal is this: Let's rename the National Institutes of Health the Reagan National Institutes of Health in honor of the fortieth president.

NIH describes itself as "the steward of medical and behavioral research for the nation." Its twenty-seven institutes and research centers include the National Cancer Center, National Center on Minority Health and Health Disparities, National Human Genome Research Institute, National Institute on Aging, National Institute of Mental Health, National Institute of Neurological Disorders and Stroke, and National Institute of Nursing Research, to name but a few.

What better way to say "thank you for a job well done" than to entrust the former president's name to the organization leading the fight against Alzheimer's, cancer, Parkinson's, and the other scourges of today?

President Reagan accepted his fate and retired from the public's view. We remember him today as a man of great strength who turned back communism. Let's also remember him in the future as a man of great faith who inspired others to find "the cure."

PRACTICE READING

The Rename Game

E. J. Dionne*

Perhaps we should simply rename ourselves the Ronald Reagan United States of America.

For the Gipper's supporters, nothing is ever enough. Congress named Washington National Airport for Reagan, but this month, Representative Bob Barr threatened federal funding for the area's Metro system because the train stop at the airport still carries National Airport's old name.

---

*E. J. Dionne is a syndicated columnist for the *Washington Post*. "The Rename Game" appears in the March 23, 2001, issue of that newspaper.

Barr said he would "take steps to tie further and future funding to Metro to make sure that the Ronald Reagan Washington National Airport is reflected correctly on all Metro maps, signs and documents." Making all these changes would cost the system $400,000. That didn't bother the fiscally conservative Barr. Barr has joined but a tiny skirmish in the overall battle plan of the Ronald Reagan Legacy Project. Grover Norquist, the project's president, recently had this to say to a congressional committee:

> It is our goal at the [Ronald] Reagan Legacy Project to preserve his legacy by encouraging governors, state legislators, and the general public to become involved in the process of naming at least one significant landmark or institution after Reagan in all fifty states and 3,067 counties as well as in former communist countries. . . . Nationally, we have also begun work on placing Ronald Reagan's portrait on the ten-dollar bill.

Where have you gone, Alexander Hamilton? The man whose portrait currently graces our ten-dollar bill was a Founding Father, an author of the Constitution and the Federalist Papers, our first Treasury secretary, and the prophet who envisioned a strong national government and the rise of the United States as an industrial nation. But Hamilton must be a chump compared with the Gipper.

And by the way, Norquist offered that testimony in support of a bill to plan a monument to Reagan on the National Mall.

Norquist is no fool. He's one of the most determined and well-connected conservative activists in the nation—the Lenin of the contemporary right. He understands the importance of creating a usable past.

If enough monuments are built to Reagan, if enough airports, highways, bridges, tunnels, parks, schools, hospitals, and subway stops are named after him, this generation will seal the Reagan Revolution as the most important moment in American history. Or so, at least, is the hope.

You can't blame an ideologue for pursuing his dream. But we can blame ourselves if we fall into line behind an effort to distort the country's history for political purposes.

Yes, Reagan had accomplishments that transcend ideology. He deserves a decent share of the credit for the end of the Cold War and the fall of the Soviet Union—even if Reagan himself did not foresee that the Evil Empire would crumble so quickly. It's fair to say that the momentum in the Cold War shifted under Reagan.

But this Reagan monument effort is driven by conservatives who care primarily about domestic policy and politics—and on those, there is no consensus on the meaning of the Reagan years. Where you stand depends on your priorities and your values.

Still, let's take the Ronald Reagan Legacy Project as an opportunity to consider whether we have given the memories of relatively recent presidents the respect they deserve. Personally, I think Harry Truman and Lyndon Johnson deserve better than they've gotten. But in deference to the party spirit behind the Reagan movement, let's narrow our focus to Republican presidents.

If you do that, the case is overwhelming that Dwight Eisenhower is the great unheralded figure of the last half-century. Even if he had never become president, Eisenhower would deserve our gratitude for his skill in leading the Allied forces against Hitler. If we had lost that one, there would be no democratic legacy, let alone a Reagan Legacy.

And despite many criticisms leveled against him during his presidency and since, Eisenhower successfully presided over the great transition in our national life from the crisis years of Great Depression and world war to the era of prosperity whose fruits we still enjoy. He got the Republican Party to make peace with the New Deal—had that not happened, Reagan would not have happened—and he kept the nation safe and out of war at a moment when neither was inevitable.

The Eisenhower Legacy Project has a nice ring to it and great bipartisan possibilities. After all, long before he became a Republican, Ronald Reagan was a member of Democrats for Eisenhower.

As in the case of the previous report, a logical step now is to formulate briefly the main idea of each article:

- Jim Martin, president of an organization of conservative senior citizens, offers two proposals for memorializing the presidency of Ronald Reagan.
- *Washington Post* columnist E. J. Dionne argues that in its zeal to create memorials, the Ronald Reagan Legacy Project has exaggerated the former president's accomplishments and minimized those of some of his predecessors.

Following the guidelines on page 222, we can now write the report:

Memorializing the Legacy of Ronald Reagan

Since 1997, the Ronald Reagan Legacy Project has been advocating various ways of honoring the former president. Jim Martin, president of an organization of conservative senior citizens, though skeptical of some of the suggestions that the Project has advanced, offers two proposals that he considers appropriate and acceptable to nearly everyone. First, Martin would put Reagan's name on the U.S. embassy in every former communist nation. This, he believes, would recognize Mr. Reagan's role in bringing about the demise of world communism. Next, he would name the National Institutes of Health for Reagan, thus honoring the former president's long and valiant struggle with Alzheimer's disease (11A).

On the other hand, Washington Post columnist E. J. Dionne argues that in its zeal to create memorials, the Ronald Reagan Legacy Project has exaggerated the former president's accomplishments and minimized those of some of his predecessors. Dionne believes that the Project's efforts are motivated more by political objectives than by reverence for the late former president. Dionne acknowledges Reagan's accomplishments in the area of foreign policy but argues that, overall, his legacy is no greater than that of Harry Truman, Lyndon Johnson, or especially Dwight Eisenhower (A25).

Works Cited

Dionne, E. J. "The Rename Game." Washington Post 23 Mar.
        2001: A25.

Martin, Jim. "Reagan Deserves Landmarks." Morning Star
        [Wilmington, NC] 17 Sept. 2004: 11A.

Three things should be noted about the way this report is written. First, it lacks a concluding paragraph or statement. Although one could have been added, a short report like this does not usually require a separate conclusion, since the reader does not need to be reminded of its purpose. Conclusions are unnecessary also when you have nothing new to add to what you already have written. Second, the report is presented in two paragraphs. Since the introduction is a single sentence, the first editorial need not be introduced with a paragraph break. There is a break for the second paragraph, however, because here the reader needs to be alerted to the change in subject. Finally, the report aims to be objective, presenting the views of both editorialists without commentary. (The statement "Jim Martin . . . offers two proposals" shows that the opinion expressed in that paragraph is not necessarily that of the person writing the report.) One question to ask, however, is whether the order in which the summaries are presented makes a difference. Would the report have a different effect if the editorials had been summarized in reverse order?

Also noteworthy is the fact that the writer has identified her sources under the heading "Works Cited." The significance of this element of the report is explained in the following section of this chapter.

 ## THE OBLIGATION OF ACKNOWLEDGING SOURCES

Whenever you compose a summary report or any other type of writing that relies on sources, you create something new for others to read. Although what you produce may seem less than earth-shaking in significance, you are nevertheless adding, in however small a way, to the sum of the world's knowledge. You are making a contribution to the domain of scholarship. That may sound lofty, yet it is still true that your writing makes you a member of the fellowship of scholars, past and present, subject to all the benefits and obligations of that august body.

One of the principal benefits of being a scholar is that you are entitled to read—as well as to use—the scholarship of others. You have a right, for example, to write a summary report based on any sources you can find. Presenting your research and ideas for others to use is in fact one of the obligations of scholarship. We must work together, sharing our findings, if humanity's search for knowledge and understanding is to progress.

Another of your obligations as a scholar is to acknowledge your sources. In the group report found on pages 218–19, even though the writers have attached copies of their sources, they are required to use parenthetical notes to make clear that the ideas and opinions presented have been expressed by others. Likewise, the objective report on sources found on pages 229–30 uses both parenthetical notes and a list of works cited, and in that regard it is typical of almost every type of research-based writing.

Whenever your writing is based on research, you should make sure that readers know which ideas and discoveries are your own and which you have taken from sources. You must give your readers accurate and complete information about what those sources are and where they can be found. Acknowledging your sources is important for two reasons:

- Credit must be given where it is due. Creators of ideas deserve to be recognized. Whenever you present material without acknowledging an outside source, readers assume that you are the author of that material. When students err in this regard, they usually do so unintentionally, because of inexperience. However, when writers deliberately present another's work as their own, they are guilty of *plagiarism*. (See pages 399–402 for a further discussion.)

- Readers need to know where they can locate your sources so they can consult the original versions. This allows them not only to check the accuracy of your citations, but also to find additional material beyond what you have presented.

The List of Works Cited

A writer adds a list of works cited to a research paper to identify sources. The list provides enough information for readers to identify each source and to locate it if they wish. Although this information might be presented in various ways, writers generally follow a standard *format*, a prescribed method of citing information. Different fields adhere to separate formats. If you are writing a paper for a psychology course, for example, you may be expected to follow a format different from the one you would use for a history paper. The lists of works cited for the two preceding summary reports follow a format known as **MLA style**, which is prescribed by the Modern Language Association, an organization of scholars in English and other literatures and languages. Research papers written for composition courses use this format more often than any other, and it is the one that we feature throughout this book. (Other widely used formats are explained in Chapters E and F in Part II.)

Each different type of source—a book, say, or a government document or a motion picture—is presented in a particular way in an MLA-style list of works cited. For now, we will examine only three of the most common types of sources: books and articles in magazines and newspapers. Formats for other sources, along with more detailed information about MLA-style documentation, can be found in Chapter A of Part II.

Suppose that you have used a passage from a book titled *Intimate Readings: The Contemporary Women's Memoir* by Janet Mason Ellerby. Here is how you would cite that source in an MLA-style list of works cited:

Author   *Title of book*

Ellerby, Janet Mason. Intimate Readings: The Contemporary

Women's Memoir. Syracuse: Syracuse UP, 2001.

  City of publication *Publisher* *Year of Publication*

The entry consists of three general categories of information, each followed by a period and presented in this order:

1. ***The author's name.*** Give the author's last name, followed by a comma, then the author's first name, followed by middle name or initial (if either is cited in the book's title page).

2. ***The complete title of the book, including any subtitle.*** Capitalize the first word of the title (and of the subtitle, if there is one) and of all subsequent words except for articles (*a, an, the*), conjunctions (*and, or, but, nor*), and prepositions (*in, from, to, between*, and so on).

3. ***Information about publication.***
   —***The city (and state, if the city is not a major one) in which the book was published.*** Follow this with a colon.
   —***A shortened form of the publisher's name.*** The shortened form always omits articles, business abbreviations (*Inc., Corp., Co.*), and words such as *Press, Books*, and *Publishers*. If the name of the publisher is that of an individual (e.g., William Morrow), cite the last name only; if it consists of more than one last name (e.g., Prentice Hall), cite only the first of them. If the name contains the words *university press*, they must be signified by the abbreviation *UP*. Follow the publisher's name with a comma.
   —***The year of publication.*** End the entry with a period.

Now suppose you have used an article in *New Scientist*. Here is how you would cite it:

Author　　　　　　　　　　　　　　　*Title of article*

Pain, Stephanie. "Why the Pharaohs Never Smiled: Life in Ancient

　　　　Egypt Was Very Civilized—Until You Needed a Dentist."

　　　　<u>New Scientist</u> 2 July 2005: 36-39.

　Name of magazine　　　*Publication date*　　　*Pages on which article appears*

This entry consists of the same three categories of information, with only slight variations in the last two. Instead of being underlined, the title of the article is placed in quotation marks. Information about publication is presented as follows:

1. *The name of the magazine.* Underline it. Do not follow it with any mark of punctuation.
2. *The publication date.* List the complete date—day, month, and year for a weekly or biweekly magazine; month(s) and year only for a monthly or bimonthly magazine; or season and year for a quarterly magazine. Abbreviate all months except May, June, and July. Follow the date with a colon.
3. *Page number(s).* List the page number(s) on which the article appears. Do not include the word *page(s)* or any abbreviation such as *pg.*, *p.*, or *pp.* If the pages are not continuous (if, for example, an article were printed on pages 34, 35, and 40), cite the number of the first page only, followed by the symbol +.

Entries for newspaper items are much the same. Following are two typical examples:

Author　　　　　　　*Title of article*　　　　　　*Name of Newspaper*

Shimron, Yonat. "Anger and Spirituality." <u>News and Observer</u>

　　　　[Raleigh] 14 June 2002: 3E.

　　　　　Publication date　　　*Page on which article appears*

Brown, Patricia Leigh. "A Push to Save Reno's Landmarks as Divorce

　　　　Capital." <u>New York Times</u> 21 Apr. 2002, natl. ed.: sec. 3: 7.

　　　　　　　　　Publication date　　　*Edition*　　　*Section*　*Page*

One difference between these entries and the example for magazine articles is that a section of the newspaper is cited. When the section is designated by a letter, as in the first instance, it is incorporated into the page number; when designated by a number, as in the second instance, it is cited separately with the abbreviation *sec.* You will also notice that the second entry cites *natl. ed.,* since the *New York Times* appears in separate late and national editions. Finally, when the title of a city newspaper (as opposed to a national paper such as the *Wall Street Journal* or *USA Today*) does not include the city in which it is published, the name of that city should be enclosed in brackets—not parentheses—after the title.

List entries alphabetically. If the author of a source is not named, introduce the entry for that work by title and alphabetize accordingly (ignoring the words *a, an,* and *the*). Do not number the items. Entries that occupy more than a single line are **outdented** (the reverse of indented); that is, the first line begins at the left margin and each subsequent line is indented half an inch. Notice how this format is applied in the following excerpt from the list of works cited in a report on the cultural implications of interstate highway construction.

Crouch, Andy. "Interstate Nation." <u>Christianity Today</u> 10 June
    2002: 55.

Finch, Christopher. <u>Highways to Heaven: The Auto Biography of</u>
    <u>America</u>. New York: Harper, 1992.

Gillespie, Angus Kress, and Michael Aaron Rockland. <u>Looking for</u>
    <u>America on the New Jersey Turnpike</u>. New Brunswick, NJ:
    Rutgers UP, 1992.

"Interstate Highway System." <u>Civil Engineering</u> Nov.-Dec. 2002:
    140.

Kilborn, Peter T. "In Rural Areas Interstates Build Their Own
    Economy." <u>New York Times</u> 14 June 2001, late ed.: A1.

St. Clair, David James. <u>The Motorization of American Cities</u>. New
    York: Praeger, 1986.

Weingroff, Richard F. "The Genie in the Bottle: The Interstate
    System and Urban Problems, 1939-1957." <u>Public Roads</u>
    Sept.-Oct. 2000: 2-25.

Consult Chapter A of Part II for more information relating to lists of works cited.

A Brief List of Works Cited

Suppose you have been asked to report on grade inflation using the following sources. Write an MLA-style list of works cited. Be careful to follow the guidelines governing format precisely.

a. A book by Alfie Kohn titled *What to Look for in a Classroom and Other Essays*, published in San Francisco, California, by Jossey-Bass in 2000.

b. An article by Gregory Stanley and Lawrence Baines titled "No More Shopping for Grades at B-Mart: Re-establishing Grades as Indicators of Academic Performance," published in the March–April 2001 issue of *Clearing House*, on pages 227–30.

c. An article titled "Who's Been Cheating?" published in the October 5, 2002, issue of *Economist*, on page 15. No author is cited.

d. An article by Richard Rothstein titled "Doubling of A's at Harvard: Grade Inflation or Brains?" published in the December 5, 2001, late edition of the *New York Times*, on page 8 of section D.

Parenthetical Notes

A list of works cited identifies your paper's sources *in their entirety*. A ***parenthetical note***—a note placed in parentheses within your paper—identifies the *specific* location within a source from which you have taken a quotation or a bit of paraphrased information. Unlike the more complicated and cumbersome footnotes and endnotes, parenthetical notes employ a clear and efficient type of shorthand: They supply the least amount of information needed to identify a source about which more detailed information can be found in the list of works cited.

The beauty of parenthetical notes is their simplicity. MLA-style notes usually contain only two items: the author's last name and the page(s) from which the quotation or paraphrased information has been taken. For example, assume that one of your sources was Stephanie Pain's article in *New Scientist*, cited on page 233 as follows:

```
Pain, Stephanie. "Why the Pharaohs Never Smiled: Life in Ancient

     Egypt Was Very Civilized--Until You Needed a Dentist."

New Scientist 2 July 2005: 36-39.
```

Any notes within your paper need only refer the reader to this citation. To indicate that the following sentence captures the main idea of that article in your own words, you would include the parenthetical note shown here:

```
Forensic evidence indicates that most ancient Egyptians

suffered from poor dental hygiene (Pain 36-39).
```

On the other hand, if you wished to paraphrase information found on page 37 of the article, you would provide a different parenthetical note:

```
The ancient Egyptians' diet contributed to severe dental

abrasion (Pain 37).
```

In either case, the note is placed at the end of the sentence but preceding the period. Observe also that in the second case, the note tells you only the *specific page* on which paraphrased information appears. (In contrast, the first parenthetical note, like the entry in the list of works cited, shows the page numbers on which the *entire article* is printed.)

When the author's name is unknown, cite instead the first word or two of the title. Suppose, for example, you wanted to paraphrase something from the fourth item in the list of sources concerning highway construction. That anonymous article is cited as follows:

```
"Interstate Highway System." Civil Engineering Nov.-Dec.

        2002: 140.
```

Your parenthetical note would look like this:

```
("Interstate" 140)
```

If you name the author (or, in the case of an anonymous article, if you cite its title) within the text of your paper, thus identifying the source, a parenthetical note provides only the page number(s). See, for example, the two notes for "Memorializing the Legacy of Ronald Reagan" on pages 229–30. As you can see, the theory behind parenthetical notes is to provide the least information needed to identify sources.

Consult Chapter B of Part II for more information relating to parenthetical notes.

EXERCISE | **Providing Parenthetical Notes**

Suppose you have written a report on interstate highway construction using the sources listed on page 234. Show what the following parenthetical notes would look like:

  a. A note referring to information on page 18 of Finch's book.
  b. A note referring to the article in *Civil Engineering* as a whole.
  c. A note referring to information taken from the last two pages of Weingroff's article.

READING SELECTION

The following chapter from the recently published book *Mosquito: A Natural History of Our Most Persistent and Deadly Foe* provides an account of the ambitious—yet unsuccessful—effort to rid the world of malaria by killing mosquitoes with dichlorodiphenyl trichloroethane (DDT), a toxic compound currently outlawed in the United States and most other developed countries. Experiences related in the first person are those of Andrew Spielman, a professor in the Harvard Medical School. Coauthor Michael D'Antonio is a journalist.

The Great Mosquito Crusade

ANDREW SPIELMAN AND MICHAEL D'ANTONIO

[Shortly after World War II,] the Greek government had begun an all-out war on malaria using the . . . super weapon, DDT. 1

Greece had a history of malaria outbreak that predated Hippocrates. Most recently, in 1942, half the country's population had been infected. In 1947, a war of eradication was declared with the goal of freeing Greece once and for all from malaria. The mosquito in question was *Anopheles sacharovi*, a notorious malaria carrier that breeds in brackish water around the Mediterranean. With DDT supplied by the United Nations and with military veterans doing the spraying, the Greeks went after the mosquito with warlike intensity. . . . 2

As far as most Greeks were concerned, the campaign was a glorious success. Spray crews were housed and fed by local villagers who welcomed them as a liberating army. Pilots in biplanes skimmed twenty feet above the ground to attack swamps with DDT fog. And where olive farmers were lucky enough to have their groves catch some of the spray, the collateral deaths of destructive caterpillars meant a much bigger haul at harvest-time. In every town, residents were thrilled to discover that flies, fleas, lice, roaches, and other pests disappeared along with their mosquitoes. DDT became so popular that a few pilots took unauthorized turns over neighborhoods where friends and family lived just to kill sand flies. 3

Except for the accidental deaths of some silkworms and honeybees, the Greek DDT offensive seemed an unblemished success. In 1948, malaria appeared to be essentially gone. Whereas sixteen percent of Greek children had previously tested positive for malaria parasites, none could then be found. Then something strange happened. The flies came back. Soon afterward a malariologist eating lunch at a country inn noticed something even more troubling: several of the dreaded *Anopheles sacharovi* mosquitoes flitting about a room that had been treated with DDT. Finally, in 1951, the men who had just sprayed a village noticed that these mosquitoes had returned in a matter of days and had recommenced biting. 4

Laboratory investigators demonstrated that *Anopheles sacharovi* could adapt, due to natural selection, to the presence of DDT. Some officials hoped that the Greek mosquitoes were somehow special, and other species might not pull off the same trick, but they were wrong. Resistance was being noted in Lebanon and Saudi Arabia. And then came the worst news of all: massive DDT resistance in *Anopheles albimanus* created by the agricultural use of DDT in cotton fields in El Salvador. In that case, the mosquitoes were adapting even before an impending antimalaria campaign could begin. 5

6   The lowly mosquito's ability to resist DDT had political as well as scientific implications. As every student of history knows, the West's cold war hostilities with the
Soviet Union began immediately after the end of World War II. As the Communists
worked to bring one nation after another into their sphere, the United States and
Western Europe responded accordingly.

7   In the geographical competition, new technologies yielded the best propaganda
material. Whether it was *Sputnik*, atomic energy, or even new vaccines, the competing
systems presented every advance as evidence of a superior political and economic system. Whenever possible, breakthroughs were delivered to allies and potential allies in
order to extend political influence. At the head of this effort, the United States,
through its Agency for International Development (AID), created countless programs
designed to use American money and know-how in this way.

8   DDT was going to be a major weapon against communism as well as mosquitoes,
bringing health to a world that would have to notice that it came from America. The
resistance problem threw an unexpected and disturbing variable into the picture—
time. Although many mosquitoes ultimately adapted to DDT, liberal and broadscale
use of this extraordinary insecticide would disrupt transmission of malaria long
enough for the disease to begin to disappear. Other forces might then break the cycle
of transmission. This is what happened in Greece, where, in the end, the mosquitoes
survived but malaria did not. . . .

9   Seven years was how long it seemed to take for resistance to arise in mosquitoes
under attack from DDT and to become an insuperable obstacle to its continued use. If
we were to employ this chemical wonder in an all-out attempt to rid the world of
malaria, our goal would have to be accomplished within that span of time. This was
the conclusion reached in 1956 in a seminal report issued by the International Development Advisory Board (IDAB) to the U.S. State Department.

10   Guided mainly by Dr. Paul Russell, Soper's* colleague and a true believer in eradication, the IDAB laid out a bold plan requiring $520 million in 1955 dollars (the
equivalent today would be many billions of dollars) to defeat malaria worldwide.
"Eradication is economically practicable today only because of the remarkable effectiveness of DDT and related poisons," the board declared. But because of resistance, it
added, in capital letters, "TIME IS OF THE ESSENCE."

11   The humanitarian reasons for a world war on malaria were obvious, but the report
suggested other justifications for America paying the bill for the assault. The first was
economic. Malaria was debilitating workers and consumers in countries that trade
with the United States. Their lost labor made goods that the United States imported
more expensive. Their malaise also retarded development, meaning fewer markets for
high-priced American goods. Ultimately, America paid a hidden, $300 million "malaria
tax"—in higher prices and lost sales—every year.

12   But beyond dollars, the board saw potential political benefit from a huge malaria
eradication initiative; it would win America friends. Unlike other development programs, which rarely lead to "visible evidence of progress," a malaria eradication project
made life better, immediately, for every family it touched. The point was obvious. DDT
spray teams that appear twice a year with mosquito-killing agents labeled "Made in
USA" would reinforce America's positive image. . . .

*Fred Soper was Regional Director of the International Health Division of the Rockefeller Foundation
from 1927 to 1942 and Director of the Pan American Sanitary Bureau from 1947 to 1959. He coordinated
an aggressive campaign to eradicate mosquito populations through massive applications of DDT. (Editor's note)

The IDAB message—that America should immediately fund a program literally to douse the world with DDT and end malaria—could not have surprised anyone who knew the board's scientific adviser, Paul Russell. Just one year before, Russell had published a book with the audacious title *Man's Mastery of Malaria*. In it, he expressed an evangelical zeal for eradication. "The verb *to master* does not imply an end to the matter," he writes, "rather it suggests that, having prevailed over an opposing force, one has moral responsibility for keeping it under control." **13**

Here was the sum of Russell's medical, scientific, and even family background coming to the fore. The son of a New England preacher, Russell had wanted to serve both God and man as a medical missionary. In his work with malaria, he found a true moral purpose. He was excited by DDT, which he called a "wonder," and his faith in eradication was all but unshakable. **14**

The DDT evangelists were persuasive enough to convince the State Department and then two prominent senators—John F. Kennedy and Hubert H. Humphrey—that victory over malaria was attainable. The timing couldn't have been better. In 1957, the Soviet's launch of the *Sputnik* satellite revved America's competitive spirit to an almost paranoid pitch. The government was ready to do anything to prove the might of American science. A project to use an American-manufactured technology (DDT) to rid the world of malaria fit perfectly. **15**

Congress approved the program and the Agency for International Development quickly organized itself to run it. USAID virtually took over the existing World Health Organization program, greatly accelerating and expanding the work underway. President Eisenhower, and later President Kennedy, delivered speeches that declared all-out war on this mosquito-borne disease. **16**

In 1958, DDT was shipped by the ton to dozens of countries that stood on the front lines in the great war against malaria. The commitment to this strategy was total, so much an article of faith in American science that grants for malaria research disappeared almost overnight. If the great solution—DDT—had been found, then what was the point of research? This became dogma, even at universities. At Harvard, for example, the faculty simply avoided teaching and doing research in malariology. To continue would have been seen as subversive. **17**

The demand for total loyalty that swept the field of tropical medicine may have been a product of the urgency felt by so many at the top. They understood best the time pressure in our gamble. Wherever DDT was applied, it would have to work its magic fast. But there was another factor to fear: recolonization. No country that rid itself of malaria would be safe if its neighbor did not join in the effort. Mosquitoes and travelers could inevitably reintroduce the infection. Here lay one final, terrible problem. A population that has been rendered malaria-free for a few years loses its immunity. And if the pathogen returns, everyone will be more vulnerable to severe disease than they were before they received the benefit of this intervention. Immunity works to modulate the symptoms of malaria but does not prevent reinfection. **18**

With the terrible possibilities of DDT resistance and recolonization hanging over their heads, the U.S. Agency for International Development and the World Health Organization worked at a fevered pitch. Training institutes were opened, malaria surveys were conducted, manuals were assembled. By 1960, sixty-six countries were embarked on the prescribed spray campaign. Another seventeen were either planning or negotiating to get involved. . . . **19**

By 1961, just three years into the offensive, the proponents of eradication were adding up their victories. More than twenty percent of the people once plagued by malaria lived in cleared areas. Wherever near total coverage was achieved, malaria was **20** beaten. And the only resistance the program officers had met was not in the mosquitoes but in the offices of the bureaucrats who managed their funds.

21   Well before the end of the five-year timetable, Americans were bragging about their role in this effort. At a mosquito-control conference in California, one federal official made the claim to glory: "Where else could sixty million pounds of insecticide be mobilized in one single year for this fight overseas?" asked Roy F. Fritz. "Where else could we obtain the number of vehicles and spray equipment which can withstand eight to ten hours a day's use, day in and day out, year in and year out? Where else could that be produced? It isn't produced anywhere else." . . .

22   Exactly one year after Roy F. Fritz crowed about American technology and the coming defeat of malaria, the Royal Society of Tropical Medicine and Hygiene met at Manson House, a brick row building in London named for Sir Patrick Manson. These scientists gathered to review the progress, or lack of it, in antimalaria battlefield reports from around the world.

23   "It appears," noted scientist M. J. Colbourne, "that resistance is seriously interfering with progress in several countries." Though he suggested that a change of insecticides might save the day, there were still other difficulties, including those dangerous "exophilic" species that flitted indoors to bite but refused to rest long enough to be killed by DDT residue. In the end, said Colbourne, "the achievement of worldwide, or even continent-wide eradication does not appear practicable in the near future." . . .

24   Failure was going to be noted, soon, all over the globe after the seven-year time span and large-scale American funding expired. Taiwan held to its eradication record, but Sri Lanka began to see the beginning of a malaria comeback that would produce half a million cases in 1969. (In the same year, the World Health Organization officially recognized the failure of eradication.)

25   In other countries the story was to be the same—the gradual appearance of resistant mosquitoes and the subsequent emergence of malaria. In Indonesia, malaria increased fourfold between 1965 and 1968. India held on longer than most, but a massive epidemic announced malaria's return in 1976, when an estimated twenty-five million people were stricken. Due to the malaria eradication effort, many people had lost all immunity to the parasite: their new infections were particularly dangerous.

26   In the early 1960s, those who pushed the military-style assault on mosquitoes with DDT clung to their strategy. If only a little more time and DDT were applied, they argued, the desired result would occur. But the money, the energy, and, most important, faith in the solution had been running out. The final blow, at least as far as public opinion in the developed world was concerned, came in the form of a book by a middle-aged biologist who once showed her students the strange mating behavior of polychete sea worms near the dock at the famous Woods Hole Marine Biological Laboratory.

27   Published in 1962, Rachel Carson's *Silent Spring* took on a host of nascent ecological issues, including problems associated with radiation, but its major effect was to challenge the widespread assertion that DDT was safe. Beginning with convincing evidence linking the pesticide to the decline of certain bird populations, Carson went on to describe health problems in workers who handled the chemical and liver cancers in exposed fish. She argued for restraint.

28   It was from Carson that the general public learned that DDT was found in mother's milk and could accumulate in the bodies of their babies. And it was Carson who told the public that as early as 1950, the federal Food and Drug Administration warned, "It's extremely likely that the potential hazard of DDT has been underestimated."

29   *Silent Spring* was one of the first popular works to bring environmental concerns to a broad audience. It also revealed that science was not a monolith. Indeed, in one

passage after another, Carson presented the work of respected researchers who challenged the DDT establishment. They described how in some cases DDT spraying killed other animals and allowed for an explosion in the abundance of certain pests. She also explained in clear terms how insecticide resistance developed.

"Spraying kills off the weaklings," she wrote. "The only survivors are insects that   **30** have some inherent quality that allows them to escape harm." These are the parents of the new generation, which, by simple inheritance, possess all the qualities of "toughness inherent in its forebears." Under Carson's guidance, it's pretty easy for any reader to understand how insect populations that give rise to new generations in a matter of days can quickly defy a pesticide.

As convincing as her science may have been, it was Carson's gift with prose that   **31** was more persuasive. "The 'control of nature' is a phrase conceived in arrogance, born of the Neanderthal age of biology and philosophy, when it was supposed that nature exists for the convenience of man," she concluded. "The concepts and practices in applied entomology for the most part date from the Stone Age of science. It is our alarming misfortune that so primitive a science has armed itself with the most modern and terrible weapons, and that in turning them against the insects, it has also turned them against the earth."

Silent Spring was published eight years before the creation of the U.S. Environmen-   **32** tal Protection Agency. But almost immediately, several states began reviewing the use of pesticides, and by 1968, half a dozen had banned particular chemicals. Four different national research commissions conducted studies on DDT and recommended that its use be phased out. A year later, the United States Department of Agriculture began banning its use on certain crops. In 1971, the EPA held hearings on DDT that resulted in nine thousand pages of testimony. On December 31, 1972, the agency issued a press release announcing that "the general use of DDT will no longer be legal in the United States after today."

DDT's supporters continue to argue that, despite the application of more than   **33** 1.3 billion pounds of the chemical in the United States, not one human death can clearly be attributed to its use. But this argument could not stand against the perceived long-term danger. And with the chemical banned in America, the prospect for its use overseas dimmed as well. How many leaders abroad would be able to assure citizens that a pesticide that Americans no longer produced, and feared using themselves, was actually safe?

Nevertheless, a worldwide ban on DDT would be a severe loss for public health   **34** workers because the pesticide has properties that render it an invaluable tool against malaria. When used for this purpose, it is applied close to where people sleep, on the inside walls of houses. After biting, the mosquitoes generally fly to the nearest vertical surface and remain standing there for about an hour, anus down, while they drain the water from their gut contents and excrete it in a copious, pink-tinged stream. If the surfaces the mosquitoes repair to are coated by a poison that is soluble in the wax that covers all insects' bodies, the mosquitoes will acquire a lethal dose.

No chemical compares to DDT as a weapon against the resting mosquito. First, it   **35** is potent. Just two grams of DDT per square meter of wall surface is more than enough to kill a mosquito within its usual one-hour resting period. Second, it is inexpensive. It is also easily stored and transported, and relatively safe for the person doing the spraying. Best of all, it remains effective for many, many months.

The total ban on DDT's use in the United States deprived American public health   **36** officials of a weapon that could have been safely used. Even today, when there are many chemicals available to kill mosquitoes, DDT retains many advantages. It is the ideal insecticide of first use. This is because the resistance that mosquitoes develop after being exposed to DDT does little to protect them against the other, more expensive insecticides that wait on the sidelines. However, mosquitoes hit first with one of those other compounds—such as malathion, sevin, or permethrin—develop a broader resistance that partially protects them from DDT as well. A spray program based on the use of chemicals in any of these alternatives also tends to be about three times as expensive as one based on DDT. When used correctly and with restraint, DDT appears to be irreplaceable in antimalaria programs.

37   In the year 2000, DDT was nearly outlawed worldwide under the terms of a United Nations Environmental Program treaty. It was to be classified as one of the unsafe "dirty dozen" of the Persistent Organic Pesticides, known as POPs. In December 2000, however, a treaty conference held in South Africa agreed to a "dirty eleven." DDT was excluded from proscription. The chemical is now manufactured only in China and India, and it is to remain available solely for use in antimalaria programs. This most recent battle over DDT's status was intense and the outcome crucial for helping to protect human health around the world.

38   By the time that the postwar effort to eradicate malaria waned, many of the important vector species had developed some degree of resistance. Where malaria workers turned to substitute insecticides, some mosquitoes learned to resist those too. At the same time, the malaria parasite itself began to demonstrate its ability to evolve resistance to our best medicines, and drug resistance accelerated as these medicines became more readily available. In too many poor households people obtain the medicine, use just enough to ease their symptoms, and then hoard the remainder for the next wave of illness. Malaria parasites frequently are exposed to sublethal doses of drug. In this manner, malaria sufferers turn their bodies into ideal breeding sites for drug-resistant parasites. . . .

39   No history of the monumental malaria eradication campaign would be completed without acknowledging several key points. Although malaria continues to destroy human lives and impede happiness, the recent eradication campaign preserved human health and lives, at least temporarily, around the globe. It's reasonable to suppose that many millions of people escaped death because they got through their vulnerable childhood years without infection. Sadly, many of their children and grandchildren will not now be spared a malarious fate, as this infection continues to stage its raging comeback.

40   It is also necessary to acknowledge America's own major failure to destroy a certain dangerous mosquito species. Under pressure from Latin American countries that had run the yellow fever vector out of their territories, the United States promised to eradicate *Aedes aegypti* from the Americas in the mid-1960s. There was more than a little irony in this situation. After all, America had gone to war with Spain, in part, because of the danger of yellow fever spreading from Cuba into nearby lands. Now the same Latin American countries that had been blamed for sending pests north were quite understandably demanding protection from the same mosquito harbored in the United States.

41   Mainly a container-breeding insect, *Aedes aegypti* would be attacked by DDT applications and by crews that located and removed disused tires, jars, and other man-made containers that collected water and supported breeding. Thousands of workers were trained for the task. Fleets of trucks were equipped with sprayers. Nine states, from Texas to South Carolina, were notified that they harbored the mosquito and would be

battlegrounds in the war against it. A determined government notified laboratories that used the mosquito for research that these colonies would be destroyed. This "guinea pig" of the medical entomology laboratory was to be lost, even in northern cities where these insects could not survive the winter.

Once the effort began in earnest, so did the opposition. Laboratories successfully   **42** fought the order to destroy the mosquito colonies that they used for experimental studies. And in one community after another, the U.S. Public Health Service encountered residents who didn't want anyone traipsing through their backyards looking for old tires or blanketing their neighborhoods with DDT. They had read (or heard of) *Silent Spring* and would have none of it.

As legal costs mounted, the eradication effort slowed. Then the EPA banned DDT.   **43** The war was over. Latin America would continue to live under the threat that the yellow fever vector could return via the United States. It was another victory for the mosquitoes. (This fact became clear to me on the day I visited the *Aedes aegypti* eradication program's headquarters near Atlanta and found the little devils breeding in a can that had been discarded near the agency's parking lot.)

When the great war on mosquitoes was begun, Fred Soper and Paul Russell de-   **44** clared victory for their theories of eradication as a solution to malaria. Generations of experts had argued over whether eradication was really feasible, and for many years those who favored more cautious "control" or "suppression" programs had prevailed. But with the U.S. government's embrace of the eradication concept, the matter seemed completely settled. It became such an article of faith that students who hoped to enter the field were warned that they had joined a dying profession. The vector mosquito was soon to be wiped off the face of the earth.

As failures mounted, however, and it became clear that worldwide eradication would   **45** never be achieved, Soper and Russell quite literally ceased discussing the matter in scientific forums. Russell, who had accepted a position at Harvard in 1959, demonstrated his disappointment by avoiding the subject altogether and steadily withdrawing from contact with students and faculty. By 1968, he had retired to an isolated village in Maine. Soper remained a heroic figure because of his work in Brazil, but he distanced himself from the global malaria initiative. Remarkably, his 1977 memoir, *Ventures in World Health*, makes no significant mention of this grand attempt to apply his theory. . . .

In reality, mosquitoes are a pest and a threat that require people to mount a con-   **46** sistent, sophisticated, and even strategic defense. The impulse to smash the enemy must be measured against the knowledge that, in the case of a weapon like DDT, it is possible to go too far. . . .

Today a map shaded to illustrate the worldwide distribution of malaria does not   **47** look much different from one drawn in 1955, before the great mosquito crusade. A few island nations, most notably Taiwan and Jamaica, have joined the nations of the Northern Hemisphere where malaria has disappeared. But across much of the tropical part of the globe, the parasite predominates. Today's map looks even more ominous when it is marked to indicate where drug-resistant parasites—entirely absent from the world scene in 1955—now roam. Chloroquine can't destroy these parasites, and even our modern multidrug cocktails are sometimes ineffective. Almost every country in sub-Saharan Africa suffers from this more deadly kind of malaria, along with half of South America and much of Asia from Afghanistan to New Guinea. Billions of people are at risk. Every year, ten percent of the world's population suffers from malaria. Every twelve seconds a malaria-infected child dies.

Freewriting

In your notebook, write for fifteen minutes about the "Great Mosquito Crusade" conducted after World War II. You may wish to consider whether, on the whole, it was a worthwhile venture, or you may want to draw connections to other human attempts to control or defy nature—cloning, genetic engineering, atomic energy, strip mining, supersonic transport, "unsinkable" ships. On the other hand, you might assess the motives and methods of Fred Soper, Paul Russell, and other advocates of mosquito eradication.

Group Work

Share both freewritings with members of your peer group by having each member read aloud as others take notes. Try to arrive at some consensus about whether any historical lesson emerges from the "Great Mosquito Crusade" and, if so, what that lesson is and the extent to which it has been understood and accepted.

Review Questions

1. What were the political implications surrounding the use of DDT to eradicate mosquito populations?
2. Why was it important to pursue the eradication campaign quickly as well as aggressively?
3. What factors contributed to the ban on DDT production and use in the United States?
4. What have been the ultimate effects of the eradication campaign on the worldwide distribution of malaria?

Discussion Questions

1. Would you say that Spielman and D'Antonio are fair and objective in their presentation of Fred Soper, Paul Russell, and their associates? If not, do you feel that they are too harsh or too lenient?
2. In one section of their book, Spielman and D'Antonio refer to the eradication campaign as "the kind of deception that people practice when they are trying their very hardest to do something good, even heroic, in the face of a terrible problem." Try to think of other possible examples of this type of deception—either public historical events or private experiences and observations. After doing so, can you say that this type of deception is ever justified? If not, do you feel that there is any moral difference between this and other types of deception?
3. Spielman and D'Antonio argue that total rejection of the production and use of DDT in the United States and most other countries was an overreaction

to the publication of Rachel Carson's *Silent Spring*. Can you account for the fact that other, more dramatic events (e.g., the nuclear accident at Chernobyl, the oil spill from the *Exxon Valdez*) have not resulted in similar consequences?

Writing

1. Write a brief summary report on one of the following sets of readings:

   a. "Learning How to Learn" (pp. 103–05), "Adapting to College Life in an Era of Heightened Stress" (pp. 105–07), and "The Challenge of First-Generation College Students" (pp. 110–14).

   b. "Another Day, Another Indignity" (pp. 146–47), "Get a Job" (pp. 149–50); and "The High Cost of Summer Cash" (pp. 150–51).

2. Using the Internet, or with the help of your instructor or a reference librarian, find two articles about one of the following technological advances: disposable diapers, enriched bread, laundry detergent, frozen or fast food, styrofoam. One article should address the benefits of this technology; the other should examine some of its unanticipated consequences. Write an objective report on sources that synthesizes the two articles.

WRITE, READ, and RESEARCH the NET

1. *Write:* Brainstorm a list of historically important inventions, beginning perhaps with those listed in the preceding writing suggestion 2.

2. *Read:* Review the two following Web sites:
   <http://www.lib.lsu.edu/sci/chem/patent/srs136.html>
   <http://www.totallyabsurd.com/>

3. *Research:* Using the internet, locate biographies of several of the inventors cited in the first of the two websites listed above. Look for similarities and differences in their backgrounds, personality traits, and personal histories. On the basis of what you find, write a short essay about what seems to foster innovative and experimental impulses.

 ADDITIONAL READING

The following chapter from *Cool Comfort: America's Romance with Air Conditioning* deals with the unanticipated consequences of a technological breakthrough that most of us take for granted.

The Air-Conditioned Nightmare

MARSHA E. ACKERMANN

1   Ten months after the outbreak of World War II had forced him to flee Paris, expatriate Brooklyn-born author Henry Miller in October 1940 set out on a ten-thousand-mile American road odyssey in an eight-year-old Buick he had just learned to drive. . . . His resulting 292-page book, published in 1945 to scant and generally scathing reviews, discovered an America in thrall to "little comforts," synthetic, sexless, anxious, sterile, terrifyingly divorced from nature. "Our instruments," said Miller, "are but crutches which have paralyzed us. We have not grown more human through our discoveries, but more inhuman. He called his extended complaint *The Air-Conditioned Nightmare.*

2   Miller's choice of air conditioning to epitomize everything he loathed about America is curious. He had begun referring to the United States as an "air-conditioned nightmare" during his decade in Paris, though at the time of his departure for France in 1930, air-conditioning had hardly begun to penetrate his New York. Air-conditioning's public presence had grown dramatically by 1940, but it was not yet a ubiquitous feature of American daily life. Perhaps air-conditioning was simply as distant as any moral climate could possibly be from the "Tropics" of Miller's two most famous books, published in France in the thirties but not until the sixties in his native land. . . .*

3   Miller's "premature" denunciation of air-conditioning represents but one of several important strands in how ideas of comfort, consumption, and the benefits of technology were evolving in American society. Air-conditioning was a highly successful instance of a mass-market product that used sophisticated technology to produce comfort. Its makers, marketers, and sometimes even its users were uneasy participants in a developing discussion that sharply questioned the habits and expectations of various groups of Americans and the proper role of technology in satisfying those expectations.

4   Such bourgeois-bashers as Henry Miller, or the more widely read H. L. Mencken and Sinclair Lewis,** focused their critical wrath on the perceived complacency of a surging middle class full of Babbitts who smugly added foolish comforts to their way of life. Increased American affluence might seem to offer a way out of the pinched self-denial these critics identified, accurately or not, with the legacy of Puritanism. Yet Miller, Lewis, and their sort of writer seemed to fear that unthinking acquisition of enslaving comforts—just as surely as Puritan prudery or Jeffersonian self-restraint—would banish from American life all that was natural, passionate, and spontaneous. Pervasive technologies, of which air-conditioning was one, presaged a totalizing uniformity that would deform social institutions and smother American individualism.

5   A broader and more overtly political critique, labeled the "new moralism" by Daniel Horowitz,*** also emerged after the First World War. This new moralism was not a call for liberation or artistic expression but an exhortation to social responsibility. Built on venerable republican forms of American self-criticism, it was willing to accept the fruits of American economic success in ways that redefined traditional republicanism's profound distaste for "luxury." . . .

Tropic of Cancer and *Tropic of Capricorn* were widely regarded as immoral at the time of their publication. (Editor's note)

**H. L. Mencken (1880–1956) was a prominent editor and social critic; Sinclair Lewis (1885–1951) was a popular novelist whose most famous work, *Babbitt,* introduced a new word to the American vocabulary. (Editor's note)

***Daniel Horowitz (1938–) is a professor of American studies at Smith College. (Editor's note)

Stuart Chase, a Thorstein Veblen**** disciple who worked in the twenties with the   6
League of Industrial Democracy, was an influential new moralist who explored connections between passive consumerism and technological dependency. Chase's 1922
attack on the perceived wastefulness of the capitalist economy, a pamphlet entitled
"The Challenge of Waste," was succeeded in 1927 by the more dramatically named
"The Tragedy of Waste." A founder of the consumers' union movement, Chase was
ideally positioned to say "I told you so" when the nation's economy declined precipi-
tously after 1929. The league re-published in 1931 two earlier Chase pamphlets as
Waste and the Machine Age. In this sixty-three-page booklet Chase assailed the "menace
of technological tenuousness" stemming from "dependence on an unknown technology." "When a fuse blows out in my suburban home," he noted, "we can neither see,
cook, nor keep warm." Chase warned that technology could produce "more geographical uniformity in dress, habits, manners, and a faster turnover in such standards." He
associated this unwelcome possibility with a "softening of racial stock due to high
levels of comfort long maintained."

As the Depression deepened, even engineers were not immune from such mis-   7
givings. "Has the Engineer Benefitted Mankind?" asked C. E. Kenneth Mees, the
British-born director of research at Eastman Kodak, in a trade journal article. He took
issue with a recent declaration by leaders of civil, mining, mechanical, and electrical
engineering groups "that the machine age has promoted human happiness." Mees
disputed the idea that happiness arose from more plentiful material possessions or
more comfortable physical conditions. Machines, he argued, had diminished the
farmer's social status and economic importance and had replaced skilled craftsmen
with interchangeable industrial laborers. . . .

Given the critique embedded in both republican tradition and the new moralism,   8
it was inevitable that air-conditioning would come in for its share of attack, by inference if not always by name. Potential accusations of luxury and demoralizing dependency were bugaboos of which air-conditioning pioneers were themselves keenly
aware. The publication of Kodak engineer Mees's criticisms in the professional journal
of the heating and cooling industry suggests that these engineers expected the critique
to be applied to their endeavors.

Questioning the "genuine need" for air-conditioning had a well-established his-   9
tory of its own. Yale geographer and part-time air-conditioning advocate Ellsworth
Huntington vacillated about the morality and desirability of comfort. Although he endorsed cooler indoor temperatures, he was equally convinced that the uniformity of
conditions promised by air-conditioning could seriously impair human achievement.
Huntington cited a 1930 Bruce Catton column on the "ideal home" that challenged
the benefits of burgeoning domestic technology:

> We seem to have made up our minds definitely that the machine is to be our salva-
> tion. The luxuries of a former day are the necessities of the present. . . . We elevate
> incidentals, meant to iron out the minor rough places in Life's pathway, into items of
> major importance, ends in themselves.

Almost a decade later, Huntington was still worrying about the effects of man's
increasing divorce from nature:

> We tend more and more to live in a purely artificial environment. We cease to in-
> crease our physiological adaptation to environmental conditions, and thereby encour-
> age the propagation of types that can live only under the optimum conditions. . . . We

---

****Thorstein Veblen (1857–1929) was an economist and sociologist. (Editor's note)

put our species more than ever at the mercy of natural disasters. . . . Thus each advance in our so-called control of nature makes us more dependent than before upon
the continued existence not only of the artificial conditions which we create, but
upon the natural conditions which alone make it possible to create the artificial
conditions.

Since the early twenties, when his invention of a new auditorium air-bypass system for
movie palaces helped air-conditioning succeed in the public comfort market, Carrier
Corporation executive Logan Lewis had fretted over the "luxury" label that he himself
tended to associate with his industry's products. In a continuing project of personal
and corporate justification, Lewis labored until his death in 1965 to link the idea of indoor comfort to the more politically and morally persuasive claims of health and
efficiency, and to answer the critics of environmental uniformity. "No, our ultimate
objective is not comfort," Lewis declared characteristically at a 1943 industry panel
discussion. "It is to give man or woman a fair chance to apply the fundamental of creating wealth by producing up to the limit of his latent capacity."

10   As the sacrificial public spirit of wartime receded in 1948, Lewis drafted a speech
entitled "Is Air-Conditioning a Luxury?" Thermal comfort, he said, might suggest
"luxury, idleness, nonproductivity" but was in fact a maximizer of human effort. In offices, said Lewis, air-conditioning would reduce errors, absenteeism, employee
turnover, trips to the water cooler, conversations about the weather, and the "nuisance
and spoilage of perspiration." Even in the home, "cooling for a bedroom looks like
pure unadulterated luxury" but must instead be understood as a wellspring of worker
renewal and reinvigoration.

11   Although the economic boom of the fifties meant that more goods came within
the reach of more Americans, shifting the boundaries between luxury, comfort, and
need, it took industry veterans like Lewis to remind his colleagues that there was nothing inevitable or irreversible about air-conditioning's migration from the realm of
desire to that of necessity. In his celebratory 1957 booklet "The Romance of Air-
Conditioning," Lewis told new hires and veteran Carrier employees that it had taken
twenty-five years of "concentrated effort" to overcome the idea that air-conditioning
was an "extravagant luxury" and "raise it up into its present state of widespread
acceptance." This effort, Lewis intimated, surely included his by now seemingly
old-fashioned insistence on staking a claim to the "virtuous" zone between need and
desire.

12   While Lewis charted the somewhat capricious course of air-conditioning's successful "romance" with the American public, the public was fulfilling the new moralists'
"worst expectations about America as a mass consumer society." An emerging generation of social critics gazed with alarm at the seeming victory of affluence in American
society. They used a neo-Malthusian language of waste and looming scarcity to attack
growing consumption and to revive the claims made by Stuart Chase and others that
deceptive advertising and other nefarious practices were victimizing the American
middle class, making it dependent on inessential products and profligate with vanish-
ing resources.

13   Historian David M. Potter in 1954 sounded a warning about American consumerism that would influence many subsequent critics. Economic abundance was altering the historical American character, he argued, and not for the better. Advertising,
although not intrinsically evil, would inevitably progress from meeting wants or needs
to creating desires in a society sated with material possessions and comforts. He raised

the specter of waste, well on its way to becoming a central complaint of the new generation of critics:

> In contrast to other peoples who keep their bodies warm primarily by wearing clothes, Americans keep their bodies warm primarily by a far more expensive and even wasteful method. . . . The oil furnace has not only displaced the open fireplace; it has also displaced the woolen undergarment and the vest.

Although Potter did not include cooling in his condemnation, the air-conditioning industry was sensitive to his study's ideological implications. In a February 1954 article, Arthur J. Hess, president of the American Society of Refrigerating Engineers, took it upon himself to debunk the debunkers, while conceding the responsibility of makers and installers to make air-conditioning work better.

Opponents of air-conditioning, wrote Hess, were a "malcontented minority." **14** They were less than twenty percent of those who had experienced the technology but "critical and vociferous" enough to create the impression of general discontent. Unfortunately, he added, the vast majority who liked air-conditioning felt no need to express themselves on the subject. The doubters, said Hess, could be divided into three basic types. "Spartans" were people, mainly men, who

> cling to the old spartan belief that discomfort without complaint proves virile manhood and superior physical power. . . . Practical women see no value in being uncomfortable as compared to bragging that one can stand discomfort. The spartans will always have a cult, and some of them will choose air-conditioning as the villain in their campaign against change.

"Nature worshipers," continued Hess, "believe that conditions of living as supplied by nature are better for mankind than any we can manufacture with machines." Although they would eventually be won over, he predicted, they would continue to object to the most recently developed product. Finally, air-conditioning "complainers" imagine they are uncomfortable owing to mental or physical problems unrelated to their actual surroundings. Hess conceded that clothing customs "make it impossible to make both men and women in the same space completely comfortable simultaneously" and proposed that men wear "proper clothing" rather than adhering to the "old, conservative, and generally uncomfortable standards." In the photograph that accompanies his essay, Hess wears a long-sleeved shirt, double-breasted jacket, and firmly knotted tie.

Hess included in his "malcontented minority" chronically dissatisfied people or **15** those easily swayed by "pseudoscientific" writers to believe any technological system inadequate or even dangerous. Hess might have been talking about notoriously quirky architect Frank Lloyd Wright who, by the mid-fifties, was joining *House Beautiful* in attacking International Style and questioning the healthfulness and desirability of air-conditioning, at least in residences. It was quite a conversion for the designer famous for the windowless S. C. Johnson & Son office building in Racine, Wisconsin, a building utterly dependent on a year-round air-conditioning system. Henry Miller had visited the ten-year-old Johnson building during his "Nightmare" tour and was both impressed and horrified. "This place is flawless—deathlike. Man has no chance to create once inside this mausoleum," he wrote in his notebook. "Down with Frank Lloyd Wright! He's an inhuman bugger masquerading as a practical aesthete. He should build Henry Ford's tomb." Instead, Wright told readers of his 1954 book, *The Natural House*, that "to me air-conditioning is a dangerous circumstance." It was "far better," he added, "to go with the natural climate than try to fix a special artificial climate of your own."

16   John Kenneth Galbraith's 1958 *The Affluent Society* took strong exception to the increasing use of technology to satisfy private wants while public needs were ignored. The Harvard economist argued that abundance was deforming American values, upsetting the balance between public good and private selfishness. His book was widely influential, going through four editions and becoming a byword in a few years as a new generation of environmentalists would denounce a polluted America as the "effluent society."

17   Affluence, said Galbraith, was a historically unprecedented economic condition peculiar to the United States and western Europe. It both fulfilled and aroused desires that were "sensuous, edifying, and lethal." In a chapter entitled "The Dependence Effect," Galbraith argued that once wants had been created by producers and their advertising minions, it was foolish to believe that the public would ever willingly "unwant" them, even in times of national crisis. As an example, he mentioned an outcry in New York City when a 1950 water shortage forced temporary limits on air cooling. The *New York Times* accorded Galbraith a reverential front-page review that asked "Are We Living Too High on the Hog?" The answer to Americans of like mine was obviously "Yes."

18   Vance Packard made this new moralist discourse of affluence and its discontents available to a mass audience. A magazine journalist turned social critic, Packard spoke to a middle class ready to be horrified and titillated by its own indulgence. During his earlier career with the middle-brow *American Magazine*, Vance Packard had asked Ellsworth Huntington for an article on the relationship between geography and American leadership. Interviewed by biographer Daniel Horowitz forty years later, Packard named Huntington's *Mainsprings of Civilization* as one of the two books that most influenced his thinking about American society in the forties.

19   Affluence, Packard suggested, was a curse of modernity from which America's sheepish consumers could save themselves and the nation only by stern vigilance. Although Packard focused on flashier consumables, like automobiles and television sets, his criticisms of waste and false pleasures were aimed at the very families most likely to use air-conditioning both to bolster their status and to overcome the comfort deficiencies of the era's mass-produced housing. Packard's 1960 "jeremiad," *The Wastemakers*, spent thirty-one weeks on the *New York Times* bestseller list, making it the third of his "scathing, nostalgic, humorous, moralistic, ambivalent, and influential" books to attract a mass readership. By 1963 Packard was one of the nation's most widely read writers of nonfiction.

20   Packard gloried in his reputation as a "public scold" and "anxiety maker." His book was a restatement, in a more popular style and more fervid tone, of the criticisms of Potter and Galbraith; it drew heavily on the admonitions of Stuart Chase, who wrote an approving blurb for *The Wastemakers*. Upton Sinclair, dean of American muckrakers, also provided a plug. Attacking the tendency to equate goods with the good life, Packard complained that two-fifths of the things the average American owns "are things that are not essential to his physical well-being. They are optional or luxury items."

21   Like the social critics he admired, Packard placed much of the blame for American consumerism on advertising, calling it the "machinery of desire stimulation," disparaging technology and desire in a single phrase. Although Packard, like Galbraith, favored the pursuit of large national objectives and public projects over the gratification of trivial and—by definition—indulgent personal desires, he warned, even these

could result in the irreversible waste of materials and energy. "If the nation's exploding population is to settle the nation's open arid areas, then air conditioners will be a required amenity of life. And air conditioners are substantial water users."

Packard was especially critical of the ways in which Americans used their newly **22** acquired houses to achieve trivial increments in social status and, in that connection, viewed air-conditioning as an expression of social climbing. A fierce critic of auto makers' superficial model changes in this era of the giant tail-fin, Packard lumped the new option of auto air-conditioning with other status add-ons designed to "blur still further the already blurred line that distinguishes Americans' luxuries and Americans' necessities."

As a popularizer of a pervasive trend in American social criticism, Packard spoke for **23** a "considerable number of puritanically minded people who stood against the tide of America's growing affluence." His distinctions between needs and desires, necessities and luxuries, were often naive and nostalgic, overstating the power of advertising, uncritically extolling small-town virtues, and understating the inconveniences of the past. Yet he helped enlarge the audience for a great deal of oppositional thinking, providing— in his 1957 *Hidden Persuaders*, according to Daniel Horowitz—the first important attack on advertising since the thirties. Many reviewers saw Packard's book as a useful corrective to what he called, with some irony, the "golden sixties" and others dubbed the "spending" or "soaring" sixties; opponents, like the *Chicago Tribune*, called it "socialistic happy talk" meant to "protect us from enjoying this lovely life too much."

The debate spearheaded by Galbraith and Packard helped popularize and refash- **24** ion republican values and virtues in a way that made sense to many in a new era of white middle-class affluence. At the same time, a developing discourse and style of "cool" would resonate in interesting ways with air-conditioning in the American social imagination. Use of the word "cool" to mean controlled composure and grace under pressure had certainly emerged by the twenties in the predominantly black and urban jazz milieu and had, by the fifties, "crossed over" to the majority white society by way of beatnik culture. By the mid-sixties, "cool" was a mainstream way of defining what Peter N. Stearns calls America's "twentieth-century emotional style." He writes:

> Cool. The concept is distinctly American, and it permeates almost every aspect of contemporary American Culture. From Kool cigarettes . . . and urban slang . . . the idea of cool, in its many manifestations, has seized a central place in the American imagination.

Steams argues that middle-class Americans have forsaken the passionate if often veiled emotionalism of the Victorian era for a disciplined impersonality that requires men, women, and children to avoid embarrassing excesses of anger, jealousy, fear, and even grief and love. Emerging in the 1920s, and achieving dominion in the 1960s, the trajectory of this notion of "cool" seems to parallel the awakening of the American public to the pleasures and possibilities of air-conditioning. Although Stearns does not propose such a literal conjunction of mental and physical states, he does suggest a correlation between the management of emotion and the discipline of bodily functions, almost all of which—think perspiration—were embarrassing to middle-class Americans by the twenties.

It seems unlikely, at least early on, that those black musicians and artists who **25** daily experienced racist provocations on the sweltering summer streets of expanding northern ghettoes associated their mode of "cool" self-presentation with actual air-conditioning. The creators of urban "cool," both black and white, rejected the proposition that it could somehow be manufactured or imposed. "Cool" emanated from the souls of truly self-possessed human beings. Southern black émigrés were developing their "cool" style at the very same time that "tropical" stereotypes were being propounded by such Anglo-Saxon climatic authorities as Ellsworth Huntington and Colum GilFillan. True "cool" came from within. Mechanical devices would not be needed to control "fiery and volatile" temperaments, nor the hot conditions encountered in the ghetto housing of crowded northern cities.

26   In his 1955 "Lament for New York's Night Life," *New York Times Magazine* writer Gilbert Millstein bemoaned the demise of city night life, done in, he said, by "television and suburbanism." Like Henry Miller, Millstein saw excessive emotional and artistic restraint as the wrong kind of "cool." Such dispassion was a bland affront to unrestrained human nature, a nature stripped of the "heat" of natural passion. The "wan gentility" of an early show at an East Side "art movie theater," said Millstein, had replaced late, hot nights of dancing and drinking in Harlem. Recalling a New York that had once been both hotter and "cooler," Millstein said, "maybe it's all these new buildings breeding more of these cool Brooks Brothers cats. They're too cool." He referred to the totally air-conditioned skyscrapers then turning Manhattan's grubby Sixth Avenue into a gentrified Avenue of the Americas where businessmen in suits could fancy that they were hip.

27   To black poet and nationalist LeRoi Jones (later Imamu Amiri Baraka) air-conditioning represented not just the manufacture of artificial "cool" but also the misapplication of technology in a larger and ultimately more dangerous project of tighter social control. Writing critically in 1963 of Martin Luther King Jr.'s nonviolent campaign for black civil rights, Jones invoked air-conditioning to describe the colonized status of American blacks. Jones, ironically like Huntington, perceived that air-conditioning was a way of erasing or trying to erase racial difference:

> The emphasis on passive resistance and moral suasion is an undiluted leftover from the missionary era, and its intentions are exactly the same. Only God has been replaced, as he has all over the West, with respectability and air-conditioning. The Negro must have both before he is "ready" for equality. . . . To enter into the mainstream of American society, the Negro must lose all identity as a Negro, as a carrier of possible dissent.

Stearns's 1994 book sees the persistence and expansion of African American emotional assertiveness, expressed in sports, religion, and politics, even in new forms of music, like rap, as a sign that the era of "American Cool" as the national emotional orthodoxy may be fraying.

28   Galbraith's and Millstein's admonishments might have sparked arguments at Manhattan cocktail parties while Vance Packard's best-sellers might motivate suburban homeowners to choose their home appliances with greater care, but few who could afford them proposed to forego conveniences and comforts altogether. While a new generation of moral muckrakers continued to question the effects of technology and rampant consumerism, air-conditioning's presence on the American landscape became ever more pervasive as makers and marketers looked for new challenges. Air-conditioning the outdoors, or at least controlling exposure to summer heat in settings previously perceived as "outdoors" was one of them. The automobile, long advertised as the means of escaping hot city streets for the presumably cooler countryside, became one such opportunity for the expansion of controlled environment.

29   R. Buckminster Fuller's air-conditioned Dymaxion car had attracted crowds but no imitators at the Chicago Century of Progress Exposition. The refrigerated car—featured in *Popular Science* at about the same time—disappeared, its grandiose marketing plans apparently a casualty of the Depression. Air-conditioning in private automobiles prior

to 1953 was a luxury that offered high status but dismal performance. The car for many years remained—in comparison to airplanes, passenger trains, and even interstate buses—the most thermally uncomfortable mode of transportation. The opulent 1939 Packard was the first production vehicle to be "cooled by mechanical refrigeration," which added about twenty-five percent to its price tag. General Motors in 1941 equipped three hundred Cadillacs with a similarly costly but flawed cooling option. Early compressor units added hundreds of pounds to the weight of vehicles, impairing style, spaciousness, and efficiency. These car air conditioners either had no controls or had controls that were virtually impossible to adjust while driving. Poorly designed seals allowed refrigerant to leak readily from auto systems, quickly incapacitating them and adding to driver expense. Between 1939 and 1953, just 10,500 air-conditioned cars were manufactured.

30   There were certainly indications that drivers wanted cars to be cooler than open windows, highly touted "flow-through" ventilation systems, and fans could make them. Some Continental Oil Company service stations in the early 1950s in Texas advertised that they would pump any car that pulled in full of cold compressed air, using a pump-side three-ton air-conditioning unit to lower the car's temperature twenty degrees in two minutes. If the driver rolled up the windows fast enough, this "free shot" of cooled air would supposedly keep the car comfortable until the next stop. As air-conditioning became more commonplace, Raymond Arsenault writes, some status-hungry Texans would keep their windows rolled up despite the heat to make people think their cars were air-conditioned.

31   *Consumer Reports* for the first time in 1954 discussed auto air-conditioning as part of its annual review of new car models. After listing all the aforementioned drawbacks, the consumer-advocacy publication declared auto air-conditioning to be well worth the money. "Members of CU's staff who have driven air-conditioned cars agree that, in very hot weather, they would rather drive the cheapest car on the market with air-conditioning, than the most luxurious car without it," the editors uncharacteristically effused.

32   There were not many "cheap" air-conditioned cars on the market and no stampede to buy those available. As *Consumer Reports* had noted, most systems added roughly an extra passenger's weight to the car and cost $600 at a time when most cars cost less than $3,000. Just fourteen percent of passenger cars sold in the United States in 1963 were equipped with factory-installed air-conditioners. Virtually all of these were in the South and the Southwest. The July 1963 issue of *Popular Science* reported that just ten percent of the two million Chevrolets sold nationwide in 1962 had air-conditioning, and almost half of them were sold to Oklahomans and Texans. Because prices and weight were down and reliability up, a boom was in the offing, the magazine predicted, adding pugnaciously: "If you're not tempted to order a cooling system for your new car . . . you're not with it, Buster."

33   The air-conditioned share of the car market passed fifty percent for the first time in 1969 even though, priced at about four hundred dollars, air-conditioning still represented a fifteen percent add-on for an average car. Auto air-conditioning grew almost continuously thereafter. By 2000, it was no longer a regional phenomenon but was installed in 98.4 percent of new cars.

34   The triumph of auto air-conditioning significantly coincides almost exactly with what a number of commentators have called the "post-love affair" era of Americans' relationship with their cars. As rising gas prices sparked new concerns for fuel economy; as safety features shouldered aside sexy styling; as the price of cars, equipped with once inconceivable amenities like cruise control, stereo systems, and carpeting, far exceeded what older drivers had once paid for their Levittown Cape

Cods, air-conditioning helped make the car a private extension of home rather than an escape from it. In these windless, gritless, and noise-free capsules, a driver could traverse the interstate, or risk the urban ghetto, but remain as if at home, making phone calls, accessing global-positioning satellites, or spinning compact discs behind locked doors and rolled-up, dark-tinted windows. Daniel L. Guillory would compare the windshield of the modem car to the living-room television screen, affording a view of pollution and crime but shielded from their effects.

35   Volkswagen, the German American automaker, in 1995 launched a "Drivers Wanted" television campaign that aimed to reglamorize the escapist, wind-in-your-hair aspects of automobile ownership and use. In the thirty-second "Windows" spot, developed for VW by Arnold Worldwide of Boston, a young executive gloats about his automated, air-conditioned skyscraper office. "I am in complete control," he declares, adding plaintively, "I just wish I could open these windows." Moments later, he escapes in a sporty red Volkswagen. "Open up a Volkswagen Jetta," the supertitles proclaim. "It invigorates, never Isolates." Ironically, as several models of the Jetta zoom by, even the quick-cut editing cannot hide the fact that their windows are rolled up, although a sunroof seems to be cracked open in several shots.

36   As air-conditioning pervaded private as well as public spaces, and the means of getting from one to the other, traditional outdoor activities fought to retain summer patronage. Air-conditioning manufacturers were quick to attribute fall-off in summer theater, big-top circus, and minor-league baseball attendance to excessive heat and propose their products as the "cure." Air-conditioning often appeared to be the simplest, and possibly cheapest, solution for providers of traditional entertainment struggling with changes in public taste, television, and suburbanization in addition to summer heat. In Connecticut, one theater manager facing summer ruin persuaded the town of Clinton to use tax money to install playhouse cooling and then economized by hiring lesser-known stars to perform in the air-conditioned space.

37   Even financially thriving summer recreations used the installation of air-conditioning to garner publicity and enhance their reputation for staying abreast if not ahead of popular preferences. In 1956, the pennant-contending Cincinnati Reds baseball club installed cooling equipment in the player dugouts, the broadcasting booths, and two-thirds of the press box "because some sports-writers still prefer to hear the noise of the crowd and feel the midsummer heat." Fans in the stands still had to be satisfied with water coolers and the breeze but, predicted a refrigerating trade journal, "ultimately, entire stadiums may be air-conditioned for the comfort of the fans as well as of the players and press."

38   The prophecy was more or less fulfilled in 1965 with the construction of the ten-acre, 56,000-seat Harris County Stadium, soon renamed the Houston Astrodome. The January 1966 meeting of the American Society of Heating, Refrigerating, and Air-Conditioning (ASHRAE) was held in Houston so members could inspect the entirely air-conditioned facility first hand. The Astrodome was built with 4,600 translucent skylights, in expectation that the light thereby admitted would allow grass to grow. It did not work. Fly balls got lost in the glare and the skylights were removed.

39   Although the Astrodome was still a Houston entertainment destination in 2001, the Houston Astros baseball club had deserted it for Enron Field. This $248 million showcase has real grass and a retractable roof that at least occasionally offers Houstonites, accustomed to air-conditioned tunnels between major downtown buildings, a rare experience with unmanufactured weather. An odd sidelight to this discussion is the case of the Carrier Dome, Syracuse University's 50,000-seat football stadium. Built, as its name implies, in the Carrier Corporation's home town with a grant from Carrier of

$2.75 million, the Carrier Dome was not air-conditioned when it opened in 1980, and so it remains. The original twenty-seven-million-dollar construction budget did not provide enough money. In 1983 the Dome hosted its first and last summer function, a Willie Nelson Fourth of July Picnic. In the wake of that sweltering experience, the facility stopped booking July and August events. Today, it would cost seven million dollars to add air-conditioning, said assistant facility director Peter E. Sala, adding, "I don't see it ever happening."

40   When Herbert L. Laube, a veteran air-conditioning engineer who saw himself as a "constructive dissenter," asked his colleagues in July 1967 "how vulnerable is today's comfort industry?" he was not defending the industry against the objections of the various "Spartans," "nature lovers," and "complainers" identified in 1954 by engineer Arthur Hess, nor the recent critics of selfish consumerism—be they artistic nonconformists or social moralists. Rather, in this article and a later book, Laube criticized his industry for disappointing a public he believed to be nearly won over to the kind of comfort that air-conditioning, properly planned, installed, and operated, could indeed provide. "Yes, warmth and coolth, as desired, should make us completely unaware of our indoor environment," Laube declared in the book. "Between them they can free our minds for more productive matters. That is the implicit promise of air-conditioning."

41   Laube understood that differing versions of thermal comfort pitted men versus women, started fights between office and shop floor mates of different races and regions, and set bosses against employees. One unnamed opera star, he reported, refused to perform at a Miami concert until the air-conditioning was shut off. Agents for Frank Sinatra and Lawrence Welk had refused to book either star at the Rochester, New York, War Memorial in the summer of 1969 because they thought the unairconditioned arena would not sell out. Laube was confident such frictions would be overcome and predicted a bright future for air-conditioning. "Confucius say 'the superior man thinks always of virtue; the common man thinks of comfort,'" the engineer concluded archly.

42   Lewis Mumford had never been the "common man" air-conditioning engineers like Laube had in mind. Mumford's view by 1970 of the prospects for the peaceful coexistence of technology and humanity had turned more darkly pessimistic than it had been in the thirties. Like Potter, Galbraith, and Packard, all of whom he cited, Mumford, in *The Pentagon of Power*, held affluence for its own sake in disdain. Far more dangerous than indulgence in petty comforts was American society's apparently willing acceptance of a monstrous technology that was being imposed on modern life by profit-seeking corporate exploiters of human invention.

43   There was little to choose, said Mumford, between environmental conditioning and psychological conditioning: both required dependence and conformity to the dictates of various machines that had "liberated" humankind from a "varied and responsive 'unprogrammed' environment, human and natural—an environment full of difficulties, temptations, hard choices, challenges, lovely surprises, and unexpected rewards."

44   This time, air-conditioning was an explicit part of Mumford's dismaying vision. In a section entitled "The Technique of Total Control," Mumford imagined how astonished Leo Tolstoy would have been by the realization of his mocking prediction:

> He pictured modem man ingeniously sealing up the windows of his house and mechanically exhausting the air so that he might, by utilizing a still more extravagant mechanical apparatus, pump air back again—instead of merely opening the window. Tolstoi did not suspect that within a generation this folly would actually be committed . . . even . . . in the midst of open country, where fresh air is available, and where the natural noises are at a lower level than that of the exhaust fans used by a ventilating system.

In his next chapter, "The Megatechnic Wasteland," Mumford called the modern sky-scraper an air-conditioned pyramid that, like those of the Pharaohs, asserted its society's false claims of divinity and immortality. Within this skyscraper and the nuclear reactor needed to power it, said Mumford, a megalomaniac technocrat class was working to impose on humanity the most tyrannical system of control ever devised. Air-conditioning was just one aspect of a larger design meant to ensure "that no part of a man's life shall be free from external control."

45   Willis Carrier's optimistic 1936 dream of the American businessman's wholly air-conditioned life had, within a generation, become Mumford's version of the "air-conditioned nightmare." Only after events of the seventies and beyond triggered global energy shortfalls, economic concerns, and health anxieties would Laube's archetypal "common man," and American society at large, begin to find reasons more compelling than virtue or civic discipline to reexamine the costs and benefits of air-conditioning.

7 *Analyzing Texts*

During a break between classes, a friend asks your opinion of the latest music video by a currently popular group. "I didn't like it," you say. "It seemed repetitive. It's like I've heard and seen it all before. They've lost their edge." After some half-hearted agreement or disagreement with this appropriately imprecise comment, the topic drifts to a recent party, an upcoming exam, the weather, or lunch. This is typical of informal conversation; it wanders from here to there, rarely pursuing any particular topic in depth.

But in a different context, your offhand comment could be disastrous. If, for example, you submitted the same response in an exam for a course in popular culture, you would fail. In that situation, your analysis would be inadequate. It has a thesis ("I didn't like it") and some support ("repetitive," "lost their edge"), but both are too superficial for formal writing.

Although the transition from the looseness of conversation to the demands of formal writing can be difficult, the distinction is critical. You rarely need to provide much support for the ideas and opinions expressed in conversation, but that is not true of writing. It is not so much a matter of right and wrong; it is, rather, that each type of communication adheres to its own conventions. As a member of an academic community, you should know and observe these conventions. When a friend casually asks your opinion of a music video, a lengthy analysis of cinematography is uncalled for; a "correct" response must be brief. In any situation, the needs and interests of your audience determine the ideas you explore, the specificity of detail you provide, and the language you choose.

As we noted in Chapter 4, the structure of most academic writing is influenced by the movement between general and specific, the process by which we make abstract ideas explicit and concrete. Writers support general statements with details, reasons, examples, and illustrations. They belong to a community of people who not only express what they think, but also explain their reasons for thinking it. In a sense, the general ideas and opinions they express are implied promises to readers, promises they fulfill by developing and linking claims and observations to specific facts and examples. When writers don't keep their promises, readers are disappointed. That's why good writers deliver.

Good readers also deliver. No educated adult wants to be a passive consumer of information. To be a contributing member of a literate community, you must be an active, analytical reader and writer. When you write about reading, you learn to read more carefully and to develop more perceptive observations. This chapter is designed to help you analyze what you read and to become a more effective interpreter of ideas and reporter of information.

ANALYZING THE PARTS

Whenever you analyze something—a chess move, an automobile engine, a political theory, or a poem—you break down its complexity by examining its components. As you look at these components individually, you observe their features and consider how they operate together.

To understand anything complex, scholars begin by analyzing its parts. Political scientists, for example, continually analyze the differences between free-market and managed economies—how they manufacture and deliver consumer goods, the profits they produce, the restrictions they impose on imports. Experts can then compare the two systems by analyzing money, people, goods, laws, attitudes, and other elements. They disassemble the whole to see how each component works; then they study the ways those components operate together.

Whenever you analyze a text, you do the same thing—you examine components separately, then see how they function together as a whole. Since writing is a flexible medium—there is no recipe for composing an essay, and success is often a function of originality—there is no formula for analyzing a text. It depends on what you read and why you read it. You look for different qualities in epic poems, satires, and scientific reports. You approach recreational reading differently than you approach sources for a research paper.

Nevertheless, some features are common to most written texts. Every piece of writing attempts to do something with concepts or information, addressing and developing a main idea in an organized sequence that helps readers comprehend and respond appropriately. The following five elements can be examined in a textual analysis:

- The *purpose* for which the text was written
- The way the author has adapted the text to an intended *audience*
- The *main idea* of the text
- The *development* or *support* for the main idea
- The *organization* and *coherence* of the text.

We will first look at each of these elements individually, then consider how they can be coordinated in a comprehensive analysis.

Purpose

Every text must be approached in terms of what it is supposed to accomplish. It is pointless to disparage a zany movie because it adopts a superficial view of human nature, an article about comparative linguistics because it lacks humor, or a fantasy adventure because it is unrealistic.

Some writers try to change our minds; others simply want to tell us something we haven't known. Some hope to provoke action; others seek to entertain, cajole, shock, or educate. As a critical reader, you must be alert to these possibilities. Misinterpreting a writer's intentions can be catastrophic—or hilarious.

Although we cannot always know exactly what an author is thinking, the basic purpose of a text is usually evident. But things are not always what they initially seem. You must be alert to satire as well as to other types of manipulation. You must detect a writer's biases and be wary of slanted evidence or outright deception. Sometimes writers are candid about where they stand; other times they expect you to read between the lines, inferring their intentions on the basis of past reading experiences and knowledge of human nature.

In the following passage, David Sacks and Peter Thiel do not conceal their bias—a disdain for the efforts of universities to raise students' consciousness of cultural diversity:

> "Orientation is designed to disorient you," announced Stanford professor James Adams to an auditorium of 1,600 puzzled freshmen at the beginning of the new school year. Assembled for one of the many orientation-week programs on "diversity," the freshmen soon learned what he meant. A lesbian activist spoke first about "challenging your sexuality" and encouraged the seventeen- and eighteen-year-old students to "overcome" their "fears of being queer." Next, a black musician performed an electric-guitar solo as police sirens wailed in the background. He concluded his demonstration by dropping suddenly to the floor and convulsing his body in a reenactment of the Rodney King beating.

After quoting Professor Adams's statement about the objectives of orientation, the authors ridicule those objectives by describing the more controversial—some might say outrageous—activities included. Various clues signal the authors' attitudes. For example, they place the word *diversity* in quotation marks and describe the audience of first-year students as puzzled. A more subtle tactic is reminding readers that some first-year college students are, legally, minors. Because they are forthright in revealing their bias (and since their article was published in the conservative *National Review*), the writers cannot be accused of deception. We may disagree with them—we may even dislike their methods of argument—but they give us every reason to expect a discussion that reflects a particular bias. An intelligent reader will examine Sacks and Thiel's article skeptically, aware that theirs is not the only perception of freshman orientation at Stanford University.

EXERCISES   **Analyzing Purpose**

1. Try to determine the author's purpose in the following paragraphs, which introduce an article in *Harper's* magazine.

Be Prepared

Lewis H. Lapham

I don't know why so many people continue to insist that we're living in a democracy that somehow would have been recognizable to Franklin D. Roosevelt or even to Richard M. Nixon. The belief is bad for their health and mental stability, in no way conducive to the upkeep of a decent credit rating or an appropriate state of personal hygiene. Or so at least it would appear if I interpret correctly what I've seen of the writers who for the last six months have been showing up in the magazine's offices with stories about the perfidy of the Bush Administration. They come forward with so many proofs of whatever crime against liberty or conscience they happen to have in manuscript or in mind (the war in Iraq, the corruption of Wall Street, the ruin of the schools, the nullification of the United States Senate, etc.) that they run the risk, as did the old Greek heroes who gazed upon the face of Medusa, of being changed into blocks of humorless stone. How can they hope to save the world from its afflictions—to stop the massacre of the innocents in Africa and Asia, preserve the Brazilian rain forest, uplift the multitudes in the slums of Las Vegas and Detroit, fight the war on terror in this darkest hour of the country's peril—if they allow themselves to become sullen and depressed, don't pay attention to their choice of adjective or to the grooming of their shoes? How can they expect to write important and financially rewarding books?

Maybe it's still worth the trouble to wonder when the American democracy lost its footing in Hollywood or Washington, but the historical fact is no more open to dispute than the extinction of the Carolina parakeet or the disappearance of Pickett's brigade on the field at Gettysburg. The setback doesn't mean that we must abandon our belief in the powers of the American imagination or the strength of the American spirit. If we have learned nothing else from the events of the last few years, it's the lesson about the facts being less important than the ways in which they're presented and perceived. Where is the joy in vain regret, where the profit to be gained by selling America short? Somewhere the sun is shining, and only a blind man doesn't look for the silver lining when clouds appear in skies of blue.

2. The following column by the chairman and chief executive officer of a major airline introduces the July 2002 issue of the company's in-flight magazine.

Control and Choice: You're in Charge When You Research and Book Your Travel Online

Leo Mullin

If you like plenty of control and choice when you're making travel plans, then online travel purchase sites may be the right place for you to shop.

At Delta's own *delta.com,* as well as through other e-travel options such as Orbitz (*orbitz.com*), Travelocity (*travelocity.com*), Expedia (*expedia.com*), and Priceline (*priceline.com*), you set the pace and decide what you want to know and when you want to know it. Because of the easy availability of Internet purchase channels, online shopping is increasingly popular. The number of U.S. online travel buyers is expected to double, growing from 18.6 million in 2001 to 38.6 million in 2007. But with so many sites to choose from, how do you decide which site is right for you?

Naturally, we think *delta.com* is a great first choice—and outside observers agree. In the latest NPD Airline Tracking Study, our site was ranked number-one in every major category, including ease of use, offers and deals, and breadth of choice. The site is easy to access and navigate, even for first-time users. *Delta.com* also allows us to expand the range of personalized services we offer our customers. Not only can you check for schedules and fares—including sales and special promotions—and make reservations, you can also review your itinerary and select your seat. But the opportunities don't stop there—you can also check current airport wait times and find links to other travel-related information. The services on *delta.com* are all are all part of Delta's commitment to minimizing potential hassles related to the travel experience—making your travel as easy as possible.

If you're a member of SkyMiles, our easy-to-join club for frequent flyers, you can also take advantage of even more time-saving services. For instance, you can:

- Check in and print your boarding card
- Redeem award tickets
- Check your SkyMiles balance online
- Sign up for fast notification of flight delays or cancellations.

Delta customers are increasingly attracted to the ease of the Internet and the personalized service we can bring to customers through its speed and power. We know, though, that when it comes to Web shopping, one size does not fit all. As a result, we've partnered with online agencies such as Orbitz, Travelocity, and Expedia as well as with Priceline to give you even more options.

Orbitz, the most recently launched online travel agency site, combines the power of a revolutionary search engine with an industry-leading customer interface that is easy to use and customize. Because of its comprehensive pricing engine—currently the best available—as well as its extensive connections throughout the travel industry, Orbitz brings customers one-stop Web shopping and more unbiased choices than any other online travel agency.

Travelocity and Expedia are two additional e-travel options providing a broad array of innovative services. And for passengers with complete flexibility in terms of both airline flown and time of travel, Priceline lets you name the maximum you're willing to pay for travel. As long as the price you name is higher than the price the site has set for the ticket, the purchase is made for you automatically.

Already, travel is the largest category of purchases made online. As more and more customers embrace the Internet as an effective means to research and purchase travel, they quickly realize the added convenience and control it provides. At Delta, we are constantly evaluating opportunities to provide customers with greater choice along with high levels of service—and continuing to offer you the best in online travel options is an important part of reaching those goals.

a. Several purposes emerge from this text. How many can you recognize?

b. Does any one purpose take priority over others? Are any in conflict with each other? Which ones are more challenging to present to an audience of passengers?

c. What strategies (e.g., phrasing, order of presentation) does the writer use to communicate information or influence the behavior of customers?

Audience

Sometimes authors write to express themselves, but more often their purpose is to influence readers. They usually have a particular audience in mind and adapt their writing to the needs and interests of those readers. Consequently, when they analyze a text, readers should consider the audience to which it was addressed and examine it accordingly.

In the following brief article from an edition of the *Weekly Reader* that targets fourth-graders, the writer considers the needs of young readers:

Maron-1: Robo Helper

When you are at school or hanging with friends, do you wonder what your dog is doing in your house? If so, a new robot might be just what you need.

The robot, called Maron-1, is made by a company in Japan. Maron-1 looks like a cartoon copy of R2-D2. It weighs about 11 pounds and stands about 2 feet high. When it goes on sale in Japan next year, the robot will cost about $1,600.

The makers of Maron-1 say their robot is better than the other kinds of robots that you can buy at toy stores. "Our robot is different from pet robots. It's useful," said a representative of the company that makes Maron-1. . . .

Maron-1 can detect whether someone or something is moving in front of it. If it "sees" something moving, it says, "An intruder found." It can also call you on a cell phone to tell you about the intruder.

The amazing computer can do many other things as well. It can turn on electronic equipment, such as a TV or VCR. Maron-1 can move around, but it cannot go up or down stairs.

Notice the clear, connected way in which information is presented. The short sentences, basic vocabulary, and lack of technical detail indicate the writer's consideration of audience.

It would be unfair to disparage this article because of its superficiality. If you were investigating robotics for a research project, you would not use it as a source. On the other hand, the following passage from *Aviation Week and Space Technology,* an engineering journal, might be equally unsuitable:

STS-111 astronauts Franklin Chang-Diaz and Philippe Perrin from France performed three extravehicular activities (EVAs) to install the new 1.5-ton $254 million MD Robotics Mobile Base System (MBS) on the [International Space] station's truss-mounted mobile transporter and to change out the wrist roll joint on the station's arm.

The starboard truss section is to be launched in late August on *Atlantis,* but engineers are checking whether the addition of the starboard, and then a port section planned in October, will stress the station's degraded attitude control gyro system. One of the station's four 800-pound control-moment gyros (CMGs) failed on June 8, the day after *Endeavour* docked. The 6,600-rpm gyros exert torque to change attitude without the use of Russian propellant. The CMGs were being used to maneuver the 700,000-pound station/orbiter stack, when CMG-1 began to fly apart in its housing in the Z-1 truss above the Node 1.

In this case, the writer's vocabulary and assumptions about what readers know, as well as the information reported, indicate an audience of experts. To characterize this passage as dense and unreadable would also be unfair.

Audience, however, is reflected in more than just vocabulary and assumptions about prior knowledge. It also involves attitudes and values that readers are expected to share. Consider, for example, the opening paragraphs of a chapter from *The Inner-Bitch Guide to Men, Relationships, Dating, Etc.,* a self-help manual by Elizabeth Hilts:

The Inner-Bitch Way of Dealing with Men
The inner-bitch deals with men who are romantic possibilities the same way she deals with anyone—which is to say honestly. It's just easier that way. It is vital, however, to recognize some simple truths about how men approach life.

Men, apparently, love a challenge. Theory has it that this is a basic biological fact, though I wouldn't know because I flunked basic biology. According to some people who seem to live in a parallel universe (you know who you are), this information entitles women who seek relationships with men to behave poorly.

Here's how it works in that parallel universe: If you want a man, you have to play hard to get.

The variations in this theme are endless—don't make it "easy" for them; men are supposed to rearrange their schedules around you, but you never do the same for them; don't ever go Dutch on a date; don't call him; and the ultimate, rarely return his calls.

There's a word for this kind of behavior—*RUDE!*

Not to mention archaic, antithetical, manipulative, and . . . RUDE! I mean, really, what are they thinking? This isn't behavior you'd put up with from other people, is it? If a man treated you this way, you'd have nothing to do with him, right? (The only correct answer to this question is "Right!") Do you honestly want to indulge in rudeness yourself?

I don't think so.

The vocabulary of this passage is unpretentious; its style is informal. The writer uses contractions, asks questions, and directs conversational asides to readers. Although the word *bitch* offends many people, the author probably assumes that women who read a book with this word in its title understand that it is used ironically. (Actually, Hilts connects the word with behavior that contradicts what overt sexists typically characterize as "bitchy.") More important than vocabulary, however, are other clues that reveal the author's assumptions about her audience. For example, when she appeals to the reader's preference for honesty and comfort in relationships, Hilts envisions an audience of women who are not naïve or blindly romantic. Without becoming jaded or cynical, these readers may be exasperated with self-defeating behaviors that frequently undermine dating relationships. Proclaiming her ignorance of biology, the author appeals to an audience that resists— or even mistrusts—academic experts while valuing the practical insights of a clear-thinking, experienced peer. Finally, Hilts skillfully allows readers to distance themselves from the foolish behavior she ridicules. Attributing this behavior to *"some people* who seem to live in a parallel universe," she adds in a sly parenthetical aside, "you know who you are." Likewise, five paragraphs later, Hilts shifts from judgmental third-person references (e.g., "I mean, really, what are *they* thinking?") to personal appeals: "If a man treated *you* this way, *you'd* have nothing to do with him, right? . . . Do *you* honestly want to indulge in rudeness *yourself?*"

These techniques contribute to a comfortable relationship, allowing Hilts to identify with an audience of forthright women who defy conventions that put them at a disadvantage. Together, they can laugh at past mistakes and brush off the stigma of "bitchiness" assigned to them by people who accept self-defeating behaviors as a normal part of dating.

Analyzing audience may entail little more than gauging how much information and terminology readers are supposed to be familiar with; more often, it involves detecting subtle clues about the attitudes, values, interests, and experiences shared by a community of readers.

EXERCISES │ Analyzing Audience

1. The following texts concern statistical correlations between mortality and left-handedness. Using clues such as style, vocabulary, content, and assumptions about what readers know, characterize the audience to which each text is addressed and explain how the author addresses the needs of that audience. It should be helpful to know that the first source appeared in the British medical journal the *Lancet,* the second in the *New York Times,* and the third in a Web site named *Lefty FAQ,* "for the left-handed population and friends and supporters."

a. Left-Handedness and Premature Death

P. J. Ellis, Eileen Marshall, Christine Windridge, Steven Jones, and Simon J. Ellis

Many studies have found less left-handedness in older age groups. This has been attributed to a more relaxed attitude to left-handedness in more recent times, to gradual adaptation to a dextral world, or to premature mortality.

We did a longitudinal study of left-handedness and mortality in a family practice. People aged between fifteen and seventy were mailed the Edinburgh Inventory, which assesses handedness. A laterality quotient (LQ) was calculated ranging from -100 (strongly left-handed) to $+100$ (strongly right-handed). Of the questionnaires which arrived at the correct address 82.17% were returned correctly, providing 6097 responses. The mean age was 41.4 years and 46% were male. Nine years later, the practice register was used to trace the patients. Those who were no longer registered were traced via death certification, through the local Family Health Service Authority, and through the Office of Population Census and Surveys register. Three hundred eighty-seven had died, 48 (0.8%) were lost to follow-up, but the remainder were known to be alive. An analysis of variance was performed with LQ as the main variable; age, gender, and whether the subject had died were built into the analysis. Age (1df, $F = 84.424$, $p < 0.001$) and gender (1df, $F = 11.505$, $p = 0.001$) were important variables. However, death was not (1 df, $F = 0.074$, $p = 0.786$).

MORTALITY IN RELATION TO HANDEDNESS IN DIFFERENT AGE GROUPS
As the majority of patients were right-handed, it is possible that we missed significant premature mortality within the left-handed minority. We reanalysed using two groups, right-handed (positive LQ) and left-handed (negative LQ). The prevalence of left-handedness was 8.00%. The fourteen cases who scored $LQ = 0$ were excluded (0.23%). We found that 6.48% of right-handers and 4.98% of left-handers had died. As a proportion, fewer left-handers died, but this was not statistically significant (difference in mortality 1.5% [95% CI 1.63%]; Z score 1.29; $p < 0.1$, two-tail). As left-handers were younger than right-handers (means 37.4 and 41.6 years respectively), this may have contributed to the survival of the left-handers and so an analysis of variance was performed with gender and age as covariables. Handedness did not make a significant contribution to the outcome of death ($F = 0.17$; $p = 0.317$).

Whilst this study does not preclude the possibility of a small effect of left-handedness on longevity, it is clearly not of the order of magnitude seen in cross-sectional or longitudinal studies.

b. Really?

Anahad O'Connor

The Claim: Right-handed people live longer than lefties.

The Facts: Look no further than the etymology of *left* to see that southpaws, who make up about ten percent of the population, have been slighted for centuries. In Latin, the word for left is *sinister*, while the word for right is *dexter*, related to dexterity. In French, the word for left, *gauche*, means clumsy; the word for right, *droit*, gives us the term *adroit*.

But the notion that lefties have a shorter life span stems largely from a popular 1991 study that found that their proportion in the population dwindles with age. Lefties live in a world designed for right-handers, the researchers explained, and are thus more prone to accidents and serious injuries.

The study, which was not peer-reviewed, has since been refuted.

In 2000, a researcher at Penn State showed that many elderly right-handed people started as lefties, but were pressured into switching as children. That practice is less common today. Two more studies, one in the *Lancet* and another in the *British Medical Journal*, studied thousands of right- and left-handed people and found similar life spans.

The Bottom Line: Right-handers do not live longer than lefties.

c. Do Lefties Die Younger Than Right-Handers?

Stanley Coren, who is the author of *The Lefthander Syndrome,* found statistical evidence of this and didn't believe it for the longest time. However, he remains unable to disprove it. He was able to demonstrate a possible reason for this might be that a left-hand startle reflex would be much more dangerous when driving a car on a U.S. or Canadian road since the car would end up pointing against traffic, while a right-hand startle reflex would simply cause the car to drive off the road. As a double check, Coren did find a statistical difference in left-handed traffic fatalities in countries where they drive on the left, such as Great Britain and Australia.

2. The following passage appeared in a syndicated newspaper column for investors. The author, Malcolm Berko, is responding to a reader who, though deeply in debt, considers using an inheritance of $105,000 to finance his son's college education. Try to infer the attitudes, values, interests, and experiences shared by Berko's audience. As much as possible, connect your inferences with specific details in the text.

> Don't be stupid. You guys are in hock up to your earballs, and soon as you get a gift from God you're hot to trot to spend it. Suckers like you who pledge their incomes ten years hence are seldom given a chance [. . .] in life. And most that do fail because they can't discipline themselves for the future. It must be genetic! . . .
>
> Forget Junior's college education. Frankly, many colleges today are nursery schools for teenage high school mutants. Most colleges have lowered their testing standards so that almost anyone with sixth-grade qualifications can get a degree. And the College Board in March 1994 made its SAT questions so simple that applicants with room-temperature IQs earn acceptable scores.
>
> In my opinion college degrees are fraudulent diplomas certifying an education that never happened. Today's students believe that paying four years of tuition entitles them to a degree, and so many colleges have acquiesced that we have created a new national social disease called the "dumbing down of America." Tell Junior to join the armed services. . . .

Main Idea

As you saw in Chapter 4, the first question a reader asks when engaging with a text is what, specifically, it is about. Writers often announce their main point in a single sentence—a thesis statement. But since many good writers develop ideas in other ways, you cannot always expect a one-sentence presentation of the main idea in an opening paragraph. Sometimes the main idea appears in the middle of a text, sometimes at or near the end, and sometimes throughout the text without being summarized in a single sentence. And since not all writers are careful, some texts wander from point to point without ever arriving at a focus.

There are, then, two questions to consider when you analyze a text: (1) What is the main idea? (2) Does the writer stay on topic, providing a coherent exploration of that main idea? The best way to determine the main idea of a text is to read it attentively and actively. Reread as necessary, using a pencil to underline key passages and to insert marginal comments. Then try to summarize the main idea in your own words.

Analyzing the Main Idea

1. Applying skills introduced in Chapter 4, underline important statements as you read the following article; then state the main idea in your own words.

Who Cares, as Long as It's Natural?

Daniel Akst

If there's a sure-fire way to sell something these days, it's to claim the thing is natural—even if it's a cigarette. "Natural American Spirit Products," the Santa Fe Natural Tobacco Company Web site, says solemnly, "were created based on our belief in the traditional Native American usage of tobacco—in moderation, in its natural state. Our brand name was chosen as a symbol of respect for this tradition."

Above those words is a row of mannered photographs showing hipsters smoking what are presumably Natural American Spirit cigarettes. It's a seductive lineup; you can just see yourself puffing away, joining this gallery of quirky individualists.

The Natural used to be Roy Hobbs, Bernard Malamud's mythic baseball player, but now it's an obsession that many of us seem to share about a life we have somehow lost. In the grip of something like lapsarian fever, people buy natural cigarettes presumably to be sure that when the cancer comes, it wasn't caused by any horrible chemical additives. They shop at health-food stores and pay outrageous prices for herbal remedies to be consumed in blissful indifference to the absence of scientific support or approval by the Food and Drug Administration. A new book, *The Soul of the New Consumer* by David Lewis and Darren Bridger, says the key to success in business is to give people authenticity, and, of course, suggests a few sophisticated techniques for accomplishing this.

Natural? Authentic? Some fairyland of trees and grass that we can traverse in our sport utility vehicles? For women, a truly natural life probably means having a dozen babies and spending all the time in between breast-feeding. For men, I imagine, it's spearing mammoths and dying at thirty of gangrene in a broken leg.

The truth is that people have never before lived so far from anything like "the natural"—or worked harder to widen the distance. And a good thing, too. The sooner we stop pretending, the sooner businesses will stop fooling us with natural folderol. I myself lead as unnatural life as possible, and I'm proud of it. If you are reading these words, you shouldn't need reminding that primitive hunter-gatherer societies had a terrible time getting home delivery of the *New York Times*.

At some level, of course, people know that they are pretending. They drive cars to natural childbirth classes. They buy natural European spring water bottled in plastic and shipped thousands of miles. They object in Internet discussion groups to genetically engineered products. Is it any wonder that businesses respond by marketing pretend "natural" products?

Oh, to wake up one day in a world that knows the state of nature is no more hospitable than the state of North Korea. Then we'll all demand hard proof that herbal remedies are safe and effective, instead of simply assuming that being herbal makes them OK. We'll recognize that some of the nastiest toxins we ingest are made by Mother Nature without capitalism's help. And we'll be open to more "unnatural" technologies that actually increase safety, like food irradiation.

For now, though, if you're selling something, natural goes with traditional, as long as the second term is used the right way. Clever marketers like Restoration Hardware, for instance, know that people hanker for "simpler times" and stock the shelves accordingly.

Among the group that David Brooks has christened Bobos (for bourgeois bohemians, from his book *Bobos in Paradise*), the natural fetish extends even to children's toys. One mother I know believed for a while that children shouldn't play with stuff made of plastic, only wood. What difference does it make? Who knows?

Personally, I'm hoping for more products like Gatorade. My favorite flavors are Riptide Rush, Alpine Snow, and, in a truly marvelous aqua hue, Glacier Freeze. Not only do they taste great, but there is no pretense whatsoever of any natural-ness about them.

Mine remains an unfashionable opinion. I bought a tasty electric-blue sports drink once from a California sales clerk who scorned its artificiality.

"But what's natural?" I asked.

"From the earth," she replied disdainfully.

Apparently she has never visited the Natural American Spirit Web site, which (at the government's behest) offers the perfect rejoinder: "No additives in our tobacco does NOT mean a safer cigarette."

2. Following is an excerpt from the opening handout for an upper-level college course. A list of class policies is not usually thought to have a purpose apart from announcing the policies themselves. Nevertheless, see if you can detect a theme, a main idea, that runs throughout the excerpt. If you can, summarize it in a sentence.

Attendance policy: Since regular attendance is an essential requirement of this course, roll is taken at each meeting. While there is no penalty for as many as three absences, each absence beyond that limit, unless excused for a legitimate reason, lowers the final course grade one letter. Students who are absent more than six times (for any reason) have missed too much to receive credit for the course and should withdraw to avoid a failing grade. Attendance is taken at the beginning of each class. (Please do *not* submit excuses for the first three absences—no matter how noble—since none is needed.)

Late arrival: You must be here on time. Since late arrival disrupts the class, it is penalized. Three arrivals after attendance has been taken are counted as one absence. Should you arrive late, it is *your* responsibility to check with me after class in order to be marked present; otherwise, you will be counted absent.

Reading assignments: You are expected and required to be well prepared for each class meeting. To contribute constructively to discussions and to benefit from lectures, you must have read assignments with care. Unannounced quizzes are fre-quent; and scores are a significant factor in final grading decisions, since they reflect your participation in the course. Continuous study is essential; this is not a course in which students can wait until exam-time to begin studying.

Exams: Four exams are given, after each quarter of the semester. Failure to take any of these exams at the assigned time results in a failing grade for the course. Make-up exams are given only in the event of a documented medical or other emergency. All make-ups are given during the final exam period (following the final exam) and are more difficult than the regularly scheduled exam. It is your responsibility to know the date and time of the final exam and to plan accordingly.

Make-up exams are *not* given to accommodate conflicting engagements, jobs, or early vacations.

Course grade: Your final grade is based principally on the four exams and a paper. Passing grades on the exams and paper range from A+ (4.33) to D– (0.67). Failing grades are F (0), F– (–1.0), and F– (–2.0). The average of the five grades determines the course grade. Quiz scores are the deciding factor when a student's average is within 0.1 of another grade. More than six absences, cheating, not taking an exam, or not submitting the paper automatically results in a failing grade for the course. Please take note: The course grade is determined strictly by a calculation based on your performance. I do not "give" grades; your grade in this course is the grade you have earned.

A final observation: You are expected to be a serious, self-disciplined, conscientious student in this class, and responsibility for your actions and performance is entirely yours, not the instructor's. In the past, students who have worked conscientiously and have consistently come to class prepared have done well. Persons with poor work habits have found themselves having to repeat it.

Development

If merely stating an idea were enough, there would be no books or essays. Every expository text could be reduced to a topic sentence. Of course, more is needed. Writers must explain, expand, and support ideas. Sometimes facts or logic is called for, sometimes narration of events, sometimes reasons and examples. A math text relies on clear, sequential explanation, with examples and exercises that reinforce each lesson. Interpretations of history demand background, evidence, and support from authoritative sources. The best way to develop a main idea depends on the purpose of a text and the audience to whom it is addressed.

Good writers develop their ideas by supporting them with specific, concrete evidence. In the following excerpt, the writer answers her opening question with a series of examples.

> Who were the influential male models of appearance and behavior in turn-of-the-century America? Sports figures like boxer John L. Sullivan were important, as were businessmen and industrialists. In addition, western cowboys were also admired. They had inherited the mantle of the frontiersman and Indian fighters after Owen Wister apotheosized their lives as cattle raisers into a saga of gun-slinging drama in his 1901 novel *The Virginian*. But there were others whose image was softer and whose aggressive masculinity was countered by sophistication and humor.
>
> Cosmopolitan men of the theater, for example, were popular. This was the age, after all, when the Barrymores first rose to prominence. In the 1890s many stationery and jewelry stores displayed in their windows photos of Maurice Barrymore holding an elegant demitasse cup and saucer in his hand and garbed in full dress as in one of his famed portrayals. . . .
>
> —Lois W. Banner, *American Beauty*

For much of the writing you do in college, you must support your ideas with research. Outside sources provide the information you need, and expert testimony lends prestige and authority to what you write. The authors of the following excerpt rely on outside sources to support their views about science education:

> The design of this science classroom . . . is also based on the notion that schools are not just buildings, and that all people are life-long learners. The need for relevance in the experiences of school children and for applicability and currency in teacher-training programs is not a new one; however, these needs are not often met.
>
> In *Educating Americans for the 21st Century,* a National Science Board Report, technology and an understanding of technological advances and applications were recognized as basic. While initial effects of the infusion of computers into instruction might not have produced desired results (Greenburg 107), the relevance of technology education is still apparent. Kids learn differently today, differently from the learning modes familiar to us. In the twentieth century people were "paper" trained. Youngsters of the twenty-first century are "light" trained, i.e., comfortable with video- and computer-based material. Matching learning styles with delivery systems is crucial for success.
>
> —Richard J. Reif and Gail M. Morse, "Restructuring the Science Classroom"

To support their thesis about classroom technology, the authors cite a report of the National Science Board. Even when they cite another source (Greenburg) that disputes some of their claims, Reif and Morse show readers that they are well informed and have considered other points of view.

EXERCISE | ## Analyzing Development

Read each of the following excerpts and respond to these questions: What is the main idea? What specific facts, ideas, or examples does the author present to support and develop that idea? What, if anything, demonstrates the author's authority to address the topic? Would a different approach (e.g., citing more sources or personal experiences) be more effective?

a. In Memory of Merry Oldsmobiles

Jerry Garrett

The only new car my grandmother bought was a dark green 1951 Oldsmobile Series 98 Deluxe with a Rocket V-8 engine. Family members proudly posed in front of it when Grandma, then forty-four, drove home from the dealership.

A few days later, she wrapped a telephone pole around it, when she couldn't stop it fast enough. No one was hurt, although the car was a total loss.

"It just had too much power," said Grandma, who never drove again. But for decades she encouraged family members to keep buying Oldsmobiles—88's and 98's, Starfires, and Cutlasses—because, she said, "It proved it's a strong car."

In 1951, it was strong enough to inspire Ike Turner and the Kings of Rhythm to immortalize Olds's amazing new V-8 engine. They arguably created rock 'n' roll in the process.

"Rocket 88" was the first hit for Sam Phillips, and the producer used money from its sales to start Sun Records, which would go on to "discover" Elvis Presley, Jerry Lee Lewis, B. B. King, Johnny Cash, and others.

"'Rocket 88' was where it all started," Phillips would say years later. "It was the first true rock 'n' roll record—the first hit record, anyway."

This was not the first time an Oldsmobile inspired a song. Vincent Bryan wrote the lyrics of "In My Merry Oldsmobile" in 1905 to pay tribute to the toast of the fledgling American auto industry, the Curved Dash runabout from the Olds Motor Works.

Olds, formed in 1897, was, until it went out of business this spring, America's oldest automaker, and the Curved Dash was the early auto sales leader and the first vehicle to be mass produced. (Henry Ford would later automate the assembly process.)

"I don't like the smell of horses," Ransom E. Olds reportedly told those who asked him why he had started his pioneering work on horseless carriages. His first vehicle, built in 1887, was steam-powered. (Gottlieb Daimler is credited with building the first gasoline-powered car about a year earlier.)

The Curved Dash's rise was fortuitous; Olds had designed and built eleven prototypes to be produced at a new factory in Detroit. But the factory burned to the ground; only the heroic act of a foreman, who dragged a lone Curved Dash to safety, kept the company going. Olds returned to his home in Lansing, Michigan, where he began reproducing the sturdy little runabout, the only car he had left.

Public demand was stoked by publicity stunts, like having Olds's associate, Roy Chapin (who later headed American Motors), drive a Curved Dash to New York City for the first auto show there, in 1901, to demonstrate the car's durability.

Olds's investors, however, would run him off in 1904. He formed Reo (named from his initials), which outsold Olds for a time. Reo would stay in business until 1975. Olds lived in Lansing until he died in 1950, but never returned to Oldsmobile. His home was later razed for construction of Interstate 496—the Olds Freeway.

Olds would become, with Buick, the cornerstone of Billy Durant's General Motors in 1908, but no one would get around to incorporating the Oldsmobile name until 1942.

Within GM, Olds was the "technology division." It was a pioneer in V-8 engines, as early as 1915. Chrome made its automotive debut on 1926 models. Olds offered the first automatic transmission (later named Hydra Matic) in 1937. The Rocket V-8 made its debut in 1949.

That high-compression engine, and the 88 model in which it was installed, created a sensation. Oldsmobile dominated Bill France's Nascar racing association in its first three seasons.

"The combination of the Oldsmobile chassis and the Rocket V-8 was unbeatable, in the hands of the right driver," France said years later.

France knew that firsthand: in 1950 he and Curtis Turner, in a Lincoln, would be beaten in the first Mexican Road Race by an Oregon lumberjack, Hershel McGriff, driving an Olds in showroom stock trim. Oldsmobile would hire Mr. McGriff to crisscross the country, making promotional appearances and racing his 88. After finishing ninth in the inaugural Southern 500 in 1950, Mr. McGriff would drive the Olds from South Carolina to Portland, arriving with 15,000 miles on the odometer.

"Those were all hard miles," Mr. McGriff, seventy-four, and still living in Oregon, remembers. "That was one tough little coupe." The prizes he won in five years of racing set him up for life in the lumber business.

Oldsmobiles helped put the Petty family on the road to racing riches, too; Lee Petty drove one to victory in the first Daytona 500, in 1959. His son Richard made his debut there in an Oldsmobile convertible.

Olds's performance image was reinforced in the 1960s by models like the turbocharged F-85; the innovative Toronado with front-wheel drive and hideaway headlights; and the 4-4-2, named for its four-on-the-floor shifter, four-barrel carburetor, and twin exhaust pipes. The Hurst/Olds, with fancy aftermarket shifter, garish paint, and removable T-top roof panels, was a common sight at American racetracks.

Through the 1970s and early 1980s, the popularity of the Cutlass Supreme made Olds the nation's third-best-selling brand. But in the mid 1980s, a sweeping reorganization ordered by GM's chairman, Roger Smith, eviscerated the close-knit Olds "family"—a completely self-contained company that designed, engineered, and produced its own cars. Olds was now folded into a new Buick-Olds-Cadillac superdivision.

Suddenly, Oldsmobiles were being built outside Lansing; the local plant was making Buicks. Olds's unique engines were even replaced by Chevy power plants. Insiders complained that Olds had lost not only its identity, but its ability to stand behind its products, address problems, and develop models. By the time the reorganization was undone, the damage was irreversible.

In the 1990s, under the outspoken leadership of John D. Rock, Oldsmobile received a last chance to re-establish its identity. New models like the Achieva, Intrigue, Aurora, and Alero replaced venerable names like Eighty-Eight, Ninety-Eight, and Cutlass. The Rocket V-8 was discontinued after a forty-year run. Extreme emphasis on motorsports produced A. J. Foyt's world closed-course speed record of 257 mph, plus an Indianapolis 500 victory on Olds's hundredth birthday in 1997 (in a predominantly Olds field). But that would not be enough to save the brand.

"Oldsmobile never had to die," an Olds historian, Helen Earley, said. "But GM seemed determined to kill it."

In an interview during a vintage car race in 2001, Robert A. Lutz, vice chairman of GM, said: "The one decision I wish hadn't been made before I got here was the decision to fold Oldsmobile. I could have done big things with it."

Mr. Lutz, who arrived a year too late, saw in Olds the "boutique car company" he'd envisioned for Plymouth, another discontinued brand, when he was at Chrysler.

"Olds had such a rich history," he said. But ultimately, it had no future.

b. The Evolution of a Daffy Species

Dave Kehr

For just about every American born since World War II, the Warner Brothers cartoons occupy a prime piece of subconscious real estate. Thanks to innumerable television showings, the Warner cartoons mean more to us now than they did to the theatrical audiences they were originally made for in the 1930s, 40s, and 50s. They are our true national fairy tales, focused on primal fears and desires and filled with archetypes of human behavior that approach the profundity of the Greek myths.

Such seminal work deserves a scholarly anthology, and while the new four-DVD box set from Warner Home Video, *The Looney Tunes Golden Collection,* is not quite the Pleaide edition of one's dreams, it will do until something else comes along.

Though it includes fifty-six cartoons, most so meticulously restored that the tiny shadows cast by the animation cels on the painted backgrounds are now visible, the set barely scratches the surface of the studio's output, which could run as high as forty short films a year.

But the selection that has been made for this edition is both informed and informative. Enlisting some of the leading scholars of animation, including Greg Ford, Michael Barrier, and John Canemaker, the producers have come up with a collection that, rather than aspiring to an impossible completeness, concentrates on the work of the three major Warner cartoon directors of the postwar period: Chuck Jones, the master of character and expression; Isidore (Friz) Freleng, the great technician of the group; and Robert McKimson, a bread-and-butter animator who nevertheless contributed several important late characters to the Warner Brothers stable like Foghorn Leghorn and Henry the Hawk.

The first two discs in the package are ostensibly devoted to "The Best of Bugs Bunny" and "The Best of Daffy and Porky," but they are in fact a panorama of some of Jones's finest work, with a few Frelengs and McKimsons tossed in. Jones, who joined the studio in 1934 as an assistant, appears here in a taped introduction shot not long before his death last year at the age of eighty-nine. By 1939, Jones had been promoted to director, signing first a serious, if somewhat painfully cute, cartoon starring the pudgy early Porky and the cloying, now forgotten Sniffles the Mouse.

The year 1940, however, found Jones working on a new character, a wise-cracking rabbit developed by the director Tex Avery for his short "A Wild Hare." In "Elmer's Candid Camera" (it is the oldest cartoon included in this collection), Jones took the still unnamed rabbit, calmed down a bit of Avery's aggressiveness and invested him with a brash, all-American optimism and resolution. The character resonated throughout an America on the brink of war, and by the time the country had entered the conflict, Bugs had become a national mascot—perhaps the first and only lasting star produced by World War II.

As developed by Jones and Freleng during the war years, Bugs Bunny became a symbol of American pluck, resourcefulness, and determination in the face of overwhelming odds. Elmer Fudd, a prewar character, proved to be too gentle, too dumb, and far too benign to provide an appropriate foil to Bugs during the war, and so Yosemite Sam, a creation of Freleng's, appeared on the scene, to take over the villainous roles with a Hitlerian rage seasoned by a strutting, comic pomposity borrowed from Mussolini (whose body type, a barrel chest poised on tiny legs, quickly became the Looney Tunes model for guest bullies, up to and including McKimso's Tasmanian Devil).

Perhaps because the rights to the films are spread among different divisions of the Time Warner empire—or perhaps because Warner Home Video didn't want to risk confusing home consumers with strange, black-and-white cartoons—the *Golden Collection* concentrates on films made after 1948. War fever had long subsided and Jones, in particular, found himself free to explore other aspects of his characters' personalities. An automatic identification with winners during the war years—epitomized by the huge popularity of Bugs—shifted in Jones's case to a deep sympathy for the underdogs.

In 1949, Jones made two transitional films, both included in this set. "For Scent-imental Reasons" introduced Pepe Le Pew, a skunk with the purring voice and seductive manner of Charles Boyer, poignantly unaware that his powerful smell might compromise his success with the ladies. And in "The Fast and the Furry-ous," the Road Runner and Wile E. Coyote made their screen debuts, in a cartoon that pushed an already abstract genre into something approaching formalism. The geometric purity of the desert landscapes, the elemental conflict between hunter (the desperate, ravenous coyote) and hunted (the insouciant, omnipotent road runner), the relentless rhythm of the simple, black-out gags all combine to create a kind of comic fable that is both modern and classical, situated somewhere between Sisyphus and Sartre. (Jones went the extra distance with his truly minimal "The Dot and the Line," in which the characters are a dot and a line—but it's not in the collection, unfortunately.)

But as Jones was refining the animated cartoon to its absolute limits, he was also building it up, bringing to the form a kind of detailed character psychology without parallel in the medium. By 1950, when Jones was making films like "The Scarlet Pumpernickel," "The Ducksters" and "The Rabbit of Seville," he had transformed the Warner stable of characters into a genuine stock company, each character playing his role in an evolving drama of interpersonal relations.

Daffy, who had been Bugs's predecessor as a force of mad, blind destructiveness, had by 1950 become the most moving of Jones's eternally frustrated second-bananas, a "we-try-harder" number-two star whose attempts to supplant the reigning bunny rabbit (whose brash self-confidence had by now become somewhat complacent and superior) met with certain humiliation. Jones's work through the 1950s, much of the best of which is included in this collection, found him developing Daffy, Bugs, Porky, and Elmer into some of the most well-rounded, psychologically vivid characters in the cinema; it becomes easy to believe in their autonomy, so fully do they exist in Jones's imagination.

Among the generous supplemental material on the *Golden Collection* disc is a two-part documentary from the 1970s, "The Boys From Termine Terrace," in which Friz Freleng twice insists that "we never made these films for children—we made them for ourselves." The adult nature of these cartoons was reinforced by Joe Dante's recent, unjustly unappreciated revival of the characters for *Looney Tunes: Back in Action,* an often brilliantly funny film that struggled to rescue the Looney Tunes from the cuteness forced upon them by franchising requirements and return them to their anarchic fury and formal sophistication. Mr. Dante's film is, in itself, one of the finest appreciations of the Warner cartoons offered to date, and a film that needs to be rescued from the Saturday morning audience to which it was mismarketed.

With perhaps five percent of the Looney Tunes output represented on the *Golden Collection,* there should be enough titles remaining to get Warner Home Video up to the Diamond-Encrusted Platinum Collection and beyond. One hopes these future collections will redress the relative neglect of three vitally important Warners directors—Bob Clampett, Tex Avery, and Frank Tashlin—in this first compendium. There is a mountain of material here, perhaps the richest vein in American humor since Mark Twain.

Organization and Coherence

Writing well involves courtesy. Like good hosts, writers are considerate of their audience. Of course, great poets and novelists often challenge readers through experimental techniques. But nonfiction writers, whose aim usually is to inform or persuade, tend to be more straightforward. They make their point and stick to it. Their readers expect clarity and logic. As one writing theorist, the late Kenneth

Burke, expressed it, writers have a duty to take readers by the hand, walking them through a text and helping them see connections among ideas, sentences, and paragraphs.

Analytical readers may consider some of the following questions about organization and coherence: Does the writer show where the text is heading? Is there a clear progression of ideas? Are you ever puzzled, lost, or taken by surprise? Is there a clear link between the main idea and supporting details? Is the supporting material arranged logically? Does the writer provide transitions when introducing new ideas?

Not every writer gives readers the help they need. The following passage, for example, leaves us to shift for ourselves; it is so poorly organized that we cannot accurately predict where it will go next. The writer arouses expectations about one topic but then veers off in other directions.

> You wouldn't believe my son Jason. He was so unbelievably wild and inconsiderate yesterday, I got one of my headaches. They come on with a vengeance, with no warning. I was so crazy with pain last week, it will be a miracle if my sister-in-law ever speaks to me again. I've been to specialist after specialist, and none of them can find the problem. A lot of money they get paid, for what? Fancy offices and fancy diplomas so they can charge fancy fees. When I think about doctors, I get another headache. My head throbs and my eyes don't focus. I don't want anything to do with people, and I'm as miserable to Jason as he is to me. Maybe Jason will be lucky enough to become a doctor someday and then the money can stay in the family.

This writer disregards organization, writing whatever comes to mind. He leads us to think the paragraph will be about Jason's behavior, but it turns into a discussion of his headaches, with frequent detours to other topics. Later, we expect to find out what he said to his sister-in-law, but that topic is abandoned with no concern for the reader's unsatisfied curiosity. The topic of doctors is introduced, then forgotten, then finally reintroduced near the end, without logical explanation.

In contrast, the essays in the following exercise are coherent, readable, and logical because the writers have considered how to present their ideas to readers. They have organized the movement of their thoughts by providing signposts. Coherence, however, is relative. Some readers may find one of the essays more carefully organized than the other.

Analyzing Organization   EXERCISE

After reading each of the following essays carefully, explain as specifically as you can how the writer has organized the text. Why is it arranged as it is? How does the writer move from one idea to the next? From general to specific? How are sentences and paragraphs linked to each other? How does the writer guide you through the text? Are there digressions or gaps in either essay? Does one essay seem more cohesive than the other?

a. Wines Have Feelings, Too

Eric Asimov

Almost from the moment humans began putting goblets to lips, they have challenged themselves to describe the experience of consuming wine. It has not been easy.

What does a wine smell like, anyway, and how does it taste? Does it remind you of fruit or flowers, or mushrooms and brambles? Possibly those metaphors are too literal. Maybe the overall effect is of a symphony, or a string quartet, or a Jimi Hendrix solo, or crumpled sheets the morning after. You could, of course, just say, "It smells like grapes and tastes like wine," but you'd be laughed out of the tasting club. And to differentiate among wines, even if just for yourself, you at least have to make the effort.

Trouble is, most efforts focus solely on aromas and flavors, which seems to make sense because they are a wine's most immediately striking characteristics. But another important distinguishing feature is not detectable by eyes, nose, or taste buds. That is texture, the tactile sense of wine on the mouth, tongue, and throat. If it's difficult to find words for the aromas and flavors of wine, how much tougher it is to describe the feel.

Think about it too much, and you might find it embarrassing to describe a liquid as crisp, or steely. But that's really no sillier than calling wines harsh or smooth; most wine drinkers know those sensations, whether the components that produce them are apparent or not.

The idea of texture in a liquid is so difficult, in fact, that wine experts cannot even agree on what to call it. You won't find the word *texture* listed in the encyclopedic *Oxford Companion to Wine,* for example. Instead, you must settle for the unwieldy term *mouthfeel* and its constituents: body, density, weight, and, for the truly geeky, viscosity. Joshua Wesson, chairman of Best Cellars, a chain of eight wine shops, uses the term *umami,* a Japanese word for the elusive, indescribably delicious quality that goes beyond salty, sweet, sour, and bitter.

Whatever you call it, great texture is a crucial though undervalued characteristic of the best wines. It's a crackling vivacity that insinuates itself in your mouth, almost demanding that you take another sip simply because it feels so good.

"It's the same seduction that one first feels when touching cashmere or fur," Mr. Wesson said. "Nobody touches fur once, or cashmere once. With wine, you want to keep it in your mouth; you want to play with it; you want to roll it around until you get it."

Almost all the most memorable wines I've tasted in the last year or so have had beautiful textures in common, wines as diverse as a '92 Puligny-Montrachet Les Pucelles from Domaine Leflaive and a '94 Hillside Select cabernet sauvignon from Shafer in the Napa Valley.

These are world-class bottles, with three-figure prices, but a wine doesn't have to be expensive to feel great in the mouth. I can think of a luscious '02 Austrian riesling from Hirsch in the Kamptal for $28, a minerally '02 Sancerre from Etienne Riffault for $20, and a smoky '98 Tuscan sangiovese from Montevertine for $27. All had a mouthwatering quality that, whatever the price, both refreshed and entranced.

It's a rare winemaker who, unbidden, actually speaks about texture, but recently Richard Geoffroy, the cellar master for Dom Perignon Champagne, told me that for him the quest for the proper texture was the supreme goal in his winemaking.

"That feel, that chew, that third dimension: that's really what I'm working on," Mr. Geoffroy said, grasping for words in English, his second language, and coming up with some evocative ones.

For Mr. Geoffroy texture is sort of a conveyor belt that carries the aromatic and flavor components through the mouth from sip to swallow and beyond. Champagne's effervescence offers a different textural experience from that of most wines, of course. Some people, trying to explain why Champagne goes so well with fried or spicy foods, talk about the bubbles' "scrubbing" the mouth. I don't know about that, but I do know you can feel the difference between a lively, vibrant Champagne and one that fatigues the mouth. It's texture.

"I'm always amused that people are so interested in aromatics," Mr. Geoffroy said.

Obtaining a deeper understanding of texture is not easy. Wine books devote scant attention to it, and a research foray can easily lead to terms like polysaccharides and anthocyanins, from which there is little hope of escape. In an effort to codify the textural experience of red wine, the Australian Wine Research Institute developed something it calls the mouthfeel wheel, with a vocabulary including words like *parching, grippy, watery,* and *sappy.* Frankly, consulting the mouthfeel wheel is about as appealing as contemplating a mouthful of polysaccharides.

A simpler way of thinking of texture is to keep in mind its integral components, which most often are acidity and, especially in red wines, tannins. Most wine drinkers are familiar with tannins. They are the astringent compounds that in a young, tannic red wine—a Barolo, say, or a Bordeaux—can seem to suck all the moisture out of your mouth. Ideally, the tannins soften over time, allowing other characteristics to emerge. Tannins come from the grapes' skins, seeds, and stems, and, if the wines are aged in new oak barrels, they can come from the wood, too.

Acidity is the juicy, zingy quality. Too much acidity, and a wine can feel harsh and aggressive. Too little, and it feels flabby and shapeless. During the making of a wine, the acidity can evolve from the crispness of malic acids in the direction of softer lactic acids. Interestingly, lactic acids often provide a creamy texture to a wine. Aging a wine without removing its yeast remnants can also add silkiness.

While descriptions of texture will never replace those of aromas and flavors in the tasting notes so dear to the hearts of consumers, the feel of a wine is worthy of more attention. Yet most people bypass texture and go directly from smelling to tasting, even well-meaning wine lovers who violently agitate the wine in their mouths before swallowing.

"When people chew wine, they don't really get a sense of its texture because they're putting it through the wash-rinse cycle of the mouth," Mr. Wesson said. "On first sip, I just let it sit there. Then I push it around with my tongue. When you push it around slowly, you get a much better sense of texture."

Then, maybe, you can figure out what to call it.

b. Forever Yours: The Best Commercial Brands Build Strong Consumer Loyalty

Daniel Gross

Few people hold up the Hare Krishna or the Unification Church of the Reverend Sun Myung Moon as models to be mimicked. After all, cults—especially religious ones—have a bad name. But when it comes to commercial cults, the reaction is different. Movies that are obscure yet profitable, like *The Rocky Horror Picture Show,* are dubbed "cult classics." Cult bands like the Grateful Dead or Phish may not get airplay on MTV, yet they attract legions of devoted fans.

In our economy of abundance, we all have infinite choices in everything from music to soft drinks—so why do some brands attract devoted customers? The question is a great commercial mystery.

In his new book, *The Culting of Brands,* advertising executive Douglas Atkin found a lot of similarities between the ways cults attract members and the ways in which companies like Harley-Davidson, Apple, Saturn, and Snapple build fanatical followings. At root, he argues, cults are the means through which people express their individuality in a group context and seek self-actualization. And in our marketing-saturated society, commercial products can increasingly serve these human needs.

Take the original American cult brand: Harley-Davidson motorcycles. In 1903, William S. Harley and Arthur Davidson built their first motorcycle. Their company immediately established itself amid brutal competition, as dozens of American motorcycle makers struggled for a place on the road. But in the decades that followed, only two survived, and when rival Indian Motorcycle Company closed shop in 1953, Harley-Davidson was the last of the Mohicans.

In the post-World War II era, Harley-Davidson motorcycles—a rumbling sign of rebellion in an age of conformity—became icons. Elvis Presley drove one, and so did tough-guy actor Steve McQueen. The large bikes appeared prominently in movies like *Easy Rider.* Groups of self-styled bikers—even outlaws—viewed their Harleys as an integral part of their identity. Many went so far as to tattoo the name of the product on their bodies. How many car owners went to such lengths?

Harley-Davidson suffered when a new corporate owner began producing inferior bikes and Japanese motorcycles took a huge market share in the 1970s. But in the 1980s, a group of HD executives bought the company back and set about retooling it, in part by copying Japanese manufacturing styles. The efforts would not have succeeded, however, had they not been able to tap into the bike's cult status. As CEO Vaughn Beals put it, Harley riders didn't just buy motorcycles; they were buying "the Harley experience." Recognizing the extraordinary loyalty of its customers—ninety-five percent of owners were repeat buyers—the company started HOG (Harley Owners' Group) in 1983. HOG offered the means for like-minded bikers to meet at local rides, and provided a point of access for newcomers. And Harley, which recovered from its near-death experience in the 1980s, still has a strong cult image. "It calls out to discontents with an accurately pitched song of recognition," Atkin notes.

Cult brands are also able to survive as niche players—in markets dominated by gigantic companies. For two decades, Apple Computer has managed to thrive in a world dominated by Microsoft's Windows-based PCs. Among the main factors: fanatical devotion to the company's charismatic founder and leader, Steve Jobs, and a sense among Apple users that they are part of a unique movement and community.

Ever since its famous anti-IBM ads in 1984, which portrayed Big Blue as an Orwellian force, Apple has inspired its adherents to "think different." One Apple ad campaign featured pictures of Picasso, Gandhi, and Einstein, with the tagline, "Here's to the crazy ones." Many devoted Apple users work in creative fields. Atkin says that "roughly thirty percent of its customers are graphic designers and artists."

Pursuing such a strategy may limit your size, but it may also enable you to roll out new products. Many companies are now selling music over the Internet. But

Apple's iTunes music store is the leader. Downloaded songs can be played on the iPod—another Apple invention. In a crowded field, Apple can tap into a highly devoted base of customers for whom using Apple products is a crucial part of their identity. As Atkin says, it "intuitively plugs into a community's distinct meaning system and corollary symbolic code." Mac users *get* the iPod in a way that Dell PC users don't.

There are other examples of cult brands that have succeeded, not because their product was somehow better than all others, but because they inspired a feeling of belonging and community among users. When Saturn launched its first car line in 1990, the cars were pretty ordinary. But its efforts to create a community of users—a cult surrounding the brand—were extraordinary. Saturn held monthly clinics to explain maintenance and invited owners to barbecues. Every year it held a reunion at its Tennessee plant for Saturn owners, drawing from around the country up to 45,000 drivers who had little else in common.

Saturn is now tightly integrated into the operations of its parent, General Motors. But cult brands don't always fare well under large corporate ownership. Snapple burst out of nowhere in the 1980s to garner a significant chunk of the highly competitive beverage market. Part of its appeal was its deliberately unslick image—its chief spokesperson was company employee Wendy Kaufman, who in TV ads answered fan mail in a thick, nasal New York accent.

But in 1994, when Quaker Oats paid $1.7 billion for Snapple, one of the first things it did was ditch cult-favorite Wendy. Sales slumped almost immediately. Even though Snapple still tasted the same, without Wendy, buying Snapple simply didn't feel the same. In 1997, Triarc bought the damaged Snapple brand for $300 million, and the new owners brought Wendy back with a parade down Fifth Avenue. The customers came back, too.

In his book, Atkin tries to lay down a process and a set of rules by which companies can enlist devoted followers to even humdrum brands. But ultimately there's no sure-fire method for turning your brand into a cult hit. The managers and owners of Harley-Davidson did not set out to build a cult brand; they tried to build motorcycles. It evolved into a cult brand over decades, and it did so as a result of popular-culture trends that the company and its ad team had little influence on.

All companies want to inspire devotion among their core customers. But not all of them can create such fierce brand loyalty. And in a way, companies that try too hard to do so may be destined to fail. Cult brands catch on because they strike psychological chords among groups of people, and for reasons that are not always clear. Proclaiming yourself to be a cult brand guarantees nothing. The savvy consumer has the final vote.

 ## WRITING A BRIEF READING ANALYSIS

Purpose, audience, main idea, development, organization, and coherence—these are the most important, but by no means the only, things to consider when you analyze a text. In addition to considering these general elements, you should approach a text on its own terms. Because texts are not all alike, and because engaged readers often respond to the same text in different ways, there is no formula for analysis. Though it is always important to read carefully and perceptively, it is also wise not to strive for a "correct" interpretation or analysis.

Having studied each of the five elements of analysis separately, you should now understand how they work together. When you analyze a complete text, you should consider all five elements. Read the following editorial carefully and analytically, contemplating each of the elements we have presented.

PRACTICE READING

"Ernie's Nuns" Are Pointing the Way

Molly Ivins

Way to go, college students!

Reebok, the sports shoe manufacturer, admitted this week that conditions at two of its factories in Indonesia were distinctly sub-par and says its subcontractors have spent $500,000 to improve them. Reebok's actions came after a boycott of its shoes on campuses around the country coordinated by United Students against Sweatshops, a nationwide student coalition. Nice going, good win.

Reebok also deserves credit: in response to the boycott and criticism from human-rights groups, the company commissioned a study of working conditions in its foreign factories fourteen months ago and has apparently followed up on the findings. "We hope that this will also break through and encourage more companies to do something like this," said a Reebok vice president.

USAS also urged students to join a new group—the Worker Rights Consortium—that will set a strict code of conduct for overseas factories that make clothes with university names.

USAS then pressed universities to withdraw from the Fair Labor Association . . . on grounds that the group's practices are insufficient. The specific criticisms of Fair Labor include letting manufacturers choose which plants will be monitored and giving advance notice of inspections. Another very smart move by the college students. In my day, we referred to this as "not getting co-opted by the Establishment."

Several human-rights groups have helped with the anti-sweatshop movement, but the bulk of the energy seems to have come from the campuses.

USAS has become quite sophisticated about how to guarantee independent monitoring and is also working for living wages for foreign workers, based on economic conditions in each country. These laptop activists have already had a major impact on the collegiate licensing industry and should in time be able to affect the entire apparel industry.

The apparel industry is—to use a word I loathe—paradigmatic, in that it is completely globalized and notoriously exploitative. Apparel manufacturers are actually design and marketing firms that "outsource" production to independent contractors all over the world. This model is increasingly copied by other industries as they seek to lower labor costs and avoid worker organizing.

Any Texan can get a look at the results by visiting the maquiladoras just on the other side of the Tex-Mex border. The toxic dump in Matamoras is worth a visit all on its own.

Tom Friedman, the *New York Times*'s foreign affairs columnist, has observed: "For many workers around the world the oppression of unchecked commissars has been replaced by the oppression of the unregulated capitalists, who move their manufacturing from country to country, constantly in search of those who will work for the lowest wages and lowest standards. To some, the Nike swoosh is now as scary as the hammer and sickle."

Middle-aged activists who waste time bemoaning apathy on campus could help by getting off their duffs and helping spread word about the USAS boycotts.

Lest you think hideous working conditions are found only in the Third World, consider the case of Big Chicken, the poultry industry in America.

Workers in chicken factories endure conditions that would shame Guatemala or Honduras. Many stand for hours on end in sheds that reek of manure, or chop chickens all day in cold, dark plants, or are constantly scratched by live chickens that have to be crammed into cages by the thousands.

The *New York Times* reported that the Reverend Jim Lewis, an Episcopal priest whose assignment is to improve the lives of poultry workers, once led a wildcat strike against a plant where a worker was fired after he had a finger cut off. The wages are so low, workers often qualify for welfare. And as Texans know from our experience with Big Chicken in East Texas, these plants are often notorious polluters as well, fouling both air and water.

The point of the *Times* article on Lewis was to demonstrate that hundreds of priests, ministers, and rabbis are involved in struggles to improve conditions for American workers on the bottom rungs of society.

This seems to me at least as newsworthy as the latest bulletin from the Christian right that Tinkie-Winkie, the purple Teletubbie, is gay or that Harry Potter books are Satanic.

If you were asked to analyze Molly Ivins's editorial, you might begin by free-writing about each of the five elements, producing preliminary notes such as these:

> <u>Purpose</u>: Ivins hopes to do more than provoke a response
> from her audience; she intends to rouse them to action.
> She talks about people "getting off their duffs," as if she
> wants to shame them into supporting boycotts. Newspaper
> opinion pieces like this often elicit a disengaged--even
> contemplative--response, asking readers to reconsider
> conventional attitudes or opinions, appealing to fairness
> and detached skepticism. But rather than urging her readers
> to consider new or controversial ideas, Ivins appeals to
> their <u>consciences</u>, almost shouting at them to take action.
> She opens her essay with an exclamation and ends with dark
> sarcasm. In the few places where she adopts the more polite,
> sophisticated language of "think pieces"--using words like
> <u>paradigmatic</u> and <u>outsource</u>--she seems at pains to distance
> herself from it.
> <u>Audience</u>: Ivins opens as though she were speaking
> directly to college students, and she continues in that vein

throughout her first two paragraphs. But in paragraph 5 it becomes clear that she really is talking <u>about</u> the actions of a <u>specific group</u> of students--"Another very smart move by the college students." The word <u>you</u> doesn't appear until paragraph 12: "Lest <u>you</u> think hideous working conditions are found only in the Third World...." Here, it sounds like she's talking down to her readers, the "middle-aged activists" she has scolded in the previous paragraph. But in spite of her exasperation with their inertia, Ivins exhorts these readers who share her values; she doesn't try to win over corporate executives or conservatives. She identifies herself as a Texan when she says "as <u>Texans</u> know from <u>our</u> experience," but I think that's because she writes a column in the Fort Worth newspaper; the issues she deals with are international in scope, and there are people throughout the world who share Ivins's concerns.

<u>Main Idea</u>: Ivins wants readers to know that savvy, committed activists are bringing abusive labor practices to light and are fighting to eliminate them. Ivins says that middle-aged, middle-class Americans who share her views ought to participate in those efforts.

<u>Development</u>: In her first seven paragraphs, Ivins presents evidence that may have come from a news story written for the Associated Press or one of the other wire services. In the next several paragraphs, she reveals knowledge of the broader economic implications of franchising and outsourcing. In paragraphs 9, 12, and 13, she leads us to understand that she has observed the inhumane working conditions in Mexico and Texas. She also quotes an article from the <u>New York Times</u> and refers to another.

<u>Organization and Coherence</u>: In her first five paragraphs, Ivins sounds triumphant, like she's gloating over the fact that someone is at last taking action. She sounds like a cheerleader: "Way to go...! Nice going, good win." The next five paragraphs place a specific event (one manufacturer's response to student activism) within a global economic context. In the following three paragraphs, Ivins alerts her audience of "middle-aged activists" to the urgency of the issue. It's not just news from some Third World country that receives brief coverage in newspaper; it's something that well-meaning Americans permit to happen within or close to their own communities. Finally, Ivins refers to one particular activist, Jim Lewis, and to the conditions he opposes and what he's doing to change them.

These notes are a beginning. You would next compose a draft to be revised and edited. Finally, a polished analysis might look like this:

Analysis: "'Ernie's Nuns' Are Pointing the Way"

Molly Ivins, a syndicated columnist for the Fort Worth Star-Telegram, addresses an audience of aging Baby Boomers, many of whom were Civil Rights activists and war protestors during their college years in the 1960s. By applauding the commitment and savvy of present-day students who have organized boycotts to improve working conditions in garment factories overseas, Ivins tries to shame readers into action. Specifically, she upbraids them for "bemoaning apathy on campus" and enjoins them to get "off their duffs" to "spread word about the . . . boycotts."

Unlike some Op-Ed authors, Ivins does not try to appear objective or disengaged from the issue. She assumes that readers share her values and political views, and she makes no effort to persuade anyone who doesn't. She appeals to our consciences rather than pursuing the kind of detached inquiry often found in journalistic think pieces. In fact, Ivins mocks the vocabulary of politically disengaged writing. She tries to distance herself from the word outsource by placing it in quotation marks and, when forced to use the word paradigmatic, she inserts a sarcastic aside: "to use a word I loathe."

To earn the moral authority to which she lays claim, Ivins must demonstrate knowledge of the issue--a challenging task in so short an essay. Her familiarity with the focusing event that introduces this essay--the successful boycott of Reebok by the United Students against Sweatshops--is a good start. However, many readers are aware that information like this is readily available through newspaper wire services, which editorial writers routinely consult. More impressive is Ivins's grasp of the economic implications of franchising and outsourcing, a preemptive response to people who might otherwise dismiss her views as naively idealistic. Ivins further enhances her credentials with specific references to working conditions in Texas and Mexico.

Ivins's essay consists of three parts. In the first five paragraphs, Ivins gloats over a successful boycott. Her tone is gleeful and exultant: "Way to go . . . Nice going, good win." The next five paragraphs demonstrate knowledge and credibility: Ivins places the boycott in a global context with heroes (labor activists) and villains (greedy corporations). Then, in her final paragraphs, Ivins appeals for action. She describes the horrible working conditions in chicken factories, tells how one person is combatting the abuse, and urges readers to join the struggle.

ASSIGNMENT   **Writing a Brief Reading Analysis**

Analyze the following essay, using this procedure:

- Read the essay twice, underlining important ideas and writing in the margins.
- Freewrite about each of the five elements of analysis.
- Compose and carefully revise a draft. Begin with a description of the essay (its purpose, audience, and main idea); then analyze development, organization, and coherence. Edit your draft thoroughly.

 READING SELECTION

The following editorial by the vice president for academic affairs at Southern Oregon University appeared in the *Chronicle of Higher Education.*

Opening Ourselves to Unconditional Love in Our Relationships with Students

SARA HOPKINS-POWELL

The concept of unconditional love may seem an unlikely topic for college faculty **1** members to consider in this time of sexual-harassment charges and consensual-relationship policies. And yet, one of the greatest gifts we have as teachers, mentors, and co-creators of learning is the ability to care so deeply for individual students that we hold them in our hearts regardless of whether we agree with their life choices.

This definition of unconditional love is not an abstract concept for me, but one **2** that I have experienced as both the receiver and the giver. My passion is the power of education to transform people's lives, and it follows that an intimacy can sometimes occur in the process that transcends the typical student-teacher relationship. I am not suggesting that faculty members establish such a relationship with every student; in fact, you are privileged if it happens more than once or twice in your lifetime.

Disturbingly, when I began research for this essay on the Internet, the most fre- **3** quent hits for the term "unconditional love" were sites related to pedophiles, who use the phrase to cloak their real intent. The second most-common use of the term was in the context of religion and theology, with emphasis on the relationship between God and humanity. It is difficult to find references to unconditional love between parents and children, and few sites use the term even remotely as an emotion between adults.

How do we experience unconditional love in our teaching? While this happens **4** with students who share our interests, one of the surprises is that frequently the student in question does not mirror our own interests or personality, although the affinity of a shared experience sparks the initial contact. The student may differ in temperament, background, or interests.

Sometimes, it's someone you initially overlooked in the classroom. These are of- **5** ten the students who are quiet in class but who ask the insightful questions. Unconditional love does not develop immediately but results from repeated interaction either in class or in other settings. Faculty members teaching large lectures may never have the time to share an intimate relationship with three hundred students, but it could be the one student who routinely comes to office hours. More likely, the possibility for this kind of friendship arises during a seminar or the supervision of thesis or dissertation work, or with a student who works in a laboratory or studio.

Let me describe my own personal experience with such a relationship. When I was **6** in graduate school, I was assigned an adviser. My first meeting with him was difficult. He found normal conversations trying, and he took an eternity to get to the point. I quickly learned that if I waited, not only would I receive an answer, but an eloquent one at that.

I took a class from him my first semester, although it was not a subject that I **7** thought would interest me. His classroom demeanor was similar to his office persona. During class, he would stare out the window, chalk dust spattered all over his clothes, and then he would turn to us and talk about the importance of social justice. I began to see him during his office hours in part because I did not quite grasp the assignments, but as the term progressed, we discovered that we enjoyed many of the same interests.

Over the next five years, our relationship grew, and he eventually became my dis- **8** sertation adviser. He bought me champagne when I passed my orals and cheered when my overseas research was arranged. He deftly guided me through the dissertation process, and then he served as an adviser as I got my first job and shared the joy of a marriage. He was always there with a ready ear to listen to whatever was plaguing me at the moment.

9   Through all of this, I learned about his family, his children and grandchildren, his love of opera and twentieth-century prints. He was one of the few people I could go to who would hear me out—without judgment. If he offered advice and I didn't take it, there was never any hint of recrimination or guilt.

10   I have also experienced the other side of the coin—as a faculty member interacting with a student. That student came to the first class I ever taught at my current institution. She was nervous and shy and would begin shaking when you asked her a question in class. Even presenting her research was enough to make her almost sick, but her writing showed great promise.

11   She began to visit me during office hours and then asked if I would be her adviser. She took every class I taught, and, as time went on, she became more confident and self-assured. She was noticed by other faculty members, who were equally impressed with her intellect.

12   As she began to contemplate her future, my behavior may have appeared less accepting—I was somewhat relentless in urging her to make plans beyond graduation. Eventually, I backed off (remembering one of the precepts of unconditional love), and she discovered her own way. She joined the Peace Corps and went to Central Asia. In an early letter to me, she wrote that she had finally found what she needed to do with her life. She is still working abroad today and routinely checks in to let me know where she is. During a rare visit home, we talked about a new relationship in her life. When I convinced her of my total acceptance, she cried. She is an exceptional young woman with a deep sense of justice and caring, and I am proud to know her.

13   Without extrapolating too much from these personal stories, I want to say that both relationships went beyond mentoring and friendship. My interactions both as receiver and giver with these two people were qualitatively different from those with other students and mentors.

14   In both cases, the relationship started out with an uneven power relationship—that of teacher-student. Over time, the nature of the connection grew first into friendship, then into unconditional love. These were not relationships in which we socialized with each other frequently. There might be an occasional lunch or something more formal, but most of the interactions took place in an office setting or a classroom. I am aware enough to realize that the needs of both the individuals and my own played into the relationships, but I have found that by careful tending, platonic love grows.

15   While discussing the joys of this sort of relationship, it is equally important to identify the potential problems. A faculty member is clearly personally vulnerable in this relationship, as is the student, but the nature of love is that you must be open to both joy and sorrow. If you are giving unconditionally, there could be a time when the other wounds you in some way.

16   Other issues to be aware of are the inherent power differential and the potential for oppression within the relationship. Faculty members must constantly remain sensitive to relationships that change from platonic to sexual—whether real or imagined—particularly with younger students or those who are mentally fragile. Boundaries need to be maintained and spoken about in an open and thoughtful way. We faculty members must also guard against pushing these students to be clones of ourselves, pursuing questions of interest only to us. That is the true test of unconditional love: the ability to let the other make different decisions.

Ultimately, I am grateful that I experienced unconditional love as a student—partly   17
so I could then share this gift as a faculty member. If we begin to model this type of relationship on our campuses, perhaps it will help us get beyond the issues of harassment
and consensual relationships that plague us. If we as faculty members are strong enough
to maintain clear boundaries, then perhaps the all-too-common yet inappropriate
sexual relationships between students and faculty members can be avoided.

Why is unconditional love so important to recognize, when it is fraught with dif-   18
ficulty and occurs so rarely? It is because we are human beings, and practicing this love
can carry us past the indifferent students and the endless meetings. It is because, as a
colleague of mine from Mexico says, "teaching is the most important work in the
world, and we do it one student at a time." When you are enriched by another's love
and friendship, it is a deep breath of life.

And there is another reason I think it is important to practice this type of rela-   19
tionship: some faculty members, out of fear of sexual-harassment charges, have completely shut students out of their lives. They have no personal interactions with
students, even with the door open. I view that as a tremendous loss, both for the
faculty members and the students. With care and maturity—and a degree of courage—
we professors can open ourselves up to deep intimacy and love with a person whom
we bring into our hearts, and hold there for a lifetime.

Freewriting

In your notebook, freewrite for at least ten minutes, making the strongest argument to support the benefits of the kind of student-teacher relationship that
Hopkins-Powell describes. Regardless of whether you agree with her views, develop a list of reasons, facts, examples, personal observations, or experiences that
lend support to her beliefs. Then freewrite for at least another ten minutes, making the strongest argument you can to support the opposite point of view (i.e.,
that this type of relationship is inappropriate).

Group Work

Share freewritings with members of your peer group by having each member read
aloud as others take notes. Try to reach some consensus about the validity of
Hopkins-Powell's claims. If you are unable to do so, try to reach a fair rendering of
two (or more) conflicting viewpoints.

Review Questions

1. How does Hopkins-Powell define unconditional love?
2. What two specific illustrations does Hopkins-Powell provide to help readers
   understand a faculty member's unconditional love for a particular student?
3. What are the potential problems with the type of student-teacher relationship that Hopkins-Powell describes?

Discussion Questions

1. How do paragraphs 15 and 16 help to support Hopkins-Powell's claims?
2. How do you suppose Hopkins-Powell would respond to the argument that what she is talking about is really nothing more than being a "teacher's pet"? Should she have anticipated and attempted to refute that argument?
3. A college instructor teaches thousands of students during her career. A typical student in a four-year degree program will take classes from thirty to forty instructors. Given these facts, how likely is it that any one student will enjoy the type of relationship that Hopkins-Powell describes? That any one instructor will do so? Is this an important consideration? That is, does it strengthen or weaken the author's case?

Writing

1. Hopkins-Powell addresses an audience of college professors and administrators. Write a summary of her ideas directed to an audience of college students, their parents, or persons who have never attended college.
2. Write a brief reading analysis of either of the additional readings in this chapter.
3. Write a brief summary report that synthesizes Hopkins-Powell's editorial with the two additional readings in this chapter.

WRITE, READ, and RESEARCH the NET

1. *Write:* Freewrite for fifteen minutes about a particularly rewarding or particularly difficult relationship you have had with a teacher.
2. *Read:* Review the following Web site:
   <http://www.ala.org/BookLinks/v09/students.html>
3. *Research:* Using the Internet, locate Web sites that deal with student-teacher relationships. Using the five elements of analysis presented in this chapter, write a brief analysis of any one of the Web sites you locate.

 ## ADDITIONAL READINGS

The following readings address issues involving relationships between teachers and students. The first, written by an English professor at Monroe Community College, was, like Hopkins-Powell's essay, an editorial in the *Chronicle of Higher Education.* The second reading, by Adam Farhi, originally appeared in the educational journal *Clearing House.*

Crossing the Fine Line Between Teacher and Therapist

M. GARRETT BAUMAN

The first day, his wheelchair was backed against the side wall, empty seats separating 1
him from his fellow students in the rest of the room. Knowing how difficult it is to
maneuver a wheelchair in cluttered classrooms, I slid some desks aside and invited
him to move nearer the others.

He wore wraparound, mirrored sunglasses and slowly panned the class, forcing 2
down curious eyes. Then he turned to me and said, "I'm OK." He looked about fifty
and wore a T-shirt whose rolled sleeves exposed tattoos of snakes and the American
flag on his thin arms. When I reached his name on the roster and called "James," he
corrected me: "The name's Jimmy."

During the first weeks of our college writing class, Jimmy slumped in his wheel- 3
chair, taking no notes, grunting minimal replies to questions directed to him. He
became animated only during a discussion of Vietnam.

Few of his classmates were even born then, so Jimmy described how his unit had 4
evacuated a flooded village. "A hundred people piled carts with stuff. Sarge says they
can bring only one thing each, 'cause the boat's overloaded. This woman has a baby
under one arm and a pig under the other. 'One thing!' Sarge says, so the woman
throws the baby into the river."

A young woman in class gasped, "What did the soldiers do?" 5

Jimmy's face was impassive, his eyes hidden behind his mirrored glasses. "Noth- 6
ing. That's the way it was in Nam. A pig was worth something." The class shrank back
as if a cobra had spit at them.

After class, Jimmy rolled to my desk. "My counselor says I got to find out why I 7
been gettin' low grades." I pointed out that his papers were much too short and suggested that he visualize more details, as he had done with his oral story. He said, "I got
nothing to say on these topics. I tell it like it is. After that it's just bullshit." I reminded
him that he chose the topics. He sighed.

"Yeah, yeah. But nothing ever happened to me my whole life but one thing." 8

I sat down to be on his level. My own distorted reflection shone in his 9
sun-glasses—bulging, insect-like. Is that how he sees me? I wondered. Or is it how I
feel—the soft professor who never saw a child thrown in a river. Vietnam was so long
ago. Yet I felt those years now, like an old shard of shrapnel under the skin. As Jimmy's
classmates were being born and I was raising a family and maturing professionally, he
was stuck in the jungle. All those years he remained a teenager serving time in a broken, old man's body. I said, "So write about that one thing."

He barked a laugh. "No way! Too much'd come out I don't want out again." He 10
clenched the wheelchair. I suggested that a good paper would make something positive of his experience, that writing might even help exorcise it. He snorted. "Nah! You
don't want that out."

Maybe not, but if education was to help him discover his strengths, it had to go 11
where the energy was. In his curved lenses I watched my lips say, "I do," and I wondered what my advice would cost him.

His next paper described his wounding, near the war's end. Jimmy was shuffling 12
to the latrine at night when the first rounds hit.

"They couldn't even see me," he wrote. A machine-gun bullet tore through his 13
kneecap. Two more shattered two vertebrae in his lower back. He collapsed like a de-
flating balloon, his kneecap gone, both legs paralyzed. Jimmy said he was "stupid" to

be crippled because he couldn't "hold a leak." He concluded, "I got a medal, but I was no hero. None of us were heroes. We were just lucky or stupid. I was stupid."

14   I puzzled over *stupid*. Wasn't *unlucky* the right word?

15   When it was time for the students to discuss their papers, I worried about how Jimmy would react to their comments about his work. A silly comment could light his fuse.

16   Yet after a few awkward moments, they began to hotly debate heroism and luck. They wanted more details to fill in their fathers' shadowy tales of Vietnam. At first, Jimmy bristled at what he took for patronizing. Yet by the end of class he seemed to sense that the students respected his authority. Nodding at their suggestions for his paper, Jimmy acted as if he owned something valuable.

17   Having a real topic led him to sharper details, bumping his grades from D-'s to C's and B's, and Jimmy tentatively edged into more of his mined landscape. His next paper described rehab and sagging through tedious years with other broken men in veterans' hospitals.

18   "All for nothing," he snarled in my office.

19   "It got you to college."

20   He shook his head. "It was college or welfare, they told me. Politicians are tired of us hardbodies. I been draining the system twenty-four years."

21   "If you can take three bullets, you can take a few D's."

22   He laughed. "You don't know what all I took, Teach. You lay flat on your back for a year. Being crippled ain't just a thing that happens to you once. I got a son. Yeah. He was born while I was in Nam. I saw him twice since I been back. The last time he was nine."

23   "Why don't you visit him?"

24   "Like this?" He slapped the chrome wheelchair. "He's better off without a daddy to shame him. I ain't dragging him down with me. The kid thinks I'm a hero. What a word. I sucked weed and got nailed going to the can. I mailed him my medals. They're better than the real me."

25   "He might see past the wheelchair," I said.

26   I was a teacher, not a therapist. Yet to treat Jimmy as a purely educational issue would be not only heartless but truly stupid.

27   While it may seem best to keep academic and personal issues separate, it's hypocritical. Personal heartaches, neuroses, and rage account for part of the vitality of great books and their best teachers. Surely it is the same for our students and their studies. Jimmy's crippled body and psyche were an unhealed wound in our collective spirit, and part of his intellectual contribution to our class.

28   Jimmy went on. "Yesterday, I was rolling to the river to fish, when I had this creepy feeling my daddy was behind me. I could hear him thinking, 'So that's my Jimmy. He looks so stupid with his fishing gear and beer strapped to that chair. He'd a been better off kilt, poor sumbitch.' I don't want my kid thinking that about me."

29   "Your son's in his twenties. How can you be bad for him? You love him." I had intruded where professors are not supposed to go, but I didn't care.

30   "I'm trash. Pin a degree on me, an' I'll still be trash."

31   "You don't have to be a rotten father because yours was."

32   He pounded his armrest. "I already am, dammit! If that's not stupid, what is? Yeah, I love the kid. I know he's a man, but he's gonna stay a kid to me! So what?" He pushed violently on his wheels and rammed the door, escaping.

33   I collapsed into my chair. How little I knew of what it was to be him. Could I really teach him unless I did? I lifted my feet and shoved my hands against the desk so I rolled in my desk chair across the office. I stranded myself in the center where I could reach nothing. I told myself to remember that feeling.

Jimmy's writing sometimes transformed his pain into insight; sometimes it en- 34
raged him. I didn't have a plan, didn't know if I pushed him to deliverance or disaster.
But we slogged together through the tangled places he'd inhabited for twenty-four
years. He was eager just to move somewhere. No matter what else he did, he wrote,
and I hoped we both might stagger into one of education's ordinary miracles, when
learning ought to be impossible but happens anyway.

I told myself that shortly after the middle of the term, when Jimmy punched a 35
police officer who had arrested him for selling pot.

He railed in my office. "Who cares if I smoke dope? Am I going to be a doctor? Fly 36
an airplane? Play shortstop?"

He was hunkering down in his miserable foxhole, and I prodded him. "You didn't 37
hit the cop because he arrested you."

He took off his purple mirrored sunglasses, and I saw his old, exhausted eyes for the 38
first time. The skin around them was sickly white from lack of sunlight. "That's right."

I rolled my chair closer and said what had been brewing in me. "Daddy's gone. 39
The cops are not the army. You can't get even with anonymous bullets. Let go of what
you were—that boy's dead. Live what's left!"

He laughed and rolled back a few inches. "This is life? See, my big problem is, 40
what's a hardbody do with a diploma? Jerk off a computer all day? Wear a suit?"

"See your son. Write your papers. It's not what it could have been, but it's better 41
than rotting in Vietnam for the rest of your life."

He sighed and nodded. 42

Jimmy's GPA turned ugly despite the C+ he was earning in my class. By December 43
he looked exhausted. During finals week, I heard the familiar whizzing, and Jimmy
rolled into my office. "I got to tell you something."

"You're dropping out?" I hate students' choosing failure, but I knew Jimmy was 44
not surrendering. He was pricking the bubble of hypocrisy that said we could help,
could atone for the loss he had suffered on behalf of all of us. And I knew he had
fought harder in college and learned more than most A students.

He shrugged. "Sure. But I finished your last paper. Here." He swallowed. "I also . . . 45
uh . . . wanted to tell you . . . I ain't been honest with you. I got some leg movement.
I can crab around with crutches; I just don't practice. Watch."

He slowly straightened one leg parallel to the floor, then the other. I had noticed 46
them twitching before, but had said nothing. "I don't have to be in this chair."

"Show me," I said. Jimmy shook his head. My hand hung in the air between us. 47

"I walk like an epileptic duck," Jimmy said. I extended my hand closer, and he 48
took it. I felt the full weight of him as I pulled.

Hollywood Goes to School

Recognizing the Superteacher Myth in Film

ADAM FARHI

"The power of cinema," says filmmaker Steven Spielberg, "is a lot stronger than the 1
power of literature" (Taylor, 1992, p. 23). Although Spielberg may be a bit biased in his
assessment, there is no denying that movies have become so embedded in our culture
that it is often difficult to determine when they are reflecting society and when they
are affecting it. Since the early 1980s, the reach of film has vastly expanded: Through

cable television and VCRs, Americans have the ability to watch a film of their choice again and again. They are bombarded with images and ideas.

2   In 1992, Elliot measured the power of the film *JFK* by having college seniors view it. He found that 68% of the audience accepted the facts presented in the film as true. A skillfully made film, he learned, can "integrate its message with existing messages and create a reality for its audience" (p. 31). That phenomenon brings up an important issue for the education community: How are teachers being portrayed to movie audiences that include impressionable students and taxpaying adults?

3   The answer is disturbing. With some exceptions, films that center around teachers tend to show them as almost superhuman, capable of permanently changing lives in a short period of time. By forcing them to compete with their cinematic counterparts, the superteacher myth places an impossible burden on real teachers.

4   The superteacher formula is fairly simple. Take one teacher, often male, ranging from someone who has "different" ideas to someone who is an outright rebel. Give him an uncaring or unwilling administration, incompetent or lackluster coworkers, and students whom everyone else has given up on. With little assistance from anyone and teaching methods that are barely existent, the teacher is able to overcome the odds and quickly transform the class. Frequently the teacher, who has no personal life of his own, becomes something of a cult figure and proceeds to solve the students' personal problems. Along the way, the teacher alienates someone in a position of power, thus putting his job on the line. The students, of course, join together to pledge their support, because the teacher has changed their lives forever. The end.

5   One of the most common elements in teacher films is the class full of unruly students. This portrayal of students has evolved over the years, from the cranky, working-class English kids in *To Sir, with Love* (1967) to the criminals who roam the halls at the start of *Lean on Me* (1989). The first line in *Teachers* (1984), which is directed at the student body, is, "All right, you little animals." Such an opening, common in the genre, is remarkably similar to the start of many western movies: The town is in chaos; the townspeople are scared; and no one is brave enough to do anything about it. Now the search is on for a gunslinger (or superteacher) who cares enough to make a difference.

6   Often, it is not only the kids who are out of control. Consider *Summer School,* a hit film from 1986. Freddy Shoop is a phys ed teacher pressed into summer duty as a remedial English teacher. Very quickly, we learn that the class is made up of kids who are "not real students." But then the film flits the odds against Mr. Shoop even further: It presents him as an untrained loser, someone who "only got into this teaching gig" to get his summers off. (As the film progresses, however, Mr. Shoop will magically be transformed into a superteacher.)

7   Then there is the film *The Principal* (1987), which revolves around James Belushi's character, whose arrest for a drunken assault leads to his being "promoted" to principal of a nightmarish urban school. The violent students are unexpellable, and the police have no jurisdiction over the school. The notion that a school like that could exist is ridiculous, but there is Belushi, about to become a hero. His secret identity as a superteacher is foreshadowed early in the film when someone tells him, "You should've worn your cape."

8   Belushi's heroic principal is rare, however; most of Hollywood's teachers are saddled with an administration that does not care about them or their students. In *Up the Down Staircase* (1968), a young teacher is warned on her first day not to "even try to communicate with these students." More often than not, the principals are presented in this stereotypical fashion, which has the effect of making the superteacher seem that much more noble. In one typically outlandish example, the principal in *Dangerous*

Minds (1995) exists for no other reason than to provide resistance to teacher Louanne Johnson. He refuses to talk to a troubled student because the student didn't bother to knock before entering his office. After being kicked out of the office, the student, who was seeking refuge, is gunned down. As a result, Ms. Johnson looks even more heroic because she is obviously the only one in the school who cares about the students.

Class of 1984 (1982) puts a rookie teacher in a school that is the ultimate urban nightmare, and when he is threatened by students, the principal does nothing about it. That situation gives the teacher a chance to utter the quintessential superteacher line: "I can't leave my job. I'm worth something as a teacher." The principal in *Teachers,* while more sympathetic, serves the same function. His philosophy is, We're here to get as many kids through the system as we can with what we've got. When John Kimble, who is actually an undercover cop, takes over a kindergarten class to track a suspect in *Kindergarten Cop* (1990), he has no educational training. Yet the principal not only gives him no help; she hopes he will fail.   **9**

There can be only one superteacher in a movie. Many times, that means that the other teachers in the school are incompetent, bitter, or drab and boring. Frequently those coworkers have given up on the students. They are burned-out individuals who warn the hero not to bother trying. "I would row home if I could," Mr. Thackary is warned at the start of *To Sir, with Love.* One of the coworkers in *Teachers* is nicknamed "Ditto" because his daily class routine is made up of the students silently completing worksheets with their chairs facing away from the teacher.   **10**

Dead Poets Society (1989) stars Robin Williams as Mr. Keating, a character who is more of an actor than a teacher. Consider the way in which Keating is introduced: We see three successive scenes at a stuffy, 1950s New England prep school. Chemistry, Latin, and calculus are all presented as deadly boring—the teachers are monotonous; they have no personality. When the audience has been sufficiently dulled, Mr. Keating wanders in, whistling, and leaves. The curious students follow as if the Pied Piper had just walked through. "Weird," one of them remarks about Mr. Keating, "but different."   **11**

That sort of portrayal is one of the major problems with the superteacher myth. It implies that a teacher has to be unconventional to be qualified, making it difficult, if not impossible, for real teachers to measure up. Anyone opposed to Mr. Keating is the enemy, even if that means creating false situations. In his essay on *Dead Poets Society,* Heilman (1991) notes, "First you've got this guy on a white horse charging in to save the place. So you need some set-up black hats to make him look like a hero instead of a moral egoist" (p. 417).   **12**

Providing another unrealistic expectation for real teachers, Hollywood's teachers are able to cause nearly instantaneous transformations for the better among their students. *Renaissance Man* (1994) is a perfect example. We are told that the soldiers in Bill Rago's class have "sawdust for brains," yet they begin to comprehend *Hamlet* immediately. How is Rago able to work such magic on his students? We never find out. The film is too busy cutting to shots of Rago beaming with pride. Instant gratification, rare in the real world of education, is common in Hollywood's classrooms.   **13**

Dangerous Minds is just as misleading. Note the steps Louanne Johnson follows to control her unruly class. On day one, she has so little control over the students that she flees the school after just a few minutes. That night, she reads a book about discipline and proclaims her new attitude: "OK, you little bastards." On day two, she has changed her outfit from a beige skirt to a black leather jacket. She gets the class members' attention by giving them a karate lesson. On day three, the same students who forced their previous teacher to quit are literally sitting with their hands folded, waiting for the class to begin.   **14**

15   This type of rapid evolution is common. Of *Dead Poets Society,* Heilman (1991) notes that "we never do see Keating *teaching anything*" (p. 418). In fact, we rarely see Hollywood's teachers teaching at all. Filmmakers tend to show the end result of the teaching process without bothering to show the process itself.

16   In many movies, superteachers don't need to teach because their students have always been smart. Their misbehavior is the fault of the previous teachers, who didn't care enough to expose the pearl in the oyster. This is why Bill Rago's students, nick-named the "Double Ds" ("dumb as dogshit"), manage to pick up Shakespeare so quickly. Sometimes, however, special measures need to be taken. When *Summer School*'s Mr. Shoop is asked how he finally got a class full of underachievers to start learning, he answers with pride, "Bribed 'em." Louanne Johnson is equally honest about her teaching methods in *Dangerous Minds*. She announces that she's "gotta find a gimmick." And she does: She tosses candy bars to the students who speak up in class.

17   So what, then, do most of these cinematic teachers actually do? Perhaps they have so little time to teach because they are too busy trying to solve all of their students' personal problems. "How you gonna save me?" a troubled student asks Louanne Johnson. The word *save* comes up two other times in the film, as Johnson makes it her mission in life to help her students.

18   Like the superteachers in *The Principal* and *Lean on Me,* she makes unannounced visits to a troubled student's home. *Summer School*'s Mr. Shoop takes the blame when two of his underage students are caught with alcohol. Shoop is arrested, but the judge lets him off without any penalty. Then he goes a step further and actually commends Shoop for his "dedication" to his students. The teacher, in other words, does not really care about his students unless he is willing to put his reputation on the line for them.

19   A great way to judge how the superteacher myth has evolved over the last thirty years is to compare *To Sir, with Love* with its made-for-TV sequel, *To Sir, with Love Part 2* (1996). The original film, on the whole, doesn't subscribe to the superteacher formula. Sidney Poitier's Mark Thackary works hard to teach his students respect. He is not a savior; he is a good teacher.

20   In the sequel, Mr. Thackary has changed. He begins making unannounced visits to his students' homes. He conceals a felony and lets himself be fired, all to protect a student with a gun. Then comes the ultimate act of heroism. He follows a troubled student into a junkyard at night, and, to protect this student, Mr. Thackary puts his own life in danger by walking into the path of a loaded gun. He manages to convince an armed thug to put down his weapon, leaving us with a disturbing question: How can real teachers be expected to match this kind of behavior?

21   With such superteachers, it should come as little surprise that the students in these films are intensely loyal. Should something happen to put their teacher's career in jeopardy, the students will be there. Inevitably, something does happen. Witness the conclusion of *Dead Poets Society,* in which Mr. Keating is blamed for a student's sui-cide and fired by the stodgy headmaster. In the final scene, some of his students (who all signed a document implicating him in the suicide) defy the headmaster and stand up on their desks in support of Mr. Keating. One by one they get up and pledge their allegiance by reciting from the poem "O Captain! My Captain!" But what, if anything, has Mr. Keating actually taught them? Film critic Roger Ebert (1996) makes an excel-lent observation: "At the end of a great teacher's course in poetry, the students would love poetry; at the end of this teacher's semester, all they really love is the teacher" (p. 142).

22   It should be noted that it is possible to make a film about a teacher that rises above the superteacher myth. Along with *To Sir, with Love, Conrack* (1974), *Stand and Deliver*

(1987), and *Mr. Holland's Opus* (1995) are all examples of films in which teachers are presented as actual human beings who work hard to teach their students. These are three excellent films that do not fall back on clichés.

It has become so easy for movies to follow the superteacher formula, however, that the formula threatens to overrun the entire teacher genre. Although unrealistic characters are not uncommon in movies, an alarmingly disproportionate number of teacher films present the protagonist as a superteacher. Never mind that schoolchildren in the audience—and their parents—are wondering why their teachers are not as funny/dedicated/charming/offbeat/devoted as the Mr. Keatings and Louanne Johnsons of the silver screen.   23

Furthermore, there is little protection against the influence of film. Any kid with cable TV or a VCR has probably seen *Summer School* at least once, which means that he or she has witnessed the film's "inspiring" ending. After being transformed into a superteacher, Mr. Shoop, using no visible teaching methods, brings about an amazing change in his students. Their test scores have soared. But the vice principal wants to see him fired, and as Mr. Shoop's students stand behind him while his job is in doubt, the principal discovers the results that Mr. Shoop has produced.   24

"Now, that's teaching!" exclaims the principal.   25

No. That's Hollywood.   26

References

Ebert, R. (1996). *Roger Ebert's movie home companion* (1996 ed.). Kansas City: Andrews McMeel.

Elliot, W. R. (1992, March). Synthetic history and subjective reality: The impact of Oliver Stone's *JFK*. Paper presented at the annual meeting of the Association for Education in Journalism and Mass Communication. Montreal (ERIC Document Reproduction Service No. ED 352 682).

Heilman, R. (1991). The great teacher myth. *American Scholar, 60* (3), 417–423.

Taylor, P. M. (1992). *Steven Spielberg: The man, his movies, and their meaning.* New York: Continuum.

8 *Beginning a Research Project*

Suppose you are a smoker who has finally decided to kick the habit. Knowing that your addiction will be hard to overcome, you wonder if you should try to cut down in successive stages, or if you should take the more drastic step of quitting cold turkey. Determined to succeed, you visit the library and find that people who quit all at once have the best results. You also learn that you can expect withdrawal symptoms, but that after seventy-two hours, the worst of these are over. You grit your teeth, toss your remaining cigarettes in the garbage, and resolve that you, not tobacco, will prevail.

In Chapter 1, you learned that research is another name for finding out what you need to know. In the case at hand, reading about nicotine addiction carries a clear personal benefit. However, research often helps others as well. A college *research project* is an undertaking that should not only satisfy your own curiosity but also inform anyone else who reads the paper in which you present your findings.

 ## THE RESEARCH PAPER

A *research paper* is one way to report your findings. However, the paper itself is only the final step in a project that seeks out and discovers information about a particular topic. After making your discoveries, evaluating and selecting among them, and then organizing the material you wish to report, you finally present what you have learned in a documented paper. Of course, not all research papers are alike; in years to come you probably will make frequent use of research in your writing, though not always in what you may think of as "research papers."

Although papers that draw on research can take many different forms, most fall into one of two categories. The more common of the two is the *research-based paper*. Papers of this type consist largely of information found through research; the writers of such papers present relatively few of their own opinions or discoveries. For example, a student seeking to learn whether the fearsome reputation of great white sharks is justified could write a paper based almost entirely on what she found from reading and from interviewing experts. Her own observations on the subject might play only a small part in her paper. In contrast, the ***research-supported paper*** presents the writer's own ideas, with research findings used to support or supplement them. Argumentative essays are frequently research-supported. For example, a student arguing for increased funding for intramural athletics could use research in part of his paper; he could demonstrate feasibility by citing published budgetary figures, and he could support his own arguments with expert testimony on the need for greater fitness. Still, his original ideas would constitute the heart of his paper.

In practice, the distinction between research-based and research-supported writing is far from absolute. It is not possible to present information in a completely impersonal or neutral way. Assume, for example, that the student writing about great white sharks tried to make her paper objective and impersonal, presenting only the facts and ideas she had learned from her reading and offering no personal opinions or speculations. Even so, the paper she wrote would be very much hers, since it was she who interpreted her sources, selected which facts and ideas to include, and shaped the material so that it represented her understanding of what great white sharks are like. Whatever type of research writing you engage in, you are expected to *think;* even research-based papers are written by human beings, not by computers.

 ## PRIMARY AND SECONDARY RESEARCH

We can also distinguish between types or methods of research. Most library research undertaken for college papers is ***secondary research***, so called because it involves the second-hand discovery of information. Through secondary research we learn what others have previously discovered or thought about a topic. In contrast, when we make our own original discoveries, we engage in ***primary research***. To give an example of primary research, an agricultural scientist might plant a standard variety of corn in one field and a new hybrid variety in another to test which provides higher yields and is more resistant to drought and disease. On the other hand, a farmer who reads a report written by that scientist to find out the best seed to plant is engaging in secondary research.

As a college student, you will have opportunities to undertake both primary and secondary research. When you conduct an experiment to test the behavior of laboratory rats or survey voter reactions to a presidential speech, you engage in primary research. When you read a history or a chemistry textbook, consult an encyclopedia, or get a printout from a computer database, you engage in secondary research.

However, not every use of a print source is secondary. Written sources can be either primary or secondary. A historian researching the slave trade in colonial America would seek sources from that era. Newspaper stories about slavery, diaries written by freed slaves and slave owners, slave auction notices and bills of sale, tracts written by abolitionists, and census figures and other records from that time are all examples of ***primary sources***. In addition, the historian would consult such ***secondary sources*** as books and articles by other historians who have also researched and written about the slave trade.

In your upcoming research project, you may have occasion to make both secondary discoveries (in library works) and primary discoveries (by interviewing or corresponding with sources). The research you do is determined by the nature of your project and the resources at your disposal.

 ## BENEFITS OF DOING RESEARCH

If research papers were not a requirement in college classes, it is doubtful that many students would have the opportunity or motivation to undertake such projects on their own. By the same token, few instructors are surprised when students, after their projects are completed, say that they were glad to have had the opportunity. Often students say they have gained more from the experience than they expected. They find that research writing can have unanticipated benefits.

Learning an Essential Skill

One aim of this book is to help you become a competent college researcher with all the tools you need to produce quality research papers. A more general—and important—aim is to give you the confidence and skills to discover and use available information about any topic that arouses your curiosity.

It is likely that you will need to write many research papers during your college career and afterward. In other classes, you may be asked to gather information on a topic and report what you discover. After college, in your professional career, you may be faced with questions that you will have to answer through research. In these cases, you will need to consult what others have written, to evaluate and select what is pertinent from this information, and to write reports on your findings.

One reason you are being asked to do one or more research projects in your current course is to give you the experience you will need to conduct future projects with confidence. Practice now will make things easier later. When you are assigned to write a research paper in an art history, marketing, or anthropology class, for example, your instructor will not have time to tutor you in the basics of research. And after you graduate, you will have no instructor at all. College students and college graduates are simply expected to have mastered these skills. Now is the time for you to become an experienced researcher.

While students in a college composition course have the opportunity to learn research skills, they are also at a disadvantage compared with other researchers. Others do research not to practice a skill but to learn about specific topics. What they are discovering is important to them, and the research process is merely a means to that end. In the composition class, however, learning about the research paper can be an end in itself, and the topic you are writing about may seem of only peripheral importance. In that regard, your research project may seem artificial to you, an exercise that is useful in teaching skills for later use but one that has no real importance of its own. This *can* happen, but it is up to you to make sure it does not. For that reason, it is essential for you to choose with care the topic that you will research and write about. Because you will be spending much time and effort on this project, you should become as involved as you can with your topic. If you pursue a topic you genuinely care about, you will gain many rewards: Not only will you spend your time profitably, but you will also write a far better paper and, in the process, learn what you need to know about research methods. If you take an interest in your topic and pursue it avidly, the skills you are seeking to acquire will take care of themselves.

Contributing to Scholarship

Although competence in research and research writing are practical skills, there is yet another reason to engage in research besides its personal usefulness to you. By doing research and then making your discoveries public in a paper, you are benefiting your readers as well.

Research is at the very heart of education—it represents the cooperation that is essential to learning. Most knowledge that you have gained is a result of such cooperation. None of us would have been able to figure out the principles of algebra, to mention just one example, if we had been left entirely on our own. Fortunately, throughout the centuries, mathematicians have shared the results of their discoveries with each other and (through our school algebra classes and textbooks) with us as well. A major function of higher education is to share with students the most important thoughts and discoveries of other scholars.

School classes are not the only means by which scholars share their work with us. They also publish their findings so that we and other scholars can have access to them. To make this sharing even easier, the books and articles they produce have been gathered in a central, accessible place: the college library. Engaging in research is simply taking advantage of what other scholars have learned. Like all scholars, you have the right to read about and learn from the discoveries of others. But scholarship is more than just passively receiving the gift of knowledge. As a scholar, you play an active role. Even when you write a research-based paper reporting on the findings of others, you are still creating something new, a fresh synthesis of information, shaped with your own wisdom and insights, a *new source* that was not available to scholars before. Every research paper makes at least a modest contribution to the domain of knowledge. As a student researcher, you are fully entitled to think of yourself as a scholar engaged in a scholarly enterprise. It is for this reason that you are expected to share your findings in a written, public form.

Gaining Personal Knowledge

In traditional college research writing, the author's aim is to report findings, to share information with readers. Authors of these papers keep their writing focused on their topic, while directing attention away from themselves as authors. (The word *I* rarely appears in conventional research writing.) But while you write such a paper to inform others, no one benefits more from your project than you yourself. Before you can inform your readers, you must first inform yourself about your topic through research. Research writing is a sharing of the knowledge you have gained.

Even the act of writing contributes to your learning. Creating a focused, unified paper forces you to see your topic in new ways. It causes you to bring together information from various sources, to make connections, to take vague ideas and make them concrete. Writing has been properly called a *learning tool;* research writers continue to gain personal knowledge while they are writing about what they have read.

On some occasions, however, personal benefit is not just a by-product but your principal motive for conducting research. At times, you need to seek answers to questions important to you personally. Writing about such privately motivated research can be just as beneficial and worthy as carrying out conventional research projects. For that reason, one type of paper that has become increasingly popular in composition courses is the **personal research paper.*** Unlike the standard research paper, this paper does not call for impersonal writing; as its name implies, it aims to be intensely personal. If you write a personal research paper, you should pick a topic that has real importance to you—or as one author puts it, you should let a topic pick you (Macrorie 66).† Perhaps your research will help you make a decision, such as what major or career to choose, or even which motorcycle to buy or what vacation to take. Perhaps it will just satisfy some strong curiosity. In any case, a personal research paper is a record of your quest for answers. You write your paper not only about *what* you found but also about *how* you went about finding it. The word *I* appears often in personal research writing. Even when such projects are approached with purely personal goals in mind, they provide far wider benefits. Besides being informative, they can be especially instructive because a strong motivation to find answers is the best teacher of research skills. Although personal research papers center on the writer's interest and focus on the writer's experiences, readers often find them interesting. The writer's deep involvement in the subject usually translates into lively writing.

THE RESEARCH PROCESS

Like all other forms of writing, a research paper does not happen all at once. Many steps are involved. Although a research paper may seem complicated and difficult, you can learn to produce one quite capably if you take one step at a time. This and the next five chapters examine each stage in the research process. To illustrate the tasks involved, we will trace the experiences of two first-year college students as they undertake research and write papers for their composition classes. By examining the steps they follow, the problems they encounter, and the solutions they discover to overcome them, you can observe the skills that go into writing a

---

*It was also given the name "I-search paper" by Ken Macrorie in his book *The I-Search Paper,* rev. ed. (Portsmouth, NH: Boynton, 1988).

†As Chapter 6 explained, "Macrorie 66" is a form of shorthand telling the reader that the authors are citing an idea by Ken Macrorie on page 66 of his book (identified in the preceding footnote).

research paper. The same procedure can be adapted for research writing in your other courses and in your future career.

 A RESEARCH ASSIGNMENT

In any given semester, students in different composition classes receive a wide variety of assignments for research projects. Some are given open-ended assignments with many options, whereas others are assigned more focused tasks, such as projects related to a particular theme the class has explored in reading and discussion.

Allen Strickland and Courtney Holbrook, first-year college students enrolled in composition courses, were given different assignments by their instructors. In Allen's class, each student was asked to write a standard college research paper. Students in Courtney's class were offered the option of writing either a standard or a personal research paper. In both classes, students were asked to choose their own topics.

Following is an assignment similar to the one that students in Courtney's class received. Your own research assignment may differ from it, and your instructor may provide additional criteria for the length, scope, and format of your paper. Make careful note of any ways in which your own instructor's assignment differs from the one given here.

Research Paper	ASSIGNMENT

Investigate a question or problem that intrigues you and write an informative essay, based on your findings from research. Observe the following guidelines, depending on the option you choose or are assigned.

Option A: The Standard College Research Paper

- *Subject*. Frame your research task in the form of a question that you want your investigation to answer. You may explore any subject that arouses your curiosity and interest. You might choose a topic related to your career goals or the field you plan to major in. Perhaps a certain topic in one of your other courses has aroused your curiosity. Perhaps an event or person from recent or earlier history would be worth learning more about. Perhaps in your reading, in conversation, or in viewing a film or television documentary, you have encountered a subject you would like to explore.

- *Audience*. Assume that the other members of your class are your audience. Write a paper that is appropriate for this audience—one that they will find informative and interesting.

- *Voice*. You are the author of this paper, and it should be an honest presentation of what you have learned. But remember that your readers' interests, not yours, should come first. Although sometimes research writers use the word *I* in their papers (e.g., when they present their personal experience as a source), the focus of the paper should be on the subject matter, not on you as a person.

- *Information and opinion.* Be certain that your paper is principally based on the findings of your research rather than on personal speculation. This does not mean, however, that your paper must avoid any ideas and opinions of your own. Your paper may adopt a point of view, but if it does, you should make it clear to your readers from the beginning.

- *Length.* A typical paper is six to twelve pages long, but the length of your paper should be determined by the nature of your subject.

- *Sources.* Your paper should be based on a variety of research, including (where appropriate) such secondary sources as books, periodicals, and newspapers. If you find that additional sources are appropriate for your topic, you should also interview or correspond with experts or participants. Most papers will cite between eight and sixteen sources. In upcoming classes, you will learn how to locate appropriate sources, how to make use of what you learn from them, and how to acknowledge them in notes and in a works-cited page—that is, how to give your sources credit for their contributions to your paper.

Option B: The Personal Research Paper

Most of the guidelines for the standard research paper apply here as well, but there are some differences.

- *Subject.* You should pick a topic that is already a personal concern in your life. That is, you should seek a question you have a good reason to answer, one that can benefit you directly. Any topic that can help you make a decision or that can provide you with information that will enhance your life in some way is likely to be a good choice.

- *Voice and audience.* You should write honestly and unpretentiously about your research experience. Since your topic is of personal interest to you, the word *I* may occur often in your paper. However, you should also write so as to inform readers who may share your interest.

- *Form.* Unlike the standard paper, which is limited to the subject of the writer's research, the personal paper tells about the writer's process of discovery as well. Although no pattern for what to include and how to arrange it is right for all papers, here is a typical pattern suggested by Ken Macrorie. If you choose, your paper can follow this general outline, found in Macrorie's book *The I-Search Paper:*

  1. What I Knew (and didn't know about my topic when I started out).

  2. Why I'm Writing This Paper. (Here's where a real need should show up: The writer demonstrates that the search may make a difference in his life.)

  3. The Search [an account of the hunt, usually in chronological order; what I did first, what I did next, and so on].

  4. What I Learned (or didn't learn. A search that failed can be as exciting and valuable as one that succeeded). (Macrorie 64)

Parts 3 and 4 can be merged if it makes sense to combine your accounts of what you found and how you found it.

• *Sources.* Interview experts, people who are likely to have the answers you want or who know where you can find answers. Consult these primary sources as well as library materials and other secondary sources.

You are also asked to keep a research notebook (explained on pages 336–37) throughout your research project. Save all your notes, outlines, and rough drafts (more about these later), and submit them in a folder with your completed paper. Your current priority is to choose one of these options and to begin focusing on a specific topic. Use the time between now and the next class to think more about potential topics for your paper.

When their instructors announced the assignment, Allen and Courtney had a reaction typical of most first-year college students in this situation: a sinking feeling in the stomach, followed by varying degrees of anxiety. It seemed more intimidating than the papers they had written before. Although both are competent writers, they weren't sure they could do it. At least momentarily, they were afraid their deficiencies would be exposed, that they would be revealed as imposters impersonating college students.

As grim as this sounds, there is nothing unusual about what Allen and Courtney felt. All writers are apprehensive at the beginning of an assignment, especially one as unfamiliar and as complex as this research paper seemed. But despite their early fears, Allen and Courtney not only wrote their papers but also received high grades for them. Afterward they admitted that the project was not the ordeal they had expected. In fact, it was not only rewarding but also interesting, informative, and, despite much hard work, even enjoyable.

What Allen and Courtney did you can do. The trick is to divide the long project into a sequence of smaller, manageable tasks. As we examine these tasks, we will consider these two students' experiences as examples—following the progress of research from chaos to clarity, from panic to finished product. Since you will be making a similar trek, the journeys of Allen and Courtney are worth your attention.

THE FINISHED PRODUCT

Before you examine all the steps Allen and Courtney took to produce their papers, first look at where they ended up. Their polished, final drafts—the completed papers that were the results of all their work—appear on the following pages.

A Sample Standard Research Paper

First is Allen's response to option A, his research paper on identical twins. Notice that Allen maintains an impersonal voice in the paper and presents multiple sides of controversial issues. Nevertheless, he shaped it to present his understanding of those issues, choosing which sources to use and how to use them. As a result, the paper is very much his, and it is presented in his voice.

Allen Strickland

ENG 12

Professor Lisa Gorman

25 July 2005

Identical Twins: Born to Be Alike?

Jim Lewis and Jim Springer, twins who were adopted as infants by different families, did not meet again until they were 39 years old. Although their hair styles were different, they were otherwise strikingly similar. Both were six feet tall and weighed 180 pounds. They had the same features, including an unusual swirl in one eyebrow and a "lazy eye" on the same side. As they were soon to learn, looking alike was just the beginning of their similarities (Watson 9-11; Wright 43-47).

Lewis and Springer are identical or "monozygotic" twins. Identical twins are created when a single egg is fertilized but then splits to form two separate embryos, which then share the same womb. Such twins are the equivalent of clones, not only looking alike but also having the identical set of genes. In contrast, non-identical twins, also known as "dizygotic" or "fraternal" twins, result from separate fertilizations of two different eggs. Non-identical twins are genetically no more alike than non-twin siblings ("Twin").

Strickland 2

Although they grew up in different circumstances, the two Jims were found to share many physical and behavioral traits. Their blood pressure was identically high, and both had suffered heart attacks, migraines, and hemorrhoids. Their scores on personality and intelligence tests were almost identical. Both are restless sleepers who grind their teeth at night, and both bite their fingernails. Psychologists who observed them found them similar in their speech patterns and even in the way they sit in chairs.

Other similarities range from the surprising to the eerie. Both had gained and then lost ten pounds during the same period in their teens, and both had vasectomies. Their wives say both are romantics who leave them love notes around the house. Both drink the same brand of beer and chain-smoke the same cigarettes. In school both loved math but hated spelling. Both follow car racing but hate baseball. Both worked in McDonald's, as part-time deputy sheriffs, and as gas station attendants. They had named their firstborn sons James Alan Lewis and James Allen Springer. Strangest of all, each got divorced from a woman named Linda and then married a woman named Betty (Watson 9-11; Wright 43-47). While some of these similarities are probably just coincidences, the pattern of these and other pairs of identical twins raised apart has led many to conclude that our genes play a large part in determining who we are and what we become.

Everyone agrees that children inherit traits such as height and hair color from their parents, but scholars have long debated the role that heredity plays in determining our personalities and behavior. Today it is still far from settled how much of our behavior can be attributed to "nature," genetic factors in our DNA, and how much to "nurture," the environment in which we are raised. To put it another way, are we "born that way" or are we shaped by our surroundings? (Powell).

Because identical twins have identical DNA, they can give us insight into the role heredity plays in our development. Psychologist Susan L. Farber calls identical twins "nature's unique controlled laboratory experiment on the interplay between heredity and environment" (5). Scientists frequently conduct studies of twins to determine if physical and emotional traits have a genetic or an environmental cause. A keyword search of "identical twins" in specialized databases such as Biological Abstracts and PsycInfo turns up hundreds of studies with serious-sounding titles such as "Homozygous Familial Hypercholesterolemia in Identical Twins" and "Discordant Identical Twins and the Genesis of the Psychoses." Most of these are of interest

Strickland 4

only to specialists, although some manage to capture the attention of the media, such as one study of female twins (683 identical pairs and 714 non-identical pairs), which reported that the ability to experience orgasm is largely genetic (Dunn, Cherkas, and Spector).

Especially interesting are twins such as the two Jims who were separated soon after birth and reared in different households. Because they share the same genes but grew up in entirely different environments, most similarities between them should be attributable to "nature" and most differences to "nurture."

The best known study was conducted by a team led by psychologist Thomas Bouchard at the University of Minnesota, which since 1979 has studied over 60 pairs of identical twins raised apart. Some of the pairs had some contact growing up while others, such as the Jims, had no contact at all. Another remarkable pair was Jack Yufe and Oskar Stohr, who were born in Trinidad before World War II to parents who then separated. Jack was taken by his mother to Germany, where he was raised as a Catholic and became a member of the Hitler Youth. His brother Oskar was raised as a Jew by his father in New York and later moved to Israel. Nevertheless, when they were reunited as adults, the twins not only had similar personality profiles, but they shared many peculiarities such as storing rubber bands on their wrists, flushing the toilet before using it, and sneezing loudly as a practical joke to startle people (Allen; Wright 53-55). The fact that they were raised in cultures that most people would regard as extreme opposites makes their similarities especially strong evidence to support the claim that nature is a major factor in determining what we become.

Stories about bizarre similarities between twins tend to capture our attention, but even the most identical of twins exhibit many differences. Caroline Clements and Sarah Heenan are identical twins raised together who consider themselves very different. In school Clements was an athlete, Heenan a cheerleader. Heenan went to a small women's college in rural Virginia, married and had children early, and was a suburban housewife until a divorce in her late thirties. Clements went to a coed university in Chicago, became a career-oriented psychology professor, and married later in life. Clements says that her sister is "a much more reactive personality; she gets angrier quicker." Compared to the more laid-back Clements, Heenan is a "neat freak" who feels compelled to clean Clements's home when she visits. In politics, Heenan is a conservative Republican, Clements a liberal Democrat, and they also have very

Strickland 6

different religious beliefs. Despite their many contrasts, the twins talk on the phone every day and are "absolutely best friends" (Clements).

One recent study has shown that the wiring in identical twins' brains is not identical (Britt), and another that the DNA of twins becomes less alike as they grow older ("Even Identical"). Many differences have been attributed to environmental factors. For example, a 2001 study showed that identical twins with different diets had significantly different cholesterol levels, and a 2002 study showed differences in emotional stress that were related to social factors such as church attendance and their relationship with their mothers (Britt). Parents of identical twins report differences in temperament between them, although some psychologists say that parents exaggerate twins' differences because they focus on slight differences as a way to tell the twins apart (Goldsmith, Buss, and Lemery 901).

In her book Not All Twins Are Alike, psychologist Barbara Schave Klein, herself an identical twin, believes that parenting is a crucial environmental factor in shaping individuals, including twins. "Parenting," she writes, "provides the substance that molds and holds together what human beings inherit and what can be changed by environmental stimulation" (6). She observed that, at the extremes, some parents treat identical twins as a single unit, two carbon copies of each other. Some other parents treat their twins as polar opposites, with a "good twin" and a "bad twin." Klein says that twins treated as one unit may develop dependence on each other and feel incomplete without the other. Twins treated as polar opposites create distinct roles for themselves but have serious identity and self-image issues. In contrast to these extremes, when each twin is treated by the parents as a unique, fully realized individual, each grows up not only with an independent personality and a healthy self-image but also with a lifelong friendship and understanding of the other twin (3).

One pair of identical twins who grew up together but who have obvious differences is Stephen and Mark O'Donnell. One is left-handed, the other right-handed. As children they had a "lazy eye" on different sides. Their hair parts naturally on opposite sides, and whorls of hair spiral clockwise for one twin, counterclockwise for the other (O'Donnell and O'Donnell). The O'Donnells are an example of "mirror-image twins," a phenomenon that results when the fertilized egg splits later than usual ("FAQ").

One of the most noteworthy differences between the O'Donnell twins is that Stephen is heterosexual and Mark

Strickland 8

is gay. Sexuality in twins has played a role in a
controversy about what causes us to have a particular
sexual orientation. On opposite sides of this controversy
are those who maintain that we are born with a fixed
sexuality and those who hold that sexual orientation is
entirely a matter of choice. Neil Whitehead, a biochemist
from New Zealand who is widely quoted in evangelical
Christian publications, argues that the existence of
identical twins with different sexual preferences, such as
the O'Donnells, proves that our genes do not determine
what our orientation will be: "Identical twins have
identical genes," Whitehead writes. "If homosexuality
was a biological condition produced inescapably by the
genes (e.g. eye color), then if one identical twin was
homosexual, in 100% of the cases his brother would
be too."

Others interpret research findings differently. Several
clinical studies have been conducted into the sexuality of
twins. Psychologist Michael Bailey and psychiatrist Richard C.
Pillard studied 161 gay men, each of whom had an identical
twin, a non-identical twin, or an adopted brother. They
found that 52% of the identical twin brothers were also gay,
but only 22% of the non-identical twin brothers and 11% of
the adopted brothers were gay (Bower). A study of lesbian

Strickland 9

women by different researchers showed similar results (Johnson). Because each pair of twins or adopted siblings was raised in the same household, they had approximately the same nurture. The fact that the more closely alike their genetic structure, the more likely siblings are to share sexual orientation points to the role of nature in determining our sexuality.

Several studies claim to have found physical differences in the brains of gay and straight men (Johnson), but most scientists doubt that there is a single "gay gene" that determines sexuality. Instead they believe that sexual orientation results from a number of factors, some of them genetic and some environmental ("Genetics"). Bailey and Pillard estimate that genes account for between 31% and 74% of male sexual orientation (Bower), and even Whitehead agrees that "genes are responsible for an indirect influence." Barbara Schave Klein is one of many psychologists who believe that both nature and nurture play important roles in determining sexual identity. She writes, "Sexual orientation cannot be specifically determined by genetics or environment. Even minute differences in genetic endowment may create differences in sexual orientation in a pair of twins" (106).

Strickland 10

Sexuality is just one of many aspects of human behavior that have been studied using twins. There appears to be a genetic contribution to such traits as alcoholism, smoking, criminality, job satisfaction, and even divorce (Wright 8). The Minnesota Twin Family Study found that if one non-identical twin got divorced, the other twin had a 30% likelihood of also getting divorced. However, if an identical twin was divorced, the other twin's chances of divorcing went up to 45% (Minnesota).

If studies of twins show that genetics is such a strong factor in shaping us, does that mean that humans have less freedom to make decisions than we suppose? In his book on twins, journalist Lawrence Wright points out that the findings can sometimes be misleading. Even if 45% of identical twins get divorced if the other twin does, that means that the majority do not. Despite genetic or environmental influences, we still remain free to make decisions (154). After studying the similarities between twins for many years, Thomas Bouchard now says:

> There probably are genetic influences on almost
> all facets of human behavior, but the emphasis on
> the idiosyncratic characteristics is misleading.
> On average, identical twins raised separately are
> about 50 percent similar--and that defeats the

widespread belief that identical twins are carbon
copies. Obviously, they are not. Each is a unique
individual in his or her own right. (Qtd. in
Allen)

Twins studies not only fascinate us but they can teach
us much about ourselves. Evidence is strong that our genes
have much to say about who we become. Nevertheless, the
degree to which we are shaped by nature and by nurture--as
well as the degree to which we are free to shape ourselves--
is likely to remain a topic of controversy for many years
to come.

Strickland 12

Works Cited

Allen, Arthur. "Nature & Nurture." <u>The Washington Post Magazine</u> 11 Jan. 1998. <u>Washingtonpost.com</u>. 11 July 2005 <http://www.washingtonpost.com/wp-srv/national/ longterm/twins/twins1.htm>.

Bower, B. "Gene Influence Tied to Sexual Orientation." <u>Science News</u> 4 Jan. 1992: 6. <u>Academic Search Elite</u>. EBSCOhost. 6 July 2005 <http://search.epnet.com>.

Britt, Robert Roy. "Identical Twins Not So Identical." <u>LiveScience</u>: Human Biology. 8 July 2005. 13 July 2005 <http://www.livescience.com/humanbiology/ 050708_identical_twins.html>.

Clements, Caroline M. Personal interview. 15 July 2005.

Dunn, Kate M., Lynn F. Cherkas, and Tim D. Spector. "Genetic Influences on Variation in Female Orgasmic Function: A Twin Study." <u>Biology Letters</u> 7 June 2005. 8 July 2005 <http://www.journals.royalsoc.ac.uk>.

"Even Identical Twins Grow Apart Genetically--Study." Reuters. <u>Yahoo News</u>. 5 July 2005. <http:// news.yahoo.com/news?tmpl=story&u=/nm/20050705/sc_nm/ science_twins_dc_5>.

"FAQ: Twin Zygosity." Proactive Genetics. 14 July 2005 <http://www.proactivegenetics.com/faqzygosity.dna>.

Strickland 13

Farber, Susan L. Identical Twins Reared Apart: A Reanalysis.
      New York: Basic Books, 1981.

"Genetics and Sexual Orientation." Answers.com. 14 July 2005
      <http://www.answers.com/topic/
      genetics-and-sexual-orientation>.

Goldsmith H. H., K. A. Buss, and K. S. Lemery. "Toddler and
      Childhood Temperament: Expanded Content, Stronger
      Genetic Evidence, New Evidence for the Importance of
      Environment." Developmental Psychology 33 (1997),
      891-905.

Johnson, Ryan D. "Homosexuality: Nature or Nurture."
      AllPsych Online. 30 Apr. 2003. 12 July 2005
      <http://allpsych.com/journal/homosexuality.html>.

Klein, Barbara Schave. Not All Twins Are Alike:
      Psychological Profiles of Twinship. Westport, CT:
      Praeger, 2003.

Minnesota Twin Family Study. "What's Special about Twins to
      Science?" 15 July 2005 <http://www.psych.umn.edu/
      psylabs/mtfs/special.htm>.

O'Donnell, Stephen, and Mark O'Donnell. "The Co-Zygotes'
      Almanac." Esquire June 1998: 132. Academic Search
      Elite. EBSCOhost. 6 July 2005 <http://
      search.epnet.com>.

Strickland 14

Powell, Kimberly. "Nature vs. Nurture." <u>About.com</u>. 9 Oct.
    2003. 10 July 2005 <http://genealogy.about.com/cs/
    geneticgenealogy/a/nature_nurture_2.htm>.

"Twin." <u>Wikipedia: The Free Encyclopedia</u>. 6 July 2005.
    9 July 2005 <http://en.wikipedia.org/wiki/Twin>.

Watson, Peter. <u>Twins: An Uncanny Relationship</u>. New York:
    Viking, 1981.

Whitehead, N. E. "The Importance of Twin Studies." National
    Association for Research and Therapy of Homosexuals.
    5 July 2005 <http://www.narth.com/docs/whitehead2.html>.

Wright, Lawrence. <u>Twins: And What They Tell Us about Who We
    Are</u>. New York: Wiley, 1997.

A Sample Personal Research Paper

True to the nature of personal research papers, Courtney's paper on whether she should pursue a career in pharmaceutical sales is more personal and informal than Allen's paper on twins. Courtney's style, however, is fully appropriate for the kind of paper she is writing.

Holbrook 1

Courtney Holbrook
English 102
Professor Richard Veit
6 June 2005

Pharmaceutical Sales: More Than Just Viagra Pens

I. Why I Am Writing This Paper

As far back as I can remember, my goal for the future has been to work in business. As a child, I would spend endless time messing around with my own makeshift store made of cardboard boxes and construction paper. Sales books and receipt papers would fascinate me. I knew even then that it was my destiny to play a key role in the business world.

My father is a pediatrician and my mother is a certified nurse, so I have also been surrounded by the medical profession from day one. But since I have an incredibly low tolerance for blood and a weak stomach for antiseptic sprays, the thought of breaking into the medical field seemed as likely as winning the lottery--that is, until two years ago, when I first encountered an occupation that combines medicine and business.

From the summer before my senior year of high school until I began college I worked in a pediatrician's office.

Holbrook 2

Day after day I would see representatives from the drug companies come into the office bringing lunch or other gifts and attempt to sell or restock samples of their drugs. Although a diverse crowd, all of the sales men and women seemed to love their job.

I have always planned on majoring in business in college, and I wanted to concentrate on marketing and advertising. Because of this, whenever the pharmaceutical representatives would come in, I wondered if that was a job I would like. When given this assignment I knew immediately that I would research pharmaceutical sales to find out what goes into the profession. I hoped by the end of my exploration to know its ins and outs and to be informed enough to decide whether it was a career I should pursue.

II. What I Knew

Going into this project I was still skeptical about pharmaceutical sales because my only knowledge of it came from my experiences at the doctor's office. Aside from my observation that all the representatives seemed to enjoy their jobs to the fullest, the actual details were fuzzy.

The salespeople never entered the office empty handed. While they always had samples of their drugs or pamphlets, there was always something more. Pens were a favorite; it

Holbrook 3

must be a requirement for drug companies to make pens with
their drug's name on them, as the reps never lacked them.
They left us calendars, mouse pads, coffee mugs, and clocks--
all advertising their companies' wares. On occasion they
would also bring lunch for the entire office with hopes of
chatting with the doctors about their drugs and other
products over the meal.

The sales representatives were always personable
people. They introduced themselves to strangers with ease
and professionalism. They also made a real effort to get to
know the office employees, and most reps knew all of us by
name. I found this both impressive and appealing, since I
want to be up front with people in whatever field I end up
choosing.

I had been thinking about an advertising/marketing
concentration in college. Having a job that put me close to
real marketing made me eager to get out of high school and
start my journey through college. Now that I am here, I must
be certain of my goals before actually declaring my major. I
knew before starting this project that I would need to focus
on all aspects of the business sales world and find out
for certain whether sales--and pharmaceutical sales in
particular--matched my capabilities, interests, and career
objectives.

Holbrook 4

III. The Search

Being the computer-savvy person that I am, I began the search process by logging on to the internet and searching the University's website. One of the first sites I came across was the marketing page posted by the Career Services office. There I found a list of personality traits that make one suited for a career in marketing as well as specific jobs in the field. Happily I also found several links at the bottom of the page related to pharmaceutical sales. The links directed me to several other sites that offered information about all aspects of being a pharmaceutical salesperson, including areas such as education, typical work day, and salary. I bookmarked the sites for future reference.

I then ventured over to the university library, where I ran searches for books on my topic. The quest proved harder than I expected. While information on being a pharmacist was readily available, pharmaceutical sales seemed nonexistent. Every search brought holdings that seemed only peripherally related. Because most of these had similar call numbers, I went to the stacks to check out that section. After searching through shelves and shelves, I found only one book with information on my topic.

Holbrook 5

    Discouraged, I put off further searching until the next
day, when a librarian spoke to our class about helpful ways
to search for career information. She showed us phrases to
use on the library search engine and key websites where
information about jobs was available. Most helpful was
a list of reference books in the library on careers.
Immediately after class I ventured upstairs to the stacks
and found the information my previous search had not
provided. I found a few books that outlined the basics
of any career you can think of, including pharmaceutical
sales.

    Wanting to gain further information, I continued
my search of the internet. On the Google search engine,
I entered phrases like "pharmaceutical career" and
"pharmaceutical representative." I found that "drug sales"
did not help me, since almost every listing related
to illegal drugs. I had most luck with the phrase
"pharmaceutical sales," which not only provided information
about the drug industry and drug sales but also led me
to several sites about a controversy over the way drug
companies market their products. These sites were the first
to give me a glimpse of some less appealing aspects of the
profession. I had similar results when I did a periodical
search using the EBSCOhost search engine.

Holbrook 6

Finally, with my father's help, I contacted an actual pharmaceutical sales representative that I knew from my work at the doctor's office. John Carter* is a salesperson for a nationwide drug company. We agreed to talk by telephone on the following day. He was very informative and helpful, answering all my questions and volunteering information I hadn't thought to ask about.

I now had an array of data from a variety of sources. I took additional notes on my reading and started narrowing down my information. I sorted my note cards and drafted a rough preliminary outline. In my mind an informed body of knowledge was beginning to take shape that would allow me to make a decision. I was ready to begin putting it all together on paper.

IV. What I Found

Most people know what a pharmacist is, but a pharmaceutical sales representative is much less familiar. Pharmaceutical reps are sales people. They try to sell their drugs and influence doctors to prescribe them to patients.

---

*At his request, I am not using his real name.

Holbrook 7

They have nothing to do with actually dispensing the drugs. They distribute samples of their products to doctors, discuss drug characteristics and what clinical studies have shown about the drugs, and takes orders ("Job Description").

Qualities needed to be hired and be successful as a pharmaceutical representative include imagination, tact, judgment, flexibility, decisiveness, maturity, and resistance to stress (Broome 27-29; Farr 125; "Job Description"). Speech clarity and command of the language are also essential. While some reps may use charts or graphs, ultimately what comes out of their mouths determines whether or not a sale is made. A salesperson must also be an active listener who gives full attention to what the client is saying and asks appropriate questions ("Job Description"). Certainly a successful rep must be personable. The key to making a sale is making the customer feel that they are the most important person alive and that they would be at a loss without the drug the representative is selling (Farr 125).

Enthusiasm, putting in the effort to learn about the drugs and ways to sell them, and willingness to work long overtime hours are what make a good pharmaceutical salesperson stand out (Malungani). The salesperson must also be a fast learner. Drug representative John Carter told me:

> Typically you are given information about a new drug two weeks before you are to start selling it. By the time you're attempting to sell the drug you should know it from front to back, top to bottom, and side to side. Your credibility is what is on the line, and not being able to answer a question about the drug you are selling lessens your credibility.

To be able to talk credibly with doctors, representatives must understand the science behind the drugs they are selling. Corey Nahman, CEO of Internet Drug News, says that representatives don't need an extensive science background. On the other hand, he says, "If you don't have an aptitude for science or don't like science, this job will not be fun."

The qualities needed to succeed in the job may lead some to picture the typical pharmaceutical salesperson as a suave mid-30s male in a business suit and imagine that no others need apply. In fact, half of all pharmaceutical reps are women (Nahman), and most defy the stereotype. As Groome states, salespeople "come in assorted shapes, sizes, hues, talents, backgrounds, philosophies, likes and dislikes" (27).

Holbrook 9

Most of the 85,000 pharmaceutical salespeople in the United States have college degrees (Goldberg, Davenport, & Mortellito). J. Michael Farr, author of America's Top Jobs for College Graduates, says that many employers give hiring preference to representatives with a bachelor's or master's degree in business administration with an emphasis on marketing. Courses in business law, economics, accounting, finance, mathematics, and statistics are highly recommended (125).

Not all representatives for drug companies, however, have business degrees, and Farr states that almost any major is suitable (123). When I interviewed John Carter, I was surprised that he had earned a degree in music education and had been a teacher for ten years. When he decided teaching was too stressful, a friend got him an interview for his current job. He says that his experience with people and his high college grades helped him. Carol Poe, territory manager with DJ Pharma, says, "Often [employers] care about your grade point average, because it shows you worked hard in school. It's the little things that add up to success in the field" (Malungani).

Pharmaceutical representatives "ride high above other salespeople when it comes to compensation," according to an article in Pharmaceutical Executive. In 2002 the average

Holbrook 10

starting salary for a pharmaceutical salesperson was $47,000 in base pay, and top primary-care representatives had a base-pay average of $82,300. Incentives add another 25-30% to the base (Goldberg, Davenport, & Mortellito). John Carter made $45,000 in his first year. He said that the main determinant of your salary is what drugs you are selling. "If the drug is in high demand, you're going to make a lot of money." If it isn't, you'll make less.

In addition to high pay, another advantage of the job is the opportunity for advancement. Carter told me that a salesperson straight out of college can be a representative for two to three years and be promoted to corporate management. He says that the CEO and other top officers in his company are in their thirties and early forties.

The job may offer great economic benefits, but it can also exact a personal price. J. Michael Farr says that "working under pressure is unavoidable as schedules change, problems arise, and deadlines and goals must be met" (124). It is not unusual for paperwork and customer interaction to spill into overtime, including nights and weekends (Carter). Selling pharmaceuticals also requires constant travel both to customers and to the company's local, regional, and

national offices. The continual travel and pressure to make
sales can cause stress and disrupt family life. Carol Poe
warns that "it's definitely not a nine-to-five job. You
pretty much eat, sleep and breathe it. Many people go in
thinking it will be the greatest job ever, and it doesn't
turn out like they expected. It's very hard work, and it's
not right for everyone" (Malungani).

While most of my sources highlighted job benefits and
personal pros and cons of the career, other sources raised
ethical questions about pharmaceutical sales practices--in
fact, about the very same lunches and giveaways that I
found so appealing when I worked in a doctor's office.
Journalist Bruce Jaspen writes, "The industry's gift-giving
practices intended to win physician loyalty to certain
drugs have been of particular concern in a climate of
growing consumer outrage over drug costs, which have risen
at an annual rate of fifteen percent during each of the last
four years, far exceeding inflation."

M. J. Fingland, director of communications for
Pharmaceutical Research and Manufacturers of America,
acknowledges that the industry has an image problem. "We're
criticized on [Capitol] Hill and in the press--put in the
category of the tobacco industry, even though we save
lives." However, he maintains that "giveaways, lavish trips

are a thing of the past. We've cleaned up the business
considerably" (qtd. in Dutka). Fingland says that the
industry adopted a new ethics policy in 2001 restricting
the types of gifts that companies can give to doctors
and limiting their monetary value to $100. Representatives
are no longer free to fly doctors to exotic conferences,
pay their hotel bills, and treat them to lavish dinners
(Dutka).

Even so, news stories report that drug companies have
forbidden their employees to talk with reporters about sales
practices (Dutka). John Carter, although otherwise a
chatterbox, said he had no comment on the matter, and he
asked me not to identify his real name or the name of his
company in this paper.

Despite the travel, the stresses, and this current
controversy, Carter remains in high spirits. While it is not
for every personality, he recommends the career to those who
are interested. "You make the job your own. You get out of
it what you put into it."

V. Conclusion

My research has greatly expanded my knowledge of
pharmaceutical sales. Certain aspects of the job are
unappealing, such as working nights and weekends. On

Holbrook 13

balance, however, the pros outweigh the cons. Potential for pay is excellent, and the substantial travel that some would find burdensome is alluring to me. Staying in one place may have its comforts, but I love being able to travel and see the world. Of my group of friends I have always been the person who welcomes going out on my own and trying new things. I enjoy meeting new people and selling products face to face. I also don't mind pressures to succeed; in fact, I thrive on them.

Equally appealing is the opportunity for rapid advancement. My goal in life is to work my way up the business chain, and pharmaceutical sales offers a greater opportunity than most professions, since it is possible to advance to a management position after as little as two or three years on the road as a sales representative. In the pharmaceutical industry, even CEOs are young.

Ethical considerations have raised doubts in my mind about the profession, but I believe each salesperson determines how he or she will behave. I was raised to have a strong moral sense, and I am confident I would steadfastly avoid the shady practices being alleged.

Pharmaceutical sales, on balance, is more appealing to me now than before I began my search, but I have not reached a final decision. This project has solidified my decision to major in business marketing and advertising. I will try to maintain a high grade average and will take science electives, which will give me background for understanding drugs and will be a valuable addition to my résumé. The knowledge and experience I gain in the next two years will further clarify my goals and desires. I hope they will take me where I need to be to fulfill my childhood dream of standing out in the business world.

Holbrook 15

Works Cited

Carter, John. Personal interview. 18 May 2005.

Dutka, Elaine. "New Michael Moore Project Gives Drug
    Companies a Sick Feeling." Los Angeles Times
    23 Dec. 2004. MichaelMoore.com. 24 May 2005
    <http://www.michaelmoore.com/words/mikeinthenews/>.

Farr, J. Michael. America's Top Jobs for College Graduates.
    3rd ed. Indianapolis: Jist Works, 1999.

Goldberg, Michele, Bob Davenport, and Tiffany Mortellito.
    "When Will the Bubble Burst?" Pharmaceutical Executive
    1 Jan. 2003. 13 May 2005 <http://www.pharmexec.com/
    pharmexec/article/articleDetail.jsp?id=42871>.

Groome, Harry C., Jr. This Is Advertising. Philadelphia:
    Ayer: 1975.

Jaspen, Bruce. "Health-Care Firms on Lookout for Planned
    Michael Moore Documentary." Chicago Tribune 30 Sep.
    2004. Newspaper Index. EBSCOhost. 16 May 2005
    <http://search.epnet.com>.

"Job Description for: Sales Representatives, Chemical and
    Pharmaceutical." CareerPlanner.com. 16 May 2005
    <http://www.careerplanner.com/Job-Descriptions/
    Sales-Representatives,-Chemical-and-Pharmaceutical.cf>.

Malungani, Megan. "Job Q&A [Interview with Carol Poe]".
    American Medical and Pharmaceutical Representatives

Association. 16 May 2005 <http://www.ampra.com/
industry_article_job_faqs.shtml>.

Nahman, Corey. "Pharmaceutical Sales; Resource Center."
CoreyNahman.com. 24 May 2005 <http://
www.coreynahman. com/practicaladvicea.html>.

Sidime, Aissatou. "Toughest Part of Pharmaceutical Sales
Rep's Job Is Getting Access to Physicians." San Antonio
Express-News 20 May 2005. Newspaper Index. EBSCOhost.
28 May 2005 <http://search.epnet.com>.

Courtney's paper is about a decision that may have important consequences for her. Personal research projects also work well with less momentous topics; any question that arouses your curiosity is a worthy candidate for such a paper. Allen's paper on twins, for example, might have worked well as a personal paper, particularly if he were a twin or had twins in his family. Certainly Courtney could have used her sources to write a standard research paper on pharmaceutical sales. In fact, the "What I Found" section of her paper would require very few changes to become an impersonal standard paper. You might try to imagine what each of these papers would have been like if its author had chosen a different format for it.

Analysis and Discussion

Before reading on to learn how Allen and Courtney went about researching and writing their papers, answer these questions about their final drafts:

a. What is your impression of the strengths and weaknesses of each paper? Does each have a clear focus; that is, can you give a brief summary of its topic or central idea? Do you find it interesting? informative? clearly written? well organized? Did the author seem to do an adequate job of researching his or her topic?

b. If you were the author's instructor, how would you respond to each paper? If you were the author, would you change it in any way to improve it?

Both Allen's paper about twins and Courtney's about her career decision impressed their instructors and classmates, but they did not get that way all at once. Many stages involving much labor, some frustrations, and many changes preceded the final versions. The history of their creation is as informative as the papers themselves.

 ## YOUR RESEARCH SCHEDULE: PLANNING IN ADVANCE

Writing a research paper is a labor-intensive project. Between now and the time you submit your final draft, you will be busy. You will be choosing a topic, exploring it, refining it, chasing down leads, riffling through sources, taking notes, thinking, jotting down ideas, narrowing your project's focus, doing more research and more thinking, writing a tentative draft, revising and revising again.

Obviously, a research project cannot be completed in a day or two. You need to plan now so that you have enough time to undertake each step in the process and so that you can make efficient use of your time. Like Allen Strickland, you may be assigned separate deadlines for the various steps in your project. Or you may be given only the final deadline for submitting the completed paper, in

---

RESEARCH PROJECT

Principal Deadlines:		Due Dates:
1.	Research prospectus due, including a statement of your research topic and a working bibliography (see page 382):	_____
2.	Note cards and preliminary outline due (see page 440):	_____
3.	In-class editing of completed draft (see pages 457–58):	_____
4.	Typed good draft due (see page 488):	_____
5.	Final draft due (see page 488):	_____

Figure 8.1 A schedule for a research project.

which case you should establish your own intermediate deadlines for completing each stage. Allen's instructor gave the class a form much like the one shown in Figure 8.1, with a date for each deadline. You can use the form for recording your own schedule.

Some instructors may supply an even more detailed schedule, which may include dates for such additional activities as library orientation, additional editing sessions, and student–instructor conferences. Whatever your schedule, your instructor will certainly concur in this advice: Budget your time wisely, and get started on your project without delay.

 ## A RESEARCH NOTEBOOK

At the beginning of your project you may already have a clear vision—or only the vaguest notion—of what your final draft will eventually look like. Nevertheless, it is probably safe to say that your final paper will be very different from anything you currently imagine. A research project involves many discoveries, and the act of writing usually inspires us to rethink our ideas. Rather than being *assembled*, research papers typically *evolve* through a process of development and change. Prepare for an adventure in which you discover what eventually emerges on paper.

Your finished paper is the end product of that adventure, the last of several stages in the research process. What you learn during that process is probably more important in the long run than the paper itself. It was for this reason that Allen's and Courtney's instructors asked each student in their classes to keep a **research notebook**. At every stage of the project, researchers were expected to keep a personal record of their progress. The research notebook is like a diary. In it Allen and Courtney recorded what they were doing and what they were expected to do. They wrote about what they had found, the problems they were facing, and their plans for their next steps. Courtney used her notebook as the raw material for the "search" section of her personal research paper.

The writing you do in a research notebook should be informal, not polished. Unlike the research paper itself, the notebook is written to yourself, not to outside readers. When you are finished, you have a record of your research process. But there is also another benefit to keeping a notebook. Both Allen and Courtney found that it helped them make decisions and focus their thoughts. In addition, many of the passages both writers used in their papers came from ideas they had scribbled in their notebooks.

You should use a spiral notepad that you can carry with you when you do research, though you may also want to use your word processor (if you have one) to record some entries. You will start using your notebook from the very beginning—now—as you select and focus your research topic.

YOUR RESEARCH TOPIC

Only on rare occasions do researchers have to *choose* a topic. Such an occasion might come about for a freelance writer of magazine articles who wants to select not only a fresh subject that will interest readers and an editor but also one about which she can find enough information through interviews, legwork, and library research.

In most cases, however, researchers already have their topics before them. A situation arises that demands exploration. For example, in order for a detective novelist to write convincingly about a counterfeiting ring, he must do research to learn how counterfeiters actually operate. A historian with a theory about the causes of the Russian Revolution would have to discover the available facts about the period as well as learn what theories other historians have proposed. A lawyer writing a brief for a criminal case must research legal precedents to know how similar cases have been decided in the past and to provide herself with convincing arguments. Most researchers begin with a strong curiosity about a topic and a need to know.

As you begin your own research project, you may already have decided on a topic. Perhaps your class has been reading and talking about an interesting issue such as nuclear policy, teenage suicide, the future of the family farm, or dating practices in foreign countries. Your discussion may have raised questions in your mind, questions that you can answer only through research. Besides satisfying your own curiosity, you can perform a service for your instructor and classmates by informing them about what you have learned. For you, a research paper is a natural.

On the other hand, you may not yet have chosen a specific topic. Perhaps your instructor, like Allen's and Courtney's, has left the selection of a topic up to you. Perhaps you have been given a choice within a limited area, such as a current event, the life and views of a public figure, or your career goals. In any case, it is important for you to select a topic you can work with. Because many hundreds of topics may appeal to you, deciding on any one can be hard.

You begin with your curiosity. Your research is aimed at answering a question in your mind, at satisfying your urge to know. For that reason, it is usually helpful at the outset of a project to state your topic in the form of a *research question*. Rather than just naming a general area for your paper, such as "racial policy in the armed forces," it is often more useful to frame your project as a question to be answered, such as "How has the military dealt with discrimination?" or "How has the struggle against discrimination in the American armed forces compared with the struggle in the civilian world?" Perhaps you have formed a *hypothesis*, a theory that you would like to test. In this case your question would begin, "Is it true that . . . ?" For example, in reading about the plagues that devastated Europe during the thirteenth century, you might have speculated that in spite of modern scientific advances, the reactions of people to epidemics have not changed much in seven hundred years. If you decided to test this hypothesis through research, your question might be, "Are effects of the AIDS epidemic on our society similar to the effects of the Black Death on medieval Europe?"

Three factors are critical in framing a good research question. Your topic should have the following qualities. It should be

1. **Appealing.** This is the most crucial factor. Your research should be aimed at answering a question that genuinely arouses your curiosity or that helps you solve a problem. If you are not involved with your topic, it is unlikely that you will write an essay that will interest readers. The interest you have in your topic will also determine whether the many hours you spend on it will be rewarding or agonizing.

2. **Researchable.** You may be curious about the attitudes of college students in Japan toward religion, for example, but if you can locate only one or two sources on the subject in your local libraries, you will not be able to write a research paper about it.

3. **Narrowed.** If your question is "What is astronomy?" you will find no shortage of materials. On the contrary, you will certainly discover that your topic is too broad. You can find hundreds of books and entire journals devoted to astronomy. However, you cannot do justice to so vast a topic in a paper of a few thousand words. You will need to narrow your topic to one you can research and cover adequately. You may decide to concentrate on black holes, for example, as a more focused topic. Later on, as you continue your research and begin writing, you may narrow the topic still more, perhaps to a recent theory or discovery about black holes.

GENERATING IDEAS

Unless you already have a question in mind that you are eager to answer, or unless you are facing a pressing decision for which you need information, you will have to do some exploring and thinking about a general subject before you arrive at a properly appealing, researchable, and narrowed research question. Several techniques for stimulating ideas can help you in your selection, including brainstorming and clustering.

Brainstorming

If you were asked right now to declare some possible research topics, you might find it difficult to do so. After a few minutes of wrestling with the problem, you might finally come up with a few topics, but you might find them to be neither original nor exciting. Yet there are literally hundreds of topics that you not only would enjoy researching but also could write about well. The trick is to stimulate your mind to think of them. *Brainstorming* is one helpful technique. It is simply a way of forcing your mind to bring forth many possible topics, under the theory that one idea can lead to another and that, if enough ideas are brought forth, at least one will click.

On the day they announced the assignment, Allen's and Courtney's instructors led their classes through several activities to stimulate their thinking. Following are some examples of brainstorming exercises.

Brainstorming: Random Listing	**EXERCISES**

1. We start with a light and unintimidating exercise. The following is a random list of concepts in no particular order and of no particular significance. Read the list rapidly and then, in your research notebook, begin your own list, adding as many items to it as you can. Give free play to your imagination. List whatever comes to mind without regard to whether it is serious or would make a reasonable research topic. Save those concerns for later. For now, write rapidly, and have some fun with your list.

surnames	water fountains	swimsuits
clowns	sea horses	salesmanship
cans	con artists	pro wrestling
lip sync	cremation	campaign buttons
lipstick	hiccups	prep schools
war paint	blueprints	sponges
juggling	Russian roulette	snuff
teddy bears	triplets	fads
cave dwellers	women's weightlifting	cavities
haircuts	chocolate	advertising jingles
ways to fasten shoes	frisbees	plastic surgery
high heels	coffins	bartending
hit men	chain letters	mirrors
cheerleaders	tanning	juke boxes
revenge	baldness	icebergs
bicycles	wigs	mermaids
televangelists	facial hair	tribal societies
silicon chips	earrings	fast food

college colors	longevity	cyclones
company logos	boomerangs	Beetle Bailey
roller skates	fuel injection	toilets
tractors	fertility	laughing
warts and birthmarks	nomads	cable cars
freckles	film editing	Mardi Gras
tattoos	spelunking	free gift with purchase

2. Because one idea leads to another in brainstorming, the ideas of other people can stimulate your own thinking. You can cross-fertilize your imagination by looking at other students' lists. After you have listed items for a few minutes, you can (a) exchange lists with one or more classmates or (b) join members of your class in calling out items (perhaps in orderly turns, perhaps randomly) as one or more people write them on the blackboard.

3. Stimulated by these new ideas, resume listing for another few minutes.

4. When you have finished, reread your list and circle the items that seem most interesting to you. What about these items stimulates your curiosity? See if you can now pose five or six questions about them for which you would like answers.

You may be concerned that some of the topics you listed or some of the questions you posed are not particularly serious or do not seem scholarly or deep. You need not worry, since any subject that provokes your genuine interest and curiosity is worth exploring and can be given serious treatment in a research paper. The item "lipstick" in the preceding list, for example, may seem frivolous at first, but it can lead to many serious questions: What is lipstick made of (now and in the past)? How long have people been using lipstick? How has society regarded its use in earlier times? Does it symbolize anything? Is its use widespread throughout the world? Is it ever prohibited by governments or by religions? Why do American women use it but not (for the most part) American men? Such questions point to an interesting and rewarding research project. A student who pursued them would find much information. In the course of research, the student could certainly narrow the topic—perhaps to "What has society thought about lipstick?"—and write an informative, worthwhile paper.

EXERCISE | **Brainstorming: Focused Listing**

This brainstorming exercise is more focused than the preceding one. In your notebook, list as many ideas as you can in response to the following questions. Write rapidly, listing whatever comes to mind. List phrases, rather than complete sentences. If one topic strikes you as having possibilities as a research topic, keep listing ideas about it until you have explored it to your satisfaction. You do not need to answer every question, but do not stop listing ideas until your instructor tells you that time is up.

- What have been your favorite courses in high school and college? What topics in those courses did you find interesting? For each topic, write as many phrases associated with it as you can.

- What major are you considering? List some particular subjects you hope to explore in your major.

- What career are you considering? What specific branches of that field interest you? What jobs can you imagine yourself holding in the future? List several possibilities.

- What recent or historical events or discoveries are associated with your career interests or major field? What notable persons are associated with these areas? List some things you know about them.

- List magazine articles, books, movies, and memorable television programs that you have encountered lately. List some specific ideas or topics that they bring to mind.

- List some events or controversies that concern you. What news stories have aroused your interest or concern? What historical events have you wanted to learn more about? What do you consider the major changes that have taken place during your lifetime in world affairs? In science and technology? In the way we lead our lives? What problems face us in the future?

- What topics have you read about because you needed or wanted to learn more about them? What problems do you now need to resolve?

- What decisions will you have to make soon? Decisions about school? career? lifestyles? morality? romance? friends? family? purchases? leisure time?

- What areas are you an expert in? What are your chief interests and hobbies?

- What are some of the major gaps in your background? What should you know more about than you do?

- What notable people do you most admire? What people have had achievements that mean something to you? Think of men, women, historical figures, living people, scientists, artists, athletes, politicians. What famous people do you pity or consider villains?

Allen's class spent about fifteen minutes listing ideas for the preceding exercise. Afterward, students shared lists with classmates and discussed their idea. They also jotted down any new ideas that came to them. Allen's list filled two pages in his notebook. Here are excerpts:

> Possible career
>   --international relations . . .
> Recent or historical events
>   --war in Iraq
>   --terrorism
>   --Palestinian-Israeli relations . . .

Articles, movies, books
 --Blue Blood, book by NYC cop
     --real cops vs. movies
     --how drug busts are made
  --internet article about twins' genes
      --identical twins different from non-twins
      --ESP in twins
  --March of the Penguins, movie about penguins
      --wild life in Antarctic
      --in extreme conditions
   --Notting Hill video
       --movie star—actual life vs. image . . .

Allen's list was not an orderly, logical outline, nor was it meant to be. However, these short excerpts show his mind actively at work, listing and shaping ideas. Clearly, he had not yet found his research topic at this point, but among the dozens of items he listed was an article on twins that, by chance, he read on the Internet the morning before his class. The twin topic was to lead to Allen's research project, but he did not yet know that. It was only one of many ideas he listed that could have become fruitful paper topics. In fact, he pursued several different topics before settling on twins.

Here are some excerpts from Courtney's list:

Favorite courses:
  art: love to draw/paint/create
                    like to showcase work
  speech: love to speak in front of groups
                    research until I'm comfortable w/ topic
                    not nervous, am comfortable
                    I like to take charge
  marketing: like to create businesses
                    really want business major
                    incorporating art (product design) w/ business . . .

Majors?
  business: marketing/advertising ——→ mainly!
                    international, love to travel
  accounting   ?

Careers?
  sales: magazine ads (marketing/design)
                    pharmaceutical sales
                    technical/IT services
                    office systems
  international   travel to promote products
  business:
  accounting: good at math/crunch numbers in my head
                    work in corporate office . . .

Decisions
    What major?
    What school to continue @ for major?
    Summer: make $ vs. leisure time vs. summer school?

In contrast to Allen, Courtney hit on her topic—her interest in pursuing a career as a pharmaceutical sales representative—almost immediately. The brainstorming question "What career are you considering?" coincided so exactly with a decision she was wrestling with that she knew instantly what she would research and write about. Courtney's certainty about her topic at this point is a rarity. In many cases, brainstorming activities do not lead directly and immediately to a topic the writer recognizes as ideal. Instead, they open up many pathways for the writer to explore. When pursued, some of those paths will lead to still other paths for the writer to take, until eventually the right destination is reached.

Developing an Idea: Clustering

A more concentrated form of brainstorming can be called *clustering* or *mapping*. It is a technique designed to stimulate the development of many ideas related to one given idea. Allen's instructor gave his class the following exercise.

Clustering Ideas	**EXERCISE**

Review the lists you have made thus far and circle all the items that look promising as research topics. If you have time, ask one or two classmates to do the same thing, each using a different color ink. Finally, select one possible topic (this is not a final commitment) and write it in the center of a blank page in your notebook. Using it as a starting point, radiate from it whatever ideas come to mind. Allen's clustering is shown in Figure 8.2.

Finally, Allen's instructor asked class members to call out question that arose from the idea they had listed (or new ones that occurred to them), while she wrote them on the board. Here are some typical questions offered by students:

- Does having a baby increase a mother's IQ?
- What effects does El Niño have on weather?
- Are big-time college athletics corrupt?
- Do high CD prices represent price fixing?
- Was Susan B. Anthony an American hero?
- How is wireless technology changing American society?
- Are violent video games harmful to children?
- What strategies work in quitting smoking?

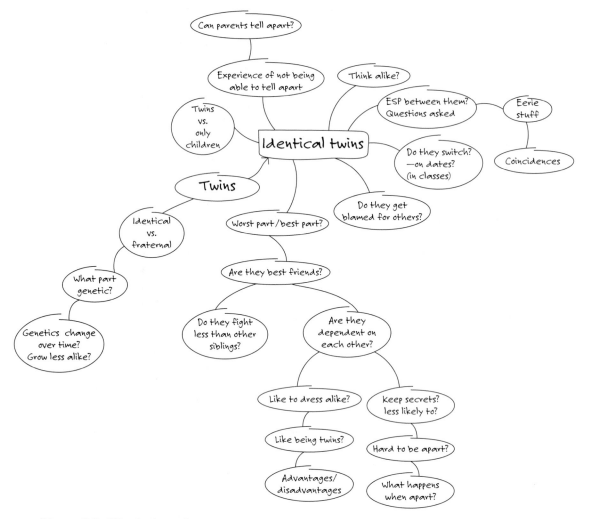

Figure 8.2 Allen's clustering.

- What are causes of body dysmorphic disorder?
- Why do wealthy people shoplift?
- Is phonics a useful strategy for teaching reading?
- What are benefits and drawbacks of state lotteries?
- What role did music play in the Civil Rights movement?

Also on the list was a question from Allen, "How alike are identical twins?"

Prewriting exercises are not magic formulas that instantly produce perfect research topics. Instead, if all goes well, they begin a chain reaction that leads you, however circuitously, to your eventual topic. The idea-generating exercises that

Allen and Courtney engaged in pointed them in helpful directions. Courtney was that rare student who knew almost immediately what would be the focus of her research. She had been giving much thought to the possibility of a career in pharmaceutical sales, and she seized on the opportunity to learn more about it through this project. In contrast, Allen was not at all sure what he would write about. His brainstorming list had included a whole variety of unrelated concepts, including an article he had read about twins. Almost on a whim, he wrote "Identical twins" in the middle of his page and began to explore ideas about it. As you can see in Figure 8.2, he was able to radiate many spokes from this hub, with one idea or question leading to another. He was sufficiently captivated that he now felt that he could enjoy learning about this topic and be able to write a paper that others would find interesting to read. His mapping raised many more questions than he would be able to answer in his paper, but it served its purpose in raising questions for his research to explore.

A research project is like a puzzle. When you begin, you never know how it will turn out. After all, the purpose of research is to answer questions for which you do not currently have answers. When you start, you cannot know what answers you will find. You cannot even be sure your questions are good ones. These discoveries are made only as you undertake the actual research and as you begin to write about your findings. You are almost certain to find that the research paper you end up writing will be quite different from your current expectations. What you learn along the way will cause you to change plans and go in new and often unexpected directions. You are sure to meet surprises. A good researcher must be flexible, able to adapt to whatever new ideas and information present themselves. For this reason you need not be concerned if you now have only a tentative idea of the topic of your paper. Your topic will take firmer shape (and perhaps a very different shape) as you undertake your research. The following chapters show you how to conduct that research.

9 *Tools for Finding Sources*

 BEGINNING YOUR RESEARCH

Having generated ideas about likely topics for papers, Allen and Courtney needed to do preliminary research to learn more about these topics and to bring their research questions into sharper focus. A visit to the library and some exploration of the resources available to them via computer were the logical next steps. From their instructors they received assignments similar to the one that follows.

ASSIGNMENT	Preliminary Research

Do some preliminary research to explore the topic you are considering.

- Learn more about your topic by reading about it in encyclopedias and other general reference sources. If the topic seems appropriate, take notes and see if you can narrow your focus to a specific question.

- See if your topic is researchable by assembling a working bibliography of about a dozen sources that you intend to consult. (Working bibliographies are further explained in Chapter 11.) Use a variety of search tools (explained in this chapter), and include books, periodicals, newspapers, and electronic media, as appropriate for your topic. If, for example, you are writing about a recent event, newspaper articles will be a significant source of information. On the other hand, if you are writing about an event from ancient history, you may not discover any newspaper sources.

- If adequate sources are not available, see if you can broaden your topic or switch to another one. If you find too many sources, read more about the subject and narrow your paper's focus within more manageable limits.

- Make sure your sources are available. Find out if the library has the periodicals and newspapers you are seeking. Check books out. If necessary, order books from other libraries through InterLibrary Loan. Ask the circulation desk to recall desired books that have been checked out by others. If most of the books are gone, however, someone else is probably writing on your topic, and the sources you need may not become available in time. If so, avoid needless frustration by switching now to another topic.

- Do some quick reading in your sources to learn more about your topic. It might be wise to ask a professor or some other authority on your subject for suggestions about the topic and for further research sources.

- Decide what additional sources can provide valuable information for your project. Write letters to request information, if necessary. Arrange interviews in advance by setting up appointments. (Letters and interviews are discussed in Chapter 10.)

- Be sure to record your discoveries, questions, and other experiences with locating sources in your research notebook.

As they begin their first research project in college, few students are experts in using the library. Many are confused and intimidated by electronic resources such as online databases and the World Wide Web. By the time students have finished the project, however, they have learned how to find information in their library as well as to access other sources throughout the world via electronic communication.

YOUR CAMPUS LIBRARY

Your purpose in conducting a research project is not only to inform yourself about your topic by discovering information but to inform others as well by making your discoveries available in a paper. Learning is, after all, a cooperative venture, and scholars have an obligation to pass on to others what they have learned. For that reason, a wealth of important information and ideas produced by scholars has been collected and located in a convenient place for your use—your college library.

As any quick browse through the library will make abundantly clear, there are a great many potential sources out there—written about an almost unlimited number of topics. Finding information about any particular topic might seem an impossible task. Fortunately, however, the means are available for locating almost anything you are looking for. Your library offers not only *research sources* themselves, such as books and periodicals, but also *search tools*, which allow you to discover what research sources are available for your topic and to locate them. These tools include the library's book catalog, online and printed guides to periodical and newspaper sources, and reference librarians. Search tools can give you a great deal of power, allowing you to discover information on almost any topic. Of immediate interest to you, of course, is that they allow you to find sources for your research paper. This chapter, with its accompanying exercises, is intended to make you proficient in the use of various search tools.

ELECTRONIC RESOURCES

A generation ago, college students searched for books about their research topics by flipping through index cards alphabetized in drawers in a library's card catalog. To find periodical and newspaper sources, they paged laboriously through dozens of bound indexes. The computer revolution changed all that, and today most library searches are conducted at a keyboard in front of a computer screen. Not only have searches become simpler and more convenient, but today's students have easy access to vastly more sources than did scholars just a few years ago.

Electronic searches have themselves undergone rapid change. A few years ago, the student researcher had to visit many different library terminals, each dedicated to a particular index or database. Today it is typical for a college library to have a **central information system**, a single online site from which a student can locate all the library's holdings, find sources in any of dozens of electronic databases, and even read many sources directly on the viewing screen. Because most library information systems are accessible on the Internet, students may avail themselves of many library resources from their home computers or at computer workstations around campus.

Being able to link up with your college library from home is only a small part of the research power now available to you through computers. For example, if you wanted, you could also search the holdings of a university library in Australia, copy a file stored on a computer in Scotland, or ask a question of a scholar in Nigeria. Before we explore the various tools for locating sources, both within and outside the library, we need some general background about electronic resources. To understand electronic resources and acquire skill in using them, there is no substitute for hands-on practice, but the following can provide a useful introduction.

A collection of material that is available electronically (by computer) is generally referred to as a **database.** Databases can be classified as either portable or online. A **portable database** is one that can reside within a particular computer, such as a program on a diskette or a CD-ROM file. In contrast, an **online database** is located at a distant site, such as a host computer or another computer on a network. For you to access it, your computer must communicate with that site. A vast and ever-growing number of databases is available online. These include valuable search tools such as indexes that enable you to locate sources, electronic encyclopedias, and whole libraries of data.

Networks

To gain access to an online database, your computer terminal needs to be connected to another computer containing the database. Such an arrangement by which a number of computers can contact each other is called a **network.** Your college is likely to have its own **local network** in which most computers on campus are connected through a central computer, known as a **server.** This connectivity allows students and faculty to share files and use e-mail to communicate. Most **college library networks** are tied in with the larger campus network, providing patrons with access to library information from classroom, office, and dormitory computers. Since colleges put restrictions on who may use their network, you may need to apply for an *account* and receive an *address* and a *password.*

Smaller networks are often joined in a larger network. For example, your college library network may be joined with networks from other regional libraries, so that you can search for works in several different libraries simultaneously. The linking of libraries in such a consortium also enables students at one campus to find and borrow works owned by another campus.

Finally, networks throughout the world, most likely including your campus network, are joined together in the largest and grandest network of them all, the *Internet.* Originally begun by the U.S. government, this network has grown to allow computer users almost anywhere on the planet to communicate and share information. Any Internet user can send and receive messages with any other user via e-mail. For example, you could direct an inquiry about your research question to a scholar in Finland, provided you knew that person's e-mail address. You could also join one of countless *discussion lists* devoted to particular topics. A message sent to a list is automatically forwarded to all its subscribers. For instance, if you were researching voting patterns of women, you might post an inquiry on the PoSciM list, which is devoted to a discussion of political science issues (and maybe also to WmSt-L, a women's studies list). Other subscribers interested in your topic would be likely to reply. To find a listserv in your area, you can do a search on Isoft.com/lists/list_q.html or search Google for a list using keywords such as "twins listserv."

Another way to follow an ongoing e-mail discussion about a particular topic is by consulting a *newsgroup* or a *bulletin board.* These are very much like actual bulletin boards, where anyone can read and post messages. Unlike discussion lists, where all items are e-mailed directly to subscribers, newsgroups and bulletin boards are "places" on the network that you can "visit" whenever you choose, but no messages are sent to your e-mail in-box.

By far the most popular component of the Internet is the *World Wide Web,* which allows users to read (and create) attractive presentations of text, graphics, and sound known as *Web pages.* Because virtually anyone can post material on the Web, there is no limit to the variety of available presentations. For example, you can explore your college's *home page,* which is linked to many other Web pages containing information about its programs, faculty, and resources. You can also read electronic "magazines" (often called *zines*) on the Web or consult the Web for instant news, weather, and sports updates. The variety is so great that "surfing the Net" has become a recreational obsession for many. However, because almost anyone can post whatever they choose on the Web without oversight or restriction, much information found on Web pages is of dubious merit. Students need to take special care in evaluating material from Web sources.

 ## USING YOUR LIBRARY'S RESEARCH TOOLS

It is worth repeating that while search tools can give you access to a vast quantity of information, the *quality* of that information varies widely. More than ever, student researchers need to use careful judgment about the reliability of their sources and the usefulness of information they encounter. Since the number of channels by which you can access research sources is so great, the following sections of this chapter will focus on those most likely to be helpful. Still, many such tools—old and new—are described, and they can seem intimidating at first. Don't allow yourself to be overwhelmed. It is not necessary for you to absorb all the information in a single sitting. Nor do you need to memorize the names of all the available reference sources and the procedures for using them. Instead, regard this chapter as a guide that you can consult whenever you need it, now and in years to come. By examining the resources that are described here one at a time and by gaining experience with their use through the practice exercises, you will soon develop a solid and confident command of the tools needed for doing college research.

Most college libraries allow you access to a great variety of resources, and you can begin your search from one convenient online screen, the home page of the library's central information system. Once you log on to this page, you are presented with a menu of choices. Different libraries set up their home pages in different ways, but most have similar features, and we will explore some typical and important research tools likely to be available through your college library's online system.

The following two menu options are a staple of most college library systems:

- **Search the library catalog.** This option allows you to find books and other items in your library's holdings.
- **Search electronic indexes and databases.** This option allows you to find articles in journals, newspapers, and other periodicals.

In addition, the menu may allow you to learn library hours, view your own library record and renew items you have borrowed, see what materials your instructor has placed on reserve, and even search catalogs at other libraries.

Finding Books and Other Library Holdings

Let us begin by examining the first of the two options just mentioned, a search of your library's catalog. The library's holdings include books, periodicals, videocassettes, sound recordings, and many other materials—and all are indexed in its online catalog. The catalog menu will present you with a number of search options, including the following:

- Author search
- Title search
- Subject search
- Keyword search
- Call number search

If you know what author or book title you are seeking, you can do an *author search* or a *title search.* Merely enter the name of the author or title, and information is displayed.

When you are engaged in a research project, you will be looking to find what books are available on a particular topic, and you will want to conduct a **subject search** or a **keyword search.** In a subject search, you enter the subject you are searching. Only particular subjects are indexed, namely the subject headings designated by the Library of Congress. Since you may not know the exact subject heading, a keyword search may be the handiest way to begin your search for books on your topic.

Doing a Keyword Search

In a keyword search, you enter one or more words that are likely to appear in a work's title, in its subject, or in catalog notes about its contents. Imagine, for example, that you are interested in researching the Boy Scouts of America. If you entered "scout," you would find that hundreds of works in your library are referenced by this keyword, most of which have nothing to do with the Boy Scouts. (In our library, the entries we found included a novel about a baseball scout and the video of a movie whose cast included an actress named Scout Taylor-Compton.) To eliminate the clutter, you can narrow your search by typing in two or more words, such as "boy scout." Most library catalogs treat two words as a phrase and will search for instances of those two words appearing side by side.

Library Catalog Searches

- Type in one or more words that may appear in the title, subject, author name, or notes.

- Multiple words are searched as a phrase: The entries "college English" and "English college" will produce different results.

- Use *AND* to search for entries containing *both* words (not necessarily together):

    alcohol AND law

- Use *OR* to search for entries containing *either* word:

    college OR university

- Use a wildcard symbol (asterisk) to represent missing letters: The entry "educat* polic*" will produce results for "educational policy" and "education policies," but also "educating police."

One limitation to keyword searches is that a computer is very literal-minded. If you include the word "scout," it will ignore instances of "scouts" or "scouting." Most catalogs allow you to use a **wildcard symbol,** usually an asterisk, to represent optional characters. For example, in a keyword search of our college catalog, we found twelve entries by entering just "boy scout" but thirty-six when we entered "boy scout*." Researchers must be judicious in their use of wildcards, because they can sometimes make a search too broad. For example, a search for "boy*" would return entries about boy scouts but also many unwanted entries containing the words "tomboy" and "boycott," as well as works by or about people named Boyle and Boykin. Partial results of our search using the keywords "boy scout*" are shown in Figure 9.1, in which the first eight of thirty-six titles are shown on the screen.

You could make a list of all the works that interest you by checking the boxes to the left of their titles. Later, when you have finished all your searches, you could ask for a display of all the works you marked. Alternatively, you could examine entries immediately. For example, if you clicked on the fourth title in Figure 9.1, *On My Honor: Boy Scouts and the Making of American Youth*, you would be shown a record, part of which is reproduce in Figure 9.2. This screen gives much information about the book, including its author, title, publisher, and length (323 pages). The fact that the book was published in 2001 tells you how current it is. The fact that the book contains "bibliographic references" tells you that you might go to pages 289–318 to find a list of other works on the topic. The information in the boxes tells you where to go to find the book (its location and call number) and that it is available (not checked out by another patron). When a book's status is "unavailable," you can ask the circulation desk to send a *recall notice* to the borrower, but you would receive no guarantee that it will be returned in time to meet your project's deadline.

Notice that in Figure 9.2, seven different items are underlined, which means that each is a computer *link* to further data, and each provides a useful way to

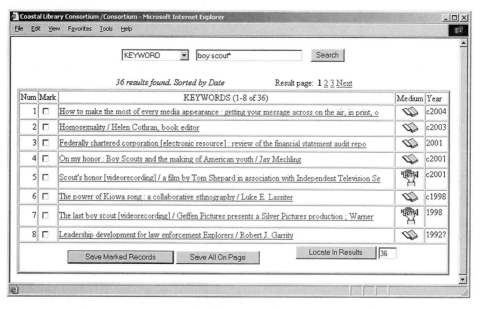

Figure 9.1 Results of a keyword search for "boy scout*" in a library catalog.

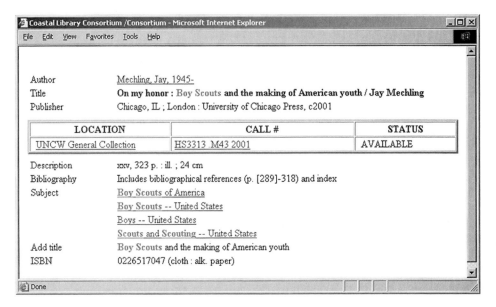

Figure 9.2 Excerpt from a book record.

find additional sources on your topic. If you were to use your mouse to click on the author's name, "Mechling, Jay," you would be shown a list of the holding in the library written by that author. If you clicked on the book's call number, you would be shown a list of works with similar call numbers. Since books are numbered according to their topic, this is a handy way to see what other related items (in this case, about clubs) are in your library. Finally, four different subject headings are listed. You could click on any one of them to do a subject search for this heading.

It should also be noted that your search need not be limited to the holdings in your own library. One useful tool for searching the holdings of over 40,000 libraries worldwide is the OCLC **WorldCat** database, which is available among the online tools on most college library Web sites. Our search on WorldCat for books using the keywords "boy scouts" found over seven thousand entries. For each entry, WorldCat noted if the work was available in our library. For a work not available locally, WorldCat provides a list of libraries in nearby states that hold the book. A work found in another library can be borrowed by your library through an **InterLibrary Loan**. You may find it useful to check the collections of libraries specializing in your subject. If you were researching automotive engineering, you would be wise to check libraries of major universities in Michigan, a state with a large automobile industry. Likewise, if you were researching manatees, you would expect to find more works on the subject at the University of Florida than, say, at the University of North Dakota. Ask your librarian for help in searching the collections of other libraries.

Using Your Library's Central Information System

Use your college library's online catalog to answer the following questions. Although these exercises may remind you of a scavenger hunt, they are intended to familiarize you with the resources in your library and to practice important research skills that you will use many times in the future.

1. These questions can be answered by doing an author search on your college library's catalog:

   a. How many authors with the surname Churchill have works in your library?

   b. How many author listings are there for Sir Winston Churchill (1874–1965)?

   c. View the record for one book by Sir Winston Churchill (and print it, if your computer terminal is connected to a printer). What is the book's full title? its call number? Is the book currently available in your library, or has it been checked out? In what city was the book published? by what publisher? in what year? How many pages long is the book? What subject headings could you use in a subject search to find similar works on the same topic?

2. Do a subject search, using one of the subject headings found in 1c, above. How many works does your library have on that subject? What are the title, author, and call number of one of those works (other than the Churchill book)?

3. Find an author whose last name is the same as or close to your own. Record the title and call number of one book by this author.

4. How would you use your library catalog to locate works *about,* rather than by, Sir Winston Churchill? How many works does your library have about him? Record the author, title, and call number of one such book.

5. How many books does your library have with the title (or partial title) *Descent of Man?* Who are the authors of these books?

6. Do a call number search to answer these questions: How many works are there in your library whose call numbers begin with TL789? What subject(s) are books with this number about? Record the author, title, and call number of one such book.

7. To answer this question, you may need guidance from your instructor or librarian: How can you limit your call number search to only those works (with call number TL789) that were published after 1990? How many such works are there in your library's collection? Can you limit your search to TL789 works with the word "flying" in the title? How many such works are in your library?

8. Do a keyword search to find works on your research project topic (or another topic that interests you). What subject headings do you find for these works? Use the most appropriate of these headings to do a subject search. Now use the WorldCat database to see what additional works on your topic are available at other libraries in your state. Record information about works likely to help you in your research project.

Encyclopedias and Other General Reference Works

General reference works, books, periodicals, newspapers, and microforms are some of the resources in college libraries. Because so many sources are available, it is helpful to approach a search for information with a strategy in mind and to turn first to resources that are most likely to be of help. Before you search in particular directions, you need a broad overview of your topic. General reference works are often a good place to begin.

General reference works, such as encyclopedias and almanacs, offer information about many subjects. They are located in the reference section of your library, where they can be consulted but not checked out. Many encyclopedias, dictionaries, and almanacs are also available online or in CD-ROM format. In addition to text and pictures, some online works allow you to view film clips and hear audio as well. Another advantage of online encyclopedias is that they are frequently updated, and the latest edition is always available to you.

General encyclopedias have alphabetically arranged articles on a wide variety of subjects. *Encyclopedia Americana* contains accessible articles that can provide you with helpful introductions to unfamiliar subjects. The print version of the *New Encyclopaedia Britannica* is somewhat more complicated to use in that it is divided into various sections, including the "Micropaedia," which consists of short articles and cross-references to other articles in the set, and the "Macropaedia," which consists of longer, more detailed articles. Encyclopedias published on CD-ROM disks or available online include *Encarta* and *Britannica Online*. Online encyclopedias, such as *Britannica Online* and *Encarta*, charge an enrollment fee, although you can gain free access to articles if your college library has subscribed. *Wikipedia* is a free online encyclopedia whose articles are contributed by readers and consequently cannot be trusted for reliability. One-volume *desk encyclopedias*, such as the *New Columbia Encyclopedia*, can be quick and handy guides to basic information about a subject. *Almanacs*, such as *Information Please Almanac, Atlas and Yearbook*, and *The World Almanac & Book of Facts*, contain tables of information and are handy sources of much statistical information.

Specialized encyclopedias, restricted to specific areas of knowledge, can provide you with more in-depth information. Many such works are available—the online catalog at the university where we teach lists over a thousand works under the subject heading "Encyclopedia." By way of example, here are just a few from the beginning of the alphabet: *Encyclopedia of Adolescence, Encyclopedia of African-American Civil Rights, Encyclopedia of Aging and the Elderly, Encyclopedia of Alcoholism, Encyclopedia of Allergy and Environmental Illness, Encyclopedia of Amazons, Encyclopedia of American Social History, Encyclopedia of Animated Cartoons, Encyclopedia of Arms Control and Disarmament*, and *Encyclopedia of Assassinations*. You can use your college catalog to locate a specialized encyclopedia dealing with your research topic. You can also browse the reference section in the appropriate stacks for your topic; sections are marked by Library of Congress call numbers (e.g., BF for psychology, HV for crime, N for art, etc.).

Using General Reference Works

1. Locate a specialized encyclopedia dealing with your research topic or another topic that appeals to you.

2. Look up that same topic in the print version of the *New Encyclopaedia Britannica* (look first in the index, which will direct you to either the "Micropaedia" or the "Macropaedia") and then in an online or CD-ROM encyclopedia. Compare the treatment and coverage of the topic in these different works.

3. Determine if information about the same topic can also be found in a print or online almanac.

4. Finally, write a one-page account of what you discovered. In particular, what kinds of information are found in the different reference works? How do the treatments of the topic differ?

FINDING ARTICLES: MAGAZINES, JOURNALS, AND NEWSPAPERS

Articles in magazines, journals, and newspapers are among the sources used most frequently by student researchers in composition classes, for several reasons: Articles are written on a variety of subjects; they make timely information available right up to the most recent issues; and, being relatively brief, they tend to focus on a single topic. Your college library is likely to have recent issues of hundreds of magazines and journals and of many local, national, and international newspapers. In addition, back issues of these publications are available either in bound volumes or on *microforms* (miniaturized photographic copies of the material). Many electronic indexes that you may use to find articles on your research topic allow you to view the articles directly on your screen, saving you the step of finding the article in print or on microform.

Locating Periodicals

If you are in doubt about whether your library has a magazine or journal you are looking for, you can consult a list of all the periodicals your library owns. Such a list is usually found in the library's online catalog. In most libraries, current issues of magazines and journals are shelved on open stacks; back issues are collected and bound by volume or copied onto microforms. Recent back issues, not yet bound, are sometimes available at a periodicals or service desk. If you have difficulty finding an article, ask at the periodicals or reference desk for assistance.

Microforms

As a space-saving device, many libraries store some printed materials on micro-forms, miniaturized photographic copies of the materials. The two principal types of microforms are *microfilm,* which comes in spools that resemble small movie reels, and *microfiche* (pronounced *MY-crow-feesh*), which comes in individual sheets of photographic film. The images they contain are so small that they can store large quantities of material. A projector is required to enlarge these images so they can be read. Most college libraries have projectors for both microfilm and microfiche. Some projectors also allow for photocopying of what appears on the projector's screen. Follow the directions on these machines or ask a librarian for assistance. Although sturdy, microforms are not indestructible, so it is important to handle them with care and to return them in the same condition as you received them.

Library Vandalism—A Crime Against Scholarship

Since scholarship is a cooperative enterprise, it is essential that all scholars have access to sources. Students who steal, deface, or mutilate library materials commit a crime against the ethics of scholarship. An unforgivable sin is to tear articles from magazines, permanently depriving others of their right to read them. Many a frustrated scholar, looking for a needed source only to find it stolen, has uttered a terrible curse on the heads of all library vandals—one that it might be wise not to incur. On the more tangible side, most states have made library vandalism a criminal offense, punishable by stiff fines and in some cases jail sentences.

Actually, there is no excuse for such vandalism. Short passages can be hand-copied. Longer excerpts, to be used for legitimate academic purposes, can be photo-copied inexpensively. Most libraries have coin-operated or debit-card photocopy machines in convenient locations. (Some photoduplication violates copyright laws; consult your instructor or librarian if you are in doubt.)

 ## USING ELECTRONIC DATABASES

Most college libraries provide links to electronic databases, which have replaced printed indexes as the most popular means for students to locate articles, elec-tronic files, and other materials related to their research topics. These databases are either online (through an electronic connection to the database host site) or portable (stored on a CD-ROM disk). *Databases* are usually accessed through the library's central information system.

College libraries allow you access to dozens of databases, and the number is in-creasing at a rapid rate. In this chapter we will introduce a few of the more popular and useful databases, but you should explore your library to learn what databases are available. Most databases work in a similar way, and you need to master only a few simple principles to conduct a successful search. Once you have practiced searching one database, you should have little trouble negotiating most other databases as well. It is usually advisable to search several different databases when you are looking for articles and other information about your research topic.

A Sample Search for Periodical Sources

Your library may subscribe to several *online reference services*, such as EBSCO-host, FirstSearch, InfoTrac, Lexis-Nexis Academic, ProQuest, and WilsonWeb. Each service allows you to search a number of databases either singly or simultaneously. As an example of how you could use an online reference service, we will demonstrate a search using the EBSCOhost service. Let us imagine you are doing a research project on college students who are binge drinkers.

Figure 9.3 shows part of the EBSCOhost menu of databases. Scrolling down the screen would reveal many other databases as well. To the left of each database

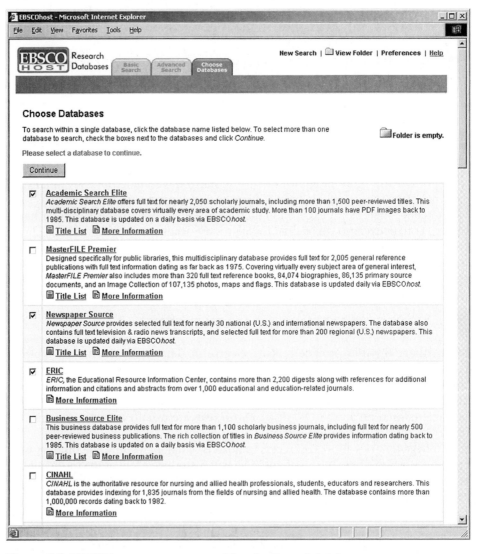

Figure 9.3 EBSCOhost menu screen with selection of databases.

is a box. As a first step in your search, you would click on the boxes of all the databases that might be pertinent. Let us assume you decided to search the Academic Search Elite database (a database of articles in scholarly journals), Newspaper Source, and ERIC (a database of education-related journals and documents). By clicking first in those three boxes and then on the *Enter* button, you bring up the search page shown in Figure 9.4.

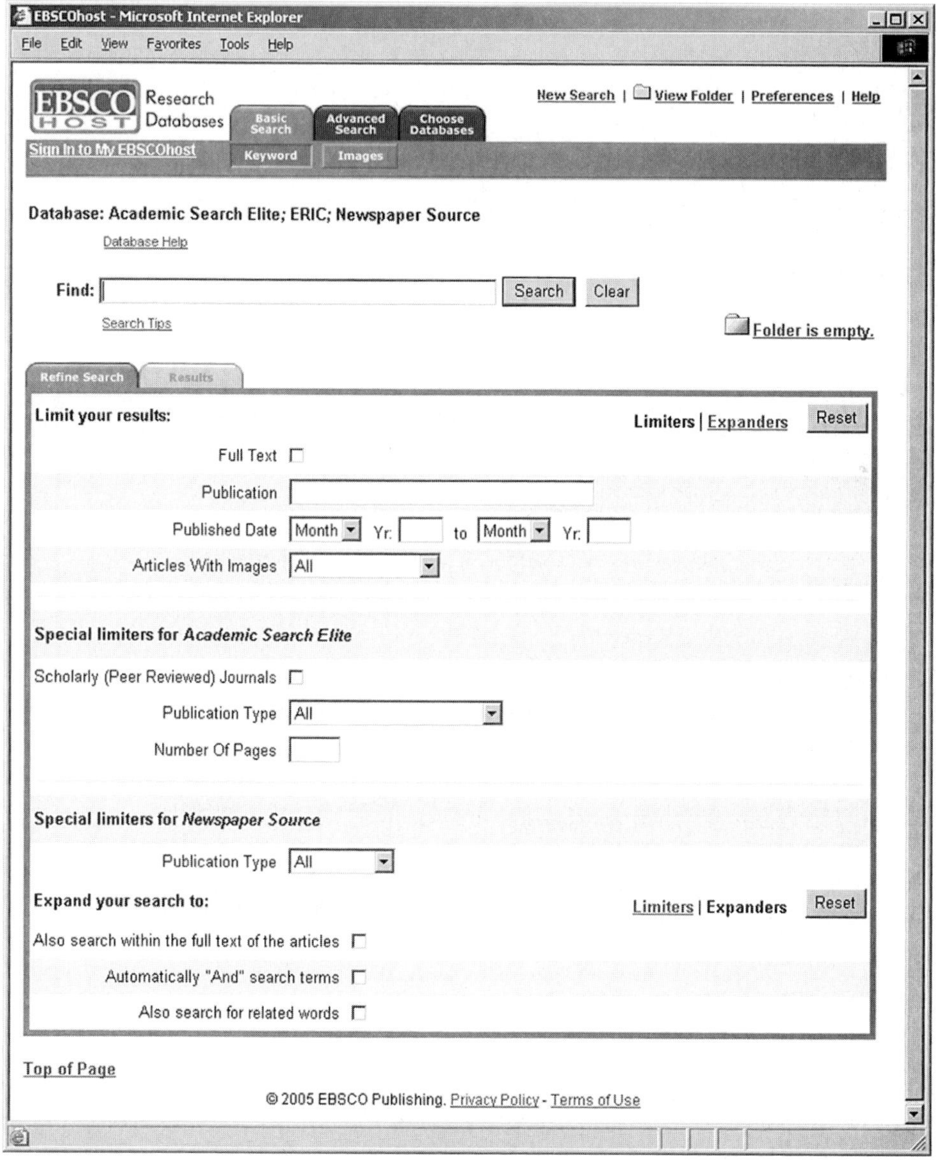

Figure 9.4 Search page in the EBSCOhost search engine.

Tips for Successful Keyword Searches

The next step in your search is to enter *keywords* on the screen in Figure 9.4 to tell the *search engine* (that's another term used to describe an online program that searches a database) what words or phrases to look for as it searches the titles and abstracts of articles. If you enter "binge drinker" in the *Find* box and then click on the *Search* button, a results list will soon appear with 154 documents, the first several of which are shown in Figure 9.5. Although this may seem a respectable

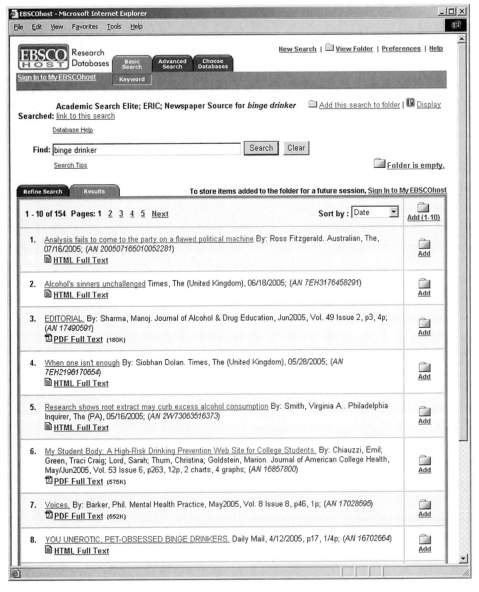

Figure 9.5 A "results list" in the EBSCOhost search engine.

return, unfortunately it does not come close to capturing all the articles available on the subject.

But wait! Computers are very literal. You have asked the search engine to restrict its search just to that one phrase, greatly limiting the results. A useful tip is to use an asterisk as a **wildcard character** to find any of several related words. Entering "binge drink*" instead of "binge drinker" will broaden your search to any phrase that begins with those characters, including *binge drinker, binge drinkers*, and *binge drinking*. Click on the *Search* button, and instead of 154 results, the search engine now reports it has found 1126 items—a more satisfactory outcome.

But perhaps a search of these keywords is still too limiting. The EBSCOhost search engine assumes that two or more words side by side constitute a phrase, and it will look only for the words *binge* and *drink** when they occur next to each other, not when they are separated by other words. A solution is to conduct what is known as a **Boolean search**, using the signals *AND, OR,* or *NOT*. For example, if you asked EBSCOhost to search for "binge AND drink*," it will look for articles that contain both of those words, even if they are separated from each other. That is, it would find articles that contain "binge drinkers" as well as those that contain "drinkers who go on a binge" and so on.

More is not always better, however, and now your search may be too broad. You aren't interested in binge drinking among business executives, just among college students, so a useful strategy is to refine your search further to eliminate unwanted articles. Make the search topic "binge AND drink* AND college*" to eliminate any documents in which the words *college* or *colleges* do not appear. However, in some articles about binge drinking, the word *university* (or *universities*) may be used instead of *college*. You can use the OR operator to search for either *college** or *universit**. That is, you might have your best results if you search for the keywords "binge AND drink* AND (college* OR universit*)." The

---

Using Boolean Operators to Refine Your Search

- The *AND* operator combines search terms to find documents that contain *both* terms:

    alcohol AND college

- The *OR* operator combines terms to find documents that contain *at least one* of the terms:

    alcohol OR drugs

- The *NOT* operator *excludes* terms:

    alcohol NOT drugs

    This will find documents on alcohol but will ignore those in which the word "drugs" appears.

search results that EBSCO host returned when different keywords were entered are shown in Figure 9.6.

The Next Step—Finding More Detail on Sources

In our sample search for articles about collegiate binge drinking, we used the keywords "binge AND drink* AND (college* OR universit*)," and EBSCOhost found 598 documents. The first screen of these results is shown in Figure 9.7. Each result gives the document's title and publication data. The next step is to examine the most promising articles to find useful sources. You can click your mouse on the title of an article to read an ***abstract*** (a brief summary) of its contents. Beneath the titles of the second article, the words "HTML Full Text" appear. If you click on these words, you can read the entire article on your screen. The fourth and fifth entries also give you the option to view photocopies of the original articles ("PDF Full Text"). For the first entry, an abstract is available online, but you would have to read the article in your library. To see if your library has back issues of the journal *International Journal of Eating Disorders*, you can click on the words "Check library catalog for title."

If you were to click on the title of the sixth item in Figure 9.7, "Editorial," you would see the detailed information shown in Figure 9.8 (page 364). In addition to the title, author, and source of the article, this screen contains several other useful items. The abstract summarizes the article and is your best guide to whether the article is likely to be a useful source for your research project. If so, you can read the full text by clicking on "PDF Full Text" above the title. If you believe the article is a useful research source, you can take notes on the article immediately if you like. You also are given several other options at the top of the page. You can *Print* it for later use; *E-mail* the article to yourself (this is especially useful if you are working in a library); *Save* it on a diskette; or *Add to folder*. The last option

Keywords entered	Number of documents found
binge drinker	154
binge drinkers	134
binge drinking	1026
binge drink*	1126
binge AND drink*	1332
binge AND drink* AND college*	475
binge AND drink* AND (college* OR universit*)	598

Figure 9.6 Number of documents found in an EBSCOhost search using different keywords.

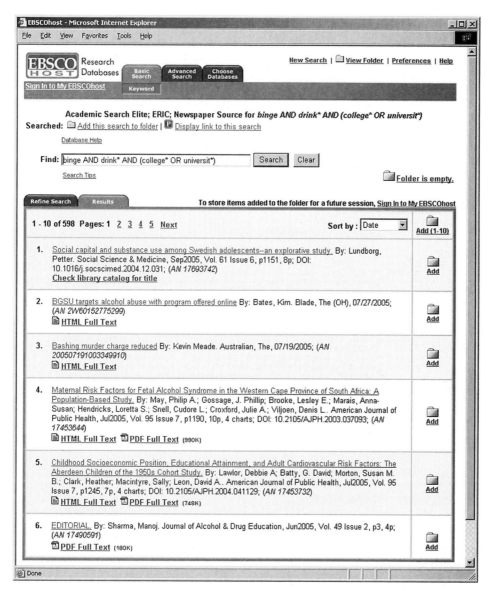

Figure 9.7 Search results for "binge AND drink AND (college* OR universit*)."

allows you to select all the articles that you have found to be likely sources for your project.

Another useful feature of Figure 9.8 is the "Subject Terms" heading. This article is indexed under six different subjects. If you were to click on the first subject, "Alcoholics," you would find additional articles related to that subject.

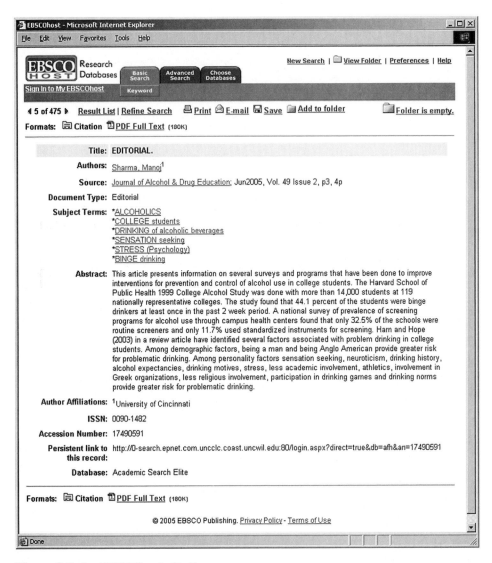

Figure 9.8 An EBSCOhost citation screen.

Using an Online Reference Service

1. In Figure 9.3, which of the databases shown would be your best source to find articles in academic journals? Which database(s) would you search if you were writing a paper on the issue of social promotion in the schools? Which database(s) would be most useful to locate sources for a research project on student

entrepreneurs who start Internet businesses? What is the difference between the MasterFILE Premier database and the Newspaper Source database?

2. Figure 9.4 shows an EBSCOhost search page. If you were looking to find articles about psychological warfare, what keywords would you enter in the "Find" box? What would you do if you were looking for articles about penguins in Chile? What if you were looking for articles about either anorexia or bulimia? If you were searching for articles about the town of Paris in Texas, how could you use Boolean operators to eliminate articles about the movie named *Paris, Texas*? What if you were looking for articles about the censorship of music or television in China or Vietnam?

3. In Figure 9.4, how could you limit your search to articles that can be read on-line? Which box would you check if you wanted to limit your search just to arti-cles that appeared in scholarly journals? What if you wanted to conduct the

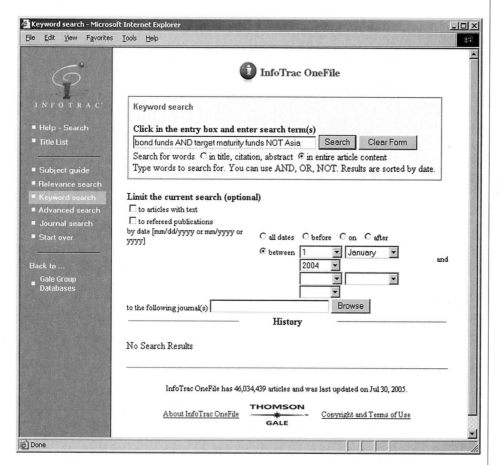

Figure 9.9 A keyword search using the InfoTrac OneFile search engine.

search for your keywords not just in the titles or abstracts of articles, but in the articles themselves?

4. In Figure 9.7, how many authors wrote the article "Maternal Risk Factors . . ."? In what publication did it appear? What is the length in pages of the article? Of the six articles listed on screen, which ones can be read online? Which would you have to look for in your library? If you wanted to return articles numbered 1, 4, and 5 at a later time, what would your first steps in the process be?

5. The page shown partially in Figure 9.7 gives the first ten of 598 documents. Where would you click with your mouse pointer to view the next ten results?

6. Figure 9.8 shows a citation page for an article. In what publication did it appear? Who is the author? How could you find additional articles by the same author? Would clicking on any of the six listed subject headings be helpful in finding additional articles about binge drinking among college students? How could you read the full article?

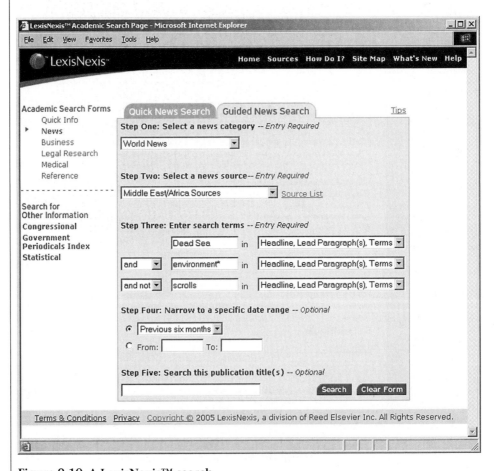

Figure 9.10 A LexisNexis™ search.

7. Figure 9.9 (page 365) shows a search screen using the InfoTrac search engine in which a student has filled in some of the boxes. What subject(s) is the student researching? In addition to entering keywords, what other limitations did the student put on the search?

8. Figure 9.10 (page 366) shows a search using the LexisNexis™ search engine. Describe what the student who filled in this page was seeking?

9. Log on to your college library's central information system. Does it allow you to search for articles online? If so, which online reference services (e.g., EBSCOhost, FirstSearch, LexisNexis, WilsonWeb) does it allow you to search? Are there other databases you can use to search for articles?

10. Use your college library's resources to find a newspaper article about Medicare fraud published within the past year.

11. Use a different database to find an article in an academic journal about the sleeping disorder known as sleep apnea. If you can, print out the citation screen for the article; if not, copy the name of the author, title, publication, date, and page numbers.

FINDING GOVERNMENT DOCUMENTS

The vast array of documents published by the U.S. government constitutes another useful resource for research in almost any field of study. Many government documents are available online. In addition, each state has at least one designated depository library that receives all documents distributed by the Government Printing Office (GPO), as well as several other partial depository libraries that receive selected government publications. Items not in your college library can usually be borrowed through the InterLibrary Loan service. Government documents are usually shelved in a special library section and identified by a call number (called a *GovDoc* or *SuDoc* number). Many library catalogs do not index all their government documents along with their book holdings. To find documents and their call numbers, you need to consult one of several indexes that can search GPO databases. The ***Catalog of U.S. Government Publications*** is a government-sponsored online search engine, located at www.gpoaccess.gov/cgp/.

Another index is the ***GPO Monthly Catalog*** available in many university libraries through the FirstSearch online reference service. Imagine, for example, that you were writing a research paper on the prevalence and causes of teenage smoking. A search of the GPO Monthly Catalog using the keywords "teen*" and "smoking" would yield many documents, including one called "Preventing Tobacco Use Among Young People: A Report of the Surgeon General: At a Glance." Clicking on the title would call up on your screen the record of that publication shown in Figure 9.11.

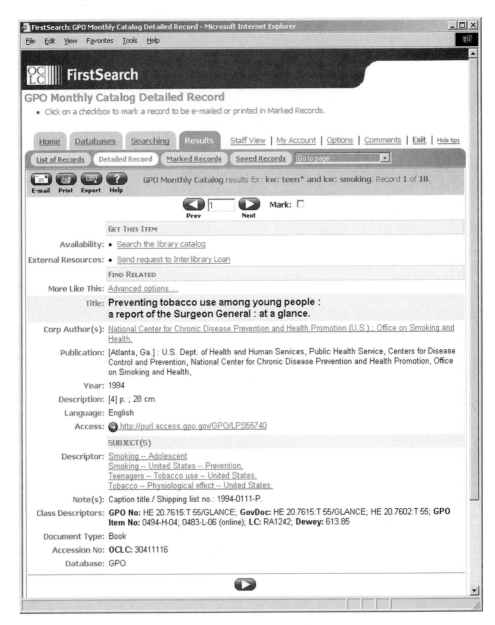

Figure 9.11 A government document record in the GPO Monthly Catalog.

EXERCISES   **Finding Government Documents**

1. This exercise can be undertaken by one or two students who can report their findings to the class. Find out if your college library is your state's regional depository for U.S. government documents or a partial depository. If the latter,

what percentage of available government items does it receive? Where are government documents shelved in the library? How can students gain access to government documents not in your library?

2. Figure 9.11 is the record of one of the government documents found from a search about teenage smoking. Which government agency authored the report? In what year was it published? On what subject heading(s) might you click to find more documents about teen smoking?

3. Use a GPO index to search for a government document related to your research topic. Report briefly on what you find.

 ## INTERNET RESOURCES

Library sources can be accessed in systematic ways; by contrast, finding sources on the Internet is much more a hit-or-miss affair. Whereas the library's staff controls its collection and creates an index of all the library's holdings (its online catalog), no one runs the Internet, much less controls access to it or creates a comprehensive index. The Internet is really a vast interconnected network of smaller networks, which virtually anyone can access and where virtually anyone can publish anything. Navigating the Internet and finding resources that can aid your research project require much practice, some skill, and considerable luck.

The best Internet tutorial comes from hands-on exploration, aided by your curiosity and an adventurous spirit. Here we can give only some brief information and hints to get you started.

Web Search Engines

When you seek Web sources for a research project, you will probably not know the addresses for specific sites. Although no comprehensive index to the millions of Web pages exists, several commercial indexes (known as *search engines*) provide access to a large number of sites.

Because different search engines provide different results, it is often best to use more than one in researching your topic. Here are the addresses of some of the more prominent search engines:

Google	google.com
AllTheWeb.com	alltheweb.com
Yahoo	yahoo.com
MSN Search	msn.com
Lycos	lycos.com
Ask Jeeves	ask.com
Dogpile	dogpile.com

One of the most popular and highly regarded search engines is Google. The Google address *www.google.com* produces the basic search screen shown in Figure 9.12. Unlike most library catalogs and periodical search engines such as EBSCOhost,

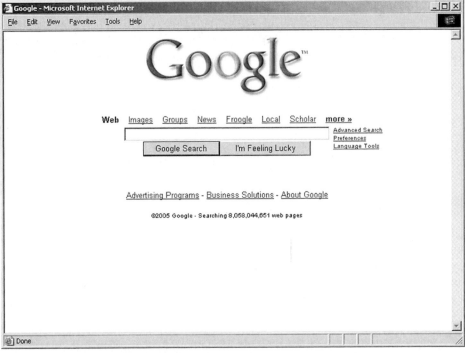

Figure 9.12 Screen for a basic Google search.

Tips for a Basic Google Search

- Google searches for entries with *all* the words listed:

    alcohol obesity
- Use quotation marks to search for phrases:

    censorship "high school"
- Google does not support wildcard characters such as *.
- Google ignores capitalization:

    pAris fraNCe
- Google ignores common words, such as *the, of, I, where,* and *how.* Entering *World War I* also provides results about World War II. Add a + sign before a common word to include it in the search, or place the word within quotation marks:

    World War +I

    "World War I"
- Use a minus sign to exclude a term. For a search on bass (the fish, not the musical term), enter

    bass −music

Google does not treat keywords as phrases; that is, it will search for sites containing all the words listed, regardless of whether they occur side by side. If you were searching for sites about the relationship between alcohol and obesity, you could enter *alcohol obesity*. You don't need the *AND* operator between the words (in fact, Google ignores *AND* or *and*). See the box at the bottom of the previous page for other tips about a basic Google search.

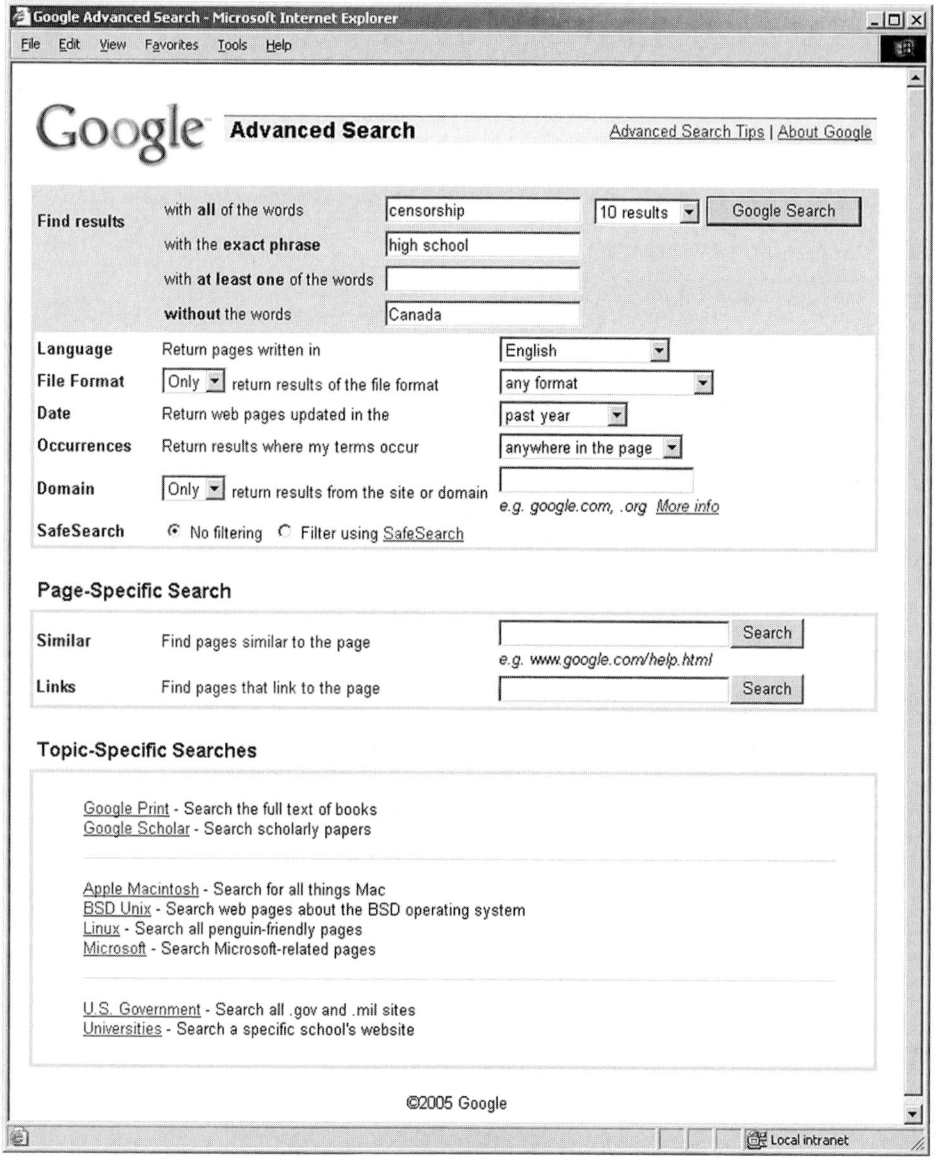

Figure 9.13 Screen for an advanced Google search.

For greater control in an Internet search, click on the "Advanced Search" link. An advanced search can allow you to return the most pertinent results while excluding unwanted sites. For example, Figure 9.13 (page 371) shows how you might search for pages in English produced within the last year about censorship in high schools, but not those in Canada. Figure 9.14 shows the results of this search. Because all search engines provide different results, it is often worthwhile to conduct searches on more than one search engine.

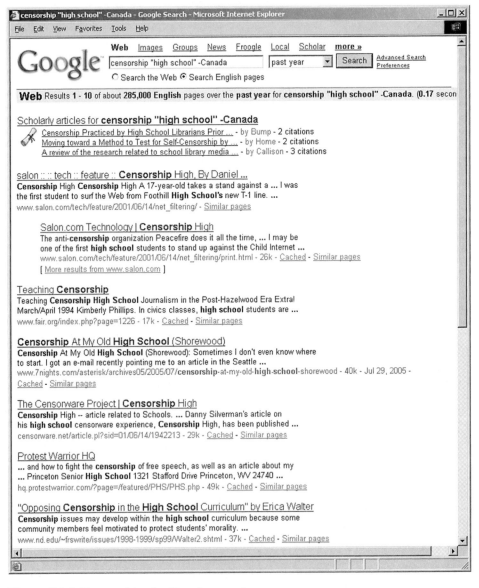

Figure 9.14 The results of a Google search.

Figure 9.15 The Yahoo Directory at dir.yahoo.com. *(Reproduced with permission of Yahoo! Inc. Copyright © 2005 by Yahoo! Inc. Yahoo! and the Yahoo! logo are trademarks of Yahoo! Inc.)*

A second option for Web searching is to consult a ***search directory***. Figure 9.15 shows the Yahoo directory at *dir.yahoo.com*. You can browse the directory by following links through relevant categories (e.g., *Science*, then *Biology*, then *Evolution*, etc.). Because items in the directory have been selected by humans (rather than a computer program), a search will provide fewer, but more selective results.

Some words of caution about Web searches are in order. Students should evaluate Web pages with a careful, critical eye. Remember that anyone can post Web pages, and so not everything on the Web is valuable or accurate. Find out who has created the document and how reliable or comprehensive it is. For example, if you are researching a scandal in the widget industry, you will likely find many widget pages. Knowing if the page is created by a widget trade organization (which would be expected to have a pro-widget bias) or by an anti-widget consumer group (with the opposite bias) is essential if you are to assess the sources and determine whether and how to use them.

Because Web searches often return hundreds, if not thousands, of results, visit only those that look promising. When you find worthwhile sites, you can take notes on them, print the pages, or bookmark them for later use.

EXERCISES

Using the World Wide Web

Do the following exercises using the World Wide Web:

1. See what you can find on the Web on the following three topics: identical twins, Peru, and archery. Use one or more of the above search engines to explore these topics. Follow links from page to page as your curiosity leads you. Write a narrative describing your search and discoveries.

2. The Yahoo directory at *dir.yahoo.com* is organized around a number of topics (business & economy, computers & Internet, etc.). Select one that interests you, and continue to choose from among options until you arrive at an interesting page. Print the page (if equipment allows) or summarize its contents.

3. Use other search engines to find Web sources on your research topic.

THE REFERENCE LIBRARIAN—THE MOST RESOURCEFUL RESOURCE

By far the most valuable resource in any library is the librarian, a professional who knows the library well and is an expert in locating information. Use the other resources in this chapter first, but if you become stuck or do not know where to look or cannot find the sources you need, do not hesitate to ask a librarian for help. College libraries have *reference librarians* on duty, usually at a station marked as the *reference desk.* Their job is to assist when you need help in finding sources. Reference librarians are almost always helpful, and they have aided many students with the same kinds of research problems and questions that you are likely to have.

There are some limits, however, to the services reference librarians can provide. One librarian requested that we mention some problems they are sometimes asked to solve but cannot. They cannot pick a topic for you, interpret your assignment, or answer questions about the format of your bibliographic citations. Those questions should be addressed to your instructor. The librarian's job is to assist when you need help locating library sources.

Although printed and electronic materials are of great value to researchers, they are not the only sources available. Chapter 10 discusses ways to use other sources in your research project.

10 *Finding Sources outside the Library: Conducting Interviews and Writing Letters*

 INTERVIEWING SOURCES

In addition to print sources, interviews with experts can provide valuable material for your paper. Because the people you interview are primary rather than secondary sources, the firsthand information they provide is exclusively yours to present—information that readers will find nowhere else. Therefore, interviewed sources can make a favorable impression, giving readers the sense that they are getting expert testimony directly and reliably. Your own reliability and credibility may also be enhanced, since you demonstrate the initiative to have extended your search beyond the usual kinds of sources.

On a college campus, professors are an accessible source of expert information. Being familiar with research in their individual fields, they also can suggest published and unpublished resources you might not have found in your library research. In his research on twins, Allen Strickland interviewed Caroline Clements, a psychology professor on his campus who is herself an identical twin. You may also find experts living in your local community. Courtney Holbrook gained valuable firsthand information about a career in pharmaceutical sales when she interviewed an actual sales representative for a drug company.

Participants and eyewitnesses are also valuable sources. If you were researching, say, biological terrorism, you could interview persons responsible for emergency preparedness in your community, such as police and hospital staff. Be resourceful in considering interviewees who can contribute to your knowledge and understanding.

Conducting interviews may not be the first order of business in your research project, but because interviews require advance planning, it is important to set up appointments as early as possible—even before you are ready to conduct them. Soon after Courtney had decided on her topic, she knew she would want to talk to a drug salesperson. She wanted to do some reading first in order to be sufficiently informed to ask intelligent questions, but she also knew that salespeople travel frequently and that it would be wise to arrange an interview well in advance.

Arranging the Interview

Like every other stage in a research project, arranging interviews can lead to inevitable frustrations. For example, if you were researching a career in psychiatry, you might find it difficult to arrange an interview with a psychiatrist. After all, psychiatrists spend their days talking with patients; they may have little interest in giving up their precious free time to talk with someone else (without compensation).

When you telephone someone you don't know, be courteous and explain your purpose simply and clearly. For example, if you were calling an executive at a computer company to ask for an interview, you might say something like this:

> Hello, Ms. Smith, I'm [your name], a student at [your school]. I'm conducting a research project concerning the future of computers in the workplace. I'm particularly interested in talking to a person in the industry with your expertise, and I would like to learn your views on the topic. I wonder if I could meet with you briefly to ask you a few questions.

You can expect the person to ask you further questions about the nature of your project and about the amount of time the interview will take. If you are courteous and open and if your purposes seem serious, people are likely to cooperate with you to the extent that they are able. Be prepared to meet at a time and place convenient to the interviewee. Many interviews can be conducted in fifteen to thirty minutes. If you wish to tape-record the interview, ask for permission at the time you arrange the meeting.

Professors are usually available to students during office hours, but business people and other professionals are usually not so easy to reach. Before talking to the executive, you might have to explain your need to a receptionist or secretary, who might be reluctant to connect you. Often a letter written in advance of your telephone call can be effective in securing an interview. For example, a student who wishes to arrange an interview with a computer executive might send a letter like this one:

```
                                202 Willow Street
                                Wilmington, NC 28401
                                2 March 2006

Ms. Denise Smith
Vice-President for Research and Development
CompuCosmos Corporation
Wilmington, NC 28401

Dear Ms. Smith:
     I am a student at the University of North Carolina at
Wilmington engaged in a research project concerning the future
of computer use in business offices. I have learned much about
the topic from written sources, but I still have some unanswered
```

questions. Your observations and expert opinions would be invaluable for my report. I know your time is valuable, and I would be grateful if I could meet with you for a brief interview. I will telephone Wednesday morning to see if I can arrange a meeting. If you wish, you can reach me by phone at 555-1893.

> Sincerely,
>
> *Blair Halliday*
>
> Blair Halliday

Conducting the Interview

Some interviews may consist of a simple question or two, designed to fill specific gaps in your knowledge about your topic. Others may be extended question-and-answer sessions about a variety of topics. The success of your interviewing depends on your preparation, professionalism, and interpersonal skills. The following guidelines should be followed when you conduct an interview:

1. *Before the interview:*

   • **Be well prepared.** The most important part of the interview takes place before the questions are posed. Become as informed about your subject as you can so that you can ask the right questions. Use your reading notes to prepare questions in advance.

   • **Dress appropriately for the interview.** How you dress can influence how the interviewee behaves toward you; people are most comfortable talking with someone who dresses as they do. Business and professional people, for example, are more likely to take you seriously if you are wearing standard business attire. On the other hand, formal attire would be inappropriate when interviewing striking factory workers, who might be reluctant to speak freely with someone who looks like management.

   • **Arrive on time for your appointment.** Not only is arriving on time a matter of courtesy, but it is essential in assuring the interviewee's cooperation.

2. *During the interview:*

   • **Take careful and accurate notes.** If you intend to quote your source, you must be certain that you have copied the person's words exactly. A tape recorder can give you an accurate transcript of your interviews.

   • **Behave politely and ethically.** Be certain you have the interviewee's permission if you tape-record the conversation. If you take notes, offer to let the interviewee check the transcript later to ensure accuracy (doing so may elicit further elaborations and additional statements that you can use).

- **Be relaxed and friendly.** People who are not accustomed to being interviewed are often nervous at first about having their comments recorded. By being friendly and relaxed, you can win their confidence and put them at ease. The most fruitful parts of interviews occur when interviewees become absorbed in what they are saying and forget they are being recorded. Begin with general questions that can be answered with ease and confidence. Later introduce more specific and pointed questions. (For experienced interviewees, these precautions may not be necessary.)

- **Make your recording as unobtrusive as possible.** Many people will not speak freely and naturally when constantly reminded that their comments are being recorded. Place the tape recorder out of the interviewee's direct line of sight. Do not write constantly during the interview; write down key phrases and facts that will allow you to reconstruct the conversation immediately after the interview.

- **Be interested in what the interviewee says.** People will speak much more freely with you if they sense that you are responsive to their comments. It is a mistake for an interviewer to read one prepared question after another, while barely listening to the interviewee's responses. Such wooden interviewing produces an uncomfortable atmosphere and strained responses.

- **Stay flexible.** Do not be a slave to your prepared questions. Listen with real curiosity to what the person says and ask further questions based on what you learn. Request explanations of what is not clear to you. Ask probing questions when a topic is raised that you would like to learn more about.

- **Let the interviewee do the talking.** Remember that it is the interviewee's ideas that you are interested in, not your own. Avoid the temptation to state your own opinions and experiences or to argue points with the interviewee.

3. *After the interview:*

- **End the interview professionally.** Check your notes and questions to determine if any gaps still need to be filled. Thank the interviewee. Ask if the person would like to check your use of statements and information for accuracy, and whether you can call again if you have further questions. Offer to send the interviewee a copy of your paper when it is completed.

- **Be fair to the source.** When you write the paper, be certain that any ideas or statements you attribute to the source are true reflections of the sound and spirit of the person's answers and comments. Be accurate in quoting the person, but eliminate slips of the tongue and distracting phrases like *uh* and *you know*.

- **Send a thank-you note.** Whether or not you send a copy of your paper to the interviewee, you should send a note expressing your appreciation for the help that the person provided.

Courtney prepared the following list of questions before she interviewed a pharmaceutical sales representative:

Possible interview questions for ["John Carter"*]

- Why did you decide to be a PS [pharmaceutical salesperson]?
- Is your job what you expected?
- What do you do on a typical day?
- How do you make contact with doctors?
- Is the job enjoyable/rewarding?
- What do you like best about it?
- Is it stressful?
- What are your major frustrations?
- Is there opportunity for advancement?
- What schooling did you have?
- What preparations would you recommend for someone planning to be a PS?
- How did your company train you for the job?
- A controversy about PS practices has been in the news. What are your thoughts?
- Would you recommend a PS career to others?

Although she used her prepared questions as a point of reference, Courtney found herself departing from them as she responded to Mr. Carter's comments. During her interview, Courtney took notes in her research notebook. Here are some excerpts. (In some cases we have recast them to make them clearer to other readers.)

Excerpt from Courtney's interview notes

—Teaching music got old, repetitive as well as stressful. Friend suggested PSR.

—Job: a lot of research

—"Sales is about business. The customer is business. The patients are Business."

—Typical day: at the computer by 6/7:30. Doing email and boss assignments. A lot of administrative work.

—By 7:30 out driving to locations – can be local or regional

—Not unusual for paperwork/customer interaction to spill into overtime, incl. nights, weekends

—CEOs in their 30s. Can be rep for only 2 to 3 yrs – be promoted (even to corp. mgt.)

—Has bach. deg. in music ed. Started pre-med classes, never finished (in physical therapy).

—Taught music 10 yrs to middle sch. Too stressful. Friend pushed him into ph. sales, got him job.

*The person whom Courtney interviewed requested that she not use his real name.

Sometimes answers to interview questions are brief. At other times, one question can lead to a long response and many new questions from the interviewer. When Allen Strickland interviewed psychology professor Caroline Clements about being an identical twin, he asked, "Are there differences between you and your sister?" Allen jotted down Professor Clements's words at a fast clip, and his notes weren't as neat, orderly, and linear as our excerpt suggests:

Excerpt from Allen's interview notes

My mom put us is separate classes
     real concerned about that
in early pictures I can't tell who's who. Now we don't look alike.
I was athlete, she wasn't
     more social, she was in cool clique, cheerleader
neat freak, basically a suburban housewife
she is much more reactive, gets angrier quicker
     me – relaxed attitude
very different life courses
     she got married earlier, divorced early, 3 kids
     became RN
different religious beliefs, conserv. Republican/lib. Dem.
     but don't fight, talk every single day
     absolutely best friends
Life experiences change you. We're just very different people.

 WRITING FOR INFORMATION

It frequently happens that information helpful to your project is unavailable in the library. For example, if you were doing a project on nutrition in children's breakfast foods, you might visit a supermarket to record nutritional information and ingredients of various brands from the sides of cereal boxes. You could also write letters of inquiry to cereal manufacturers, such as the one that follows.

November 3, 2006

Public Relations Officer
Breakfast Foods Division
General Foods Corporation
250 North Street
White Plains, NY 10625

Dear Public Relations Officer:
    As a student at [your university], I am undertaking
a research study of nutrition in breakfast cereals. I am
particularly interested in learning if there is a market for
low-sugar cereals targeted specifically for the children's
market. Could you please tell me the sales figures for your

```
low-sugar Post Crispy Critters cereal? I would also appreciate
any additional information you could send me related to this
subject.
      I would be grateful if you could respond before [date], the
deadline for my research paper.

                              Sincerely,
                              [your signature]
                              [your name]
```

Business directories in the reference section of your library, such as the *Directory of Corporate Affiliations*, can help you find company addresses. Your library may also subscribe to online databases that provide corporate information, such as *Dow Jones Interactive*. You can also consult a "yellow pages" search engine, such as www.switchboard.com. If you need further assistance, consult with the reference librarian.

It is wise to tell correspondents how you plan to use the information you are requesting. They are more likely to respond if convinced that your project will not be harmful to their interests. (Some businesses, such as tobacco or liquor companies, are understandably leery about supplying information for studies that may attack them.) You can increase your chances of getting a response by including a self-addressed stamped envelope with your letter. If time is short, a telephone call, e-mail message, or a fax may get a speedier response than a letter.

 ## STILL OTHER SOURCES

Researchers can avail themselves of many other sources besides library materials, interviews, and letters. *Lectures, films, television programs*, and *audio recordings* are among the sources often cited in student research projects. In your paper, for example, you might quote a person who appeared in a television documentary, or you might describe an event portrayed in a news program. A song lyric or a line from movie dialogue might effectively illustrate a particular theme.

On many campuses there is a *media center* in which videotapes (including television documentaries), DVDs, and various audio recordings are available. It may be housed in the library or in a separate building. Some campuses belong to a regional network of media centers that share their materials, usually with little or no charge to the borrower. If your campus has a media center, ask how you can find what sources are available on your topic and whether it is possible for you to gain access to materials from other campuses.

11 *Putting Your Sources to Work*

◼ A RESEARCH PROSPECTUS

A *prospectus* is a statement of your plans for a project. During the early stages of their projects, Allen Strickland and Courtney Holbrook were asked by their instructors to submit a research prospectus. Allen's class received the following assignment.

ASSIGNMENT   **Research Prospectus**

Bring to our next class a prospectus of your research project. It should consist of the following elements:

1. **A statement of your research question.** Your topic may be tentative at this point, so you needn't feel locked into it. In upcoming days, you may decide to alter your question or shift its focus as you conduct further research and learn more about the subject.

2. **A paragraph or two about your progress so far.** You can summarize why you chose your topic, what you already know about it, and what you hope to discover. You can also discuss any problems or successes you have had with focusing your topic and finding sources.

3. **A working bibliography (a list of the sources you have located so far).** Use the MLA format (explained in Chapter A of Part II) for your bibliography. This is a list of raw sources—sources you have not yet had much chance to examine and evaluate—so it is likely to contain some items that you will not use in your paper and therefore will not appear in the works-cited page of the final draft.

Allen and Courtney by now had a general idea of their topics. They had done some browsing in encyclopedias and other reference works, and each was beginning to assemble a list of potential sources. Following are some excerpts from

Allen's research notebook, written as he was beginning his search. Allen's notes are informal, in the style of journal entries. We have edited them somewhat to make them clearer for other readers. Allen made his first journal entry on the day his class did the invention exercises in Chapter 8:

> Today I just happened to read an article on Yahoo about
> identical twins. I looked at it because I've always been
> fascinated by twins, even though I'm an only child. I've
> often wished I had a twin and have fantasized about being an
> identical twin. The article said that [identical] twins have
> identical genes but these genes don't always act in the same
> way. This accounts for the differences in twins. It was on my
> mind, so when we did the mapping exercise I wrote about
> twins . . .

Here are two more entries from Allen's notebook a few days later:

> I was mostly interested in how twins behave and how different
> it is to be a twin rather than a non-twin or an only child. I
> searched Yahoo for news stories on twins and got more
> articles that were mostly about differences between twins.
> One was on why twins have different fingerprints. Another was
> about twins that are different in sexuality, one gay and one
> straight. I googled identical twins and found several sites,
> one posted by two twins who are identical but also opposites--
> one left-handed, one right-handed, one gay, one straight . . .
> I checked the library catalog and only found one book on
> twins, but when I went to the stacks I found five books next
> to each other on twins. Most of them are old. I also checked
> EbscoHost and found many articles . . . I didn't find anything
> yet about ESP in twins. Most of the sources are about twin
> differences, so I will probably focus on that instead of
> twins vs. non-twins.

> I used "identical twins" as keywords in searching the
> PsychInfo database, but didn't get great results. Articles in
> journals seem to use "monozygotic" rather than "identical" to
> describe them, and I had much better results with the
> keywords "twins and (identical or monozygotic or MZ)."

After more searching with their college library's central information system and on-line databases, Allen and Courtney has settled on their topics and were ready to write their prospectuses. Allen's prospectus and working bibliography are shown in Figure 11.1. His paper would not turn out exactly as he predicted here, nor would he use all the sources he found in his early searches. The shape of a research paper is never final until the actual writing—and further research—are done, but Allen's prospectus shows he was engaged in a process that would continue to take him to a final result.

Strickland 1

Allen Strickland
Research Prospectus

1. Research question: How alike are identical twins, and how are twins different from other siblings?

2. Although I am an only child, I have long been interested in identical twins, particularly about how their lives differ from non-twins like myself. I have been curious about what it is like to have a mirror image of oneself and whether twins have a different relationship with others as a result.

From my research so far I have learned that identical twins have identical genes, which makes them behave in eerily similar ways, but they are not identical in all respects. I am especially interested in studies of identical twins who were raised apart from each other and in studies of telepathy in twins.

I have found numerous books and articles. I have more work to do in finding scholarly sources, but the number of sources available seems great. I expect to write about what twins are, how they differ socially from non-twins, and what studies of twins can show about the role of our genes in shaping us.

Figure 11.1 Allen's research prospectus.

Strickland 2

3. Working bibliography

Bower, B. "Gene Influence Tied to Sexual Orientation."
    Science News 4 Jan. 1992: 6. Academic Search Elite.
    EBSCOhost. 6 July 2005 <http://search.epnet.com>.

"Even Identical Twins Grow Apart Genetically--Study."
    Reuters. Yahoo News. 5 July 2005. 5 July 2005
    <http://news.yahoo.com/news?tmpl=story&u=/nm/20050705/
    sc_nm/science_twins_dc_5>.

"Findings Shed Light on Why Identical Twins Differ." Reuters
    Health. Yahoo News. 5 July 2005. 5 July 2005
    <http://news.yahoo.com/news?tmpl=story&u=/nm/20050705/
    hl_nm/twins_differ_dc_1>.

Goldberg, Alan B. "Identical Twins Become Brother and Sister:
    Female Twins Become Sister and Brother after Sex-Change
    Surgery." ABC News. 19 Nov. 2004. 5 July 2005
    <http://abcnews.go.com/2020/story?id=267325&page=1>.

O'Donnell, Stephen, and Mark O'Donnell. "The Co-Zygotes'
    Almanac." Esquire June 1998: 132. Academic Search
    Elite. EBSCOhost. 6 July 2005 <http://search.
    epnet.com>.

Richards, Edward P. "Phenotype v. Genotype: Why Identical
    Twins Have Different Fingerprints." Forensic-
    Evidence.com. 5 July 2005 <http://
    www.forensic-evidence.com/site/ID/ID_Twins.html>.

Strickland 3

Sandbank, Audrey C., ed. Twin and Triplet Psychology: A
    Professional Guide to Working with Multiples. New York:
    Routledge, 1999.

"Twin." Wikipedia: The Free Encyclopedia. 5 July 2005
    <http://en.wikipedia.org/wiki/Twin>.

Whitehead, N. E. "The Importance of Twin Studies." National
    Association for Research and Therapy of Homosexuals.
    5 July 2005 <http://www.narth.com/docs/whitehead2.html>.

Wright, Lawrence. Twins: And What They Tell Us about Who We
    Are. New York: Wiley, 1997.

 ## THE WORKING BIBLIOGRAPHY

A *bibliography* is a list of research sources. One of the last tasks in your search project is to type a *list of works cited* at the end of your paper—a formal bibliography or listing of all the sources you have used in writing it. But this occurs much later in the research process. For now, your task is to continue gathering sources; that is, you need to use the library databases and other research tools described in Chapter 9 to locate books and articles for your paper. The list of possible sources you draw up as you begin your search is your *working bibliography.* You add to the working bibliography during the course of your project as you discover additional sources, and you subtract from it as some sources on the list turn out not to be helpful.

A working bibliography is tentative, informal, and practical. The only requirement for a good working bibliography is that you are able to use it conveniently. Since it is for your own use—not part of the paper itself—you can record the information you need any way you like. For example, when you find a likely book from a subject citation in the library catalog, you can jot down in your notebook the key information that will enable you to locate it—perhaps only its title and call number. On the other hand, there are advantages to including more complete information in your working bibliography, as Allen did, in that you will use this information later, at the end of the project, when you type your works-cited page. Therefore, you can save considerable time by including all the information you may need later. For that reason, it is important for you to be acquainted with the standard conventions for citing sources. Those conventions are detailed in Chapter A of Part II.

Once you have completed your prospectus and have had it approved by your instructor, you are ready to put your sources to work.

 ## USING YOUR SOURCES

The early stages of your project may have been easier than you expected. You selected a topic, did some preliminary browsing in the library, and assembled a list of sources to work with. So far so good. But now what? Is there some simple technique that experienced researchers use to get ideas and information *out* of their sources and *into* their writing?

In fact, there is a reasonably uncomplicated and orderly procedure for putting your sources to use, but it isn't exactly simple. You can't just sit down before a stack of sources, read the first one and write part of your paper, then read the second one and write some more, and so on until you are finished. Obviously, such a procedure would make for a very haphazard and disjointed paper.

You can't write your paper all at once. Because you have a substantial body of information to sort through, digest, select, and organize, you have to use good management skills in your project. Your course of action needs to consist of manageable subtasks: You need to (1) *read* your sources efficiently and selectively and (2) *evaluate* the information you find there. As you learn more about your topic, you should (3) *narrow your focus* and (4) *shape a plan* for the paper. And to make use of new ideas and information, you need to (5) *take notes* on what seems important and usable in the sources. Only then are you ready to begin the actual drafting of the paper.

This chapter examines each of these tasks in turn, but do not think of them as separate operations that you can perform one after the other. They must interact. After all, how can you know what to read and take notes on unless you have some plans for what your paper will include? On the other hand, how can you know what your paper will include until your reading reveals to you what information is available? In working on your paper, you can never put your brain on automatic pilot. As you read and learn from your sources, you must continually think about how you can use the information and how using it will fit in with (or alter) your plan for the paper.

Allen and Courtney received an assignment like the following from their instructors.

Continue your research by reading your sources, evaluating them, taking notes on note cards, narrowing your focus, and shaping a plan (a preliminary outline) for your paper. This is the most time-consuming stage of your research project, so be sure to begin working on it right away. Continue to record your experiences and observations in your research notebook.

Reading Your Sources

At this stage, you need to undertake several tasks, the first of which is to *read your sources.* A research paper should be something new, a fresh synthesis of information and ideas from many sources. A paper that is largely a summary of only one or two sources fails to do this. Become well informed about your topic by reading widely, and use a breadth of information in your paper. Most likely you have found many sources related to your topic, and the sheer volume of available material may itself be a cause for concern. Because your time is limited, you need to use it efficiently. Following are some practical suggestions for efficient reading:

- **Read only those sources that relate to your topic.** Beginning researchers often try to read too much. Do not waste valuable time reading sources that do not relate specifically to your topic. Before reading any source in detail, examine it briefly to be sure of its relevance. Chapter titles in books and section headings or even illustrations in articles may give you a sense of the work's usefulness. If you find dozens of books devoted solely to your topic, that topic probably is too broad to treat in a brief paper, and your focus should be narrowed. (Narrowing your paper's focus is discussed later in this chapter.)

- **Read each source selectively.** Do not expect to read every source from cover to cover; rather, read only those passages that relate to your topic. With a book, for example, use the table of contents in the front and the index in the back to locate relevant passages. Skim through promising sections, looking for passages relating directly to your topic—only these should you read carefully and deliberately.

- **Think as you read.** Ask yourself if what you are reading relates to your topic. Is it important and usable in your paper? Does it raise questions you want to explore further? What additional research do you need to do to answer these questions? Find new sources as needed, discard unusable ones, and update your working bibliography.

- **Read with curiosity.** Do not let your reading become a plodding and mechanical task; don't think of it as plowing through a stack of sources. Make your reading an act of exploration. You want to learn about your topic, and each source holds the potential to answer your questions. Search out answers, and if you don't find them in one source, seek them in another. There are many profitable ways for researchers to think of themselves: as explorers discovering unknown territory, as detectives following a trail of clues, as players fitting together the pieces of an intriguing puzzle.

• **Use your hand as well as your eyes when you read.** If you have photocopied an article or book chapter, underline important passages while reading, and write yourself notes in the margins. (Of course, don't do either of these things unless you own the copy; marking up material belonging to the library or to other people is a grave discourtesy.) Getting your hand into action as you read is a good way of keeping your mind active as well; writing, underlining, and note-taking force you to think about what you are reading. An article from *The Washington Post Magazine* that Allen photocopied and then annotated is shown in Figure 11.2.

• **Write notes about your reading.** Use your research notebook to "think on paper" as you read. That is, write general comments about what you have learned from your sources and the ideas you have gained for your paper. Use note cards to write down specific information that you might use in writing your paper. (Note cards are discussed in detail later in this chapter.)

Evaluating Your Sources

All sources are not equally reliable. Not all writers are equally competent; not all periodicals and publishers are equally respected; and not all statements from interviewees are equally well informed. Certainly not every claim that appears in print is true. Because you want to base your paper on the most accurate, up-to-date, and authoritative information available, you need to exercise discretion in *evaluating your sources*. Following are some questions you can ask about a source:

Print Sources

• **Is the publication respectable?** If you are researching flying-saucer sightings, for example, an article in an astronomy or psychology journal commands far more respect than an article like "My Baby's Daddy Came from a UFO" in a lurid supermarket tabloid. Between these two extremes are popular magazines, which cover a wide range of territory. Information that appears in a news magazine such as *Newsweek* or *U.S. News & World Report* is more likely to be accepted as balanced and well researched than information taken from a less serious publication such as *People* or *Teen*. You must use your judgment about the reliability of your sources. Because sources differ in respectability and prestige, scholars always identify their research sources so as to allow readers to make their own judgments about reliability. (Acknowledging sources is discussed in Chapter B of Part II.) As a general rule, works that identify their sources are more likely to be reliable than those that do not.

• **What are the author's credentials?** Is the author a recognized authority? An astrophysicist writing about the possibility of life in other galaxies will command more respect than, say, an amateur flying-saucer enthusiast who is

Nature & Nurture: The Mysteries of Twins

The nature-nurture debate, a scientific controversy that has been raging for more than a century, is all about our limits—about whether they come from outside or within. Whether we are what we are because our genes programmed us that way, or because environment—be it womb, home, neighborhood or nation—shaped us.

[margin: Debate: whether genes or environment shapes us]

It is a debate that has often been tipped one way or another by shifts in public opinion. There was a time early this century when scientists tried to create a kind of animal husbandry for humans that aimed, in the words of its founder, Sir Francis Galton, to 'check the birth rate of the unfit' and 'improve the race' by promoting 'early marriages of the best stock.' The Nazis took Galton's idea, which was called eugenics, to its notorious extreme, and in the horrific failure of their master race rendered the idea of tinkering with the human gene pool unfit for a generation. In the postwar era, bolstered by the ideas of anthropologist Franz Boas and psychologist B.F. Skinner, among others, nurture took over. People weren't intrinsically good or bad stock; it was how mama raised the kids, and the social context she raised them in, that accounted for whether they became bums or angels.

[margin: Early nature advocates were racists ↑↓ then nurture ↑↓ now nature again]

Now the pendulum has swung again. Nurture is out, nature is back. And science is largely the reason why.

Every week, it seems, comes a new revelation about who we are and why we are, all attributable to our genetic code. So amazing are these discoveries that they seem in need of exclamation points and screaming headline type: We've isolated the gene that determines sexual orientation! We've isolated the gene that causes breast cancer! We've isolated the gene that determines whether we will become substance-addicted! It's as if we are on the brink of being able to alter fate through genetic engineering, one person at a time.

In truth, the discoveries have proved to be more complicated than they might appear at first glance, but they portend an ability to unlock in the laboratory some of the mysteries of life. Well before molecular genetics gained center stage, however, scientists had—and continue to have—another way of approaching these mysteries, and that's through the mysteries that are twins.

For behavior geneticists like Lindon J. Eaves, who do the nitty-gritty work in the nature-nurture debate, twins are the perfect people on whom to test hypotheses about what is molded by life's pressures and what is inborn. But such scientists wage the battle from a distance, using statistics to describe the behavior of populations—of aggregates, in other words— rather than individuals.

[margin: Twins provide answers]

These statistics have shown that on average, identical twins tend to be around 80 percent the same in everything from stature to health to IQ to political views. The similarities are partly the product of similar upbringing. But evidence from the comparison of twins raised apart points rather convincingly to genes as the source of a lot of that likeness. In the most widely publicized study of this type,

[margin: (!)]

[margin: twin studies support nature]

Figure 11.2 Annotation of a photocopied source.

a retired dentist. Expert sources lend authority to assertions you make in your paper—another reason for the standard practice of identifying your sources to your readers.

- **Is the source presenting firsthand information?** Are the writer's assertions based on primary or secondary research? For example, articles about cancer research in *Reader's Digest* or *Time* may be written with a concern for accuracy and clarity, but their authors may be reporters writing secondhand on the subject—they may not be experts in the field. You can use these sources, but be certain to consider all factors in weighing their reliability.

- **Does the source demonstrate evidence of careful research?** Does the author show by way of notes and other documentation that the statements presented are based on the best available information? Or does it appear that the author's statements derive from unsupported speculation or incomplete research? A source that seems unreliable should either not be used at all or else be cited as an example of one point of view (perhaps one that you refute using more reliable sources).

- **Is the source up-to-date?** Clearly, you do not want to base your paper on information that is no longer considered accurate and complete. For example, a paper on a dynamic field such as nuclear disarmament or advances in telecommunications would be hopelessly out-of-date if it is based on five-year-old sources. If you are writing a paper on a topic about which new findings or theories exist, your research should include recent sources. Check the publication dates of your sources.

- **Does the source seem biased?** Writers have opinions that they support in their writing, but some writers are more open-minded than others. Is the author's purpose in writing to explain or to persuade? Does the author provide a balanced presentation of evidence, or are there other perspectives and evidence that the author ignores? Be aware of the point of view of the author and of the publication you are examining. An article in a magazine of political opinion such as *National Review* can be expected to take a conservative stance on an issue, just as an article in *The Nation* will express a more liberal opinion. Your own paper, even when you are making an argument for a particular viewpoint, should present evidence for all sides. If you use opinionated sources, you can balance them with sources expressing opposing points of view.

- **Do your sources consider all viewpoints and theories?** Because many books and articles are written from a single viewpoint, it is important to read widely to discover if other points of view exist as well. For example, several works have been written claiming that ancient monuments such as the pyramids are evidence of past visits to our planet by extraterrestrials. Only by checking a variety of sources might a student discover that scientists have discredited most of the evidence on which these claims are based. Students writing about such topics as astrology, subliminal advertising, Noah's flood, holistic healing, Bigfoot, or the assassination of President Kennedy should be aware that these areas are controversial and that they should seek out diverse points of view in their research so they can be fully informed and present a complete picture of the topic to their readers.

Internet Sources

All of the criteria for evaluating print sources apply equally to Internet sources. In fact, it is even *more* important to be critical in evaluating sources on the Web, where anyone can post anything. For example, on the Internet anyone who wishes to can post **blogs** (journal entries or "web logs") expressing their personal stories and opinions. Some writers are serious and informed, while others are not. Malicious persons sometimes post false information disguised to look reputable. Here are some additional questions you should ask in evaluating Internet sources:

- **What is the source of the page?** Is the page posted by an individual? If so, you may not be able to vouch for that person's reliability. Is it the Web version of a reputable print source, such as the online edition of the *New York Times*? Is it an online journal? Web magazines can be reliable or not; do you know anything about it? Is the page posted by an advocacy group, such as a trade organization with a financial stake in presenting a product in the best possible light? Is it posted by a political organization seeking to foster its viewpoint?

- **Can you tell who wrote it?** Is the page signed? Do you know anything about the author? Did the author post the page or is the author writing for a sponsoring organization, such as an Internet journal? Look for information on the page describing the author and sponsor. The URL, including the domain (*.edu, .org,* and so on) may give information that can help you evaluate the source.

- **How recent is the page?** See if the page is dated, and check whether the date describes when the page was written or when it was most recently updated. Knowing the date is particularly important for information subject to change.

Of course, as a student researcher, you cannot be expected to be able to authoritatively rate each source you encounter. Still, it is important to look at unfamiliar sources with a skeptical eye and to reject sources that seem dubious and untrustworthy.

Narrowing Your Paper's Focus

If you are like most students, the research paper assigned in your composition course may be the longest paper you have had to write, so you may feel worried about filling enough pages. Most students share that concern at this stage, but they soon find so much material that having *too much* to say (not too little) becomes their concern.

The ideal topic for your paper is one to which you can do justice—one you can write about with some thoroughness and completeness—in a paper of the length you are assigned. Most student researchers start out with a fairly broad conception of their topic and then make it more and more limited as their research and writing progress. As you learn how much information is available about your topic and as you discover through your reading what aspect most intrigues you, you should *narrow your paper's focus*—that is, bring your topic into a sharper and more limited scope.

From your first speculations about a topic until the completion of your final draft, your topic will probably undergo several transformations, usually with each new version more narrowly defined than the one before. For example, a student might begin with the general concept of her major, oceanography, and narrow it through successive stages as follows:

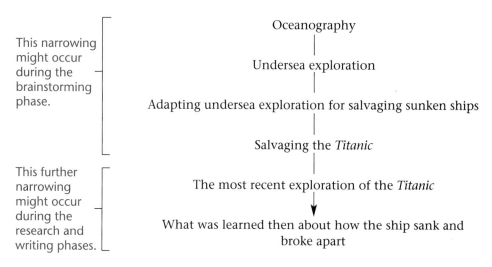

This narrowing might occur during the brainstorming phase.

Oceanography

Undersea exploration

Adapting undersea exploration for salvaging sunken ships

Salvaging the *Titanic*

This further narrowing might occur during the research and writing phases.

The most recent exploration of the *Titanic*

What was learned then about how the ship sank and broke apart

The journey from the original germ of an idea to an eventual paper topic often involves a sorting out process. For example, Allen Strickland quickly settled on the general topic of identical twins, but his early plans were quite broad. He expected to write about many aspects of the twins phenomenon, including their experiences, the comparison of their social lives to non-twins, the role of genes in making them alike, and even whether twins are able to communicate via telepathy. Allen soon found that he was attempting too much and that any one of these topics would make a paper in itself, and he eventually settled just on the question of why twins are alike.

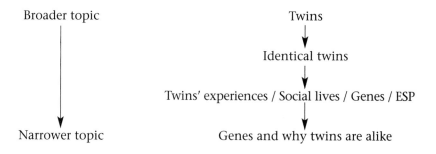

Broader topic

Twins

Identical twins

Twins' experiences / Social lives / Genes / ESP

Narrower topic

Genes and why twins are alike

The path to a final topic, however, isn't always a matter of successive narrowing. Once Allen reached the narrow topic of the role of genes, he then *broadened* his topic in a sense by considering the larger question of what twins can tell us about the nature–nurture debate—whether our genes or our experiences are more important in making us what we are. Do not be surprised, or discouraged, if, like Allen, the path to your topic takes similar twists and turns. Just keep in mind that *narrowing* your paper's focus is generally the best advice for making your project manageable and for producing the best result.

EXERCISES | **Narrowing a Topic**

1. Speculate on how each of the following general topics might be successively narrowed during the course of a research project. Write each topic in your notebook, and beneath it give three or four additional topics, each more specific and more narrowly focused than the one above it. (For example, if you were given the topic *oceanography*, you might create a list something like the one given on the facing page.)

   warfare   music   famous people   luxury goods

2. Now take your own research topic and make a general-to-specific list of its successive stages. First list the most general idea you started with and show how it narrowed to your present topic. Then speculate on how your topic might be narrowed even further as you complete work on your project.

Formulating and Refining a Plan

Writing is never an exact science or a tidy procedure, and the business of planning and organizing is the untidiest part of all. It would be nice if you could start by creating a full-blown outline of your paper, then take notes on the areas you have outlined, and finally write your paper from your notes, exactly as first planned. However, any writer can tell you it rarely if ever works that way.

Research papers evolve as you do research, and they continue to evolve as you write them, so it is important to remain flexible. As you learn more about your subject—as you read and take notes, and even as you begin writing—new directions will suggest themselves to you. Be prepared to adjust the focus and organization of your paper at every stage, right up to your final revision. Many a student has expected to write one paper, only to discover something quite different actually taking shape on the page. There is nothing wrong with making these changes—they are a natural part of the writing process. Writing is as much a process of discovery for the writer as it is a medium for communicating with readers.

As you start examining your sources, you may have only a hazy notion of the eventual contents of your paper, but the beginnings of a plan should emerge as you learn more and more. Shortly into your research you should be ready to pause and

Twins

Background information

　　—Types of twins: identical, fraternal

　　—Cause of twin births

　　—Statistics on twins

Experience of twins

　　—Difference from non-twins

　　—Relationship with each other

　　—Separation problems

　　—Telepathy

Role of genes

　　—Identical twins raised separately

　　　　—How alike

　　　　—How different

　　—Role of environment

Conclusions

Figure 11.3 Allen's rough outline.

sketch a very general ***informal preliminary outline*** of where your paper seems to be going. Allen's first rough outline, shown in Figure 11.3, makes no pretense of being complete or final or even particularly pretty—nor should it at this stage. Allen was "thinking on paper," making sense of his own thoughts and trying to bring some vague ideas into focus. He was doing it for his own benefit, not trying to impress any outside readers. Having established some sense of his paper's parts, Allen was then able to resume reading and taking notes with greater efficiency. He now had a clearer idea of what he was looking for. He was also aware that the organization of his paper would probably change as he continued writing.

Begin with a very general outline, perhaps listing just a few of the main topics you expect your paper to include. As you continue reading, taking notes, and thinking, your outline may become more fleshed out, as you continue to refine your preliminary plans. Remember that an informal outline is an aid to you in organizing and writing your paper. It is not a part of the paper and does not need to be in any kind of polished, orderly form. A formal outline, if you do one, can be written as one of the last steps of your project. (Formal outlines are discussed in Chapter C of Part II.)

Taking Notes on Note Cards

Clearly, you cannot put into your paper everything you read during the course of your research. Some sources will be more useful than others, but still you will use only a small portion of any one source. Note-taking is a way of selecting what you can use. It is also a way of aiding your memory and storing the information and ideas you find in a convenient form for use when you write the paper.

Good notes, then, have the virtue of being both selective and accessible. You could take notes in your notebook, but a notebook is far less easy to work with than *note cards,* which have the advantage of flexibility. Unlike entries in notebooks or on long sheets of paper, notes on index cards can be easily sorted, rearranged, and weeded out. When you are ready to write, you can group note cards according to topics and arrange them in the order in which you expect to use them in the paper. This greatly simplifies the task of writing.

Besides being selective and convenient, good notes have another quality—accuracy. You are obliged as a scholar to be scrupulously accurate in reporting and acknowledging your sources. In research writing, you must quote your sources accurately and paraphrase them fairly. (Quoting and paraphrasing sources are discussed more fully in Chapter 12.) Moreover, you should give credit to sources for their contributions and make it clear to your readers which words in the paper are your own and which are taken directly from sources. You can use your sources fairly and accurately only if you write from notes that you have taken with great care.

For an example of how a writer take notes, look first at excerpts from one of Courtney's sources, an article by Michele Goldberg, Bob Davenport, and Tiffany Mortellito that appeared in *Pharmaceutical Executive*, an online magazine.

> Years ago, a cereal maker ran a commercial in which children who'd eaten oatmeal for breakfast floated to school, snug in a protective bubble of warmth. Today, the same imagery comes to mind with respect to the country's 85,000 pharmaceutical salespeople. They are protected to a certain extent from the chilling winds of the economy, and they ride high above other salespeople when it comes to compensation. . . .
>
> An entry-level primary care sales rep earns an average of $47,000 in base pay—up from $45,800 in 2001—and a top-level primary care sales rep earns an average of $82,300 in base pay, compared with $81,000 for 2001. Oncology sales reps and their district managers are the clear winners in the base pay department. Compared with their counterparts in primary care, oncology sales reps earn 30 percent more, and oncology district managers earn 13 percent more than their reps. . . .
>
> Incentive pay is, on average, 25–30 percent of sales employees' base salary. Because 75 percent of companies target above the 50th percentile of sales rep salaries in other industries in total cash, they put a lot of emphasis on their incentive plans as the means for employees to reap the rewards of successful performance.

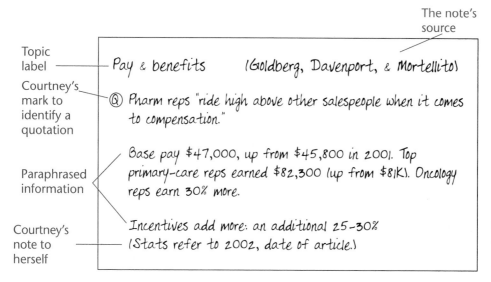

Figure 11.4 A note card.

These three paragraphs were found in different parts of the article, separated by other text. Figure 11.4 is a notecard that Courtney made from these excerpts. Later, when she wrote her paper, she used this card to write the following:

> Pharmaceutical representatives "ride high above other salespeople when it comes to compensation," according to an article in Pharmaceutical Executive. In 2002 the average starting salary for a pharmaceutical salesperson was $47,000 in base pay, and top primary-care representatives had a base-pay average of $82,300. Incentives add another 25-30% to the base (Goldberg, Davenport, & Mortellito).

There are various systems for taking notes on cards, and you should use consistently a system that meets your needs. All good note-card systems have several features in common. In making note cards, you should follow these guidelines:

• **Put only related information on a note card.** That is, use one card for each important fact or idea. If you try to economize by crowding many unrelated notes from a source onto a single card, you will sacrifice flexibility later when you try to sort the cards by subjects. Some cards may contain long notes, whereas others may contain only a word or two. One source may provide you with notes on a dozen different cards, whereas another may give you only a single note (or no notes at all).

- **Label each card by topic.** A topic label helps you remember what a note card is about so that after you have finished taking notes from all your sources, you can easily arrange your cards according to topic. Courtney selected the label *Pay & benefits*, writing it in the upper left corner of the card. Similar labels appeared on two other cards that Courtney prepared while reading different sources. When she was ready to organize her notes, Courtney gathered these three cards together, discarded one of them that she knew she would not use, and arranged the remaining two in the order she was likely to use them in a first draft of her paper.

  You should consider following a procedure similar to Courtney's. Whenever you take a note, consider where within your subject the information might fit and give the note a label. The label may correspond to one of the divisions in your preliminary outline. If it does not, this may suggest that the organization of your paper is developing and changing and that you need to expand or revise your outline to reflect those changes.

- **Identify the source of each note precisely.** In the upper right corner of her note card, Emily identified her note's source: *(Goldberg, Davenport, & Mortellito)*. This is an example of a parenthetical note (explained in Chapter B of Part II), and its purpose is to tell Courtney that the information on the card comes from the article written by those three writers. Courtney had recorded the full information about that source in her working bibliography, so she needed only the authors' last names to identify it.

  It is important for each note card to contain all the information you will need in order to cite its source when you write your paper—so you can give the source credit in a parenthetical note. You will find nothing more frustrating as a researcher than having to search through sources at the last minute to find a page reference for a passage that you forgot to identify on a note card. It is smart to identify each source, as Courtney did, just as you will identify it in the paper itself—with a parenthetical note. For that reason, you should consult Chapter B before you begin taking notes.

- **Clearly identify the kind of information your note contains.** Three principal kinds of information can appear on note cards; you must make it clear which is which, so you do not get confused later if you use the card in writing the paper:

  Direct quotations. The passage "ride high above . . ." on Courtney's card is quoted directly from the article's authors. *Any time you put a source's own words on a note card, place them within quotation marks.* Do so even if everything on the card is a quotation. It is essential that when you read a note card later, you can tell whether the words are a direct quotation or your own paraphrase of the source. For this reason, you might even use a backup procedure for identifying quotes, as Courtney did. She put a circled Q next to each quotation on her cards to be doubly sure she knew these were her source's exact words.

  Your own comments. When you write a note from a source, it may inspire some additional thoughts of your own that you will want to jot down. You may also want to remind yourself later of how you intend to use the note in your paper. *Put your own comments in parentheses.* For example, at the bottom of Courtney's note card, she wrote a note to herself to remind herself of the year that the statistics refer to "(Stats refer to 2002 . . .)." She placed these comments in parentheses to alert herself that these were her own ideas, not those of her source.

Paraphrase. Like Courtney's, your cards should consist largely of paraphrases of what you have found in your sources. *Anything on a card that is not in quotation marks or in parentheses is assumed to be your paraphrasing of the source.* To paraphrase, recast the source's words into your own language, using your own phrasing and style.

- **Be selective in your note-taking.** Because many beginning researchers fear they will not have enough material to use in writing their papers, they often take too many notes. When it comes time to write the paper, they soon discover that if they were to make use of every note, their paper would be dozens of pages long. In fact, for each student who cannot find enough source material for a paper, many others discover to their surprise that they have more than enough.

With experience, researchers learn to be selective, restricting their note-taking to material they stand a good chance of using. Of course, no one makes use of every note card. Especially in the early stages of reading, a researcher does not have a clear notion of what the paper will include or of what information is available. As reading continues, however, hazy notions become more substantial, and the researcher can take notes more selectively.

Figure 11.5 shows two cards that Allen Strickland wrote when he read the article by Arthur Allen in *The Washington Post Magazine* shown in Figure 11.2.

 ## AVOIDING PLAGIARISM

To ensure that you use your sources fairly and accurately, you should observe one additional guideline when you take notes: *Do your paraphrasing on the note card, not later.* If you do not intend to use a source's exact words, do not write those words on your card. (When you should and should not quote a source directly is discussed on pages 426–30.) It is wise to translate important information into your own words right after you read. This will save time and help you avoid unintentional *plagiarism*—using the source's words without quotation marks—when you begin to write from your notes. Paraphrasing and summarizing your sources now will also give you more focused notes, as well as force you to read and analyze your sources more carefully.

Since you cannot use everything in your sources, no matter how interesting, it is often necessary to boil down what you find into brief summaries of what is

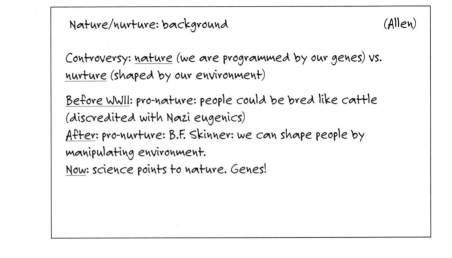

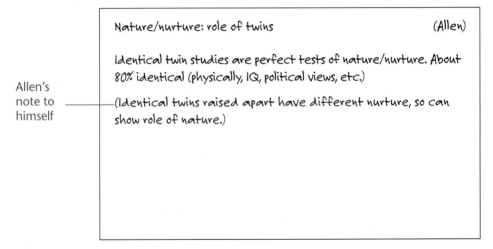

Allen's note to himself

Figure 11.5 Two additional note cards.

important. In general, the procedure for paraphrasing and summarizing a source is as follows:

1. When you have discovered a passage that you may want to use in your paper, reread it with care.

2. After you have reread it, put it aside and think about the essential idea you have learned. Then write that idea on your card in a brief version, using your own words and style. It is often best not to look at the passage while you write the note, so as to be less likely to plagiarize the original language.

Do not forget to indicate on your note card the specific source of the paraphrase.

Consider how Allen used material from one of his sources. First he read this passage from Lawrence Wright's book *Twins: And What They Tell Us about Who We Are*:

> If genes account for half the development of the personality, then environment must account for the remainder. Using increasingly sophisticated models to analyze the data, behavioral geneticists were able to ask a new and highly pertinent question: what, exactly, in the environment shapes personality? Their answer is that the common shared environment—the family, the neighborhood, the parents' income and level of education, their way of raising children—has essentially no effect on the development of personality. Identical twins who have been reared apart are not much different in various personality measurements than twin reared together.

The original source

If Allen had written a note like the following, he might have plagiarized the passage when he used the note card to write his paper:

> If genes are responsible for 50% of the personality, the environment must be responsible for the other 50%. Behavioral geneticists then wonder how environment shapes personality. The surprising answer is that environmental factors such as family, parental income and education, and even their child rearing, have almost no effect in shaping personality. Identical twins raised apart are as close in personality measures as twins raised together.

Note too close to the original

Notice how the passage—while it selects from the original, changes some words, and rearranges phrases—relies too closely on Wright's original wording. Now look at the note Allen wrote from this passage:

> Genes and environment each account for 50% of the personality. Twins reared apart are not much different than those raised together, so the environmental half is <u>not</u> caused by family life.

A legitimate note

In this note, Allen succinctly summarized his understanding of Wright's ideas in his own words.

Putting source information into your own words does *not* mean substituting a few synonyms now and again as you copy your source's sentence onto your note card. For example, consider how it would be possible to misuse the following sentences from Barbara Schave Klein's book *Not All Twins Are Alike*:

> Twins face the triumphs, trials, and lingering after-effects of a childhood shared as each begins a separate life. The cuteness of having an ever-present companion and the attention of curious onlookers wears thin. An adult twin has to learn to live without her sister to function somewhat normally in the world.

The source's words

> Twins encounter the triumph, tribulations, and consequences of their shared childhoods as they begin to live separately. Although it is cute to have a nearby companion and to receive

A plagiarized note

> attention from curious strangers, that quickly grows old. A
> grown-up twin needs to live without the sibling to be able to
> function in the real world.

Observe that this is really the Klein passage with a few word substitutions (*tribulations for trials*, *consequences for after-effects*, etc.). Putting sources aside when you write note cards is one way to avoid this plagiarism by substitution. It also ensures that your paraphrase will be a genuine expression of your own understanding of a source's idea. Of course, if the exact words are particularly memorable or effective, you may wish to copy them down exactly, within quotation marks, for possible use in your paper.

The foregoing can be summed up in the following guidelines.

GUIDELINES | **Avoiding Plagiarism**

1. Whenever you use ideas or information from a source but do not intend to quote the source directly, paraphrase the source. You must restate the material in your own words, using your own phrasing and style. Merely substituting synonyms for the source's words or phrases is not acceptable. Do your paraphrasing at the time you take notes.

2. Whenever you intend to use the source's words, copy those words exactly onto a note card and place them within quotation marks. To be doubly sure that you will not later mistake the author's words for your own, place a circled letter *Q* (or some other prominent device) on the card next to the quotation.

3. For any borrowed material—whether a direct quotation or your paraphrase of it—carefully note the source and page number(s) on your note card so that you can cite them in your paper.

4. In your paper, you will give full credit to the sources of all borrowed material, both those you quote directly and those you paraphrase. The only exception is for commonly available factual information. (For further guidelines, see the section "When Are Notes Needed?" in Chapter B of Part II.)

5. Observe the rules for acknowledging sources in your paper by providing acknowledgment phrases, parenthetical notes, and a list of works cited. (Further information about giving credit to sources can be found in Chapter 6 and Chapter B.)

EXERCISES | **Note-Taking**

Imagine that, in doing a research project on the subject of urban legends, you discovered the following sources. Using the guidelines provided in this chapter, write notes from these sources. On your note cards, you may want to paraphrase some passages, quote others, and offer your own comments or responses. You may take more than one note from a passage.

1. The following appeared on page 175 in an essay by Richard A. Reuss titled "Suburban Folklore." Write one note card that captures an explanation of what is meant by the term "urban legend." Then write a second card whose heading is "Urban legend: example." Include at least one passage that you might want to quote in your paper.

   Another major component of the verbal lore of contemporary suburbia is the so-called urban legend, which perhaps deserves equal billing in the folklorist's lexicon as the "suburban legend," since so large a percentage of these narratives are set, either explicitly or implicitly, in a suburban locale. These narratives typically are brief accounts of anonymous people caught up in bizarre and traumatic, occasionally supernatural or humorous, circumstances because of the violation of some unspoken community or social norm. They are most intensively communicated among teenagers but are widely disseminated throughout the rest of the suburban population as well. One cycle of these stories revolves around babysitters left alone with their young charges. In one narrative the parents call to notify the sitter of a later returning time only to be informed by the teenager spaced out on LSD that all is well and "the turkey is in the oven." Knowing no such food is in the house, the parents speed home to find their baby roasting in the oven.

2. Darcy Lockman wrote an article titled "What Fuels Urban Legends?" for *Psychology Today*. The following paragraph appeared on page 21. Write a note card that summarizes the researchers' discovery about what causes urban legends to succeed.

   Psychologists at Stanford and Duke universities had another theory. "We proposed that ideas are selected and retained in part based on their ability to tap emotions that are common across individuals," explains Chip Heath, Ph.D., an associate professor of organizational behavior at Stanford. Heath and his colleagues decided to examine anecdotes that inspire disgust (some 25 percent of urban legends fit the bill). They took 12 urban legends and presented undergraduates at Duke University with three increasingly revolting versions of each story. . . . Amused undergrads consistently repeated the version that elicited the most disgust. "Emotion matters," says Heath. "It's not informational value alone that causes these things to succeed."

12 *Reporting on Sources: Paraphrase and Quotation*

Mostly when you *do* research on sources, you find out what other people have thought, discovered, said, or written. When you *report* on your research, you tell your readers what you have learned. The following very different passages could all be called examples of reporting on research sources:

1. My old man says he can lick your old man.

2. "If man does find the solution for world peace," wrote General George C. Marshall in 1945, "it will be the most revolutionary reversal of his record we have ever known.

3. Senator Woodling made it clear today that she would shortly declare herself a candidate for the presidency.

4. The first words ever transmitted by telephone were spoken by Bell to his assistant: "Mr. Watson, come here, I want you."

5. The Stoics argued that it was the highest wisdom to accept triumph without elation, tribulation without regret.

6. V. O. Key, Jr., a leading political scientist, offered this positive assessment of the role played by interest groups in American politics:

   > At bottom, group interests are the animating forces in the political process. . . . The chief vehicles for the expression of group interest are political parties and pressure groups. Through these formal mechanisms groups of people with like interests make themselves felt in the balancing of political forces. (Qtd. in Lowery 63–64)

These six passages all report on sources, since each of them communicates what has been learned from someone else. They certainly do so in different ways and with different effects. The first statement, you might guess, is spoken by one child to another, reporting on what he learned from his father. As for its authority, a listener might be wise to doubt that his father said any such thing. The last statement, in contrast, is surely an example of writing, not speech, since it has all the earmarks of a passage from a scholarly paper or article. Its very form, its direct quotation, its acknowledgment of its source and claim for his expertise (*V. O. Key, Jr., a leading political scientist*), and its careful source citation (*Qtd. in Lowery*

63–64; i.e., the quotation was found on those pages in a work by Lowery) all lend it an impressive authority. The four middle passages could be either spoken or written.

There are other differences among them as well. Passages 2, 4, and 6 all present their sources' words through **direct quotation**, with the original language repeated in a word-for-word copy. Passages 1, 3, and 5, on the other hand, **paraphrase** their sources, with the source's ideas and information recast in different words. The identity of the sources in each statement is generally clear, although we are not told where the author of passage 5 learned about the Stoic philosophy; still, it is evident that the ideas presented are those of the Stoics and not the author. Of all these passages, however, only number 6 with its **parenthetical note** gives a careful **citation** of its source, the exact location from which the quotation was taken.

 ## THE CONVENTIONS OF REPORTING

Like the reporting of journalists, the reporting of scholars aims to get at and present the truth. To ensure accuracy and clarity, both types of writing follow careful rules and procedures.

Often these practices are identical in both fields. Both journalism and scholarship, for example, require that sources be acknowledged and identified. Both pay scant attention to unsupported opinions. On the other hand, both pay great respect to expert testimony. In reporting on sources, both fields observe the same time-honored conventions, including rules for paraphrasing, quoting, and even punctuating quotations. If there is one outstanding difference between scholarship and journalism, however, it is that scholarly writing, with its careful conventions of documentation, follows even more stringent procedures for identifying the precise sources from which ideas and information are taken.

This chapter is in large part devoted to these conventions. While some of it involves technicalities (e.g., does a comma go to the left or right of a quotation mark?), even they are important extensions of the care that researchers take to be accurate and truthful. While you are expected to become familiar with most of the conventions here, you should also regard this chapter as a resource that you can turn to often throughout your college career for guidance in presenting the results of your research.

 ## OPTIONS FOR PRESENTING SOURCES

Whenever you report on your research, you need to find a way of presenting to your readers what you have learned from your sources. Sometimes the appropriate method will be paraphrase; at other times, quotation. In fact, you have several options.

Imagine, for example, that in an introductory anthropology course, your instructor has assigned a research paper in which you are to analyze some aspect of

American culture. You have chosen to write about the way Americans express their emotions, and in your research you come upon the following passage from page 248 of Ashley Montagu's book, *The American Way of Life*:

> To be human is to weep. The human species is the only one in the whole of animated nature that sheds tears. The trained inability of any human being to weep is a lessening of his capacity to be human—a defect which usually goes deeper than the mere inability to cry. And this, among other things, is what American parents—with the best intentions in the world—have achieved for the American male. It is very sad. If we feel like it, let us all have a good cry—and clear our minds of those cobwebs of confusion which have for so long prevented us from understanding the ineluctable necessity of crying.

The passage expresses an interesting opinion—that American men have been trained, unnaturally, not to cry—and you want to use it in your paper. You can do so in many ways; the following are examples of your options.

Paraphrase

You can restate an author's ideas in your own words:

```
Montagu claims that American men have a diminished capacity
to be human because they have been trained by their culture
not to cry (248).
```

Direct Quotation of a Sentence

You can quote an author's exact words, as in these three examples:

```
In his book, The American Way of Life, Ashley Montagu writes,
"The trained inability of any human being to weep is a
lessening of his capacity to be human--a defect which usually
goes deeper than the mere inability to cry" (248).

According to Montagu, "To be human is to weep" (248).

"If we feel like it," writes Ashley Montagu, "let us all have
a good cry--and clear our minds of those cobwebs of confusion
which have for so long prevented us from understanding the
ineluctable necessity of crying" (248).
```

Quoting Part of a Sentence

You can incorporate part of an author's sentence into a sentence of your own:

> One distinguished anthropologist calls the American male's
> reluctance to cry "a lessening of his capacity to be human"
> (Montagu 248).

> Montagu finds it "very sad" that American men have a "trained
> inability" to shed tears (248).

Quoting Longer Passages

You can quote more than one sentence:

> Anthropologist Ashley Montagu argues that it is both
> unnatural and harmful for American males not to cry:
>> To be human is to weep. . . . The trained
>> inability of any human being to weep is a
>> lessening of his capacity to be human--a defect
>> which usually goes deeper than the mere inability
>> to cry. . . . It is very sad. (248)

In this chapter, we will study these options in some detail. We will first examine the precise methods of presenting sources through paraphrase and quotation. Afterward, we will look at strategies for using sources: when and where to use the options at our disposal. Chapter B of Part II considers the techniques for citing these sources in parenthetical notes.

 ## ACKNOWLEDGING SOURCES

Whether you paraphrase or quote an author, it is important that you make it clear that it is the author's ideas, not your own, you are presenting. This is necessary for the sake of clarity and fairness—so that the reader knows which words, ideas, and discoveries are yours and which are your source's. Parenthetical notes, which cite a page reference and, if needed, the author's name, do that. Notice, too, that each of the preceding examples makes its indebtedness to its source clear through an *acknowledgment phrase*, such as "Montagu claims that. . . ." Other acknowledgment phrases that we might have used include the following:

Acknowledg-
ment phrases

> Ashley Montagu maintains that . . .
>
> Ashley Montagu, author of The American Way of Life,
>
> says that . . .
>
> Montagu also believes that . . .
>
> Professor Montagu argues that . . .
>
> According to Ashley Montagu, the eminent
>
> anthropologist, American men . . .

A quotation should never be placed in a paper without acknowledgment. Even a parenthetical note is not enough to identify a quotation. You must always introduce a quotation, telling your readers something about it. Avoid writing passages like this with a "naked" quotation in the middle:

Bad: un-
acknowledged
quotation

> When my grandfather died, all the members of my family--men
>
> and women alike--wept openly. We have never been ashamed to
>
> cry. "To be human is to weep" (Montagu 248). I am sure we are
>
> more human, and in better mental and physical health, because
>
> we are able to express our feelings without artificial
>
> restraints.

Even though the parenthetical note identifies the source, readers find it awkward to read a quotation without knowing its origin in advance. Forcing them to skip ahead to find the note creates an undesirable interruption of the flow of the paper. These problems would not arise if the writer had used a simple phrase (e.g., *As anthropologist Ashley Montagu observed,*) to introduce the quotation:

Better:
acknowledged
quotation

> When my grandfather died, all the members of my family--men
>
> and women alike--wept openly. We have never been ashamed to
>
> cry. As anthropologist Ashley Montagu observed, "To be
>
> human is to weep" (248). I am sure we are more human,
>
> and in better mental and physical health, because we are
>
> able to express our feelings without artificial
>
> restraints.

Not only does the reader better understand the quotation's function with the introductory phrase, but the quotation has more impact as well because it has been attributed to a recognized authority.

Always give your readers enough information to identify your sources. The first time you refer to a source, give both the person's first and last names. Unless the source is a well-known figure, identify him or her so that the reader can understand why this particular person is being quoted.

> ```
> Winston Churchill said,...
> ```
> ```
> Cynthia Bathurst, author of The Computer Crisis,
>         believes that ...
> ```
> ```
> According to Valerie Granville, British ambassador to
>         Bhutan during the Sherpa Riots, ...
> ```
> ```
> Rock star Mick Jagger gave a flip answer: ...
> ```

First references

After the first reference, the source's last name is sufficient:

> ```
> Churchill said that ...
> ```
> ```
> Later Jagger remarked,...
> ```

Subsequent references

Although acknowledgment phrases almost always introduce quotations, they are sometimes unnecessary with paraphrased material. As a general rule, use an acknowledgment phrase when the paraphrased material represents an original idea or opinion of the source, when the source's credentials lend the material authority, or when you wish to distance yourself from opinions with which you disagree.

> ```
> Anthropologist Ashley Montagu argues that crying is a
> distinctively human activity--as appropriate and necessary
> for males as for females (248).
> ```

Acknowledgment phrase for paraphrased material

However, an acknowledgment phrase is not needed for largely factual information, as in these passages:

> ```
> At one point in his life, even Alex Haley, the author of
> Roots, possessed only eighteen cents and two cans of sardines
> (Powell 179).
> ```

No acknowledgment phrase is needed for factual information

One study has found that firstborns score better in
achievement tests that measure language and mathematics
skills (Weiss 51).

In such cases, the parenthetical notes provide adequate recognition of sources.
(Parenthetical notes are discussed in Chapter B of Part II.) Use your best judgment
about whether an acknowledgment phrase is called for with paraphrased material.
When in doubt, however, provide the acknowledgment phrase. It is better to err
on the side of *over-* rather than *under-* recognition of your sources.

 ## RELYING ON EXPERTS

Besides being fair, acknowledging the contribution of a source can also add force
to your own writing. In most cases, the sources you present will have greater expertise than you on the subject; a statement from one of them can command
greater respect than an unsupported statement from you, a nonexpert. To illustrate this, assume that, in writing a research paper, you quote Montagu on the
subject of crying and identify him to your readers as an eminent anthropologist.
Could you have made the point equally effectively if instead you had written the
following?

I think it is wrong that men in America have been brought
up to think it is not manly to cry. Crying is natural.
Our macho-man mentality takes a terrible toll on our
emotions.

While you are entitled to your opinions, a reader who doubts your expertise on
the subject is likely to question whether you have considered all aspects and implications of your position. After all, what reason does the reader have to trust
you? However, when an expert such as Montagu is quoted, many of the doubts
are removed and the statement carries greater weight.

This is not to say that experts are automatically right. Experts do not always
agree with each other, and progress in humanity's quest for truth often comes as
new ideas are introduced to challenge old ones. What it does mean is that experts
are people who have studied their subjects thoroughly and have earned the right
to be listened to with respect. Since you will not often begin with a thorough
knowledge of the subjects you write about in research papers, your writing will
rely heavily on what you have learned from expert sources.

PARAPHRASING SOURCES

Most of the time when you present ideas or information from sources, you will paraphrase them. To *paraphrase* a statement or a piece of writing is to recast it into different words. Paraphrase is the least cumbersome way of communicating what a source has said, as well as the easiest to read. Often the source is too technical for your readers or too wordy; you can present the source's point more clearly and succinctly using your own words. When you paraphrase a source, be accurate and faithful to what your source wrote, but use your own style and phrasing. Imagine, for example, that you wished to make use of this passage as a research source:

> Nearly forty years ago Damon Runyon nearly collapsed in laughter when he covered the trial of George McManus, a gambler, who was accused of shooting Arnold Rothstein, another gambler, who thereupon died. The cause of Damon Runyon's mirth was the sight of the witnesses and jurors in the case running out into the halls during court recesses to place bets with their bookies—even as they considered the evils of gambling in the city.
>
> —Edwin P. Hoyt, *The Golden Rot*

You can paraphrase this information in a briefer version, using your words:

```
According to Edwin P. Hoyt, Damon Runyon was highly amused        Good

that both witnesses and jurors in a gambling trial would

place bets with their bookies during court recesses.
```

What you must *not* do is simply change a word or two while keeping the structure of the original intact:

```
Edwin P. Hoyt writes that about forty years ago Damon Runyon       Bad

almost fell down from laughing when he was a reporter for the

trial of gambler George McManus, accused of murdering another

gambler, Arnold Rothstein.
```

You can avoid word-substitution paraphrase, as well as unintentional plagiarism, if you paraphrase from memory rather than directly from the original copy. Chapters 3 and 11 describe the best method as follows: *Read the passage so that you understand it; then put it aside, and write your recollection of its meaning on a note card, in your own words.* Be certain to observe the guidelines for avoiding plagiarism (see pages 401–02).

Paraphrasing a Source   **EXERCISE**

Imagine that each of the following is a source for a research project. Write a paraphrase of important information from each quotation as you would on a note card. Then write it as you would in the paper itself, giving credit to your source with a suitable acknowledgment phrase. (*Note:* You do not need to present all of the information from each passage in either your paraphrases or your acknowledgments.)

a. *Source:* Linus Pauling. He won Nobel Prizes for both Chemistry (1954) and Peace (1962).

Quotation
Science is the search for truth—it is not a game in which one tries to beat his opponent, to do harm to others. We need to have the spirit of science in international affairs, to make the conduct of international affairs the effort to find the right solution, the just solution of international problems, not the effort by each nation to get the better of other nations, to do harm to them when it is possible.

b. *Source:* Edwin P. Hoyt. This quotation is from his book, *The Golden Rot: A Somewhat Opinionated View of America,* published in 1964.

Quotation
Let there be no mistake, the pressures on government for destruction of wilderness areas will grow every time the nation adds another million in population. The forest service has been fighting such pressures in the West for fifty years. Any national forest visitor can gauge the degree of success of the "multiple use program" of the forest service very nicely by taking a fishing rod and setting out to catch some trout. He will find mile after mile of the public waters posted by private landowners who do not allow fishing or hunting on their property—or on the government property they lease. Inevitably this includes the best beaver dams and open stretches of water along the streams.

c. *Source:* Marvin Harris. He is an anthropology professor and author of several books on human behavior throughout the world.

Quotation
The trouble with the "confessions" is that they were usually obtained while the accused witch was being tortured. Torture was routinely applied until the witch confessed to having made a pact with the Devil and having flown to a sabbat [a witches' meeting]. It was continued until the witch named the other people who were present at the sabbat. If a witch attempted to retract a confession, torture was applied even more intensely until the original confession was reconfirmed. This left a person accused of witchcraft with the choice of dying once and for all at the stake or being returned repeatedly to the torture chambers. Most people opted for the stake. As a reward for their cooperative attitude, penitent witches could look forward to being strangled before the fire was lit.

d. *Source:* Jessica Mitford. She was a well-known muckraker, an investigative journalist who specialized in exposing scandals and abuses.

Quotation
True, a small minority of undertakers are beginning to face the facts and to exhibit more flexibility in their approach to customers, even to develop some understanding and respect for people who as a matter of principle do not want the full funerary treatment ordinarily prescribed by the industry. But the industry as a whole, and particularly the association leaders, are unable to come to grips with the situation that confronts them today because their whole operation rests on a myth: the assumption that they have the full and unqualified backing of the vast majority of the American people, that the costly and lavish funeral of today, with all its fabulous trimmings, is but a reflection of American insistence on "the best" in all things. It is particularly hard for them to grasp the idea that a person who has lived well or even luxuriously might *prefer* the plainest disposition after death.

QUOTING SOURCES

In research writing, sources are quoted less often than they are paraphrased, but quotation is more complicated and requires more explanation.

Punctuating Quotations

The conventions of punctuation have driven many a student nearly to distraction. They seem arbitrary and often illogical. If you were to set about tinkering with the rules of punctuating, you could very likely make some worthwhile improvements in the current system. Nonetheless, the system as it stands is well established and unlikely to change. Your consolation is that, even if it is complicated, it can be mastered, and it does serve its purpose of giving readers helpful signals that make reading easier. In the case of quotations, punctuation makes it clear just which passages are your own and which belong to your sources.

The following are the most important punctuation conventions for presenting sources. You should learn these guidelines and follow them carefully.

1. *Use double quotation marks (" ") before and after a source's words when you copy them directly.*

> At the Battle of Trafalgar, Admiral Nelson exhorted his
> fleet: "England expects every man to do his duty."
>
> The phrase "bats in the belfry" was coined by the writer Eden
> Phillpotts.

Double
quotation
marks

2. *Use single quotation marks (' ') before and after quoted material when it occurs within other quoted material—that is, when it occurs inside double quotation marks.*

> Charles and Mary Beard contend that the American government
> was not established as a <u>democracy</u>: "The Constitution did not
> contain the word or any word lending countenance to it,
> except possibly the mention of 'We, the people,' in the
> preamble."
>
> We used this example earlier in the chapter: "According to
> Ashley Montagu, 'To be human is to weep.'"

Single
quotation
marks

3. *Indent a quotation that takes up more than four lines in your paper.* In typing, indent one inch (ten spaces) from the left margin. Do not indent any additional

spaces from the right margin. If you are quoting a single paragraph or less, do not indent the first line of the quotation any additional spaces:

> The millionaire Andrew Carnegie believed that free enterprise
> and private charity, not government social programs, offered
> the best solution to the problem of poverty:
>
>> Thus is the problem of Rich and Poor to be solved.
>> The law of accumulation will be left free; the laws
>> of distribution free. Individualism will continue,
>> but the millionaire will be but a trustee of the
>> poor; entrusted for a season with a great part of
>> the increased wealth of the community, but
>> administering it for the community far better than
>> it could or would have done for itself.

Indent the left margin one inch (ten spaces). Do not indent the right margin.

However, if the indented quotation consists of two or more paragraphs, indent the first line of each paragraph an additional quarter inch or three spaces:

> Florence Nightingale questioned the unequal treatment of men
> and women in Victorian England:
>
>> Now, why is it more ridiculous for a man than
>> for a woman to do worsted work and drive out
>> everyday in the carriage? Why should we laugh if we
>> see a parcel of men sitting around a drawing room
>> table in the morning, and think it all right if
>> they were women?
>>
>> Is man's time more valuable than woman's? Or is
>> the difference between man and woman this, that
>> women have confessedly nothing to do?

Indent paragraphs an additional quarter inch (three spaces)

These passages demonstrate other guidelines as well:

- **An indented quotation is never placed within quotation marks.** Quotation marks are unnecessary since the indenting already makes it clear that the passage is a quotation.
- **When typing, do not skip extra lines before or after an indented quotation.** The entire paper, including such quotations, is double-spaced.

4. *Accuracy is essential in quoting a source.*

- **Copy a quoted passage exactly as it is printed.** The only exception is for obvious typographical errors, which you should correct. Otherwise, make no changes in a quoted passage, even if you disagree with its wording or punctuation. For example, if you, rather than Andrew Carnegie, had been the author of the quotation that concludes on the top of the previous page, you might have used a colon or dash after the word *poor* instead of a semicolon. But since Carnegie used a semicolon, that is the way it must appear when you copy it.

- **Insert *[sic]*, the Latin word meaning "thus," in brackets, immediately after an apparent error.** Do so only if you feel it necessary to identify it as your source's error, not your error in copying the passage.

```
The régime posted a proclamation on every streetcorner:
"Amnesty will be granted all mutineers who lay down their
arms. Die-heart [sic] traitors who persist in rebellion
will be shot."
```

This device should be used only rarely. Avoid using *sic* to belittle a source with whom you disagree.

5. *Use punctuation to separate a quotation from an acknowledgment phrase or sentence.*

- **Use a comma or colon when the phrase comes before the quotation. A comma is preferred when the introduction is not a complete sentence:**

```
Jacques Delille wrote, "Fate chooses our relatives, we
choose our friends."

As Al Jolson remarked, "You ain't heard nothin' yet, folks."
```
The introduction is not a complete sentence

- **A colon is preferred when the introduction is a complete sentence:**

```
Edmund Burke believed that sadism is a component of human
nature: "I am convinced that we have a degree of delight
and that no small one, in the real misfortunes and pains
of others."
```
The introduction is a complete sentence

```
The last words in Act II are spoken by Hamlet: "The
play's the thing / Wherein I'll catch the conscience of
the King."
```
Colon

- **Use a colon to introduce an indented quotation:**

From his jail cell Martin Luther King wrote about the law:

> An unjust law is a code that a numerical or power
> majority group compels a minority group to obey
> but does not make binding on itself. This is
> <u>difference</u> made legal. By the same token, a just
> law is a code that a majority compels a minority
> to follow and that it is willing to follow
> itself. This is <u>sameness</u> made legal.

- **However, no punctuation is needed when a quotation is a continuation of the introductory sentence:**

According to the Library Bill of Rights, libraries are

No colon   forums for information and ideas, and they have

> ...the responsibility to provide ... all points
> of view on all questions and issues of our times,
> and to make these ideas and opinions available to
> anyone who needs or wants them, regardless of
> age, race, religion, national origin, or social
> and political views.

- **Use a comma when the acknowledgment phrase comes after the quotation, unless the quotation ends in a question mark or exclamation point:**

Comma   "When you have nothing to say, say nothing," wrote Charles
Caleb Colton.

But:

No comma   "Who can refute a sneer?" asked William Paley.

- **When the acknowledgment phrase is inserted within a quoted sentence, begin and end it with commas:**

Commas   "Politics," said Bismarck, "is not an exact science."

- Use no punctuation at all (other than quotation marks) when you make quoted words part of your own sentence:

Robert E. Rogers's advice to the Class of 1929 at MIT was   No comma

to "marry the boss's daughter."

The word *that* incorporates a quotation that follows it into your sentence. Note carefully the difference in punctuation among the following three sentences:

–Quotation treated as an independent sentence:

Henry Ford said, "History is more or less bunk."   Comma

–Quotation incorporated into the sentence:

Henry Ford said that "history is more or less bunk."   No comma

–Quotation paraphrased:

Henry Ford said that history is nonsense.   No comma

6. *Capitalize the first word of a quotation when it is treated as an independent sentence. Do not capitalize it when it is incorporated into your own sentence.*

Margaret Hungerford gave us the famous saying, "Beauty is   Uppercase
letter
in the eye of the beholder."

Like Margaret Hungerford, many psychologists believe that   Lowercase
letter
"beauty is in the eye of the beholder."

7. *The trickiest rules apply to punctuation at the close of a quotation. Refer to the following examples whenever necessary.*

- Commas and periods are always placed inside a closing quotation mark:

"From the sublime to the ridiculous is but a step," wrote   Comma inside
the quotation
Napoleon.   mark

Martin Joseph Routh offered timeless advice over a century   Period inside
the quotation
ago: "You will find it a very good practice always to   mark

verify your references, sir."

Period inside single and double quotation marks

Judge Learned Hand wrote, "I should like to have every court begin, 'I beseech ye in the bowels of Christ, think that we may be mistaken.'"

- **Colons, semicolons, and dashes are placed outside a closing quotation mark:**

Colon outside the quotation mark

"Blood, toil, tears and sweat": these were the sacrifices Churchill promised to his country.

Semicolon outside the quotation mark

On his deathbed, O. Henry said, "Turn up the lights--I don't want to go home in the dark"; then he expired.

- **Question marks and exclamation points go inside the closing quotation mark when they belong to the quotation, but outside when they do not:**

Question mark belongs to quotation

Macbeth asked, "What is the night?"

Question mark does not belong to quotation

Who said, "Cowards die many times before their deaths"?

Exclamation point belongs to quotation

Colonel Sidney Sherman first shouted, "Remember the Alamo!"

Exclamation point does not belong to quotation

How dare you respond, "No comment"!

- **For punctuation following a parenthetical note, see pages 565–66 or the quick reference guide on the inside back cover.**

8. *Follow these conventions for quoting poetry:*
   - **Use a slash with a space before and after it to divide quoted lines of poetry:**

Space, slash, space

Ogden Nash wrote, "Candy / Is dandy / But liquor / Is quicker."

   - **Longer passages of poetry are indented:**

Indent the left margin ten spaces

Emily Dickinson wrote

> "Faith" is a fine invention
> When Gentlemen can <u>see</u>--
> But <u>Microscopes</u> are prudent
> In an Emergency.

Like other indented passages, poetry is not placed within quotation marks. The word *"Faith"* is in quotation marks because Dickinson punctuated it that way in her poem.

Punctuating Quotations

1. The following passages that appear in brackets are quotations, printed with their original capitalization and punctuation. Remove the brackets and add whatever punctuation is necessary. Make whatever additions and changes are necessary to put each sentence into proper form.

   a. Anne Morrow Lindbergh wrote [The wave of the future is coming and there is no fighting it.].

   b. Rachel Carson was among the first to warn against the pollution of the environment [As crude a weapon as the cave man's club, the chemist's barrage has been hurled against the fabric of life.].

   c. [Gentlemen of the old régime in the South would say, "A woman's name should appear in print but twice—when she marries and when she dies."] wrote Arthur Wallace Calhoun in 1918.

   d. [Gentlemen] wrote Anita Loos [always seem to remember blondes.].

   e. How many students today believe with James B. Conant that [He who enters a university walks on hallowed ground.]?

   f. William Morris called this a [golden rule] [Have nothing in your houses that you do not know to be useful, or believe to be beautiful.]; a rather different conception of what a house should be is presented in a statement of architect Le Corbusier [A house is a machine for living in.].

   g. Freud never underestimated the role of religion in human culture [If one wishes to form a true estimate of the full grandeur of religion, one must keep in mind what it undertakes to do for men. It gives them information about the source and origin of the universe, it assures them of protection and final happiness amid the changing vicissitudes of life, and it guides their thoughts and motions by means of precepts which are backed by the whole force of its authority.].

   h. Poverty is not portrayed as romantic in Keats's poem "Lamia" [Love in a hut, with water and a crust, Is—Love, forgive us!—cinders, ashes, dust.]

   i. Gloating on his pact with the devil, Doctor Faustus asked [Have not I made blind Homer sing to me?].

   j. [We was robbed!] shouted manager Joe Jacobs into the microphone in 1932, when the decision went against his fighter, Max Schmeling.

2. Create sentences that incorporate quotations according to the following guidelines:

   a. Use this quotation by Mark Twain in a sentence that begins with an acknowledgment phrase:

      Man is the only animal that blushes. Or needs to.

b. Use the following quotation by Havelock Ellis in a sentence that ends with an acknowledgment phrase:

The place where optimism most flourishes is the lunatic asylum.

c. Use the following quotation by George Santayana in a sentence with an acknowledgment phrase inserted within it:

Fanaticism consists in redoubling your efforts when you have forgotten your aim.

d. Incorporate a paraphrase of this quotation into a sentence that acknowledges its author, Congressman Grimsley Buttersloop:

My opponents have accused me of embezzlement, drinking, fooling around, and falling asleep during committee meetings. The only thing they haven't accused me of is not loving my country, and that they can never do.

e. When you quote the following, let the reader know that its author, Frank Winslow, deliberately misspelled the word *souperior* in a letter to his aunt, Martha Fleming:

All I can say of your clam chowder is that it was positively souperior.

Altering Quotations

Sometimes when you write about your research, you will want to use a quotation that does not precisely fit. Either it lacks a word or a phrase that would make its meaning clear to your readers, or else it contains too much material— unnecessary words that are not relevant to your point. For example, imagine that you found this quotation from a person named Vanessa O'Keefe:

I absolutely long to prove to the world, as I said in an interview yesterday, that a perpetual motion machine is not an impossibility.

Assume you wanted to introduce it with the phrase *Vanessa O'Keefe announced that she. . . .* Fortunately, there are methods that allow you to alter such a quotation to fit your needs. By using them, you can write

```
Vanessa O'Keefe announced that she "absolutely long[ed] to

prove to the world . . . that a perpetual motion machine is

not an impossibility."
```

As you can see, you can make certain alterations in quotations to suit your needs. When you do so, however, you must obey these two guidelines:

1. You must make it completely clear to your readers precisely what changes you have made.

2. Your alterations must not distort the meaning or essential phrasing of a quotation or make it appear to say something other than what the author intended.

The following methods may be followed to alter quotations.

Adding to Quotations: Brackets [ ]

Whenever a word, phrase, or suffix needs to be added to a quotation to make its meaning clear, you may insert it within **brackets**. Brackets are most commonly used to explain a reference. For example, it would not be evident to a reader of this quotation that it was the United States that José Martí was referring to as "the monster":

> I have lived in the monster and I know its insides; and my
> sling is the sling of David.

By using brackets when you quote this sentence, you can make the reference clear:

> In a letter to Manuel Mercado, Martí wrote, "I have lived in
> the monster [the United States] and I know its insides; and
> my sling is the sling of David."

Insertion in brackets

Similarly, you can insert modifiers in brackets. The following insertion makes it clear which frontier is being referred to:

> Churchill said, "That long [Canadian-American] frontier from
> the Atlantic to the Pacific Oceans, guarded only by
> neighborly respect and honorable obligations, is an example
> to every country and a pattern for the future of the world."

Another use for brackets is to provide brief translations of foreign or archaic words:

> Chaucer wrote, "A fol [fool] can not be stille."

Unusual terms may also require explanation. For example, if you used the following quotation in writing about doctors performing unnecessary operations, you might need to explain the term *arthroscopic surgery* to your readers.

> According to Dr. Robert Metcalf, who teaches orthopedic
> surgery at the University of Utah, the problem exists in his
> field as well: "There's considerable concern that
> arthroscopic surgery [a technique for repairing damaged
> knees] is being overutilized and is sometimes being done in a
> manner damaging to healthy cartilage."

When the unclear term is a simple pronoun, you can replace it altogether with the noun it refers to. For example, in the following quotation, instead of "They [the Americans] are the hope of the world," you can write

> Baron de l'Aulne expressed a more favorable opinion in 1778:
> "[The Americans] are the hope of the world."

Instead of brackets, however, sometimes the simplest solution is to incorporate the unclear portion into your own sentence:

> Writing about Americans in 1778, Baron de l'Aulne expressed
> the more favorable opinion that "they are the hope of the
> world."

Or better still:

> In 1778, Baron de l'Aulne expressed the more favorable
> opinion that Americans are "the hope of the world."

The best rule is to use brackets when they provide the simplest way of making the source's meaning clear to your readers. As you can see, bracketing is a useful tool that can solve several writing problems. At the same time, it should not be overused. As with other devices, when brackets appear again and again in a paper, readers will find them distracting.

Subtracting from Quotations: Ellipsis Dots (. . .)

You can omit irrelevant parts of a quotation and replace them with *ellipsis dots*, three typed periods separated by spaces. The part you omit can be a word, a phrase, one or more sentences, or even a much longer passage. As with everything you alter, there is one important condition: You must not distort the author's meaning or intentions.

Good writers edit their writing, paring away what is unnecessary, off the point, or distracting. Quotations are used most effectively when you select them carefully and when you keep only the pertinent parts and omit what is not needed. As an example, consider again the passage by Ashley Montagu quoted earlier:

> To be human is to weep. The human species is the only one in the whole of animated nature that sheds tears. The trained inability of any human being to weep is a lessening of his capacity to be human—a defect which usually goes deeper than the mere inability to cry. And this, among other things, is what American parents—with the best intentions in the world—have achieved for American males. It is very sad. If we feel like it, let us all have a good cry—and clear our minds of those cobwebs of confusion which have for so long prevented us from understanding the ineluctable necessity of crying.

As interesting as this passage is, you might be best able to make your point if you quote only parts of it. For example:

> Anthropologist Ashley Montagu argues that it is both
> unnatural and harmful for American males not to weep:
>> To be human is to weep. . . . The trained
>> inability of any human being to weep is a lessening
>> of his capacity to be human--a defect which usually
>> goes deeper than the mere inability to cry. . . .
>> It is very sad.

Ellipsis dots indicate a deletion

Whole sentences have been removed from the passage and replaced with ellipses. Parts of a sentence can also be omitted, as follows:

> Montagu feels that "the trained inability . . . to weep is
> a defect which usually goes deeper than the mere inability
> to cry."

As with brackets, there is a danger in overusing ellipses. Not only can they become distracting to the reader, but they can also defeat your purpose in quoting, as with this monstrosity:

> Montagu feels that "the . . . inability . . . to weep is
> a defect which . . . goes deeper than the . . . inability
> to cry."

The preceding sentence makes so many changes in the original quotation that it can no longer be said to communicate Montagu's phrasing, and the point of using direct quotation is lost. Paraphrase would make much more sense; for example:

> Montagu feels that the inability to cry is a more significant
> defect than many realize.

Ellipsis dots are not needed when it is already obvious that the passage you have quoted is only a part of the original:

> A man's inability to cry, according to Montagu, is a
> "lessening of his capacity to be human."

Ellipsis dots are not needed

You should use ellipses, however, when it is not obvious that you are quoting only a portion of the source's complete sentence:

```
Montagu wrote, "The trained inability of any human being to

weep is a lessening of his capacity to be human. . . ."
```

When the omission comes at the front of a quoted sentence, you may capitalize the first word if you put the first letter in brackets:

```
Montagu offered this advice: "[L]et us all have a good

cry. . . ."
```

EXERCISES   **Using Brackets and Ellipsis Dots**

1. The following is part of the transcript of a reporter's interview with a political candidate, Paul Shawn. Read it and comment on the quotations that follow.

    Q: Your opponent, Darla Stowe, says you hunger for money. Is that true?
    A: If you mean, do I want to earn enough for my family to live decently, then yes, I hunger for money. I think that's true of almost everyone. But I hunger for other things as well: peace, justice, brotherhood, and national prosperity.
    Q: Your opponent also says you are using this race as a stepping-stone to higher office. Is this true?
    A: Actually, I'm quite certain I have no more desire for higher office than she has.

    Which of the following quotations can be justified on the basis of this interview? Explain why each of them is fair or unfair, and discuss its use of brackets, ellipses, and paraphrase.

    a. Paul Shawn says he "hunger[s] for . . . peace, justice, brotherhood, and national prosperity."
    b. Shawn admitted, "[Y]es, I hunger for money."
    c. Shawn's opponent accuses him of using this race to seek further political advancement, but he responds, "I have no more desire for higher office. . . ."
    d. Shawn believes that a "hunger for money" is "true of almost everyone."
    e. Quick in responding to an opponent's accusation, Shawn retorted that he has "no more desire for higher office than [Darla Stowe] has."
    f. While admitting he has the same interest as most people in earning a comfortable living for his family, Shawn says he has other goals as well: "peace, justice, brotherhood, and national prosperity."

2. Use quotations from the following passages according to the instructions given for each. Introduce each quotation with an acknowledgment phrase.

a. Quotation

I always dreamed of it as being a kind of earthly paradise where no troubles ever intruded.

Speaker: Linnea Aycock

Instructions:
(1) Introduce the quotation with the acknowledgment phrase *Linnea Aycock said,* and use brackets to show that Aycock is talking about Tahiti. (2) Write another version, this time quoting only part of her sentence. Without using brackets, show that she is talking about Tahiti.

b. Quotation

Our inspiration was a cartoon that appeared in a children's magazine.

Speaker: A NASA scientist

Instruction:
Use brackets to indicate that the cartoon inspired the design of a new space helmet.

c. Quotation

My generation never thought of college in terms of making ourselves employable. It was OK to be interested in Plato or T. S. Eliot or Freud, but never in IBM or General Mills. It was easy then to regard jobs with contempt since there were so many of them. It is very different with today's job-conscious generation. The response to Shakespeare now is likely to be, "How will he help me in my job?"

Writer: Ronni Jacobsen

Instruction:
Quote two or three sentences that communicate the main idea of this passage. Use ellipsis dots to represent what you omit.

d. Quotation

My message to all you students is that hard work and self-discipline are the keys— and you should never forget this—to success in your college and business careers.

Speaker: Cyrus T. Pierpont

Instruction:
Begin with *Cyrus T. Pierpont told students that.* Omit unnecessary parts of the quotation, including the first eight words and the part that is surrounded by dashes. Although it is not necessary, you can change *your* to *their.*

e. Quotation

If idiots drive motor vehicles when they are drunk, this should happen: they should lose their licenses and be sent to jail—for 90 days or longer.

Speaker: Sergeant Robert Symmes

Instruction:
Introduce the quotation with the words *Sergeant Robert Symmes said that.* Alter the quotation by deleting the word *if,* inserting *who* after *idiots,* omitting *this should happen:,* and making whatever other changes are necessary.

 ## WHEN TO QUOTE AND WHEN TO PARAPHRASE

One of the questions beginning research writers often ask their instructors is: "How many quotations should I put in my paper?" Their uncertainty is not usually allayed by the appropriate answer: "It depends." What it depends on are the circumstances of the individual case—and your own good judgment. While there is no easy answer to the question, some useful guidelines can help you decide how to use your sources.

1. ***Do not overquote.*** In fact, do not quote very much at all. Most beginning researchers quote far too much in their papers. Quotations should be saved for special occasions, and with good reason: Readers find papers that are filled with quotation after quotation unpleasant and hard to read. (By now you are probably tired of reading quotations in this chapter!) When they encounter a great many quotations, readers will often skim them or skip them entirely. No one likes to read a passage like this:

Bad (too many quotations)

> "Early [Roman] amphitheaters," according to Fredericks, "were temporary wooden structures that often collapsed under the weight of spectators, with the result of great loss of life" (40). Bennett reports:
>
> > The most famous of all buildings of this kind was the Flavian Amphitheater in Rome. Also called the Colosseum because of its size, it was begun by the emperor Vespasian and dedicated by his son Titus in A.D. 80. . . . After the 6th century it was used as a fortress and a quarry. (101)
>
> Fredericks says, "Although accounts of the time report it held more than 80,000 spectators, modern estimates place

its capacity at 50,000" (42). The architectural historian
Anne Ramsey wrote:

> Structurally and functionally, the Roman Colosseum
> has been rivaled by no comparably sized arenas
> until the most recent age. Even today it remains a
> model of planning for rapid crowd access and exit
> and for unobstructed spectator sight lines. (17-18)

Of these four quotations, piled one on the other, all but the last, which expresses the opinion of an authority, should be rephrased in the writer's own words. The passage then becomes much more readable:

The first Roman amphitheaters were temporary structures   Better
built of wood. Because they could not long support the great
crowds who attended the spectacles, they often collapsed in
terrible disasters (Fredericks 40). Later they were replaced
by permanent facilities, the most famous of which was the
Flavian Amphitheater, better known as the Colosseum. Begun by
the emperor Vespasian, it was dedicated in A.D. 80 by his
son, Titus. It served as a sports and gladiatorial arena with
a capacity of 50,000 spectators until the sixth century. It
was then allowed to deteriorate, being used occasionally as a
fortress and frequently stripped of its stone for use in
other buildings (Bennett 101). Nevertheless, it survived and
remains today one of the most widely admired Roman buildings.
Architectural historian Anne Ramsey writes:

> Structurally and functionally, the Roman Colosseum
> has been rivaled by no comparably sized arenas
> until the most recent age. Even today it remains a
> model of planning for rapid crowd access and exit
> and for unobstructed spectator sight lines. (17-18)

The rule can be restated as follows: *If you have a choice between quoting and paraphrasing a source, paraphrase it.*

2. *Always paraphrase a source, except when a direct quotation is needed.* You should paraphrase most of your sources most of the time, especially under the following conditions.

- **Paraphrase if the source provides factual information.** Avoid quotations like the following:

Unnecessary
quotation

The collapsing of bridges was a considerable problem in the past: "In the latter half of the 19th century, American bridges were failing at the rate of 25 or more per year!" (Worth 29).

Instead, state this factual information in your own words:

Better

A century ago American bridges were far more dangerous than today, collapsing at an annual rate of 25 or more (Worth 29).

- **Paraphrase if you can say it more briefly or clearly in your own words.**

Wordy

Sun worshiper Andrea Bergeron claims that "Solists face grave and persistent discrimination, not the least of which is that which prohibits a fair hearing for our beliefs. Because our beliefs are not traditional we are dismissed as cultists" (202).

Very likely, you would need nothing more elaborate than this brief paraphrase to make your point:

Better

Andrea Bergeron feels that she and her fellow Solists (sun worshipers) are discriminated against and their religious views are not taken seriously (202).

3. *Quote a source directly when the source's words work better than your own.* If you use them sparingly, quotations can be effective in your research writing. Use them in the following cases:

- **Quote when the source's words are phrased in a particularly eloquent or memorable way.** Paraphrase could not do justice to the following quotations:

General Patton wrote, "A pint of sweat will save a gallon of blood" (987).

In 1947, physicist J. Robert Oppenheimer expressed the
unease felt by many scientists about their role in
developing the atom bomb: "In some sort of crude sense
which no vulgarity, no humor, no overstatement can quite
extinguish, the physicists have known sin; and this is a
knowledge which they cannot lose" (1055).

You may not always find it easy to decide whether a statement from a
source is so well phrased that it should be presented to readers directly. Use
your best judgment. In cases where you are in doubt, the wisest course is to
paraphrase.

- **Quote when you are writing about the source or the source's words:**

Ginter was never modest in his self-descriptions: "When I
was born 42 years ago to a family of humble asparagus
farmers, none suspected I would one day be the world's
leading transcriber of baroque music for the
banjo" (37).

The advertisement promised "luxury villas with a
spectacular ocean view," but only by leaning far out the
windows of our ancient bungalow could we gain even a
distant glimpse of the sea.

Victor Hugo called Jean Henri Fabre "the Homer of the
Insects" with good reason. Few naturalists wrote such
vivid metaphors as Fabre does in this description of the
praying mantis:

> To judge by the term Prègo-Diéu, we should look
> to see a placid insect, deep in pious
> contemplation; and we find ourselves in the
> presence of a cannibal, of a ferocious spectre
> munching the brain of a panic-stricken victim.
> (Qtd. in Lynch and Swanzey 51)

- **Quote when the source is an expert whose exact words will lend authority to a claim that you make:**

Paratrupus schusterensis, the common swamp frogwort, is a
delicacy among scavenger gourmets. Florence Demingo, author
of A Field Guide to Edible Weeds, exclaims: "Ah, the frogwort! No other plant offers such a thrill to the palate
while fortifying the liver with such potent dosages of
Vitamin B-8" (188).

The public is often outraged when technicalities decide the
outcome of important court cases, but as Justice Felix
Frankfurter observed in 1943, "The history of liberty has
largely been the history of the observance of procedural
safeguards" (37).

As anthropologist Ashley Montagu observed, "To be human is
to weep" (248).

Usually, however, you can paraphrase an authority with the same good
results:

Florence Demingo, author of A Field Guide to Edible Weeds,
finds the frogwort both tasty and rich in Vitamin B-8
(188).

And one final consideration for quotation in research papers:

- **Do not restrict your quoting to already quoted material.** Many students
quote only passages that appear within quotation marks in their sources;
that is, they quote writers they have found quoted by other writers. It
never occurs to them to quote their sources directly. Of course, you should
not overquote, but on the other hand, do not be afraid to quote your
sources themselves. If, for example, you were using this very paragraph as a
research source, you could quote from it:

Veit and Gould advise, "Do not restrict your quoting to
already quoted material" (460).

Judging When to Paraphrase and Quote	**EXERCISE**

Decide if any of the quotations in the following passages should instead have been paraphrased by the writers. For those quotations, write a paraphrase that could be substituted for the inappropriate quotation. Omit any notes that you decide are unnecessary.

a. Pott's disease is "tuberculosis caries of the vertebrae, resulting in curvature of the spine. It was named after the physician who described it, Percival Pott (1714–88)" (Gleitman 110).

b. Geologists and seismologists are uncertain how to interpret the cryptic note found in McPhilibar's hand after the cave-in: "Major discover [sic]—8th strata, fault line demarcation—earthquake predictor. Eureka!" (Donnelly 192).

c. Harris argues that the animal-powered agriculture of India is not necessarily a problem to be corrected:

   To convert from animals and manure to tractors and petrochemicals would require the investment of incredible amounts of capital. Moreover, the inevitable effect of substituting costly machines for cheap animals is to reduce the number of people who can earn their living from agriculture. . . . Less than 5 percent of U.S. families now live on farms, as compared with 60 percent about a hundred years ago. If agribusiness were to develop along similar lines in India, jobs and housing would soon have to be found for a quarter of a billion displaced peasants. (12)

d. Humans are not entirely logical creatures. Often we take our guidance from emotional and spiritual voices within us. As the philosopher Pascal observed, "The heart has its reasons which reason knows nothing of" (40).

e. "The word *ain't*," says Phillips, "has generated its share of controversy" (64). Frelling writes, "*Ain't* is widely accepted in casual conversation. It is rarely used in formal discourse and in writing" (6). A controversy arises especially over its use as a contraction for *am not*. Dwight Macdonald speaks in its behalf, noting that "there is no other workable contraction, for *amn't* is unpronounceable and *aren't* is ungrammatical" (144). Theodore Bernstein, on the other hand, says, "There can be no doubt that *ain't I* is easier to say than *aren't I* and *amn't I,* and sounds less stilted than *am I not.* Nevertheless, what should be not always is" (13–14).

◼ A FURTHER NOTE ON PLAGIARISM

Undoubtedly, the most often repeated exhortation in this book is your obligation as a scholar to acknowledge your sources. The message is so important that we don't want to risk its being missed. Feel free to make use of sources (after, all, that is what research is all about), but give them full credit when you do so. Failure to acknowledge a source, thereby making someone else's work appear to be your own, is plagiarism.

The most glaring cases of plagiarism are deliberate acts of cheating: students handing in papers that they did not write or copying articles from magazines and passing them off as their own work. These are dishonest acts that rank with library vandalism as among the most serious breaches of the code of scholarship. They are dangerous as well, since penalties for them are understandably severe, and instructors are much better than most plagiarists realize at spotting work that is not a student's own.

A less serious offense, but also one to be avoided, is an unintentional act of plagiarism. Most of the time when students plagiarize, they do so innocently, unaware that they are violating the rules of scholarship. They copy a sentence or two from an article, not knowing that they should either quote or paraphrase it. They change a few words in copying a sentence, sincerely believing that they are paraphrasing it. They do not provide a parenthetical note because they do not know that one is needed. They are not trying to cheat; they are not even aware that they are cheating. It is just that no one ever told them to do otherwise. Perhaps when they were in the fifth grade, they wrote papers that consisted of copying out passages from encyclopedia articles. That may have gone unreprimanded in grade school. It is never tolerated in college.

There is certainly no need to plagiarize, because you are allowed to use sources provided that you acknowledge them. In fact, there is no advantage in it either: Papers based on expert sources, fairly acknowledged, are what is wanted of scholars. They are exactly what instructors are looking for.

PRACTICE WITH USING SOURCES

The first part of this chapter—in which you learned to paraphrase and quote individual sources—can be compared to the on-the-ground instruction given to would-be parachutists. It is essential background, but the real learning doesn't take place until the first jump. In the rest of this chapter, we intend to push you out of the plane. Your jump will involve taking a selection of sources and using them to write a brief research-based essay.

Writing a Brief Objective Research Essay

When you do research, you have a purpose in mind: You are seeking to learn more about a certain topic and, often, to inform others about what you have discovered. As an example to illustrate the process involved in a brief research project, imagine that you have been assigned to report briefly to your political science class on a controversy surrounding the Constitution's Bill of Rights. Let's suppose that, having narrowed your topic, you decide to review the "Schillinger case." Here are excerpts from five (fictitious) sources that you have discovered in your research.

The following is a news article from the *Essex Herald-Journal*, 5 August 2006, on page 6:

> #### State Seeks to Force Cancer Treatment
> State authorities have asked the courts to grant them custody over the 13-year-old daughter of a clergyman so that she can receive the anti-cancer treatment doctors say she needs to stay alive.

The Rev. and Mrs. Paul Schillinger and their daughter, Cathy, are members of the Children of Prophecy church, which rejects all medical treatment and relies on faith to cure ailments. The Schillingers are contesting the state's attempt to force Cathy to undergo chemotherapy. Doctors say that she suffers from leukemia and will die within six months without treatment.

Claiming in his brief to the court that "the first duty of the state is to protect its citizens," State's Attorney J. Walker Dodson says he is "reluctantly" undertaking the action to save the girl's life.

At a press conference outside the courthouse, Cathy Schillinger affirmed her own opposition to the state's action. "I know there is a better place waiting for me in heaven. If God calls me, I am ready to die," she said.

If the court rules in favor of the state, the girl will be placed in Memorial Hospital until the course of treatments can be completed.

A ruling is expected later this month.

This excerpt is from an article by Cathy's father, the Rev. Paul Schillinger, "Leave Our Daughter Alone," printed on page 20 of the *Lexington Post,* 9 August 2006:

. . . I know in my heart I am doing God's will. He holds the power of life and death, and if in His infinite goodness and wisdom He wants us to live we will live, and if He wants us to die we will die. No state and no court can say otherwise. The judge and the doctors are trying to play God, and they are committing a damnable blasphemy. My daughter is willing to die if she must, because she knows there is a better place for her waiting in heaven.

The following is an excerpt from page 67 of the September/October 2006 issue of *American Religion.* It appeared in an article by Mark Signorelli, "A Church-State Battle over Child Custody," printed on pages 65–67:

Interviewed outside court, State's Attorney Dodson said, "Cathy Schillinger's life is in imminent danger, and only this action can save her. If it were her father or any other adult, we would not intervene. But Cathy is a minor, not yet able to make an informed decision about a complicated matter, nor is there evidence that she fully understands the issues involved. It is our policy not to interfere with the parents' raising of their children as they see fit unless the child is abused or in danger. Here the child's right to life takes priority."

This is a letter to the editor of *National News Weekly,* appearing in the 16 August 2006 edition, on page 17:

Dear Editor:

Once again our fundamental American rights and freedoms are being trampled by the very government that was established to protect them. Freedom of religion and the right of parents to raise their children in their own beliefs and values mean nothing to the prosecutors. As a neighbor, I have known the Schillingers for years. They are a loving family, and the parents want Cathy to live. But they and Cathy believe that medical treatment is sinful, and the government must respect that. People must respect the beliefs of others, even if they do not agree with them.

Helen Bridgeman

This is the first sentence from a front-page article in the 17 August 2006 *Essex Herald-Journal.* The headline is "Girl's Death Ends State Attempt at Custody":

> The state's effort to gain custody over 13-year-old Cathy Schillinger was made moot this morning when the girl died of leukemia in her sleep.

No one can read about this case without having an opinion, very likely a strong emotional one. You probably also recognize with the rational part of your brain that the issues here are complicated ones with profound implications and that there is much to be considered on both sides before you can reach a wise decision about their merits.

You can use these sources to write either *subjectively* or *objectively* about the case; that is, you can express your opinion, or you can simply present information to the reader without offering views of your own. As an example of the difference between objective and subjective writing, note that the reporter who was the author of the first source wrote objectively. By reading that article, you cannot tell the reporter's personal feelings about the case. On the other hand, there is nothing objective about Helen Bridgeman's letter to the editor. You know exactly where she stands. She and the reporter were clearly writing for two different purposes.

Often it is wise to write objectively about a controversial matter before expressing an opinion. This ensures that you at least examine the merits of both sides before rushing to a judgment.

In this imaginary paper, let's assume that you have decided first to present the facts from the case objectively and afterward to draw subjective conclusions from what you have found. For this earlier part of the paper, then, you will write a brief objective report on the Schillinger case, informing your readers of the nature of the case and the issues involved.

How do you begin writing an objective report from the five sources that you have discovered? They consist of two tersely written news stories, quotations from some of the principal participants on opposing sides, and an opinion from an outside reader. All of them might offer material you can use. But what do you do with them?

Unlike the summary reports you produced in Chapter 6, you cannot simply summarize each source individually and then present the summaries one after the other. Instead you must interweave your materials. Since you have important statements from participants, you will also want to quote some of their words. You will need, then, to select material from your sources and produce a synthesis. Here is how one student, Keith Pearsall, Jr., wrote a report from these five excerpts:

Keith's paraphrase of a source

> The Schillinger case, another prominent instance of conflicting rights and freedoms, involved a 13-year-old girl with leukemia. On one side of the case stood the girl and her parents, who rejected all medical treatment on religious grounds. On the other stood the state, which sought to force the medical care doctors say she needed to remain alive

("State" 6). Parental and religious rights were in conflict with the right to life itself and with the obligation to protect minors.

> Keith's thesis statement

One question that is raised by the case is the extent to which parents have the right to raise their children in their own religious beliefs and practices. The father of the girl, a minister in the Children of Prophecy church, believed that God alone "holds the power of life and death, . . . and if He wants us to die we will die." The minister also believed that in seeking to counteract the divine will, the state was committing a "damnable blasphemy" (Schillinger 20). The daughter, Cathy, subscribed to her parents' beliefs and expressed her willingness to die if necessary rather than undergo treatment they believed to be sinful ("State" 6).

> Quoting a source directly

> A note for paraphrased material

According to State's Attorney J. Walker Dodson, on the other hand, the issue was not one of religious freedom but of the state's "first duty . . . to protect its citizens" (qtd. in "State" 6). Dodson argued that the girl was too young to make an informed decision about a matter of vital interest to her and that the state was obliged to protect her right to life (Signorelli 67).

> A note for quotation

Legal questions in this controversial case have still not been answered, since the girl died before the courts could reach a decision.

> No note for widely available information

Keith has taken five sources and from them has written something that is new and his own. The report is objective, since nowhere are Keith's opinions evident, but he still remains in control throughout. He is aware of the point of the entire report, and he shapes it with several of his own sentences. For example, the last sentence of the first paragraph and the sentence following it are topic sentences, expressing his summary of the main ideas of the passage.

In his handling of sources, Keith avoids three mistakes often made by inexperienced research writers; that is, he observes three important rules:

1. **Don't just quote.**
2. **Don't just quote quotations.**
3. **Don't just note quotations.**

Examples from Keith's report can demonstrate what the rules mean:

Don't Just Quote

Many beginning researchers quote too much, tediously stringing together one quotation after another. Keith avoids that mistake. His three direct quotations all make perfect sense in his report. In addition, he selects only the words from his sources that are most relevant, and he introduces them so that the reader always knows who is being quoted and why. More often than quoting, however, Keith paraphrases his sources. For example, in the first three sentences of his report and the last sentence of his second paragraph, he has rephrased material from his sources into his own words. The result is a clear, readable, effective report.

Don't Just Quote Quotations

Some students quote only material that appeared within quotation marks in their sources. It never occurs to them to quote the sources themselves. Note that Keith does both: The first source contains quotations, and Keith uses them in his report. Although the second source does not quote any other authors, Keith quotes from it as well. This may seem obvious, but many students are unaware of this valuable way researchers can use their sources.

Don't Just Note Quotations

Another mistake made by inexperienced research writers is to give parenthetical notes only for direct quotations. Notice that Keith provides notes not only for sources he has quoted, but also for sources he has paraphrased, such as his citation of the first source in his opening paragraph.

Not every source you use will receive mention in notes. Each of the sources played a role in Keith's writing of the report, but only three of them are noted in parentheses. The fourth source, the neighbor's letter, gave Keith some general ideas, but since it did not provide him with any specific information, he decided not to paraphrase it or quote from it. Therefore, it did not receive a note. Although the fifth source, the mention of Cathy's death in a news story, did contain the information used in Keith's last paragraph, that information is so readily available (found in news accounts throughout the country) that acknowledgment is not necessary.

Because Keith quoted or paraphrased only three of his five sources (and cited them in parenthetical notes), he omitted the two other sources from his list of works cited, which follows:

```
                         Works Cited
Schillinger, Paul. "Leave Our Daughter Alone." Lexington Post
        9 Aug. 2006: 20.
Signorelli, Mark. "A Church-State Battle over Child Custody."
        American Religion Sept./Oct. 2006: 65-67.
"State Seeks to Force Cancer Treatment." Essex Herald-Journal
        5 Aug. 2006: 6.
```

Writing an Objective Research Essay

EXERCISES

Imagine that in writing a paper about how Americans have kept track of time through the years, you discovered the following (purely fictitious) sources. Part of your paper will concern a recent proposal to change our current time zones. Use these sources to write a brief objective report on what you have learned. Acknowledge your sources with parenthetical notes and provide the list of works cited that you would include in your final paper.

1. This news story appeared last year in the May 22 issue of the *Birmingham Star-News* in section B, page 4. Dina Waxman wrote the article under the headline, "Parent Tells Dangers of Time Zone Change."

Congressional hearings on a proposal to have all the country's clocks tell the same time continued today with testimony from a parents' group opposed to the plan.

The proposal, put forth by Edna Odom of Muscatine, Iowa, would eliminate the four time zones that now divide the country. She would replace them with a single nationwide zone.

Testifying against Odom's plan was Floyd Rugoff, president of the Eureka, California, PTA. He argued that it would endanger schoolchildren, who would travel to or from school in darkness.

Under the proposal, clocks in the Eastern zone would be set back one and a half hours, while Pacific zone clocks would be set ahead by the same period. Central and Mountain zone clocks would receive half-hour adjustments. Alaska and Hawaii would be exempt from the proposal.

In his testimony Rugoff said, "In December it's already dark in the morning when children leave for school. If we change, California children won't see the sunrise until 8:30, and in New England it will have set by the time children come home from school. We're going to see a big increase in accidents involving children."

2. These excerpts are from Edna Odom's article, "It's About Time," in *Future and Change* magazine. It appeared in last year's January issue on pages 76–78.

If all of the country operated by the same clock, businesses would reap an enormous advantage. Communication from coast to coast would be simplified. Now, with four time zones, companies operating from nine to five on the two coasts have only five working hours in common, and only three if you remove the two lunch hours. Under my proposal, if an executive in Tucson needs to reach her main office in New York at

4 P.M., she can call and get through. The way it is now, the time in the East would be 7 P.M., and she'd have to wait until Monday morning for the New York office to re-open. Television networks, airlines, and neighboring communities that now straddle time zones would all reap enormous benefits. [page 77]

. . . It isn't as if we were being asked to switch day with night. An hour and a half change isn't that big. The claims of opponents are vastly exaggerated. We already move the clocks an hour twice each year, and everyone adjusts easily. There is nothing that says that the sun has to be overhead at noon. If it's dark at 6 A.M., why can't a farmer milk the cows at 8 instead? Schools could open later or earlier to accord with the sunlight. Why are people so hidebound? If the human race isn't flexible enough to make small adjustments, heaven help us when a major catastrophe strikes. [page 78]

3. "Farmer Ticked by Time Scheme" is the headline for an article that appeared without a byline last May 23 on page 24 of the *Riverside Ledger:*

In his testimony against the OUT (Odom Unified Time) proposal, farmer Duane Went-worth of Millinocket, Maine, argued that the proposal would wreak havoc with live-stock producers.

"Animals operate by the sun, not the clock," he said, "and we can't convince them otherwise. If we have to get up at 4 in the morning to tend them, we'll be eating lunch at 9 and going to bed by 8. We'll be out of sync with the rest of the country."

Writing a Brief Subjective Research Essay

Not all writing is objective writing; sometimes your purpose is to express your own opinion in order to convince others. Chapter 14 considers argumentative writing in detail, but here we will take a brief look at how writers can use research sources to support and strengthen an argument. Of course, you are always free to offer an opinion without any outside support at all, but the support of experts can greatly help your case. By taking your facts from sources, you also show your readers that you have gone to the trouble of researching the issue, and you make yourself seem more worthy of their trust. When you quote or paraphrase authorities in support of your opinions, those opinions seem much more impressive than they otherwise would.

For a brief example of how subjective writing can be supported by sources, imagine that you are arguing your own views on the unified time zone plan that was introduced in the exercise above. You can use those sources effectively to support your argument:

Edna Odom's proposal to synchronize all the nation's clocks within a single time zone may seem attractive at first glance, but closer inspection of the scheme reveals serious flaws. Although Odom rightly points out the benefits to TV networks and airlines of eliminating time zone differences, she is too quick to dismiss her plan's opponents as "hidebound" and its problems as "exaggerated" (77–78).

The proposed change would have the most impact on the two coasts, where clocks would be altered by an hour and a half from current settings.

While Odom sees this as small, the effects would be considerable for farmers and schoolchildren, to take only two examples. Since livestock regulate their lives by the sun, farmers on the east coast would need to rise as early as 4 A.M. to tend animals at sunrise ("Farmer" 24). And as the president of a California PTA chapter observed in testifying before Congress, it would be dark in winter as western children traveled to school and as eastern children returned home from school. He predicted that the number of auto accidents involving children and pedestrians would increase sharply (Waxman 4).

A principal advantage that Odom claims for her scheme is that it would aid communication by standardizing business schedules. But she also recommends that schools and other institutions adjust their opening and closing times to conform with the sun (77–78). She can't have it both ways. If California schools open according to the sun, three hours after New York schools, parents will demand that businesses where they work do likewise, and the uniformity that Odom promises will be lost.

While it would be wonderful if time were the same in all parts of the country—and of the world, for that matter—the fact is that the sun refuses to cooperate. Any proposal that is based on human wishes, without regard for the realities of nature, is doomed to certain failure. Imperfect as our current time system is, it is at least preferable to the alternative.

The list of works cited for this essay would be the same one that you listed for the objective essay in the exercise.

The writer of this essay argues the case against the plan. The sources he uses buttress his arguments and lend it authority. For example, because he has supported it with sources, readers are more likely to accept his claim that the plan would hurt farmers and schoolchildren; the reader can see that this is not just the writer's unfounded speculation.

Notice that the writer has used sources to help make his point. At the same time, he has not been a slave to the sources. While he takes several arguments from sources, much of the language and thought behind the paper is entirely his own. His introduction and conclusion are original, and in the third paragraph he has applied his own logical twist to turn Edna Odom's argument against her.

Sources, in other words, are tools that require the ingenuity of writers to make use of them. There is nothing in the three sources that led inevitably to this paper. In fact, another writer with different views about time zones could use them to write an equally effective paper supporting Edna Odom's proposal.

Writing Subjective Research Essays   EXERCISES

1. Write a subjective essay arguing your views on the Schillinger case. Use the five sources found on pages 432–34 to support your essay. Acknowledge your sources in notes and include a list of works cited.

2. Write a subjective essay that argues in favor of Edna Odom's time zone proposal. Support your position, using the sources in the exercise on pages 437–38.

13 Writing and Revising the Research Paper

GETTING ORGANIZED

Once Allen Strickland and Courtney Holbrook had gathered material from their sources and taken notes on index cards, they were ready for the next step: the actual writing of their papers. While writing proved less time-consuming than source-gathering, it was no less important, and, like earlier stages of the research process, it consisted of several substeps. Allen and Courtney each received an assignment similar to the following for the first of these substeps:

ASSIGNMENT   **Preparing to Write**

Do the following before our next class meeting in preparation for writing your first draft:

- Complete your note-taking on index cards.
- Formulate a thesis statement; that is, state in a sentence or two your concept of the main idea of your paper.
- Sort your note cards by topic.
- Prepare an updated informal working outline for your first draft.
- Put new topic titles on your note cards as necessary, arrange them in the order suggested by your outline, and put aside (but do not discard) the ones you do not expect to use.

Formulating a Thesis Statement

When Allen began his project, he was afraid he would not have enough to say about his topic. However, halfway through his first source, he had fifteen cards' worth of notes. Aware that he was taking too many notes, Allen concluded that he would need to be more selective. Like almost every other student researcher, he found that a shortage of material would not be a problem for him after all. He sharpened his focus and began to take fewer but more carefully chosen notes. Even so, he ended up taking notes on over a hundred cards, several dozen more than he would end up using.

When Allen began his search for sources, he was thinking about the topic of identical twins broadly and, as far as he knew, might write about many, perhaps even all, aspects related to twins. As a result, he began taking many notes about topics he would not end up using, such as twins and ESP, identical twins who switched places with each other, and the preference of twins for dressing or not dressing alike. Before long, however, he realized that his original broad topic was leading in too many directions that were far too diverse for one research paper. His topic, he realized, needed to be more specific, and he soon narrowed it to just what identical twins can show about the nature-nurture debate—a decision made easier by the abundance of sources he found on that topic. Even so, he discovered many different aspects to this narrowed topic, and he did not become entirely sure of his paper's thesis or organization until he was well into an early draft of the paper itself. He was then able to formulate a ***thesis statement***, a brief summary of what he expected to be his main focus:

> Thesis: Identical twins can give us insights into the extent to which nature and nurture make us who we are.

Allen was not writing an argumentative paper, and his thesis does not come down squarely on either side of the nature-nurture debate. His purpose was not to argue for a particular point of view but to discover what he could about the question. He found sources that supported both the nature and the nurture view of human development, and he also found sources that pointed to both our genes and our upbringing as powerful forces shaping us. Consequently, he keeps an open mind in his thesis, just as he later did in writing his paper.

Students are sometimes misled by the advice to *start* a research project with a thesis that is clear, unified, and restricted. Like an outline, a thesis ought to assist the process of searching, thinking, and composing; it should never become a straightjacket. As we have seen, Allen's preliminary research caused him to narrow his focus. Courtney, however, was quite certain of her topic, and formulating a thesis statement presented little difficulty. She simply expressed in plain language the goals of her project:

> Thesis: I am attracted to pharmaceutical sales as a potential profession, and I want to know the pros and cons of the job and to discover if it suits my abilities.

As we have seen, premature commitment to a thesis can become a hindrance to thorough, objective inquiry. Nevertheless, many writers prefer to develop a cohesive theme during the early stages of research. They have found that keeping such a theme in view—often in form of a preliminary thesis statement—can help focus their work. If you have difficulty finding such a focus, try the following procedure:

Tips for Formulating a Thesis Statement

1. **Think about your project in general terms.** In your notebook, write a quick informal paragraph describing what you expect your paper to say and do. It may help to respond to these questions: What main topic have your efforts become focused on? What question(s) have you been trying to answer? What have you learned from your research? Do you now have a point of view about your topic—a conclusion or insight that you want to express in your paper?

2. **Make your general idea specific.** Review the paragraph you have written, and see if you can summarize its main idea in a single sentence.

As you continue your work, you should think often about how each part of your paper supports your focus. Be prepared to eliminate any sections that stray from the main topic. You may, of course, adjust your focus as you proceed with your project. In the final draft of her paper, Allen introduced his readers to his subject with this summary of his thesis:

```
. . . [S]cholars have long debated the role that heredity
plays in determining our personalities and behavior.
Today it is still far from settled how much of our
behavior can be attributed to "nature," genetic factors
in our DNA, and how much to "nurture," the environment in
which we are raised.
     Because identical twins have identical DNA, they can
give us insight into the role heredity plays in our
development.
```

Sorting Your Note Cards

With an evolving conception of his topic, Allen recorded in his notes material that he thought was usable. While his note cards were a distillation of all he had learned from his reading, they still represented a formidable mass of data. He now had to select and arrange his cards in an order he could use. He read through them and sorted them by topic.

Since Allen had written a topic label at the top of each note card, he was able to group many of his cards together by subject. He found that most of his cards fell into a half-dozen general categories: "twins alike," "twins different," "free will," "nature/nurture: background," and so on. As he sorted, he also set aside many discards—notes it was now clear he could not use. There were also many strays—single cards that did not fit conveniently into categories with any others. Allen had to decide if these belonged in his paper and, if so, how he might use them. In some cases, he would not know for sure until the actual writing.

Even with a good plan and a working outline, the final form of a paper can rarely be predicted in advance. Like Allen, you might follow this procedure:

1. **Read through and sort your note cards.** Sorting you cards into piles on a large table or on the floor can be helpful. Be sure you sort the cards by *topic* (not by any other principle, such as by source). Some piles will contain note cards from several different sources.

2. **When your cards are sorted, think about how they can be used and arranged.** Write about your ideas in your research notebook; think as you write, using the opportunity to work out ideas for organizing your paper. But do not be dismayed if you encounter loose ends at this stage. You will make many further decisions about your paper's organization as you write it.

3. **Put aside any cards you do not expect to use.** The best way to create an organizational plan for a paper is to think first in terms of the most general categories. The following is one of several excerpts from Allen's research notebook that reveals his thoughts about shaping and organizing his project:

> Twins reared apart having amazing similarities—much material. Many sources describe them. Begin with some anecdotes or too common? Fewer stories about identical twins who are different. O'Donnell twins are gay/straight but also mirror-image twins with many similarities. Talk first about similar twins, then different twins. Twins similar in similarity related to ESP abilities.

Allen did not yet have a clear organization in mind for his paper, but we can see his mind working here—even making decisions as he wrote. He was confident he had good materials to work with, and he had enough ideas for at least a tentative organization that he could try out.

Updating Your Outline

Having thought about the parts of his paper and how he might put those parts together, Allen needed a clearer idea—a diagram of what his paper might look like. That is, he needed an ***informal working outline***, an updated plan for organizing his paper.

When you create an outline, the headings you use will correspond, in theory, to the topic labels on your note cards. In reality, though, you will need to make adjustments to both the cards and the outline as a clear conception of the shape of your paper gradually forms in your mind. Try to put your ideas on paper in a handy visual form: A working outline is nothing more than a way of making these ideas visible and concrete.

Checking and rechecking his note cards, Allen developed the parts of an outline and, after several revisions, created an informal scheme, shown in Figure 13.1, to use in writing his first draft. Although some of the details would change in the final version of his paper, Allen found this outline helpful as he wrote, especially in getting started.

During his next class, Allen showed his outline and note cards to the other students in his editing group. He discussed his plans, received suggestions, and—even more valuable—answered questions. Explaining and defending his outline helped Allen notice strengths and weaknesses in his plan. An added benefit of the session was that it familiarized everyone in each editing group with classmates' projects.

Allen Strickland

Thesis and Working Outline

           Identical Twins: Nature or Nurture?

<u>Thesis</u>: Identical twins can give us insights into the extent to which nature and nurture make us who we are.

Introduction

    Explanation of twins

        Identical, non-identical, mirror-image

        Genes and environment

    Nature vs. nurture

        Controversy and history

    Role of twins in solving nature/nurture controversy

Evidence for nature

    Anecdotes: three pairs of identical twins raised apart

    ESP in twins

    Twins grow less alike genetically as they age

    Studies showing similar IQ, habits, etc.

Evidence for nurture

    Anecdotes: identical twins who are different

    Role of free will

Sexual orientation in twins: mixed picture

    Evidence for nurture

    Evidence for nature

Conclusion: experts believe both play role

Figure 13.1 Allen's thesis and working outline.

WRITING THE FIRST GOOD DRAFT

Having a tentative plan for organizing their papers, Allen and Courtney received an assignment like the following from their instructors:

ASSIGNMENT   **Writing the Paper**

You are now ready to write a careful draft of your paper. Do so, and revise it until you are satisfied that it is as clearly written, well organized, interesting, and informative as you can make it. Be sure to document your sources carefully with parenthetical notes and include an updated list of works cited. You should also consult the guidelines for editing and revising that begin on page 454.

Allen soon discovered that his outline was only a starting point. In fact, he made changes in his organization from almost the moment he began his actual writing. He encountered difficulties with his opening, and, as his rough drafts would show, he went through at least six versions of the introductory section before he felt ready to move on. His preliminary outline rapidly became obsolete, but it had served its purpose. It had forced Allen to think about his paper as a whole—about how the individual parts might work together. Once he had made the outline, his concept of what he would accomplish in his writing became considerably less vague.

Although later parts of his draft went more smoothly, Allen discovered there is more to writing a paper than following a plan. Certainly, it is not just a matter of first writing about note 1, then about note 2, and so on throughout the paper. It will help to consider the following guidelines in writing your paper

GUIDELINES | **Research Writing**

1. Keep your goals in mind. Novices can easily be overwhelmed by the procedures and details of research writing. Because of the many steps—all the procedures for assembling a list of sources and making note cards, outlines, and parenthetical notes—it is easy to lose sight of what a research paper is really about. The goal of your research is to learn something, to discover truth. In writing your paper, your goal is to present what you have learned so that your readers can also become informed. It follows that your writing should be readable and honest, informative and interesting. Never lose sight of these important goals as you write. Do not be blinded by procedures for their own sake.

2. Remember that principles of good writing apply to research writing, too. Like any other type of paper, a research paper should be clear and lively, not stodgy and pompous. It should be written so it can be read with enjoyment and without difficulty. Quotations and other source material should be neatly integrated into your writing so they are not obtrusive or awkward.

Like any other author, you have a responsibility to make the reader's job easier. Use topic sentences to help the reader know what to expect. Provide paragraph breaks to signal changes in topic or emphasis. Where appropriate, use transitional words and phrases (such as *on the other hand, also, for example*, and *consequently*) to make clear the relationship between successive sentences and paragraphs.

3. Most of your paper should be you, not your sources. While your sources may provide you with most of the information that you present, in your paper *you* are the one writing it. Write in your own voice. Your research paper should communicate what you have to say—just like any other paper you write. Remember, too, that your use of sources is simply a means of reaching the goal of informing your readers; it is not an end in itself. Don't let your paper become simply a vehicle for presenting sources. Don't let your sources get in the way of clear writing.

4. Don't be a slave to your note cards and outline. Whenever you use a note from one of your cards, think about how it contributes to the point you are making. If a note isn't useful, don't include it. If it isn't clear, explain it. If you realize that your paper would be improved by adding new topics or rearranging your outline, by all means do so.

5. Don't rely too heavily on one or two sources. Inevitably, a few of your sources will have proved more helpful than the rest, and you will rely on these more than the others in writing your paper. Remember, however, that it is not your paper's purpose to restate what has already been said by another source or two. A research paper should present something new, a fresh synthesis of information and ideas from many sources. A paper that is largely a summary of only one or two sources fails to do this. A variety of sources should make substantial contributions to your paper. On the other hand, the opposite extreme—where it becomes an end in itself to squeeze in material from every source you find—should also be avoided. Let common sense guide you between these two extremes.

Some Practical Writing Tips

Following are some practical tips on the act of writing itself.

Don't Put Off Your Writing

Although the pressure of an impending deadline may stimulate great energy, it is unwise to begin writing your paper the night before it is due. You will produce a far better paper if you allow time for careful writing and revision. Start writing as soon as possible. Finishing ahead of your deadline will allow you the valuable opportunity to put the paper aside for a day or so, at which time you can take it up again, read it with fresh eyes, and gain new perspectives for improving it further.

Adopt Methods That Work for You

All writers are different. Use your past experience to decide what writing practices give you the best results.

Write in a place you find comfortable. A quiet library setting may free you from distractions and give you ready access to additional sources. On the other hand, you may prefer sitting at your computer keyboard at home. Or perhaps settling into a comfortable easy chair, writing with a pad on your lap and with your note cards on a table by your side, may allow you to do your best work.

Find ways to overcome obstacles. When you get stuck in your writing, perhaps it may help you to pause for a snack or a brief break to recharge your mental batteries—or you may find it best to shift gears, perhaps rereading what you have written or redirecting your attention to another part of the paper.

Adopt Positive Attitudes

Recognize that writing is hard work. Good writers work hard enough to make it *look* easy. Don't be discouraged by the snags that inevitably arise, and be prepared to give your project the time and energy it deserves.

Be persistent in writing. During the hard work of writing, writers are often visited with thoughts of more pleasant things they could be doing. At such times it is tempting to put down the pen or turn off the computer, promising yourself to resume writing later. Such temptations pose stern challenges to one's character and moral fiber. To be a successful writer is to develop self-discipline and to continue when one would rather not. As with any discipline you develop (from quitting smoking to mastering the cello to training for a triathlon), it is important to set realistic goals and to stick with them. At each writing session, set a goal of writing a certain number of pages or working for a certain number of hours—and meet it faithfully. Writing isn't usually fun, although at times it can be. But writing *is* very satisfying, especially when you know you have worked hard and produced a work you are proud of.

Have confidence in yourself. Even if this is your first research project, there is no reason to think you can't achieve admirable results. Remember, there are no secret formulas that others know and you don't. A paper is nothing more complicated than this: You have learned some information and are simply explaining it to readers who are much like yourself. Keep that in mind, tell your story clearly, let your own interest in the topic come through—and you will write a successful paper.

Getting Started

By the time you are ready to write, the hardest work should be behind you. You have plenty to say, as well as a plan for how you want to say it. You have a stack of note cards, arranged in the order in which you expect to use them. Once you are a page or two into your writing, the work should start to flow more smoothly. After students get past the initial unfamiliarity of working with source material, they usually find research writing little different from any other kind. In fact, because they are so well prepared, it is often easier.

Frequently, the most difficult part is simply getting started. In writing his first draft, Allen began by composing his opening section. He decided that his readers would need background about the nature-vs.-nature controversy that was at the heart of his paper, and, after several drafts, he composed the paragraph shown in the following section as Option 1. However, as he received feedback from classmates and then revised his paper in subsequent drafts, Allen decided that he could better capture the interest of his readers if he first began with an anecdote about twins raised apart (his new opening is shown below in Option 3), and he moved what had been his original opening to follow this anecdote in his paper.

Struggling with an opening is not uncommon. Often it is best to wait until after you have drafted the body of a paper before even attempting to write the beginning. Writers sometimes waste time by overlooking the fact that the parts of a paper do not have to be written in the order in which they are to be read. If you are having difficulty getting started or are unsure about where to begin, start with a section that especially interests you or that seems easiest to write. Once you are successfully under way, composing the rest of the paper may be easier.

Writing the Opening

After you have written a draft of the body of your paper, you are in a better position to see what type of opening is most effective. An introductory section can serve many purposes: to inform readers of what your paper is about and where it is going, to generate interest, and to create a smooth transition into the body of the paper. There are many ways to begin a research paper; the following strategies are among those most frequently used.

Option 1: Begin with a Summary of the Paper's Main Idea

The purpose of beginning with a summary of the main idea is to tell your readers immediately what the paper is about. A version of your thesis statement will figure prominently in the opening, which serves as a summary of the entire paper to come.

In his first draft, Allen began his paper with this paragraph:

> Everyone agrees that children inherit traits such as
> height and hair color from their parents, but scholars
> have long debated the role that heredity plays in
> determining our personalities and behavior. Today it is still
> far from settled how much of our behavior can be attributed
> to "nature," genetic factors in our DNA, and how much to
> "nurture," the environment in which we are raised. To put it
> another way, are we "born that way" or are we shaped by our
> surroundings? (Powell). Because identical twins have
> identical DNA, they can give us insight into the role
> heredity plays in our development.

In this paragraph, Allen first explained the question about nature and nurture, and he then stated his main idea: how identical twins can help answer this question. When you begin with a summary, your reader's job is made easier because you have given them a clear expectation of what will follow in the paper.

Option 2: Begin with Background

Because your readers may not be well informed about your topic, you can provide them with information that will create a context for your thesis. For example, Allen might have begun with background information about twins:

> Unlike fraternal twins, who result when eggs from two different fertilizations are implanted in the mother's uterus at the same time, identical twins result when a single egg is fertilized and then splits to form two separate embryos. Unlike fraternal twins, identical twins have identical genes and generally look very much alike. Such twins are separate individuals with separate personalities, however, and they are not identical in all of their characteristics. By comparing what is alike or different about identical twins, scientists can gain insights into how much of our development is shaped by genetics.

Alternatively, historical background can also be used to introduce your topic:

> In the first half of the twentieth century, the belief was widespread that our ancestry was the principal determinant of what individuals became. One unfortunate outcome of this view was the development of racist ideologies such as the Nazi belief in a "master race" with a duty to exterminate "inferior races." After the war, the dominant school of psychology became behaviorism, which downplays genetics and holds that our actions can be shaped almost entirely by our environment. In the twenty-first century, however, most philosophers and psychologists now believe that both genetics and the environment play a role in shaping us. Identical twins, who share identical DNA, can be especially useful in providing insights into the role of "nature" and "nurture" in human development.

In both of these openings, background information leads to a statement of the paper's thesis in the final sentence.

Option 3: Begin with an Interesting Anecdote

Starting with a specific story can capture your readers' interest immediately and prepare them for your thesis statement. Allen chose to begin his paper with an extended anecdote:

> Jim Lewis and Jim Springer, twins who were adopted as infants by different families, did not meet again until they were 39 years old. Although their hair styles were different, they were otherwise strikingly similar. Both were six feet tall and weighed 180 pounds. They had the same features, including an unusual swirl in one eyebrow and a "lazy eye" on the same side. As they were soon to learn, looking alike was just the beginning of their similarities (Watson 9-11; Wright 43-47).

An anecdote is often a very specific case that readers can visualize. With a story in mind, readers are then better prepared to understand and take interest in the general thesis that the anecdote illustrates.

Courtney also began her personal research paper with an anecdote from her own experience:

> As far back as I can remember, my goal for the future has been to work in business. As a child, I would spend endless time messing around with my own makeshift store made of cardboard boxes and construction paper. Sales books and receipt papers would fascinate me. I knew even then that it was my destiny to play a key role in the business world.

Courtney's story also captures our interest. Her purpose, however, is not to exemplify a thesis but to give us background in how she became interested in the career she researched and wrote about.

Option 4: Begin by Explaining Your Purpose for Writing

A personal research paper often begins with a section headed "Why I Wrote This Paper" or "What I Wanted to Find Out." Courtney could have begun her paper with a direct statement of her purpose, such as this:

> I have always planned on majoring in business in college, and I wanted to concentrate on marketing and advertising. Because of this, whenever pharmaceutical sales representatives came into the doctor's office where I worked during high school, I wondered if that was a job I would like. When given this assignment I knew immediately that I would research pharmaceutical sales to find out what goes

> into the profession. I hoped by the end of my exploration to
> know its ins and outs and to be informed enough to decide
> whether it was a career I should pursue.

Many scientific papers also begin by stating specifically what is to come in the rest of the paper. Conventional research papers, however, generally avoid direct statements by the author about purpose. A rule of thumb in writing for the liberal arts is that papers should avoid talking about themselves. That is, they should not contain statements such as "In this paper I will . . ." or "The rest of this paper will examine. . . ." (Note how the other sample beginnings make the theme evident without any such statements.) The personal research paper is an exception to this rule.

Writing the Conclusion

The one section of the research paper that can be even more troublesome than the opening is the conclusion. After all, once you have said what you have to say, what else remains to be done? Fortunately, it is not as hopeless as that. The principal purpose of a conclusion is not to say something new but to draw the ends of the paper together and to leave the reader with a satisfying sense of closure. Simply put, an ending should feel to the reader like an ending.

One strategy, appropriate for a long paper, is to tie together what you have written by summarizing the paper's content. A summary serves no purpose, however, if it merely rehashes what has already been made evident to the alert reader, but it can be effective if you summarize the paper in a fresh and insightful way, as Allen did in concluding his paper:

> Twins studies not only fascinate us but they can teach
> us much about ourselves. Evidence is strong that our genes
> have much to say about who we become. Nevertheless, the
> degree to which we are shaped by nature and by nurture--as
> well as the degree to which we are free to shape ourselves--
> is likely to remain a topic of controversy for many years
> to come.

Sometimes a paper explores many aspects of a topic and is only ready to draw final conclusions at the end. After Courtney researched the facts about a pharmaceutical sales career and weighed its pros and cons in her paper, she had not reached an ironclad decision about her future, but she was able to state her judgment about what she had learned in her final paragraph:

> Pharmaceutical sales, on balance, is more appealing to
> me now than before I began my search, but I have not reached
> a final decision. This project has solidified my decision to
> major in business marketing and advertising. I will try to

maintain a high grade average and will take science
electives, which will give me background for understanding
drugs and will be a valuable addition to my résumé. The
knowledge and experience I gain in the next two years will
further clarify my goals and desires. I hope they will take
me where I need to be to fulfill my childhood dream of
standing out in the business world.

A word of caution: Strategies such as these are offered as helpful possibilities, not as
rules or boundaries. Good writing resists formulas, and good writers continually
find original ways of achieving their goals. Adopt whatever strategies work for
you, and consider new approaches. That is the best way to extend your range as a
writer.

Giving Your Paper a Title

Giving your paper a title may be the final stage of your project. Ideally, your title
should both indicate to your readers what your paper is about and arouse their
interest. In his first draft, Allen gave his paper the title "Identical Twins: Nature or
Nurture?" This title certainly captured the theme of his paper, but he realized it
would not mean much to readers who were unaware of the nature/nurture debate
that his paper would describe. In later drafts, he changed the title to something
he considered clearer: "Identical Twins: Born To Be Alike?" For her paper about
her career search, Courtney considered the straightforward title "Should I Be a
Pharmaceutical Representative?" but finally chose the more playful title "Pharmaceutical Sales: More than Just Viagra Pens."

Arresting, clever, or witty titles are not easy to create—and not always desirable, as there is a fine line between originality and cuteness. Start with a simple,
direct title that captures your theme. If later on you are inspired with a better
choice, fine, but if not, no one should object to a plain but clear title.

EDITING AND REVISING

Writers differ in their work habits. Allen is a constant reviser. Composing, rearranging, and editing at the keyboard of his computer, Allen tends to write a little,
pause to read what he has produced, make changes, and then move on. Courtney,
on the other hand, is more of an all-at-once reviser: She generally writes long
passages straight through, forging ahead while ideas are still fresh in her mind.
Only after she has written several pages will Courtney pause to reread and make
changes.

Because of their different work habits, Allen and Courtney produced very different kinds of preliminary drafts. Courtney wrote several complete drafts, each
more polished than the previous one. Allen, on the other hand, emerged with
something very close to a final draft after having gradually reached the concluding

section of his paper. To call Allen's final paper a single "perfect" draft, however, would be very misleading. Since Allen was constantly rereading, revising, and editing earlier parts of his paper, these parts had actually gone through several drafts by the time he reached his conclusion. His success was due partly to productive work habits and partly to the fact that Allen kept the structure of his paper clearly in view from the outset.

Both writers achieved success by using methods that worked for them. You, too, should feel free to adopt practices that work for you. Basically, though, you can be an effective editor of your own work if you approach it like a reader. Put aside what you have written for a day or more until you can read it with a fresh perspective. Put yourself in your readers' place, trying to anticipate whether they will find it clear, readable, and effective. You may find it helpful to consult the checklist that begins below, considering each question as if you were responding to a paper someone else has written.

Reworking Your Paper

After completing preliminary drafts, both writers put aside what they had written for a while, then came back and reread them with a pencil in hand. A page from Courtney's early draft in which she made particularly extensive changes appears in Figure 13.2. Although Courtney makes handwritten corrections on pages composed at a word processor, other writers prefer working entirely on paper, while still others make all their revisions directly at the computer keyboard.

CHECKLIST | **Editing and Revising**

Topic, Focus, and Support

- Is it clear what the topic of the paper is? Does the writer provide a thesis statement or otherwise make it evident, early in the paper, what the paper is about? Is any further help needed for the reader to see the paper's point?

- Is the topic adequately narrowed—that is, neither too broad nor too limited for the writer to do it justice in a paper of this length?

- Has the writer kept the promises made by the thesis statement? That is, does the paper remain focused on its thesis? Does it stick to the point?

- Is the thesis supported with a variety of details or evidence?

- Is this support clear and convincing?

- In reading the paper, have you learned what you were expecting to learn from it? What questions remain in your mind? What needs to be developed more? What seems to be missing?

Audience, Style, and Readability

- Is the writing style appropriate for its intended audience? What passages do you have trouble understanding?

The qualities needed to succeed in the job may lead some to
the typical
When ~~someone~~ pictures ~~a~~ pharmaceutical salesperson ~~they~~
as   *male*   *in a*   *and that*
~~probably imagine~~ a suave mid-30s ~~gentleman with~~ business suit~~,~~   *no others*
                              In   *half of all*   *s are women (Nahman),*   *need apply.*
~~like attire. But in~~ fact, pharmaceutical represen~~tatives have no~~
and most defy the   *As Groome states,*
stereotype. "They come in assorted shapes, sizes, hues, talents,

backgrounds, philosophies, likes and dislikes" (~~Groome~~ 27).

                                                                          have college
~~According to pharmaceutical.com, today there are approximately~~ *degrees*
¶ Most of the 85,000   *people*   *(Goldberg...).*
~~eight-five thousand~~ pharmaceutical sales~~men~~ in the United States

~~of America.~~ /Courses in business law, economics, accounting,

finance, mathematics, and statistics are highly recommended.
                                                  Author J. Michael Farr says,
College-level education is also suggested. "For marketing and

and sales, some employers prefer a bachelor's or master's degree in

business administration with an emphasis on marketing" (~~Farr~~ₑ

125).
       N   *representatives for drug companies, however,*
~~But~~ not all ~~pharmaceutical salesmen~~ have ~~a~~ business degree~~.~~ₛ, *and*
Farr says that
"~~A college degree with~~ almost any major is suitable ~~for~~ₑ
                                                          When I interviewed
~~entering"~~ pharmaceutical ~~sales~~ (~~Farr~~ 123). ~~Upon interviewing~~

John Carter, I was surprised ~~to find out~~ that ~~his degree was not~~

~~in advertising or marketing, but rather~~ he had earned a ~~four~~
                                              and
~~year~~ degree in music education. ~~Carter~~ had been a teacher for
           When he decided teaching   *got him*
ten years ~~before deciding it~~ was too stressful, ~~and~~ a friend
an interview for his current job. He says that his experience with people and
~~helped him get a job in pharmaceutical sales. His high grade~~
his high college grades   *Carol Poe, territorial manager with DJ Pharma, says,*
~~point average~~ helped him out. "Often ~~they~~ [employers] care about

your grade point average, because it shows you worked hard in

school. It's the little things that add up to success in the

field" (Malungani).

Figure 13.2 Courtney's editing of a draft.

- Does the paper read smoothly and easily? Does the paper's use of sources and quotations ever become distracting or interrupt the smooth flow of your reading?
- Is the paper free from awkward phrasing, misspellings, typographical errors, and other mechanical flaws?
- Does the paper conform to MLA format (see Chapter C in Part II)?

Organization

- Is the paper organized in a way that makes sense? Can you understand why topics come where they do in the paper? Could any parts be rearranged for greater logic and clarity? Are there passages in different parts of the paper that should be brought together?
- Does the paper begin with a helpful general introduction to the topic? Can you tell from the introduction where the paper is going? Does the paper capture your interest right from the beginning? Could it be made more lively and interesting?
- Does the writer provide smooth and helpful transitions between subjects? Can you always tell how the part you are reading fits into the paper as a whole?
- Does the paper end with a satisfying conclusion?

Use of Sources

- Is the paper based on a variety of sources? Is the use of sources balanced, or is most of the information taken from only one or two sources?
- Is most of the information from sources paraphrased, rather than quoted directly? Are quotations used excessively? When sources are quoted, is there a reason for doing so? (See pages 406–07 for the proper use of quotations.)
- Does the writer avoid "naked quotations"? That is, is each quotation introduced by a phrase or sentence? When sources are referred to in the paper, are they adequately identified in acknowledgment phrases? That is, are you given enough information about them so that you can tell who they are and whether they are experts on the subject? (See pages 407–10)
- Are sources documented? Does the paper credit its sources within parenthetical notes? Does it credit paraphrased material as well as direct quotations? (Consult the Quick Reference Guides on the inside covers of this book.)
- Does the writer avoid overnoting (unnecessary notes for commonly available information) as well as undernoting (paraphrasing a source's ideas without providing a note)?
- Is it clear what each note refers to? That is, can you tell what information goes with what note?
- Are the sources listed in a works-cited page following the paper? Are the number and types of sources adequate for the paper?

- Does each note provide the least amount of information needed to refer you to the works-cited page and to identify the specific pages being referenced by the note?

- Except for longer, indented passages, are the notes placed inside the sentences with the period after, not before, the note?

- Does the punctuation in each note and in each entry in the works-cited page follow the prescribed format exactly? (Check the Quick Reference Guides on the inside covers.) Are items in the works-cited page listed in alphabetical order? Has the writer remembered that in MLA format these items should not be numbered?

Getting Advice from Other Readers

No matter how good a job writers do at editing their own writing, they can always benefit from outside help as well. Writers become so closely involved with their work that they can lose the ability to observe it from the reader's perspective. For that reason, good editing often requires advice from a reader who can point out flaws and possibilities that have escaped the writer's notice.

When she was satisfied with her revisions, Courtney brought her printed paper to class for editing. (Students in Allen's class met with partners outside of class time to edit each other's papers.) Courtney and her classmates were given the following assignment:

Group Editing   ASSIGNMENT

Read the papers written by members of your editing group and offer them the most helpful advice you can give.

Your Role as Editor
- Read each paper with care and interest, as if it were written with you as its intended audience.

- In responding to the paper, think of yourself as a friend trying to help, not as a judge providing a grade or evaluation.

The Editing Procedure
Read each paper at least twice, first for a general impression, then for specific details.

- The first time, read it straight through to gain a general impression. Do not stop to ask questions or write comments. When you have completed your first reading, pause to write a paragraph or two about the paper in general, including the following:

  —State what the paper's main idea seems to be.
  —Describe your general reaction to the paper. What did you learn from it?

—Tell the author how the paper worked for you. Where was the best writing in the draft? Did the paper develop as you expected it to? As you were reading, did questions arise in your mind that the author answered or failed to answer? Did you ever have trouble following it?

—Ask any other questions and make any other general comments about the paper as a whole.

- Now read the paper a second time, paying greater attention to specifics. Pause at any time to write comments, according to the following guidelines:

—Write comments, questions, or ideas in pencil in the margins of the paper. Put checkmarks by passages that you want to talk with the writer about.

—Point out the paper's strengths (note passages you especially like) as well as weaknesses, but be honest. You will not be much help to the author if you say that everything is wonderful when you think the paper might be improved. You are not insulting the writer by offering ideas to improve it. Specific suggestions are much more helpful than vague comments like "?" or "Needs work."

—If you are in doubt about an editing or proofreading matter, consult with your instructor.

- Finally, talk with the paper's author. Explain your comments. Describe your response to the paper, what problems or questions you had while reading it, and what suggestions you have for making it better.

Courtney received editing suggestions from the two other students in her editing group. The following pages show the comments of Laura, one of her peers.

Holbrook 1

Courtney Holbrook

Editing Draft

I love your title.

It's clever and gets my attention.

Pharmaceutical Sales: More Than Just Viagra Pens

I. Why I Am Writing This Paper

From as far back as I can remember my goal for the future has been to be involved with business. As a child I would spend endless amounts of time messing around with my own makeshift store made out of cardboard boxes and some construction paper. Sales books and receipt papers would fascinate me. I knew that it was my duty to one day play a key role in the business world.

My father is a pediatrician and my mother is a certified nurse so I have been surrounded by the medical profession from day one. Having an incredibly low tolerance for blood and a weak stomach for antiseptic sprays, the thought of breaking into the medical field seemed about as likely as me winning the lottery. That is until about two years ago. *—Comma?*

From the summer before my senior year of high school through the end of the grade I worked in a pediatric doctor's office. Day to day I would see representatives from the drug companies come into the office, either bringing lunch or other goods, and attempt to sell or

Holbrook 2

restock samples of their drug. Although a diverse crowd,
each salesman or saleswoman seemed to really enjoy their
job. *So this job combines both business and medicine.*

I have always planned on majoring in business in
college and I have wanted to concentrate on marketing and
advertising. Because of this, whenever the pharmaceutical
representatives would come in, I would wonder to myself if

Haven't you already done the research?

or pursue?

that would be a job I would like to peruse. In my paper I

Why caps?

plan to research Pharmaceutical Sales and find out just what
goes into the profession. I hope by the end of my research
journey I will have a better outlook on all sides of what
pharmaceutical sales is about and if the career is one I
still wish to pursue.

You come across as a real person. I want to read on.

II. What I Knew

Going into this project I was hesitant to concentrate
on pharmaceutical sales because all the knowledge I have on
it so far has been from observations at the pediatric
doctor's office. Aside from seeing that all the
representatives seemed to enjoy their jobs to the fullest,
the actual details were fuzzy.

The representatives never entered the office empty
handed. While they always had samples of their drugs or
pamphlets with information, there was always something else

Holbrook 3

attached. Pens were a favorite; it must be a requirement for drug companies to make pens with their drug's name on them for the reps were never lacking them. They would also on occasion bring lunch for the entire office with hopes of talking over new facts about their particular drug with the main doctor over the food.

The sales representatives were very personable people. I noticed that they appeared to introduce themselves to strangers with ease as well as professionalism. The representatives also made a real effort to get to know the employees at the office. The majority of them, or at least the more successful ones, knew all of the employees by name.

This was very appealing to me. I want to be up front with people in whatever field I end up choosing. Being that close to real advertising sales made me anxious to get out *is "eager" better?* of high school and start my journey in college. Now that I am here, I must make the decision of whether advertising/ marketing is the right thing for me before I choose my major, and even more specifically, pharmaceutical sales. I knew before starting this paper that I would need to focus on all key characteristics of the business sales world and find out for certain whether my capabilities, interests, and career objectives fit in with it.

Holbrook 4

III. The Search

Being the computer savvy person that I am, my first step in the search process was to log on to the internet and search the University's website. I came across the marketing page run by the career services branch. There I found a list of several qualities that one must have to purse the *(a?)* marketing career as well as perspective *(pro)* jobs available in the area. *(Do you mean they list local job openings? I'm confused.)* I also found an abundance of links at the bottom of the page that were directly related to pharmaceutical sales. By following those links I was directed to several other websites that contained key information about all aspects of being a pharmaceutical saleswoman, *(Was it a site for woman, or do you mean salespeople?)* including areas such as education, typical work day, and salary. I bookmarked the sites for future reference.

I then ventured over to the university's library where I ran searches for books related to pharmaceutical sales. This served *(Maybe proved or turned out?)* to be harder than I imagined. While information on being a pharmacist was readily available, pharmaceutical sales seemed almost nonexistent. Almost every search was a hit and miss situation. *(Are you saying you struck out?)* I eventually kept receiving similar call numbers on the book*(s)* that appeared to be useful, so I wrote this number down and checked out the section. After searching through selves and shelves, I found only one book to satisfy my objective.

Holbrook 5

Discouraged, I then put off my search until the
following class where we met with a librarian [as a class] *needed?*
to find out specific ways to search for career information.
The librarian informed the class of many helpful processes
to aid in our finding of information. She showed us phrases
to use on the library search section and key websites to
find information about top jobs. But the most helpful was a
list of books on careers located in the library. Immediately *You can move*
this so
it doesn't
after class I ventured upstairs to the books and found the *seem to be*
about "careers
information my previous library search had not provided. I *in the library."*
found a few books that outlined the basics of any career you
can think of, including pharmaceutical sales.

Wanting to gain further information, I continued my
search from before on the internet. I did a search with the
Google search engine using phrases like "pharmaceutical
career," "pharmaceutical sales," and "pharmaceutical
representative." The phrase "pharmaceutical sales" led me to *I am curious*
several sites on a current controversial issue. These sites *and I'd like*
a hint about
were both interesting and informing on the possible cons of *what this is?*
the industry. At this point I also did a periodical search
using the EBSCOhost search engine, with similar results.
basic?
Finally, after gaining enough background and basis
information, I interviewed an actual pharmaceutical sales
representative that I used to see at the doctor's office. I

Holbrook 6

spoke with John Carter*, a sales representative for a major

nationwide pharmaceutical company. We made an appointment

omit? seems obvious

for the following day [at a time that would work for both of

us]. The next afternoon we telephone conferenced and I asked

him my questions. Carter was very informative and answered

You mean he told you useful things

all my questions and then some. *you didn't ask about?*

By the time I ended my interview, I had an array of

information from my various sources. I felt confident that

You use this word a lot.

my information had given me a great idea of whether or not

pharmaceutical sales was right for me. I started narrowing

down my information and sorted my note cards and made an

outline for my paper. This allowed me to get down to the

actual information that I needed, rather than just pages of

words. I was ready to write my paper. *I found your description of your search process very clear.*

IV. What I Found

Most people may know what a pharmacist is, but being a

pharmaceutical sales representative is quite different.

Pharmaceutical reps are sales people. They try to contract

companies and individual people to buy their specific wares.

The sales representatives have nothing to do with actually

---

*At his request, I am not using his real name.

Holbrook 7

dispensing the drugs. According to Paul Phifer, author of

College Majors and Careers: A Resource Guide for

Effective Life Planning, being a sales representative

to
This seems
in deal
with sales
* general,*
rather
than with
pharmaceutical
sales.

"involves the study of consumer needs and desires for

products and services, the consumer's willingness and

ability to pay for those needs and desires, and the

geographical vicinity in which they reside." Pharmaceutical

sales representatives must not only be knowledgeable about

their products, but be able to sell them to as many customers

as possible within their sales region (87).

    Every aspect of sales is seen in the skills a

pharmaceutical sales representative must have.

Representative must be personable. The key to making a sale

is persuading the customer to feel like they are the most

important person alive and that they would be at a loss

without the drug the representative is selling (Farr 125).

The representative must also be a fast learner. ∧"Typically

you are given information about a new drug two weeks before

you are to start selling it. By the time you're attempting

to sell the drug you should know if from front to back, top

to bottom, and side to side. Your credibility is what is

on the line, and not being able to answer a question

about the drug you are selling lessens your credibility"

(Carter).

This is a little unclear.
Do you mean that these
reps need all the skills
other sales reps need?

Should you give his name here
so we know
who is saying
this?

Holbrook 8

Speech clarity is key to being a pharmaceutical

This sentence isn't as clear as the next one. representative. [Oral expression and oral comprehension are

all the customer has to go on.] While some representatives

may use charts or graphs, ultimately what comes out of their   *This is clear.*

mouths determines whether or not a sale is made ("Job

Description"). Desire is also highly advantageous. "Having a

high level of desire for the success of one's client and

I'm confused. Isn't this about advertising, rather than drug sales? their products which the company advertises" can lead

to being very successful in the business world"

(Groom 27-9).

Just like any job, pharmaceutical sales can be very

stressful. A representative must be able to handle the day

to day stress of working in sales. It is not unusual for

office work as well as customer interaction to spill over

into overtime, including nights and weekends (Carter). All

in all, the desire to succeed is what a pharmaceutical sales

representative must have. Enthusiasm and willingness to put

in the effort of learning about the drugs and ways to sell

them, and to work overtime are what really make a good

pharmaceutical salesman stand out (Malungani).

When someone pictures a pharmaceutical salesperson they

probably imagine a suave mid-30s gentleman [with business   *in a business suit?*

suit-like attire]. But in fact, pharmaceutical

You mean the stereotype isn't accurate, right? representatives have no stereotype. "They come in assorted

Holbrook 9

shapes, sizes, hues, talents, backgrounds, philosophies,
likes and dislikes" (Groom 27). According to
pharmaceutical.com, today there are approximately eight-five
thousand pharmaceutical salesmen in the United States of
America. Courses in business law, economics, accounting,
finance, mathematics, and statistics are highly recommended.
College-level education is also suggested. "For marketing
and sales, some employers prefer a bachelor's or master's
degree in business administration with an emphasis on
marketing" (Farr 125).

These sentences don't seem to go with the ones before them.

y [inserted in "eight-five"]

Should you paraphrase here instead of quote?

But not all pharmaceutical salesmen have a business
degree. "A college degree with almost any major is suitable
for entering" pharmaceutical sales (Farr 123). Upon
interviewing John Carter, I was surprised to find out that
his degree was not in advertising or marketing, but rather
he had earned a four-year degree in music education. Carter
had been a teacher for ten years before deciding it was too
stressful, and a friend helped him get a job in pharmaceutical
sales. His high grade point average helped him out. "Often
they [employers] care about your grade point average,
because it shows you worked hard in school. It's the little
things that add up to success in the field" (Malungani).

Now we're back to challenging the stereo-types.

Here too

This is a good fact. Surprising

Who is saying this?

The average starting salary of a pharmaceutical
salesman straight out of college varies. John Carter started

Starting salaries vary, but there must be an average. Maybe that figure is available.

Holbrook 10

out making $45,000 in his first year, but he says that
it's not uncommon for salaries to range anywhere from
pretty good money $35,000 to $150,000 per year. The main factor in what your
salary is is what drugs you are selling. "If the drug is in
high demand, you're going to make a lot of money." If it
isn't, you'll make less (Carter).

I think this could be clearer. [One's salary can also be based on what type of working
conditions they are in.] Pharmaceutical sales requires a lot
of travel. There's everyday travel to national, regional, and
local offices. This abundance of travel, as well as
pressure, can cause stress and disrupt family life.
J. Michael Farr says that "working under pressure is
unavoidable as schedules change, problems arise, and
deadlines and goals must be met" (124). But, at the end of
the day all that effort can pay off. According to John
Carter, there is a high opportunity for advancement in
pharmaceutical sales. A salesperson straight out of college
can be a representative for two to three years and be
promoted to corporate management. Shockingly, the CEOs *Isn't there just one CEO? May be "top executives"?*
in his company are mostly in their thirties or close
to it (Carter). *Do you need this since you used his name?*

     While everything seems pretty glamorous so far, a
current issue has lit a fire under the pharmaceutical sales
world and has nothing to do with new drugs or medical

Holbrook 11

Is there an author? The paper didn't write it.

treatments. The Chicago Tribune writes, "The industry's gift-giving practices intended to win physician loyalty to certain drugs have been of particular concern in a climate of growing consumer outrage over drug costs, which have risen at an annual rate of fifteen percent during each of the last four years, far exceeding inflation" (Jaspen).

This is very interesting, and I'd like to know more. Are they claiming bribery? Are the drug companies defending themselves?

The fear of bad publicity has spread all the way down to the local level. When I interviewed John Carter, although otherwise a chatterbox, he stayed closed lipped on the matter, and he asked me not to use his real name or his company in this paper. *It sounds like they feel guilty.*

Despite this current controversy, John Carter still feels ~~like~~ *that* pharmaceutical sales is a career that anyone interested should get into. While the stress and travel does sometimes get out of control, Carter remains in high spirits. "You make the job your own. You get out of it what you put into it" (Carter). *This section jumps around a bit. I'd suggest a little reorganizing.*

V. Conclusion

My research has taught me a great deal about pharmaceutical sales. While certain aspects of the job, like working nights and weekends, are unappealing, the pros outweigh the cons. The substantial travel that a pharmaceutical sales representative endures is alluring to

Holbrook 12

me. While staying in one place is enticing, being able to travel and see the world would be a wonderful career. I've always been the person out of my group of friends that welcomes going out on my own and trying new things. [I believe that being a sales rep would allow me to be an individual.] *I'm not sure exactly what you mean.*

The high prospect for advancement is also very appealing. The opportunity, with a college degree and two years of being a representative, of being able to become a CEO is unbelievable. My goal in life is to work my way up the business chain, and pharmaceutical sales appears to be an easy way to do that.

Whether?
or have you
made up your
mind?

My research solidified my decision to purse a career in business marketing and advertising, and I'm closer to deciding (that) I will concentrate on pharmaceutical sales. I am now very hopeful the next two years will bring me where I need to be to stand out in the business world.

It sounds like a worthwhile career but not as perfect as you first thought.
It also sounds like you are still very interested in it, you didn't say whether
the money was an important factor for you. What about the controversy?
Does that affect your decision? You made this surprisingly interesting.

—Laura

Holbrook 13

Works Cited

Is this an actual author, or is this source anonymous?

Carter, John. Personal interview. 18 May 2005.

CareerPlanner.com. "Job Description for: Sales

    Representatives, Chemical and Pharmaceutical."

    16 May 2005 <http://www.careerplanner.com/

    Job-Descriptions/Sales-Representatives,-Chemical-

    and-Pharmaceutical.cfm>.

Farr, J. Michael. America's Top Jobs for College Graduates.

    3rd ed. Indianapolis: Jist Works, 1999.

Goldberg, Michele, Bob Davenport, and Tiffany Mortellito.

    "When Will the Bubble Burst?" Pharmaceutical

    Executive 1 Jan. 2003. 13 May 2005 <http://

    www.pharmexec.com/pharmexec/article/

    articleDetail.jsp?id=42871>.

Groome, Hurry C., Jr. This Is Advertising. Philadelphia:

    Ayer: 1975.

Jaspen, Bruce. "Health-Care Firms on Lookout for Planned

    Michael Moore Documentary." Chicago Tribune 30 Sep.

    2004. Newspaper Index. EBSCOhost. 16 May 2005

    <http://search.epnet.com>.

Malungani, Megan. "Job Q&A" [Interview with Carol Poe].

    American Medical and Pharmaceutical Representatives

Association. 16 May 2005 <http://www.ampra.com/
industry_article_job_fags.shtml>.

Phifer, Paul. <u>College Major and Careers: A Resource Guide
for Effective Life Planning</u>. 3rd ed. Chicago:
Ferguson, 1997.

Courtney found Laura's comments valuable because they revealed another reader's response to her paper as well as useful ideas for improving it. Several of Laura's remarks highlight what worked well for her ("I found your description of your search process very clear"). Others inform Courtney about a passage she found unclear ("This sentence isn't as clear as the next one"). Remarks that specify her difficulty and suggest clarifications are particularly useful ("Do you mean they list local job openings? I'm confused"). In some of her remarks Laura responds on a personal level to what Courtney is saying ("You come across as a real person. I want to read on"). In her longer commentary at the end of the paper Laura responds on a personal level to Courtney's search ("It sounds like a worthwhile career but not as perfect as you first thought. It also sounds like you are still very interested in it"), but it also gives helpful suggestions that can help Courtney in later drafts of the paper.

Note that Laura's comments are framed in a positive and nonintrusive way. When she offers suggestions, she usually does so in the form of questions, making it clear that the paper belongs to Courtney and that final editing decisions rest with her ("Should you paraphrase here instead of quote?"). Even when Laura notes a surface error, she asks rather than tells ("Comma?"), and it is clear that Laura's goal is to be as helpful to Courtney as possible as she undertakes her revision. Laura's comments are constructive, useful, and confidence-building.

Allen Strickland also received valuable suggestions from his classmates and instructor. Each time he reread his draft, Allen noticed new possibilities for revising it. He spent many hours rephrasing, clarifying, and even rearranging sections of the paper, until he was ready to submit the polished draft that you read in Chapter 8, which is reprinted, with annotations, on the following pages.

Strickland 1

Allen Strickland

ENG 12

Professor Lisa Gorman

25 July 2005

The title is not underlined, italicized, or placed within quotation marks.

Identical Twins: Born to Be Alike?

Jim Lewis and Jim Springer, twins who were adopted as infants by different families, did not meet again until they were 39 years old. Although their hair styles were different, they were otherwise strikingly similar. Both were six feet tall and weighed 180 pounds. They had the same features, including an unusual swirl in one eyebrow and a "lazy eye" on the same side. As they were soon to learn, looking alike was just the beginning of their similarities (Watson 9-11; Wright 43-47).

The writer begins with an anecdote to capture readers' interest. For other opening strategies, see pages 479–82.

A parenthetical note is used to identify the source of paraphrased material.

Lewis and Springer are identical or "monozygotic" twins. Identical twins are created when a single egg is fertilized but then splits to form two separate embryos, which then share the same womb. Such twins are the equivalent of clones, not only looking alike but also having the identical set of genes. In contrast, non-identical twins, also known as "dizygotic" or "fraternal" twins, result from separate fertilizations of two different eggs. Non-identical twins are genetically no more alike than non-twin siblings ("Twin").

A note identifies an anonymous source by the first word or two from the title.

Strickland 2

Although they grew up in different circumstances, the two Jims were found to share many physical and behavioral traits. Their blood pressure was identically high, and both had suffered heart attacks, migraines, and hemorrhoids. Their scores on personality and intelligence tests were almost identical. Both are restless sleepers who grind their teeth at night, and both bite their fingernails. Psychologists who observed them found them similar in their speech patterns and even in the way they sit in chairs.

Other similarities range from the surprising to the eerie. Both had gained and then lost ten pounds during the same period in their teens, and both had vasectomies. Their wives say both are romantics who leave them love notes around the house. Both drink the same brand of beer and chain-smoke the same cigarettes. In school both loved math but hated spelling. Both follow car racing but hate baseball. Both worked in McDonald's, as part-time deputy sheriffs, and as gas station attendants. They had named their firstborn sons James Alan Lewis and James Allen Springer. Strangest of all, each got divorced from a woman named Linda and then married a woman named Betty (Watson 9-11; Wright 43-47). While some of these similarities are probably just coincidences, the pattern of these and other pairs of identical twins raised apart has led many to

Notes are used for paraphrased as well as quoted material from sources.

Notes for print sources identify the specific page(s) where the information was found. Information preceding this note was taken from both sources.

Strickland 3

conclude that our genes play a large part in determining who we are and what we become.

Everyone agrees that children inherit traits such as height and hair color from their parents, but scholars have long debated the role that heredity plays in determining our personalities and behavior. Today it is still far from settled how much of our behavior can be attributed to "nature," genetic factors in our DNA, and how much to "nurture," the environment in which we are raised. To put it another way, are we "born that way" or are we shaped by our surroundings? (Powell).

Because identical twins have identical DNA, they can give us insight into the role heredity plays in our development. Psychologist Susan L. Farber calls identical twins "nature's unique controlled laboratory experiment on the interplay between heredity and environment" (5). Scientists frequently conduct studies of twins to determine if physical and emotional traits have a genetic or an environmental cause. A keyword search of "identical twins" in specialized databases such as Biological Abstracts and PsycInfo turns up hundreds of studies with serious-sounding titles such as "Homozygous Familial Hypercholesterolemia in Identical Twins" and "Discordant Identical Twins and the Genesis of the Psychoses." Most of these are of interest

Following the anecdotes the writer introduces his paper's theme.

The opening sentence in this paragraph summarizes the paper's main idea.

The author integrates part of a quotation into his own sentence.

Strickland 4

only to specialists, although some manage to capture the
attention of the media, such as one study of female twins
(683 identical pairs and 714 non-identical pairs), which
reported that the ability to experience orgasm is largely
genetic (Dunn, Cherkas, and Spector).

Especially interesting are twins such as the two Jims
who were separated soon after birth and reared in different
households. Because they share the same genes but grew up in
entirely different environments, most similarities between
them should be attributable to "nature" and most differences
to "nurture."

The best known study was conducted by a team led by
psychologist Thomas Bouchard at the University of Minnesota,
which since 1979 has studied over 60 pairs of identical
twins raised apart. Some of the pairs had some contact
growing up while others, such as the Jims, had no contact at
all. Another remarkable pair was Jack Yufe and Oskar Stohr,
who were born in Trinidad before World War II to parents who
then separated. Jack was taken by his mother to Germany,
where he was raised as a Catholic and became a member of the
Hitler Youth. His brother Oskar was raised as a Jew by his
father in New York and later moved to Israel. Nevertheless,
when they were reunited as adults, the twins not only had
similar personality profiles, but they shared many

Notes for sources with multiple authors list all the last names that appear in the Works Cited listing.

A note for an online source with no identifiable page numbers lists only the author(s).

peculiarities such as storing rubber bands on their wrists, flushing the toilet before using it, and sneezing loudly as a practical joke to startle people (Allen; Wright 53-55). The fact that they were raised in cultures that most people would regard as extreme opposites makes their similarities especially strong evidence to support the claim that nature is a major factor in determining what we become.

   Stories about bizarre similarities between twins tend to capture our attention, but even the most identical of twins exhibit many differences. Caroline Clements and Sarah Heenan are identical twins raised together who consider themselves very different. In school Clements was an athlete, Heenan a cheerleader. Heenan went to a small women's college in rural Virginia, married and had children early, and was a suburban housewife until a divorce in her late thirties. Clements went to a coed university in Chicago, became a career-oriented psychology professor, and married later in life. Clements says that her sister is "a much more reactive personality; she gets angrier quicker." Compared to the more laid-back Clements, Heenan is a "neat freak" who feels compelled to clean Clement's home when she visits. In politics, Heenan is a conservative Republican, Clements a liberal Democrat, and they also have very

Having given examples of similar twins, the writer now describes twins with notable differences.

Strickland 6

different religious beliefs. Despite their many contrasts, the twins talk on the phone every day and are "absolutely best friends" (Clements).

> An interview source is identified in a note.

One recent study has shown that the wiring in identical twins' brains is not identical (Britt), and another that the DNA of twins becomes less alike as they grown older ("Even Identical"). Many differences have been attributed to environmental factors. For example, a 2001 study showed that identical twins with different diets had significantly different cholesterol levels, and a 2002 study showed differences in emotional stress that were related to social factors such as church attendance and their relationship with their mothers (Britt). Parents of identical twins report differences in temperament between them, although some psychologists say that parents exaggerate twins' differences because they focus on slight differences as a way to tell the twins apart (Goldsmith, Buss, and Lemery 901).

> Two notes identify which information in the sentence is from which source.

> Acknowledgment phrases identify unfamiliar sources and allow the reader to judge their authority.

In her book Not All Twins Are Alike, psychologist Barbara Schave Klein, herself an identical twin, believes that parenting is a crucial environmental factor in shaping individuals, including twins. "Parenting," she writes, "provides the substance that molds and holds together what human beings inherit and what can be changed by

Strickland 7

environmental stimulation" (6). She observed that, at the extremes, some parents treat identical twins as a single unit, two carbon copies of each other. Some other parents treat their twins as polar opposites, with a "good twin" and a "bad twin." Klein says that twins treated as one unit may develop dependence on each other and feel incomplete without the other. Twins treated as polar opposites create distinct roles for themselves but have serious identity and self-image issues. In contrast to these extremes, when each twin is treated by the parents as a unique, fully realized individual, each grows up not only with an independent personality and a healthy self-image but also with a lifelong friendship and understanding of the other twin (3).

The author's name is not given in the note since she is identified in the text.

One pair of identical twins who grew up together but who have obvious differences is Stephen and Mark O'Donnell. One is left-handed, the other right-handed. As children they had a "lazy eye" on different sides. Their hair parts naturally on opposite sides, and whorls of hair spiral clockwise for one twin, counterclockwise for the other (O'Donnell and O'Donnell). The O'Donnells are an example of "mirror-image twins," a phenomenon that results when the fertilized egg splits later than usual ("FAQ").

One of the most noteworthy differences between the O'Donnell twins is that Stephen is heterosexual and Mark is gay. Sexuality in twins has played a role in a controversy about what causes us to have a particular sexual orientation. On opposite sides of this controversy are those who maintain that we are born with a fixed sexuality and those who hold that sexual orientation is entirely a matter of choice. Neil Whitehead, a biochemist from New Zealand who is widely quoted in evangelical Christian publications, argues that the existence of identical twins with different sexual preferences, such as the O'Donnells, proves that our genes do not determine what our orientation will be: "Identical twins have identical genes," Whitehead writes. "If homosexuality was a biological condition produced inescapably by the genes (e.g. eye color), then if one identical twin was homosexual, in 100% of the cases his brother would be too."

Others interpret research findings differently. Several clinical studies have been conducted into the sexuality of twins. Psychologist Michael Bailey and psychiatrist Richard C. Pillard studied 161 gay men, each of whom had an identical twin, a non-identical twin, or an adopted brother. They found that 52% of the identical twin brothers were also gay, but only 22% of the non-identical twin brothers and 11% of the adopted brothers were gay (Bower). A study of lesbian

The writer first presents support for one side of a controversy.

The writer then presents support for the opposing side.

Strickland 9

women by different researchers showed similar results (Johnson). Because each pair of twins or adopted siblings was raised in the same household, they had approximately the same nurture. The fact that the more closely alike their genetic structure, the more likely siblings are to share sexual orientation points to the role of nature in determining our sexuality.

Several studies claim to have found physical differences in the brains of gay and straight men (Johnson), but most scientists doubt that there is a single "gay gene" that determines sexuality. Instead they believe that sexual orientation results from a number of factors, some of them genetic and some environmental ("Genetics"). Bailey and Pillard estimate that genes account for between 31% and 74% of male sexual orientation (Bower), and even Whitehead agrees that "genes are responsible for an indirect influence." Barbara Schave Klein is one of many psychologists who believe that both nature and nurture play important roles in determining sexual identity. She writes, "Sexual orientation cannot be specifically determined by genetics or environment. Even minute differences in genetic endowment may create differences in sexual orientation in a pair of twins" (106).

Having presented both the "nurture" and "nature" positions, the writer then presents the views of those who support a balance between them.

Strickland 10

The writer uses a transition phrase to guide readers to a new topic.

Sexuality is just one of many aspects of human behavior that have been studied using twins. There appears to be a genetic contribution to such traits as alcoholism, smoking, criminality, job satisfaction, and even divorce (Wright 8). The Minnesota Twin Family Study found that if one non-identical twin got divorced, the other twin had a 30% likelihood of also getting divorced. However, if an identical twin was divorced, the other twin's chances of divorcing went up to 45% (Minnesota).

A period usually follows a parenthetical note.

If studies of twin show that genetics is such a strong factor in shaping us, does that mean that humans have less freedom to make decisions than we suppose? In his book on twins, journalist Lawrence Wright points out that the findings can sometimes be misleading. Even if 45% of identical twins get divorced if the other twin does, that means that the majority do not. Despite genetic or environmental influences, we still remain free to make decisions (154). After studying the similarities between twins for many years, Thomas Bouchard now says:

An acknowledgment phrase marks the beginning of a passage.

A note marks the end of the passage.

Longer quotations are indented one inch. No quotation marks are used.

> There probably are genetic influences on almost all facets of human behavior, but the emphasis on the idiosyncratic characteristics is misleading. On average, identical twins raised separately are about 50 percent similar--and that defeats the

Strickland 11

When one source is quoted in another source, give the source where the quotation was found.

widespread belief that identical twins are carbon copies. Obviously, they are not. Each is a unique individual in his or her own right. (Qtd. in Allen)

A note following an indented quotation comes after the period.

The writer concludes by summarizing the paper's main idea.

Twins studies not only fascinate us but they can teach us much about ourselves. Evidence is strong that our genes have much to say about who we become. Nevertheless, the degree to which we are shaped by nature and by nurture--as well as the degree to which we are free to shape ourselves-- is likely to remain a topic of controversy for many years to come.

Strickland 12

Works Cited

Sources are listed in alphabetical order.

Sources are not numbered.

Allen, Arthur. "Nature & Nurture." The Washington Post
     Magazine 11 Jan. 1998. Washingtonpost.com. 11 July 2005
     <http://www.washingtonpost.com/wp-srv/national/
     longterm/twins/twins1.htm>.

Bower, B "Gene Influence Tied to Sexual Orientation."
     Science News 4 Jan. 1992: 6. Academic Search Elite.
     EBSCOhost. 6 July 2005 <http://search.epnet.com>.

Britt, Robert Roy. "Identical Twins Not So Identical."
     LiveScience: Human Biology. 8 July 2005. 13 July 2005
     <http://www.livescience.com/humanbiology/
     050708_identical_twins.html>.

Give a publication date for an online source if one is shown. Also give the date when you consulted an online source.

For a source with multiple authors, only the first has the first and last names inverted.

Clements, Caroline M. Personal interview. 15 July 2005.

Dunn, Kate M., Lynn F. Cherkas, and Tim D. Spector. "Genetic
     Influences on Variation in Female Orgasmic Function: A
     Twin Study." Biology Letters, 7 June 2005. 8 July 2005
     <http://www.journals.royalsoc.ac.uk>.

"Even Identical Twins Grow Apart Genetically--Study."
     Reuters. Yahoo News. 5 July 2005. <http://
     news.yahoo.com/news?tmpl=story&u=/nm/20050705/sc_nm/
     science_twins_dc_5>.

"FAQ: Twin Zygosity." Proactive Genetics. 14 July 2005
     <http://www.proactivegenetics.com/faqzygosity.dna>.

Strickland 13

Farber, Susan L. <u>Identical Twins Reared Apart: A Reanalysis</u>.
    New York: Basic Books, 1981.

"Genetics and Sexual Orientation." <u>Answers.com</u>. 14 July 2005
    <http://www.answers.com/topic/
    genetics-and-sexual-orientation>.

Goldsmith H. H., K. A. Buss, and K. S. Lemery. "Toddler and
    Childhood Temperament: Expanded Content, Stronger
    Genetic Evidence, New Evidence for the Importance of
    Environment." <u>Developmental Psychology</u> 33 (1997),
    891-905.

Johnson, Ryan D. "Homosexuality: Nature or Nurture."
    <u>AllPsych Online</u>. 30 Apr. 2003. 12 July 2005
    <http://allpsych.com/journal/homosexuality.html>.

Klein, Barbara Schave. <u>Not All Twins Are Alike:
    Psychological Profiles of Twinship</u>. Westport, CT:
    Praeger, 2003.

<u>Minnesota Twin Family Study</u>. "What's Special about Twins to
    Science?" 15 July 2005 <http://www.psych.umn.edu/
    psylabs.mtfs/special.htm>.

O'Donnell, Stephen, and Mark O'Donnell. "The Co-Zygotes'
    Almanac." <u>Esquire</u> June 1998: 132. <u>Academic Search
    Elite</u>. EBSCOhost. 6 July 2005 <http://
    search.epnet.com>.

This source is attributed to an organization or group, rather than an individual.

A line break in a URL can be made following a backslash. Do not add a hyphen.

Give the online location of electronic databases.

Strickland 14

Powell, Kimberly. "Nature vs. Nurture." <u>About.com</u>. 9 Oct.
    2003. 10 July 2005 <http://genealogy.about.com/cs/
    geneticgenealogy/a/nature_nurture_2.htm>.

"Twin." <u>Wikipedia: The Free Encyclopedia</u>. 6 July 2005.
    9 July 2005 <http://en.wikipedia.org/wiki/Twin>.

Watson, Peter. <u>Twins: An Uncanny Relationship</u>. New York:
    Viking, 1981.

Whitehead, N. E. "The Importance of Twin Studies." National
    Association for Research and Therapy of Homosexuals.
    5 July 2005 <http://www.narth.com/docs/whitehead2.html>.

Wright, Lawrence. <u>Twins: And What They Tell Us about Who We
    Are</u>. New York: Wiley, 1997.

TYPING AND PROOFREADING YOUR POLISHED DRAFT

Allen and Courtney benefited from the comments and suggestions they received from classmates in their editing groups and from their instructors. They made further revisions in their papers and submitted them in polished form, in accordance with the assignment they had been given, which follows.

ASSIGNMENT   **Submitting Your Portfolio**

Submit the following items in your folder:

- Your typed polished draft
- All earlier drafts and outlines
- Your note cards in two packets:

  —those you used in your paper, in the order you used them
  —those you wrote but did not use

- Your research notebook

When you prepare your final draft, be sure that you observe formatting conventions described in Chapter C of Part II, along with any others your instructor may specify. Before you submit your paper, read it through several times, slowly and carefully, looking for errors. Look for typing mistakes, misspellings, missing words, punctuation problems, and any other surface errors that may have escaped your notice in earlier readings. It is especially useful to have a friend proofread the paper as well, because by now you have become so familiar with what you have written that you may have difficulty noticing surface details.

Neatly cross out a minor error with a single line and write the correction above it. Never erase, and do not use correction fluid for making handwritten changes. Any page with a major error or numerous minor errors should be reprinted.

After proofreading their final drafts, Allen and Courtney brought them to class, where their instructors gave them one final assignment:

ASSIGNMENT   **Final Proofreading**

Read the final drafts of the other students in your editing group. Do not mark on their papers, but if you find an error, point it out to the author so that it can be corrected.

At last, Allen and Courtney submitted their final drafts. For both, the project had been difficult but rewarding work. Like their classmates, they had struggled with the previously unfamiliar process of research and research writing. They had uncovered and managed a large body of research materials. From these sources, they had created essays that had substance, form, and interest—essays they were proud of. They had also learned a great deal, not only about their particular topics, but also about research, about college scholarship, and even about the meaning of an education itself. It is likely that after the hard work of your own research project is completed, you too, like Allen, Courtney, and many thousands of other students before you, will feel a well-deserved sense of satisfaction with what you have accomplished.

14 *Argument: Reading, Writing, and Research*

You don't have to be hostile or arrogant to argue effectively. You don't even have to be an expert or have firsthand experience with your topic. In fact, in writing a college-level argument, you should avoid sounding overconfident, too sure you have found the truth. You are expected to be reasonable, fair-minded, and logical. In a way, that may be a relief, since you don't face the pressure of needing to win at any cost. Unlike a debater, to whom winning is everything, a writer engaged in a serious argument should be above mere victory. The goal is more important—an honest search for truth in a world where we must acknowledge and respect competing representations of reality. Of course, you always want to make your case convincing enough to have an impact on an audience, but you "win" in argumentative writing when you are fair, thorough, and clear. The challenge of argument is to place ideas in a public forum to see if they stand up under scrutiny. College students construct arguments not to trick or outmaneuver others, but to test the validity of ideas. This is the intellectual excitement and ethical challenge of argument.

Of course, not every form of persuasion adheres to these ideals. Most advertisements, for example, are designed to stimulate purchases rather than to discover truth. And, in some cases, fairness and ethics have little to do with how advertisers influence consumers.

If you visualize argument as a horizontal line or continuum, at one end you would place the rigorous logic and impersonal language of the physical sciences—for example, a geologist's efforts to demonstrate to professional colleagues that her experimental findings challenge accepted theories of beach erosion. At the other end of the spectrum, you might place a richly colored photograph of a vacation fantasy that tries to persuade us to book reservations at an exclusive beach resort. The two extremes of this continuum would look like this:

Logical reasoning ⟵──────────────⟶ *Emotional appeal*

EMOTIONAL PERSUASION

Although emotional appeals are not the primary concern of this chapter, we begin by examining the tactics of advertisement. At times, these tactics seem obvious. But even though we understand that ads are designed to manipulate consumers,

490

most of us are influenced by them. They succeed because most people observe ads casually, if not subconsciously, on billboards and in magazines; rarely do we analyze them systematically. In their appropriate context, ads are evidently effective, since people spend billions of dollars on products and services that are not necessities.

When we study advertising techniques, we discover how ads and other forms of emotional persuasion can motivate people to behave and believe in accordance with the desires of others. Awareness is the best defense against manipulation.

The advertisement in Figure 14.1 (page 492) illustrates this type of persuasion. Like most other magazines ads, it is concerned more with stimulating desires than with explaining the features of a product or service. In fact, the advertisement illustrates a formula developed by Hugh Rank, a prominent analyst of advertising and propaganda. First comes *attention-getting*. When readers first encounter this ad, they are likely to notice the pristine mountain landscape and close-up image of a bear, which evoke a unique and intimate encounter with nature and its wildlife. Second comes *confidence-building*. Traveling to this region in the small ships of Cruise West is bound to get readers "close enough to see bears on a shoreline, and the barnacles on a humpback's tail." Presumably, it is truly an "up-close, casual, and personal" experience. Third comes *desire-stimulating*. The advertisement speaks of "the magic" of traveling from "the outermost reaches of Alaska to the wildlife-rich jungles of Costa Rica and Panama." Fourth comes *urgency-stressing*. Since this could be the only "travel experience [that] can bring you closer to a region's wildlife, culture, and natural history," failing to contact Cruise West to make a booking may lead to regret. Finally comes *response-seeking*. Readers are encouraged to call the number provided or visit the Web site for brochures and availability before it is too late.

Few ads illustrate Rank's formula quite so clearly as the one in Figure 14.1. However, many ads maximize the emotional appeal of products without providing specific information about ingredients, specifications, or cost. Ads are subject to constant testing and research to make sure that the emotions and desires they evoke actually motivate consumers. As you study the following ads, try to decide whether you are among the audience that their creators have targeted.

Emotional Persuasion

EXERCISE

After carefully examining the advertisements on the following pages (Figures 14.2 and 14.3), freewrite for five to ten minutes about each of them. What audience do the advertisers have in mind, and what responses do they hope to stimulate? How does the advertiser expect people to be persuaded by the appeal? Is one ad more logical than the other? Is emotional appeal a component of either or both ads? Now try to envision ads that seek the same results without resorting to emotional appeals. How would they differ from the ads pictured here? Would they be more or less effective in furthering the advertisers' goals?

Figure 14.1 Ad illustrating the Hugh Rank formula.

Figure 14.2 Ad using emotional persuasion.

Figure 14.3 Ad using emotional persuasion.

LOGICAL ARGUMENT

In contrast to emotional persuasion, formal argument relies primarily on facts and logic. Some arguments, like the following passage from a book by a noted biologist and conservationist, adhere to a tightly organized pattern:

> For species on the brink, from birds to fungi, the end can come in two ways. Many, like the Moorean tree snails, are taken out by the metaphorical equivalent of a rifle shot—they are erased, but the ecosystem from which they are removed is left intact. Others are destroyed by a holocaust, in which the entire ecosystem perishes.
>
> The distinction between rifle shots and holocausts has special merit in considering the case of the spotted owl *(Strix occidentalis)* of the United States, an endangered form that has been the object of intense national controversy since 1988. Each pair of owls requires about three to eight kilometers of coniferous forest more than 250 years old. Only this habitat can provide the birds with both enough large hollow trees for nesting and an expanse of open understory for the effective hunting of mice and other small mammals. Within the range of the spotted owl in western Oregon and Washington, the suitable habitat is largely confined to twelve national forests. The controversy was first engaged within the U.S. Forest Service and then the public at large. It was ultimately between loggers, who wanted to continue cutting the primeval forest, and environmentalists determined to protect an endangered species. The major local industry around the owl's range was affected, the financial stakes were high, and the confrontation was emotional. Said the loggers: "Are we really expected to sacrifice thousands of jobs for a handful of birds?" Said the environmentalists: "Must we deprive future generations of a race of birds for a few more years of timber yield?"
>
> Overlooked in the clamor was the fate of an entire habitat, the old-growth coniferous forest, with thousands of other species of plants, animals, and microorganisms, the great majority unstudied and unclassified. Among them are three rare amphibian species, the tailed frog and the Del Norte and Olympic salamanders. Also present is the western yew, *Taxus brevifolia*, source of taxol, one of the most potent anticancer substances ever found. The debate should be framed another way: what else awaits discovery in the old-growth forests of the Pacific Northwest?
>
> This cutting of primeval forest and other disasters, fueled by the demands of growing human populations, are the overriding threat to biological diversity everywhere. But even the data that led to this conclusion, coming as they do mainly from vertebrates and plants, understate the case. The large, conspicuous organisms are the ones most susceptible to rifle shots, to overkill and the introduction of competing organisms. They are of the greatest immediate importance to man and receive the greater part of his malign attention. People hunt deer and pigeons rather than sowbugs and spiders. They cut roads into a forest to harvest Douglas fir, not mosses and fungi.
>
> Not many habitats in the world covering a kilometer contain fewer than a thousand species of plants and animals. Patches of rain forest and coral reef harbor tens of thousands of species, even after they have declined to a remnant of the original wilderness. But when the *entire* habitat is destroyed, almost all of the species are destroyed. Not just eagles and pandas disappear but also the smallest, still uncensused invertebrates, algae, and fungi, the invisible players that make

up the foundation of the ecosystem. Conservationists now generally recognize the difference between rifle shots and holocausts. They place emphasis on the preservation of entire habitats and not only the charismatic species within them. They are uncomfortably aware that the last surviving herd of Javan rhinoceros cannot be saved if the remnant woodland in which they live is cleared, that harpy eagles require every scrap of rain forest around them that can be spared from the chain saw. The relationship is reciprocal: when star species like rhinoceros and eagles are protected, they serve as umbrellas for all the life around them.

—Edward O. Wilson, *The Diversity of Life*

The Structure of Logical Argument: Claims, Evidence, and Values

Although environmental issues often arouse an emotional reaction, Edward O. Wilson appeals to reason by adopting the techniques and strategies of formal argument. He advances a central point, an ***argumentative assertion*** or ***claim:*** that environmental debates oversimplify or ignore transcendent issues when they focus on the fate of one or two "charismatic species." Wilson supports this claim with various types of ***evidence:*** demonstrable ***facts*** (e.g., "patches of rain forest and coral reef harbor tens of thousands of species"), opinions or ***inferences*** derived from facts ("the cutting of primeval forests and other disasters, fueled by the demands of growing human populations, are the overriding threat to biological diversity everywhere"), and ***judgments*** based on ethical values or political views (e.g., "the debate should be framed another way"). Because his argument seems logical and his tone is calm and confident, many readers may conclude that Wilson has authority and reason on his side.

Presented in the abstract, the rules of argument seem straightforward and unambiguous. However, anyone who has witnessed a vigorous discussion among friends, colleagues, or family members who hold contradictory views can testify to the difficulty of distinguishing facts from opinions or claims from truth. Nevertheless, a few basic guidelines should serve your needs as a reader and writer of arguments in college. First, a valid argument is one that advances a claim about which reasonable, educated adults can disagree. You cannot base a worthwhile argument on an assertion of fact (e.g., *The Adventures of Huckleberry Finn* reveals Mark Twain's disapproval of slavery) or an expression of individual taste (e.g., *The Adventures of Huckleberry Finn* is the greatest American novel).

An effective argument does not, however, evade or ignore individual ***values***. On the contrary, responsible writers acknowledge their own attitudes and predispositions as they appeal to those of a particular audience. Jim Martin, for example, appeals to the values of conservative readers by giving Ronald Reagan full credit for the fall of European Communism: "Thanks to Mr. Reagan's leadership, vision, and gutsy determination, tens of millions of men and women are free today because he refused to accept the status quo of the Cold War" (page 227). E. J. Dionne, on the other hand, addresses a more liberal audience. Although he concedes that Reagan "deserves a decent share of the credit for the end of the Cold War and the fall of the Soviet Union," he contends that Reagan's admirers "care primarily about domestic policy and politics—and on those, there is no consensus on the meanings of the Reagan years" (page 228). Although they may not change many minds, both writers resist irresponsible claims. Martin, for example, does not suggest that those who disagree with him are trying to belittle Ronald Reagan. Dionne, likewise, does not dismiss the Reagan presidency as a failure.

Varieties of Evidence

Perhaps the most common obstacle to productive argument is disputed or misleading evidence. Writers undermine their credibility when they insist on the authority of their claims, belittle or ignore competing claims, or misrepresent evidence. On the other hand, uncritical readers can be misled by careless inferences or hasty judgments when they are asserted as self-evident truth.

Facts

Facts, though they offer convincing proof, are sometimes hard to come by. Few arguments can be supported entirely with indisputable facts: for example, alcohol acts as a depressant. Other facts, though not universally acknowledged throughout history, are nonetheless authoritative: for example, motorists are more likely to cause accidents when they drive under the influence of alcohol. Still other facts require proof: for example, Festerhagen was intoxicated when he swerved to miss the neighbor's cat and collided with a police car. This last fact demands verification (visual evidence based on the testimony of witnesses, the results of a breathalizer test, or a blood-alcohol reading) that may hinge on legal definitions that vary from one state to another.

One impediment to fair, logical argument is confusing facts with inferences: for example, since Festerhagen was intoxicated, he caused the accident that injured Officer Reilly. Although this is a reasonably persuasive inference—an opinion based on the fact that Festerhagen was legally under the influence of alcohol—a competing fact to consider is that drunk drivers are sometimes involved in accidents caused by others. Likewise, writers often err by mistaking correlations for causes. For example, there is a well-known correlation between the incidence of Down syndrome and the age of a mother during pregnancy. However, it has yet to be proved that a mother's age is a direct *cause* of Down syndrome. Moreover, the fact that an overwhelming majority of babies born to women over the age of thirty-five do not have birth defects, along with the fact that many children who have Down syndrome are born to women under that age, seems to weaken a causal argument.

Inferences

Important as they are in validating claims, facts usually are not the crux of an argument. More often, people argue issues of interpretation—inferences or conclusions drawn from factual evidence. Chapter 4 introduced **inductive** and **deductive** reasoning as organizational patterns. These terms apply also to formal argument.

An inductive argument arrives at an inference or judgment after weighing specific facts. For example:

- **Fact.** Professor Fangle permitted Bushrod to enroll in his American literature class after the published deadline for adding courses—with the strict understanding that he would make up the work that other students had already completed.
- **Fact.** By the end of September, Bushrod still had not submitted any of this work.
- **Fact.** At the urging of his instructor, Bushrod scheduled an office conference to discuss the assignments and to agree on a reasonable deadline for submitting them. However, he did not keep his appointment.
- **Fact.** By fall break, Bushrod had accumulated six more absences and failed three daily quizzes.
- **Fact.** Explaining that his return flight from Bermuda had been delayed, Bushrod was absent from class the day after fall break and therefore missed an opportunity to review material covered on the midterm examination, which he subsequently failed.
- **Fact.** At this point, Professor Fangle offered Bushrod the option of withdrawing from the course without failing, but he rejected the offer indignantly.
- **Fact.** Although Bushrod submitted the two essays assigned during the second half of the semester, both were late. One of them dealt with an eighteenth-century French play, and the other plagiarized an article about Edgar Allan Poe published in a well-known literary journal.
- **Fact.** Confronted with this evidence, Bushrod became verbally abusive and threatened to assault his instructor physically. He refused to leave Professor Fangle's office and was escorted away by the campus police.
- **Inference.** Bushrod has no legitimate basis for appealing his grade in Professor Fangle's class.

Unlike a deductively organized paragraph, a deductive argument does not necessarily open with a summarizing assertion or conclusion. Instead, it is distinguished by the logical relationship between two statements (both facts, or a fact and an inference) that support an argumentative claim. The preceding argument about Festerhagen's accident, for example, is actually based on deductive reasoning:

- **Fact.** A motorist is more likely to cause an accident while driving under the influence of alcohol.
- **Fact.** According to the results of an on-site breathalyzer test, Festerhagen was legally intoxicated when he swerved to miss the neighbor's cat and collided with a police car.
- **Claim.** Festerhagen bears responsibility for the accident that injured Officer Reilly.

Presented fairly, as a logical conclusion, the claim that Festerhagen bears responsibility for the accident is more persuasive and ethical than it would be if it were presented as fact.

Analogy

An argument based on *analogy* makes a comparison. The following condensation of Edward Wilson's argument (pages 495–96) provides an illustration:

> For species on the brink, from birds to fungi, the end can come in two ways. Many, like the Moorean tree snails, are taken out by the metaphorical equivalent of a rifle shot—they are erased, but the ecosystem from which they are removed is left intact. Others are destroyed by a holocaust, in which the entire ecosystem perishes.
>
> The distinction between rifle shots and holocausts has special merit in considering the case of the spotted owl (*Strix occidentalis*) of the United States, an endangered form that has been the object of intense national controversy since 1988. . . .
>
> Overlooked in the clamor was the fate of an entire habitat, the old-growth coniferous forest, with thousands of other species of plants, animals, and microorganisms, the great majority unstudied and unclassified. . . .
>
> The large, conspicuous organisms are the ones most susceptible to rifle shots, to overkill and the introduction of competing organisms. They are of the greatest immediate importance to man and receive the greater part of his malign attention. . . .
>
> But when the entire habitat is destroyed, almost all of the species are destroyed. Not just eagles and pandas disappear but also the smallest, still uncensused invertebrates, algae, and fungi, the invisible players that make up the foundation of the ecosystem. Conservationists now generally recognize the difference between rifle shots and holocausts. They place emphasis on the preservation of entire habitats and not only the charismatic species within them.

Because most people regard genocide as a more heinous crime than homicide, many readers will accept Wilson's argument that preserving entire ecosystems is a more urgent priority than protecting any one individual plant or animal species.

Testimony

Writers often support their arguments with the *testimony* of acknowledged experts. As we noted in Chapter 3, the most persuasive, reliable sources for research writing are persons with recognized authority in an appropriate field. Notice how James Surowiecki uses testimony in the following passage from his article about conflicts of interest in the stock trade:

> This outbreak of straight talk is Wall Street's way of addressing the collapse of its credibility. Everyone agrees that conflicts of interest riddle the securities and accounting industries—research analysts touting dubious companies to win their business, auditors signing off on dubious numbers to keep it—and that something must be done, so Wall Street has decided to adopt the talking cure. The problem with the conflicts of interest, the argument goes, is that no one knows about them. Fess up, and the problem goes away.

It's a nice thought, but the diagnosis is facile, and the remedy won't work. Start with the central tenet: that during the boom the conflicts of interest were kept secret. The truth is, people knew more than they like to admit. Back in 1998 a *Business Week* cover story called "Wall Street's Spin Game" put the matter succinctly: "The analyst today is an investment banker in sheep's clothing." When Merrill Lynch hired Henry Blodget as an Internet analyst in 1999, the media explained the decision by saying that Blodget, with his rosy predictions, would help the firm bring in more investment-banking business. Jack Grubman, the former Salomon Smith Barney analyst, bragged of his intimate relationship with the companies he was supposed to be evaluating objectively. And the problems in the accounting industry were even more obvious. Though the firms maintained their game face, it was no secret, by the late 1990s, that the game itself was rigged. Most investors accepted this state of affairs with the genial tolerance of pro-wrestling fans.

Why? One reason, clearly, was the boom itself—people didn't care why an analyst recommended a stock, as long as it went up. But there was something else: it turns out that people think conflicts of interest don't much matter. "If you disclose a conflict of interest, people in general don't know how to use that information," George Lowenstein, an economics professor at Carnegie Mellon, says. "And, to the extent that they do anything at all, they actually tend to underestimate the severity of these conflicts."

Usually, conflicts of interest lead not to corruption but, rather, to unconscious biases. Most analysts try to do good work, but the quid-pro-quo arrangements that govern their business seep into their analyses and warp their judgments. . . . "People have a pretty good handle on overt corruption, but they don't have a handle on just how powerful these unconscious biases are," Lowenstein says.

Ethical and Emotional Appeals

Earlier in this chapter we contrasted the emotional appeals of advertisements with the logical evidence presented in formal argument. This, like many other distinctions, can be oversimplified and exaggerated. The fact is that while writers who argue effectively rely on sound reasoning (sometimes called *logos*), they also recognize that the minds of readers are not impassively mechanistic. Classical rhetoricians understood that effective argument also appeals to the emotions of an audience (*pathos*) and rests on the character (*ethos*) projected by a speaker or writer, often referred to as a *persona*.

Ethos

Writers use *ethical appeals* to project a credible, trustworthy persona. Credibility and trust are earned through careful research, clear writing, and humility. Notice how historian Lawrence Stone creates such a persona in the following passage from "A Short History of Love" (pages 49–51):

Historians and anthropologists are in general agreement that romantic love—that usually brief but intensely felt and all-consuming attraction toward another person—is culturally conditioned. Love has a history. It is common only in certain societies at certain times, or even in certain social groups within those societies, usually the elite, which have the leisure to cultivate such feelings. Scholars are, however, less certain whether romantic love is merely a culturally induced psychological overlay on top of the biological drive for sex, or whether it has biochemical roots that operate quite independently from the libido. Would anyone in fact "fall in love" if they had not read about it or heard it talked about? Did poetry invent love, or love poetry?

Some things can be said with certainty about the history of the phenomenon. The first is that cases of romantic love can be found in all times and places and have often been the subject of powerful poetic expression, from the Song of Solomon to Shakespeare. On the other hand, as anthropologists have discovered, neither social approbation nor the actual experience of romantic love is common to all societies. Second, historical evidence for romantic love before the age of printing is largely confined to elite groups, which of course does not mean that it may not have occurred lower on the social scale. As a socially approved cultural artifact, romantic love began in Europe in the southern French aristocratic courts of the twelfth century, and was made fashionable by a group of poets, the troubadours. In this case the culture dictated that it should occur between an unmarried male and a married woman, and that it either should go sexually unconsummated or should be adulterous.

By the sixteenth and seventeenth centuries, our evidence becomes quite extensive, thanks to the spread of literacy and the printing press. We now have love poems, such as Shakespeare's sonnets, love letters, and autobiographies by women concerned primarily with their love lives. The courts of Europe were evidently hotbeds of passionate intrigues and liaisons, some romantic, some sexual. The printing press also began to spread pornography to a wider public, thus stimulating the libido, while the plays of Shakespeare indicate that romantic love was a concept familiar to society at large, which composed his audience.

Whether this romantic love was approved of, however, is another question. We simply do not know how Shakespearean audiences reacted to *Romeo and Juliet*. Did they, like us (and as Shakespeare clearly intended), fully identify with the young lovers? Or, when they left the theater, did they continue to act like the Montague and Capulet parents, who were trying to stop these irresponsible adolescents from allowing an ephemeral and irrational passion to interfere with the serious business of politics and patronage?

Stone projects authority by explaining historical facts and trends, summarizing scholarly research, and alluding to literary texts. Yet he concedes the limits of his knowledge by posing questions at various points. Another impressive ethical appeal is the clarity and careful organization of Stone's writing.

Similarly, Edward O. Wilson tries to project objectivity in the following paragraph from his book *The Diversity of Life* (pages 495–96):

The controversy [surrounding the spotted owl] was first engaged within the U.S. Forest Service and then the public at large. It was ultimately between loggers, who wanted to continue cutting the primeval forest, and environmentalists determined to protect an endangered species. The major local industry around the owl's range was affected, the financial stakes were high, and the confrontation was emotional. Said the loggers: "Are we really expected to sacrifice thousands of jobs for a handful of birds?" Said the environmentalists: "Must we deprive future generations of a race of birds for a few more years of timber yield?"

Wilson establishes credibility by summarizing two conflicting arguments without endorsing either. Rejecting both arguments as extreme and simplistic, he projects a cautious, deliberate persona.

Stone and Wilson each adopt a persona that is effective in specific ***rhetorical situations***. Molly Ivins, on the other hand, projects a very different persona in the following passage from "'Ernie's Nuns' Are Pointing the Way" (pages 280–81):

> Middle-aged activists who waste time bemoaning apathy on campus could help by getting off their duffs and helping spread word about the USAS boycotts.
>
> Lest you think hideous working conditions are found only in the Third World, consider the case of Big Chicken, the poultry industry in America.
>
> Workers in chicken factories endure conditions that would shame Guatemala or Honduras. Many stand for hours on end in sheds that reek of manure, or chop chickens all day in cold, dark plants, or are constantly scratched by live chickens that have to be crammed into cages by the thousands. . . .
>
> The wages are so low, workers often qualify for welfare. And as Texans know from our experience with Big Chicken in East Texas, these plants are often notorious polluters as well, fouling both air and water.

Ivins presents herself as a morally outraged citizen. She invokes stark contrasts—right and wrong, heroes and villains. She tries to goad people into immediate action and is prepared to shame them if necessary. Individual readers may disagree about whether a more deliberate, objective persona would have been more effective in this rhetorical situation. However, the fact that Ivins's syndicated column appears in daily newspapers throughout the United States indicates that many readers respect or at least enjoy her persona. Whether Ivins alters the opinions of readers is, of course, not so clear.

Pathos

Individual readers will not agree about the appropriateness of emotional appeals in specific rhetorical situations. For example, some may argue that the word *holocaust* conjures up such dreadful associations that Edward O. Wilson's use of the term (page 495) is unwarranted or irresponsible. Others may feel that it is a uniquely effective means of arousing the attention of apathetic readers who do not fully recognize what is at stake.

E. V. Kontorovich goes a step further when he assails a court decision prohibiting discriminatory practices by the Boy Scouts:

> Recently, a New Jersey appellate court forced the Boy Scouts to give a scoutmaster post to James Dale, a gay activist and editor at *Poz*, a magazine for HIV-positive people. . . .
>
> The wave of litigation against the Scouts is not ultimately about the rights of gays, or atheists, or females. It is a challenge to the BSA's right to exist in its present form. Such an attack should not be surprising; if anything, it's odd that the Boy Scouts have hung on for so long. . . .
>
> The existence of the Scouts irritates the ideologues of modernity—and so hordes of litigators, the antibodies of a dissolute culture, have responded by attacking the foreign body. If the courts find in favor of the plaintiffs in the undecided cases, the meaning of the Boy Scouts will be greatly eroded. The

organization will become the Gay Godless Girl/Boy Scouts of America. It is only the right to restrict membership and insist that members follow rules that can give a civic group definition.

For example, the Scout's oath has a clause about "keeping myself . . . morally straight," a provision the BSA says is on its face incompatible with homosexual activity. "There is nothing in [the Scout's oath] about homosexuality," says Timothy Curran, the California gay seeking reinstatement as a scoutmaster. "It says you must be 'morally straight,' but you can define that any way you want." Which is precisely what New Jersey's jurisprudes chose to do.

Kontorovich engages in name-calling—comparing plaintiffs' attorneys to microbes and implying that his opponents are "dissolute." Likewise, his reference to judges as "jurisprudes" (a word that Kontorovich has apparently coined) slyly invokes another label—*prude*, a self-righteous person who tries to control the manners and behaviors of other people.

Dubious emotional appeals appear in arguments from every point along the ideological spectrum. The prevalence of such appeals has led some commentators to deplore the "declining civility" of contemporary discourse. Reviewing the political rhetoric of past eras indicates that these expressions of alarm lack perspective. But whether or not reckless emotional appeals are effective is a different question, and they are clearly out of bounds in most of the arguments you read and write as a college student.

 ## AN INFORMAL ANALYSIS OF ARGUMENTS

Having considered the elements and techniques of argument, you should now be prepared to examine an argumentative text by analyzing its components. Most arguments can be assessed in terms of the following five elements:

- **Purpose.** What audience does the writer seem to have in mind; that is, whom does he intend to influence? What attitudes do his readers (or listeners) probably share? How and why does the writer want to influence this audience? What does the writer want them to do in response to his message?

- **Thesis** (also called the *assertion, claim,* or *proposition*). What main point or idea is the writer trying to persuade readers to accept or act on? Is this point clearly and explicitly stated? Does the writer present it as the only reasonable view of the issue at hand?

- **Evidence.** What kinds of evidence does the writer use to support the thesis? facts? inferences? analogies? expert testimony? Is the evidence appropriate, credible, and sufficient? Is the argument based on logic, emotion, or both? How is the evidence arranged or organized?

- **Refutation.** Are opposing views presented fairly? Would opponents feel that their opinions have been stated accurately? Does the writer effectively show that opposing views are inadequate or invalid? Does the writer overlook any opposing arguments?

- **Persona.** How would you characterize the writer's attitude and credibility? Does the writer seem hostile? conciliatory? reasonable? sarcastic? Is the writer obviously biased or bound by a narrow perspective? Does the language sound reasonable? conciliatory? pedantic? aggressive? Do you trust the writer to argue fairly and objectively?

These questions can be applied to any persuasive text, providing a valuable way to analyze argumentative techniques and to assess their effectiveness.

To trace the process of informal analysis, start by reading the following essay by William Safire, editorialist for the *New York Times* and former speech writer for President Richard Nixon.

PRACTICE READING

Abolish the Penny

William Safire

Because my staunch support of the war in Iraq has generated such overwhelming reader enthusiasm, it's time to re-establish my contrarian credentials. (Besides, I need a break.) Here's a crusade sure to infuriate the vast majority of penny-pinching traditionalists.

The time has come to abolish the outdated, almost worthless, bothersome, and wasteful penny. Even President Lincoln, who distrusted the notion of paper money because he thought he would have to sign each greenback, would be ashamed to have his face on this specious specie.

That's because you can't buy anything with a penny any more. Penny candy? Not for sale at the five-and-dime (which is now a "dollar store"). Penny-ante poker? Pass the buck. Any vending machine? Put a penny in and it will sound an alarm.

There is no escaping economic history: it takes nearly a dime today to buy what a penny bought back in 1950. Despite this, the U.S. Mint keeps churning out a billion pennies a month.

Where do they go? Two-thirds of them immediately drop out of circulation, into piggy banks or—as the *Times*'s John Tiemey noted five years ago—behind chair cushions or at the back of sock drawers next to your old tin-foil ball. Quarters and dimes circulate; pennies disappear because they are literally more trouble than they are worth.

The remaining 300 million or so—that's ten million shiny new useless items punched out every day by government workers who could be more usefully employed tracking counterfeiters—go toward driving retailers crazy. They cost more in employee-hours—to wait for buyers to fish them out, then to count, pack up, and take them to the bank—than it would cost to toss them out. That's why you see "penny cups" next to every cash register; they save the seller time and the buyer the inconvenience of lugging around loose change that tears holes in pockets and now sets off alarms at every frisking-place.

Why is the U.S. among the last of the industrialized nations to abolish the peskiest little bits of coinage? At the G-8 summit next week, the Brits and the French—even the French!—who dumped their low-denomination coins thirty years ago, will be laughing at our senseless jingling.

The penny-pinching horde argues: those $9.98 price tags save the consumer two cents because, if the penny were abolished, merchants would "round up" to the nearest dollar. That's pound-foolish: the idea behind the 98-cent (and I can't even find a cent symbol on my keyboard any more) price is to fool you into thinking that "it's less than ten bucks." In truth, merchants would round down to $9.95, saving the consumer billions of paper dollars over the next century.

What's really behind America's clinging to the pesky penny? Nostalgia cannot be the answer; if we can give up the barbershop shave with its steam towels, we can give up anything.

The answer, I think, has to do with zinc, which is what pennies are mostly made of; light copper plating turns them into red cents. The powerful, outsourcing zinc lobby—financed by Canadian mines as well as Alaskan—entices front groups to whip up a frenzy of save-the-penny mail to Congress when coin reform is proposed.

But when the penny is abolished, the nickel will boom. And what is a nickel made of? No, not the metallic element nickel; our five-cent coin is mainly composed of copper. And where is most of America's copper mined? Arizona. If Senator John McCain would get off President Bush's back long enough to serve the economic interests of his Arizona constituents, we'd get some long-overdue coin reform.

What about Lincoln, who has had a century-long run on the penny? He's still honored on the five-dollar bill, and will be as long as the dollar sign remains above the four on keyboards. If this threatens coin reformers with the loss of Illinois votes, put Abe on the dime and bump FDR.

What frazzled pollsters, surly op-ed pages, snarling cable talkfests, and issue-starved candidates for office need is a fresh source of hot-eyed national polarization. Coin reform can close the controversy gap and fill the vitriol void. Get out those bumper stickers: Abolish the penny!

The following brief extemporaneous notes demonstrate how the questions on pages 503–04 might be used to analyze Safire's argument:

Purpose: Ostensibly, Safire seems to be appealing to political decision makers, urging them to stop minting pennies. His flippant comments in the opening paragraph (e.g., "Besides, I need a break"), however, suggest that he's not particularly committed to this proposal and that he doesn't think that there's a great deal at stake. In fact, his stated aim of "re-establish[ing] my contrarian credentials," is not completely tongue-in-cheek: Safire appears to enjoy challenging accepted, conventional beliefs, perhaps only for the sake of doing so. He may get a little more serious in paragraph 10, where he takes a swipe at "the outsourcing zinc lobby." But his suggestion, in the following paragraph, that Senator McCain ought to adopt the same tactics in behalf of Arizona copper mining seems intentionally ironic. And in the final paragraph, where Safire characterizes his proposal as "a fresh source of hot-eyed national polarization" to "fill the vitriol void," it becomes clear that the author has been adopting a somewhat playful stance throughout his essay.

Thesis: Safire presents his thesis explicitly in the first sentence of paragraph 2.

Evidence: Safire presents facts in paragraphs 5 and 6 (two thirds of all newly minted pennies never circulate, and the remaining third number more than 300 million a year); paragraph 7 (the U.S. is the last industrialized nation that still produces pennies); and paragraphs 10 and 11, where he talks about the metallic content of pennies and nickels. Safire reasons inductively in paragraphs 3 and 4, listing things that can't be bought with a penny, to draw an inference: "There is no escaping history. . . ." Safire also cites the testimony of a fellow journalist, John Tierney, and suggests that Abraham Lincoln himself would want to abolish the penny. Much of his argument, however, rests on abstract reasoning and informal observation (paragraphs 6 and 8), which seems appropriate to the light-hearted tone of the essay.

Refutation: Safire makes extensive use of refutation--perhaps even too much so, given his meager commitment to winning an argument or influencing policy in regard to the issue. Here, too, Safire may be engaging in playful overstatement. In paragraph 8, he refutes the argument that abolishing the penny would raise the price of goods; in paragraph 9, he dismisses the notion that nostalgia explains the survival of the penny; and in paragraph 12 he rejects the claim that abolishing the penny would dishonor Abraham Lincoln.

Persona: Safire presents himself as a gadfly, a provocateur who's kind of amused by the "frazzled pollsters, surly op-ed pages, snarling cable talkfests, and issue-starved candidates for office. He seems to be above it all, at least for the time being. This, along with his use of wordplay (e.g., "specious specie," "pass the buck," "penny-pinching") creates. He seems to be having fun with the topic, treating it as an escape, perhaps only temporary, from more controversial issues.

Informal Analysis of Argument

1. Two differing approaches to argument are named *Aristotelian* and *Rogerian* (for the ancient philosopher Aristotle and the modern psychologist named Carl Rogers. Adopting an Aristotelian approach, you try to influence readers by citing authorities and presenting overwhelming evidence to support your views. You silence the opposition by building an irrefutable case. Projecting confidence in your views, you assume that reasonable people will all agree with you. You win; the opposition loses. Adopting a Rogerian approach, you listen to opponents, trying to understand their values and assumptions. According to this view neither side is all wrong; there are various reasonable positions. Therefore, you try to paraphrase your opponents' opinions in a way they can accept. You try to engage in dialogue, seeking a partial solution. You enlist mutual respect and find common goals rather than seeking victory.

   a. What elements of each appeal do you find in William Safire's essay?

   b. What might you change in Safire's essay to make it more Rogerian or more Aristotelian?

2. You are now ready to analyze an argument. Keeping in mind the previous example, read the following editorial by *Newsweek* columnist Robert Samuelson. After reading it, respond to the questions on pages 503–04.

A Cell Phone? Never for Me

Robert Samuelson

Someday soon, I may be the last man in America without a cell phone. To those who see cell phones as progress, I say: they aggravate noise pollution and threaten our solitude. The central idea of cell phones is that you should be connected to almost everyone and everything at all times. The trouble is that cell phones assault your peace of mind no matter what you do. If you turn them off, why have one? You just irritate anyone who might call. If they're on and no one calls, you're irrelevant, unloved or both. If everyone calls, you're a basket case.

I'm a dropout and aim to stay that way. I admit this will be increasingly difficult, because cell phones are now passing a historic milestone. As with other triumphs of the mass market, they've reached a point when people forget what it was like before they existed. No one remembers life before cars, TVs, air conditioners, jets, credit cards, microwave ovens, and ATM cards. So, too, now with cell phones. Anyone without one will soon be classified as a crank or member of the (deep) underclass.

Look at the numbers. In 1985 there were 340,213 cell-phone users. By year-end 2003 there were 159 million. (These figures come from the Cellular Telecommunications and Internet Association, or CTIA.) I had once assumed that age, orneriness, or hearing loss would immunize most of the over-60 population against cell phones. Wrong. Among those 60 to 69, cell-phone ownership (60 percent) is almost as high as among 18- to 24-year-olds (66 percent), though lower than among 30- to 49-year-olds (76 percent), according to a recent survey from the Pew Research Center. Even among those 80 and older, ownership is 32 percent.

Of course, cell phones have productive uses. For those constantly on the road (salesmen, real-estate agents, repair technicians, some managers and reporters), they're a godsend. The same is true for critical workers (doctors, oil-rig firefighters) needed at a moment's notice. Otherwise, benefits seem murky.

They make driving more dangerous, though how much so is unclear. The Insurance Information Institute recently summarized some studies: the Harvard Center for Risk Analysis blamed cell phones for 6 percent of auto accidents each year, involving 2,600 deaths (but admitted that estimates are difficult); the AAA Foundation for Traffic Safety studied videotapes of 70 drivers and concluded that cell phones are distracting, though less so than many other activities (say, stretching for an item in the glove compartment).

Then, there's sheer nuisance. Private conversations have gone public. We've all been subjected to someone else's sales meeting, dinner reservation, family feud, and dating problem. In 2003 cell-phone conversations totaled 830 billion minutes, reckons CTIA. That's about 75 times greater than in 1991 and almost 50 hours for every man, woman, and child in America. How valuable is all this chitchat? The average conversation lasts two-and-a-half to three minutes. Surely many could be postponed or forgotten.

It's true that lots of people like to gab. Cell phones keep them company. Count that as a plus. But it's also true that lots of people dislike being bothered. These are folks who have cell phones but often wish they didn't. A recent poll, sponsored by the Lemelson-MIT program, asked which invention people hated most but couldn't live without. Cell phones won, chosen by 30 percent of respondents.

Some benefits may be overstated. Cell phones for teens were sold as a way for parents to keep tabs on children. That works—up to a point. The point is when your kids switch off the phones. Two of my teens have cell phones (that was Mom's idea; she has one, too). Whenever I want them most, their phones are off. Hmm. Similar advantages are claimed for older people. They have cell phones to allow their children to monitor their health. This may spawn gallows humor on voice-mail messages. (For example: "Hi, Sonny. If you get this, I'm dead.")

Cell phones—and, indeed, all wireless devices—constitute another chapter in the ongoing breakdown between work and everything else. They pretend to increase your freedom while actually stealing it. People are supposed to be always capable of participating in the next meeting, responding to their e-mails or retrieving factoids from the Internet. People so devoted to staying interconnected are kept in a perpetual state of anxiety, because they may have missed some significant memo, rendezvous, bit of news or gossip. They may be more plugged in and less thoughtful.

All this is the wave of the future or, more precisely, the present. According to another survey, two thirds of Americans 16 to 29 would choose a cell phone over a traditional land line. Land lines have already dropped from 189.5 million in 1999 to 181.4 million at the end of 2003, says the Federal Communications Commission. Cell phones, an irresistible force, will soon pull ahead. But I vow to resist just as I've resisted ATM cards, laptops, and digital cameras. I agree increasingly with the late poet Ogden Nash, who wrote: "Progress might have been all right once, but it's gone on too long."

A CRITIQUE OF AN ARGUMENT

As you probably noticed in the previous section, analyzing another writer's argument is an effective way to understand how persuasive texts are constructed. But it can also help you analyze and clarify your own positions and provide the motivation and ideas to compose arguments of your own. Good writers of arguments are good *readers* of arguments.

Before composing an argument, it may be useful to engage in another kind of reading analysis—***critique***. A critique is more formal and objective than the type of analysis described and illustrated in the previous section, though it too expresses opinions. You begin composing a critique by addressing the same questions, but you try to move beyond personal responses and to become more detached and analytical. After expressing your initial reaction to the argument you wish to critique, try to stand back and examine more deliberately the writer's claims and evidence. Above all, try to judge fairly.

To critique is not to find fault. It involves weighing strengths and weaknesses in order to reach a balanced assessment. Of course, it may turn out that, in your judgment, a particular argument is not very sound. That's fine. All you can do is make a sincere effort to analyze its strengths and weaknesses. Your purpose is first to search for the truth and then to write a clearly organized evaluation of the entire argument. Not only does critiquing an argument help you see more clearly what a writer is saying; it also prepares you to write capable, cogent arguments yourself.

The following procedure can be used to critique an argument. Notice how the developing dialogue between you and the writer can lead naturally to a written critique.

Writing a Critique of an Argument   GUIDELINES

Preparation

1. Read the text twice. The second time, read with a pencil, underlining important ideas and writing comments in the margins.

2. Respond to the text subjectively. Freewrite for five minutes, recording any personal responses: agreement, anger, bewilderment, engagement, or any other reaction.

3. Write a brief objective summary of the text without inserting your own ideas.

Analysis

Responding to the questions on pages 503–04, consider each of the following five elements:

- Purpose
- Thesis

- Evidence
- Refutation
- Persona

Writing the Critique

1. Begin with a brief objective summary of the argument and a thesis statement that presents your judgment of the text.

2. Support your thesis by analyzing the evidence presented in the text.

3. Comment on any of the five elements that you consider noteworthy.

Revision

Reread and edit your critique. Ask others to read it. Consider their suggestions as you revise. Prepare your polished draft and proofread it with care.

To observe how this procedure can lead to an effective critique, read the following article by Michelle Cottle, published in the *New Republic*, a magazine of opinion. Cottle disputes the perception that violence in the workplace is a growing menace in the United States. After reading the article, observe how one writer uses the recommended sequence to critique Cottle's argument.

PRACTICE READING

Workplace Worrywarts
The Rise of the "Going Postal" Industry

Michelle Cottle

Look over at the colleague toiling in the next cubicle. Is he a white man in his thirties or forties? Does he seem stressed out? Does he suffer from low self-esteem? Do people suspect he's experiencing personal problems—tiffs with the wife, attitude from the kids? If so, you should start being really, really nice to this guy, because he fits the profile of someone at risk to go berserk one day soon and start blowing away his coworkers like a character in a Tarantino flick.

Don't take my word for it: I learned these tips from a new newsletter called *Workplace Violence Briefings: News You Need to Know*. For $195 a year, you too can receive a monthly dose of anxiety-inducing stats, headlines, and snippets such as "Routine HR Activities Can Trigger Violence" and "Why the Risk of Workplace Violence Will Increase." Also included are quickie articles on prevention: "Watch for These Subtle Warning Signs of Impending Violence," "Similarities in the Backgrounds of Those Who Erupt in Violence," "How to Say 'No' Diplomatically." Most valuable of all, the newsletter provides contact info for myriad experts in the now white-hot field of workplace violence prevention.

It was bound to happen. In response to growing fear of high-profile workplace tragedies—the most sensational recent example being [the] Atlanta massacre, in which day trader Mark Barton went on a shooting spree that left nine dead and thirteen wounded—a cottage industry of consultants has sprung up, pledging to protect your organization from a similar fate. While such rampages may seem frighteningly random, consultants insist they are able to employ a variety of tools to identify and defuse potentially bloody situations: employee background checks, profiles to screen out unbalanced job applicants, manager training to help spot on-the-edge employees, security systems to keep out angry people with weapons, and so on. Costs vary depending on what you want and how many employees will participate: basic training videos are a few hundred dollars, while comprehensive programs and security systems can easily hit six figures.

Companies of every size and flavor are signing on: Mazda, CalTrans, the city of San Francisco, the state of New Jersey—even the U.S. Air Force. Some clients want help addressing an existing "situation"—a disgruntled ex-employee or friction among coworkers. Others simply hope to guard against the chaos they're seeing on television; most consultants say that in the wake of media events such as Columbine and Atlanta, demand for their services rises dramatically.

Such a response is understandable—but unfortunate. Many prevention programs are a monumental waste. Sure, there's a chance your organization can reduce—though never eliminate—the risk of "an incident." But, for the vast majority of businesses, the additional margin of safety will not be worth the necessary investment of time, money, and emotional energy. And that doesn't even factor in the intangible social cost of promoting the idea that employers are somehow responsible for shielding us against not only foreseeable hazards such as shoddy equipment or toxic substances but also the most irrational, unpredictable tendencies of our fellow man.

Forget what you think you know from the media. There is no epidemic of deadly workplace violence; in fact, fatalities are down almost twenty percent from 1992. Last year, the Bureau of Labor Statistics put the total number of workplace homicides at 709—just seven more than the number of workers killed by falling from a roof, scaffold, or other lofty perch. Still, if that figure makes you nervous, there are basic steps you can take to safeguard your person. Number one: Don't drive a taxi. Cabbies have long endured the highest death rate of any occupation: between 1990 and 1992, forty-one of every 100,000 were killed on the job. You should also steer clear of jobs at liquor stores or gas stations. More than seventy-five percent of workplace homicides in this country occur during the commission of another crime, such as robbery. Referred to as Type I violence, these attacks are perpetrated by strangers seeking money, not coworkers seeking vengeance.

Other employees at increased risk of violence are police officers, prison guards, security guards, and health care workers. They face what the state of California calls Type II violence, "an assault by someone who is either the recipient or the object of a service provided by the affected workplace or the victim" (e.g., getting injured or killed while trying to restrain a violent convict or mental patient).

Obviously, we don't want to downplay these dangers. There are concrete precautions that employers can and should take to improve worker safety in high-risk fields: installing security cameras, additional lighting, bulletproof partitions, lock-drop safes, and panic buttons. Similarly, the Occupational Safety and Health Administration (OSHA) has violence-prevention guidelines for the health-care industry.

More and more, however, what companies are angsting about—and what consultants are focusing on—is Type III violence, which consists not only of coworker rampages but also of instances in which domestic discord spills over into the workplace, and a crazed husband storms into the office itching to teach his woman (and anyone else who crosses his path) a brutal lesson. "Companies are looking to prevent the sensational stuff," says Richard Fascia, president of Jeopardy Management Group in Cranston, Rhode Island.

For consultants, the advantages of specializing in Type III violence prevention are clear. Although Type III episodes occur far less frequently than do other types, their random nature means that essentially any organization is a candidate for prevention counseling. ("Everyone needs it—absolutely," says Dana Picore, a Los Angeles cop-turned-consultant.) Moreover, while the owner of the corner liquor store might be loath to drop big bucks on violence prevention, the management of a large accounting firm might not even blink at the cost. Thus, instead of targeting the industries hardest hit by violence, the market is becoming saturated with employment attorneys, clinical psychologists, and retired law-enforcement agents clamoring to advise you on how to keep the Mark Bartons at bay. There has been "an explosion of training, an explosion of consultants," says Joseph A. Kinney, president of the National Safe Workplace Institute, a consulting firm in Charlotte, North Carolina.

So why should we care if some hysterical human-resources managers fall for the latest consulting craze? Put aside the practical matter that there are almost certainly better ways to spend corporate (or government) resources. In a broader sense, this trend just isn't healthy: bringing in a high-paid consultant to talk at length about what to do if a colleague decides to try a little target shooting in the executive washroom is just as likely to exacerbate our collective fears as to alleviate them. "If we have big programs to counter a danger, then the danger must be large—or so our reasoning goes," says Barry Glassner, a professor of sociology at the University of Southern California and the author of *The Culture of Fear*. "The more programs we have and the bigger they get, the bigger the problem seems. . . . In fact, we're living in about the safest time in human history."

Consultants counter that they're concerned with preventing not only homicides but also the more common eruptions of low-level violence: shouting matches in the boardroom, abusive language, fistfights on the loading dock. But it's clearly the sensational killings they want employers to think of. The Web site of one Sacramento consultant features graphics depicting bullet holes and exploding bombs and cautions: "We often hire the person that kills us. It is the killer in our ranks that we must address. . . ." Another firm's ad sucks you in with the words "HE'S GOT A GUN!" in bold red letters.

Then, of course, there are the two words guaranteed to make any manager's blood run cold: *legal liability*. Consultants note that, while they cannot guarantee you a violence-free work environment, they can protect you from lawsuits if something does occur. They are quick to cite the "general duty" clause of the Occupational Safety and Health Act, which requires employers to guard against "recognized hazards" in the workplace. All Safety Training's Web site shrieks, "If you have employees, you have a Workplace Violence problem! Because you are required to provide a safe workplace, you can be held liable, and your costs can run into the MILLIONS of dollars!"

But this threat, too, is wildly overstated. OSHA has no specific guidelines on the Type III violence most companies fear. The agency has issued safety recommendations for high-risk workplaces, such as late-night retail establishments, but it is exceedingly vague about what it expects from, say, brokerage firms. "It's very rare that workers are able to sue employers for workplace violence," says Charles Craver, a professor of employment law at George Washington University. Because of the broad immunity workers'-comp laws provide employers, "in most assault-type cases, the recourse against an employer is solely workers' compensation," he explains. There are rare exceptions—if, for example, there's proof that an employer deliberately injured workers or that the company negligently brought someone on board whom they knew, or suspected, to be prone to violent behavior. But the burden of proof is high. As long as a company behaved with "reasonable care," says Craver, the suit will likely go nowhere.

This is not to imply that consultants are preying on our fear simply to make a fast buck. Many of them got into the field after years in law enforcement and are painfully aware of the dark side of human nature. They speak movingly of the tragedies they have witnessed on the job and of lives shattered by violence. But do we really want to adopt their understandably paranoid perspective in our workplaces? This seems an unreasonably high price to pay to combat what is, in reality, a blessedly marginal danger.

Here is a freewritten response to Cottle's article:

> Cottle pooh-poohs the popular belief that workplace violence has reached epidemic proportions. Writers for magazines like the New Republic often display skepticism of widely held views and disdain for conventional wisdom. I kind of admire that stance because, in this case, a writer who scoffs at our fears of violence or questions the reactions of people who have been affected by violence will be suspected of insensitivity. So I see Cottle as kind of gutsy. However, I find myself irritated by her heavy sarcasm and mocking tone. I resist her assertion that safety carries a self-evident price tag—her confidence that a cool-headed reckoning of costs and benefits can lead us to a fair, cheap, and easy solution to the problem. She belittles her opposition, dismissing their fears as hysterical. Frankly, I'm even inclined to mistrust her use of statistics and expert opinion. Near the end of her article, she seems concerned mainly with the bottom line for employers: Don't worry, you won't get sued.

Freewritten response

This freewriting explores an initial, subjective response. The following objective summary provides perspective:

> Michelle Cottle argues that experts in the field of violence prevention are exaggerating the dangers posed by employees who carry personal stress into the workplace. Cottle suggests that consulting firms exploit fears aroused by the Columbine massacre and the shooting spree in an Atlanta office building. She also implies that these firms offer false hope that random, irrational acts of violence can be anticipated and prevented. Cottle distinguishes violence that occurs in dangerous working environments, like liquor stores and prisons, from violence caused by stress and other factors affecting the personal lives of mentally unstable employees. She claims that some consultants have used scare tactics to persuade companies to waste time and money on services of dubious value.

Objective summary

An informal analysis of the article helps prepare the writer to draft a formal critique:

Informal
analysis

Purpose: Cottle tries to persuade employers that irrational violence is, by its very nature, random and unpredictable. She urges them not to overestimate the likelihood that this type of violence will erupt in any given workplace and warns of the scare tactics that consulting agencies use to market their services as an effective deterrent to violence. She argues that the advertising claims of consultants are misleading, that the costs of their services exceed any plausible benefit, and that they deliberately exaggerate dangers in hopes of gaining clients. She ridicules the fear of violence, characterizing it as the "hysterical" response of "worrywarts" influenced by a current "craze." However, Cottle is so derisive of both the fear of violence and the methods of consultants that it is not completely clear whether she is more committed to persuading readers than she is to winning an argument by belittling her opponents.

Thesis: Cottle states her thesis in paragraph 5: "Many prevention programs are a monumental waste," adding that "for the vast majority of businesses, the additional margin of safety will not be worth the investment of time, money, and emotional energy."

Evidence: Cottle quotes the newsletters and advertising literature of consulting agencies, comparing their exaggerated claims to data provided by the U.S. Bureau of Labor Statistics (from which she also derives the classifications of violence discussed in paragraphs 6-10). Is this fair? Advertising, in general, appeals to the emotions and rarely provides thorough, objective facts about products or services. For example, does anyone expect TV ads for children's cereal to offer detailed, reliable information about nutrition or preservatives? (Perhaps Cottle would argue that consultants, many of whom are former police officers, ought to uphold a higher standard of ethics.) She seeks to buttress her criticism of consultants by quoting two university professors (Glassner and Craver), though the first of these sounds like it may have been taken out of context. However, she undermines the appearance of fairness and objectivity by introducing one quotation from a consulting firm's brochure with the word shrieks.

Refutation: Cottle seems more concerned with destroying the arguments of her opponents than with affirming her own point of view. The first instance of refutation appears in paragraph 5 when she concedes that fear of violence is "understandable--but unfortunate." She also acknowledges that organizations can reduce safety risks, though she adds that the possibility of violence is never eliminated. But she dismisses these reservations by arguing that the cost of any "additional margin of safety" far outweighs the benefits. In her next paragraph, Cottle anticipates and refutes the argument that news reports offer proof of a rise in workplace violence: "Forget what you think you know from the media." (A familiar ploy: "the media" are constantly blamed for exaggerating problems while overlooking the "real" story.) In paragraph 8, Cottle deflects accusations of insensitivity by saying, "Obviously, we don't want to downplay" the risk of Types I and II violence. But she cleverly uses this concession to trivialize Type III violence, the kind that "companies are angsting about" (another derisive phrase). In paragraph 11, Cottle addresses the why-should-we-care argument. In this case, her tactic is to pass over or "put aside" a supposedly stronger argument in support of her position (there are better ways to spend money than to hire consultants) in favor of a simpler, presumably irrefutable assertion (validating fears of violence "isn't healthy"). It's as if she's saying, "Let me save time here." Also, any skeptics inclined to quibble are served warning that she's holding more powerful ammunition in reserve. Cottle then refutes the claim that consultants may alleviate less ominous types of workplace stress by citing the emotional appeals found in some of their advertisements. (But does this really prove that consultants <u>can't</u> help companies reduce the likelihood of verbal abuse and fistfights?) Concluding her argument, Cottle adopts the "I'm-not-saying-that..." strategy: "This is not to imply that consultants are preying on our fear simply to make a fast buck." Though she seems to acknowledge the sincerity of "many" consultants, Cottle asks readers whether "we really want to adopt their understandable paranoid perspective." (Are "paranoid" views <u>ever</u> understandable? Isn't this another instance of loaded diction?)

<u>Persona</u>: Cottle relies on some of the emotional appeals that she imputes to consultants. Her language is inflated. "Hysterical" personnel managers are falling prey to a momentary "craze"; advertisements for consulting services "shriek"; former law enforcement officers are "paranoid"; attorneys and clinical psychologists "clamor" to offer their services. She tries to belittle consultants, portraying them as hucksters who hope to "suck you in" with "quickie" answers and describing their services as a new "cottage industry" in "the now white-hot field of workplace violence prevention."

On the other hand, when Cottle refers to acts of violence, she uses understatement and euphemism--words like "situation" and "incident," placed in quotation marks as if to distance herself from popular jargon. In paragraph 6, she adopts a condescending tone: among the "basic steps you can take to safeguard your person" is not to drive a taxi. In other words, causes and remedies are so self-evident that no one needs to hire a consultant to recognize what they are.

Having developed some ideas, the writer is ready to draft her critique. Notice that she begins objectively with a summary and explanation of Cottle's argument, then examines its persuasiveness, and finally expresses reservations and disagreement.

A Critique of Michelle Cottle's "Workplace Worrywarts"

Michelle Cottle, writing for the New Republic, argues that news reports often sensationalize the menace of the deranged office employee and thereby exaggerate the danger of workplace violence. Fears aroused by these reports play into the hands of consultants who offer programs aimed at minimizing the risk of violence perpetrated by stressed-out workers. Cottle believes that hiring these consultants wastes money and jeopardizes employee morale by propagating the mistaken belief that workplace violence has reached epidemic proportions. While Cottle may be correct in claiming that violence is sensationalized, she weakens her argument by adopting a contentious stance, ridiculing the fears of employers and attributing greedy opportunism to consultants.

To show how consulting agencies exploit fears of workplace violence, Cottle cites ominous headlines from a trade publication that she derides as "a monthly dose of anxiety-inducing stats, headlines, and snippets." She

acknowledges, however, that these scare tactics fuel a demand
for programs, often expensive, that are supposed to
anticipate and prevent seemingly random acts of violence.
Cottle finds this demand "understandable--but unfortunate"
because it causes companies to waste money and encourages
workers to blame employers for hazards that no one can
foresee. She also contends that the fear-mongering of
consultants has obscured a statistical decline in workplace
violence and diverted attention from the more preventable
hazards of truly dangerous work like driving a taxi or
working in a liquor store or a prison. Cottle distinguishes
between reasonable efforts to enhance the security of workers
who are logical targets of crime and futile attempts to avoid
violence brought on by stress or mental illness. She
concludes that consultants exaggerate the danger of these
random, unpredictable events and mislead employers about
their responsibility to prevent them. Cottle is most
persuasive when she supports her case with data provided by
the Bureau of Labor Statistics. However, the fact that 709
homicides occurred on the job last year is not reassuring,
even though it is "just" seven more deaths than were caused
by falling. Cottle responds to this objection glibly: persons
troubled by the statistic should consider the risks of
driving a cab or working in a liquor store--as if concern for
personal safety were unjustified so long as anyone else has
to face greater danger. Police officers, prison wardens,
security guards, and others who perform hazardous work
usually enter their careers conscious of the risks;
persons who choose other fields of work cannot be blamed
for wanting to avoid comparable, or even lesser,
dangers.

More troublesome are the logical fallacies in Cottle's argument. Having argued that office work is safer than many other types of employment, Cottle sets up a false dilemma: "instead of targeting the industries hardest hit by crime," consultants are exploiting a "market saturated with employment attorneys, clinical psychologists, and retired law enforcement agents clamoring to advise" companies about the less urgent needs of office workers. Shouldn't we find ways to improve everyone's security? A similar fallacy appears in Cottle's quotation from Barry Glassner's book The Culture of Fear, which blames programs designed to remedy problems for magnifying public perceptions of problems. Assuring modern workers that they live "in about the safest time in human history" is hardly different from telling coal miners and factory workers of the nineteenth century that, compared to the Middle Ages, they lived during a time of extraordinary comfort, security, and opportunity.

Another weakness in Cottle's argument is the assumption that we can calculate the value of safety. When Cottle says that any "additional margin of safety will not be worth the necessary investment of time, money, and emotional energy," she speaks for employers; workers might hold a different view. Later, disputing claims that safety programs reduce the risk of liability, Cottle offers reassurance in Professor Craver's statement that employees are not likely to win lawsuits involving workplace violence. If the danger has been so irresponsibly exaggerated, why does Cottle go to such pains to show how companies are not liable?

Finally, Cottle seems too intent on overwhelming opponents in a debate that need not end with a triumphant victor and a silenced loser. She alienates uncommitted readers by denigrating the field of consulting as a "craze" or "a cottage industry" in a "white-hot field," consultants as opportunists who "clamor" and "shriek," managers of human resources as "hysterical," and much of the public as "worrywarts." Readers who come to the article with little prior knowledge are offered a polarized view in which the author concedes only that her opponents are "understandably paranoid." Most fair-minded readers will recognize that few issues are quite so clearcut.

You may not agree with this critique. Although the writer attempts to weigh the strengths and weaknesses of "Workplace Worrywarts," she is influenced by what she considers an unfair presentation of opposing arguments and is alienated by Cottle's combative, Aristotelian approach to argument. Note that the critique acknowledges these subjective responses (biases, perhaps) yet strives to be fair and logical and that some of the writer's irritation, expressed in the informal analysis, is removed or modulated in the critique. Any analysis of an argument should be rigorous and balanced, but in writing a critique, you should be clear about your own views. An issue worth debating has more than one side, and not everyone can be brought to the same position. Another reader might find Cottle's argument valid and therefore view this critique as unduly harsh. A critique of an argument balances objective and subjective judgments. You may want to try your own critique of Cottle's essay.

EXERCISES | Writing a Critique of an Argument

1. How successful is this critique of Michelle Cottle's argument? Has the writer been fair in her judgments? Are her arguments reasonable? Did she miss something that you would have commented on? Which writer do you find more convincing, Cottle or the author of the critique? Is there a part of each writer's opinion that makes sense to you? How might each be made more persuasive?

2. Now it is your turn. Use the procedures presented in this section to compose a polished written critique of the following essay by George C. Edwards, III, Distinguished Professor of Political Science at Texas A&M University and author of the recently published book *Why the Electoral College Is Bad for America*. Use your own ideas to evaluate the author's arguments. Remember that a critique is not necessarily an attack on another person's argument; you may find yourself agreeing with someone whose writing you critique. Your critique should address whatever successes and flaws you find in the text you analyze.

It's Really the Selectoral or Ejectoral College and Needs to Go

George C. Edwards, III

It is difficult to imagine a definition of democracy that does not include equality in voting as a central standard for a democratic process. Because political equality is central to democratic government, we must evaluate any mechanism for selecting the president against it.

In 2000, the presidential candidate who received the most votes lost the election. In 2004, a switch of fewer than 60,000 votes in Ohio from George W. Bush to John Kerry would have elected Kerry, even though Bush would still have had a majority of the national vote and a margin of more than 3 million votes. The Electoral College is a capricious system favoring the votes of some citizens over others, depending solely upon the state in which they live.

All but two states award all their electoral votes to the plurality winner of the state. Nearly 3 million people voted for Al Gore for president in Florida in 2000. Because George W. Bush won 537 more statewide votes than Gore, however, he received all of Florida's electoral votes; the votes for Gore played no role in the national election.

In multiple-candidate contests (as in 1992, 1996, and 2000), this system may suppress the votes of the majority as well as the minority. In 2000, pluralities rather than majorities determined the allocation of electoral votes in nine states, including Florida. In each case, a minority of voters determined how all of their state's electoral votes would be cast.

A candidate thus can win some states by very narrow margins, lose other states by large margins, and win the electoral vote while losing the popular vote. The votes for candidates who do not finish first in a state election play no role in the outcome of the election, since they are not aggregated across states. The winner-take-all system takes the electoral votes allocated to a state based on its population and awards them all to the plurality winner of the state. In effect, the system gives the votes of the people who voted against the winner to the winner.

VOTE VALUES VARY

The Constitution allocates electoral votes to each state based on that state's representation in Congress. Each state receives two electoral votes corresponding to its number of U.S. senators. When states with unequal populations receive similar numbers of electoral votes, states with smaller populations gain a mathematical advantage. Thus, every voter's ballot does not carry the same weight. The typical citizen of Wyoming has on average four times as much influence in determining an electoral vote for president as the typical citizen of California and twice as much influence as the typical citizen of Texas.

In addition, under the Electoral College third-party candidates like Ralph Nader in 2000 may actually determine the outcome of the election. There is little question that Nader cost Gore the election in 2000. Most Nader voters would have voted for Gore in the absence of a Nader candidacy. Gore lost Florida by 537 votes, while Nader received 97,488 votes in that state. Pat Buchanan and the Libertarian candidate Harry Browne received a total of only 33,899, which were more likely to have otherwise gone to Bush.

Similarly, Gore lost New Hampshire by 7,211 votes while Nader received 22,198 votes. Buchanan and Browne together received 5,372 votes. Gore would have been elected if he had won either state.

THIS HOUSE IS NOT YOUR HOUSE

If no candidate receives a majority of the Electoral College vote, the House of Representatives selects the president. In this selection, every state has one vote. It would be possible for the seven members of the House representing the seven smallest states, with a combined population of about 4.9 million Americans, to have more say in the selection of the president than the 177 members representing the six largest states, with a combined population of 119 million people. The selection of the president by the House is the most egregious violation of democratic principles in American politics.

One net result of these distorting factors is that the candidate who receives the most votes in the country may not win the election, as happened in 1824, 1876, 1888, 1960 (as I demonstrate in my book *Why the Electoral College Is Bad for America*), and 2000.

The Electoral College distorts the preferences of Americans and thus the results of presidential elections. It violates political equality, favoring some citizens over others, depending solely upon the state in which people cast their votes for president. Can we reconcile such a selection system with the ideal of political equality, one of the most deeply ingrained of democratic principles? We cannot.

CONSENSUS WINNERS?

According to its supporters, one of the primary virtues of the Electoral College is that candidates must obtain concurrent majorities from around the country in order to win. In other words, these advocates argue, by guaranteeing a specific number of electoral votes to each state, the Electoral College forces the winner to pay attention to all regions of the country and to build broad coalitions by winning a wide geographic distribution of states that helps his coalition mirror the nation.

If states did not employ the unit rule by allocating all their electoral votes as a bloc, the argument goes, candidates might appeal to clusters of voters whose votes could be aggregated across states and regions. This could be potentially divisive and lead to discord because the coalition behind a candidate might represent only one part of society.

Electoral College advocates build their case about its virtues on a set of faulty premises. Do candidates try to build broad national coalitions by appealing to voters throughout the nation? Except in a superficial fashion, the candidates of both parties virtually ignore large sections of the country.

For example, in the presidential election of 2000, one of the most competitive elections in history, the Electoral College distorted the political system by providing incentives for candidates to campaign actively in only 17 "battleground" states, and largely to ignore the other 33 states and Washington, D.C. The candidates made few visits and did little or no advertising in the Great Plains, the Rockies, the Deep South, and the Southwest—except for New Mexico. The candidates displayed a similar pattern in 2004.

With a few exceptions, small states were not among the "battleground" states. Indeed, it is difficult to imagine how presidential candidates could be less attentive to small states. Under direct election of the president, candidates would be much more attentive to small states. They would have incentives to appeal to all voters, not just those strategically located in swing states.

Do candidates actually win support across regions? Anyone examining the red and blue states on an election-night map knows that candidates tend to win with regional support. John Kerry and Al Gore won the West Coast, the Northeast and the Upper Midwest, while George W. Bush won the South, the Mountain States and the rural Midwest.

Do winning candidates receive majority support across social strata? In 2000, George W. Bush did not win a larger percentage than Al Gore of the votes cast by women, blacks, Hispanics, Asian-Americans, the elderly, the poor, members of labor unions, those with a high-school education or less, those with postgraduate education, Catholics, Jews, liberals, moderates, urbanites, those with less than $50,000 of household income, voters aged 18 to 29 and 60 and older—in addition to those living in the East and West. It is no criticism of the winner, but his vote simply did not represent winning concurrent majorities across the major strata of American society.

Is there a chance that a candidate under direct election could win a plurality of the vote by carrying one big state by a large margin but win no other states? Could a candidate enjoy extraordinary support in a state as diverse as, say, California, and lack substantial support in other areas of the country? Such a scenario is quite farfetched. There is nothing in American history that would lead one to believe that such an outcome is a realistic possibility.

The Electoral College did not prevent class appeals by Democratic candidates such as Franklin D. Roosevelt in 1936 or Harry Truman in 1948. Nor did it prevent the election of ideologues on the right such as Ronald Reagan in 1980 and 1984 and George W. Bush in 2000 and 2004. These, and others, were polarizing elections in which differences of opinion among the coalitions supporting the candidates were considerable.

If Al Gore had received 538 more votes in Florida in 2000, he would have been elected president. If Ralph Nader had not been on the ballot in either Florida or New Hampshire in 2000, Gore would have won.

Advocates of the Electoral College are in the position of having to argue that Bush was the proper winner but that if either of these changes had occurred, Gore would have been the proper winner—proper because the Electoral College elected him—even though Bush's coalition would not have changed by one vote. Such an argument is simply nonsense.

STATES' INTERESTS

Some argue that the Electoral College balances local and national interests, protecting small states from majoritarian politics. It is not clear what might be protected.

States do not embody coherent, unified interests to protect. Even the smallest state has substantial diversities of interest and opinion within it. Thus, Alaska may have a Democratic governor and two Republican senators, and Montana and North and South Dakota can vote for Republican presidential candidates and then send two liberal Democrats—now minus one, Tom Daschle—to the U.S. Senate.

Nor is there a need for protection. Given the many constraints the Constitution places on the actions that simple majorities can take, the Senate's extraordinary representation of small states, the power of the Senate filibuster to thwart majorities, and the difficulty of changing these rules, it strains credulity to argue that certain geographically concentrated interests require additional protection from the majoritarian political process.

States with small populations do not have common interests to protect. Instead, they represent a great diversity of core economic interests, including mining, gambling, chemicals, tourism, energy, and agriculture, ranging from grain and dairy products to hogs and sheep. Most farmers live in states with large populations, such as California, Texas, Florida, and Illinois. It is not surprising that small-state representatives don't vote as a bloc in Congress or that their citizens don't vote as a bloc for president. The great political battles of American history have been over ideology and economic interests rather than between small and large states.

Do presidents focus on local interests in building their electoral coalitions? They do not. We have seen that candidates ignore most of the country in their campaigns. In addition, I have shown in my book that candidates do not focus on local interests in the states in which they do campaign.

Nowhere in the vast literature on voting in presidential elections has anyone found that voters choose candidates on the basis of their stands on state and local issues. Indeed, candidates avoid such issues, because they do not want to be seen in the rest of the country as pandering to special local interests. In addition, once elected the president has little to do with local issues. There is no reason and certainly no imperative to campaign on these issues.

Two of the most important architects of the Constitution, James Wilson and James Madison, understood well the diversity of state interests and the protections of minorities embodied in the Constitution. They saw little need to confer additional power to small states through the Electoral College. "Can we forget for whom we are forming a government?" Wilson asked. "Is it for men, or for the imaginary beings called States?" Madison was equally dubious, proclaiming that experience had shown no danger of state interests being harmed and that "the President is to act for the people not for States."

Congress is designed to be responsive to constituency interests. The president, as Madison pointed out, is to take a broader view. When advocates of the Electoral College express concern that direct election of the president would suppress local interests in favor of the broader national interest, they are supporting a presidency responsive to parochial interests in a system that is already prone to gridlock, and that offers minority interests extraordinary access to policymakers and opportunities to thwart policies they oppose.

The Electoral College violates basic democratic principles and does not offer the country benefits to compensate for this disadvantage. We do not require a runoff between the top two candidates. We elect presidents without majority votes all the time (as in 1992, 1996 and 2000).

What we need to do is to count all the votes and declare the candidate who receives the most votes the winner.

 AN ARGUMENTATIVE RESEARCH ESSAY

In writing a critique, you respond to another writer's argument. You express agreement or disagreement—or some of each. In any case, you cannot avoid an argumentative approach. Still, you are responding to an argument rather than making one. This section will prepare you to write an argument of your own, perhaps one that others will want to critique. In particular, we will focus on writing an argumentative essay that is also a research paper—that is, one that uses sources to inform and support its argument, thereby gaining authority and credibility.

Dozens of books are devoted exclusively to the complexities of argumentative writing. The subject has a long scholarly tradition that goes all the way back to Aristotle's *Rhetoric*, a study of argument still used as a text to teach theories and tactics for persuading audiences.

Arguments take so many forms—writers can find so many different ways to persuade readers—that there is no easy formula for argumentative writing. We can offer suggestions, however. Like other types of academic writing, an argumentative research paper can seem intimidating if you have had little experience in composing one before. With practice, however, you can learn to argue effectively and persuasively. As you did when you critiqued the arguments of others, you need to pay attention to the principal elements that constitute an argument. The following sections discuss important ideas to consider whenever you write an argument.

Purpose

The best advice is to have a genuine reason to persuade others and to keep that reason in mind as you write. Argue about a topic you care about and believe in. Argue because you feel it is important for others to learn the truth. Argue to make the world a better place. Without commitment, argument becomes an empty exercise, offering little prospect for success or satisfaction. But when you pursue an objective you care about, argument can be an exciting, fulfilling activity—and one at which you are likely to succeed.

Although commitment is important, it is also wise to keep an open mind, willing to be persuaded yourself when better ideas and new information present themselves. The purpose of college writing, as we have suggested, is not to win a contest or wield power; rather, it is to test ideas in a sincere search for truth. To that end, you must be honest and fair, while upholding your duty to present the views you believe in as effectively as possible.

Thesis

Although writers of arguments may feel at times that they can be more effective by disguising actual objectives, college writers should make their aims clear to readers. State your thesis in a sentence or two, early in your paper.

Not every thesis is worth arguing. The thesis you write about should meet the following criteria:

- It should be **controversial**. You should argue a claim about which reasonable people can disagree. Instead of claiming that pollution is dangerous (a point that few people would dispute), you could argue for or against restricting the production of vehicles with internal-combustion engines.

- It should be **arguable**. Argue a thesis that is open to objective analysis. Instead of arguing that racquetball is more fun than tennis (a matter of personal taste), you could argue that racquetball promotes cardiovascular health more effectively than tennis does. Research can examine this claim, evidence can be collected, and readers can draw conclusions based on objective criteria.

- It should be **clearly defined**. Words and phrases like *freedom, law and order, murder,* and *obscenity* may seem perfectly clear to you, but friendships and even lives have been lost over differing interpretations of "obvious" terms.

You can argue for removing pornography from television, but if you do, you must make very clear what you mean by pornography and propose some reasonable method of testing whether a show is pornographic.

Audience

Construct your argument with a particular audience in mind. Whom do you want to persuade? Who will be reading your argument? What do your readers expect from you and you from them? Why might they ignore you, and what can you do to avoid that? The tone of your writing, the language you use, and the sophistication of your evidence must all be adjusted to the interests, values, and education of your readers. What appeals to first-year college students may fail miserably with students in either junior high or graduate school. Arguments must be tailored to specific audiences.

It is not dishonest to write in different ways for different readers. Sometimes it is important to withhold a belief that you know will offend or alienate readers. Mature people know not to utter every thought that comes to mind. If diplomats at the United Nations said exactly what they thought of each other, there would be few civil discussions. You cannot get people even to listen to your argument if you threaten them or make them feel defensive. If you are addressing readers who disagree with you, try to understand their point of view, to view reality from their perspective. Not only will this allow you to explore issues more thoroughly; it will also help you present your own argument more effectively.

Persona

When you write an argument, you should be acutely aware of how you sound to your audience. You want to project an image appropriate to the situation at hand. You may adopt the role of a concerned environmentalist, a crusading member of the student senate, or a frustrated commuter campaigning for additional parking places. Each of these personas can be adopted sincerely at various times by the same writer. Being yourself means being flexible as well as honest.

Regardless of how well researched and carefully constructed your arguments are, you must sound trustworthy in order to appear credible. To establish trust, you must maintain a reasonable tone. Extreme statements and emotional rhetoric work fine at pep rallies or in sermons to the already converted, but they can repel the undecided as well as those who disagree with you. You should resist the temptation to belittle your opponents or to engage in name-calling. Shocking an audience may make you feel better, but rarely does it help you appear balanced and fair. Readers need to feel rapport with a writer before they will alter their opinions.

Evidence

In supporting your thesis, you can make emotional appeals, as advertising does, or you can present facts and logical inferences, as participants in scientific debates strive to do. Argumentative writing often presents both kinds of support.

What you should avoid, however, is the kind of emotional appeal that aims only at the fears and insecurities of readers. On the other hand, you should avoid a persona so coldly impersonal that your essay may as well have been written by a computer.

Since the ideas you present in an argumentative essay reflect your thinking and personality, your own voice should come through. On the other hand, it is important to win your readers' trust through the authority of your evidence. Research can help. Sources lend support to your thesis, but they also provide evidence, convincing readers that you have studied your topic carefully enough to be trusted. Library research may be most appropriate when you are arguing about a controversy that has received public attention, such as gun control or drunk-driving laws. Observation, interviews, or questionnaires may be appropriate in researching a local issue or original proposal, such as a plan to improve food services on your campus.

Opposition

Remember that any point worth arguing will arouse opposing points of view. You must acknowledge this in your essay. And you must do so in a way that is fair to those with whom you disagree. People do not usually cooperate or alter their beliefs when they feel threatened; instead, they become defensive and rigid. You increase your credibility when you admit that those who differ with you are reasonable. You should also realize that since alert readers will think of counter-arguments, it is wise to anticipate any objections and try to refute them. Experienced writers do this briefly, realizing that they don't need to devastate their opponents. Let readers see that you understand the complexity of an issue; then give a reasonable, brief response to opposing arguments. You will seem more trustworthy if you acknowledge other points of view as well as defending your own.

Organization

You can organize your essay in various ways, but you may find the following arrangement helpful, particularly in a first attempt at argumentative writing:

1. *Introduction.* Provide background information so that your readers are informed about the controversy; then state your thesis.
2. *Evidence.* Support your thesis. (This will be the longest part of your essay.)
3. *Opposition.* Acknowledge and refute opposing points of view.
4. *Conclusion.* Draw conclusions from the evidence so as to reaffirm your thesis.

You are now ready to research and write an argumentative essay.

Write an argumentative essay in support of a thesis that you believe in. It can be about a national controversy, a local issue, or a proposal. Support your thesis with evidence from research as well as your own reasoning. You can invent a purpose and an audience for your essay if you choose. For example, you can write it in the form of a letter to your college board of trustees, petitioning greater support for the women's intramural program. Acknowledge your sources with parenthetical notes and provide a list of works cited.

 ## A SAMPLE ARGUMENTATIVE ESSAY

Following is an argumentative research essay written by a first-year college student named Ellie Stephens. Ellie wrote on the topic of Title IX, a milestone in gender equity. You may not agree with Ellie's conclusions, but notice how she has used research to explore ideas and bolster her opinions. The result is a paper with great credibility. As readers, we cannot dismiss Ellie's opinions as uninformed; instead, we note the care she has used to research the topic, and we are obliged to treat her presentation with respect.

Stephens 1

Ellie Stephens

English 201

Professor Kathleen Hallmark

14 March 2003

Title IX: Leveling the Playing Fields

The signing of Title IX on June 23, 1972, is now regarded as a milestone in gender equity. At the time of its adoption, few people anticipated the impact that this federal law would have on sports and recreation in the United States. But in the years that followed, thousands of female athletes enjoyed opportunities unavailable to their mothers. Today, Title IX is under attack, accused of promoting the very thing it was intended to prohibit: discrimination based on gender. As unfair and exaggerated as these accusations are, the best strategy for preserving the benefits of Title IX is to support proposed modifications aimed at appeasing its most vocal critics. Suitably amended, Title IX can still carry out its fundamental purpose of leveling the playing field for men and women. Its repeal would be a severe setback.

Critics of Title IX often overlook the discriminatory conditions that the law was designed to remedy. George Bryjak, Professor of Sociology at the University of San Diego, details some of those conditions:

Stephens 2

In 1961, nine states prohibited interscholastic sports for females. On the eve of Title IX in 1971, a mere 7.5% of the almost 4,000,000 high-school student-athletes were girls. . . . Prior to Title IX, women comprised 15% of college athletes, but received 2% of the total athletic budget. While male teams often traveled via first-class accommodations paid for by the athletic department, women's teams were forced to make expenses by way of bake sales, car washes, and raffles.

Since they cannot dispute the historical record, critics of Title IX focus their attacks on the use of "proportionality" as a measure of compliance. One provision of the law stipulates that the ratio of male to female athletes should correspond (within one to three percent) with the proportion of men and women enrolled in the institution. Critics stigmatize this provision of Title IX as an imposition of mandatory quotas. Such quotas, they claim, ignore relative levels of interest among men and women and thus promote gender equity at the expense of popular, well-established programs for men. They cite, for example, curtailed funding for male wrestling and gymnastics teams in some colleges.

Stephens 3

This, admittedly, has been an unfortunate consequence of Title IX, but it results from voluntary choices by athletic directors in response to the law's mandates, rather than from any directives contained in the law itself. Title IX does not require colleges to reduce their support for men's teams. Instead, says Peg Bradley-Doppes, president of the National Association of Collegiate Women Athletic Directors: "Institutions have made such decisions based on a number of factors. . . . Athletics departments could provide more money to preserve opportunities for men, but some of them have spent excessively on a few sports--namely football and basketball--to the detriment of others" (qtd. in Robinson et al. B7).

The cost of football, in fact, is a particularly sensitive issue in the controversy. While many of Title IX's supporters regard the elimination of excellent men's programs in gymnastics, wrestling, and soccer as a mistake, they blame college administrators for squandering resources on football programs, which consume the largest part of the athletic budgets of most colleges and universities (Young). For example, the University of Southern California, which recently dropped men's swimming and gymnastics for an annual saving of $250,000, spends $5.5 million on football (Boyce 6). The elimination of two nationally distinguished athletic programs at USC is something to lament, but to attribute it to Title IX is to ignore alternatives available to the athletics department.

A weaker argument advanced by critics of Title IX is that relatively few women are "really interested" in sports. Granting, for the sake of argument, the validity of this dubious claim, one must still consider the influence of cultural conditioning in a society that has often discouraged, if not stigmatized, most forms of athletic achievement and competition among women. The best way to perpetuate any supposed lack of interest is to tell women athletes that gender equity shouldn't apply to them because they are too small a minority. As law professor Robert Farrell has observed, "It is hard to have a high level of interest in a sports program that does not exist" (qtd. In Bryjak). It is a curious irony that sports enthusiasts who eagerly embrace the popular notion that "if you build it they will come" rarely apply it to women's athletics.

Although critics of Title IX have not always argued logically or fairly, provisions of the law can be improved. Definitions of proportionality, in particular, bear review. One proposed amendment is to allow a variance of seven percent. Thus, a college that enrolls an equal number of men and women would remain in compliance so long as forty-three

Stephens 5

percent (or more) of its athletes were female. Another
proposal would treat <u>opportunities</u> for team membership as
equivalent to actual participation. If, for instance, a
men's and a women's soccer team each provided thirty
opportunities for membership, but only twenty women tried
out while walk-ons increased the men's roster to forty, both
teams could claim thirty participants (Brady). Either of
these "close-is-good-enough" policies would facilitate
compliance with Title IX, encouraging colleges to serve the
interests of prospective athletes without being forced to
recruit equal numbers of men and women.

Other recommendations also deserve consideration. Some
have suggested that colleges conduct surveys to determine
relative levels of interest in athletics. The results of
these surveys would determine thresholds of compliance. Some
have suggested that nontraditional-age students, many of
whom are older women with less interest in athletics, should
be excluded from calculations of proportionality (Davis 22).

Title IX, whatever its flaws, has been too successful
to warrant repeal. The year it was enacted, only 32,000
women participated in intercollegiate sports; today the
number exceeds 163,000 (Schneider 40). Criticism of Title IX
is often uninformed, specious, or downright sexist.
Nevertheless, the best strategy for advocates of gender

equity is to acknowledge the problems surrounding strict
quotas and to support the proposed amendments currently
before Congress. After all, the purpose of this law is not
just to increase women's participation in athletics but also
to dispel negative beliefs about the role of women in
sports. Supported by a majority of the American public, an
amended Title IX can keep the playing field level.

Stephens 7

Works Cited

Boyce, B. Ann. "Title IX: What Now?" Journal of Physical
     Education, Recreation, and Dance 73.7 (2002): 6-7.

Brady, Erik. "Proposal to Revamp Title IX Focuses on
     'Proportionality.'" USA Today 5 Dec. 2002: 1C.
     MasterFILE Premier. EBSCOhost. 6 Mar. 2003
     <http://web3.epnet.com>.

Bryjak, George J. "The Ongoing Controversy over Title IX."
     USA Today July 2000: 62-63. Lexis-Nexis. 2 Mar. 2003
     <http://www.lexisnexis.com>.

Davis, Michelle. "Title IX Panel Contemplates Easing
     'Proportionality' Test." Education Week 11 Dec.
     2002: 22.

Robinson, J., et al. "Gender Equity in College Sports: Six
     Views." Chronicle of Higher Education 6 Dec. 2002:
     B7-10.

Schneider, Jodi. "A Face-Off over Title IX." U.S. News and
     World Report 27 Jan. 2003: 40.

Young, Cathy. "Good Sports?" Reason Nov. 2001: 22-24.
     MasterFILE Premier. EBSCOhost. 6 Mar. 2003
     <http://web3.epnet.com>.

EXERCISE

Critiquing an Argumentative Essay

Using the procedure outlined on pages 509–10, critique Ellie Stephens's essay "Title IX: Leveling the Playing Fields." In particular, consider the following: Ellie resists an opinion that many people hold. Are her arguments sufficient to make others consider her position? If you did not begin the essay in agreement with Ellie, were your views altered as you read her arguments? What kinds of arguments and evidence does she use to make her case? Does she give a fair presentation of opposing arguments? Does she seem interested in fair play? Does she use her research effectively? What kind of persona does she project? Does her style contribute to the effectiveness of her argument?

PART II

Research Paper Reference Handbook

A   *List of Works Cited (MLA Format)*

A *list of works cited*, placed at the end of a research paper, identifies all the sources you have quoted, paraphrased, or referred to. A *working bibliography* is a list of possible sources that you draw up as you begin your research and that you revise and update throughout your research project. You should provide your readers with citations of your sources to give the authors rightful credit for their contributions to your work and to allow your readers the opportunity to consult your sources directly. Consequently, it is important that you cite sources with care.

 BIBLIOGRAPHIC FORMATS

A list of works cited is expected to conform to a certain *bibliographic format*—a prescribed method of listing source information. Every academic field, such as English, sociology, or mathematics, has a preferred format that dictates not only what information about sources should be in the list of works cited but also how it should be arranged and even punctuated.

Unfortunately, each format has its own quirks and peculiarities. Which one you use will depend on the academic discipline in which you are working. If you are writing a paper for a psychology course, for example, you may be required to use a different format than you would use in a chemistry paper. The research papers in Part I follow the *Modern Language Association (MLA) format*, which is widely used in humanities courses (courses in such fields as literature, history, philosophy, theology, languages, and the arts), and it is frequently accepted for use in other courses as well. Two other formats widely used in the social and applied sciences—that of the *American Psychological Association (APA)* and the *numbered references* system—are presented in Chapters E and F. Fortunately, you do not need to memorize the details of these various formats. However, it is important that you know they exist, that you know how to find and use them, and that you follow whatever format you use with care. These chapters can serve as a reference guide to the various bibliographic formats you may encounter throughout your college career.

GENERAL GUIDELINES—MLA FORMAT

The following general guidelines apply to MLA-style bibliographies. Notice how Allen Strickland followed the format in his working bibliography on pages 385–86 and in his list of works cited on pages 315–17.

1.   **What to include?** Allen's working bibliography listed the sources he had discovered during the preliminary stages of his project. He had not yet examined all of them, and some he would not use in his paper. Later, in his list of works cited, he would include only the sources he used in writing the paper. You should include a source in your list of works cited if you have quoted or paraphrased from it or if you have made reference to it. Do not list a work if you consulted it but did not make use of it in writing the paper.

2.   **In what order?** Sources are presented in alphabetical order, *not* in the order in which they are used in the paper. Do not number the items in your list.

3.   **What word first?** Each entry begins with the author's last name. When a work is anonymous—that is, when no author's name is given—the title is listed first. If the first word is *a*, *an*, or *the*, put that word first, but use the next word of the entry to determine its place within alphabetical order.

4.   **What format for titles?** In typed or handwritten papers, titles of longer works, such as books and magazines, are *italicized* or <u>underlined</u>. Do not underline the period that follows a title. Titles of shorter works, such as articles and book chapters (which are published as subparts of longer works), are printed within quotation marks (" "). Thus in Figure A.1 we observe that the article "When Will the Bubble Burst?" was published in the online journal *Pharmaceutical Executive*.

5.   **What format for publishers?** Publishers' names are shortened in MLA style. If a publishing firm is named after several persons, only the first is used (e.g., *Houghton* instead of *Houghton Mifflin Co.*). Omit first names (write *Knopf* instead of *Alfred A. Knopf, Inc.*), and omit words such as *Books*, *Press*, and *Publishers*. Use the abbreviation *UP* to represent *University Press* (e.g., *Indiana UP*, *U of Michigan P*, and *UP of Virginia*). When questions arise, use your judgment about identifying a publisher accurately. For example, you may write *Banner Books* to distinguish it from *Banner Press*.

6.   **What margins?** The first line of each entry begins at the left margin (one inch from the left edge of the page). The second and all following lines are indented one-half inch. In other words, each entry is "*out*dented" (also called a *hanging indent*), the reverse of the way paragraphs are *in*dented. The purpose is to make it easy for readers to find the first word of the entry so they can quickly locate individual items from a long list.

7.   **What spacing?** Double-space throughout, both within and between entries. Do not skip extra lines between entries.

Holbrook 15

Works Cited

Carter, John. Personal interview. 18 May 2005.

Dutka, Elaine. "New Michael Moore Project Gives Drug
        Companies a Sick Feeling." Los Angeles Times
        23 Dec. 2004. MichaelMoore.com. 24 May 2005
        <http://www.michaelmoore.com/words/mikeinthenews/>.

Farr, J. Michael. America's Top Jobs for college Graduates.
        3rd ed. Indianapolis: Jist Works, 1999.

Goldberg, Michele, Bob Davenport, and Tiffany Mortellito.
        "When Will the Bubble Burst?" Pharmaceutical Executive
        1 Jan. 2003. 13 May 2005 <http://www.pharmexec.com/
        pharmexec/article/articleDetail.jsp?id=42871>.

Groome, Harry C., Jr. This Is Advertising. Philadelphia:
        Ayer: 1975.

Figure A.1 Sample works cited page.

8. What punctuation? Punctuation conventions, however inexplicable they may seem, should be observed with care. Follow the models in this book whenever you create a list of works cited, paying close attention to periods, commas, parentheses, underlining, quotation marks, and spaces. In MLA style, most entries have three principal components, each one followed by a period: the author, the title, and the publication information. The most common oversight is to omit the period at the end of each entry.

9. What heading? Informal bibliographies do not require any special heading. A formal list of works cited, except in short papers with few sources, should begin on a separate page at the end of your paper. Center the heading:

Works Cited

(or *Bibliography*, if you prefer) and double-space (skip one line within and between entries). Do not skip an extra line between the heading and the first entry.

Citing Electronic Sources

Not many years ago, students who wrote research papers encountered almost all of their written sources in print form. Today, many research sources are likely to be gathered electronically. These might include a newspaper article retrieved from an online database, an entry from an encyclopedia on a CD-ROM, a Web page on the Internet, even a play by Shakespeare stored on some distant computer. As with other sources, you are expected to cite electronic sources so as to give credit to their authors and to allow your readers to retrieve and consult them directly.

A problem peculiar to electronic sources, particularly online sources, is that many of them are subject to being updated without notice or moved to another electronic address or even withdrawn altogether, so that someone seeking to consult a source next week may not find it in exactly the same form as another person who consulted it last week—or perhaps may not find it at all. In contrast, a printed work, such as a book, can be cited in the certainty that others who consult it will be able to find exactly the same text that you encountered. Although thousands of copies may be printed, all of them have the same words on the same pages. A book may be updated (e.g., the book you are now reading has been updated six times since its initial publication), but each update is identified with a new edition number. (This is the seventh edition of *Writing, Reading, and Research.*)

Being able to identify electronic sources accurately is not a great problem with ***portable electronic sources*** such as software programs on CD-ROM or diskette, which, like books, are identified with edition or version numbers. ***Online sources*** such as World Wide Web pages and some databases, however, are subject to frequent updating and revision. For such sources, it may not be possible to provide a citation that will allow others to consult the source in exactly the same form it took when you consulted it. In your citation of such sources, you should give information that is as adequate as possible, as well as the date when you consulted the source. Consult the models that follow for citing both portable and online electronic sources.

 ## MODEL ENTRIES—MLA FORMAT

You are likely to encounter many different kinds of sources in your research. When you compile a list of works cited using MLA style, you should find the appropriate model for each source from the samples that follow and copy its format with care. If you still have questions about a source you wish to list, consult the latest edition of *MLA Handbook for Writers of Research Papers*, which can be found in the reference section of most college libraries, or ask your instructor for assistance.

Examine the following model entries and read the explanatory notes. For quick reference later on, you can consult the model MLA citations printed on the inside front and back covers.

Sources in Books

Citations for books have three main divisions:

```
Author's name. The title of the book. Publication information.
```

For the ***author's name***, list the last name first, followed by a comma, followed by the author's other names. Abbreviations such as *PhD* and titles such as *The Rev.* are omitted from citations. The ***book title*** is underlined. List the full title, including any subtitle. When there is a subtitle, place a colon immediately following the main title and then list the subtitle. ***Publication information*** is cited in this format:

```
City of publication: publisher, year of publication.
```

You can find this information on the book's title page and its copyright page (usually the page following the title page). Use the shortened version of the ***publisher's name***. If the ***year of publication*** is not recorded on the title page, use the most recent year on the copyright page. If more than one ***city of publication*** is listed, give the first. If the city is not widely known, you can also list the state (using standard post office abbreviations—two capital letters, no periods) or foreign country.

Books

Following are sample entries for books (accessed in print form). For online books, see Internet and Electronic Sources on pages 556–57.

A Book with One Author

Walt, Stephen M. <u>Taming American Power: The Global Response to</u>
  <u>U. S. Primacy</u>. New York: Norton, 2005.

Wheelock, Arthur K., Jr. <u>Vermeer and the Art of Painting</u>. New
  Haven: Yale UP, 1995.

In the first example, a colon is placed between the book's title and its ***subtitle***. Publishers' names are abbreviated: *Norton* is short for the publishing company W. W. Norton & Company. *UP* is the standard abbreviation for University Press, as in *Yale UP*. However, you may give the publisher's name in a more complete form, particularly if you are in doubt (*Hill and Wang* rather than *Hill*, to avoid confusion with Ernest Hill Publishing or Lawrence Hill Books).

A Book with Two or Three Authors

Dingman, Robert L., and John D. Weaver. <u>Days in the Lives of</u>
  <u>Counselors</u>. Boston: Allyn, 2003.

Reid, Jo Anne, Peter Forrestal, and Jonathan Cook. <u>Small Group</u>
  <u>Learning in the Classroom</u>. Portsmouth, NH: Heinemann, 1990.

The first book is written by Robert L. Dingman and John D. Weaver. Note that only Dingman's name is inverted (last name first), since only the first author's last name is used to determine the work's alphabetized placement in the list of sources. In the second book, the three authors' names are not listed alphabetically; they are listed in the order in which their names appear on the title page. You may use the state abbreviation when you consider it helpful in identifying a city of publication that is not well known, such as *Portsmouth, NH.*

A Book with More Than Three Authors

Courtois, Stéphane, et al. <u>The Black Book of Communism: Crimes,</u>

    <u>Terror, Repression</u>. Cambridge, MA: Harvard UP, 1999.

Courtois is one of six authors of this book. The term *et al.* is a Latin abbreviation meaning "and others." It is not italicized or underlined in lists of works cited. You may also list all the authors, if you consider it desirable to acknowledge them by name.

Two or More Works by the Same Author

Asimov, Isaac. <u>Adding a Dimension</u>. New York: Discus, 1975.

---. "Fifty Years of Astronomy." <u>Natural History</u> Oct. 1985: 4+.

---. The New Intelligent Man's Guide to Science. New York:

    Basic, 1965.

Asimov, Isaac, and John Ciardi. <u>A Grossery of Limericks</u>. New

    York: Norton, 1981.

The first three works (two books and a magazine article) are written by the same author, Isaac Asimov. The fourth work is written by Asimov and another author. When you have used more than one work by the same author, your works-cited list should arrange the works alphabetically by title. (In our example *Adding* comes before *Fifty*, which comes before *New*.) Replace the author's name for all but the first work with three hyphens followed by a period. The reader can then see at a glance that the author is represented more than once and is alerted not to confuse one work with another. Use hyphens only when works have identical authors; notice that Asimov's name is not replaced for the fourth work, since its authors (Asimov and Ciardi) are not identical with the author of the first three works (Asimov alone).

A Book with No Author Listed

<u>Addison Wesley Longman Author's Guide</u>. New York: Longman, 1998.

In the works-cited list, give the book alphabetically according to the first main word of the title.

A Book with a Corporate or Group Author

Sotheby's. <u>Nineteenth Century European Paintings, Drawings and</u>

>   <u>Watercolours</u>. London: Sotheby's, 1995.

U of North Carolina Wilmington. <u>2005-2006 Code of Student</u>

>   <u>Life</u>. [Wilmington, NC]: n.p., [2005].

Cite the group as author, even if it is also the publisher. Publication information that can be inferred but is not printed in the publication is placed in brackets. If publication information is not known, use *n.p.* for "no place" or "no publisher," and use *n.d.* for "no date." Note that these abbreviations do not require italics or underlining.

A Book by a Government Agency

United States. Congress. House. Committee on Government Reform.

>   Subcommittee on Energy and Resources. <u>America's Energy</u>

>   <u>Needs As Our National Security Policy</u>. Washington:

>   GPO, 2005.

For a work produced by a government, first state the name of the government (e.g., *United States*), followed by the agency (and subgroup, if any) authoring the work. *GPO* stands for the Government Printing Office.

A Book with a Translator

Ramos, Julio. <u>Divergent Modernities: Culture and Politics in</u>

>   <u>Nineteenth-Century Latin America</u>. Trans. John D. Blanco.

>   Durham: Duke UP, 1999.

Ramos's book was translated into English by Blanco. Note that *translator* is capitalized and abbreviated as *Trans.*

A Book with an Author and an Editor

Shakespeare, William. <u>Henry V</u>. Ed. T. W. Craik. New York:

>   Routledge, 1995.

Shakespeare is the author of the play, which is published in an edition edited by Craik. Note that *edited by* is capitalized and abbreviated as *Ed.*

A Book with an Editor

> Stimpson, Catherine R., and Ethel Spector Person, eds. <u>Women:</u>
>
>   <u>Sex and Sexuality</u>. Chicago: U of Chicago P, 1980.

Stimpson and Person edited this book, an **anthology** of essays by various writers. Note that *editors* is lowercased and abbreviated as *eds*. It should be noted that occasions when you refer to such a collection *as a whole* in your research will be relatively rare. More frequently, you will use material from a selection in the collection, and you will cite that specific work (rather than the collection as a whole) in your list of works cited. See "A Selection from an Anthology" on pages 547–48.

A Book in a Later Edition

> Skinner, Ellen. <u>Women and the National Experience</u>. 2nd ed. New
>
>   York: Longman, 2003.

Skinner's book is in its second edition. Use *3rd*, *4th*, and so on for subsequent editions. Abbreviate *edition* as *ed*.

A Book in a Series

> Matthee, Rudolph P. <u>The Politics of Trade in Safavid Iran: Silk</u>
>
>   <u>for Silver, 1600-1730</u>. Cambridge Studies in Islamic
>
>   Civilization. New York: Cambridge UP, 2000.

Matthee's book is one of several books published by Cambridge University Press in a series entitled Cambridge Studies in Islamic Civilization. Note that the series title follows the book title and is neither italicized or placed within quotation marks.

A Multivolume Book

When an author gives different titles to individual volumes of a work, list a specific volume this way:

> Brinton, Crane, John B. Christopher, and Robert Lee Wolff.
>
>   <u>Prehistory to 1715</u>. Vol. 1 of <u>A History of Civilization</u>.
>
>   6th ed. 2 vols. Englewood Cliffs, NJ: Prentice, 1984.

When individual volumes do not have separate titles, cite the book this way:

> Messenger, Charles. <u>For Love of Regiment: A History of British</u>
>
>   <u>Infantry, 1660-1993</u>. 2 vols. Philadelphia: Trans-Atlantic,
>
>   1995.

If you use only one of these volumes, cite it this way:

Messenger, Charles. <u>For Love of Regiment: A History of British Infantry, 1660-1993</u>. Vol. 1. Philadelphia: Trans-Atlantic, 1995.

Note that when citing a specific volume, *volume* is capitalized and abbreviated to *Vol.* When citing the number of volumes that exist, *volumes* is lowercased and abbreviated to *vols.*

A Book Published before 1900

Nightingale, Florence. <u>Notes on Nursing: What It Is, and What It Is Not</u>. New York, 1860.

The publisher's name may be omitted for works published before 1900. Note that a comma, instead of a colon, follows the place of publication.

A Paperback or Other Reprinted Book

Horwitz, Tony. <u>Confederates in the Attic: Dispatches from the Unfinished Civil War</u>. 1998. New York: Vintage, 1999.

The book was originally published (in hardcover, by a different publisher) in 1998. Note that the copyright year of the original publication follows immediately after the book title and is punctuated with a period.

Selections from Books

A Selection from an Anthology

Leifer, Myra. "Pregnancy." <u>Women: Sex and Sexuality</u>. Ed. Catherine R. Stimpson and Ethel Spector Person. Chicago: U of Chicago P, 1980. 212-23.

Lichtheim, George. "The Birth of a Philosopher." <u>Collected Essays</u>. New York: Viking, 1973. 103-10.

Rushdie, Salman. "A Pen Against the Sword: In Good Faith." Newsweek 12 Feb. 1990: 52+. Rpt. in <u>One World, Many Cultures</u>. Ed. Stuart Hirschberg. New York: Macmillan, 1992. 480-96.

Leifer's article "Pregnancy" is one of the essays in the collection *Women: Sex and Sexuality* edited by Stimpson and Person. Leifer's essay appeared on pages 212 to 223 of the book. (See the "Page Numbers" box on page 551 for information on how to list pages.) The Lichtheim book in the example does not have an editor; he is the author of all the essays in the book. Rushdie's article originally appeared in *Newsweek;* the person who wrote this listing found it in Hirschberg's book, where it had been ***reprinted*** (*rpt.*).

Several Selections from the Same Anthology

If several essays are cited from the same collection, you can save space by using ***cross-references***. First, include the entire collection as one of the items in your list of works cited, as follows:

```
Stimpson, Catherine R., and Ethel Spector Person, eds. Women:
     Sex and Sexuality. Chicago: U of Chicago P, 1980.
```

Then you are free to list each article you refer to in your paper, followed by an abbreviated reference to the collection—just the last names of the editors and the pages on which the articles appear, as follows:

```
Baker, Susan W. "Biological Influences on Human Sex and Gender."
     Stimpson and Person 175-91.
Diamond, Irene. "Pornography and Repression: A Reconsideration."
     Stimpson and Person 129-33.
Leifer, Myra. "Pregnancy." Stimpson and Person 212-23.
```

An Article in an Encyclopedia or Other Reference Work

```
Harmon, Mamie. "Folk Arts." The New Encyclopaedia Britannica:
     Macropaedia. 15th ed. 2002.
"Morrison, Toni." Who's Who in America. 60th ed. 2006.
"Yodel." The Shorter Oxford English Dictionary. 5th ed. 2002.
```

The *Britannica* is a printed encyclopedia. Pages need not be listed for reference works whose entries are arranged alphabetically (and can therefore easily be found). In many reference works, such as *Who's Who in America*, no authors are named for individual entries. Publishers need not be cited for well-known reference books. Provide publisher information for ***lesser-known reference works***:

```
Hames, Raymond. "Yanomamö." South America. Vol. 7 of
     Encyclopedia of World Cultures. Boston: Hall, 1994.
```

For a reference work that you have accessed on the Internet, see Internet and Electronic Sources on page 558.

A Preface, Introduction, Foreword, or Afterword

> Bradford, Barbara Taylor. Foreword. Forever Amber. By Kathleen
>
> Winsor. 1944. Chicago: Chicago Review, 2000.

The entry begins with the author of the preface, introduction, foreword, or afterword. The book's author follows the title (preceded by the word *by*).

Sources in Periodicals and Newspapers

Following are entries for a periodical and newspaper (when accessed in print form). Periodical entries are also summarized in Figure A.2. For articles accessed online, see Internet and Electronic Sources on pages 557–58.

An Article in a Magazine

> Block, Toddi Gutner. "Riding the Waves." Forbes 11 Sept. 1995:
>
> 182+.
>
> Fletcher, Winston. "The American Way of Work." Management Today
>
> Aug. 2005: 46-49.
>
> Schwartz, Deborah F. "Dude, Where's My Museum? Inviting Teens to
>
> Transform Museums." Museum News Sep./Oct. 205: 36-41.

This format is used for all weekly, biweekly, monthly, or bimonthly periodicals, except for scholarly journals. The Fletcher article appears on pages 46 through 49. The Block article is not printed on continuous pages; it begins on page 182 and is continued further back in the magazine. For such articles, only the first page is listed, immediately followed by a plus sign (+). Although some magazines may show a volume or issue number on the cover, these are not needed in the entry. Names of months, except for May, June, and July, are abbreviated. Note that there is no punctuation between the periodical's name and the publication date. For a magazine article that you have accessed on the Internet, see various entries under Internet and Electronic Sources on pages 557–58.

An Article in a Journal

> Gerson, Lloyd P. "What Is Platonism?" Journal of the History of
>
> Philosophy 43 (2005): 253-76.

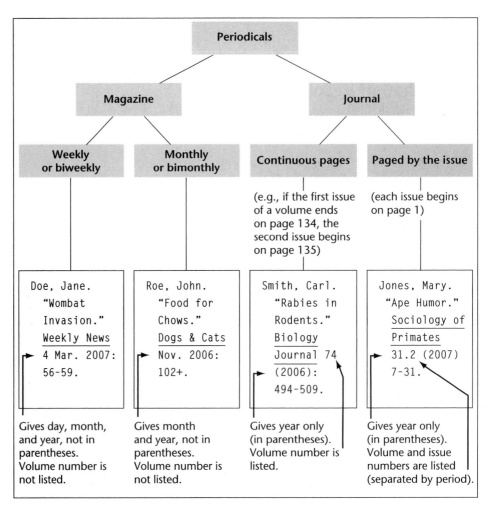

Figure A.2 Periodical listings for an MLA works cited list.

Journals are usually scholarly publications and are typically published three or four times yearly. Each year begins a new volume. The volume number (43 in this case) is included in the entry for a journal article. It is not necessary to include the seasonal designation (Winter, Spring, etc.). Pages in many journals are numbered according to the volume, not the issue. For example, if the Winter issue of volume 43 of *Journal of the History of Philosophy* ended on page 222, the Spring issue would begin on page 223. The paging of the next volume (44) would begin again with page 1. Some journals, however, begin each issue on page 1; for

---

Page Numbers

Book. Do not give page numbers when citing a book in a works-cited list.

An article or a selection from a book. Give the page numbers on which an essay or article appears within a larger work, such as a book or periodical. List the pages for the *entire* selection, not just pages cited in your paper.

Page number style. In listing page numbers, omit all but the last two digits of the final page number, unless they are different from those of the first page. *Examples:*

> 5–7
>
> 377–79 (not –9 or –379)
>
> 195–208
>
> 1006–07 (not –7 or –1007)
>
> 986–1011

Noncontinuous pages. For articles that are continued on pages further back in the publication, list only the first page and a plus sign. For example, for an article that appears on pages 45 to 47 and continues on pages 123–130, list the following:

> 45+

---

these, add a period and the issue number following the volume number, as follows:

> Anderson, Rebecca, and Jane Puckett. "The Usefulness of an
>
> Online Platform for Capturing Literacy Field Experiences:
>
> Four Lessons Learned." Reading Instruction & Research
>
> 23.4 (2005): 22–46.

The number 23.4 tells you that the article appeared in volume 23, issue 4, of *Reading Instruction & Research.* Periodical listings are also shown in the chart on page 550. For a journal article that you have accessed on the Internet, see various entries under Internet and Electronic Sources on pages 557–58.

An Article in a Newspaper

> Cauvin, Henri E. "Lawyers Seek Release of U.S. Detainee in
>
> Iraq." Washington Post 31 Aug. 2005: A19.

Leonhardt, David. "Defining the Rich in the World's Wealthiest
Nation." <u>New York Times</u> 12 Jan. 2003, natl. ed.:
sec. 4: 1+.

Ranii, David. "Adding a Different Symbol." <u>News and Observer</u>
[Raleigh] 9 Sep. 2005: 3D.

The article *The* is omitted from citations of newspapers such as the *Washington Post*. When the newspaper's name does not include the city (e.g., *News and Observer*), provide the city name in brackets; however, do not give a city for national newspapers like the *Wall Street Journal* and *USA Today*. Number pages as they appear in your source. The number on the page of the newspaper where the Cauvin article appears is A19 (i.e., page 19 of section A), while the newspaper where the Ranii article appeared has the section and page numbers reversed (it appear on page 3D). When both the section and pages are numbered, present them as in the second example (*sec. 4: 1+*). Because the *New York Times* publishes two different editions (called the late and the national editions), it is necessary to specify which edition you used. For a newspaper article that you have accessed on the Internet, see various entries under Internet and Electronic Sources on pages 557–58.

An Editorial

"Oil for Food as Usual." Editorial. <u>Wall Street Journal</u> 9 Sep.
2005: A16.

A Letter to the Editor

Brewer, Jack. Letter. <u>U.S. News & World Report</u> 5 Sep. 2005: 16.

A Review

Benfey, Christopher. "An Illustrated Woman." Rev. of <u>The Tattoo
Artist</u>, by Jill Ciment. <u>New York Times Book Review</u> 21 Aug.
2005: 8.

Glenn, Kenny. Rev. of <u>Man on the Moon</u> [film]. <u>Premier</u> Jan. 2000:
20.

Rev. of <u>Going to the Territory</u>, by Ralph Ellison. <u>Atlantic</u> Aug.
1986: 91.

Stearns. David Patrick. Rev. of <u>The Well-Tempered Clavier</u>, by
J. S. Bach [CD]. Angela Hewitt, piano. <u>Stereophile</u> Dec.
1999: 173+.

The first and third reviews are of books; the second is of a film; the fourth is of a music recording on CD. Information in review listings appears in this order: the reviewer's name; the title of the review; the work reviewed; its author; performers and performance information, if applicable; and the publication information. Notice that only the first review was published under a title. In the third review, Ralph Ellison is the author of the book reviewed; the review itself is published anonymously. If the medium of the reviewed work is not obvious, it can be added in brackets after the name of the work (e.g., *[CD]*).

Other Sources

An Audio Recording

> Dickinson, Dee. <u>Creating the Future: Perspectives on Educational Change</u>. Audiocassette. Minneapolis: Accelerated Learning Systems, 1991.
>
> Mahler, Gustav. Symphony No. 7. Michael Tilson Thomas, cond. London Symphony Orch. CD. RCA Victor, 1999.
>
> Shuster, George N. Jacket notes. <u>The Poetry of Gerard Manley Hopkins</u>. LP. Caedmon, n.d.

Audio recordings vary greatly in type and purpose, so do not hesitate to exercise judgment about what information is important. In general, label each recording by medium (CD, audiocassette, LP, etc.), although the label is optional for compact discs, which are assumed to be the standard audio medium. For a musical recording, list first the name of the composer or performer or conductor, depending on what aspect of the recording you are emphasizing. Recordings are produced by print-media publishers as well as traditional record companies, with the line separating them increasingly blurred; list either the manufacturer and year (as in the second example) or city, publisher, and year (as in the first example). Cite jacket or liner notes as in the third example. When a date is unavailable, as in the last example, use *n.d.* for "no date." For a multidisc publication, follow the medium with either the total number of discs included or the specific disc number being cited.

A Film, DVD, or Video Recording

> <u>Downfall</u>. Dir. Oliver Hirschbiegel. Screeplay by Bernd Eichinger. Newmarket Films, 2005.

For a film, give the title, the director, the distributor, and the year of release. You may include other information you consider pertinent, such as the screenwriter and principal performers. For a film viewed on videocassette, DVD, or videodisc, provide that same information, but also identify the medium, the distributor, and the video release date:

<u>All about Eve</u>. Dir. Joseph L. Mankiewicz. Perf. Bette Davis,

Anne Baxter, and George Sanders. Fox, 1950. DVD. Studio

Classics, 2003.

Cite a nontheatrical video as follows:

<u>The Classical Hollywood Style</u>. Program 1 of <u>The American Cinema</u>.

Prod. New York Center for Visual History. Videocassette.

Annenberg/CPB, 1995.

A Government Document

See "A Book by a Government Agency" on page 545.

A Lecture

Granetta, Stephanie. Class lecture. English 315. Richardson

College. 7 Apr. 2006.

Kamenish, Eleanor. "A Tale of Two Countries: Mores in France and

Scotland." Public lecture. Friends of the Public Library.

Louisville, 16 Apr. 2006.

A Pamphlet

Golden Retriever Club of America. <u>Prevention of Heartworm</u>.

n.p.: GRCA, 2006.

<u>Who Are the Amish?</u> Aylmer, Ont.: Pathway, n.d.

Pamphlets are treated like books. Use these abbreviations for unknown information: *n.p.* for both "no place" or "no publisher," *n.d.* for "no date," and *n. pag.* for "no pagination" (when the source lacks page numbers). Because pamphlets vary widely, you should exercise judgment to make your listing clear.

An Interview

Clements, Caroline M. Personal interview. 15 July 2005.

Maher, Bill. Interview with Terry Gross. <u>Fresh Air</u>. Natl. Public

Radio. WHQR, Wilmington, NC. 9 Aug. 2005.

Trump, Donald. "Trump Speaks." Interview with Aravind Adiga.
Money Feb. 2003: 28.

All interviews begin with the name of the person being interviewed, not the interviewer. Label an interview that you conduct as *Personal interview*. Label a broadcast or print interview as *Interview with [interviewer]*. Only those print interviews that are presented in a question-and-answer format are listed in this way; other print sources in which a person is quoted are listed in a standard format (author's name first).

A Television or Radio Program

The Crossing. Dir. Robert Harmon. Screenplay by Sherry Jones and
Peter Jennings. History Channel. 1 Jan. 2000.
Garcia-Navarro, Lourdes. Report on illegal immigration.
All Things Considered. Natl. Public Radio. 8 Sep. 2005.

An Unpublished Essay

Strickland, Allen. "Identical Twins: Born to Be Alike?" Essay
written for Prof. Lisa Gorman's English 12 class. Summer
term 2005.

An Unpublished Letter

Cilano, Cara. Letter to author. 5 Mar. 2006.

See also "E-Mail" on page 560.

An Unpublished Questionnaire

Questionnaire conducted by Prof. Barbara Waxman's English 103
class. Feb. 2006.

A citation for a project or paper written for a college class needs be no more formal than this. An essay meant for wider circulation, however, would need to include the title of the course and the name of the college. Common sense is your best guide in these matters.

Internet and Electronic Sources

A basic principle for citing a print source found online is to provide the information one would supply for the print source, followed by information about the online source. Unlike citations for books that have three major divisions, a citation for an electronic publication may have up to five:

```
Author's name. "Title of document." Information about print

     publication. Information about electronic publication.

     Access information.
```

Access information include the date of access and the URL. Following are examples of both print and nonprint sources found online.

An Online Book

```
Calvin, William H. How Brains Think: Evolving Intelligence Then

     and Now. New York: Basic Books, 1996. 1 Oct. 2005

     <http://www.williamcalvin.com/bk8/>.
Conrad, Carl W. A Brief Commentary on the Book of Mark, 2004. 1

     Oct. 2005 <http://www.ioa.com/~cwconrad/Mark/>.
Wollstonecraft, Mary. Vindication of the Rights of Women. 1792.

     Bartleby.com, 1999. 1 Oct. 2005 <http://www.bartleby.com/144/>.
```

For an online book that first appeared in print, such as the first and third examples, provide standard information for the print source of the reproduced text, if available. Then provide the name of the online "publisher" and the date of the online publication (not known in the first example; *Bartleby.com, 1999* in the third). Finally, give the date you consulted the online work, immediately followed (no period) by the online address within angle brackets. If an online address cannot fit completely on one line, you can break it following a slash (/), but do not use a hyphen to show the break. Conrad's book did not first appear in print and is available on a personal Web page. Because electronic sources vary widely, you may need to use your judgment about how best to identify your source.

A Part of an Online Book

```
Speed, Harold. The Visual Memory. The Practice and Science of

     Drawing. 1913. Project Gutenberg, 2004. 1 Oct. 2005

     <http://www.gutenberg.org/files/14264/14264-h/

     14264-h.htm#CHAPTER_XVIII>.
```

Note that if the selection is a standard part of the book such as a chapter, preface, or introduction, the title does not need to be placed within quotation marks. However, when the selection is a poem or essay, then quotation marks are needed. Also note that the URL should indicate the specific location of the part of the book you are citing.

A Print Periodical (Newspaper, Magazine, or Journal) Accessed on the Publication's Web Site

The following works appeared in print but were accessed on the Web sites of the publications. See also "A Work Accessed in an Online Database" below.

Hopfensperger, Jean. "Wal-Mart Debate Gains Momentum across
    Minnesota." Minneapolis Star Tribune 12 Sep. 2005.
    1 Oct. 2005 <http://www.startribune.com/stories/1405/
    5608958.html>.

Hopkins, Philip F., et al. "Black Holes in Galaxy Mergers:
    Evolution of Quasars." Astrophysical Journal 630.2 (2005):
    705-15. 1 Oct. 2005 <http://www.journals.uchicago.edu/
    ApJ/journal/issues/ApJ/v630n2/62521/62521.html>.

Hosenball, Mark. "Iraq: Planning for Pullout." Newsweek 19 Sep.
    2005. 1 Oct. 2005 <http://msnbc.msn.com/id/9285511/
    site/newsweek/>.

For online periodical articles that also appeared in print, first provide the same information as for the print article, including the publication, the date of print publication, and the articles' pages, if available. Finally, give the date you consulted the online work, immediately followed (no period) by the online address, within angle brackets.

A Nonprint Periodical Accessed on the Publication's Web Site

"Cellular's Unhappy Customers." Red Herring 7 Sep. 2005. 1 Oct.
    2005 <http://www.redherring.com/>.

The essay was published in the exclusively online magazine *Red Herring*. The Internet address for an article is often a lengthy temporary address that cannot be used on later occasions, so you can list the general address for the online magazine.

A Work Accessed in an Online Database

Use the following format when you access a work in an online database such as EBSCOhost, InfoTrac, LexisNexis, ProQuest, or WilsonWeb.

```
Ernst, Steve. "Pandemic Fever." Bioscience Technology July

    2005: 6. InfoTrac OneFile. 1 Oct. 2005 <http://

    infotrac.galegroup.com/>.

Parks, Noreen. "Dolphins in Danger." Science Now 17 Dec. 2002:

    2-3. Academic Search Elite. EBSCOhost. 1 Oct. 2005

    <http://web3.epnet.com/>.

"Ukraine Foreign Minister Says 'No Alternative' to Constructive

    Ties with Russia." Global News Wire 28 July 2005.

    LexisNexis Academic Universe. 1 Oct. 2005 <http://

    web.lexis-nexis.com/universe>.
```

Provide the standard publication information, including the pages of the original publication, if available. Include the name of the database and underline it (in the first example, InfoTrac OneFile) and the name of the database family if not included in the database name (in the second example, EBSCOhost). Because the Internet address of an individual citation is often a very long temporary address that cannot be used on later occasions, give only the general address of the database or of the library where you accessed the database.

An Online Encyclopedia Article

```
"Humpback Whale." Encyclopaedia Britannica 2005. Encyclopaedia

    Britannica Online. 1 Oct. 2005 <http://

    0-search.eb.com.uncclc.coast.uncwil.edu/eb/>.
```

An Online Review

```
Ebert, Roger. Rev. of The Constant Gardener, dir. Fernando

    Meirelles. RogerEbert.com 1 Sep. 2005. 1 Oct. 2005

    <http://rogerebert.suntimes.com>.
```

Maslin, Janet. "Back to '68: Radicals, Chemicals and Patty
    Hearst." Rev. of <u>Backward-Facing Man</u>, by Don Silver.
    <u>New York Times on the Web</u> 12 Sep. 2005. 1 Oct. 2005
    <http://www.nytimes.com/2005/09/12/books/12masl.html>.

In Ebert's movie review, the director's name (preceded by *dir.*) follows the movie's title. In Maslin's book review, the name of the book's author (preceded by the word "by") follows the book title.

An Organization's Web Site

<u>The Coral Reef Alliance</u>. "Major Mesomerica Initiative
    Underway." 1 Oct. 2005 <http://www.coralreefalliance.org/
    parks/mar/>.

Note that the name of the site is <u>underlined</u>. And, if available, the editor (*Ed.*) of the site immediately follows it.

A Course Web Page

Reilly, Colleen. English 313: Writing about Science. Course home
    page. U of North Carolina at Wilmington. Spring 2003.
    1 Oct. 2005 <http://people.uncw.edu/reillyc/313/>.

The course title is not underlined or placed within quotation marks.

An Academic Department Page

Dept. of English home page. U of North Carolina at Wilmington.
    1 Oct. 2005 <http://www.uncwil.edu/english/>.

A Personal Web Page

Hemming, Sally. Home page. 1 Oct. 2005 <http://
    www.sallyhemming.com>.

If the page has a title, it is <u>underlined</u> and placed before the word Home page.

Khan, Genghis. <u>Latest Conquests</u>. Home page. . . .

Weblog (Blog) or Online Posting

```
Lessig, Lawrence. "Gifts from the Other Side." Weblog
        entry. Lessig Blog 11 Sep. 2005. 1 Oct. 2005
        <http://www.lessig.org/blog/>.
Newlin, Keith. "McTeague's Tooth," Online posting, 22 Mar. 2003.
        1 Oct. 2005 <http://people.uncw.edu/newlink/tooth.htm>.
```

E-Mail

```
Wilkes, Paul. E-mail to author. 29 Dec. 2005.
```

Computer Software

```
ChemSketch. Vers. 8.0. Software. 2005 <http://www.acdlabs.com/
        download/chemsk.html>.
Twain's World. CD-ROM. Parsippany, NJ: Bureau Development,
        1993.
```

The first example is of software downloaded from the Internet; the second is software published on a CD-ROM. The boundary between pure software and a book or other work that is published in an electronic medium is not a distinct one.

EXERCISE | **A List of Works Cited**

This exercise practices many types of bibliographic entries. Imagine that (in a temporary lapse from sanity) you have written a paper called "The Shoelace in History" and you have made use of the following sources. Compile your list of works cited, paying close attention to proper MLA format.

As a first step, circle the word in each of the following items that would begin the listing. Second, order the entries alphabetically. Third, put each listing in proper MLA form. (*Warning:* Some listings contain irrelevant information that you will not use in your works-cited list.) Finally, prepare the finished list.

1. The book *Sandals in Greece and Rome* was written by Sally Parish and published in 2000 by Wapiti Press in Omaha.

2. You found Walter Kelly's article "Shoelaces" on page 36 of volume 12 of the 1997 edition of *Encyclopedia of Haberdashery*, published in New York by the Buster Green Company.

3. During World War II, Fiona Quinn wrote *Knit Your Own Shoelaces* as part of the Self-Reliance Series printed in Modesto, California, in 1942 by Victory Press.

4. On page 36 of its July 23, 1977, edition, *Time* magazine published "Earth Shoes Unearthed in Inca Ruins." No author is given.

5. Two days ago, using the Internet, you consulted an online book by Imelda Markoz, *Never Too Many Shoes*. Two years ago, it had appeared in print, published by Converse Press in Wichita. You found the book at the address http://www.shoebooks.umanila.edu.

6. Constance Jowett translated a book by Max Philador and Elisaveta Krutsch, *Shoelaces in Africa and the Far East 1800–1914*. It was published in 2002 by Vanitas Publishers, Inc. Cities listed on the title page for Vanitas are Fort Worth, Texas; Chicago; Amsterdam; and Sydney, Australia.

7. On January 5 of this year Louise K. Frobisher wrote you a letter about her father's shoelace research.

8. You found volume 3 of Fiona Quinn's six-volume work of 1950: *The Shoe in the English-Speaking World*, published by S. T. Bruin & Sons of Boston.

9. On pages 711 and 712 of volume 17 of the *Indiana Journal of Podiatry* (November 1974) appears an essay, "Solving the Loose Shoe Problem" by Earl Q. Butz.

10. Leon Frobisher, Werner Festschrift, Ella Fitsky, and Ian McCrimmer published the twelfth edition of *Shoemaking with a Purpose* in 2005. The publisher, Hooton-Muffin of Boston, has published editions of the book since 1939.

11. The Society of Legwear Manufacturers wrote a book, *Laces, Gaiters, and Spats*, in 1901. Provolone-Liederkranz Publishers, Ltd., of Toronto reprinted it in 1955.

12. Mr. O. Fecteau and Ms. Mary Facenda edited a 1996 anthology, *An Ethnography of Footwear*, published in New Orleans by Big Muddy Publications. You found an article on pages 70–81, "Footloose and Sandal-Free," by J. R. R. Frodobaggins.

13. Norman Zimmer thoroughly explores "The Shoelace Motif in Finno-Latvian Sonnet Sequences" in the Fall 1999 edition (volume 43), pages 202 through 295, of a scholarly journal called *PMLA*.

14. Theodore and Louisa Mae Quinn edited a book written by their mother, Fiona Quinn, shortly before her death. The book, *Old Laces and Arsenic*, is published by Capra Press of Los Angeles. Copyright dates given are 1947, 1952, and 1953.

15. In the February 4, 1968, *Hibbing Herald* newspaper, the article "Lace, Lady, Lace" appeared under Robert Dylan's byline. A week ago today, you printed out a copy of the article online in the MasterFile Premier database by using the EBSCOhost search engine. EBSCOhost's homepage is http://www.epnet.dome/ehost/.

16. You draw on information from a television exposé, "The Shoelace Coverup," which appeared last Sunday on the CBS show *60 Minutes*. Leslie Stahl is the narrator.

17. *Dog's Life* is a monthly magazine published in Atlanta. In volume 16, number 3, of that publication (whose date is August 2003), Walter Kelly's article "Little

Laces for Little People" appeared. It began on pages 32 to 37 and continued on pages 188 and 189. You found it using the ProQuest reference service (homepage: http://www.bellhowell.infolearning.com/proquest/).

18. You used the World Wide Web to read an article, "Tasteless Laces" by M. R. Blackwell. It appeared this year in the January issue of *Cyberlace*, which calls itself "the e-zine for the well shod." The address of the article is http://www.knotco.edu/cyberlace/notaste.html.

Congratulations. Having completed this exercise, you are now prepared for almost any situation that you may face as you prepare lists of sources in the future.

Remember, for quick reference, consult the summary of MLA bibliographic models on the inside front covers.

B *Parenthetical Notes (MLA Format)*

Research writing has two principal devices for giving detailed information about sources: lists of works cited and notes. The former is a *general*, alphabetized list of all the sources you used in your writing. A ***note***, in contrast, acknowledges the *specific location* within a source of a *specific quotation* or bit of information in your paper. For example, if you quoted this very sentence in a paper you were writing, you would include the seventh edition of *Writing, Reading, and Research* in your list of works cited. A note, however, would also be needed with the quotation to tell your readers that it came from page 563 of this book.

TYPES OF NOTES

Notes are of three principal kinds: parenthetical notes, footnotes, and endnotes. Parenthetical notes are by far the simplest kind of notes to use, and they are the standard method for documenting sources in MLA style. Footnotes and endnotes, however, are sometimes used by scholars in such fields as history, theology, and the fine arts. The following case illustrates the differences among these three types of notes.

Imagine that you included the following source in your list of works cited:

> Sternberg, Robert J., and Todd I. Lubart. <u>Defying the Crowd:</u>
>
> <u>Cultivating Creativity in a Culture of Conformity</u>. New
>
> York: Free, 1995.

A works-cited listing

Suppose you made use of the following passage about the invention of Post-it® Notes, which appeared on page 4 of that book:

> Consider, for example, the Post-its on which many people jot reminders of things they need to get done. These "stick-ums" were created when an engineer at the 3M Company ended up doing the opposite of what he was supposed to. He created a weak adhesive, rather than the strong one that was the goal of his working division. But instead of throwing out the weak adhesive, he redefined the problem he was trying to solve: namely, to find the best use for a very weak adhesive. . . . Some of the greatest discoveries and inventions happen when people do just the opposite of what they have been told to do!

A passage from that source

Assume you paraphrased material from this passage in your paper as follows:

Your
paraphrase of
the source

```
Creativity consists in seeing possibilities where others
see only dead ends. For example, the discovery of a weak
adhesive by an engineer who was actually looking for a
strong adhesive led to the invention of Post-it® Notes.
```

It is your obligation to identify the specific source you used in writing this paraphrase. Here it is done with a *parenthetical note:*

```
Creativity consists in seeing possibilities where others
see only dead ends. For example, the discovery of a weak
adhesive by an engineer who was actually looking for a
strong adhesive led to the invention of Post-it® Notes
```

A parenthetical
note

```
(Sternberg and Lubart 4).
```

The note tells your readers that you discovered this information on page 4 of the Sternberg and Lubart book, the complete citation for which can be found in your list of works cited.

By contrast, if you use the footnote or endnote system, you mark your paraphrase with a raised number:

```
Creativity consists in seeing possibilities where others
see only dead ends. For example, the discovery of a weak
```

Reference to a
footnote or
endnote

```
adhesive by an engineer who was actually looking for a
strong adhesive led to the invention of Post-it® Notes.[1]
```

The raised number refers the reader to the following note:

A footnote or
endnote

```
[1] Robert J. Sternberg and Todd I. Lubart, Defying the Crowd:
Cultivating Creativity in a Culture of Conformity (New York:
Free, 1995), 4.
```

As a *footnote*, it would be typed at the bottom of the page on which the reference appeared. As an *endnote*, it would be typed in a list of notes at the end of the paper.

Unless you are using a word processor that automatically formats and arranges your footnotes for you, you will find endnotes easier to type than footnotes. Both, however, involve redundancy; notice that the sample footnote repeats all the information already found in the works-cited listing. In contrast, parenthetical notes are far simpler and more economical than either footnotes or endnotes. In this chapter, we will focus on the MLA parenthetical style, but a full discussion of footnotes and endnotes can be found in Chapter D, and still other styles of notation are explained in Chapters E and F.

 ## PARENTHETICAL NOTES

The rationale for parenthetical notes is that a note should give the least amount of information needed to identify a source—and give it within the paper itself; readers who want to know more can consult the list of works cited for further information. Different academic fields use slightly different formats for parenthetical notes. We consider here one general-purpose format, but you should be aware that papers written for other classes may require some adjustment in their note form. Always ask your instructor for format information if you are in doubt.

In the style used here as a model—the MLA style—a note is placed in the paper at the point where it is needed to identify a source. A typical note consists of two bits of information, in this format: (author pages). That is, the author's last name and the pages from which the information is taken are placed in parentheses. Here is an example of how a parenthetical note is used with a quotation:

One textbook defines <u>false arrest</u> as "an intentional, unlawful, and unprivileged restraint of a person's liberty, either in prison or elsewhere, whereby harm is caused to the person so confined" (Wells 237).

Observe that the note follows the quotation and that the period is placed *after* the parentheses, not at the end of the quotation. In other words, the note is treated as a part of the sentence. If a quotation ends with a question mark or exclamation point, add a period after the note, as follows:

Schwitzer taped a quotation from Thoreau to the wall above his desk: "I have never yet met a man who was quite awake. How could I have looked him in the face?" (Johnson 65).

Period follows the note

If the author's name already appears in your sentence, it can be omitted from the note. For example:

Wells writes that "a false arrest or false imprisonment is an intentional, unlawful, and unprivileged restraint of a person's liberty, either in prison or elsewhere, whereby harm is caused to the person so confined" (237).

For a longer, indented quotation, the note can be placed immediately following the acknowledgment phrase, as follows:

```
Historians of the last century maintained a firm belief in
human progress, according to British historian Edward Hallett
Carr (324):
        The liberal nineteenth-century view of history had a
        close affinity with the economic doctrine of laissez-
        faire--also the product of a serene and self-confident
        outlook on the world. Let everyone get on with his
        particular job, and the hidden hand would take care of
        the universal harmony.
```

Alternatively, the note can be placed at the quotation's end, as in this example:

```
Although the earth is a small planet in a remote corner of a
minor galaxy, there are reasons for arguing its importance:
        One should not be impressed too much by mere quantity;
        great dimensions and heavy mass have no merit by
        themselves; they cannot compare in value with
        immaterial things, such as thoughts, emotions, and
        other expressions of the soul. To us the earth is the
        most important of all celestial bodies, because it has
        become the cradle and seat of our spiritual values.
(Öpik 9)
```

Period precedes the note in an indented quotation

Notice one oddity of the parenthetical style: When a note is placed after an indented quotation, it follows the final period. (In the other cases we have seen, the period follows the parenthetical note.)

Many students mistakenly assume that notes are used only for quotations, but they are used for paraphrased ideas and information as well. For example:

Note for paraphrased material

```
John Huston's first movie, The Maltese Falcon, is a faithful
adaptation of Dashiell Hammett's novel (Fell 242).
```

Fell's book is the source of the information, but the sentence is not a direct quotation. This point is important and needs to be stressed: *Use notes whenever you make use of a source's ideas and information, whether you quote the source's words directly or paraphrase them.* Since your research paper will contain more paraphrasing than direct quotation, most of your parenthetical notes will follow information written in your own phrasing.

The beauty of parenthetical notes is their simplicity: They provide the *least* amount of information needed to identify a source from the list of works cited, and the same form is used whether the source is a book, a periodical, or a newspaper. Only a few special cases require any variation from this standard form.

Some Special Cases

Notes should be as unobtrusive as possible; therefore, they should contain the least information needed to identify the source. In the following special cases, you will have to include additional information in your notes.

An Anonymous Work (Unidentified Author)

For works where no author is given, substitute the title (the item that comes first in the entry for that work in the list of works cited; remember that the point of notes is to refer your readers to the list of works cited if further information is needed). For example, consider a note for an anonymous article listed like this:

> "An Infant's Cries May Signal Physiological Defects." Psychology
>
>   Today June 1974: 21-24.

A parenthetical note referring to this article might look like this:

> ("An Infant's" 22)

Notice that when a title is long, only the first word or two should be given in the note, with no ellipsis dots. Also notice another difference: The list of works cited locates the complete text of the article, pages 21 through 24, whereas the note lists only page 22. The reason is that a list of works cited gives *all the pages* on which an article appears, whereas a note refers to the *specific page* or *pages* from which a quotation or piece of information is taken.

Works with Two or More Authors

Notes for works with multiple authors list their names just as they appear in your list of works cited. (You can find the works-cited entries for these two sources on pages 543–44.)

> (Reid, Forrestal, and Cook 52-54)
>
> (Courtois et al. 112)

Two or More Works by the Same Author

When two or more works by the same author appear in your list of works cited, add the first word or two from the title to your note to distinguish one work from another. For example, if your paper uses both a book by Isaac Asimov, *Adding a Dimension*, and a magazine article by him, "Happy Accidents," notes for those two sources might look like this:

```
(Asimov, Adding 240-43)
(Asimov, "Happy" 68)
```

Two Authors with the Same Last Name

When two authors with the same last name are cited in a paper, include their first names in notes so as to distinguish between them. For example:

```
(George Eliot 459)
(T. S. Eliot 44)
```

A Multivolume Work

If you are citing a book published in more than one volume, you do not need to list the volume number in the note if it is shown in the list of works cited.

Take, for example, the following entry:

```
Agus, Jacob Bernard. The Meaning of Jewish History. 2 vols.
      London: Abelard, 1963. Vol. 2.
```

Since your list of works cited shows that only this one volume is used in your paper, your notes should not list the volume number. For example:

```
(Agus 59)
```

If, on the other hand, your paper uses more than one volume of a work, each note needs to specify the volume as well, as in these examples:

```
(Agus 1: 120)
(Agus 2: 59)
```

A Reference to an Entire Work

When you refer to a work as a whole, rather than to a specific passage, no page numbers are needed, as in this example, which refers readers to three different sources found in the list of works cited:

```
At least three full-length biographies of Philbin have been
written since his death (Brickle; Baskin; Tillinghast).
```

More often, when a work as a whole is referred to, the author's name is mentioned in the paper itself, so no note is needed. For example:

```
Fermin's book on wine-making is sold only by mail-order.
```

A Reference to More Than One Work

Sometimes a note needs to refer to more than one work. You can list multiple sources in a note, separated by semicolons:

```
Broadwell's controversial theory about the intelligence of

lizards has been disputed by eminent herpetologists

(Matsumoto 33; Vanderhooten 7; Crambury 450).
```

A Reference to Discontinuous Pages

When you have taken source material from discontinuous pages of a work, list the pages, separated by commas:

```
(Witanowski 47, 103)
```

An Interview or Other Source without Pages

Many sources, such as recordings, television programs, and interviews, have no pages. For example, suppose you have conducted an interview for your paper and have this entry in your list of works cited:

```
Philcox, Arthur C. Personal interview. 17 Oct. 2005.
```

Information from the interview can be cited simply with the interviewee's name:

```
During World War II, children in Hadleyville played at being

civil defense spotters on the levee, searching the skies for

German aircraft (Philcox).
```

If the interviewee's name appears in the passage, no note at all is needed, as shown here:

```
Retired teacher Arthur Philcox says that ballpoint pens did

not replace fountain pens in Hadleyville's grade schools

until the mid-1950s.
```

References with Other Forms of Page Numbering

Page references in parenthetical notes should use the same numbering system as in the text being referred to. For example, a reference to pages with Roman numbering would look like this:

```
(Bullock iv-viii)
```

Reference to a newspaper article uses the system employed by that newspaper:

```
(Carlton B17-B18)
```

An Electronic Source

Some electronic texts look much like their printed versions, and the text appears on numbered pages. An example is David Irving's book *Hitler's War*, which you would list on a works-cited page like this:

```
Irving, David. Hitler's War. New York: Viking, 1977. 20 Jan.

    2000 <http://www.focal.org/books/hitler/HW.pdf>.
```

Because page numbers are visible on screen, you would cite a reference to this book as you would to any other—for example:

```
(Irving 166)
```

Some works, however, display no page numbers on screen, such as Kenneth Robinson's online book *Beyond the Wilderness*. Consequently, a parenthetical note referring to that work as a whole or to any part of the work would simply be:

```
(Robinson)
```

The same is true for periodical articles that you have not consulted in their original print forms but only as reproductions, without page numbers, in an electronic database. For example, the newspaper article in the following works-cited listing was consulted online through the Newspaper Source database, where it was reproduced without page numbers:

```
Yue, Lorene. "Economists Expect Federal Reserve to Leave Rates

    Unchanged." Detroit Free Press 20 Dec. 1999. Newspaper

    Source. EBSCOhost. 14 Jan. 2005 <http://www.epnet.com>.
```

Since it was consulted online and not in its original print form, a parenthetical note would not list page references:

(Yue)

One Source Cited in Another

Sometimes you wish to quote a source whom you have found quoted in *another* source. In such a case, your note should cite the actual source from which you take the material you are using. Imagine, for example, that in reading a book by an author named Robinson, you encounter a quotation from an article by another author named Amoros. Robinson provided a note (*Amoros 16*), to cite the quotation's location in Amoros's article. However, unless you actually then go to Amoros's article to look up the quotation, you would list Robinson as your source, preceded by *qtd. in* (an abbreviation for "quoted in"):

Amoros writes that "successful politicians, like successful actors and teachers, always stay in character" (qtd. in Robinson 199).

Quoting a print source found in another source

Also use *qtd. in* for notes when the person being quoted was an interview source. For example, if Robinson had interviewed and then quoted someone named Reese, you would give Robinson as your source for the Reese quotation:

Reese said, "The secret to life is learning how to write off your losses" (qtd. in Robinson 208).

Quoting an interview source found in another source

However, if you paraphrased Reese, you would omit *qtd. in:*

Reese believes that people should not dwell on past setbacks (Robinson 208).

Paraphrasing one source found in another source

Once you have practiced citing sources in your own research writing, you will quickly become familiar with the techniques involved. Observe the way notes are used in the works that you read, as in Allen's and Courtney's papers on pages 304–34. In writing your own research papers, refer to the Quick Reference Guide on the inside back covers of this book as needed, and use this chapter for fuller explanations. When unusual situations arise and you are uncertain how to cite a source, the wisest course may be to improvise, guided by your common sense. Always keep in mind that the purpose of notes is to acknowledge your sources in a clear, brief, consistent, and unobtrusive way.

Using Parenthetical Notes

Assume that the following passages are all taken from the same research paper. Parenthetical notes have been omitted, but information about their sources is given in brackets following each passage. First, write the list of works cited that would appear at the end of the paper (assuming that these are the paper's only sources). Second, insert parenthetical notes in the passages.

1. The world's most advanced bicycle was invented in 1997 by Swiss inventor Ugo Zwingli.

   [You discovered this information on page 33 of Vilma Mayer's book, *101 Offbeat Ideas*, published by the Phantom Company of Chicago in 2004.]

2. When he first encountered Zwingli's invention, cyclist Freddie Mercxx exclaimed: "This will either revolutionize road racing or set it back a hundred years!"

   [Mercxx wrote this on page 44 of his column, "New Products," which appeared on pages 44 and 45 of the November 1998 *Cyclist's World*.]

3. According to Rupert Brindel, president of the International Bicycle Federation, "The cycling world was in a tizzy about the Zwingli frame. Supporters called it 'the bike of the future,' while detractors said it removed the sport from the sport of cycling."

   [You found this in Melba Zweiback's book, *Two Wheels*, on page 202. She is quoting from Brindel's article, "The Zwingli Fiasco," which appeared on page 22 of the *Sporting Times* newspaper, April 13, 2003. *Two Wheels* was published in Montreal by Singleday in 2005.]

4. Zwingli had discovered a revolutionary way to reinforce tissue paper. The result was a frame so lightweight that it would actually gain speed while coasting uphill.

   [This too was taken from Mayer's book, page 36.]

5. In his Memoirs, Zwingli wrote, "I was overjoyed by how strong the tissue-paper frame was. The first prototype held up well under every test--until the first rainstorm."

   [He wrote *Memoirs* in 2003; the quotation is from the bottom of page 63 and the top of page 64. Zigurat Press of Zurich published it.]

6. Zwingli's bicycle was a mere curiosity until the following year, when he made his second brilliant discovery: waterproof tissue paper.

[You paraphrased this from "And Now: Non-Absorbent T.P.," an anonymous brief article on page 416 of the July 1998 *Applied Chemistry Bulletin* (volume 28), a journal with continuous paging.]

7. The twin brother of Freddie Mercxx, also a world-class cyclist, wrote:

> With all other bicycles, the strongest and fittest cyclist wins the race. With the Zwingli bike, the lightest racer wins. I'm tired of being wiped off the track by skinny guys on tissue paper.

[Otto Mercxx wrote this in a letter to his brother dated 28 January 2000.]

8. The fate of the Zwingli bicycle was sealed in 2001 when it was outlawed for competition by a vote of 70 to 3 of the International Bicycle Federation.

[You found this information on page 54 of Melba Zweiback's magazine article, "IBF Disposes of Tissue Paper 10-Speed," published on pages 54, 55, and 56 of the August 2001 *Newsmonth*.]

9. Although the following week's Tour de Finland race was marred by protests from newly unemployed lightweight riders, the cycling world soon returned to normal.

[This information appeared on page C17 of the *New York Times-News-Post* newspaper dated August 22, 2000, in an article by Greg LeMoon under the headline "Feather-weight Furor in Finland." You read the article last Tuesday in the AllSports-News online database, using the BOSCOworld online reference service at http://www. BOSCO.com.]

When Are Notes Needed?

It is your privilege as a scholar to make use of the scholarship of other people in your writing. It is your obligation as a scholar to make it clear to your readers which words and ideas in your writing are your own and which ones came from your sources. The general rule for when notes are needed is this: *Provide notes for all quotations; provide notes for all paraphrased information that is not commonly available knowledge.* The examples that follow illustrate this rule.

A frequent mistake made by beginning scholars is to give notes only for quotations. Remember that you need to acknowledge your debts to your sources, whether you quote their exact words or only borrow their ideas. You should give a note for information you have used, even if you have phrased it in words entirely your own. For example, assume you are writing an article on the Black Death, the plague that devastated medieval Europe, and one of your sources is Barbara Tuchman's book *A Distant Mirror*. Imagine that you found this passage on page 94:

> . . . Although the mortality rate was erratic, ranging from one fifth in some places to nine tenths or almost total elimination in others, the overall estimate of modern demographers has settled—for the area extending from India to Iceland— around the same figure expressed in Froissart's casual words: "a third of the world died." His estimate, the common one at the time, was not an inspired guess but a borrowing of St. John's figure for mortality from plague in Revelation, the favorite guide to human affairs in the Middle Ages.
>
> A third of Europe would have meant about 20 million deaths. No one knows how many died. Contemporary reports were an awed impression, not an accurate count.

If you wrote any of the following sentences based on this passage, you would need to give credit to Tuchman in a note.

```
It is widely accepted that about one third of Europe's
population died from the Black Death (Tuchman 94).
```

```
Although a mortality of 20 million Europeans is usually
accepted for the Black Death, no accurate figures exist to
confirm this estimate (Tuchman 94).
```

```
Even if the usual mortality estimate of one third of Europe
(Tuchman 94) is not accepted, the Black Death still exacted a
horrendous toll of the population.
```

None of these passages is a direct quotation, but since they are based on your source, they require notes. In the first two examples, by placing the note at the end of the sentence, you signal that all the information is from Tuchman's book. In the third example, by placing the note in the middle of the sentence, you indicate that only the material preceding the note is from that source.

You do not need to note information from a source if it is widely available and generally accepted. For example, you might have learned this information in an encyclopedia or almanac: *Oklahoma became a state in 1907*. Although you did not know this fact before you looked it up, it is such common information that it is in effect public property, and you need not acknowledge a source in a note. The facts on the Black Death in Tuchman's article, on the other hand, represent her own research findings, and she deserves full acknowledgment when her ideas are used.

The distinction being drawn here may not always be an obvious one. As is often the case with research writing, your best practice is to let common sense be your guide. You can usually tell when information is public property and when a source deserves credit for it in a note. But when you are in doubt, the safest course is to provide the note.

How Many Notes Are Enough?

In writing a research paper, you are creating something new, even if almost all the ideas and information in it are from your sources. At the very least, your contribution is to synthesize this information and to present it in a fresh way. For this reason your research paper will be based on a variety of sources. A long paper based on only one or two sources serves little purpose since it does nothing new. Consequently, your research papers are likely to have a number of notes, indicating the contributions of your various sources.

Sometimes you will have to use many notes to acknowledge a complex passage that is developed, quite legitimately, from several different sources. For example:

```
Herbal folk remedies have been imported to the West with

mixed results. An East African tea seems to be effective

against cholera ("Nature's" 6), while moxibustion, a Chinese

remedy for diarrhea, is still largely untested ("Burning" 25).

A Chinese arthritis medicine called "Chuifong Toukuwan," on

the other hand, is a positive danger to health (Hunter 8).
```

The second sentence requires two notes because it is based on two separate sources.

On the other hand, there can be a danger in overloading your paper with notes. One reason the format of notes is so brief is to keep them from getting in the way of what you are saying in the paper. When a paper is filled with note after note, even brief notes call attention to themselves, and they distract and annoy readers. With notes—as with quotations, brackets, and ellipsis dots—there can be too much of a good thing. Avoid passages like this in your writing:

```
In 1948, Isaac Stork ran for president (McCall 80) on the          Bad (too many

Anti-Vice ticket (Sullivan 42). His platform included a            notes)

prohibition on all sweetened or alcoholic beverages (McCall

80), fines for wearing brightly colored outfits (Stokes 124),

and the clothing of naked cats, dogs, and horses (McCall 81).
```

The notes here are annoying, not only because they interrupt the passage so often but also because they are unnecessary. It is evident that the writer has done some research and is eager to show off. The writer is deliberately juggling three sources, all of which contain the same information. The first sentence would seem to state commonly available information that does not require acknowledgment. Information in the second sentence might also be considered public property, but to be safe, the writer might provide a single joint note after the final sentence like this:

```
...cats, dogs, and horses (McCall 80-81; Stokes 124).
```

EXERCISE **Judging When Notes Are Needed**

Imagine that it is some time in the near future and that you are writing a brief research report. Imagine too that, having found the following six passages in your research, you have then written the report that follows them. What remains for you to do is to supply notes for the report.

1. Horseradish (*Armoracia lapathifolia*), a plant of the mustard family, is grown for its pungent, white fleshy root. [*Source:* Elizabeth Silverman's book, *Common Plants of North America*, page 208.]

2. I first met Mr. Finnahey when I stopped by his farm to get forms filled out for his medical benefits. When I asked him his age, he said, "I forget the exact year I was born. It was the same year the Brooklyn Bridge was built." Naturally I didn't believe him since he didn't look a day over 40, and his wife, Becky, was 26. Imagine my surprise when he brought out his birth certificate. [*Source:* social worker Marlys Davenport, quoted on page 35 of a newspaper article written by Lester Grady.]

3. The Brooklyn Bridge was built in 1883. [*Source:* an anonymous article in *Encyclopedia Galactica*, volume 4, page 73.]

4. When I arrived to examine Julius Finnahey, he was eating a lunch of peanut butter and horseradish sandwiches. "Best thing for you," he said. "I eat 'em every day—always have." This was my first clue to the cause of his longevity. My research into his diet led to a discovery that may provide humans of the future with lifetimes lasting perhaps two centuries. [*Source:* Chester Vinneman writing on page 19 of his article, "Radish-Legume Combination Slows the Aging Process," in the *New England Medical Report*.]

5. Chester Vinneman discovered that the combination of the trace element *vinnemanium*, which occurs in the common horseradish root, with amino acids in the common peanut retards the decay of the cell wall lining in human tissue. To Vinneman, the increased longevity which his discovery will provide is a mixed blessing: "I find the prospect both thrilling and frightening. The questions and problems that it raises stagger the mind." [*Source:* an unsigned article, "Life Everlasting Now a Reality?" in *Timely* magazine, page 78, continued on page 80.]

6. Chester Vinneman won the Nobel Prize for medicine for his discovery of the miracle age retardant. He is a professor of biochemistry at the University of Manitoba. [*Source: Who's Who,* page 993.]

Here is a section of your report, which is based on the preceding list of sources. Supply the appropriate parenthetical notes.

Important discoveries are often the result of chance occurrences. If it had not been for a routine inquiry by social worker Marlys Davenport, Chester Vinneman might never have won the Nobel Prize for medicine. It was Davenport who confirmed Julius Finnahey's amazing statement that he was born in 1883, "the year the Brooklyn Bridge was built."

Professor Vinneman made the connection between Finnahey's extraordinary youthfulness and his diet of peanut butter and horseradish sandwiches. Horseradish (Armoracia lapathifolia) was not previously thought to have benefits beyond the flavor of its pungent root. Through extensive tests, however, Vinneman discovered a previously unreported trace element in horseradish, which he named vinnemanium. This element, when combined with amino acids such as those found in peanuts, prevents human cell walls from decaying.

Vinneman predicts that as the result of his discovery, human lifetimes may extend in the future to as many as two centuries. He finds the prospect of such longevity "both thrilling and frightening. The questions and problems that it raises stagger the mind." It remains to be seen how wisely humankind will cope with greatly extended lives.

Finally, explain why you placed notes where you did and why you provided notes for some statements and not others.

How Much Material Can One Note Cover?

A parenthetical note comes after borrowed material, but how can a writer make clear *how much* of the preceding material is referred to by the note? The following passage illustrates the problem:

> Haagendazs was considered one of Denmark's premier
> eccentrics. He continually wore the same heavy woolen
> sweater, regardless of the occasion or season. Former
> colleagues attest that he worked in near darkness, and he
> reportedly kept exotic spiders and beetles as pets
> (Noland 18).

The extent of the reference is not clear. Is Noland the source for all three examples of Haagendazs's eccentricities or just the latter two (or the last one)? The ambiguity could be avoided, perhaps, by placing a note after each paraphrased sentence. But the paper would then be overloaded with notes, and readers would find it annoying to meet with identical notes sentence after sentence.

A somewhat clearer way to define a long borrowed passage is to mark its beginning with an acknowledgment phrase. For example:

The acknowledgment phrase marks the beginning of the borrowed passage

> Noland reports that Haagendazs was considered one of
> Denmark's premier eccentrics. He continually wore the same
> heavy woolen sweater, regardless of the occasion or season.
> Former colleagues attest that he worked in near darkness, and

The note marks the end of the passage

> he reportedly kept exotic spiders and beetles as pets (18).

Here it is clear that the entire passage is taken from page 18 of a work by Noland. However, acknowledgment phrases are not commonly used with factual information, and an excess of acknowledgment phrases can be as distracting to readers as an excess of parenthetical notes. Alas, some ambiguity in the scope of your references is probably unavoidable. Rely on your judgment about whether a borrowed passage is adequately marked, but if you are in doubt, supply the acknowledgment phrase. You may also ask your instructor for advice.

EXERCISE   **Judging When Borrowed Material Is Adequately Marked**

Examine the parenthetical notes in the research papers by Allen and Courtney on pages 304–34. For each parenthetical note, is it clear how much material is borrowed from the source? If not, can you suggest a way to make it clearer?

INFORMATION FOOTNOTES

Even when you use parenthetical notes to acknowledge sources, you can still use footnotes to supply information that you feel does not belong in the text of your paper. To mark an *information footnote*, place a raised asterisk (*) in the place where you invite the reader to consult the note, like this:

```
...domesticated animals such as dogs, cats,* and...
```

At the bottom of the same page, type ten underline bars and present your footnote on the next line, beginning with a raised asterisk, like this:

———————

```
    * Witherspoon does not classify the common house cat as a
"domesticated" animal but as a "wild" animal that merely
"coexists" with humans (16).
```

Typing footnotes can be cumbersome. Fortunately, most word-processing programs can place footnotes automatically at the bottom of the proper page.

If you use a second information footnote on the same page, mark it with a double asterisk (**) or dagger (†). You should, however, use information footnotes rarely. Almost always when you have something to tell your readers, it is better to say it within the paper itself. This is in line with the general rule that anything which interrupts the reader or makes reading more difficult should be avoided.

C *Research Paper Format (MLA Style)*

 FORMAT FOR YOUR POLISHED DRAFT

The polished draft of your paper should be printed (using word processing software on a computer). A neatly handwritten paper may be allowed in rare cases, but only a printed paper presents a professional appearance. When you are communicating with others, appearance counts. Although the paper's appearance does not alter the content of your writing, it most certainly does affect the way your writing is received. Instructors try to be as objective as possible in judging student work, but they are still swayed, like all other humans, by appearances. Computer-printed papers give the impression of more serious, careful work, and they are certainly more inviting and easier to read. In the professional world, reports and correspondence are always computer-printed; anything less would be unthinkable. There is no reason to treat your college writing with any less respect.

Computer word processing offers the greatest benefits for composing, revising, copyediting, and printing your paper. With a word processor, you can make additions, deletions, corrections, and rearrangements of passages easily and at any time. The spell-check feature can identify errors in spelling and typing that you might otherwise miss. And, of course, the finished product has a polished, professional appearance.

When you compose your paper, follow the format exemplified by one of the sample papers in Chapter 8. The following are standard format guidelines for research paper. Individual instructors may wish to modify some of them according to their preferences. Check with your instructor if you have questions about the required format.

Margins and Alignment

Set your **page margins** at one inch at the top, bottom, right, and left of your paper. For a Word document, select "Page Setup" from the "File" menu, and set up your margins as in Figure C.1.

For the **alignment** of your paper, choose "Align left" on the Formatting toolbar; do not select "Justify." Research papers have a "ragged" right margin, unlike books such as this one, which set their type with a justified right margin. Do not have the computer divide words with hyphens to achieve a straighter right margin.

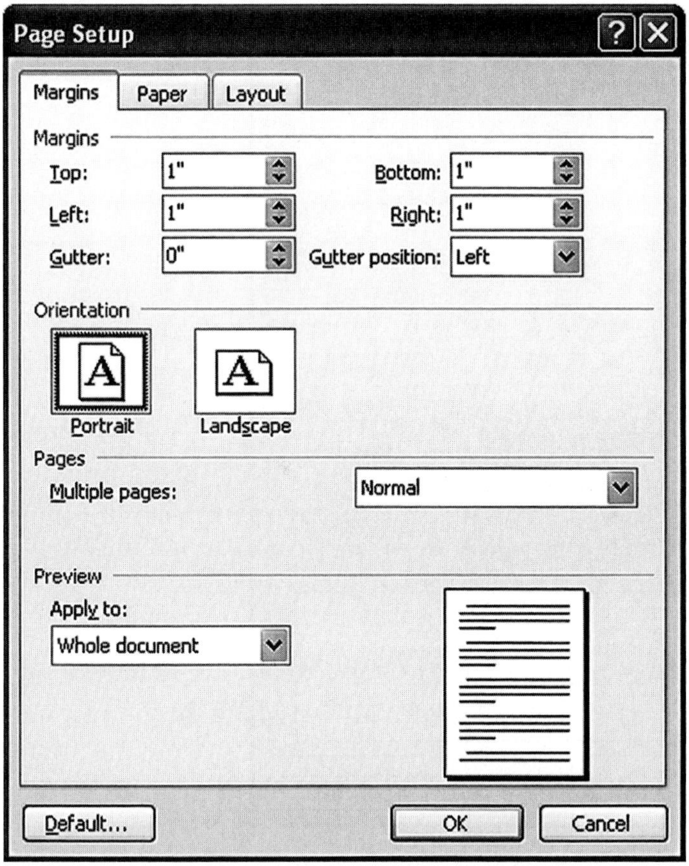

Set all margins at one inch.

Figure C.1 Margin settings in a Word document.

Your computer may allow you to avoid a ***widow line*** or an ***orphan line***—the typesetting terms for stranded lines. An orphan is the first line of a new paragraph printed as the last line of page. A widow is the final line of a paragraph printed as the first line of a page. In Word, choose "Paragraph" from the "Format" menu, and click on the "Line and Page Breaks" tab. Select "Widow/Orphan control" as in Figure C.2. Notice how Allen Strickland avoided a widow at the top of page 306.

Spacing

Double-space (leave every other line blank) throughout the paper. This includes indented quotations and the list of works cited, which are also double-spaced. Do not skip additional lines between paragraphs, although it is acceptable to skip extra lines before a new section that has a heading. Notice how Courtney Holbrook skipped extra lines before the "What I Found" section on page 324. In Word, you can either set the line spacing at "2" on the Formatting toolbar, or you can set line spacing as "Double" in the "Paragraph" menu, as in Figure C.3.

Select widow/
orphan control
for your paper.

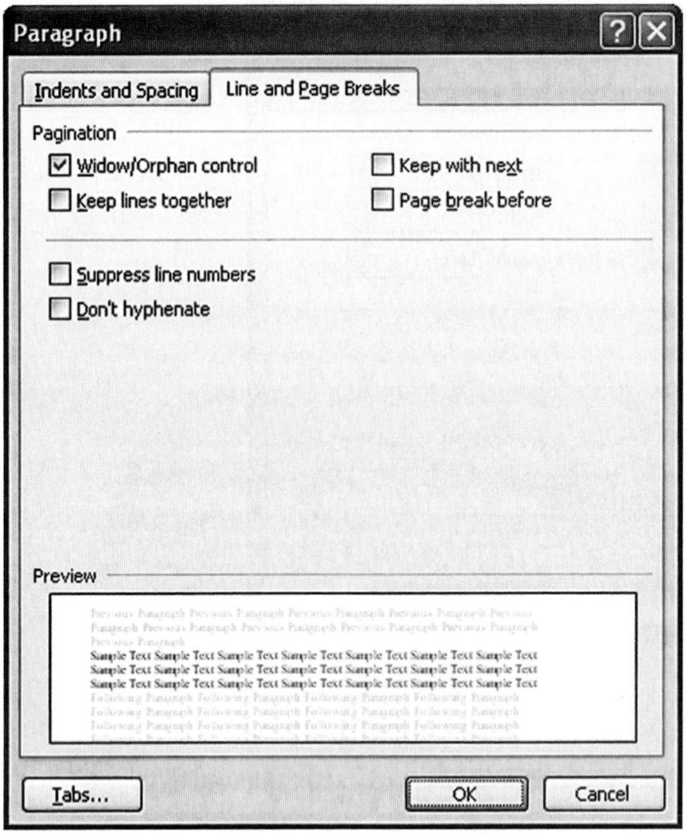

Figure C.2 Setting widow/orphan protection.

Indenting

Indent the first line of each **new paragraph** one-half inch from the left margin.
You can have Word do this automatically by setting the indentation from the
"Paragraph" menu, as in Figure C.3.

For **long quotations**, indent one inch from the left margin. In Word, with
your cursor in the quotation, select "Paragraph" from the "Format" menu, and set
indentations as in Figure C.4.

Figure C.5 shows an excerpt from a research paper demonstrating the standard format for margins, alignment, spacing, and indentation.

Type Font

If your software allows a choice of **fonts**, choose Times Roman, a proportional-
space font, or a monospaced font such as Letter Gothic or Courier. You can also
use a sans-serif font such as Arial if your instructor approves. Never use a fancy
font such as script. Set the **font size** at 12.

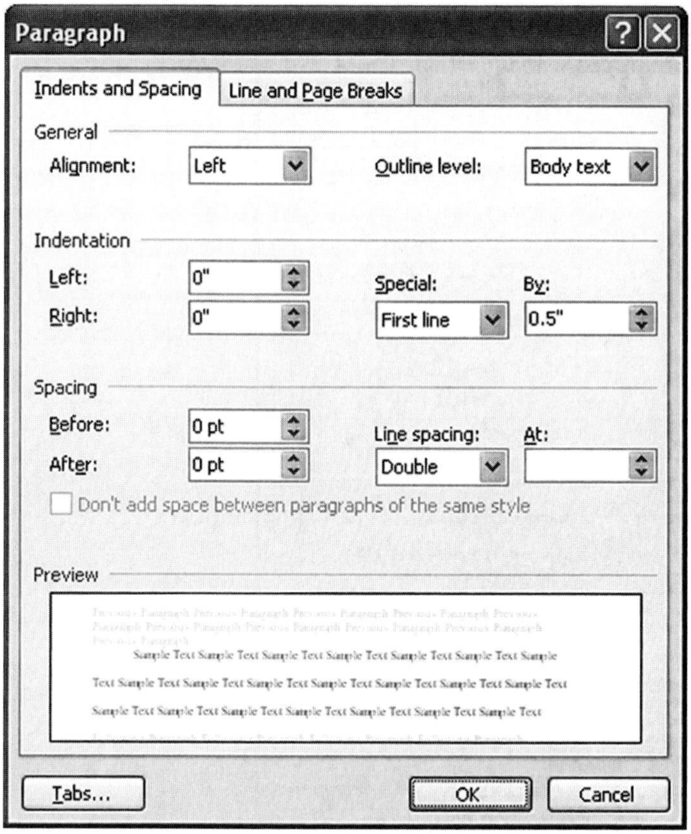

You can set first-line indentation at a half inch.

Set line spacing at "Double."

Figure C.3 Setting line spacing and paragraph indentation.

For **book titles** you can use either italics (*Moby Dick*) or underlining (<u>Moby Dick</u>), but be consistent throughout. Do not use boldface (**bold**) for titles or section headings or for emphasis.

Standard Fonts for Research Papers
Times Roman   (a proportional font)
Letter Gothic (a monospaced font)
Arial   (a sans-serif font)

Nonstandard and Usually Unacceptable Fonts
Any script font
Any other fancy font

Indent a long quotation one inch from the left margin.

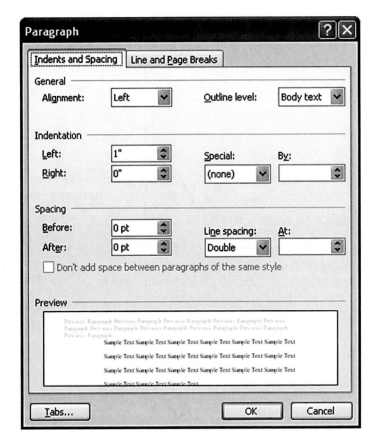

Figure C.4 Setting the indentation for a long quotation.

The First Page

The format of your first page should resemble that of Allen's paper in Figure C.6.

- **Page header.** Your last name and the page number go at the top of the first page and each subsequent page. In a Word document, to set up a header that will automatically run at the top of every page, select "Header and Footer" from the "View" menu. A header box will appear on the page, as in Figure C.7. Type your last name in the box, and then click on "Align Right" on the Formatting toolbar. Skip a space after your name and click on the "Insert Page Number" icon in the popup "Header and Footer" box. Finally, click on "Close."

- **Author information.** Type your full name, course information, and the date in the upper-left corner of the first page, about one inch from the top of the page. If you use an automatic header the author information goes on the first line of the paper itself, immediately below the header. A separate title page is needed only for lengthy reports (see page 591).

- **Title.** The title follows immediately under the author information. Writers have the option of whether or not to skip additional lines before and after the

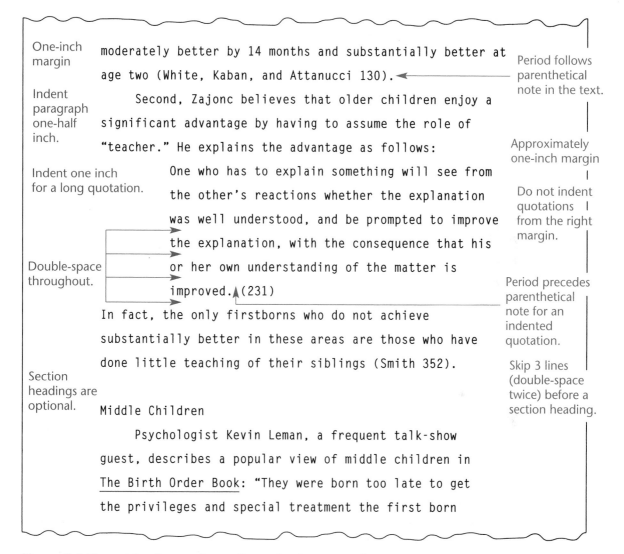

One-inch margin

moderately better by 14 months and substantially better at age two (White, Kaban, and Attanucci 130).

Period follows parenthetical note in the text.

Indent paragraph one-half inch.

Second, Zajonc believes that older children enjoy a significant advantage by having to assume the role of "teacher." He explains the advantage as follows:

Indent one inch for a long quotation.

One who has to explain something will see from the other's reactions whether the explanation was well understood, and be prompted to improve the explanation, with the consequence that his or her own understanding of the matter is improved. (231)

Approximately one-inch margin

Do not indent quotations from the right margin.

Double-space throughout.

Period precedes parenthetical note for an indented quotation.

In fact, the only firstborns who do not achieve substantially better in these areas are those who have done little teaching of their siblings (Smith 352).

Section headings are optional.

Middle Children

Psychologist Kevin Leman, a frequent talk-show guest, describes a popular view of middle children in The Birth Order Book: "They were born too late to get the privileges and special treatment the first born

Skip 3 lines (double-space twice) before a section heading.

Figure C.5 Format for the spacing and margins in a research paper.

title. Only the first letter of each important word in the title should be capitalized; do not capitalize a word such as *the* (article), *and* (conjunction), or *of* (preposition) unless it is the first word of the title or the first word following a colon. Do not use underlining, italics, or bold for the title and do not enclose it in quotation marks. Of course, you should use standard punctuating conventions for titles of works that you include within your own title. For example:

The Depiction of Old Age in King Lear

and in "The Love Song of J. Alfred Prufrock"

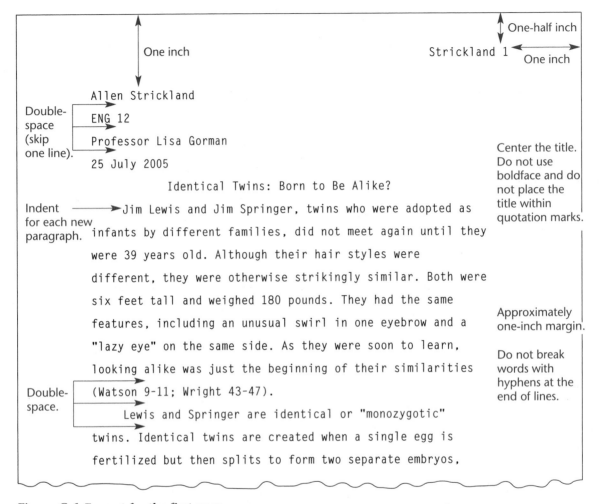

One-half inch

One inch   Strickland 1

One inch

Double-space (skip one line).

Allen Strickland

ENG 12

Professor Lisa Gorman

25 July 2005

Identical Twins: Born to Be Alike?

Indent for each new paragraph.

Jim Lewis and Jim Springer, twins who were adopted as infants by different families, did not meet again until they were 39 years old. Although their hair styles were different, they were otherwise strikingly similar. Both were six feet tall and weighed 180 pounds. They had the same features, including an unusual swirl in one eyebrow and a "lazy eye" on the same side. As they were soon to learn, looking alike was just the beginning of their similarities (Watson 9-11; Wright 43-47).

Double-space.

Lewis and Springer are identical or "monozygotic" twins. Identical twins are created when a single egg is fertilized but then splits to form two separate embryos,

Center the title. Do not use boldface and do not place the title within quotation marks.

Approximately one-inch margin.

Do not break words with hyphens at the end of lines.

Figure C.6 Format for the first page.

Header   Strickland 1

Header and Footer

Insert AutoText ▼   Close

Figure C.7 Setting an automatic page header in Word.

> • **Body.** Indent the first line of each new paragraph and double-space throughout. Do not skip additional lines between paragraphs.

Subsequent Pages

The format of subsequent pages is shown in Figure C.8. If you use an automatic header, have the computer automatically place your last name and page number

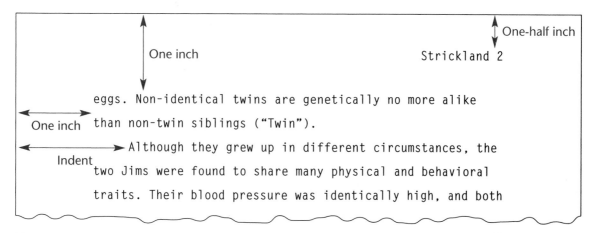

Figure C.8 Format for subsequent pages.

at the top right of each page (see Figure C.7). If not, type this information at the top right, and then double-space twice (skip three lines); the first line of text should begin one inch from the top of the page.

Tables and Figures

You can include **tables**—the presentation of data in columns—and **figures**—drawings, graphs, photographs, or other inserts—in your paper. Tables and figures can be either of your own creation or copied from a source (and duly acknowledged). A sample page from a research paper that includes a table is illustrated in Figure C.9. Figure C.10 shows a figure that the writer photocopied from a source he acknowledged.

Observe the following guidelines when you include tables and figures:

1. All tables and figures should be referred to within the paper (e.g., "Table 1 shows the variation among . . . ," ". . . as can be seen in Figure 6," etc.). Place the table or figure as close as possible following its mention in the paper.

2. Tables and figures should be numbered consecutively (Table 1, Table 2, Table 3, . . . ; Figure 1, Figure 2, . . .). Each table should be given a clear explanatory label on the following line, and each figure should have an explanatory caption typed on the same line and placed below the figure. Each line begins at the left margin; it is not centered.

3. Double-space throughout, but skip three lines (double-space twice) both before and after a table or figure.

4. Lines may be drawn across the page (as in Figure C.9, e.g.) to set a table or figure apart from the rest of the paper.

5. A table or figure may be photocopied from a source and pasted onto your page (see Figure C.10). You may then wish to photocopy the entire page again.

Reagan 8

Other statistics show that although the number of medical students in their thirties and forties is increasing, one's chances of being admitted to medical school decrease with age, as Table 1 demonstrates:

The table is referred to within the paper.

Each table or figure is given a number and a label.

Quadruple-space before and after each table or figure.

Table 1

Percentages of Men and Women Accepted by Medical Schools (1989)[a]

Raised lowercase letters are used for footnotes within tables and figures.

Age	Men	Women
21-23	73	67
24-27	58	55
28-31	49	53
32-34	46	51
35-37	41	46
38 and over	27	34

Each line of a table begins at the left margin (it is not centered).

Double-space throughout the table.

Source: Plantz, Lorenzo, and Cole 115

[a] The chart is based on data gathered by the American Medical Association.

The table ends with the source and footnotes (if any).

I have learned that there are many criteria other than age that medical schools consider when reviewing applications.

The paper resumes following the table.

Figure C.9 Sample page with table.

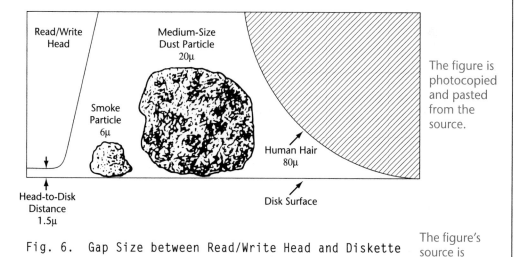

Shriver 10

material off the diskette and avoids several potential
hazards. The gap between the read/write head and the
diskette is incredibly small, as can be seen in Figure 6.
The figure also shows some of the "gremlins" that cause
disk problems.

Read/Write
Head

Medium-Size
Dust Particle
20μ

The figure is
photocopied
and pasted
from the
source.

Smoke
Particle
6μ

Human Hair
80μ

Head-to-Disk
Distance
1.5μ

Disk Surface

Fig. 6.   Gap Size between Read/Write Head and Diskette
          (Smith-Richardson 62).

The figure's
source is
acknowledged.

Figure C.10 Sample page with a figure.

6. If the table or figure is taken from a source, acknowledge the source on a line following the table or figure.

7. If you use footnotes (as in Figure C.9), assign them raised lowercase letters (a, b, c, etc.) and place the notes below the table or figure (and source citation, if given).

List of Works Cited

Begin the list of works cited on a new page. The exception is a very brief list, which you can begin by skipping three lines (double-spacing twice) from the end of the text.

- **Title.** Center the title *Works Cited* (or *Bibliography*) at the top of the page (the same top margin of one inch as you use the throughout the paper).

- **Spacing.** Double-space between throughout. That is, double space between the title and the first entry and throughout the list. Do not skip additional lines between entries.

- **Indentation.** Follow the guidelines in Chapter A. Remember to use a "hanging intent" for each entry; that is, begin each entry at the left margin and indent the second and subsequent lines one-half inch. To set up automatic indentation for entries in a Word document, selection "Paragraph" from the "Format" menu and choose settings as in Figure C.11.

- **Order of entries.** List items in alphabetical order. Do not number your entries. The list of works cited should include only works that you quoted or paraphrased in writing the paper, not works you consulted but did not use.

Refer to Figure C.12 for a sample works-cited page.

Use hanging indentation for a works cited list.

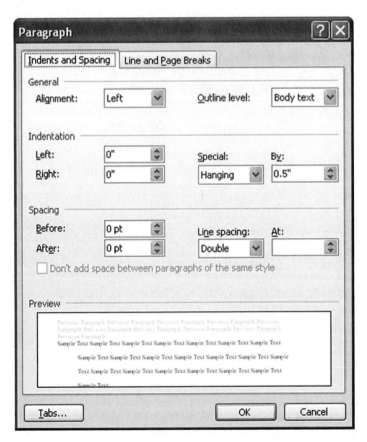

Figure C.11 Setting indentation for a works-cited list in a Word document.

Holbrook 1

Works Cited

Double-space throughout.

Carter, John. Personal interview. 18 May 2005.

Dutka, Elaine. "New Michael Moore Project Gives Drug

Indent the second subsequent lines one-half inch.

Companies a Sick Feeling." Los Angeles Times 23 Dec.

2004. MichaelMoore.com. 24 May 2005 <http://

www.michaelmoore.com/words/mikeinthenews/>.

Break URLs only after a backslash. Do not use a hyphen.

Farr, J. Michael. America's Top Jobs for College Graduates.

3rd ed. Indianapolis: Jist Works, 1999.

Figure C.12 Sample works-cited page.

Identical Twins:

Born to Be Alike?

by

Allen Strickland

ENG 12

Professor Lisa Gorman

25 July 2005

Figure C.13 Sample title page.

Title Page

A title page is standard only for a book-length report, a paper with multiple chapters, or a paper with preliminary material such as a formal outline or preface. If you use a title page, it should follow the format shown in Figure C.13. Title-page information is typed in the center of the page. In Word, create your title page in a separate file. Select "Page Setup" from the "File" menu. Click on the "Layout" tab and set the vertical alignment to "Center," as in Figure C.14. To center each line horizontally, choose "Center" alignment from the Formatting toolbar.

Printing the Paper

- **Paper.** Use plain white, heavyweight, $8^1/_2 \times 11$-inch paper. Print on one side of the paper only.
- **Ink.** Use only black ink. Replace the cartridge in your printer if it no longer produces a dark legible copy.
- **Fastening.** Fasten your paper with a paper clip in the upper left-hand corner. Do not staple or rivet pages together or place your paper in a cover unless you are requested to do so by you instructor.

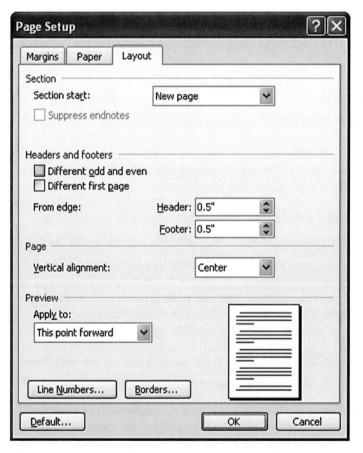

Set vertical alignment to "Center" for a title page.

Figure C.14 Page setup for a title page.

Errors

Use the spell-check feature of your word-processing program and proofread to make your paper as error-free as possible before you print your final draft. For errors discovered during proofreading, neatly cross out a minor error with a single line, and write the correction above it. Never erase, and do not use correction fluid for making handwritten changes. Any page with a major error or numerous minor errors should be corrected on the computer and reprinted.

 A FORMAL OUTLINE

The general, *informal outlines* that Allen Strickland used in writing his early drafts (see pages 395 and 445) helped him organize his research materials. The length and complexity of a research paper require writers to have a plan for arranging it—one that is general and flexible enough so that they can develop and alter it as they discover new ideas.

Informal outlines are valuable, but most writers—both beginners and professionals alike—find it difficult and limiting to create a detailed, formal outline *before* they write. As you have now read many times in this book, writing is a learning process. Writers rarely know exactly how a paper will turn out before they write it. Even the best-prepared writers are usually surprised by the final form their writing takes. This occurs because our minds are actively at work when we write, and writing stimulates new thoughts that can take our writing in unforeseen directions.

Although a *formal outline* is limited in usefulness when it is prepared before you begin writing, it *can* be useful as part of the revision process—when it is written *after* you have completed a preliminary draft. As a scaled-down map of your paper, the formal outline allows you to see its organization with clarity. It can point out the flaws of your arrangement and suggest new possibilities. Some instructors require that a printed, formal outline be included as a part of the research paper to make sure that their students have considered organization carefully. The detailed formal outline that Allen submitted with his paper is printed on the following page.

Identical Twins: Born to Be Alike?

I. Introduction
   A. Anecdote of Jim twins (beginning)
   B. Cause of twin births
      1. Identical
      2. Non-identical
   C. Anecdote of Jim twins (continued)
   D. Thesis: questions about role of genes in shaping us

II. Controversy: nature vs. nurture
   A. Statement of the controversy
   B. Twin studies in science
   C. Different perspectives on identical twins
      1. Similarities between twins
         a) Studies of identical twins reared apart
         b) Jack/Oskar anecdote
            (1) Similar nature, different nurture
            (2) Support for role of nature
      2. Differences between twins
         a) Caroline/Sarah anecdote
            (1) Similar nurture, different nature
            (2) Support for role of nurture
         b) Studies of differences in twins
         c) Theory of role of parenting

III. Controversy: determinism vs. free will
   A. Arguments about role of genetics in sexuality
      1. O'Donnell twins anecdote
      2. Positions
         a) Choice argument
         b) Genetics argument
         c) Combined view: role for both nature and nurture
   B. Arguments about role of genetics in divorce

IV. Conclusion
   A. Importance of genetics
   B. Controversy likely to continue

An outline can be as detailed—or as general—as you wish. Allen's outline is reasonably complete, but he could have made it either shorter or longer if he wished. Compare it to this less detailed version of Allen's outlined:

    I. Introduction: Role of identical twins in genetics controversy
   II. Controversy: nature vs. nurture in twin studies
      A. Similarities between twins: case of Jack/Oskar
      B. Difference between twins: case of Caroline/Sarah
         1. Studies of differences in twins
         2. Role of parenting
  III. Controversy: determinism vs. free will
      A. Arguments about role of genetics in sexuality
      B. Arguments about role of genetics in divorce
  IV. Conclusion: controversy likely to continue

On the other hand, Allen could also create a far more detailed outline of his paper. For example, he could expand Section III-A of his outline as follows:

  III. Controversy: determinism vs. free will
      A. Arguments about the role of genetics in sexuality
         1. O'Donnell twins anecdote
            a) Mirror-image differences
            b) Different sexual orientations
         2. Positions
            a) Choice argument
               (1) Different orientations despite identical genes
               (2) Conclusion that orientation not genetic
            b) Genetics argument
               (1) Greater probability of same orientation for identical twins
               (2) Conclusion that orientation is genetic
             c) Combined view: contribution of multiple factor
               (1) No "gay gene"
               (2) Gene role estimated at 31–74%
               (3) Role for both nature and nurture

When you are revising your paper, a detailed outline can help you see how each part fits into the whole. When you have difficulty in creating an outline, the cause is often a problem with organization of your paper. Your attempts to create a logical outline can often suggest a workable arrangement of material within your paper. For example, in an early draft of his paper, Allen wrote about differences between identical twins in several sections throughout his paper. As he created an outline, however, he decided the paper would work better if he grouped a discussion of twin differences into a single section.

On the other hand, a writer should not be a slave to a rigidly symmetrical outline. In the final analysis, the nature of your material and not form-for-form's sake should determine your outline.

Standard Numbering System

Formal outlines usually follow the format that Allen used. Notice that each major part of Allen's outline is divided into subparts. These subparts are indented and marked with numbers and letters, following this *standard system:*

Paper Title

    I. First major part of the paper
       A. First subpart of I
       B. Second subpart of I
          1. First subpart of B
          2. Second subpart of B
   II. Second major part
       A. First subpart of II
          1. First subpart of A
          2. Second subpart of A
       B. Second subpart of II
          1. First subpart of B
          2. Second subpart of B
 III. Third major part
       A. First subpart of III
          1. First subpart of A
          2. Second subpart of A
          3. Third subpart of A
       B. Second subpart of III
          1. First subpart of B
          2. Second subpart of B
             a. First subpart of 2
             b. Second subpart of 2
             c. Third subpart of 2
          3. Third subpart of B

Decimal System

The *decimal system* is also widely used for outlines, particularly for scientific papers.

  1. First major part
  2. Second major part
     2.1 First subpart of 2
     2.2 Second subpart of 2
         2.2.1 First subpart of 2.2
         2.2.2 Second subpart of 2.2
             2.2.2.1 ...
             2.2.2.2 ...
  3. ...
     3.1 ...
     3.2 ...
     3.3 ...

Some instructors who assign formal outlines require, in the interest of symmetry, that whenever a part is to have subparts, there must be at least two of them; that is, they prefer that there not be a part 1 without at least a part 2, and so on. For example, they would find level IA(1) in the following to be faulty because it is the only entry on its level—there is no IA(2):

      I. Nature vs. nurture in twin studies
         A. Similarities between twins
            (1) Case of Jack/Oskar
         B. Differences between twins
            (1) Case of Caroline/Sarah

It should be stressed that not everyone objects to lone subparts. For those who do, the preceding can be adjusted easily by incorporating the subparts into the parts above them:

     II. Nature vs. nurture in twin studies
         A. Similarities between twins: case of Jack/Oskar
         B. Differences between twins: case of Caroline/Sarah

Formal Outlines

EXERCISES

1. Following are the parts of an outline for an argumentative paper. They appear in the proper order, but they have not been numbered or indented. Number them according to the *standard system* for outlining.

The Case against Saturday Morning Cartoons

Introduction
Background: description of current situation
Thesis: harm to children by Saturday morning cartoon shows
Counterarguments (those favoring these shows)
Positive-benefit arguments
Benefit to parents: babysitting
Benefits to children
Cartoon violence a harmless outlet for children's aggression
Children taught about life from cartoons
Free-market arguments
Programming determined by ratings, sponsors
Children's viewing up to parents, not networks
Censorship dangerous to our way of life
Refutation of counterarguments
Refutation of positive-benefit arguments
Damage to parents: deprived of interaction with their children
Damage to children
Shown only violent solutions to problems
Shown only the worst aspects of life
Refutation of free-market arguments
Morality, not only profits, a responsibility of networks
Parents unable to judge and screen all programming

> Voluntary controls, not censorship, requested
> Additional argument: danger to society of children's viewing
> A nation of antisocial zombies
> A nation of viewers, not doers
> Conclusion: a call for reform

2. Renumber the preceding outline entries using the decimal system.

Topic and Sentence Outlines

The preceding formal outlines are examples of ***topic outlines***, in which all the parts consist of phrases rather than complete sentences. In a ***sentence outline***, the parts consist of complete sentences. For example:

> III. Another philosophical debate is between determinism and free will.
>   A. Is our sexual orientation determined by our genes?
>   (1) The identical O'Donnell twins have different sexual orientations.
>   (2) Three different positions have been argued.
>   (a) Some use twin data to argue against the role of genetics.
>   (b) Some use the data to argue for the role of genetics.
>   (c) Most researchers argue that both nature and nurture play a role in determining sexual orientation.
>   B. Similar arguments have been made about divorce. . . .

You can use either the topic or sentence outline method, but whichever you choose, be certain that you follow it consistently.

Like some of the other steps in research writing, the details of outline-writing may strike you as complicated—as undoubtedly they are—but they do serve a purpose. Use your informal and formal outlines to help you organize, write, and revise your paper. But remember that an outline is a tool to help you produce a better paper and not an end in itself. It is important at all times to remember the central goal of your research writing: to communicate what you have discovered in an effective way. Like all parts of the research process, the outline will work best and be of most help to you if you approach it with common sense.

EXERCISES | **Sentence Outlines**

1. Continue revising Allen Strickland's outline on page 594 to make it a sentence outline.

2. Rewrite the outline in the preceding exercise beginning on the previous page to make it a sentence outline. Each line of the outline should be a complete sentence.

Footnotes and Endnotes

Scholars in the fields of art, dance, history, music, religion, and theater often use footnotes and endnotes, instead of parenthetical notes, to document sources. Although it should not be necessary for you to memorize the details of the format, you should know how to use this chapter as a reference guide whenever you need to write footnotes or endnotes. When you do, consult it carefully and be certain to follow the format exactly, paying special attention to the mechanics of arrangement and punctuation.

Figures D.1 and D.2 show how a portion of Allen Strickland's research paper would have looked if he had used footnotes instead of parenthetical notes. (Compare them with his use of parenthetical notes on page 309.) The excerpt in Figure D.3 shows what his "Notes" page would have looked like if he had used endnotes. To insert a footnote or endnote in a Word document, place the cursor where you wish the first note to go, select Insert, "Reference" and then "Footnote" from the "Insert" menu and then choose either "Footnotes" or "Endnotes."

Footnotes and endnotes serve the same purpose as parenthetical notes—to identify and give credit to your sources for their specific contributions to your paper. In the same place in your paper where you would put a parenthetical note, put a raised number to refer your readers to the note. Number your notes consecutively throughout the paper, starting with number 1. For footnotes, type each note at the bottom of the same page where the reference occurs. For endnotes, type all notes, in numerical order, on a separate page following the paper but preceding the list of works cited.

SAMPLE FOOTNOTES AND ENDNOTES

The models in this chapter show the footnote/endnote format for works cited in Chapter A. Note that complete information about a source is required only the first time it is cited in a note. Subsequent notes use an abbreviated format. (See sample footnote 11 in Figure D.1.)

contrasts, the twins talk on the phone every day and are "absolutely best friends."[8]

One recent study has shown that the wiring in identical twins' brains is not identical,[9] and another that the DNA of twins becomes less alike as they grown older.[10] Many differences have been attributed to environmental factors. For example, a 2001 study showed that identical twins with different diets had significantly different cholesterol levels, and a 2002 study showed differences in emotional stress that were related to social factors such as church attendance and their relationship with their mothers.[11]

arents of identical twins report differences in

[8] Caroline Clements, personal interview, 15 July 2005.

[9] Robert Roy Britt, "Identical Twins Not So Identical," LiveScience: Human Biology, 8 July 2005, 13 July 2005 <http://www.livescience.com/humanbiology/050708_identical_twins.html>.

[10] "Even Identical Twins Grow Apart Genetically-- Study," Reuters, Yahoo News, 5 July 2005, 5 July 2005 <http://news.yahoo.com/news?tmpl=story&u=/nm/20050705/sc_nm/science_twins_dc_5>.

[11] Britt.

Notes are numbered consecutively throughout the paper. The numbers are super-scripts (raised slightly above the line).

Double-space twice (skip 3 lines).

Double-space within and between footnotes.

After the first refer-ence to a source (see footnote 9), the abbrevi-ated form is used (see footnote 11).

Figure D.1 A sample page from a paper that uses footnotes.

One is left-handed, the other right-handed. As children they
had a "lazy eye" on different sides. Their hair parts
naturally on opposite sides, and whorls of hair spiral
clockwise for one twin, counterclockwise for the other.[14]

    [12] Barbara Schave Klein, Not All Twins Are Alike:
Psychological Profiles of Twinship, Westport, CT: Praeger,
2003: 6.

    [13] Klein 3.

    [14] Stephen O'Donnell and Mark O'Donnell, "The Co-
Zygotes' Almanac," Esquire June 1998: 132, Academic Search

Footnote 14 must be continued on the following page.

sexuality of twins. Psychologist Michael Bailey and
psychiatrist Richard C. Pillard studied 161 gay men, each of
whom had an identical twin, a non-identical twin, or an

Elite, EBSCOhost, 6 July 2005 <http://search.epnet.com>.

    [15] "FAQ: Twin Zygosity." Proactive Genetics. 14 July
2005 <http://www.proactivegenetics.com/faqzygosity.dna>.

A line drawn on the page signals that the first footnote beneath it is continued from the previous page.

Figure D.2 Format for a footnote continued on the following page.

Strickland 12

Notes

[1] Peter Watson, Twins: An Uncanny Relationship (New York: Viking, 1981) 9-11; Lawrence Wright, Twins: And What They Tell Us about Who We Are (New York: Wiley, 1997) 43-47.

[2] "Twin," Wikipedia: The Free Encyclopedia, 6 July 2005, 9 July 2005 <http://en.wikipedia.org/wiki/Twin>.

[3] Watson 9-11; Wright 43-47.

[4] Kimberly Powell, "Nature vs. Nurture," About.com 9 Oct. 2003, 10 July 2005 <http://genealogy.about.com/cs/geneticgenealogy/a/nature_nurture_2.htm>.

[5] Susan L. Farber, Identical Twins Reared Apart: A Reanalysis (New York: Basic Books, 1981) 5.

[6] Kate M. Dunn, Lynn F. Cherkas, and Tim D. Spector, "Genetic Influences on Variation in Female Orgasmic Function: A Twin Study," Biology Letters 7 June 2005, 8 July 2005 <http://www.journals.royalsoc.ac.uk>.

[7] Arthur Allen, "Nature & Nurture," The Washington Post Magazine 11 Jan. 1998, Washingtonpost.com, 11 July 2005 <http://www.washingtonpost.com/wp-srv/national/longterm/twins/twins1.htm>; Wright 53-55.

[8] Caroline M. Clements, personal interview, 15 July 2005.

[9] "Even Identical Twins Grow Apart Genetically--Study."

Figure D.3 Sample notes page from a paper that uses endnotes.

Books

Following are sample entries for books (accessed in print form). For online books, see Internet and Electronic Sources on pages 609–10.

A Book with One Author

> [1] Stephen M. Walt, <u>Taming American Power: The Global Response to U.S. Primacy</u> (New York: Norton, 2005) 123-26.

Footnotes/endnotes differ from works-cited entries in several particulars. The first line of each footnote/endnote is indented; the author's first (not last) name comes first; the publisher and date are enclosed in parentheses; and commas (not periods) separate major items. Also, unlike works-cited entries (but like parenthetical notes), footnotes/endnotes give the specific page or pages from which the cited information is taken.

Second and Subsequent References—All Sources

After a work has been cited in one note, you do not need to repeat all the same information in subsequent notes that refer to that same source. For second and subsequent references to a source, footnotes/endnotes should contain the least amount of information needed to identify the source (usually the author and page number).

> [2] Walt 45.

A Book with Two or Three Authors

> [3] Robert L. Dingman and John D. Weaver, <u>Days in the Lives of Counselors</u> (Boston: Allyn, 2003) 88-103.

> [4] Jo Anne Reid, Peter Forrestal, and Jonathan Cook, <u>Small Group Learning in the Classroom</u> (Portsmouth, NH: Heinemann, 1990) 110.

A Book with More Than Three Authors

> [5] Stéphane Courtois, et al., <u>The Black Book of Communism: Crimes, Terror, Repression</u> (Cambridge, MA: Harvard UP, 1999) 248-49.

A Book with No Author Listed

> [6] <u>Addison Wesley Longman Author's Guide</u> (New York: Longman, 1998) 11.

A Book with a Corporate or Group Author

[7] Sotheby's, Nineteenth Century European Paintings, Drawings and Watercolours (London: Sotheby's, 1995) 306.

[8] U of North Carolina Wilmington, 2005-2006 Code of Student Life ([Wilmington, NC]: n.p., [2005]) 23-31.

A Book by a Government Agency

[9] United States, Congress, House, Committee on Government Reform, Subcommittee on Energy and Resources, America's Energy Needs As Our National Security Policy (Washington: GPO, 2005) 3-4.

A Book with a Translator

[10] Julio Ramos, Divergent Modernities: Culture and Politics in Nineteenth-Century Latin America, trans. John D. Blanco (Durham: Duke UP, 1999) 97-199.

A Book with an Author and Editor

[11] William Shakespeare, Henry V, ed. T. W. Craik (New York: Routledge, 1995) 88.

A Book with an Editor

[12] Catherine R. Stimpson and Ethel Spector Person, eds., Women: Sex and Sexuality (Chicago: U of Chicago P, 1980), 11.

A Book in a Later Edition

[13] Ellen Skinner, Women and the National Experience, 2nd ed. (New York: Longman, 2003) 206-21.

A Book in a Series

[14] Rudolph P. Matthee, The Politics of Trade in Safavid Iran: Silk for Silver, 1600-1730, Cambridge Studies in Islamic Civilization (New York: Cambridge UP, 2000) 368.

A Multivolume Book

Volumes individually titled:

[15] Crane Brinton, John B. Christopher, and Robert Lee Wolff, Prehistory to 1715, vol. 1 of A History of Civilization, 6th ed., 2 vols. (Englewood Cliffs, NJ: Prentice, 1984) 303.

Volumes not individually titled:

[16] Charles Messenger, For Love of Regiment: A History of British Infantry, 1660-1993, vol. 1 (Philadelphia: Trans-Atlantic, 1995), 388.

A Book Published before 1900

[17] Florence Nightingale, Notes on Nursing: What It Is, and What It Is Not (New York, 1860) 27.

A Paperback or Other Reprinted Book

[18] Tony Horwitz, Confederates in the Attic: Dispatches from the Unfinished Civil War (1998; New York: Vintage, 1999) 177.

Selections from Books

A Selection from an Anthology

[19] Myra Leifer, "Pregnancy," Women: Sex and Sexuality, ed. Catherine R. Stimpson and Ethel Spector Person (Chicago: U of Chicago P, 1980) 215.

[20] George Lichtheim, "The Birth of a Philosopher," Collected Essays (New York: Viking, 1973) 109.

[21] Salman Rushdie, "A Pen Against the Sword: In Good Faith," Newsweek 12 Feb. 1990: 52+, rpt. in One World, Many Cultures, ed. Stuart Hirschberg (New York: Macmillan, 1992) 487-88.

An Article in an Encyclopedia or Other Reference

[22] Mamie Harmon, "Folk Arts," The New Encyclopaedia Britannica: Macropaedia, 15th ed., 2002.

23 "Morrison, Toni," Who's Who in America, 60th ed., 2006.

24 "Yodel," The Shorter Oxford English Dictionary, 5th ed.,
2002.

25 Raymond Hames, "Yanomamö," South America, vol. 7 of
Encyclopedia of World Cultures (Boston: Hall, 1994).

A Preface, Introduction, Foreword, or Afterword

26 Barbara Taylor Bradford, foreword, Forever Amber, by
Kathleen Winsor, 1944 (Chicago: Chicago Review, 2000) iv-viii.

Sources in Periodicals and Newspapers

For articles accessed online, see Internet and Electronic Sources on pages 610–611.

An Article in a Magazine

27 Toddi Gutner Block, "Riding the Waves," Forbes 11 Sept.
1995: 182.

28 Winston Fletcher, "The American Way of Work," Management
Today Aug. 2005: 48.

29 Deborah F. Schwartz, "Dude, Where's My Museum? Inviting
Teens to Transform Museums," Museum News Sep.-Oct. 2005: 39.

An Article in a Journal

Pages numbered continuously throughout a volume:

30 Lloyd P. Gerson, "What Is Platonism?" Journal of the
History of Philosophy 43 (2005): 267-70.

Each issue begins on page 1:

31 Rebecca Anderson and Jane Puckett, "The Usefulness of an
Online Platform for Capturing Literacy Field Experiences: Four
Lessons Learned," Reading Instruction & Research 23.4 (2005): 22.

An Article in a Newspaper

32 Henri E. Cauvin, "Lawyers Seek Release of U.S. Detainee
in Iraq," Washington Post 31 Aug. 2005: A19.

33 David Leonhardt, "Defining the Rich in the World's Wealthiest Nation," <u>New York Times</u> 12 Jan. 2003, natl. ed.: Sec. 4: 1.

34 David Ranii, "Adding a Different Symbol," <u>News and Observer</u> [Raleigh] 9 Sep. 2005: 3D.

An Editorial

35 "Oil for Food as Usual," editorial, <u>Wall Street Journal</u> 9 Sep. 2005: A16.

A Letter to the Editor

36 Jack Brewer, letter, <u>U.S. News & World Report</u> 5 Sep. 2005: 16.

A Review

37 Christopher Benfey, "An Illustrated Woman," rev. of <u>The Tattoo Artist</u>, by Jill Ciment, <u>New York Times Book Review</u> 21 Aug. 2005: 8.

38 Kenny Glenn, rev. of <u>Man on the Moon</u> [film], <u>Premiere</u> Jan. 2000: 20.

39 Rev. of <u>Going to the Territory</u>, by Ralph Ellison, <u>Atlantic</u> Aug. 1986: 91.

40 David Patrick Stearns, rev. of <u>The Well-Tempered Clavier</u>, by J. S. Bach [CD], Angela Hewitt, piano, <u>Stereophile</u> Dec. 1999: 185.

Other Sources

An Audio Recording

41 Dee Dickinson, <u>Creating the Future: Perspectives on Educational Change</u>, audiocassette, Minneapolis: Accelerated Learning Systems, 1991.

[42] Gustav Mahler, Symphony No. 7, Michael Tilson Thomas, cond., London Symphony Orch., CD, RCA Victor, 1999.

[43] George N. Shuster, jacket notes, The Poetry of Gerard Manley Hopkins, LP, Caedmon, n.d.

A Film, DVD, or Video Recording

[44] Downfall, dir. Oliver Hirschbiegel, screenplay by Bernd Eichinger, Newmarket Films, 2005.

[45] All about Eve, dir. Joseph L. Mankiewicz, perf. Bette Davis, Anne Baxter, and George Sanders, Fox, 1950, DVD, Studio Classics, 2003.

[46] The Classical Hollywood Style, program 1 of The American Cinema, prod. New York Center for Visual History, videocassette, Annenberg/CPB, 1995.

A Government Document

See "A Book by a Government Agency" on page 604.

A Lecture

[47] Stephanie Granetta, class lecture, English 315, Richardson College, 7 Apr. 2006.

[48] Eleanor Kamenish, "A Tale of Two Countries: Mores in France and Scotland," public lecture, Friends of the Public Library, Louisville, 16 Apr. 2006.

A Pamphlet

[49] Golden Retriever Club of America, Prevention of Heartworm (n.p.: GRCA, 2006) 4.

[50] Who Are the Amish? (Aylmer, Ont,: Pathway, n.d).

An Interview

[51] Caroline M. Clements, personal interview, 15 July 2005.

[52] Bill Maher, interview with Terry Gross, <u>Fresh Air</u>, Natl. Public Radio, WHQR, Wilmington, NC, 9 Aug. 2005.

[53] Donald Trump, "Trump Speaks," interview with Aravind Adiga, <u>Money</u> Feb. 2003: 28.

A Television or Radio Program

[54] <u>The Crossing</u>, dir. Robert Harmon, screenplay by Sherry Jones and Peter Jennings, History Channel, 1 Jan. 2000.

[55] Lourdes Garcia-Navarro, report on illegal immigration, <u>All Things Considered</u>, Natl. Public Radio, 8 Sep. 2005.

An Unpublished Essay

[56] Allen Strickland, "Identical Twins: Born to Be Alike?" essay written for Prof. Lisa Gorman's English 12 class, summer term 2005.

An Unpublished Letter

[57] Cara Cilano, letter to author, 5 Mar. 2006.

An Unpublished Questionnaire

[58] Questionnaire conducted by Prof. Barbara Waxman's English 103 class, Feb. 2006.

Internet and Electronic Sources

An Online Book

[59] William H. Calvin, <u>How Brains Think: Evolving Intelligence Then and Now</u> (New York: Basic Books, 1996), 1 Oct. 2005 <http://www.williamcalvin.com/bk8/>.

[60] Carl W. Conrad, <u>A Brief Commentary on the Book of Mark</u>, 2004, 1 Oct. 2005 <http://www.ioa.com/~cwconrad/Mark/>.

[61] Mary Wollstonecraft, <u>Vindication of the Rights of Women</u>, 1792, Bartleby.com, 1999, 1 Oct. 2005 <http://www.bartleby.com/144/4.html> ch. 4, para. 14.

Part of an Online Book

[62] Harold Speed, The Visual Memory, <u>The Practice and Science of Drawing</u>, 1913, Project Gutenberg, 2004, 1 Oct. 2005 <http://www.gutenberg.org/files/14264/14264-h/14264-h.htm#CHAPTER_XVIII>.

A Print Periodical (Newspaper, Magazine, or Journal) Accessed on the Publication's Web Site

[63] Jean Hopfensperger, "Wal-Mart Debate Gains Momentum across Minnesota," <u>Minneapolis Star Tribune</u> 12 Sep. 2005, 1 Oct. 2005 <http://www.startribune.com/stories/1405/5608958.html>.

[64] Mark Hosenball, "Iraq: Planning for Pullout," Newsweek 19 Sep. 2005, 1 Oct. 2005 <http://msnbc.msn.com/id/9285511/site/newsweek/>.

[65] Philip F. Hopkins, et al, "Black Holes in Galaxy Mergers: Evolution of Quasars," <u>Astrophysical Journal</u> 630.2 (2005): 710, 1 Oct. 2005 <http://www.journals.uchicago.edu/ApJ/journal/issues/ApJ/v630n2/62521/62521.html>.

A Nonprint Periodical Accessed on the Publication's Web Site

[66] "Cellular's Unhappy Customers," <u>Red Herring</u> 7 Sep. 2005, 1 Oct. 2005 <http://www.redherring.com/>.

A Work Accessed in an Online Database

[67] Steve Ernst, "Pandemic Fever," <u>Bioscience Technology</u> July 2005: 6, <u>InfoTrac OneFile</u>, 1 Oct. 2005 <http://infotrac.galegroup.com/>.

[68] Noreen Parks, "Dolphins in Danger," Science Now, 17 Dec. 2002: 2-3, Academic Search Elite, EBSCOhost, 1 Oct. 2005 <http://web3.epnet.com/>.

[69] "Ukraine Foreign Minister Says 'No Alternative' to Constructive Ties with Russia," Global News Wire 28 July 2005, LexisNexis Academic Universe, 1 Oct. 2005 <http:// web.lexis-nexis.com/universe>.

An Online Encyclopedia Article

[70] "Humpback Whale," Encyclopaedia Britannica 2005, Encyclopaedia Britannica Online, 1 Oct. 2005 <http:// 0-search.eb.com.uncclc.coast.uncwil.edu/eb/>.

An Online Review

[71] Ebert, Roger, rev. of The Constant Gardener, dir. Fernando Meirelles, RogerEbert.com 1 Sep. 2005, 1 Oct. 2005 <http://rogerebert.suntimes.com>.

[72] Janet Maslin, "Back to '68: Radicals, Chemicals and Patty Hearst," rev. of Backward-Facing Man, by Don Silver, New York Times on the Web 12 Sep. 2005, 1 Oct. 2005 <http:// www.nytimes.com/2005/09/12/books/12masl.html>.

An Organization's Web Site

[73] The Coral Reef Alliance, "Major Mesoamerica Initiative Underway," 1 Oct. 2005 <http:// www.coralreefalliance.org/parks/mar/>.

A Personal Web Page

[74] Sally Hemming, home page, 1 Oct. 2005 <http:// www.sallyhemming.com/>.

Weblog (Blog) or Online Posting

[75] Lawrence Lessig, "Gifts from the Other Side," weblog entry, Lessig Blog 11 Sep. 2005, 1 Oct. 2005 <http://www.lessig.org/blog/>.

[76] Keith Newlin, "McTeague's Tooth," online posting, 22 Mar. 2003, 1 Oct. 2005 <http://people.uncw.edu/newlink/tooth.htm>.

E-Mail

[77] Paul Wilkes, e-mail to author, 29 Dec. 2005.

Computer Software

[78] ChemSketch, vers. 8.0, software, 2005 <http://www.acdlabs.com/download/chemsk.html>.

[79] Twain's World, CD-ROM (Parsippany, NJ: Bureau Development, 1993).

E *APA Format*

FORMATS OTHER THAN MLA

Although you will use the MLA parenthetical or footnote/endnote format to acknowledge sources in papers that you write for humanities courses (such as research papers in a composition class), other disciplines may require you to use different formats. Since many journals establish their own conventions for documenting sources, you are also likely to encounter various other formats when you conduct library research. A glance through scholarly journals in your college library will show you that dozens of different formats are in use—usually varying only in minor ways from MLA format or the formats described in this chapter.

Although it is not practical to describe all the different formats here, you should be familiar with the most commonly used formats for citing sources. It is probably unnecessary for you to memorize the details of any of them, but when you use a particular format, you should be prepared to model your own references carefully on sample entries, such as those in this chapter. Note the ways in which these formats differ from MLA format and pay close attention to the information that is presented in each entry, the order in which it is presented, and the punctuation used to denote and separate items.

Two principal formats, besides the MLA, are in wide use among scholars. The APA format (described in this chapter) gives special prominence to the source's publication date in all citations. In the numbered references format (described in the following chapter), each source is assigned a number in the list of works cited; each note in the paper refers to a source by its assigned number.

APA STYLE

Next to the MLA style, the most common format for documenting sources is that of the American Psychological Association—*APA style*. This format (or a variation of it) is widely used for course papers and journal articles in psychology but also in many other disciplines in both the social and natural sciences. Although APA format differs in many particulars from MLA format, the main difference is the prominence its citations give to the source's publication date. In fields where new theories and discoveries are constantly challenging past assumptions, readers must know if a writer's sources are up-to-date. Note how the date is featured in the following sample APA citations. Parenthetical notes in APA style always include the date, as in the following:

```
...tendency of creative people to be organized (Sternberg &
Lubart, 1995, p. 246).
```

Following is the listing for that same source, as it appears in the references page (list of works cited). Notice that the date is given in parentheses immediately following the author's name.

```
Sternberg, R. J., & Lubart, T. I. (1995). Defying the crowd:
    Cultivating creativity in a culture of conformity. New
    York: Free Press.
```

The particulars of APA reference style are explained in the following sections.

APA Bibliographic Citations (Reference List)

At the end of the paper, all sources are listed on a separate page, under the title *References* (not *Works Cited*). Like the MLA format, the APA also arranges works alphabetically, according to the first word in each item. See, for example, Figure E.1 on the following page.

In addition to the prominence given to publication dates, bibliographic citations in APA style differ from MLA listings in three principal ways:

1. In APA style, only the author's last name is given in full. Initials are used for first and middle names. Thus, an author who would be listed in MLA style as *Sternberg, Robert J.* is listed as *Sternberg, R. J.* in APA style.

2. Except for proper names, only the first word of the work's title (and, if there is a subtitle, the first word following the colon) is capitalized. Thus, a book title that would be listed in MLA style as *Defying the Crowd: Cultivating Creativity in a Culture of Conformity* is listed in APA style as *Defying the crowd: Cultivating creativity in a culture of conformity.*

3. Titles of periodical articles (and other works shorter than book-length) are not enclosed in quotation marks as they are in MLA style.

Other differences can be seen in the following sample entries.

Model Entries

Punctuation following italicized text is also italicized in APA style.

Fast Food 13

References

Author's last
names and
first initials
are given.

Article titles
are not placed
in quotation
marks.

Ayoub, N. C. (May 25, 2001). Nota bene. [Review of the
book *Youth at Work: The unionized fast-food and
grocery workplace*]. *Chronicle of Higher Education*,
p. A20.

Broydo. L. (1999, January/February). Worked over. *Utne
Reader, 16*, 20-21.

General information on the fair labor standards act (FLSA).

Online sources
are cited in this
format.

(n.d.). U.S. Department of Labor Employment Standards
Administration Wage and Hour Division. Retrieved
September 29, 2002, from http://www.dol.gov/esa/
regs/compliance/whd/mwposter.htm

Hamstra, M. (1998, September 7). Unions seek momentum from
Canadian McD's certification. *Nation's Restaurant
News, 32:* 3. Retrieved September 15, 2002, from
MasterFILE Premier database (Item 1099749).

Titles are
capitalized
according to
the rules for
sentence
capitalization.

Figure E.1 Sample APA references page.

Books

Following are sample APA entries for books (accessed in print form). For online
books, see Internet and Electronic Sources on page 622.

A Book with One Author

Walt, S. M. (2005). *Taming American power: The global response
to U.S. primacy.* New York: W. W. Norton.

Wheelock, A. K., Jr. (1995). *Vermeer and the art of painting.*
New Haven, CT: Yale University Press.

The complete names of publishers are given. Words like *University* and *Press* are not abbreviated.

A Book with Two to Six Authors

> Reid, J. A., Forrestal, P., & Cook, J. (1990). *Small group*
>
>   *learning in the classroom.* Portsmouth, NH: Heinemann.

All authors, not just the first, are listed last name first, followed by initials. An ampersand (&) is used before the name of the last author.

A Book with More Than Six Authors

> Martin, S., Smith, L., Forehand, M. R., Mobbs, R., Lynch, T. F.,
>
>   Renfrew, E. J., et al. (2003). *Migratory waterfowl.*
>
>   Lincoln, NE: Wendell Press.

List only the first six authors, followed by *et al.*

Two or More Works by the Same Author, Different Years

> Irwin, E. (2003). *New...*
>
> Irwin, E. (2006). *Lessons...*

When two or more works have the same author(s), arrange the works chronologically, not alphabetically by title.

Two or More Works by the Same Author, Same Year

> Bushman, D. E. (2006a). *Development...*
>
> Bushman, D. E. (2006b). *Lessons...*

When the author(s) has two or more works in the same year, arrange the works alphabetically by title, and place lowercase letters (*a, b, c,* etc.) immediately after the year.

A Book with No Author Listed

> *Addison Wesley Longman author's guide.* (1998). New York: Longman.

A Book with a Corporate or Group Author

> Sotheby's. (1995). *Nineteenth century European paintings,*
>
>   *drawings and watercolours.* London: Author.

A Book by a Government Agency

United States. Congress. House. Committee on Government Reform. Subcommittee on Energy and Resources. (2005). *America's energy needs as our national security policy.* Washington: Government Printing Office.

A Book with a Translator

Ramos, J. (1999). *Divergent modernities: Culture and politics in nineteenth-century Latin America* (J. D. Blanco, Trans.). Durham, NC: Duke University Press.

A Book with an Author and Editor

Shakespeare, W. (1591). *Henry V* (T. W. Craik, Ed.). New York: Routledge. (Edition published 1995)

A Book with an Editor

Stimpson, C. R., & Person, E. S. (Eds.). (1980). *Women: Sex and sexuality.* Chicago: University of Chicago Press.

A Book in a Later Edition

Skinner, E. (2003). *Women and the national experience* (2nd ed.). New York: Longman.

A Book in a Series

Matthee, R. P. (2000). *The Politics of trade in Safavid Iran: Silk for silver, 1600-1730.* Cambridge Studies in Islamic Civilization. New York: Cambridge University Press.

A Multivolume Book

Messenger, C. (1995). *For love of regiment: A history of British infantry, 1660-1993* (Vol. 1). Philadelphia: Trans-Atlantic Publications.

List all volumes of the work that you cite; for example, *(Vols. 2–3).*

A Paperback or Other Reprinted Book

Horwitz, T. (1999). *Confederates in the attic: Dispatches from the unfinished Civil War.* New York: Vintage. (Original work published 1998)

Selections from Books

A Selection from an Anthology

Baker, S. W. (1980). Biological influences on human sex and gender. In C. R. Stimpson & E. S. Person (Eds.), *Women: Sex and sexuality* (pp. 212-223). Chicago: University of Chicago Press.

Rushdie, S. (1992). A pen against the sword: In good faith. In Hirschberg, S. (Ed.), *One world, many cultures* (pp. 480-496). New York: Macmillan. (Reprinted from *Newsweek, 115,* February 12, 1990: 52-57)

An Article in an Encyclopedia or Other Reference

Harmon, M. (2002). Folk arts. In *The new encyclopaedia Britannica: Macropaedia* (15th ed., Vol. 19, pp. 306-338). Chicago: Britannica.

Morrison, T. (2006). In *Who's who in America* (60th ed.). Chicago: Marquis.

Hames, R. (1994). Yanomamö. In South America. *Encyclopedia of world cultures* (Vol. 7, pp. 374-377). Boston: G. K. Hall.

A Preface, Introduction, Foreword, or Afterword

Bradford, B. T. (2000). Foreword. In K. Winsor, *Forever amber* (pp. iii-xi). Chicago: Chicago Review.

Periodicals and Newspapers

Following are APA entries for periodicals and newspapers (when accessed in print form). For articles accessed online, see Internet and Electronic Sources on pages 622–23.

An Article in a Magazine

> Block, T. G. (1995, September 11). Riding the waves. *Forbes,*
>   *156,* 182, 184.
>
> Fletcher, W. (2005, August). The American way of work.
>   *Management Today,* 46-49.
>
> Schwartz, D. F. (2005 September/October). Dude, where's my
>   museum? Inviting teens to transform museums. *Museum News,*
>   *84,* 36-41.

The date of a periodical is given (year first) immediately following the author's name. Months are not abbreviated. Neither quotation marks nor italics are used for article titles. All important words in a periodical's title are capitalized (*Opera News*). The volume number of a periodical is italicized and follows the name of the periodical (*Forbes,* 156). All page numbers are given immediately afterward. For magazine and journal articles (unlike newspaper articles), neither *p.* nor *pp.* is used. The Block article appeared on pages 182 and 184.

An Article in a Journal

A journal whose pages are numbered continuously throughout a volume:

> Gerson, L. P. (2005). What is Platonism? *Journal of the History*
>   *of Philosophy, 43,* 253-276.

A journal, every issue of which begins on page 1:

> Anderson, R., & Puckett, J. (2005). The usefulness of an online
>   platform for capturing literacy field experiences: Four
>   lessons learned. *Reading Instruction & Research 23*(4),
>   22-46.

The number *23*(4) tells you that the article appeared in volume 23, issue 4, of *Reading Instruction & Research.* Only the volume number is italicized. Page numbers are not shortened, as they are in MLA style; pages in the Gerson article are written 253–276 (not 253–76).

An Article in a Newspaper

> Cauvin, H. E. (2005, August 31). Lawyers seek release of U.S.
>   detainee in Iraq. *Washington Post,* p. A19.

Leonhardt, D. (2003, January 12). Defining the rich in the world's wealthiest nation. *New York Times,* national edition, section 4, pp. 1, 8.

An Editorial

Oil for food as usual. (2005, September 9). [Editorial]. *Wall Street Journal,* p. A16.

A Letter to the Editor

Brewer, J. (2005, September 5). [Letter to the editor]. *U.S. News & World Report,* p. 16.

A Review

Benfey, C. (2005 August 21). An illustrated woman. [Review of the book *The tattoo artist*]. *New York Times Book Review,* p. 8.

Glenn, K. (2000, January). [Review of the film *Man on the moon*]. *Premiere, 13,* 20.

[Review of the book *Going to the territory*]. (1986, August). *Atlantic, 120,* 91.

Stearns, D. P. (1999, December). [Review of the CD *The well-tempered clavier*]. *Stereophile,* 10, 173, 175.

Other Sources

An Audio Recording

Dickinson, D. (Speaker). (1991). *Creating the future: Perspectives on educational change* [Audiocassette]. Minneapolis, MN: Accelerated Learning Systems.

Mahler, G. (1999). Symphony No. 7 [CD]. United States: RCA Victor.

A Film, DVD, or Video Recording

Hirschbiegel, O. (Director). (2005). *Downfall* [Film]. Germany: Newmarket Films.

Mankiewicz, J. L. (Scriptwriter and director). (2003). *All about Eve*. [DVD]. Hollywood, CA: Studio Classics. (Film produced 1950).

The classical Hollywood style [Videocassette]. (1995). Program 1 of *The American cinema*. Washington, DC: Annenberg/CPB.

A Lecture

A source that cannot be retrieved by your readers, such as a classroom or public lecture which is not available in print or on recording, is not listed among your paper's references. However, it is cited in the paper in a parenthetical note: (*S. Granetta, classroom lecture, April 7, 2006*).

A Personal Interview

A personal interview that you conduct cannot be retrieved by your readers, so it is not listed among your paper's references. However, it is cited in the paper in a parenthetical note: (*C. Clements, personal communication, July 15, 2005*).

A Broadcast or Published Interview

Adiga, A. (2003, February). Trump speaks. [Interview with Donald Trump]. *Money, 32,* 28.

Gross, T. (2005, August 9). [Interview with Bill Maher]. In *Fresh air*. National Public Radio. Wilmington, NC: WHQR.

A Television or Radio Program

Garcia-Navarro, L. (Reporter). (2005, September 8). [Report on illegal immigration]. In *All things considered*. Washington, DC: National Public Radio.

Harmon, R. (Director). (2000, January 1). The crossing [Television program]. Stamford, CT: History Channel.

An Unpublished Essay

Strickland, A. (2005). Identical twins: Born to be alike? Unpublished essay for Prof. Lisa Gorman's English 12 class, University of North Carolina Wilmington.

An Unpublished Letter or E-Mail

Unpublished correspondence cannot be retrieved by your readers, so it is not listed among your paper's references. However, it is cited in the paper in a parenthetical note: (*C. Cilano, personal communication, March 5, 2006*).

An Unpublished Questionnaire

Doe, J. (2006). [Survey of student attitudes on dating].
Unpublished raw data.

Internet and Electronic Sources

An Online Book

Calvin, W. H. (1996). *How brains think: Evolving intelligence
then and now.* New York: Basic Books. Retrieved October 1,
2005, from http://www.williamcalvin.com/bk8/

A Print Periodical Accessed Online

Cellular's unhappy customers. (2005, September 7). *Red
Herring.* Retrieved October 1, 2005, from http://
www.redherring.com/

Hopfensperger, J. (2005, September 12). Wal-Mart debate gains
momentum across Minnesota. *Minneapolis Star Tribune.*
Retrieved October 1, 2005, from http://www.startribune.com/
stories/1405/5608958.html

Hopkins, P. F., Hernquist, L., Cox, T. J., Di Matteo, T.,
Martini, T., Robertson, B., et al. (2005). Black holes in
galaxy mergers: Evolution of quasars. *Astrophysical Journal
630* (2): 705-715. Retrieved October 1, 2005, from
http://www.journals.uchicago.edu/ApJ/journal/issues/
ApJ/v630n2/62521/62521.html

Hosenball, M. (2005, September 19). Iraq: Planning for pullout.
Newsweek. Retrieved October 1, 2005, from
http://msnbc.msn.com/id/9285511/site/newsweek/

A Work Accessed in an Online Database

Use the following format when you access a work in an online database such as EBSCOhost, InfoTrac, LexisNexis, ProQuest, or WilsonWeb.

> Ernst, S. (2005, July 6). Pandemic fever. *Bioscience Technology,*
> *30*, 6. Retrieved October 1, 2005, from InfoTrac OneFile
> database (Item A134910272).

> Global News Wire. (2005, July 28). Ukraine foreign minister says
> 'no alternative' to constructive ties with Russia.
> Retrieved October 1, 2005, from LexisNexis Academic
> Universe database.

Include an item number for the article, if available.

An Online Encyclopedia Article

> Humpback whale. (2005). Encyclopaedia Britannica 2003. Retrieved
> October 1, 2005, from Encyclopaedia Britannica Online.

An Organization's or Individual's Web Site

> The Coral Reef Alliance. (n.d.). Major Mesoamerica initiative
> underway. Retrieved October 1, 2005, from
> http://www.coralreefalliance.org/parks/mar/

> Hemming, S. (n.d.). [Home page]. Retrieved January 21, 2003.
> from http://www.sallyhemming.com/

Use (*n.d.*) for "no date."

Weblog (Blog) or Online Posting

> Lessig, L. (2005, September 11). Gifts from the other side.
> [Weblog entry]. Retrieved October 1, 2005, from
> http://www.lessig.org/blog/

> Newlin, K. (2005, March 22). McTeague's tooth. [Online posting].
> Retrieved October 1, 2005, from http://people.uncw.edu/
> newlink/tooth.htm

Treatment of other sources, as well as detailed information about APA format, can be found by consulting the latest edition of the *Publication Manual of the American Psychological Association.* You can find the book in the reference section of most college libraries.

Notes in APA Style

Parenthetical notes in APA format are handled similarly to the MLA method, but with three notable differences:

1. The year of publication is included in the note.
2. All items are separated by commas.
3. Page numbers are preceded by the abbreviation *p.* or *pp.*

When a work is referred to as a whole, no page numbers are needed:

```
In a study of reaction times (Sanders, 2006),...
```

Only the year is needed when the author's name appears in the sentence:

```
Sanders (2006) studied reaction times ...
```

Include pages when the source can be located more specifically:

```
"...not necessary" (Galizio, 2005, p. 9).
```

Give the first word or two from the title when the author's name is unknown. Book titles are italicized; periodical titles in notes (unlike in the reference list) are enclosed in quotation marks; all important words are capitalized (also like reference-list citations):

```
...the book (Culture, 2005).
...the article ("US policy," 2001).
```

Only the year, not the complete date, is given in notes referring to periodical articles.

For a work with six or fewer authors, the note lists all authors' last names:

```
(Andrulis, Beers, Bentley, & Gage, 2005)
```

However, only the first author's name is given for a work with more than six authors:

```
(Sabella et al., 2006)
```

When the reference list cites two or more works written by the same author in the same year, use lowercase letters to differentiate them, as in reference-list citations:

```
(Bushman, 2006a)
```

```
(Bushman, 2006b)
```

These two notes cite different works by Bushman, both written in 2003.

When a note refers to more than one work, list the references alphabetically and separate them with a semicolon:

```
(Earle & Reeves, 1999; Kowal, 2004)
```

Sample Pages in APA Style

Any paper written using MLA format can also be written in APA format. For example, Allen Strickland could have used APA style for his paper on twins.

A cover page is typically used for APA papers. The cover page is numbered as page 1, and a shortened version of the title precedes the page number on each page, as in Figure E.2.

The title is repeated on the opening page of the paper, numbered as page 2. Compare Figure E.3 and E.4 with pages from Allen's MLA-style paper on pages 304–14. Compare Figure E.1 with Allen's list of works cited on page 315.

```
                                         Identical Twins 1


                   Running head: IDENTICAL TWINS



                 Identical Twins: Born to Be Alike?
                         Allen Strickland
            University of North Carolina Wilmington



                     Professor Lisa Gorman
                            ENG 12
                         Section 23
                       July 25, 2005
```

Figure E.2 Sample APA cover page.

Identical Twins 2

Identical Twins: Born to Be Alike?

Jim Lewis and Jim Springer, twins who were adopted as infants by different families, did not meet again until they were 39 years old. Although their hair styles were different, they were otherwise strikingly similar. Both were six feet tall and weighed 180 pounds. They had the same features, including an unusual swirl in one eyebrow and a "lazy eye" on the same side. As they were soon to learn, looking alike was just the beginning of their similarities (Watson, 1981, pp. 9-11; Wright, 1997, pp. 43-47).

Figure E.3 Sample APA opening page.

Identical Twins 10

divorced, the other twin's chances of divorcing went up to

45% (Minnesota Twin Family Study, n.d.).

Citation of a
source without
date or pages.

If studies of twins show that genetics is such a

strong factor in shaping us, does that mean that humans

have less freedom to make decisions than we suppose? In his

book on twins, journalist Lawrence Wright (1997, p. 154)

Citation of a
source with a
page reference.

points out that the findings can sometimes be misleading.

Even if 45% of identical twins get divorced if the other

twin does, that means that the majority do not. Despite

genetic or environmental influences, we still remain free

to make decisions. After studying the similarities between

twins for many years, Thomas Bouchard (Allen, 1998)

Citation of a
source follow-
ing author's
name.

now says:

There probably are genetic influences on almost

all facets of human behavior, but the emphasis on

Figure E.4 Sample APA notes.

Format Featuring Numbered References

Another common bibliographic format uses **numbered references** to identify sources. Variations on this format are used most widely in fields such as mathematics, computer science, finance, and other areas in the applied sciences.

Sources are assigned a number in the references page (list of works cited) and are referred to in the paper by that number rather than by the author's name. Items in the references list can be arranged either in alphabetical order or in the order in which references occur within the paper. Figure F.1 shows how the references list at the end of Allen Strickland's paper might have looked if he had used this style. In this case, the references are numbered in the order in which they first appear in the paper.

Here is how the first five sentences with notes in Allen's paper would have appeared if he had used the numbered-references style:

The paper's first note is numbered 1.

As they were soon to learn, looking alike was just the beginning of their similarities [1, pp. 9-11; 2, pp. 43-47].

Note for a source without pages.

Non-identical twins are genetically no more alike than non-twin siblings [3].

A later reference to a source cited earlier in the paper.

Strangest of all, each got divorced from a woman named Linda and then married a woman named Betty [1, pp. 9-11; 2, pp. 43-47].

To put it another way, are we "born that way" or are we shaped by our surroundings? [4].

Psychologist Susan L. Farber calls identical twins "nature's unique controlled laboratory experiment on the interplay between heredity and environment" [5, p. 5].

The page reference follows the number note.

Apart from the use of reference numbers, there is no uniform style for citing bibliographic sources in this format. Individual items in the bibliography could follow the principles of MLA format, APA format, or yet some other format. If you are required to use numbered references for a course paper, be sure to check with your instructor for specific format details.

Another characteristic of papers using this format is that citation of page references is far less common than in either MLA or APA style. Usually, sources are

---

Strickland 12

References

1. Watson, Peter. Twins: An Uncanny Relationship. New York: Viking, 1981.

2. Wright, Lawrence. Twins: And What They Tell Us about Who We Are. New York: Wiley, 1997.

3. "Twin." Wikipedia: The Free Encyclopedia. 6 July 2005. 9 July 2005 <http://en.wikipedia.org/wiki/Twin>.

4. Powell, Kimberly. "Nature vs. Nurture." About.com. 9 Oct. 2003. 10 July 2005 <http://genealogy.about.com/cs/geneticgenealogy/a/nature_nurture_2.htm>.

5. Farber, Susan L. Identical Twins Reared Apart: A Reanalysis. New York: Basic Books, 1981.

Figure F.1 Sample list with numbered references.

referred to in the paper solely by their reference numbers, which are usually written within brackets:

```
Smith and Gurganus [6] showed that . . .
```

Often even the authors' names are omitted:

```
Other examples of this approach are [1, 4, 5]. In 1996, [3]
analyzed . . .
```

Instead of brackets, alternative formats that use numbered references place them either within parentheses:

```
Fort (7) disputes the findings of Byington (3) . . .
```

or as raised numbers:

```
It has been demonstrated[1] that artifacts that occur . . .
```

The raised number *1* in the preceding example refers not to a footnote or endnote but directly to the first source in the references list.

Credits

Text

PHOTOS

Index

Parenthetical Notes (MLA Style): Quick Reference Guide

Detailed information on parenthetical notes can be found on pages 563–78.

PURPOSE

Use a note to identify the specific source location for a specific idea, piece of information, or quotation in your paper.

FORMAT

Give the specific page reference, preceded by the *least* amount of information needed to identify the source in your list of works cited.

PLACEMENT

Place the note following the passage.

MODEL ENTRIES

Standard Reference

Give the author and page(s):

> A fear of thunder is common among dogs (Digby 237).

Author Identified in the Passage

Omit the author's name in the note:

> Digby noted that dogs are often terrified of thunder (237).

An Anonymous Work (Unidentified Author)

Use the first word or two from the title:

> ("An Infant's" 22)

A Work with Two or Three Authors

> (Reid, Forrestal, and Cook 48-49)

A Work with More Than Three Authors

> (Courtois et al. 112)

Two or More Works by the Same Author

Add the first word(s) from the title:

> (Asimov, Adding 240-43)
> (Asimov, "Happy" 68)

Two Authors with the Same Last Name

Include the authors' first names:

> (George Eliot 459)
> (T. S. Eliot 44)

A Multivolume Work

The volume number precedes the page number(s):

> (Agus 2: 59)

Exception: Omit the volume number if only one volume is identified in your list of works cited:

> (Agus 59)